DORNDEN GU[...]

(AA Listed & R[...])

Church Lan[...]

[...]
[...]
C[...]
be[...]
pea[...]
is an   ..dar,
Wells   .. Laycock all
nearby,   . route to Wales or
Cornwa[...]   walk of 100 miles from
Chipping   ..r runs through the village. Please
        rea[...]   ..w advert for more information.

moorlands

· MENDIP · COUNTRY · GUEST HOUSE ·

HUTTON, AVON
Nr. WESTON-SUPER-MARE

This attractive Georgian House stands in
extensive grounds with peaceful views
of nearby wooded hills. The pretty village
. of Hutton is just four miles from
Weston's centre.

Moorlands is personally run by the family; our
daughter is a trained pâtisserie chef. Children
are most welcome; we offer reduced rates and
pony rides. Some rooms have en-suite
facilities, one of which is a ground floor room
suitable for the less mobile. We are open from early February to early November for a family
holiday and Bed and Breakfast. Write or phone for a brochure from:

GOOD
ROOM
AWARD

MARGARET AND DAVID HOLT, MOORLANDS, HUTTON,
Nr WESTON-SUPER-MARE, AVON BS24 9QH. TEL: (0934) 812283.

* RESIDENTIAL LICENCE   * ETB ♛♛ APPROVED

THAMES VALLEY HOLIDAY HOMES

Two country holiday homes overlooking the Thames Valley

Overleigh sleeps 2-6 people. Underleigh sleeps 1-4 people. Both
properties are fully equipped – central heating, colour TV, tele-
phone, pretty gardens/orchard, plenty of parking. Situated in a
picturesque village a short distance from the famous Cliveden
Estate, within easy reach of London 25 miles and Windsor 10 miles.
Registered with Tourist Board.
**For further information see classified entry under
Wooburn Green, Bucks.**
Send for free colour brochure: Mrs E.G. Griffin
MYOSOTIS, WIDMOOR, WOOBURN GREEN, BUCKS HP10 0JG
Tel: Bourne End (06285) 21594   Fax: 0628 850471

BOARD

BOSSINEY HOUSE HOTEL

Tintagel
Cornwall PL34 0AX
Tel: 0840 770240

Perched on the cliffs overlooking one of the finest stretches of National Trust coastline in Cornwall. ½ mile from Tintagel.

★ 20 bedrooms including family suite, pleasant sea or country views and nearly all en-suite.

★ Residents' lounge, TV lounge, spacious dining room & cocktail bar.

★ Renowned cuisine with varied menus.

★ 2½ acres of lawns and gardens including putting green.

★ Scandinavian log chalet in the grounds with heated swimming pool, sauna and solarium.

★ Magnificent cliff walks and nearby facilities including surfing, horse riding, golf, squash, pony-trekking and fishing.

★ Reduced prices for longer stays. Dinner, bed & breakfast.

AA
★★
RAC

For details and our colour brochure please contact resident proprietors C. & R. Savage, The Bossiney House Hotel.

Enjoy a holiday by the sea in the heart of King Arthur's kingdom.

ETB

A REAL COUNTRY HOUSE HOTEL JUST OUTSIDE OF FALMOUTH

THE HOME
PENJERRICK, FALMOUTH

Telephone: Falmouth (STD 0326) 250427 and 250143

Situated in lovely unspoilt countryside, yet only 2½ miles from Falmouth.
Ideal for lovers of the country, yet within 18 minutes' walk of Maenporth Beach.

An Ashley Courtenay Recommended Hotel

Our house, in its large garden, has lovely views over tree-clad countryside to
Maenporth and the bay. Close to the Helford River with its beautiful walks and
boating facilities. Ideal base for touring.

All bedrooms have H&C, razor points, bedside lights, tea/coffee making
facilities and heaters. A number of bedrooms with shower or en suite facilities
available. Our home is graciously furnished and carpeted to a high standard.
All beds are modern divans. Partial central heating.

Our elegant dining room has separate tables. Large lounge with colour TV.
In addition there is a spacious sun lounge overlooking the garden.

★

TABLE LICENCE   GOOD ENCLOSED CAR PARK   BUS SERVICE

★

Mr & Mrs P. Tremayne have welcomed guests to their lovely house for the past 26 years

★

Dinner, Room and Breakfast from £100 per week, including 15% VAT.
Illustrated brochure from: Mrs. T. P. Tremayne

We are of a farming family and our visitors' book is blushingly complimentary
over the home-cooked food and its presentation. This is our home and as such
we welcome you to it and hope you will enjoy it as much as we do.

Also Self-Catering Furnished Farmhouse and Cottage at Constantine, Falmouth

BOARD

BOARD

TREGADDRA FARMHOUSE

Tregaddra is an early 18th century farmhouse set in half-an-acre of well-kept gardens, providing high class accommodation. Ideally situated in the centre of the Lizard Peninsula with views of sea, coast and country-side for 15 mile radius. Sandy beaches, golf and horse riding all nearby. Good farmhouse cooking and own produce used. All double rooms are en-suite. Lounge has inglenook fireplace with log fires early/late season. Large games room. Heated swimming pool with slide. Children welcome but sorry, no pets. Evening Dinner, Bed and Breakfast or Bed and Breakfast, English Tourist Board ❤❤ Commended. Helston six miles, Mullion three miles, Helford River seven miles, The Lizard six miles. Open all year. Send for colour brochure. Mrs H. LUGG, TREGADDRA, CURY, HELSTON, CORNWALL TR12 7BB. Tel: Mullion (0326) 240235.

"Halwyn"

Manaccan, Helston, Cornwall
Mr & Mrs H. Donald
Tel. 0326 280359
Delightful farmhouse and
cottages in tranquil surroundings.
Open all year.
*Indoor swimming pool, sauna
and solarium.*
For full details see SELF CATERING
SECTION – CORNWALL – HELSTON.

AA** 𝕽osemundy 𝕳ouse 𝕳otel RAC**

Telephone St. Agnes (087-255) 2101

Rosemundy House is a delightful Georgian residence set in its own sheltered and attractive grounds in the village of St. Agnes and within a mile of Trevaunance Cove beach. Rosemundy is family owned and run and we take pride in the quality of food, service and accommodation we offer. St. Agnes is an unspoilt village on the north Cornish coast between St. Ives and Newquay and is an ideal centre for touring.

* Family-run Hotel
* Attractive licensed bar
* Good home cooking
* Colour TV lounge
* 43 en-suite bedrooms

* Colour TV in all bedrooms
* Tea/coffee making facilities in all bedrooms
* Ample parking space
* 45ft heated swimming pool

* Games room with table tennis, pool, snooker, darts etc.
* Badminton, Croquet, Putting
* Horse riding, golf, tennis, surfing, gliding, fishing nearby

Dinner, Bed and Breakfast from £125 to £200 per week (including VAT).
Bed and Breakfast from £100 to £175 per week (including VAT). We make no service charge.
Write or phone for full colour brochure and tariff:
Rosemundy House Hotel, Rosemundy, St. Agnes, Cornwall TR5 0UF

SELF-CATERING

BOARD

Crantock Plains Farm

Relax in this charming character farmhouse in peaceful countryside and combine comfort, home cooking and personal service for an enjoyable holiday. Crantock Plains Farm is situated two and a half miles from Newquay and half a mile off the A3075 Newquay–Redruth road. Picturesque village of Crantock with Post Office, village stores, tea rooms, two pubs and beautiful sandy beach is nearby, as are riding stables and many sporting activities. Three doubles, one single, three family (two en-suite), shower room; two toilets, bathroom; sittingroom; central heating, log fire. No smoking in dining-room and bedrooms. Table licence. Home grown vegetables when available. No pets. Open all year. Please send SAE for brochure with details of prices.

**Mr and Mrs Rowlands, Crantock Plains Farm, Near Newquay, Cornwall
Tel. Crantock [0637] 830253.**

SELF-CATERING

Picturesque group of 17th century cottages overlooking beautiful National Trust Valley with fabulous views of the sea. All our cottages are individually furnished and equipped to a very high standard. All have colour TV etc. Cottages are warm and comfortable and are open all year. Wonderful walks, peace and quiet and unspoilt beaches are on our doorstep. Our cottages offer you quality and comfort at a reasonable cost. Please write or phone any time for our free colour brochure.

Mrs Russell-Steel, Courtyard Farm, Lesnewth, near Boscastle, Cornwall. Tel: 084-06 256.

SELF-CATERING

Helman Tor Cottages, Lanlivery

Overlooking Redmoor Nature reserve and set within peaceful surroundings, Higher Trevilmick Farm is within easy reach of both coasts and offers easy access to Cornwall's many tourist attractions.

The Accommodation: *DOVECOT . . . Sleeps two in a beautiful 4-poster bed. Open plan living room. Shower room with wc and wash basin. This cottage is separated from the other cottages by a short flight of stairs and is designed for quiet romantic holidays.* FOXES COTTAGE . . . Ground floor, sleeps four, in two bedrooms with a double in one bedroom and two single beds in the other. BADGERS SET and RAVENS CROFT (pictured) . . . Ground floor, both sleep four, in two bedrooms with a double in one, and bunk beds in the other. KESTREL CORNER . . . Ground floor, the largest cottage, sleeps 4/5, in two bedrooms, with a double in one and 2/3 single beds in the other. The cottages have own car park, play area and lawn and have carpeted living area, well equipped kitchens, modern bathrooms, duvets and colour TV. Cot, high chair available. Laundry with payphone.
Apply Mr & Mrs C.D. Girdler, Higher Trevilmick, Lanlivery, Bodmin, Cornwall PL30 5HT. Tel: 0208 872372.

"HIDE-A-WAY", Tregaddra, Helston, Cornwall

This luxury mobile home is tucked away in the grounds of Tregaddra farmhouse in the centre of the Lizard Peninsula. Surrounded by garden of half an acre and having magnificent views over the rolling countryside. Use of heated outdoor swimming pool & games room. Furnished to a high standard, one double bedroom, one twin-bedded. Bathroom with shower and basin, separate toilet. Kitchen, dining area. Lounge with colour TV. Linen/gas/electric included in rental. Open all year. Terms from £100 per week. Mullion 3 miles, Helston 6 miles. Send for colour brochure to:

Mrs Hilary Lugg, Tregaddra, Cury, Helston, Cornwall TR12 7BB. Tel: Mullion (0326) 240235.

BLIGHT'S MANOR FARM

Wheal Buston, St. Agnes,
Cornwall TR5 0PT   Tel: 087-255 3142

Situated amidst 22 acres of rolling country-side just one mile from St. Agnes and four from Perranporth, Blight's Manor is ideally placed for visiting superb beaches, quaint fishing villages and all the best tourist attractions. Facilities at this renovated Cornish farmhouse include outdoor heated pool, games room, stables, fitness room and grassed area for football etc. Guests are comfortably accommodated in tastefully furnished bedrooms, most with private facilities.

Contact Mrs Welsby for colour brochure.

Trencreek Farm

HOLIDAY PARK
AA ▸▸▸
Hewaswater, St Austell
Telephone 0726 882540
RAC

Trencreek is a small working farm with a real farm atmosphere. Most small animals roam freely around the site – a wonderful place for young children and adults who want peace and quiet. *The bungalows and caravans are modern, comfortable and serviced. *3 camping fields with large pitches (Spaced around field edges only). *Electrical hook-ups. *Lots of recreational space. *Modern washroom facilities. *Laundry and dishwashing rooms. *TV and table tennis. *Adventure barn. *Playground. *Heated swimming pool. *Well-behaved dogs welcome. *Tennis Court. *Pitch & Putt. *Fishing.
'The' Holiday for families with 'young' children

Patterdale Hall Estate

GLENRIDDING · PENRITH · CUMBRIA · CA11 0PT
Telephone: Glenridding (07684) 82308

In a magnificent mountain setting at the southern end of Ullswater, Patterdale Hall Estate is ideally situated for holidays and outdoor activities. Its spacious wooded grounds reach from the shores of the lake to the lower slopes of the Helvellyn range. The 300 acres contains a working hill farm, own private section of foreshore and 100 acres of private woodland and gardens for walks. Sailing, fishing, canoeing, windsurfing and steamer trips on Ullswater, and the Estate makes an ideal base for touring the whole of the Lake District.

There are 11 self-catering units in various parts of the Estate including:

Three	Two	Six
Apartments	*Cottages*	*Pine Chalets*

Terms are from £121 to £305 per week including central heating and one tank of hot water per day. Other electricity metered. Linen hire available. Children welcome. Sorry, no animals. Patterdale Hall itself also offers accommodation for groups, with meals provided.

Last minute (within 2 weeks) "Short Breaks" and special offers available. Telephone for detailed brochure.

WINDERMERE

10 minutes' walk from lake or village.
Open all year. 10 fully equipped spacious
apartments sleep 2-6.
Pool, colour TV, central heating.

All Apartments have ♀ ♀ ♀ gradings –
some 'Commended' the others 'Approved'.

**For brochure contact:
Bruce and Marsha Dodsworth,
Birthwaite Edge, Birthwaite Road,
Windermere LA23 1BS
Telephone: 09662 2861**

*See self catering section –
Windermere, Cumbria.*

Come to the White House
A small licensed Guest House for Non-Smokers

Would you like the opportunity to be thoroughly
spoiled in our comfortable and attractive 17th
century converted farmhouse? Our home and
gardens are situated in a fascinating rural area
close to Ullswater and Haweswater. We can give
you the holiday you deserve – your children too
are particularly welcome. Bed and Breakfast from
£12.00, Evening Meal £8.50. Special reductions
for children. Are you tempted? To find out more,
contact *Anne and Chris Broadbent at The White House,
Clifton, Near Penrith CA10 2EL (0768 65115).*

Between Kendal and Windermere

Open All Year
6 Spacious Flats – Garden Chalet
Sleep 2-7, Central Heating,
Col.TV, 3 acres secluded grounds.

**Jonathan and Fidelia Somervell,
Crook, Kendal, Cumbria LA8 8LE
Tel: Staveley (0539) 821325**

**For full details see:
Self-Catering Section – Cumbria: Kendal**
Founder Member Cumbria & Lakeland
Self-Caterers' Association
ETB ♀ ♀ ♀ ♀ Commended.

Plumgarths Holiday Flats

HOLMHEAD FARM
♛♛♛ GUEST HOUSE   ♀ ♀ ♀

Holmhead Farm sits on the line of Hadrian's Wall and makes an ideal
base for historical Northumberland, The Lakes and Scotland. Flights
over the Wall, Slide Shows and Tours can all be arranged. The
modernised farmhouse offers bedrooms with shower/toilet and lovely
views. Residents' lounge with colour TV and tea/coffee facilities.
Guests choose from **"The Longest Breakfast Menu in the World"** and
in the evening they dine together by candle-light, dinner-party style, at
the round oak dining table. Home cooking, all freshly prepared. Diets
catered for. B&B £17.50. EM £10. Sorry, no pets. Open all year. Also
well-equipped S/C flat available, sleeps 4 (circled in picture). Approach from Greenhead Village on A69/B6318 over Ford or Private Bridge
and farm road behind the garage. M6 Exit 43. A68 exit "Stagshaw"

**Apply: Mrs Pauline Staff, Holmhead Farm Guesthouse, Hadrian's Wall, Greenhead-in-Northumberland,
Via Carlisle CA6 7HY   Telephone Gisland (0697) 747402 or (06972) 402**

BOARD

SELF-CATERING

SELF-CATERING

RADFORDS
DAWLISH

In beautiful unspoilt countryside not too far from the beach

Chosen by the independent 'Peaudouce Guide' to Hotels as the very best Hotel for Children that they visited, 1988.

FOR THE PERFECT FAMILY HOLIDAY

Come and relax at Radfords in one of our chintzy old world lounges, our comfortable bar or our six acres of lovely garden – or come and enjoy an active action-packed holiday swimming in our heated indoor pools, playing badminton outdoors or enjoying a game of table tennis or skittles or one of the many other games in our large indoor games room. Squash, indoor badminton, golf, tennis, fishing and horse riding are all available close by. We have our own solarium for that essential sun tan.

We have family bedrooms or two room family suites available, all with a private bathroom, to accommodate a total of about thirty families. All bedrooms have tea/coffee making facilities.

THE CHILDREN will love their special heated indoor pool, the outdoor playground, the freedom of our large gardens and the assorted ponies and dogs there are to talk to. In the evenings they can look forward to a swimming gala, live entertainment, a party and their own cartoon show etc. Playroom now available.

THE ADULTS can look forward to superb food lovingly cooked and served and the various entertainments we arrange for them – from skittle tournaments to live entertainers. We also have a fully equipped laundrette and an evening babysitter to help make your holiday as relaxing as possible. We have a playgroup several mornings a week. Mothers can bring babies and small children here with every confidence. Radfords has been featured on TV by Judith Chalmers and holds the Farm Holiday Guide Diploma.

MEMBER WEST COUNTRY TOURIST BOARD.
Please telephone or send for an illustrated brochure to:

Mr and Mrs T. C. Crump, MHCI
RADFORDS, DAWLISH, SOUTH DEVON EX7 0QN
(Dawlish 863322. STD 0626-863322)

BOARD

Seclusion and Peace at
THE COVE GUEST HOUSE, TORCROSS

As the pace of modern life increases so does the need for people to use available holiday periods to get away from it all. Torcross, a small seaside village and The Cove House are a combination which can serve to be one of the most relaxing holidays you have ever had. The only sound you hear will be that of the sea as it kisses the shore only 25 yards from the house. The Cove House is situated in $3\frac{1}{2}$ acres of its own coastline; there can be no better place from which to enjoy the pleasures the sea can give, whether it be fishing, swimming or just strolling along the beach. By night one can indulge in romantic gazes at starlit skies or looking at uninterrupted views of both rises of sun and moon.

Within one hour by car one can visit the following places, Dartmouth, Torquay, Paignton, Plymouth or Dartmoor.

Visitors to The Cove House can be assured of excellent food both in quality and quantity, served in the Diningroom which immediately overlooks the sea. There is an attractive licensed Bar Lounge. The Proprietors and Staff are always on hand and they care about your holiday. Accommodation is excellent. All bedrooms have TV sets installed and basins with hot and cold water. Some have private showers. There is ample free car parking in the grounds. A car is desirable but not essential. A Fire Certificate is held. Children under 8 years of age and pets are not catered for.

The Cove House is open for visitors from March 1st to November 30th offering Dinner, Bed and Breakfast. Price reductions apply during March, April, May and from mid-September to end of November.

Please send postage stamp only for free coloured brochure and tariff to:

**MR & MRS K. SMALL
THE COVE GUEST HOUSE
TORCROSS, NEAR KINGSBRIDGE
South Devon. Telephone Kingsbridge 580448 (STD 0548)**

For the widest choice of cottages in Devon...

Luxury Exmoor hideaway with jacuzzi and private indoor pool. Sleeps 5/7. From £50 per person per week.

...and the best value you'll find anywhere

Contact us now for a free copy of our guide to the 500 best value cottages around Devon's unspoilt National Trust Coast. Spring and Autumn breaks in delightful Exmoor farm cottages from only £55 to luxury beachside homes with swimming pools at over £550 p.w. in Summer. All are regularly inspected and guaranteed to offer first class value.

Free leisure guide and £75 worth of discount shopping vouchers with every booking. Cottages for sale details and free hotel accommodation also available.

North Devon Holiday Homes
**18 Boutport Street, Barnstaple EX31 1SE
Tel (0271) 76322 (24 hrs)**

West Ridge, Devon

Seaton EX12 2TA "West Ridge", Harepath Hill, Mrs E. P. Fox (Seaton [0297] 22398).

"West Ridge" bungalow stands on elevated ground above the small coastal town of Seaton. It has 1½ acres of lawns and gardens and enjoys wide panoramic views of the beautiful Axe Estuary and the sea. Close by are Axmouth, Beer and Branscombe. The Lyme Bay area is an excellent centre for touring, walking, sailing, fishing, golf etc. This comfortably furnished accommodation (including the spacious kitchen/living room on the right of the picture) is ideally suited for 3 to 5 persons. A cot can be provided. Available March to October. £95 to £275 weekly (fuel charges included). Full gas c/h; Colour TV. AA Listed and British Tourist Board Approved. ♀♀♀ Approved S.A.E. for brochure.

SMYTHEN FARM COASTAL HOLIDAY COTTAGES

Superior holiday cottages on this Devon family farm with many animals. Situated overlooking the picturesque Sterridge Valley with superb views across the sea to Wales and ships on the Bristol Channel. Central for miles of golden sands and coves and Exmoor touring; olde worlde village two miles with shops and inn. Plenty of sports in the area – surfing, fishing, golf, pony trekking. Guests may enjoy free pony rides and walks over the farm and in the woods to see the badgers. Large gardens and indoor games area. Heated swimming pool in a sun trap enclosure. One, two, three bedroom cottages to suit any size family. Modernised and regularly updated. Fully equipped. Free colour TV, cleanliness guaranteed. Special out of season rates. Member West Country Tourist Board. ETB Approved.

For brochure and terms apply to: Mrs F. M. Irwin, Smythen Farm, Sterridge Valley, Berrynarbor, Ilfracombe, Devon EX34 9TB. Combe Martin (0271) 883515.

MAELCOMBE HOUSE

A small coastal working farm nestling beneath wooded cliffs overlooking Lannacombe Bay. Beach one minute from comfortable farmhouse which is nearly the most southerly in Devon. Choice of family, double or single rooms. Excellent food, much being produced on farm; freshly caught seafood is a speciality. Activities include fishing, tennis (new hard court), bathing, spectacular walking, exploring, climbing or just relaxing in the gardens. Prices from £79.50 per week for Bed & Breakfast or £123.50 for Bed, Breakfast & Evening Meal, with special reductions for children. Also self-catering flat to sleep 6; limited camping facilities are provided. Telephone or write for colour brochure.

Mr and Mrs C. M. Davies, Maelcombe House, East Prawle, Near Kingsbridge, Devon TQ7 2DA. (Chivelstone [054-851] 300).

COTMORE FARM

Chillington, Near Kingsbridge, Devon TQ7 2LR
Felicity Moody: (0548) 580374

OPEN ALL YEAR. Delightful period farmhouse in 15 acres. South-facing. Magnificent unbroken views across South Devon countryside to the sea. Spectacular coastal and country walks. Sandy coves. Sailing, fishing, diving, windsurfing, riding, golf, birdwatching and other recreations readily available. Comfortable guests' sittingroom and sun lounge. Well appointed bedrooms with washbasins and tea-making facilities. Family suite with private bathroom. Excellent home cooking. Friendly atmosphere. Ample parking for cars and boats. Pets welcome. Bed and Breakfast from £80 per week. Evening Meals optional. Reductions for children. For the perfect break send for a brochure. Tourist Board Listed. Also self-catering cottage available.

BEADON FARMHOUSE

Beadon Road, Salcombe TQ8 8LX
Telephone: 054 884 3020

This Victorian farmhouse set in 3½ acres is in a quiet position overlooking a peaceful valley. Situated on the outskirts of a boating/fishing town with a mild climate, it is ideal for early or late holidays. Coastal path, beaches and beautiful walks within easy reach.

3 bedrooms – one double en suite, and 2 twin bedded, with washbasins. Separate tables in dining room. Tea and coffee always available and often homemade cakes. Sitting room with colour TV. Central heating. Cot and highchair if required. Children's Evening Meals and babysitting by arrangement. Ample parking. Terms from £12 per night or £80 per week per person.

Adjoining self-contained flat – see self catering section for details.

Torcross Apartment Hotel

At the water's edge on Slapton Sands overlooking the blue waters of Start Bay

Family self-catering in our Luxury Apartment Hotel. Ranging in size from our ground floor Beachside apartments for two, to our really spacious Family apartments. Superb sea views. Family owned and supervised ensuring a high standard of cleanliness. Village Inn and Waterside Family Restaurant with an extensive Menu including fresh local fish and a 'Sunday Carvery'. Light entertainment some evenings. Baby listening. Games room. Launderette/drying/ironing room. Bargain breaks. Central heating. Car Park. Colour brochure with pleasure.

Torcross Apartment Hotel, Torcross,
near Kingsbridge, South Devon
Telephone: (0548) 580206

Northcote Farm Cottages

Surrounded by natural gardens, woodlands and streams, three charming character cottages set together with 17th century farmhouse around delightful courtyard. One a traditional Devon farm cottage; 2 beds, sleeps 4. Also two tastefully converted stone barns, both sleep 5. 2/3 beds respectively. Sorry, no pets in these two. All equipped to a very high standard, each with colour TV, electric cooker, fridge, etc. Cot and high chair available. Ample car parking. Central for touring. Exmoor National Park 2 miles. Sandy beaches, lovely walks, riding, fishing and golf, all only minutes away.

For details contact Mrs D. Heath & Family, Northcote Farm, Patchole, Kentisbury, Barnstaple, Devon EX31 4NB or phone (Combe Martin) 0271 882376

Buckland Court, Slapton

ETB 🌸🌸🌸🌸

Set in nine acres of beautiful South Hams countryside, with ponds and stream, seven luxury cottages created from 17th century barns and arranged around the courtyard of an old South Devon farm. Situated two miles from Slapton Sands and close to Dartmouth, Dartmoor and Salcombe, the opportunities for all types of outdoor pursuits are endless. The cottages carry the English Tourist Board's highest grade for self-catering accommodation. Central heating. Colour TV, telephone and laundry rooms. Linen, cots and high chairs by arrangement. Pets welcome. For colour brochure please write or phone:

Mrs Sarah Hanmer, Buckland Court, Slapton, Near Kingsbridge, South Devon TQ7 2RE.
Telephone 054 852 366.

**Raddicombe Lodge
South Devon**

Set in peaceful surroundings overlooking sea and country, midway between the picturesque harbour towns of Brixham and Dartmouth. The Lodge has a charm and character of its own, with pitched ceilings and lattice windows. Scrumptious traditional English Breakfast, well appointed bedrooms with tea making facilities and colour TV; en suite rooms available. AA & RAC listed. – Les Routiers recommended. English Tourist Board 2 Crowns. Offering room and breakfast only. For prices see our classified entry.

Phone or write to Graham and Yvonne Glass, Raddicombe Lodge, 102 Kingswear Road, Brixham, Devon TQ5 0EX. Tel: 0803 882125.

MANOR FARM HOLIDAY CENTRE
CHARMOUTH, BRIDPORT, DORSET

WCTB   *ETB*

Situated in rural valley of outstanding natural beauty, Manor Farm has all the requisite amenities for an exciting yet carefree holiday. Shop, launderette, licensed bar with family room, swimming pool and children's pool, play area. Ten minutes' level walk to beach, safe for bathing and famous for its fossils. Golf, riding, tennis, fishing and boating all nearby. Accommodation in 3 bedroomed bungalow, 2 and 3 bedroomed houses, and luxury caravans. All units sleep six, and are equipped with colour TV, fitted carpets and parking/garage.

**SAE to Mr. R. B. Loosmore
or Telephone 0297-60226**

COTSWOLDS

Mrs A. E. Hughes, Ham Hill Farm,
Whittington, Cheltenham, Gloucestershire
Telephone 0242 584415

This 160-acre farm has a new farmhouse built in 1983 in true traditional Cotswold style, with beautiful views of the Cotswolds and only about two miles from the town of Cheltenham. All visitors will be made welcome and everything will be done to make their stay enjoyable. Leisure activities nearby – riding, golf, walking (Cotswold Way). Rooms available, one family, one single, one double and two twins, all with washbasins, TV, Teasmades. Three en-suite rooms, bathroom, two toilets; sittingroom and diningroom. Central heating. Open all year round. Children over seven years welcome. Bed and Breakfast from £12.50. Brochures available. **No smoking.**

HOLIDAY IN OUR ENGLISH COUNTRY GARDEN

2 ACRES IN RURAL NORFOLK WITH RIVER NEARBY.

10 select and spacious family-run bungalows and lovely country farmhouse. Peacefully set in 2 acres of delightful gardens with Games room, Heated pool, Children's play area. Fishing, Boating, Riding and Golf nearby. Only 50 yards from river staithe with access to Broads and well situated for touring. Car essential.

HEDERA HOUSE & Plantation Bungalows

For full details & colour brochure contact:
H. G. Delt, Thurne Cottage,
The Staithe, Thurne, Norfolk
NR29 3BU. Tel. (0692) 670242
or (0493) 844568.

NORFOLK

GARDEN HOUSE HOTEL
Salhouse Road, Rackheath, Near Norwich, Norfolk NR13 6AA
Telephone: 0603 720007

Superb food, comfortable accommodation, relaxed, informal atmosphere and lovely surroundings – the Garden House recipe for a really enjoyable holiday.

Ideally situated for Norwich City, the Norfolk Broads and Coast. With adequate parking, the hotel boasts a restaurant renowned in the area for its classical English cooking, specialising in beautifully prepared, fresh local vegetables, and game and shell fish when in season. All rooms have telephones, colour TV, and beverage making facilities and are mostly en suite. There is a large lounge with bar and two diningrooms, one of which overlooks our lovely garden. Details on request.

ETB LISTED AA LISTED FIRE CERTIFICATE

TOR FARM – near Cheddar

Working Farm. Set in 33 acres this working mixed farm is situated on the Somerset Levels. Ideal base for exploring Cheddar Gorge/caves; Roman Bath; Wells and mystic Glastonbury; beach 20 minutes. The farmhouse offers one family room, 2 twin rooms, and 5 double rooms. Some en-suite. Lounge with colour TV; separate dining room. Fully centrally heated with log fires on colder evenings. Open views from every window. Large lawn and ample car parking. Private fishing. Children welcome. Tea/Coffee on arrival as well as hot beverages at bedtime. Sorry no pets in house. B&B from £10-£16. Evening Meal (bookable) using home produced meat and vegetables. Weekly reductions.

Mrs C. Ladd, Tor Farm, Nyland, Cheddar, Somerset BS27 3UD.
Cheddar (0934) 743710.

WITHY GROVE FARM HOLIDAYS

HEATED SWIMMING POOL LICENSED

A warm welcome awaits you at Withy Grove Farm which is a working farm adjoining River Huntspill, famous for its coarse fishing and central for touring Somerset's beauty spots. We can offer accommodation in six self-catering Bungalows and a large Barn Flat which are fully furnished and equipped and sleep 5/6 or Bed, Breakfast and Evening Dinner in the farmhouse where generous helpings of traditional home-cooking are served with cream desserts a speciality. Guests can enjoy themselves in the outdoor heated swimming pool, licensed bar, games room or badminton court or just enjoy the friendly and relaxed atmosphere. Off peak short breaks welcome.

Please write or phone Mrs Wendy Baker, Withy Grove Farm, East Huntspill,
Nr. Burnham-on-Sea, Somerset TA9 3NP. (0278 784471).

EMMETTS GRANGE

Listed Farmhouse and Self Catering Cottages in the heart of Exmoor National Park

ETB ♛♛♛ Commended
AA Listed

* Large hill stock farm – 1,200 acres
* Near to North Devon and Somerset Coast
* En-suite Bedrooms with Colour TV
* Table Licence
* Beautiful Moorland and Coastal Walks
* Marvellous Riding and Trekking Country
* Local River, Reservoir and Sea Fishing
* Stabling available
* Farmhouse open March to October. Self-catering Cottages March to November.

THE FARMHOUSE is in a quiet situation with lovely views. Comfortably furnished. Centrally heated. Attractive sittingroom with log fire. We are renowned for our delicious country cooked food which is all home-made. Four-course Dinners and large English Breakfasts. Tea and coffee making facilities. Well behaved dogs welcome.

ETB APPROVED 2/3 KEYS SELF-CATERING COTTAGES. Two cottages, one bungalow and one flat sleeping 4-8. All centrally heated. Colour TV. Micro-ovens. Dinners are available in farmhouse when open. Apply for detailed brochure, stating which property required.

Mrs F. H. Brown, Emmetts Grange, Simonsbath, Minehead, Somerset TA24 7LD.
Tel: Exford (064-383) 282.

BATCH FARM

COUNTRY HOTEL
LYMPSHAM,
Nr. WESTON-SUPER-MARE
SOMERSET

Telephone: Weston-Super-Mare (0934) 750371

Fully Licensed Bar   AA**RAC**
Egon Ronay Recommended
W.S.M. Hotels and Restaurants
Merit Award
Ashley Courtenay Recommended

A charming spot in a lovely part of England

There is an air of old world charm that still pervades Batch Farm Hotel lending atmosphere to the modern accommodation. Situated midway between the resorts of Weston and Burnham-on-Sea, three miles to sea and sands. Ideal centre for touring. Easy reach of Cheddar Gorge, Wells, Longleat, Bristol and Bath. Hotel surrounded by spacious lawns away from busy main roads and traffic yet only five to ten minutes by car to local resorts. Acres of land for children to play games in safety. Guests have freedom of the farm. Fishing in River Axe in grounds. Riding school, swimming, tennis, golf, available locally.

Guests welcome all year, except Christmas. 10 bedrooms, family, doubles, singles, all with tea/coffee facilities, colour TV, vanity units with H&C, shaver sockets and bathrooms en suite. All bedrooms have panoramic views of countryside and hills. Fully licensed lounge bar, also three lounges, one with colour TV and large diningroom with separate tables.

Traditional home cooking with variation of menus. Home reared beef and local produce used when available. Personal attention by Resident Proprietors and their family combined with their staff whose ambition is to make your holiday a happy one. Visa, Access, American Express, Diners Club Cards accepted.

Colour brochure and terms on request.

Mr and Mrs D. J. Brown, Batch Farm Country Hotel, Lympsham, Nr. Weston-Super-Mare, Somerset   Phone Weston-Super-Mare [0934] 750371.

WOODLANDS HOTEL

Woodlands Hotel, a beautiful old house, brick built and ivy clad, has been converted to a hotel which offers every modern comfort yet loses none of its country house atmosphere. Set in its own wooded grounds, it looks out across open country to the Quantock Hills. Secluded gardens provide delightful sun traps. Most bedrooms with private shower and toilet. Real home cooking. Horse riding arranged. Cocktail bar. Heated swimming pool. Free holidays to those organising parties. Also bargain breaks and special hunting weekends. Livery arranged. Terms on application.

Mr and Mrs Gibson, Woodlands Hotel, Hill Lane, Brent knoll, Somerset TA9 4DF
(Brent Knoll [0278] 760232).

Rossmoor Park

Rossmoor Park is a lovely new farmhouse standing in large gardens amidst 30 acres green fields and woodlands, 10 miles from York. Accommodation is offered to guests in three luxury en-suite rooms with colour TV, central heating and tea/coffee facilities. There are separate tables in the diningroom which overlooks gardens, park and woodland. Children welcome and there is swimming, riding, fishing available locally. Lovely walks on the farm and lots of wildlife. Easy reach Yorkshire coast, moors, wolds and dales. Open all year except Christmas. Bed & Breakfast from £15 per person with reductions for children.

Mrs Brenda Lazenby, Rossmoor Park, Melbourne, York YO4 4SZ
Telephone: 0759 318410

Spring Time

**4½ miles from the City . . .
alongside the River Ouse . . .
and right at the heart of
YORKSHIRE – and quiet,
homely and spacious
that's . . .**

THE MANOR
COUNTRY GUEST HOUSE

**ACASTER MALBIS,
YORK YO2 1UL**

Telephone (9 am to 9 pm): York (0904) 706723
(To speak to a guest at The Manor dial 0904 707534)

Peacefully and restfully situated in the countryside amidst 6 acres of delightful grounds and woodland, THE MANOR is away from all main roads; but York is only 12 minutes or so away by car or local bus. Easily reached from York or from the A64 (Leeds – Tadcaster section) via Tadcaster, Copmanthorpe or Bishopthorpe; and from the A64 (York) Ring Road via either Copmanthorpe or Sim Balk Lane and Bishopthorpe.

Part of the Garden

Join us if you like it really quiet!

Chapel in the Wood

TV lounge with open coal fire. Carport and large car park. 12 bedrooms, some en-suite and all with tea/coffee making facilities. One ground floor room suitable for the disabled. Stairlifts to both floors. Open all year except Christmas. Unlicensed.

For details send SAE or telephone Mrs C.P. Dale.

Enquiries from overseas send four International Reply Coupons.

TYGLYN HOLIDAY ESTATE (Dept. FHG)
CILIAU AERON, NEAR LAMPETER, DYFED SA48 8DD
Telephone: Aeron (0570) 470684

SELF-CATERING

Tyglyn Holiday Estate nestles in the heart of rural Wales and yet is only 4 miles from the pretty little seaside town of Aberaeron.

From your holiday bungalow the views up and down the Aeron Valley are awe inspiring. Beautiful rolling hills rise from the valley through which the River Aeron flows. It passes through the estate for almost a mile and its outfall is at Aberaeron where day or fishing trips can be taken.

The bungalows take pride of place overlooking most of the 110 acre farm and in sight of some of the woodland.

Buzzards nest on the farm, Ravens are regular visitors, Dippers can be seen on the river, Kestrels and the rare Red Kite can be seen in the air. We have Badgers and Foxes breeding on the estate and Otters have been seen in the river; there are rare butterflies and an abundance of wild flowers.

Riding can be arranged locally, bowling, tennis, golf and swimming can all be found within a few miles.

While at Tyglyn your accommodation will be provided by one of only 20 award-winning brick built semi-detached two bedroom bungalows which include all modern facilities and colour TV. Your pets are welcomed as warmly as you.

For further details contact Nigel Edkins for a free colour brochure on Aeron (0570) 470684.

4/6 Berth
£100-£200

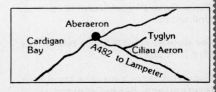

SOLVA ♣♣♣

Lochmeyler is a 220-acre dairy farm situated in centre of St. David's Peninsula, 2½ miles from coastal path, 4 miles from Solva Harbour, 6 miles from St. David's – Grid Number FM855 275. The 11th century farmhouse has been modernised but still retains its olde worlde character with beams, and open fires in early and late season. There are five en-suite bedrooms with colour TV, video – video library available. Tea-making facilities, electric blankets, clock radios, hairdryers and telephones. Some rooms have four-poster beds. Two lounges (one for smokers). Spacious dining room with separate tables. Children 10 years and over welcome. Choice of menu. Dinner served 7pm. Traditional farmhouse fare, and vegetarians can be catered for. Plenty of wildlife with farm trails, pond and streams. Open all year round. Brochure from Mrs M. Jones, Lochmeyler Farm, Pen-y-Cwm, Near Solva, Haverfordwest, Pembrokeshire SA62 6LL. Telephone (0348) 837724 or (0348) 837705.

SOLVA – Upper Vanley Farm

Welsh Tourist Board ♣♣♣.   AA Listed and RAC Acclaimed.
Enjoy an informal and relaxed holiday in a happy atmosphere at our comfortable old farmhouse surrounded by a working farm, fields and hedgerows full of wild flowers. Close to spectacular coastline with safe sandy beaches, coastal path, castles, lovely Solva harbour and St David's. Our traditional Breakfasts and Evening Meals are farmhouse cooked and freshly prepared. Sunny diningroom and cosy, quiet lounge with log fire. Plenty for the children – large garden and play room. Some small farm pets. All the homely bedrooms have private bathroom, colour TV and teamaking facilities. Run by a young family, we welcome children and quiet pets. Bed and breakfast from £13.50. Weekly rates. Reductions for children sharing. Licensed.

Kevin and Carol Shales
Upper Vanley Farmhouse, Pen-y-Cwm, Near Solva
Pembrokeshire SA62 6LJ   Tel: 0348 831418

· MYDROILYN ·

Stone farm buildings, newly converted into 4 cottages, providing modern standard of comfort in traditional setting. Sleep 2/3 (terms £70-£160) or 4/8 (terms £110-£280). Gas, electricity, linen included. All have shower room; fully equipped kitchen; colour TV available; laundry room; facilities for children. Secluded rural area, abundant with wildlife and flowers; 5 miles from sandy beaches, picturesque harbours of Cardigan Bay. National Trust coastal paths; breathtaking mountain scenery; birdwatching, fishing, pony trekking nearby.

WTB and AA Approved.   Open Easter to October.
Gil & Mike Kearney, Blaenllanarth Holiday Cottages, Mydroilyn, Lampeter, Dyfed SA48 7RJ. Telephone: Lampeter (0570) 470374.

CHAPEL FARM

Guests are assured of a warm welcome when they visit this 15th century, renovated farmhouse and many return each year. The house has oak beams in lounge and family room and there is an Inglenook fireplace. Hot and cold showers. Panoramic views overlooking local towns and villages. Lovely walks. Good base for touring Big Pit Blonovan, Bryn-Bach Park, Brecon Beacons, Abergavenny. Pony trekking within easy distance. Only four miles from the 1992 Garden Festival site. Packed lunches available. Evening meal on request. There is a drinks licence but no bar, though there is an unusual drinks cupboard. Full details from Malcolm & Betty Hancocks, Chapel Farm, Blaina, Gwent NP3 3DJ. Telephone (0495) 290888.

BOARD

Treat yourself to a relaxing break amongst gloriously peaceful surroundings at our country house. All bedrooms en-suite with coffee/tea-making facilities, separate tables in diningroom, comfortable lounge with separate TV room. Central heating. We pride ourselves on our reputation for good, wholesome cooking using local produce. Ideal rambling/birdwatching centre. Golf, swimming pool, beach two miles. Children under 12, free accommodation if sharing. Special rates OAP's out of season. Tourist Board ♥♥♥. AA Listed. Brochure sent with pleasure. Proprietor. Mrs G. J. Williams.

GWRACH YNYS
Country Guest House, Ynys, Talsarnau, Gwynedd LL47 6TS. Tel: (0766) 780 742.

BOARD

TYDDYN DU FARM
Gellilydan, Near Blaenau Ffestiniog LL41 4RB
Telephone: 0766 85281

Relax in the comfortable, homely Welsh atmosphere of our delightful 16th century historic farmhouse. Situated in the heart of Snowdonia National Park – ideal for exploring the whole of North Wales. Easy to find, just 300 yards off the A470. Inglenook fireplace and a wealth of beams and exposed stonework throughout. Private family unit and some en suite rooms, all with tea/coffee/hot chocolate facilities and TV. Non-smoking areas in farmhouse. Good wholesome food with home made soups, buns, etc. Pets area with rabbits, ducks, bottle-fed lambs and goats, free pony rides. Conservation walk on farm. Within easy reach of many tourist attractions, beaches and walks. Bed and Breakfast from £12. Dinner, Bed and Breakfast from £126 weekly. Dinner from £6. Reduced rates for children. *Telephone or SAE please, for brochure to Mrs Paula Williams.*

BOARD

GORWEL DEG
Gorwel Deg farmhouse, cleverly converted from farm buildings, provides super accommo-dation. A working farm with a Welsh-speaking family, situated in a rural position in the heart of the Snowdonia National Park in a wealth of unspoilt beauty overlooking Cardigan Bay. The popular golden sands of Harlech and shells of Shell Island beaches are within easy reach. Convenient for golf, fishing, walking etc. An ideal spot for countryside tranquillity and peace. Provides good farmhouse cooking, and guest accommodation in one family, one double and one bunk room. Colour TV. Lounge. Evening Meal optional. Children under ten reduced rates. From £10.50 per person per night.

Mrs E.L.L. Williams, Gorwel Deg, Hen Dy Farm, Llanbedr LL45 2LT (Llanbedr [034 123] 263)

BOARD

VICTORIA WELLS
FOREST CABIN HOLIDAY MOTEL · POWYS
Arguably as like the Canadian Rockies as you'll find in this country
BARGAIN BREAKS – 3 DAYS £55
which includes accommodation, full English breakfast and evening meal
WEEKLY TARIFF ALSO AVAILABLE

High in the verdant mountains of Central Wales, situated in 24 acres of woodlands and with miles of natural parkland and riverside walks Victoria Wells is the ideal holiday location for those who want to unwind and shed the tensions of modern living. ● Three-quarters of a mile of private fishing ● Heated swimming pool ● Restaurant and bar ● Horse riding and pony trekking centres nearby. All accommodation with en-suite, colour TV and tea-making facilities. Children and pets welcome.

BOOK BY PHONE ON CARDIFF 0222 340558
Victoria Wells Booking Office, Grosvenor House, 20 St. Andrews Crescent, Cardiff CF1 3DD. Fax: 0222 223692

Farm Holiday Guide

ENGLAND, WALES & IRELAND
AND THE CHANNEL ISLANDS

1991

The Farm Holiday Guide to
HOLIDAYS
IN
ENGLAND, WALES & IRELAND
AND THE CHANNEL ISLANDS

Farms, guest houses and country hotels.
Cottages, flats and chalets.
Caravans and camping.
Activity Holidays.

FHG Publications 1991

Farm Holiday Guide to Holidays in England, Wales, Ireland and the Channel Islands
Farm Holiday Guide to Holidays in Scotland
Britain's Best Holidays — A Quick Reference Guide
FHG Self-Catering & Furnished Holidays
Guide to Caravan & Camping Holidays
Bed & Breakfast Stops

ISBN 1 85055 123 5 © FHG Publications Ltd. 1991
Cover photograph: Farm Harvesting supplied by Visionbank.
Design by Edward Carden (Glasgow).

Typeset by R.D. Composition Ltd., Glasgow.
Printed and bound by Benham's Ltd., Colchester.

Distribution – **Book Trade**: Moorland Publishing, Moor Farm Road, Ashbourne, Derbyshire DE6 1HD
(Tel: 0335 44486. Fax: 0335 46397).
News Trade: UMD, 1 Benwell Road, Holloway, London N7 7AX (Tel: 071-700 4600. Fax: 071-607 3352).

Published by FHG Publications Ltd.,
Abbey Mill Business Centre, Seedhill, Paisley PA1 1JN   (041-887 0428).
A member of the U.N. Group.

———

US ISBN 1-55650-285-0
Distributed in the United States by
Hunter Publishing Inc., 300 Raritan Center Parkway CN94,
Edison, N.J., 08818, USA

FOREWORD

The Farm Holiday Guide to
Holidays in
ENGLAND, WALES
IRELAND & THE CHANNEL ISLANDS 1991

Choosing a holiday is never easy. *Farm Holiday Guide* will help solve some of your problems with our large range of illustrated and well-described entries of all sorts of holiday opportunities throughout the country. Why not phone and have a talk with one or two different proprietors before deciding. Ask questions about any special facilities or other points not mentioned in the description which are important to you.

We cannot help you with your final choice but we suggest that you bear the following in mind.

ENQUIRIES AND BOOKINGS. Give full details of dates (with an alternative), numbers and any special requirements. Ask about any points in the holiday description which are not clear and make sure that prices and conditions are clearly explained. You should receive confirmation in writing and a receipt for any deposit or advance payment. If you book your holiday well in advance, especially self-catering, confirm your arrival details nearer the time. Some proprietors, especially for self-catering, request full payment in advance but a reasonable deposit is more normal.

CANCELLATIONS. A holiday booking is a form of contract with obligations on both sides. If you have to cancel, give as much notice as possible. The longer the notice the better the chance that your host can replace your booking and therefore refund any payments. If the proprietor cancels in such a way that causes serious inconvenience, he may have obligations to you which have not been properly honoured. Take advice if necessary from such organisations as the Citizen's Advice Bureau, Consumer's Association, Trading Standards Office, Local Tourist Office, etc., or your own solicitor.

COMPLAINTS. It's best if any problems can be sorted out at the start of your holiday. If the problem is not solved, you can contact the organisations mentioned above. You can also write to us. We will follow up the complaint with the advertiser – but we cannot act as intermediaries or accept responsibility for holiday arrangements.

FHG Publications Ltd. do not inspect accommodation and an entry in our guides does not imply a recommendation. However our advertisers have signed their agreement to work for the holiday-maker's best interests and as their customer, you have the right to expect appropriate attention and service.

HOLIDAY INSURANCE. It is possible to insure against holiday cancellation. Brokers and insurance companies can advise you about this.

We hope that *Farm Holiday Guide 1991* will bring you many happy holidays. Don't forget our **Farm Holiday Guide Diploma.** Every year we award a small number of Diplomas to holiday proprietors who have been specially recommended to us by readers. Your hosts will appreciate your recommendation and we are always pleased to hear from you.

On page 87 you'll see a list of the **Farm Holiday Guide Diploma** winners for 1990. We'd welcome your suggestions for 1991!

We would also appreciate your mentioning *Farm Holiday Guide* whenever you make an enquiry or booking.

Peter Clark
Publishing Director

CONTENTS

ENGLAND

ENGLAND

CONTENTS

WALES

IRELAND

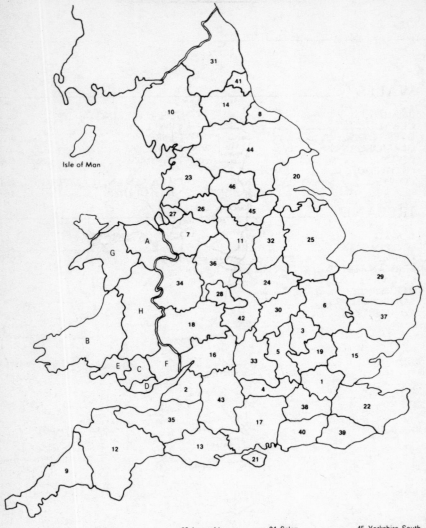

ENGLAND & WALES COUNTIES

Isle of Man

1 London	12 Devon	23 Lancashire	34 Salop	45 Yorkshire, South
2 Avon	13 Dorset	24 Leicestershire	35 Somerset	46 Yorkshire, West
3 Bedfordshire	14 Durham	25 Lincolnshire	36 Staffordshire	
4 Berkshire	15 Essex	26 Manchester, Greater	37 Suffolk	A Clwyd
5 Buckinghamshire	16 Gloucestershire	27 Merseyside	38 Surrey	B Dyfed
6 Cambridgeshire	17 Hampshire	28 Midlands, West	39 Sussex, East	C Glamorgan, Mid
7 Cheshire	18 Hereford & Worcester	29 Norfolk	40 Sussex, West	D Glamorgan, South
8 Cleveland	19 Hertfordshire	30 Northamptonshire	41 Tyne & Wear	E Glamorgan, West
9 Cornwall	20 Humberside	31 Northumberland	42 Warwickshire	F Gwent
10 Cumbria	21 Isle of Wight	32 Nottinghamshire	43 Wiltshire	G Gwynedd
11 Derbyshire	22 Kent	33 Oxfordshire	44 Yorkshire, North	H Powys

ENGLAND & WALES
TOWNS AND MAIN ROADS

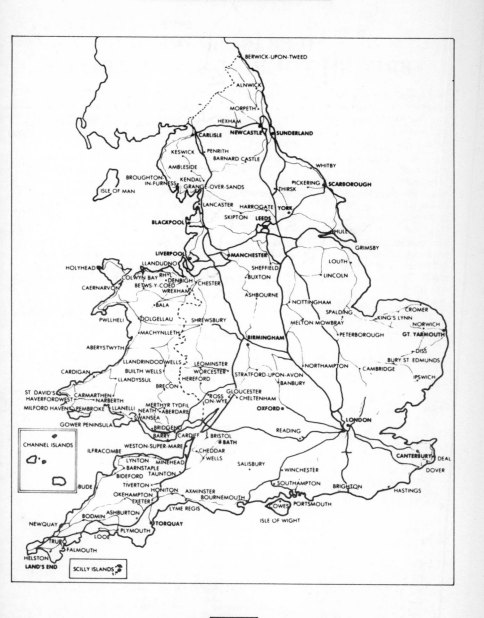

THE FHG DIPLOMA

HELP IMPROVE
BRITISH TOURIST STANDARDS

You are choosing holiday accommodation from our very popular FHG Publications. Whether it be a hotel, guest house, farmhouse or self-catering accommodation, we think you will find it hospitable, comfortable and clean, and your host and hostess friendly and helpful.

Why not write and tell us about it?

As a recognition of the generally well-run and excellent holiday accommodation reviewed in our publications, we at FHG Publications Ltd. present a diploma to proprietors who receive the highest recommendation from their guests who are also readers of our Guides. If you care to write to us praising the holiday you have booked through FHG Publications Ltd. – whether this be board, self-catering accommodation, a sporting or a caravan holiday, what you say will be evaluated and the proprietors who reach our final list will be contacted.

The winning proprietor will receive an attractive framed diploma to display on his premises as recognition of a high standard of comfort, amenity and hospitality. FHG Publications Ltd. offer this diploma as a contribution towards the improvement of standards in tourist accommodation in Britain. Help your excellent host or hostess to win it!

FHG DIPLOMA

We nominate ....

....

Because

Name ....

Address ....

.... Telephone No. ....

LONDON

LONDON. Queens Mansions, 33 Anson Road, Tufnell Park N7 0RB (071-607 4725/7277). Large double fronted Victorian house standing in own grounds. Quiet, residential area. Tree lined, close to Hampstead Heath and Highgate Village, very convenient for public transport into City and West End. 36 rooms most with private facilities. Radio, TV and tea making facilities in rooms. 24 hour reception. Our rates start from £14 to £20 single and £24 to £30 double. Family rooms arranged on contact. These prices include English Breakfast and VAT. Parking space available outside the Hotel. The house has full central heating. Special rates for low season.

LONDON. Mr Marios Stavrou, 129 Sussex Gardens, Hyde Park W2 2RX (071-262 2262/3). Victorian building in central London, close to shops, tubes, buses, etc. Near Hyde Park and Bayswater. The Hotel has 21 bedrooms (singles, doubles, twins and family) all with private facilities, TV, radio and telephone. Centrally heated. Free tea/coffee making facilities. Singles from £20 to £32, doubles from £30 to £42, family rooms arranged on contact. Reception open 24 hours. Off the road parking. English Breakfast included. Family run business. Madame Tussaud's and many theatres nearby.

AVON

BATH. Mr and Mrs John and Daphne Paz, Dornden Guest House, Church Lane, Old Sodbury, Near Bristol BS17 6NB (Chipping Sodbury [0454] 313325). A lovely Cotswold stone house beautifully situated. We have nine bedrooms, five of which are en-suite, all with washbasins and razor points; all have colour TV. Comfortable lounge with colour TV. We serve English breakfast and home cooked dinner using free range eggs and produce in season from our well stocked vegetable garden. Children are welcome — cot and high chair available if needed. Reduction for children sharing parents' room and also for four-day stays. Please write or phone for brochure.

BATH. Mrs T.C. Shellard, Manor Cottage, Combe Hay, Bath BA2 7EG (Combe Down [0225] 837437). Combe Hay is a small quiet picturesque village, four and a half miles south of Bath off the A367 Exeter road. An ideal centre from which to tour Somerset, Gloucester or Wiltshire and several National Trust properties. Highly recommended. Manor Cottage is a small Georgian farmhouse accommodating four to six persons. Full English Breakfast. Tea-making facilities. Car essential. Ample parking. No pets in the house. Open Easter to September. ENGLISH COUNTRYSIDE AND HOSPITALITY AT ITS BEST. The 17th-century Wheatsheaf Inn in the village serves excellent lunches and evening meals. Horse riding and trekking available.

BATH. Geoff and Avril Kitching, Wentworth House Hotel, 106 Bloomfield Road, Bath BA2 2AP (0225 339193). ♛♛♛ *Commended*. AA Listed; RAC acclaimed. Traditional Bed and Breakfast in comfortable imposing Victorian house, set in large gardens within walking distance of the Roman Baths and Abbey. Large car park. Outdoor swimming pool which is open in the summer. There are 20 comfortable bedrooms, some with private bath or shower. All rooms have tea/coffee making facilities and telephones. Excellent base for touring. Licensed. Double or twin rooms £17 to £24 per person per night including Full English Breakfast.

BATH near. Mrs B.M. Martin, The Old Inn Guest House, Farmborough, Near Bath BA3 1BY (Timsbury [0761] 70250). The Old Inn Guest House is very attractive, built 1684, and was at one time a Coaching Inn, but extensively modernised to offer every comfort, though retaining its charm and character. It stands on the side of a hill overlooking the valley on the edge of Farmborough Village. Attractive landscaped garden. It is highly recommended and maintains a high standard of home cooked food; a family atmosphere, with personal attention. All bedrooms (doubles, twins, and family size) have washbasins. Lounge with TV. Ample parking space. Very central for touring Bath, Wells, Cheddar, Wookey Hole, Longleat, Chew Lake, Wye Valley. Open all the year. Evening Meal, Bed and full English Breakfast. Fire Certificate held. SAE or telephone for terms.

BATH near. Mrs Pam Wilmott, Pool Farm, Wick, Bristol BS15 5RL (Abson [027 582] 2284). Working farm, join in. May we welcome you to our 350 year old farmhouse, a listed building on a working dairy farm. We are on the A420, only six miles from Bath, nine miles from Bristol, and a few miles from exit 18 on the M4. This makes us an ideal touring centre for these cities and places of interest such as the Cotswolds, Wells, Badminton, etc. Nearby is a shop with newspapers, local pub with good food, Golf and Country Club with squash, tennis, croquet and open air pool. TV lounge, central heating. Parking. Open all year except Christmas. Terms for Bed and Breakfast on request.

BRISTOL near. Mrs Delia Edwards, Brinsea Green Farm, Brinsea Lane, Congresbury, Near Bristol BS19 5JN (Churchill [0934] 852278).

Comfortable 18th century farmhouse on a 360 acre dairy and sheep farm, situated one-and-a-half miles from village with views of the Mendip Hills. The farmhouse is located at the end of a quiet country lane surrounded by open fields. Easy access from M5 (approximately 12-15 minutes, Exit 21), and centrally situated between Bath, Bristol, Weston-super-Mare, Wells, Cheddar Caves and Blagdon Lake (fishing). The village has nine inns, many serving food. Bed, Breakfast with home-made marmalade and jams, offered to guests all year round. In keeping with their character, both the sittingroom and diningroom in the farmhouse have inglenook fireplaces. Three double bedrooms, with hot drinks facilities, two with vanity units. Bathroom, plus shower, toilet. Central heating. Children welcome at reduced rates. Cot and babysitting. Car essential — ample parking. Tourist Board Registered. Also self-contained luxury flats in barn conversion sleeping 4-6.

BRISTOL near. Mrs Colin Smart, Leigh Farm, Pensford, Near Bristol BSI8 4BA (Compton Dando [0761] 490281). 🐄 Working farm.

Off A37 Bristol/Shepton Wells road. Leigh Farm is a beef and sheep farm enjoying all the advantages of COUNTRY life, yet close to many tourist attractions such as Bath, Bristol, Cheddar, Wells and Glastonbury and the famous Stanton Drew Stone Circles. Access to the bedrooms at all times. Breakfasts are served in the farmhouse kitchen complete with its pine dresser and guests are made to feel at home in their own lounge where log fires burn during cold evenings. Large lawns surround the farmhouse and visitors can relax and enjoy the view and the peaceful surroundings. One double, one single and one family rooms all with washbasins and some additional bedrooms with private shower room; bathroom, toilet. Car essential, parking. Rainbow trout fishery within 25 yards of farmhouse; chill and freezing facilities.

CHIPPING SODBURY near. Mrs J. Pye, Elmlea, King Lane, Horton, Near Chipping Sodbury BS17 6PF (Chipping Sodbury [0454] 312295).

Secluded detached bungalow in one acre garden with scenic views over unspoilt countryside. Beautiful spot for walking and birdwatching. Ideal for touring Cotswolds. Easy reach Bristol and Bath. Three miles from Chipping Sodbury where there is a choice of pubs. Elmlea offers one double room and one twin bedroom with tea/coffee making equipment (tea/coffee supplied). Comfortable lounge/diner with log stove for chilly evenings. Bathroom, toilet. All tastefully furnished. A warm welcome and personal service. April to mid-October. Car essential. Ample parking. Sorry, no children or pets. Bed and Breakfast from £12.50, Evening Meal available if ordered. Weekly bookings welcome.

LANGFORD. Mrs I.M. Griffin, Stoneycroft House, Langford, Stock Lane, Bristol BS18 7EX (Churchill [0934] 852624).

Stoneycroft House is a small country house situated deep in the Wrington Valley. Most rooms have en-suite bathrooms; exceptional family room with four-poster on request. Log fires ensure a cosy atmosphere for guests, either stopping off en-route to the Cornish Riviera or staying to enjoy the many local attractions. Explore Cheddar Gorge, Wookey Hole, Wells Cathedral, the cities of Bath and Bristol, or just enjoy walking in the quiet English countryside. A short car ride brings skiing, horse riding, fly fishing, shooting, golf, tennis, bowls etc within easy reach. Guests are made welcome all year round.

WESTON-SUPER-MARE. Valerie and Keith Brandon-Wilson, The Orchards, Hewish, Weston-super-Mare BS24 6RQ (0934 876178). A 200-year-old character residence with 12 acres and easy access M5 Junction 21. Ideal touring spot and short drive to the beach. Full Enlgish Breakfast with free range eggs. Guests' lounge with inglenook, beams and colour TV. Diningroom with separate tables. All bedrooms have colour TV, vanitory units and tea-making facilities. En-suites available. Large garden and conservatory to relax in. Ample private parking. Children over seven years welcome. Pub within walking distance serves excellent food. Also available two newly converted character holiday cottages sleeping two/four each and one well equipped mobile home. Tourist Board registered.

WESTON-SUPER-MARE. Mrs T.G. Moore, Purn House Farm, Bleadon, Weston-super-Mare BS24 0QE (Bleadon [0934] 812324). Seventeenth-century creeper-clad house standing on a 400-acre mixed farm at the foot of Purn Hill where there are panoramic views of the Bristol Channel, Glastonbury Tor in the east to Exmoor and the Welsh Mountains in the west. The house contains some period furniture in day rooms. Tastefully decorated bedrooms — three double, one single, three family, all except single room have washbasins; en-suite available; modern conveniences; sittingroom, diningroom and games room for use of visitors. Excellent home cooking with traditional menus using home produce when possible. Special diets by arrangement. No pets. Open February to December, a car not essential, parking provided. Evening Dinner, Bed and Breakfast. Fire Certificate held. Miles of sandy beaches a short distance at Uphill, Weston, Berrow and Brean. Fishing, golf, sailing available; also riding and pony trekking locally. En route for the West Mendip Way walk. Milking may be watched through observation window in very modern milking parlour. SAE for brochure, please. Les Routiers recommended. Merit award from local Tourist Board.

BEDFORDSHIRE

PULLOXHILL. Mrs J. Tookey, Pond Farm, Pulloxhill MK45 5HA (Flitwick [0525] 712316). Working farm. Pond Farm, an arable farm, is an ideal base for touring Woburn Abbey and Safari Park, Whipsnade Zoo, Luton Hoo, Luton Airport, Dunstable Downs and Shuttleworth Collection of Historic Aircraft. Three double, one single, two family bedrooms (all with TVs); bathroom, toilet; diningroom. Children welcome at reduced rates. Babysitting most evenings. Open from January to December for Bed and Breakfast from £12; Evening Meal on request from £8.50 or meals at the local inn. Ample parking. Further details on request. Tourist Board listed.

BEDFORDSHIRE – RURAL AND INDUSTRIAL ASPECTS!

The River Ouse, The Dunstable Downs and Bedford on the rural side and Luton and Dunstable on the industrial constitute the two different aspects of Bedfordshire. Worth a visit are Dunstable Downs, Whipsnade Zoo, Stockgrove Park and the French style garden at Wrest Park.

BERKSHIRE

ALDWORTH, near Reading. Mrs B.M. Chapman, Woodrows Farm, Aldworth, Near Reading RG8 9RS (Compton [0635] 578 336). Working farm. This attractive farmhouse is set in peaceful Berkshire countryside, near the River Thames and the Ridgeway. Within easy reach of Oxford, Newbury and Henley-on-Thames. Old world pub within half-a-mile serving excellent evening meals. Accommodation comprises one family or double room, twin room and one single room; two bathrooms, three toilets. Bed and Breakfast from £15 per person per night. Open April to October. Tourist Board registered.

STREATLEY. Mrs P.J. Webber, Bennets Wood Farm, Southridge, Streatley RG8 9ST (Goring-on-Thames [0491] 872377). Working farm. Situated high above the Thames Valley, the farm holds a unique position in peaceful wooded countryside free from noise and traffic. It is a homely farm of 80 acres. Lovely walks include the famous Ridgeway. Oxford, Windsor and London easily visited by train or car. Golf course two miles. One double, one family bedrooms with washbasins; bathroom, toilets; sitting/diningroom. Children over five welcome. Sorry, no pets. Open from May to September. Car essential, parking. SAE, please, for terms for Bed and Breakfast.

CAMBRIDGESHIRE

CAMBRIDGE. Mrs M. Quintana, Segovia Lodge, 2 Barton Road, Cambridge CB3 9JZ (Cambridge [0223] 354105). ❀ ❀ ❀ Detached residence known as Segovia Lodge, nicely situated in this highly regarded west-side of the City and within walking distance of City centre and Colleges. Splendid facilities are offered — parking in own grounds. TV, washbasins, tea-making facilities, pleasant atmosphere. Children of all ages are welcome. Sorry, no pets. Very close to M11, A604, A603, A45. Bed and Breakfast from £17. Registered with ETB.

ELY. Mrs Jennifer Farrow, Laurel Farm House, 8 High Street, Mepal, Ely CB6 2AW (Ely [0353] 778023). Spacious old Georgian farmhouse in small quiet fen village. One double, one twin, one single bedrooms; two bathroom and toilets for guests' use. Tea/coffee making facilities. Elegant diningroom and comfortable sittingroom with TV. Cathedral city of Ely seven miles, Cambridge 16 miles. Near RSPB and Wildfowl Reserves and Duxford Imperial War Museum. Please write or ring for brochure. Bed and Breakfast only. Good food available at local riverside inn. (No pets).

ELY. Mrs Margaret Thurnham, The Laurels, 104 Victoria Street, Littleport, Ely CB6 1LZ (0353 861972). Visit Ely Cathedral (known as the ship of the Fens), stained glass museum, Cromwell's House, Welney Wildfowl Trust (floodlight feeding of the swans), Denver Sluice — the 300-year-old drainage system — also local boating, fishing on the Ouse. Twin/double bedrooms with shower/hand basins, one room en-suite; all rooms have tea/coffee facilities, radios, central heating, TV. Sitting and diningrooms. Delicious breakfasts and imaginative four course evening meals, served with a pre-meal glass of sherry in the sub-tropical garden room. Cot/high chair, ample parking. NON-SMOKING guests only. SAE, please for terms or telephone.

LITTLE EVERSDEN. Mrs Chambers, Church Farm, Little Eversden, Cambridge CB3 7HQ (0223 262228). ❀ ❀ ❀ Working farm. Working farm. A 300-year-old listed farmhouse in beautiful quiet gardens overlooking an old Saxon church. We offer double, twin and family accommodation in quaint comfortable rooms, some en-suite. We are next to Wimpole Hall estate, a National Trust property once occupied by Rudyard Kipling's daughter, Lady Bambridge. Six miles south of historic Cambridge and five miles from the Imperial War Museum at Duxford. Children by arrangement. Open all year for Bed and Breakfast. Also family accommodation in very comfortable and spacious flat which is also available for self catering holidays.

CHESHIRE

CHESTER. Mrs Joan Critchley, Roslyn Guest House, 8 Chester Street, Near Saltney, Chester CH4 8BJ (Chester [0244] 682306). ♛♛ Situated conveniently one-and-a-quarter miles from the centre of Chester, this traditional guest house is bright, clean and comfortable, with personal attention from the owner. Two twin, four double, two single and three family bedrooms, all with hot and cold water, and central heating. Shower and bathroom, three toilets (showers and baths free). Diningroom, sittingroom with colour TV. Children welcome — cot and high chair. Pets permitted. Open all year, except Christmas season. Car parking. Ideal base for exploring Cheshire, North Wales and Liverpool area. Bed and Breakfast from £11 — including tea making facilities. Reduced rates for children.

Mrs S. Woolley
HATTON HALL, HATTON HEATH, CHESTER CH3 9AP
Telephone (0829) 70601

Situated on a 200 acre dairy farm, this elegant Georgian farmhouse with its Norman moat is ideally placed just off the A41, five miles from the Roman walled city of Chester. Luxury Bed and Breakfast is offered here for the discerning guest. Centrally heated throughout, bedrooms have electric blankets, colour TVs and tea/coffee facilities, not to mention en suite bathroom and fine quality linen and towels. Guests also have access to gardens.

Open all year. Bed and Breakfast from £15 daily; Evening Meal from £8 (for unaccompanied ladies only).

Write or telephone for details.

English Tourist Board

CONGLETON. Mrs Sheila Kidd, Yew Tree Farm, North Rode, Congleton CW12 2PF (0260 223569).

Yew Tree Farm is a working farm set in the peaceful village of North Rode, amidst beautiful scenery. It is conveniently placed for exploring Cheshire and the Peak District. 20 minutes from M6. Ideal for touring and walking, surrounded by numerous beauty spots and places of interest e.g., Jodrell Bank, Gawsworth Hall, Alton Towers, Chatsworth Hall and Gardens, etc. Children are welcome and guests are invited to look around the farm and get to know the animals. Lounge with open log fire. Bed and substantial cooked Breakfast from £11; optional Evening Meal. Reduced rates for children.

HYDE. Mrs Freda Beaumont, Beaumonts-Upland Farm, Werneth Low, Gee Cross, Hyde SK14 3AG

(061-368 6559). Step back in time into this 18th century stone-built farmhouse with wooden beams, stripped pine, log fires, brass beds and feather mattresses. This is a non-working mixed farm of four acres, commanding panoramic views of Cheshire, Derbyshire and Staffordshire. Convenient for Manchester (city and Airport) and Stockport. The centrally heated accommodation comprises one single, one twin-bedded and two family rooms (most with TV and wash-basin); two bathrooms. Children welcome, cots, babysitting. Ample parking. Pets welcome. Open all year. Bed and Breakfast from £12.50. Good basic home cooking or five minutes to "pub grub".

HYDE, Near Manchester. Mrs Charlotte R. Walsh, Needhams Farm, Uplands Road, Werneth Low, Gee Cross, Near Hyde SK14 3AQ (061-368 4610). ♛♛♛ **Working farm.** A cosy 16th century farmhouse set in peaceful, picturesque surroundings by Werneth Low Country Park and the Etherow Valley, which lie between Glossop and Manchester. The farm is ideally situated for holidaymakers and businessmen, especially those who enjoy peace and quiet, walking and rambling, golfing and riding, as these activities are all close by. At Needhams Farm everyone, including children and pets, receives a warm welcome. Good wholesome meals available in the evenings. Residential licence and Fire Certificate held. Open all year. Single Bed and Breakfast from £14; Evening Meal from £6 – £7.50. AA listed. RAC acclaimed. See Bed and Breakfast Stops, refer to entry under DERBYSHIRE.

MACCLESFIELD. Mrs P.O. Worth, Rough Hey Farm, Leek Road, Gawsworth, Macclesfield SK11 0JQ (02605 2296). Delightfully situated overlooking the Cheshire Plain and on the edge of the Peak National Park, Rough Hey is an historic former hunting lodge dating from before the 16th century. Tastefully modernised yet retaining its old world character. This 300 acre sheep farm consists of wooded valleys and hills with plenty of wildlife and lovely walks. In the locality there are numerous old halls and villages to visit. Family/double, twin and single rooms all with tea/coffee making facilities; family/double and twin rooms with washbasins and TV. Large comfortable lounge with TV. A warm and traditional welcome is assured. Terms from £11.

MACCLESFIELD. Mrs Irene Kennerley, Sandpit Farm, Messuage Lane, Marton, Macclesfield SK11 9HS (0260 224254). 🐾🐾 A friendly welcome to our 200 acre arable farm in peaceful surroundings. Well maintained farmhouse with washbasins in all bedrooms, visitors' bath/shower room. Separate diningroom, TV lounge. Heated throughout. Tea/coffee making facilities. Excellent touring centre for the Peak District, Chester and Potteries. Manchester Airport 14 miles. National Trust properties, stately homes and Jodrell Bank radio telescope nearby. Children and pets welcome. Bed and Breakfast from £12.

MACCLESFIELD near. Mrs M.M. Birch, High Low Farm, Langley, Near Macclesfield SK11 0NE (02605 2230). 🐾🐾 Working farm. This 17th century farmhouse pleasantly situated on the outskirts of the Peak Park in beautiful countryside, overlooking reservoir, offers comfortable and spacious accommodation for a maximum of six guests. Within easy reach of Buxton, Chester and Manchester, it is ideally placed for tourist or walker. With a lovely country inn 200 yards away, evening meals are easily catered for. Open all year except Christmas and New Year. Bed and Breakfast from £12.

HOLIDAY ACCOMMODATION
Classification Schemes in
England, Scotland and Wales

The National Tourist Boards for England, Scotland and Wales have agreed a common 'Crown Classification' scheme for **serviced (Board)** accommodation. All establishments are inspected regularly and are given a classification indicating their level of facilities and services.

There are six grades ranging from 'Listed' to 'Five Crowns 🐾🐾🐾🐾🐾'. The higher the classification, the more facilities and services offered.

Crown classification is a measure of *facilities* not *quality*. A common quality grading scheme grades the quality of establishments as 'Approved', 'Commended' or 'Highly Commended' according to the accommodation, welcome and service they provide.

For **Self-Catering**, holiday homes in England are awarded 'Keys' after inspection and can also be 'Approved', 'Commended' or 'Highly Commended' according to the facilities available. In Scotland the Crown scheme includes self-catering accommodation and Wales also has a voluntary inspection scheme for self-catering grading from '1 (Standard)' to '5 (Excellent)'.

Caravan and Camping Parks can participate in the British Holiday Parks grading scheme from 'Approved (√)' to 'Excellent (√ √ √ √ √)'. In addition, each National Tourist Board has an annual award for high-quality caravan accommodation: in England – Rose Awards; in Scotland – Thistle Commendations; in Wales – Dragon Awards.

When advertisers supply us with the information, FHG Publications show Crowns and other awards or gradings, including AA, RAC, Egon Ronay etc. We also award a small number of Farm Holiday Guide Diplomas every year, based on readers' recommendations.

MALPAS. Mrs Margaret Davies, Millhey Farm, Barton, Malpas SY14 7HU (Broxton [0829] 782209). ✤✤ Working farm. Charming black and white

half-timbered farmhouse on a 140 acre farm, situated approximately one and a half miles off A41 road to Chester, on A534 road to Wrexham and North Wales. Bed and Breakfast accommodation provided all year round in one double, two family bedrooms, all with washbasins; bathroom, two toilets; sittingroom; diningroom. Children welcome and babysitting arranged. Many interesting places to visit within easy driving distance including Beeston and Peckforton Castles, Erdigg Hall, Chester Zoo, Chondeley Castle and gardens; golf courses and many lovely walks. Excellent centre for touring the Welsh border country and North Wales. Good food served in an interesting country inn just across the road. Tourist Board listed. Bed and Breakfast from £10. Children £5. Car essential — parking.

MALPAS. Mrs Angela Smith, Mill House, Higher Wych, Malpas SY14 7JR (Redbrook Maelor [094-873] 362). ✤✤ Situated in a peaceful rural valley with the Welsh border running through the grounds, Mill House is ideally placed for touring North Wales and for visiting historic Chester and Shrewsbury. The accommodation is available all year round with central heating for cold weather comfort. One double bedroom with en-suite shower/WC and one twin bedroom with washbasin; radio and tea making facilities; TV lounge with open log fire; diningroom. Children welcome, cot and babysitting available. Garden with small stream and walled patio. Car essential; parking. Bed and Breakfast from £11. Evening Meal from £5.

MIDDLEWICH. Mrs M. Williams, Curtis Hulme Farm, Bradwall Road, Middlewich CW10 0LD (Middlewich [060-684] 3230). Working farm, join in.

Relax on a 160 acre dairy farm situated along a quiet country lane, midway (three miles) between junctions 17 and 18 of M6. The 17th century oak beamed farmhouse is comfortable and spacious and surrounded by gardens. Set in lovely Cheshire countryside, it is ideal for touring the many local attractions. Diningroom, sittingroom, lounge with colour TV. Tea and coffee available at all times. One family, one double and one twin room, all with washbasins. Shower in bathroom. Bed and Breakfast from £12; children sharing family room from £6. Tourist Board listed.

NANTWICH. Mrs Jean E. Callwood, Lea Farm, Wainehill Road, Wybunbury, Nantwich CW5 7NS (0270 841429). ✤✤ Working farm, join in. A charming

farmhouse set in landscaped gardens where peacocks roam on 150 acre dairy farm. Spacious bedrooms with vanity units, colour TV and tea/coffee making facilities. Family, double and twin bedrooms. Luxury lounge, diningroom overlooking gardens. Pool/snooker and fishing available. Children welcome, also dogs if kept under control. Help to feed the birds and animals and see the cows being milked. Near to Stapeley Water Gardens, Bridgemere Garden World and Wild Life Park. Also Nantwich, Crewe, Chester, the Potteries and Alton Towers. Bed and Breakfast from £11 per person; Evening Meals £6. Weekly terms available.

CORNWALL

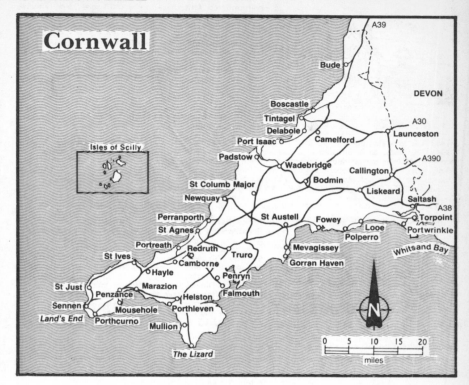

BODMIN. **Mrs B.P. Harris, Tredarrup Farm, Treveighan, St. Teath, Bodmin PL30 3JN (0208 850324).** The farmhouse is about 300 years old, with modern conveniences. Situated in lovely countryside, not far from Wadebridge and Bodmin, central to lovely beaches and rugged North Cornwall coast. Guests are free to walk round the 280 acre working farm which carries beef cattle, sheep, cereals and horses. Home grown vegetables, clotted cream, milk and a homely atmosphere. TV. Tea/coffee available in bedrooms. Cot, high chair, babysitting and reduced rates for children. Terms and further details on application, SAE please.

BODMIN. **Mrs Daphne Eddy, Trehannick Farm, St. Teath, Bodmin PL30 3JW (Bodmin [0208] 850312). Working farm.** First mentioned in Domesday in 1086, Trehannick is a 180-acre family farm consisting of dairy cows, beef cattle and cereals. The tastefully and comfortably furnished farmhouse stands in an acre of garden overlooking the beautiful Allen Valley. Safe sandy beaches, sailing, fishing, surfing and golf all within eight miles. One family, three double (one twin-bedded) and one single bedrooms, all but single room with handbasins. Bathroom, two toilets; lounge with colour TV; diningroom with separate tables. Electric blankets. Children welcome. Sorry, no pets. Varied menu of good farmhouse cooking using mainly all home produce including beef, milk and cream. Car essential. Open Easter to October for Bed and Breakfast and Evening Meal, or Bed and Breakfast only. Reductions for children. SAE for terms.

BODMIN. Mrs Joy Rackham, High Cross Farm, Lanivet, Near Bodmin PL30 5JR (Lanivet [0208] 831341). Working farm. High Cross is a 91 acre dairy farm

situated in the village of Lanivet which is the geographical centre of Cornwall and therefore central to beaches on the North and South Coast, the Moor and other places of interest. Riding and fishing available in the area. Please come only if you enjoy appetising food. Vegetarian diets catered for with prior notice. The two family rooms and one twin bedroom are centrally heated and have vanity units; TV lounge and separate diningroom. Bed and Breakfast, optional Evening Meal. Approved by the Cornish Tourist Board. SAE, please, or telephone.

BODMIN. Mrs P.A. Smith, Treffry Farm, Lanhydrock, Bodmin PL30 5AF (Bodmin [0208] 74405).

🐌🐌 A warm welcome is guaranteed at our 200 acre dairy farm with lovely Georgian farmhouse in mid-Cornwall. National Trust Lanhydrock with its stately home and glorious parkland, with miles of scenic walks, is just next door. We pride ourselves on our plentiful and delicious farmhouse cooking and home from home atmosphere. Visitors are welcome to explore and help on the farm. Treffry is just seven miles from the sea, ideally situated for touring the whole of Cornwall. There is a safe play area for children, and a farm pony. Good facilities for fishing, sailing, riding and windsurfing nearby. One twin room fully en-suite, one double with en-suite shower and washbasin, one single room with washbasin. Bed, Breakfast and Evening Meal from £130 per week. Reductions for children. AA; Cornwall Tourist Board listed.

BODMIN near. Mrs K. Botterill, Little Rylands Farm, Redmoor, Near Bodmin PL30 5AR (0208 873123). A small working farm idyllically set in mid-Cornwall adjoining a wildlife conservation area — ideal for exploring north and south coasts. One double room with en-suite facilities, one twin/double room with adjacent bathroom; TV and tea/coffee making facilities. Residents' lounge and diningroom, tastefully decorated and furnished; real fire for those chillier days. Conservatory and patio take full advantage of Cornwall's mild climate and early spring. Open all year. Pets welcome. Ample parking. Bed and full English Breakfast from £10; five course Evening Meal £7. Organically grown home produce used wherever possible in imaginative menus.

Terms quoted in this publication may be subject to increase if rises in costs necessitate

BODMIN MOOR, near Altarnun. Mrs Sheila J. Charman, Westermoorgate, Trewint, Altarnun, Launceston PL15 7SF (Pipers Pool [0566] 86727).

Westmoorgate is a working smallholding set in a peaceful situation with stream, yet only one mile off A30 between Launceston and Bodmin. Golf and horse riding within easy reach; central for touring both coasts. Birdwatchers and walkers will encounter old tin streamings and archaeological sites right on the doorstep. A warm welcome awaits guests in the beamed granite farmhouse, part of which dates back to 1650, with two double bedrooms having colour TV and tea/coffee facilities. Bed and Breakfast from £9 daily. Also available: six-berth, fully equipped caravan, £60 to £95 weekly. Please phone for further details or SAE.

BOSCASTLE. Sue and Allan Miller, The Old Coach House, Tintagel Road, Boscastle PL35 0AS (Boscastle (08405) 398). ♛♛♛ AA and RAC listed.

Relax in a 300-year-old former coach house now tastefully equipped to meet the needs of the 90's with all rooms en-suite, colour TVs, radios, tea/coffee makers and central heating. Good cooking, optional Evening Meal, vegetarians catered for. This picturesque village is a haven for walkers with its dramatic coastal scenery, a photographer's dream, and an ideal base to tour both the north and south coasts. The area is famed for its sandy beaches and surfing whilst King Arthur's Tintagel is only three miles away. Come and enjoy a friendly holiday with people who care. Brochure on request. Bed and Breakfast from £15 to £20.

BOSCASTLE. Mrs J. Grinsted, Tredole Farm, Trevalga, Boscastle PL35 0ED (Boscastle [08405] 495). Working farm, join in. The farmhouse, part of which is 300 years old, is situated on the coast in a beautiful valley in an area of outstanding natural beauty. From the farm we run horse and pony trekking, riding out in small groups, with personal attention assured. Tredole Farm is well placed for beaches, touring, walking, fishing and visiting places of interest. Guests are served good home cooking using fresh vegetables and dairy produce. We offer a relaxed and informal holiday and visitors are welcome to lend a hand with the farm chores, ponies and other farm animals. Tea making facilities; shower/bath; television/video lounge; games room; gardens. Children and pets welcome. Open all year for Bed, Breakfast and Evening Meal.

BUDE. Mrs Rosina Joyner, Penrose, Dizzard, St. Gennys, Bude EX23 0NX (08403 318). Penrose is a

delightful 17th century cottage with beamed ceilings and inglenook fireplaces. Tastefully modernised, yet retaining all its olde worlde charm. Set in one and a half acres of lawns and gardens within the National Trust area close to the coast path. It is ideal for those seeking peace and quiet. Nearby is the beautiful beach of Widemouth Bay. The views from the cottage are extensive. All rooms have four-poster beds, tea making, en-suite facilities. Good breakfast; optional Evening Meals. Open all year. Car essential. Also available mobile home, cottage annexe for self-catering. SAE for booking form and brochure. Terms from £87 weekly per person. Room suitable for disabled.

BUDE. Mrs Monica Heywood, Cornakey Farm, Morwenstow, Bude EX23 9SS (Morwenstow [028-883] 260). Working farm. This is a 220-acre mixed

farm on the coast, with lovely views of sea and Lundy Island. Good touring centre, within easy reach of quiet beaches. The farmhouse offers two family bedrooms; bathroom, toilet; sittingroom; diningroom. Children welcome at reduced rates; cot, high chair, babysitting. Good home cooking. Colour TV. Sorry, no pets. Car essential — parking. SAE, please, for terms. Evening Meal, Bed and Breakfast or Bed and Breakfast only.

BUDE. Michael and Pearl Hopper, West Nethercott Farm, Whitstone, Holsworthy (Devon) EX22 6LD (Week-St-Mary [028884] 394). Working farm, join in. A warm welcome awaits you on this dairy and sheep farm. Watch the cows being milked, help with the animals. Free pony rides, scenic farm walks. Short distance from sandy beaches, surfing at Bude and Widemouth Bay, and the rugged North Cornwall coast. Ideal base for visiting any part of Devon or Cornwall. We are located in Cornwall though our postal address is Devon. The traditional farmhouse has five bedrooms; diningroom and separate lounge with colour TV. Plenty of traditional home cooking. Baby sitting available. Bed and Breakfast from £9, four-course Evening Meal available. Children under 10 years reduced weekly terms available. Open all year, except Christmas.

FOR THE MUTUAL GUIDANCE
OF GUEST AND HOST

Every year literally thousands of holidays, short-breaks and overnight stops are arranged
through our guides, the vast majority without any problems at all. In a handful of cases, however,
difficulties do arise about bookings, which often could have been prevented from the outset.

It is important to remember that when accommodation has been booked, both parties —
guests and hosts — have entered into a form of contract. We hope that the following points will
provide helpful guidance.

GUESTS: When enquiring about accommodation, be as precise as possible. Give exact
dates, numbers in your party and the ages of any children. State the number and type of rooms
wanted and also what catering you require — bed and breakfast, full board, etc. Make sure that
the position about evening meals is clear — and about pets, reductions for children or any other
special points.

Read our reviews carefully to ensure that the proprietors you are going to contact can
supply what you want. Ask for a letter confirming all arrangements, if possible.

If you have to cancel, do so as soon as possible. Proprietors do have the right to retain
deposits and under certain circumstances to charge for cancelled holidays if adequate notice is
not given and they cannot re-let the accommodation.

HOSTS: Give details about your facilities and about any special conditions. Explain your
deposit system clearly and arrangements for cancellations, charges, etc, and whether or not
your terms include VAT.

If for any reason you are unable to fulfil an agreed booking without adequate notice, you
may be under an obligation to arrange alternative suitable accommodation or to make some
form of compensation.

While every effort is made to ensure accuracy, we regret that FHG Publications cannot
accept responsibility for errors, omissions or misrepresentation in our entries or any
consequences thereof. Prices in particular should be checked because we go to press early. We
will follow up complaints but cannot act as arbiters or agents for either party.

BUDE. Mrs Sylvia Lucas, Elm Park, Bridgerule, Holsworthy, Devon EX22 7EL (Bridgerule [028-881] 231). ♛ ♛ Working farm, join in. Elm Park is a 205 acre dairy and mixed farm, six miles from surfing beaches at Bude and half a mile from the village. Guests are welcome to wander over the farm and watch the milking, animals etc. Pony rides and a tractor and trailer ride are given. Large lawn with golf putting. There are three family rooms (two en-suite) and a twin room, all with tea/coffee making facilities. Mainly roast four course dinners served using fresh produce. Bed, Breakfast and Evening Meal from £15; Bed and Breakfast from £10. Big weekly and children's reductions.

BUDE near. Mrs J. Cholwill, Tackbeare Farm, Marhamchurch, Near Bude (028 881 264). Tackbeare Farm is our own home and we wish guests to enjoy its peaceful comfortable surroundings. It is ideally situated for touring and within easy reach of sandy beaches, golf and fishing. The 16th century farmhouse comprises three family bedrooms, two double and one single. There are washbasins in all rooms, colour TV in lounge. Good home cooking with fresh farm produce. Bed and Breakfast and Bed, Breakfast and Evening Meal. Bedtime drinks provided. Visitors are welcome to view any of the farm activities. Children welcome, babysitting, cots, highchairs available. Mrs Cholwill assures you of a pleasant and relaxing holiday. SAE for terms.

TACKBEARE FARM

BUDE. Mrs V.M. Hale, The Villa, Bridgerule, Holsworthy, Devon EX22 7TA (Bridgerule [028-881] 452). Working farm, join in. An attractive old farmhouse with an acre of gardens plus a safe children's play area. Comfortable rooms. Excellent meals including some regional dishes prepared by qualified cook using fresh home produce. The family-run dairy farm is within walking distance. Private fishing is available on one mile of River Tamar. Situated in the picturesque village of Bridgerule which has an Inn, Antique Shop and a General Store. Only five miles from the sandy beaches and surfing of the North Cornwall coast, or the popular market town of Holsworthy; also ideal for touring Dartmoor and Bodmin Moor. One family, one double, one twin and one single bedrooms; bathroom; lounge; diningroom. Attractive rates. Children welcome at reduced terms; cot, high chair and babysitting available. On bus route. Parking. Evening Meal, Bed and Breakfast or Bed and Breakfast only. Further details on request.

BUDE near. Mrs D. Stripp, Week-Ford, Week St Mary, Holsworthy EX22 6XW (028884 364). Week-Ford is situated in a delightful wooded valley growing Christmas trees, being one mile from the village of Week St. Mary, seven miles from Bude and three miles from the coast, making this an ideal spot for beaches and touring inland. We are an ideal base for riding, fishing, golf, walks and many other recreational activities throughout North Cornwall. Doreen and Roy Stripp invite you to their friendly and comfortable countryside accommodation. Open all year. En-suite facilities available. Large car park in own grounds. Daily and mid-week bookings accepted. Reductions for children. For full details write or telephone.

CAMBOURNE. Mrs Christine Peerless, Cargenwen Farm, Blackrock, Praze, Cambourne TR14 9PD (0209 831442). A small family-run farm set on lovely hillside enjoying beautiful extensive country views towards St. Ives and Carbis Bay. Ideally situated for both north and south coast beaches, places of interest, etc. whatever your taste. Within easy reach of Penzance, St. Michael's Mount, Land's End, Truro, St. Ives and Helston. We offer traditional cooking; TV lounge; tea/coffee making facilities and washbasins in all bedrooms. Easy parking available. Children welcome. Our aim is to make your holiday one to remember. Bed and Breakfast; Evening Meal optional.

FUN FOR ALL THE FAMILY IN CORNWALL

Woolly Monkey Sanctuary, Murrayton, Looe; *Padstow Bird & Butterfly Gardens*, Fentonluna, Padstow; *Bird Paradise*, Hayle; *Bodmin Farm Park*, Fletchers Bridge, Bodmin; *Newquay Zoo*, Trenance Park, Newquay; *Cornish Seal Sanctuary*, Gweek, Helston; *Mevagissey Model Railway*, Mevagissey; *The Forest Railroad Park*, Dobwalls, near Liskeard; *Age of Steam*, Crowlas, near Penzance; *Lappa Valley Railway*, Benny Halt, Newlyn East; *Poldark Mining & Wendron Forge*, Wendron, near Helston; *Cornwall Aero Park*, Royal Naval Air Station, Culdrose; *Museum of Nautical Art*, Chapel Street, Penzance; *St. Agnes Leisure Park*, St. Agnes.

FALMOUTH. Mrs Deborah Bennetts, Gadles Farm, Laity Moor, Ponsanooth, Truro TR3 7HS (0872 863214) A modern dairy farm with traditional Cornish farmhouse which offers vanity units with H&C and tea making facilities in all rooms. Separate bathroom, toilet and shower. Each family occupies a separate table in the diningroom. Comfortable TV lounge with video. Children welcome at reduced rates. Free babysitting. A 15-minute drive from Falmouth town and sandy beaches. Pets welcome by arrangement. Spacious garden, ample parking. Cornwall Tourist Board registered. Bed and Breakfast or Bed, Breakfast and Evening Meal. Terms on application.

FALMOUTH. Mrs John Myers, Dolvean Hotel, 50 Melvill Road, Falmouth TR11 4DQ (Falmouth [0326] 313658). ✿ ✿ This small family-run hotel faces due south and is only 250 yards from the sea front and sandy Gyllyngvase Beach with safe bathing. The fascinating old town with its fine harbour is within walking distance. Good food, varied menu, table licence, cheerful service assured. Four double, five twin and five single bedrooms all with washbasins, radio-intercom and automatic tea and coffee makers (seven with bathroom en-suite). Nine bathrooms, eleven toilets; diningroom with separate tables; lounge with TV. Fire Certificate granted. Central heating. Car not essential, but ample parking. Dogs welcome. Open Easter till October for Evening Dinner, Bed and Breakfast from £110 to £165 per week or Bed and Breakfast from £75 to £145. Stamp, please, for colour brochure. ETB; Cornwall TB; Fal Hotels registered, RAC listed.

FOWEY. Mrs S.C. Dunn, Menabilly Barton, Par, Fowey PL24 2TN (Par [072-681] 2844). Working farm. MENABILLY BARTON is a secluded farmhouse set in wooded valley leading to a quiet cove, accessible by footpath and safe for bathing. Farmhouse with spacious diningroom and large lounge with TV, also peaceful garden available during the day. Good traditional farmhouse cooking. National Trust cliff walks round the coast. Fowey, 10 minutes by road, offers fishing, sailing, quaint shops, etc. Golfing on the coast nearby. North coast about 40 minutes' drive; Land's End two and a half hours. Several National Trust properties in the area. Open March to October with accommodation in three family bedrooms with washbasins and one single bedroom; bathroom with shower, toilet. Facilities for making drinks. Cot, high chair, babysitting. Pets allowed. Bed and full English Breakfast only from £11 per adult; reductions for children.

GORRAN HAVEN. Mr and Mrs A. Pike, Tregillan Guest House, Trewollock Lane, Gorran Haven PL26 6NT (0726 842452). ✿ ✿ Tregillan is situated in a beautiful rural area perfect for a relaxing holiday. This small family guest house is only minutes from the picturesque harbour of Gorran Haven, with its safe, clean, sandy beaches; ideal for swimming, boating and fishing trips. Three guest rooms all en-suite with colour TV and tea/coffee making facilities. Children and pets welcome. Parking available. Open Easter to October. Bed and Breakfast from £12 per person; optional Evening Meal. SAE please for brochure. Mr and Mrs Pike have a modern house near Fowey available for self-catering holidays. Sleeps six maximum. Details on request.

GORRAN HAVEN. Diana and Graham Allen, Pine Ridge, Trewollock Lane, Gorran Haven, St. Austell PL26 6NT (Mevagissey [0726] 843551). Large modern house standing in spacious private grounds with superb sea and country views. Gorran Haven is a small village with a quiet and relaxed atmosphere, ideal for a peaceful holiday. Safe sandy beaches 600 yards away with launching facilities. An ideal centre to explore the north and south coasts of Cornwall. Three double/twin bedrooms, all with washbasins and sea views, two with showers. Diningroom overlooks the garden and sea. TV lounge. Fully centrally heated. Swimming pool is solar heated. Plenty of parking. Pets welcome by arrangement. Bed and Breakfast from £11 per person per night.

GORRAN HAVEN. Mr and Mrs A. and B. Butterworth, "Mellins Close", Trewollock Lane, Gorran Haven, St. Austell PL26 6NT (Mevagissey [0726] 843318). "Mellins Close" is situated in its own grounds on the edge of the small fishing village of Gorran Haven. Safe, sandy beaches just a few minutes' walk away. Come and relax in pleasant comfortable surroundings. Good food, sea and country views. Ideally situated to explore the beautiful Roseland Peninsula with its many coves, beaches and coastal walks. Three double bedrooms with washbasins; two bathrooms (one with shower). Lounge; diningroom with separate tables. Private parking. Sorry, no pets. Open Easter to October. Bed and Breakfast (Evening Meal optional). Tourist Board listed. SAE for terms, please.

CORNWALL – SOMETHING FOR EVERYONE!
Sea, sand, cliffs and quite often the sun, but that's not all you will find in this interesting county. Cornwall has many fascinating places to visit, such as the Charlestown Shipwreck Centre, the Tropical Bird Gardens at Padstow, Cornwall Aeronautical Park near Helston, Botallack Tin Mine, The Cornish Seal Sanctuary, Perranporth and of course, St. Michael's Mount.

Perhaver

THE HOUSE ON THE CLIFF
GORRAN HAVEN
(Licensed)

Perhaver is a delightful Guest House where you can relax in a pleasantly informal atmosphere. The house occupies a commanding cliff-top position above the most attractive unspoilt fishing village of Gorran Haven. In an area designated as being of outstanding natural beauty, Perhaver is situated at the end of the cliff road away from all the traffic and stands on a small headland with the sea on two sides and open country at the rear. All the rooms have lovely views of the sea and coastline. The bedrooms have hot and cold running water, shaver points, reading lamps, fitted furniture and fitted carpets and are most attractive and comfortable. The lounge has colour television and is tastefully decorated and furnished. The Residents' bar and the diningroom have the same magnificent views as the lounge. An excellent standard of food is maintained and served at tables for two. Personal attention is given to everyone and you can be assured of absolute comfort.

A small quiet beach below the house is reached by a natural cliff path starting at the stile at the top of the drive and there are other beaches within a few minutes' walk. All are sandy and ideal for sailing, fishing and safe swimming. Fishing trips may be taken from the quay in the summer. Some beautiful walks can be enjoyed and the path over the cliffs to Mevagissey begins at the entrance to Perhaver. This is a perfect place to spend a honeymoon. Parking space for vehicles not exceeding 7' in height. Mr and Mrs Bolt regret they are unable to accommodate persons under 18 years of age or pets. There is no accommodation for single persons. The standards at Perhaver comply with those of the British Travel Association and the Guest House is registered with both the English Tourist Board and Cornwall County Tourist Board. Mr and Mrs Bolt will be pleased to forward a brochure showing the magnificent position. Please send SAE for reply.

Evening Dinner, Bed and Breakfast £110 per person weekly, no VAT. Please confirm price when enquiring as this may alter due to any inflationary increase. Mevagissey 3 miles, St. Austell 10 and Truro 14.

Mr and Mrs I. W. Bolt (Mevagissey [0726] 842471)
Perhaver Guest House, Perhaver Point, Gorran Haven, Cornwall

HELSTON. Mrs D.J. Hill, Rocklands Guest House, The Lizard, Helston (0326 290339). Mixed farm carrying pigs and beef cattle. Rocklands is situated away from the farm, overlooking uninterrupted sea views. There are five double rooms and two family rooms; two toilets, bathroom. Diningroom with separate tables; lounge with colour TV and sun lounge. Visitors are made to feel at home. Good farmhouse cooking, fresh cream, eggs, vegetables. The Lizard is well known for its lovely scenery and walks along the cliff tops. Good fishing, safe beaches. Golf at Mullion five miles, horse riding. Open Easter to October. Children welcome. Dogs welcome if well trained. Shingle and sand beaches half a mile distant. Bed and Breakfast from £12. Evening Meal available. Reductions for children under 12 years.

HELSTON. Mrs P. Roberts, Hendra Farm, Wendron, Helston TR13 0NR (Falmouth [0326] 40470). Working farm. Hendra Farm, just off the main Helston/Falmouth road, is an ideal centre for touring Cornwall; three miles to Helston, eight to both Redruth and Falmouth. Safe sandy beaches within easy reach — five miles to the sea. Beautiful views from the farmhouse of the 60-acre beef farm. Two double, one single, and one family bedrooms; bathroom and toilets; sittingroom and two diningrooms. Cot, babysitting and reduced rates offered for children. No objection to pets. Car necessary, parking space. Enjoy good cooking with roast beef, pork, lamb, chicken, genuine Cornish pasties, fish and delicious sweets and cream. Open all year except Christmas. Evening Dinner, Bed and Breakfast from £70 per week which includes cooked breakfast, three course evening dinner, tea and homemade cake before bed. Bed and Breakfast only also available.

HELSTON. Mrs Maureen Dale, Polgarth Farm, Crowntown, Helston TR13 0AA (Helston [0326] 572115). Working farm. Polgarth Farm is central for touring West Cornwall. Three miles from the market town of Helston (home of the famous Furry Dance — 8th May) on the main Helston-Camborne road (B3303). Market gardening includes early potatoes and cabbage; we invite children to help with the feeding of calves, pigs and chickens. Maureen Dale, having cooked at The London Dairy Show, Ideal Home Exhibition, on TV, and broadcast on local radio, takes great pleasure in producing sumptuous meals for all her guests and, with her husband, welcomes you to their home. Babysitting available and pets welcome by prior arrangement. Open all year. Registered with the English and Cornwall Tourist Boards. SAE, please, for terms.

HELSTON. Mrs H. Lugg, Tregaddra, Cury, Helston TR12 7BB

(Mullion [0326] 240235). ☙☙ *Commended.* Tregaddra is an early 18th century farmhouse set in half-a-acre of well-kept gardens, providing high-class accommodation. Ideally situated in the centre of The Lizard Peninsula with views of the sea, coast and countryside for 15 miles radius. Sandy beaches, golf and horse-riding all nearby. Good farmhouse cooking and own produce used. All double rooms are en suite. Lounge has inglenook fireplace with log fires early/late season. Large games room. Heated swimming pool with slide. Children welcome, but sorry no pets. Evening Dinner, Bed and Breakfast or Bed and Breakfast. AA Commended. Helston six miles, Mullion three miles, Helford River seven miles, The Lizard six miles. Open all year. Send for colour brochure.

HELSTON. Mrs Alice Harry, Polhormon Farm, Polhormon Lane, Mullion, Helston TR12 7JE (0326

240304). ☙ Polhormon is a dairy farm with magnificent coastal and country views, overlooking sandy Poldhu Cove. Situated half a mile from charming and unspoilt Mullion Village on "The Lizard" — Cornwall's most southerly peninsula. The Victorian farmhouse is comfortably furnished in keeping with that period. New guest bathroom and separate WC. Central heating. Access at all times. Tea/coffee making facilities in all bedrooms. Children welcome, babysitting by arrangement. Pony riding, golf, fishing trips nearby. Sailing on the Helford River plus glorious cliff walks. Bed and Breakfast from £12.

HELSTON. Mrs Kathleen Worden, Anhay Farm, Gunwalloe, Helston TR12 7QF (Helston [0326] 572114). Working farm. Anhay consists of 74 acres of dairy farm and market gardening and is situated about five minutes' walk from the sea. Three family rooms and two double, all with hot and cold water; diningroom and sittingroom. Gunwalloe is within reach of many beauty spots: Church Cove which has an adjoining 18-hole golf course and St. Ives, Land's End, Helford River and The Lizard. Helston is the home of the "Furry Dance" which takes place on the 8th May every year. Bed, Breakfast and Evening Meal or Bed and Breakfast. Children taken. Terms on request. Open Easter to October.

HELSTON. Mrs Margaret Jenkin, Boderloggan Farm, Wendron, Helston TR13 0ES (0326-572148). Working farm. "Boderloggan" is a 120-acre dairy farm, ideally situated for touring the main towns and beauty spots of South and West Cornwall. Within easy reach of the coast, Newquay, Falmouth, St. Ives, Penzance, Truro; Helston three miles. A well known holiday attraction for all the family within walking distance at "Poldark Mine", Halfpenny Park. Two double (family) bedrooms with washbasins; bathroom; diningroom, lounge with TV. Mrs Jenkin will give her guests a value-for-money holiday with plenty of fresh vegetables, clotted cream with a three-course Evening Meal. English Breakfast. Friendly homely atmosphere, children welcome, babysitting if required.

HELSTON. Mrs Gillian E. Lawrance, Longstone Farm, Trenear, Helston TR13 0HG (Helston [0326]

572483). ☙☙ **Working farm.** A warm welcome is extended to guests at this modernised farmhouse situated on a 62 acre dairy farm set in peaceful countryside, ideal for touring and within easy reach of West Cornwall's beautiful beaches. All bedrooms have washbasins, spring interior mattresses, carpeted throughout. Separate tables in dining-room, colour TV in lounge, large sunlounge provides additional relaxation area, either for reading or games. Full electric central heating. Good farmhouse fare served, milk and cream produced on farm, with Cornish eggs, meat and vegetables. SAE for terms. Special rates in low season. Fire Certificate. AA listed. Cornish Tourist Board approved. Open February to November for Evening Dinner/Meal, Bed and Breakfast or Bed and Breakfast only. Reductions for children and Senior Citizens. Babysitting by arrangement.

KINGSAND. Mrs Ann Heasman, Cliff House, Devonport Hill, Kingsand, Near Torpoint, Cornwall PL10 1NJ (Plymouth [0752] 823110). 🐛🐛 A delightful

listed Grade 2 Regency house on the outskirts of a small picturesque fishing village on the unspoilt Rame peninsula. It is only a few yards from the sea, and there are superb views of Cawsand Bay and Plymouth Sound. There are ample opportunities for walking, sailing, fishing and windsurfing as the house lies on the South Cornwall coastal path and Mount Edgecumbe Country Park. Plymouth is eight miles away, many pubs and restaurants nearby. Accommodation comprises three double bedrooms (one with en suite bathroom) with washbasins, tea making facilities, central heating. Log fires. Super home cooked wholefood, including vegetarian. Bed and Breakfast; Evening Meal by arrangement. Non-smoking.

LAUNCESTON. Mrs Kathryn Broad, Lower Dutson Farm, Launceston PL15 9SP (0566 776456).

Lower Dutson is two miles from Launceston, ancient capital of Cornwall with its Norman castle. We are a 200 acre mixed farm on the Cornwall/Devon Border. Ideal for touring both counties and moors. We are about two miles from the golf course (18 hole) and riding stables. We have a well established coarse fishing lake which borders our fields. You can fish the River Tamar as well. Washbasins in most bedrooms, guests' own bathroom; TV lounge. Bed and Breakfast from £10 per person; Evening Meal £5. We also have a self catering cottage which sleeps six. Price from £100.

LAUNCESTON. Mrs Valerie Griffin, Wheatley Farm, Maxworthy, Launceston PL15 8LY (056681-232). 🐛🐛🐛 *Highly Commended.* **Working farm.** The

warmest of welcomes awaits you at Wheatley Farmhouse nestling in the quiet heart of Cornwall. Wheatley offers you a real Cornish farm holiday with all the comforts of home. The farm has been in the possession of the Griffin family for five generations and Raymond and Valerie are proud to share their heritage with you. It is ideally situated for touring the magnificent Cornish countryside and only ten minutes from the best beaches. Watch the busy farm activities. Children have exciting indoor and outdoor play areas, plus pony rides. Comfort and charm abound in the bedrooms, which have en-suite bathrooms and colour TV. We offer tempting menus using fresh local produce: Bed, Breakfast and Evening Meal. For self-catering holidays, we also offer two luxury cottages. Brochure available.

LAUNCESTON. Mrs A. E. Werren, Waterloo Farm, North Petherwin, Launceston PL15 8LL (North Petherwin [0566-85] 386). Family accommodation provided in our comfortable, six-bedroomed farmhouse situated amid peaceful countryside overlooking the beautiful Ottery Valley. The river, ancient county boundary, offers lovely walks and one and a half miles of good, private trout fishing. Shooting and sea fishing trips can be arranged. The village Post Office/stores and Otter Sanctuary are ten minutes' walk from farm. Thriving market town of Launceston (four and a half miles) has 18-hole golf course, Norman Castle and Steam Railway. Excellent farmhouse cooking and a relaxed, friendly atmosphere make Waterloo an ideal touring centre for the Moors and coasts of Devon and Cornwall. Bed and Breakfast from £9.00 per night; Evening Meal optional. Reductions for children. SAE please for terms.

LAUNCESTON near. Mr and Mrs R.P. Irving, The Old Station, Egloskerry, Near Launceston PL15 8ST (North Petherwin [0566-85] 492). This former village railway station makes an interesting base for exploring the area: within half an hour's drive are the splendid North Cornwall coast, Bodmin Moor and Dartmoor, and there are fine historic houses and gardens (National Trust, etc). The setting is rural, the large garden, partly wild, overlooks open grazing land. There is a spacious sittingroom (formerly booking hall) for guests' use and a separate diningroom. One bedroom with twin beds, one with single bed and bunk beds, both with washbasins; guests' bathroom. Bed and Breakfast from £10.50; optional Evening Meal £4.50. Mid-week and one night bookings accepted.

· HURDON FARM ·

AA & RAC LISTED
FARM HOLIDAY GUIDE DIPLOMA WINNER 1988

This 400-acre mixed working farm and its gracious 18th century stone farmhouse is situated 1½ miles from the ancient market town of Launceston and within one mile of leisure centre with heated swimming pool. Great priority is placed on the use of our own farm and garden produce to create sumptuous dinners, home made rolls, soups and starters. Traditional and original main courses, delicious desserts and our own home made clotted cream, and to start the day a hearty four-course English Breakfast. Most of the bedrooms have bathroom en suite. Log fire in the lounge for those colder evenings. Tea on arrival. Morning tea and evening drinks provided as part of the service. Fire certificate issued. Reductions for senior citizens and children. Bed and Breakfast or Bed, Breakfast and Evening Meal. Brochure on request from:

**Mrs Margaret Smith, Hurdon Farm, Launceston, Cornwall PL15 9LS
or Telephone: 0566 772955.**

LISKEARD. Mrs Stephanie Rowe, Tregondale Farm, Menheniot, Liskeard PL14 3RG (Liskeard [0579] 42407). ✿ ✿ Working farm, join in. Tregondale is

situated in an attractive valley, with woodland walks. Set back in a walled garden with a swing and see-saw. Mixed farm of 180 acres with a pony; easily located between A38 and A390. This characteristic farmhouse provides a high standard of comfort, good home produced food, friendly atmosphere with personal attention. Close to coast, Looe, Plymouth, the moors, National Trust properties, golf, fishing. Children's amusements, heated swimming pool at the market town of Liskeard. Local pub. Three double rooms with washbasins, bathroom/toilet, lounge, diningroom, log fires, colour TV, sun porch, picnic table. Reduced rates for children, babysitting. Bed and Breakfast, optional Evening Meal. AA listed. Open all year. Brochure available — good value.

LISKEARD. Mrs Bridget Endacott, Upton Farm House, Upton Cross, Liskeard PL14 5AZ (0579 62689). ✿ ✿ Old Duchy Farmhouse situated in beautiful

countryside on the eastern side of Bodmin Moor. Ideal for visiting both the rugged north and popular south coasts, Plymouth, Launceston, our National Trust properties and Dobwalls Theme Park (six miles). Sports available include golf, horse riding, swimming, wind surfing, fishing and canoeing. The house is elegant and spacious comprising one family room and two double rooms en-suite. Enjoy your evenings relaxing in the beamed lounge with open fireplace, TV and video, an excellent library and many board games. Children are well catered for with a cot, high chair and push chair provided. Also available are high teas, babysitting plus toys. Parents can enjoy the nearby famous Caradon Inn (50 yards) or other excellent restaurants nearby. Brochure available.

LISKEARD. Mrs A.R. Hawke, Cartuther Barton, Liskeard (Liskeard [0579] 43244). Cartuther Barton is a pleasant Cornish manor farmhouse, situated one mile from Liskeard on the A38 Plymouth road. Within easy reach of Looe, Polperro and many other coastal resorts. Ideal for touring. Lounge with TV; diningroom with separate tables, and hot and cold water in bedrooms. Ample free parking space. Bed, Breakfast and Evening Dinner. Terms on application.

LISKEARD. Mrs Elizabeth Rowe, Trewint Farm, Menheniot, Liskeard PL14 3RE (Liskeard [0579] 47155 or 62237). Working farm, join in. Trewint Working

Farm is situated about one and a half miles off the A38. Set in peaceful, rural surroundings, four miles from old market town of Liskeard, local popular attractions and National Trust. The 200 acre farm has attractive valley walks, cattle, sheep, pigs; pony for children, play area and they may also help feed the lambs, calves. Ideal for touring Cornwall and South Devon. The south coast is within easy reach with fishing harbours Looe, Polperro, Mevagissey. Bodmin Moor four miles and St. Mellion Golf Course eight miles. Vegetables and naturally fed meat, all home produced, provides a delicious four course Evening Meal. Full English Breakfast, bedtime drink, packed lunches if required. Double, twin and family rooms, all with washbasin, toilet and shower en-suite. Tea/coffee making facilities, electric blankets. Cot, high chair, babysitting (reductions for children). Lounge with colour TV, large open fire for the cooler evenings. Five minutes' walk from popular village pub. Sorry, no pets. Open all year. SAE for brochure or ring for a chat about your requirements. Cornwall Tourist Board registered. RAC listed.

LISKEARD. Mrs Lindsay M. Pendray, Caduscott, East Taphouse, Liskeard PL14 4NG (Liskeard [0579] 20262). Working farm. Down the lane where the

wild flowers nod in passing; to relax and unwind in attractive 17th century listed farmhouse peeping over the valley where streams converge to make the 10 mile journey to the sea at Looe. Double room (en-suite toilet/shower), adjoining twin-bedded room. Traditional Bed and Breakfast with Evening Meal served in a large lounge/diningroom where a log fire assures you of a warm welcome, also central heating. Children especially welcome; cot, high chair and open spaces to play in with swing and climbing frame. The Pendray family have farmed Caduscott for over 60 years and will make every effort to ensure that you discover Cornwall.

LISKEARD. Mrs E.R. Elford, Tresulgan Farm, Horningtops, Liskeard PL14 3PU (Widegates [050-34] 268). 🐑🐑 Working farm, join in. Tresulgan is a 115-acre

dairy farm situated on the Plymouth/Liskeard road, set in quiet surroundings. The attractive farmhouse, built in the 1700s, still retains its quiet character and original beams. Modernisation over the past few years, including double glazing, has added to its comfort. The bedrooms (two en-suite), which overlook the large enclosed garden, have picturesque views of the wooded Seaton Valley. Nearest beach at Seaton (four miles), and the popular fishing village of Looe is six miles away (shark fishing and boating). Sailing, golf, riding, Woolly Monkey Sanctuary, Forest Railway, National Trust properties and other attractions within a few miles. Friendly accommodation — two double, one single, one family bedrooms, all with washbasins; bathroom/toilet and shower; separate toilet, shower and washbasin. Children welcome. Colour TV in guests' lounge. Price includes cooked Breakfast, three-course Evening Meal and Light Supper. SAE, please, for terms and Brochure.

THE LIZARD PENINSULA. Mr and Mrs Barbara and John Rosindale, Treworder Farm, Ruan Minor, Helston TR12 7JL (The Lizard [0326] 290970). Only

three miles from England's most southerly point. A converted barn, in a quiet and secluded courtyard, yet within 75 yards of centre of village. Ideal location for a relaxing holiday with the emphasis on an informal and friendly atmosphere. Well situated for all beaches, touring, walking, sailing and fishing. One double, one twin-bedded rooms (with extra bed if required). Tea/coffee making facilities and TV in both rooms. Bathroom, two toilets. Bed and Breakfast, Dinner optional. Weekly terms. Children over five years welcome. Sorry, no pets. Good food, home grown vegetables whenever possible. Ample parking. Tourist Board registered. Brittany Ferries recommended. Brochure available.

WHEN MAKING ENQUIRIES PLEASE MENTION
FARM HOLIDAY GUIDES

WIDEGATES, Nr. LOOE
CORNWALL PL13 1QN
Tel: Widegates (05034) 223

A delightful country house, furnished with antiques, set in ten acres of lawns, meadows, woods, streams, and ponds with superb views down wooded valley to sea. Log fires. Delicious home cooking. Candlelit dining. Licensed.

In the grounds – many birds, animals and flowers, a lovely heated swimming pool, a croquet lawn and a stone barn for games including snooker and table tennis.

Nearby – golf, fishing, tennis, horse riding, glorious walks and beaches.

The perfect centre for visiting all parts of Cornwall and Devon.

WINNER AA Guest House of the
Year Award West of England

Bed and Breakfast from £16.50.
Four course dinner from £10.00.

Special Short Break discounts.

Open March to October

Please send for our free brochure.

A warm welcome assured by Alexander and Sally Low

THE LIZARD PENINSULA. Mrs Joan Gilbert, Erisey Barton, Ruan Minor, Helston TR12 7LJ (Mullion [0326] 240296). Working farm. Erisey Barton is a 500-acre beef and sheep farm with a historic 17th century farmhouse set in walled gardens. Guests can enjoy peaceful and relaxed walks on the farm which borders the Goonhilly Downs. There is a Nature Reserve and Farm Museum. Sandy beaches, golf and horse riding within a three mile radius. Two double (family) rooms with tea/coffee making facilities. Large beamed lounge with piano and TV. Bed and Full English Breakfast only, served in separate Breakfast Room from £10 per adult; special rates for children who are very welcome. Babysitting if required. Mrs Gilbert will welcome her guests for a friendly, homely and comfortable holiday.

LOOE. Mrs D. Eastley, Bake Farm, Pelynt, Looe PL13 2QQ (Lanreath [0503] 20244). Working farm. This is an old farmhouse, bearing the Trelawnay Coat of Arms (1610) situated midway between Looe and Fowey. There are three double bedrooms all with washbasins; bathroom, two toilets; combined sitting/diningroom. Children welcome at reduced rates, babysitting available. Sorry, no pets. Open from May to September. Plenty of fresh farm food, a lot of home produce including Cornish clotted cream, an abundance of roasts including home-bred chicken. A car is essential for touring the area, ample parking. There is much to see and do here — horse riding four miles, golf seven. The sea is only five miles away and there is shark fishing at Looe. SAE, please for terms for Evening Meal, Bed and Breakfast. Cleanliness guaranteed.

LOOE. A.F. Tomkinson, Pixies Holt, Shutta, East Looe PL13 1JD (Looe [05036] 2726). ✿✿ An

old-world house converted into a small, comfortable, centrally heated hotel in grounds of one acre with private car park. Peacefully situated with magnificent views over rivers, woodlands and countryside, yet just seven minutes' walk to picturesque Looe and beaches. All seven bedrooms have radio, TV, tea-making facilities and washbasins, and most have their own private bathroom/toilets. There is a comfortable lounge with colour TV and residential licence. RAC listed. Access, American Express and Visa welcome. Bed and Breakfast from £13.50 to £21 per person per day according to season.

LOOE. Mrs Jean Henly, Bucklawren Farm, St. Martin, Looe PL13 1NZ (Widegates [05034] 738).

✿✿✿ **Working farm.** Bucklawren is situated deep in the unspoilt countryside yet only one mile from the beach, two and a half miles from Looe and only one mile from the Woolly Monkey Sanctuary. It is mentioned in the Domesday Book, but the manor house is now replaced by a 19th century spacious farmhouse, which has a large garden and beautiful sea views. We offer excellent accommodation with en-suite and family rooms, with farmhouse cooking in a friendly relaxed atmosphere. There is ample parking. Open all year. Reduced rates for children. Terms from £12 for Bed and Breakfast; Evening Meal £7 (optional). Brochure on request. Farm Holiday Bureau member.

MARAZION near. Mrs N.J. White, Ennys, St. Hilary, Penzance TR20 9BZ (Penzance [0736]

740262). ✿✿✿ **Working farm.** Beautiful 16th century manor farm in idyllically peaceful surroundings. Imaginative candlelit suppers from our own produce. Comfort guaranteed in tastefully decorated surroundings, overlooking walled garden with patio area and grass tennis court. Within easy reach of many lovely beaches and coves and the famous St. Michael's Mount. Log fires. Bread baked daily. Three double bedrooms with en-suite facilities, one with romantic four-poster bed. Two family suites. Games room. Coarse fishing, pony trekking, golf and windsurfing nearby. Car essential. Dinner, Bed and Breakfast from £28 per person; Bed and Breakfast from £17. Children's and special weekly rates. As featured in Country Living Magazine.

MEVAGISSEY. Mrs Jane Youlden, Steep House, Portmellon Cove, Mevagissey PL26 2PH (0726

843732). ✿✿ Steep House stands in an acre of ground by the sea, in a natural cove which has a safe, sandy beach 20 yards from the large garden. Comfortable, centrally heated double bedrooms all having washbasins and sea or beach views, colour TV and tea/coffee maker, some en-suite. Full English Breakfast and imaginative home cooked dinners of a very high standard served in wood panelled diningroom overlooking Portmellon Cove. All meals include as much home grown produce as possible and barbecue evening meals by the heated swimming pool are a popular event during the summer months. Guests welcome all year. Modest prices, special weekly and winter break rates. Private parking. Fire Certificate. All enquiries welcomed.

MEVAGISSEY. Mrs Anne Hennah, Treleaven Farm, Mevagissey PL26 6RZ (Mevagissey [0726] 842413). Working farm. Treleaven Farm is situated in quiet, pleasant surroundings overlooking the village and the sea. The 200-acre mixed farm is well placed for visitors to enjoy the many attractions of Mevagissey with its quaint narrow streets and lovely shops. Fishing and boat trips are available and very popular. The house offers a warm and friendly welcome with the emphasis on comfort, cleanliness and good food using local produce. A licensed bar and solar heated swimming pool add to your holiday enjoyment, together with a games room and putting green. Tastefully furnished throughout, with central heating, there are five double bedrooms and one family bedroom, all en-suite with tea/coffee making facilities and TV; bathroom, two toilets. Sittingroom and diningroom. Open February to November for Evening Dinner, Bed and Breakfast or Bed and Breakfast. Sorry, no pets. SAE, please, for particulars or telephone.

MEVAGISSEY. Mrs J. Rowe, Rosedale, Valley Park, Tregony Hill, Mevagissey PL26 6RS (Mevagissey [0726] 842769). This is the beautiful view from the sittingroom of "Rosedale", an attractive modern farmhouse with its own market garden. It is approached by a private road — no sound of passing traffic — and guests are assured of a warm welcome, good food and home produced vegetables and fruit, with strawberries in the summer. Three minutes' walk from shops and picturesque harbour with fine beaches nearby and pleasant walks in the area. Two double bedrooms, one bedroom with twin beds, all with washbasins. Dining/sittingroom with colour TV. Bathroom with shower, two toilets. Children seven years and older welcome, babysitting by arrangement. Sorry, no pets. Ample free parking at the house. Open Easter to October. Reductions for children under 10. Evening Dinner, Bed and Breakfast from £90 per week. Enquiries welcome (SAE please). Cornwall Tourist Board registered.

MEVAGISSEY. Mrs Diana Owens, Mevagissey House, Vicarage Hill, Mevagissey PL26 6SZ (Mevagissey [0726] 842427). 🐾🐾🐾 Georgian Country House restored to its original elegance. Log fires, home cooking and licensed bar add to the comfort. Each bedroom has washbasin, colour TV; some rooms with en-suite facilities. Surrounded by four acres of lawns, shrubs and woodland setting, together with three self-catering cottages. An ideal centre for fishing, with nearby coves, beaches, golf, riding and National Trust properties. Open March to October. Children over seven years welcome with reductions for families sharing. Regret no pets. Bed and Breakfast from £16; optional Evening Meal. RAC Acclaimed. AA Listed. Telephone or write for brochures.

MEVAGISSEY. Mrs Linda Hennah, Kerry Anna Country House, Treleaven Farm, Mevagissey PL26 6RZ (Mevagissey [0726] 843558). Working farm. 🐾🐾🐾 The Hennah family invite you to enjoy the peace and tranquillity at Treleaven Farm, a working farm overlooking the quaint fishing village of Mevagissey. Surrounded by beautiful countryside, abundant wild life and flowers. All rooms en-suite and have welcome tray and colour TV. Family room with en-suite bathroom. Licensed bar, games barn, outdoor swimming pool heated in season, putting green. Creative and traditional food with choice of menu. Colour brochure available.

MEVAGISSEY near. Mrs Sally Wade, Tregidgeo Farm, Grampound, Truro TR2 4SP (St. Austell [0726] 882450). Working farm. Tregidgeo is a comfortably furnished farmhouse in a beautifully secluded and peaceful setting. On the edge of the unspoilt Roseland Peninsula and within easy reach of the main St. Austell to Truro road, it is ideally situated for touring and any part of the county is easily reached on a day's excursion. There are several sandy beaches and the fishing village of Mevagissey is nearby. Good home cooking. Children welcome at reduced rates; cot and babysitting offered. Bedrooms with washbasins, continental quilts and tea-making facilities, also separate shower room. One en-suite bedroom available. Lounge, diningroom and snooker room. Evening Dinner, Bed and Breakfast or Bed and Breakfast. Terms on request with SAE please.

MULLION. Mrs L.M. Curnow, Nanfan Farm, Cury, Helston (0326 240413). Friendly family-run dairy farm located in a lovely rural valley only one and a half miles from popular Poldhu Cove, ideal for touring all the local attractions and towns. Accommodation is in three comfortable double rooms and two spacious family rooms all with washbasins; two bathrooms with showers, two toilets, one bath; TV lounge and attractive diningroom, both of which face into the orchard and garden where children are very welcome to play. Regret no pets. Open from May to October. Reduced rates for children. Half Board or Bed and Breakfast available. Terms on request.

See also Colour Display Advertisement **NEWQUAY near. Mr and Mrs Rowlands, Crantock Plains Farm, Near Newquay TR8 5PH (Crantock [0637] 830253).** Charming character farmhouse in peaceful countryside. Comfort, home cooking and personal service combine to make an enjoyable, relaxing holiday. Crantock Plains Farm is situated two and a half miles from Newquay and half a mile off the A3075 Newquay-Redruth road. One and a half miles to the village of Crantock with Post Office, village stores, tea rooms, two pubs and beautiful sandy beach. Riding stables and many sporting activities nearby. Choice of double, single and family bedrooms, two en-suite bedrooms; shower room, toilets. Sittingroom and diningroom. Home grown vegetables where available. Table licence. Sorry, no pets. Bed, Breakfast and Evening Meal or Bed and Breakfast. Terms and brochure on request with SAE please.

NEWQUAY. Mrs K. Woodley, Degembris Farmhouse, St. Newlyn East, Newquay TR8 5HY (Mitchell

[0872] 510555). 💘💘 *Commended.* Degembris is a listed Cornish farmhouse built in the 18th century on the site of the old manor. Overlooking a beautiful wooded valley the house, set on a 165 acre working farm, still retains much of its character to the present day. Our country trail will take you through natural woodland and fields visiting the pond and exploring the valley of the bluebells. Degembris is ideally situated in the centre of Cornwall enabling you to explore easily from coast to coast and from Land's End to the Tamar. All rooms have washbasins and tea/coffee making facilities. Open Easter to October for Bed, Breakfast and Evening Meal or Bed and Breakfast only. We will provide you with comfort, home cooking and a taste of country life. OS Ref: SW852568. AA Listed; Cream of Cornwall; FHB Member.

NEWQUAY. Mrs J.C. Wilson, Manuels Farm, Newquay TR8 4NY (Newquay [0637] 873577). 💘💘

Commended. **Working farm.** Built in the early 17th century on a site mentioned in Domesday Book, "Manuels" is situated two miles inland from Newquay on the A392. In a sheltered wooded valley it offers peace of the countryside with charm of traditional Cornish farmhouse. Emphasis placed on comfort, good farm produced food and a friendly relaxed atmosphere. Pets galore and a games room with table tennis, etc. Children especially welcome, free baby-sitting every night. Two double, one single and two family bedrooms; plus cot and two high chairs available. Open all year except Christmas. Log fires and storage heating. Reduced rates for children. Pets accepted but not in the house. Terms from £11 per night per person for Bed and Breakfast; Evening Meal from £7. Packed lunches and suppers also available. Farm cottage for self-catering also available. AA listed.

NEWQUAY. Mrs S. C. Coombe, Legonna Farm, Newquay (Newquay [0637] 872272). Legonna is

situated in a pleasant valley two miles from Newquay. An ideal centre for visiting all the beaches and beauty spots of Cornwall. Open Easter until end of October, the house is large and has been tastefully furnished and fully carpeted throughout. All bedrooms have washbasins, razor sockets. Large diningroom with separate tables, TV lounge and sun lounge; also a small licensed bar for guests only. Legonna also has a swimming pool, hard surface tennis court, table tennis and snooker. Swings for the young children, and plenty of play area. Babysitting available and is included in terms. Cot and high chair. Pets welcome. Bed, Breakfast and Evening Dinner. Reductions for children — for Senior Citizens early and late season. Terms from £95. Fire Certificate.

NEWQUAY near. Mr & Mrs Alan Grateley, Trewerry Mill, Trerice, St. Newlyn East, Near Newquay

TR8 5HS (Mitchell [0872] 510345). A picturesque 17th century listed water mill situated in quiet peaceful countryside. Attractive gardens, trout stream, variety of birds, and a donkey. Open 24 March — 31 October. Three doubles, one single and two family bedrooms with washbasins and shaver points. Bathroom/shower, two toilets. Fully carpeted and centrally heated. Unusual Mill lounge with log fire. Diningroom with individual tables. Delicious home cooking using home grown fruit and vegetables. Licensed with interesting wine list. Car essential — FREE parking. No Smoking in any part of the house. Children over 7 years only welcome. Lovely sandy beaches — four miles. Ideal base for touring Cornwall. Brochure available.

NEWQUAY. Mrs O.B. Dunn, "Heidelberg," Gaverigan, Indian Queens, St Columb TR9 6HE (St

Austell [0726] 860392). This small, quiet guest house is just off the A30, a quiet spot but convenient for touring the whole of Cornwall, with numerous beaches nearby and Newquay seven miles. Five double and two family bedrooms with washbasins; TV lounge; diningroom with good varied food; bathroom and shower; two toilets. Children welcome at reduced rates; cot and babysitting. Car essential — good parking. Coarse fishing; riding in the area. Cornwall Tourist Board registered; Fire Certificate. Cheerful service, with every attention to your comforts, will ensure an enjoyable holiday. Evening Dinner, Bed and Breakfast; or Bed and Breakfast. SAE, please.

Shepherds Farm
Newlyn East, Newquay TR8 5NW

A warm welcome awaits you at Shepherds, a 500-acre working farm situated between Newquay and Perranporth and close to 5 large, sandy beaches. OS Ref: SW8 16545. The house is pleasantly decorated and furnished. En suite bedrooms and tea-making facilities. Large diningroom and comfortable lounge. Free horse riding. Games room. Good home cooking with personal service. Bed and Breakfast from £9, Evening Meal £6.50. Open all year.

For further details contact Heather Harvey (087254) 340/502.

NEWQUAY near. Newquay Holiday Motel, Porth, Near Newquay. Ideally situated in a peaceful valley about one mile from Newquay. Set in five acres of its own grounds. One, two and three room suites. All en-suite with tea making facilities and colour TV. Plenty of car parking space. Newquay overlooks a succession of fine beaches (11 in all) and is a major centre for surfing. There is sea fishing, wind sailing, boat hire, sea trips, diving, sports centre, coastal footpaths, a fine golf course, variety theatre, leisure park, zoo/animal park, nightlife, bowls, ten-pin bowling, swimming pools. Newquay Holiday Motel is ideal for the exploration of Cornwall, the coves and caves, the harbours and fishing villages and the country lanes and woodlands for which Cornwall is famed. Three-day Breaks only £55 which includes suite, English Breakfast and Evening Meal. Full colour brochure on request. All bookings through **Booking Office, Grosvenor House, 20 St. Andrews Crescent, Cardiff, Glamorgan CF1 3DD (0222 387070. Fax: 0222 223692).**

See also Colour Display Advertisement **NEWQUAY near. Dalswinton Country House Hotel, St. Mawgan, Near Newquay TR8 4EZ (St Mawgan [0637] 860385).** An old Cornish house of immense character in one and a half acres of secluded grounds, overlooking the beautiful Valley of Lanherne with views to the sea. Ideally situated between Newquay and Padstow, reputed to be the finest coastline in Europe. Superb beaches and coastal walks within two miles. The hotel has been completely refurbished and offers superb cooking and comfort in a friendly atmosphere. Open all year. Colour brochure available.

NEWQUAY near. Cy and Barbara Moore, The Ranch House, Trencreek, Newquay TR8 4NR (Newquay [0637] 875419). A detached licensed bungalow one and a half miles from Newquay set in two and a half acres outside the village of Trencreek with views overlooking countryside, Newquay and the sea beyond. Lovely gardens. Open Easter to October. Accommodation comprises three doubles (one en-suite), two family, one single; two shower rooms, three separate toilets; two lounges (one with TV); diningroom with separate tables. Ample parking. Pets welcome by arrangement. Good wholesome home cooking. Full English Breakfast and five course Evening Dinner offered. Cot and high chair available. Bed and Breakfast from £77 weekly; Bed, Breakfast and Evening Meal from £105 weekly. Reduced rates for children sharing. Phone or send stamp only for brochure.

See also Colour Display Advertisement **NEWQUAY near. Marian and Derrick Molloy, Tregurrian Hotel, Watergate Bay, Near Newquay TR8 4AB (St. Mawgan [0637] 860280).** Peaceful position between Newquay and Padstow — 100 yards from glorious sandy beach and spectacular Atlantic coastline. Open Easter to November, 27 rooms (most en-suite) have tea makers, radio/listening, colour TV available. Heated pool, sun patio, games room, solarium. Licensed. Central for touring Cornwall; parties and coaches by arrangement. Spring and Autumn Breaks. Dinner, Bed and Breakfast £110 to £200 inclusive. Children welcome at reduced rates. Brochure from resident proprietors **Marian and Derrick Molloy.**

PADSTOW near. Mrs Ethel Dennis, Tregavone Farm, St. Merryn, Near Padstow PL28 8JZ (Padstow [0841] 520148). This 120-acre beef and sheep farm is open for guests from March to October. It is set in peaceful surroundings in an area of great scenic beauty. Situated near the coast road to Treyarnon, Porthcothan, Constantine, Harlyn and Trevose Head. Golf, surfing and sailing can be enjoyed. Shops one mile at St. Merryn. One double and two family bedrooms; one bathroom, toilet; sitting room with colour TV; diningroom. All rooms are carpeted. Children over five welcome at reduced rates. Good home cooking served in friendly atmosphere, with eggs, milk, cream and vegetables fresh from the farm. **Full English Breakfast from £10.** Car essential, ample parking space. Sorry, no pets. This farm is just two miles from the sea. SAE for terms, please.

PADSTOW near. Andrew and Sue Hamilton, Trevone Bay Hotel, Trevone, Near Padstow PL28 8QS (Padstow [0841] 520243). ♛♛ A friendly, family-owned and run hotel with panoramic views of the superb coastline. Ideally situated in a quiet village, two miles from Padstow and 500 yards from beautiful, sandy Trevone beach. There are 14 comfortable bedrooms with tea-making facilities, most en-suite. Three lounges, bar and spacious diningroom. Excellent home cooked food with a choice for all courses. Within easy reach of most of Cornwall's tourist attractions, or suitable for a relaxing holiday walking the coastal paths or lazing on the beach. All ages very welcome. Dogs accepted. Tourist Board registered. From £20 Dinner, Bed and Breakfast. Open Easter to October. Please contact us for further details and a colour brochure.

PENZANCE. Mrs Penny Lally, Rose Farm, Chyanhal, Buryas Bridge, Penzance TR19 6AN (0736 731808). Working farm, join in. Rose Farm is a small working farm close to the picturesque fishing villages of Mousehole and Newlyn and seven miles from Land's End. The 200 year old granite farmhouse has two en-suite rooms, one double and one family suite. Adjacent to the main house is the barn room with a romantic 15th century four-poster; this suite is ideal for a honeymoon (first or second!). We have all manner of animals from pedigree cattle to pot-bellied pigs! Rose Farm is cosy and relaxing and a warm welcome awaits you. Bed and Breakfast from £16.

PENZANCE. Mrs R. Warren, Tredinney Farm, Crows-an-Wra, St. Buryan, Penzance TR19 6HX (St. Buryan [0736] 810352). Working farm. Tredinney is a working dairy farm five miles from Penzance and Land's End. Immediately behind the farm is Bartinney hill with magnificent unspoiled views. Ideal for touring, country walks and close to pretty coves and sandy beaches. Variety of sports nearby. Accommodation consists of one family bedroom and one double bedroom, both with washbasins and tea making facilities; bathroom/toilet, separate shower room; diningroom with colour TV. Cot and high chair available. Car advisable. Bed and Breakfast from £56 per week, Evening Meal optional. Also very clean, well-equipped self-catering cottage to let; sleeps seven plus cot. Pleasant garden. Terms from £80 per week. Tourist Board registered.

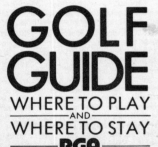

PENZANCE. Mrs Monica Olds, Mulfra Farm, Newmill, Penzance TR20 8XP (Penzance [0736] 63940).

This 20 acre smallholding on Mulfra Hill on the edge of the Penwith Moors has panoramic views and provides a rare opportunity to stay in an area of historic and natural beauty. Over 300 years old the farmhouse, which is attractively furnished and decorated, offers a double room en-suite, twin/family room with washbasin and colour TV; bathroom; sun porch; diningroom; lounge with colour TV, inglenook fireplace and Cornish stone oven. Tea/coffee facilities in bedrooms. Plenty of good food. Warm, friendly atmosphere with dogs, horses, cows and calves. Car essential — ample parking. Three miles to Penzance and seven miles to St. Ives. Bed, Breakfast and Evening Meal from £82 per week. Further details sent with pleasure.

PENZANCE. Mrs A. Rowe, Higher Crankan Farm, Newmill, Penzance TR20 8UT (0736 63636). Solid granite farmhouse overlooking Mount's Bay and most certainly "off the beaten track". If you can navigate the rough farm lane you are assured of good company, good food and good views of this area of outstanding natural beauty. Situated between Penzance and St. Ives, there are many sandy beaches within easy reach. Family, double, twin and single rooms. Children most welcome. Bed and Breakfast from £7 to £10. Children under five years FREE, five to 15 years at two third adult rate. Family rates available.

PENZANCE. Mrs A.R. Blewett, Menwidden Farm, Ludgvan, Penzance TR20 8BN (Penzance [0736] 740415). Working farm, join in.

Menwidden Farm is centrally situated in west Cornwall four miles from St. Ives north coast and three miles from Marazion (south coast). Within easy reach of Land's End and The Lizard. It is a dairy and market gardening farm of 40 acres. Comfortable bedrooms and good home cooking including Roast Meats, pasties and Cornish Cream. Four double, two family bedrooms, one with washbasin; bathroom, shower room and toilet; sittingroom, diningroom. Cot, high chair, reduced rates for children. Pets allowed. Open February to November. Car essential — parking. Lots of interesting places nearby including many beaches and coves, St Michael's Mount, Bird Paradise, model village. Fire Certificate held. Tourist Board listed and winner of Farm Holiday Guide Diploma 1986. Evening Meal, Bed and Breakfast from £85 per week or Bed and Breakfast from £10 per night.

PERRANPORTH. Mrs Thelma Hawkey, Lambourne Castle Farm, Penhallow, Truro TR4 9LQ (Truro [0872] 572365). Working farm.

Lambourne Castle Farmhouse is stone-built and adjoins a tarmacadam council road only 200 yards from the main Newquay to Redruth road. It is just two miles from the golden sands at Perranporth which is ideal for surfing, also 18-hole golf course, pottery and horse riding. An ideal centre for the whole of Cornwall, there are beautiful local walks. Plenty of good wholesome food much of which is produced on the farm. The comfortable accommodation comprises two double and two family rooms (three with washbasins); bathroom, toilet; sittingroom; diningroom. Children welcome. Regret no dogs. A car is essential — ample parking space. Open Easter to end of October. Fire Certificate held. SAE, please for terms for Evening Dinner, Bed and Breakfast or Bed and Breakfast. Reductions for children sharing parents' room.

PERRANPORTH. Alan and Janet Lambeth, Perrancourt Hotel, 27 Tywarnhayle Road, Perranporth TR6 0DX (Truro [0872] 572151).

This attractive private hotel, quietly situated near beach, shops, cliff walks is open from March to November. Residential Licence. Tourist Boards registered. Well appointed single, double and family rooms all have washbasins (some with private WC and bath/shower), tea-making facilities, radio/intercom/baby listening service. Lounge with colour TV or TV in own room optional extra. Car parking. Children at reduced rates if sharing parents' room. Pets accepted. Central heating. Access at all times. Concessionary rates at local golf course. Alan and Janet concentrate on personal service, relaxed family atmosphere and exceptionally good value. Evening Dinner, Bed and Breakfast from £110 weekly, £15.90 daily. Bed and Breakfast from £11 per day, £77 weekly. Please write or phone for colour brochure.

PLEASE ENCLOSE A STAMPED ADDRESSED ENVELOPE WITH ENQUIRIES

POLZEATH. Mrs B. Dally, Tredower Barton, St. Minver, Wadebridge PL27 6RG (Wadebridge [020-881] 3501). Working farm. Tredower Farm is situated in pleasant position, near Rock and Polzeath on the Cornish coast, where there are ample opportunities available for swimming, sailing, surfing, riding, squash and golf; also numerous lovely walks along the golden sandy beaches and the cliff tops. Open moors nearby for rambles and picnics. Nearest town is Wadebridge, three miles. The mixed farm is 141 acres. Tredower Barton has one family room, and one double room. Diningroom/lounge and TV. Guests' bathroom and toilet. Children welcome, cot, high chair. Babysitting if requested. Sorry, no pets. Homely atmosphere and good food assured. Open May to October. Car essential, ample parking. Bed, Breakfast and Evening Meal (optional). Evening hot drinks included. Reductions for children. Terms on request with SAE, please.

PORT ISAAC. Mrs Pamela Richards, Bodannon Farm, Trewetha, Port Isaac PL29 3RU (Bodmin [0208] 880381). Working farm. Guests are catered for all year round at Bodannon Farm, half-a-mile from the picturesque village of Port Isaac and the sea on 100-acre mixed farm. The house has all modern conveniences. Two family and two double bedrooms, all with washbasins; bathroom, two toilets; lounge with TV; diningroom with separate tables. Children welcome — cot available; occasional babysitting. Ample parking space for cars which are necessary here. The menu includes roast chicken, pork, lamb, beef; fresh farm eggs, cream etc., home grown vegetables. Pets are permitted. Fire Certificate held. SAE, please, for terms for Evening Dinner, Bed and Breakfast or Bed and Breakfast only. Cornwall Tourist Board registered.

PORT ISAAC. Mr and Mrs D. Phelps, Trewetha Farm, Port Isaac PL29 3RU (Port Isaac [0208] 880256). ♛♛ 18th century traditionally Cornish Farmhouse with 20 acres of grazing land in "Betjeman country", on the Heritage Coast. Superb sea and countryside views. Poultry, sheep, miniature Shetland ponies kept. Ideal area for surfing, wind-surfing, trout and sea fishing, bird-watching and walking, footpath to beach from the farm. Two double, one family bedrooms all with washbasins; separate diningroom and lounge with colour TV. Access to house throughout day. Tea-making facilities. Reductions for children, babysitting by arrangement. Bed and full English Breakfast or vegetarian breakfast. Fire Certificate held. Also available, holiday bungalow. For terms and further details, SAE please.

ROSELAND PENINSULA. Mrs Shirley E. Pascoe, Court Farm, Philleigh, Truro TR2 5NB (Portscatho [087-258] 313). Working farm, join in. Situated in the heart of the Roseland Peninsula at Philleigh, with its lovely Norman church and 17th century Roseland Inn, this spacious and attractive old farmhouse, set in over an acre of garden, offers Bed and Breakfast accommodation. There are double, single and family bedrooms with washbasins and tea making facilities; bathroom, separate toilet; large comfortable lounge with colour TV. Enjoy a full English breakfast in the traditional farmhouse kitchen. Children welcome, cot, high chair, babysitting available. Sorry, no pets indoors. Car essential — ample parking. The family livestock and arable farm includes 50 acres of woodlands which border the beautiful Fal Estuary providing superb walking, picnic areas and bird-watching, whilst the nearest beaches are just over two miles away. Tourist Board Registered. Please write or telephone for brochure and terms.

See also Colour Display Advertisement **ST. AGNES. Mrs D. Welsby, Blights Manor Farm, Wheal Butson, St. Agnes TR5 0PT (St. Agnes [087-255] 3142).** Situated amidst 22 acres of rolling countryside just one mile from St. Agnes and four from Perranporth, Blight's Manor is ideally placed for visiting superb beaches, quaint fishing villages and all the best tourist attractions. Facilities at this renovated Cornish farmhouse include outdoor heated pool, games room, stables, fitness room and grassed area for football, etc. Guests are comfortably accommodated in tastefully furnished bedrooms, most with private facilities. Contact **Mrs Welsby** for colour brochure.

See also Colour Display Advertisement **ST. AGNES. Mr S. Manico, Rosemundy House Hotel, St. Agnes TR5 0UF (St. Agnes [087 255] 2101).** Rosemundy House Hotel occupies a most sheltered and secluded position in the village of St. Agnes and within a mile of Trevaunance Cove beach. Built around 1780, Rosemundy has been tastefully extended to provide a charming diningroom and many bedrooms with en-suite facilities. Our amenities include an attractive licensed bar, 45ft outdoor heated swimming pool and a large games room with table tennis, pool, snooker, darts, etc. The informal grounds comprise some four acres of gardens and woodland secluding the property and making Rosemundy ideal for a restful holiday. Badminton, croquet and putting may be enjoyed in the grounds. Our hotel boasts a warm and friendly atmosphere with good, home English cooking. Dinner, Bed and Breakfast from £125 to £200, Bed and Breakfast from £100 to £175.

FHG PUBLICATIONS LIMITED publish a large range of well-known accommodation guides. We will be happy to send you details or you can use the order form at the back of this book.

ST. AGNES. Mrs Dorothy Gill-Carey, Penkerris, Penwinnick Road, St. Agnes TR5 0PA (St. Agnes [087-255] 2262).  Enchanting Edwardian country residence on outskirts of village, fields on one side, but pubs and shops only 100 yards on the other. Open all year. Beautiful diningroom and lounge with colour TV and video, piano and open log fires. Central heating. Single, double, twin and family rooms available all with TV, tea making facilities, radios, washbasins, shaver points. There is a shower room as well as bathrooms. Large lawn with garden chairs and tables. Ample parking. Delicious meals, traditional roasts with fresh vegetables and home made fruit tarts. There are three beaches nearby for swimming and surfing. Superb cliff walks. Tennis, riding and gliding locally. Good touring centre. Bed and Breakfast from £10; Evening Meal from £6.50.

ST. BURYAN. Mrs S.N. Hosking, Boskenna Home Farm, St Buryan, Penzance TR19 6DQ (St Buryan [0736] 810250). Boskenna is a working dairy farm situated about five miles from Land's End. Lovely sandy beaches within a four miles radius, beautiful coastal path walks, old Cornish stones and legends, Minack Theatre, St Michael's Mount within easy reach. Car essential. Only six guests taken at any one time. One double bedroom and two twin bedded rooms; bathroom; sittingroom with colour TV; diningroom with separate tables. High chair and cot available. Rooms available at all times. Children welcome, no dogs. Parking. Bed and Full English Breakfast only. Open Easter to end September. SAE for terms.

ST. COLUMB. Mrs Mary Hobson, Brentons Farm, Goss Moor, St. Columb TR9 6HR (0726 860632). Working farm. Brentons Farm is a small farm close to the A30, an ideal place for touring Cornwall being only eight miles from St. Austell, 12 miles from Padstow, nine miles from Newquay. There is always a warm friendly welcome with full English breakfast and a chance to relax in our beautiful south-facing garden or stroll down the Cornish country lanes. Three bedrooms — one twin, two double, all with washbasin and central heating. Bathroom with shower. Open first February to 30th November. Bed and Breakfast from £10 per person. Morning tea if required. Member Cornwall Tourist Association.

ST. IVES. Miss B. Delbridge, Bella Vista Guest House, St. Ives Road, Carbis Bay, St. Ives TR26 2SF  **(0736 796063).** Bella Vista occupies an ideal position on the main road to St. Ives, with its superb beaches and cobbled streets, and is conveniently situated one minute from bus service and ten minutes from beach. All rooms have washbasins, shaving plugs and interior sprung mattresses. Colour TV lounge, central heating. Radio intercom and baby-listening service in all rooms. Own key and access to rooms at all times. Guests are assured of a homely welcome and good, plentiful cooking with farm fresh produce. Fire Certificate held. Les Routiers recommended, ETB Listed. Bed and Breakfast from £11, Evening Dinner (optional) £7.

ST. IVES. Mrs N.I. Mann, Trewey Farm, Zennor, St. Ives TR26 3DA (Penzance [0736] 796936). Working farm. On the main St Ives to Land's End road, this attractive granite-built farmhouse stands among gorse and heather-clad hills, half-a-mile from the sea and five miles from St Ives. The mixed farm covers 300 acres, with Guernsey cattle and fine views of the sea; lovely cliff and hill walks. Guests will be warmly welcomed and find a friendly atmosphere. Menus include beef, duck, pork and Cornish cream. Five double, one single and three family bedrooms (all with washbasins); bathroom, toilets; sittingroom, diningroom. Cot, high chair and babysitting available. Pets allowed. Car essential — parking. Open all year. Electric heating. Evening Dinner, Bed and Breakfast or Bed and Breakfast only. SAE for terms, please.

ST. IVES near. Mrs H.L. Blight, Trencrom Farm, Lelant Downs, Hayle, Near St. Ives TR27 6NU (Cockwells [0736] 740214). Situated half-way between Hayle and St. Ives, Trencrom Farmhouse offers guests a really homely atmosphere, comfortable rooms and excellent home cooking. Commanding magnificent views of Cornwall, the house is open from Easter to end of October. Pony rides available from adjoining stables, many wonderful walks and good, safe sandy beaches abound. St. Ives three mile, Carbis Bay one-and-a-half miles, Lelant one-and-a-half miles and Hayle two miles. Accommodation comprises two double and one family bedrooms, all with washbasins; bathroom and shower, toilet; sittingroom with TV, diningroom with separate tables. Children welcome, cot, high chair and babysitting available. Sorry, no pets. Car essential — parking. Bed and Breakfast or Bed, Breakfast and Evening Meal. Reductions for children sharing parents' room. Reductions for senior citizens (not in high season). Further details on request.

CORNWALL – SOMETHING FOR EVERYONE!

Sea, sand, cliffs and quite often the sun, but that's not all you will find in this interesting county. Cornwall has many fascinating places to visit, such as the Charlestown Shipwreck Centre, the Tropical Bird Gardens at Padstow, Cornwall Aeronautical Park near Helston, Botallack Tin Mine, The Cornish Seal Sanctuary, Perranporth and of course, St. Michael's Mount.

Tregoad Farm
St. Martins-by-Looe, Cornwall

This farm Guest House is one and a half miles from Looe. It is a lovely old Georgian farmhouse, set atop a hill, overlooking Looe Bay. Guests can enjoy the view of the bay from bed! Mrs Hembrow does all the cooking and provides large nourishing breakfasts and five-course dinners. There are tea/coffee facilities and colour TV in all rooms. It is open from April to October.

TOURIST BOARD REGISTERED (3 Roses).

Dinner, Bed and Breakfast is £20 low season and £27 high season and rates are reduced for children. Bed and Breakfast only £15 to £20 according to season. A warm welcome is assured at all times from:

Mr & Mrs K. J. Hembrow, Tregoad Farm Guest House, St. Martins-by-Looe PL13 1PB. Telephone Looe (05036) 2718.

ST. JUST. Mrs Joyce Cargeeg, Manor Farm, Botallack, St. Just TR19 7QG (0736 788525). ✿✿

Commended. Manor Farm is an attractive 17th century granite manor featured in BBC TV's Poldark and Penmarric series. Tastefully modernised with central heating and bedrooms (two en-suite) having tea/coffee making facilities. Guests have their own diningroom and lounge with TV. The house has sea views, with Geevor tin mine and its museum in easy reach. Children welcome. Bed and Breakfast from £12 to £15.

ST. JUST (Penzance). Ronald and Jean Jarratt, Kenython, St. Just, Penzance TR19 7PT (Penzance [0736] 788607). ✿✿

We welcome you to our Guest House, situated in peaceful, large grounds; pool. Guests will find a warm welcome, good home cooking and friendly service. Some en-suite bedrooms; comfortable lounge, diningroom and sun lounge with views over St. Just. Just towards Land's End and to the Isles of Scilly. Kenython makes an ideal base for people of all ages to visit the many and varied attractions of this outstandingly beautiful area, others find it provides peace and quiet to relax and do nothing. Open all year. Central heating. Children welcome, reduced rates, provision made. Bed and Breakfast from £13; with Dinner from £21. Also a self-contained bungalow for self-caterers — accommodates six. Dinner available. AA listed. Brochures with pleasure.

The Weary Friar

Pillaton
Saltash
Cornwall PL12 6QS

Mr & Mrs R. Sharman   Tel: Liskeard (0579) 50238

This twelfth-century hotel of character, which was once a resting place for travelling Friars, is set in beautiful surroundings and is famous for good food, be it a bar snack or a meal in our à la carte restaurant and real ales from a well-stocked bar, served in an atmosphere of traditional comfort. All the bedrooms are en-suite. This is an excellent touring centre, being only 2½ miles from St. Mellion Golf Course, with fishing and riding available locally. Plymouth 8 miles, Looe 13 miles.

SUMMERCOURT. Mrs Rachael Wimberley, Resurrance Farm, Carnego Lane, Summercourt, Near Newquay TR8 5BG (Mitchell [0872] 510338). Working farm, join in. A warm welcome awaits you at our dairy, beef, sheep and arable farm of 194 acres. Traditional Cornish Cob farmhouse set in the quiet of the country but with easy access to the major towns and resorts of Cornwall, just off the A30. Enjoy the peace and quiet of farm and country. Guided tour of farm, when work permits. Two double rooms, sharing bathroom and toilet. Large open beamed lounge/diner for your relaxing evenings, colour TV. Sorry, NON-SMOKING household. Children and pets not permitted. Bed and Cornish Breakfast from £10 per person.

TINTAGEL. Mrs A. Jones, Grange Cottage, Bossiney, Tintagel PL34 0AX (Camelford [0840] 770487). If you enjoy beautiful scenery, Grange Cottage is a

picturesque Cornish cottage. Part of the cottage dates back to the 16th Century — complete with low beamed ceilings. It retains its character, despite modernisation over the years. Situated on the North Cornwall Heritage Coast and within easy walking distance of Tintagel Castle, the Coastal Path and Bossiney Cove, with its surfing, sandy beach and rock pools. Two large comfortable double/family bedrooms with tea making facilities and a small single bedroom. Hot and cold washbasins in all rooms. Diningroom, lounge with colour TV. Excellent area for walking and an ideal base for touring. Open Easter to October for Bed and Breakfast, Evening Meal optional. Reduced rates for children under 12 years. Telephone or SAE for brochure.

See also Colour Display Advertisement

TINTAGEL. C. and R. Savage, Bossiney House Hotel, Tintagel PL34 0AX (Tintagel [0840] 770240). An ideal base to tour and explore an area packed with interest and beauty. Bossiney House is situated about half a mile from Tintagel on the cliffs overlooking a magnificent stretch of coastline. Nearly all of the 20 bedrooms have sea or country views. Spacious diningroom and cocktail bar; three lounges. Colour TV. Good English cooking with excellent choice of menu. Personal attention. Indoor heated pool, sauna, solarium. Nearby activities include surfing, riding, golf, squash, pony trekking and shark fishing. Reductions for children. Open Easter to end of October.

TREGONY. Mrs Shirley E. Green, "Carveth", Tregony, Truro TR2 5SE (Tregony [087-253] 250).

"Carveth" is an elegant listed farmhouse with beautifully decorated, spacious rooms. A warm welcome awaits you along with superb home cooking, optional Evening Meal. No longer a working farm, it is set in its own lovely gardens and orchard, is surrounded by farmland and is accessible along a farm lane. This peaceful setting on the fringe of the Roseland Peninsula is central for exploring the golden sandy beaches of both the north and south coasts of Cornwall. There are golf courses, National Trust gardens, sailing, riding etc all within easy reach. Open all year. Bed and Breakfast £13.50, Evening Meal £7.00 per person. Weekly terms available.

TROON, near Camborne. Mrs S. Leonard, Sea View Farm, Troon, Near Camborne TR14 9JH (Praze [0209] 831260).

🐄 Farmhouse on small horticultural holding, one mile from Troon village. Six double, one single and three family bedrooms, all with individual heating, washbasins etc. Large lounge with colour TV; bathroom, two shower rooms, three toilets; two diningrooms. Good home cooking. Heated swimming pool. Well recommended by previous guests. Cot, high chair, babysitting and reduced rates for children. Pets permitted. Panoramic views from some bedrooms. Within easy reach of north and south coasts, only 15 minutes by car. Open all year round for Bed and Breakfast from £60 weekly. Dinner £6 per night. English Tourist Board registered. AA.

TRURO. Mrs Margaret Opie, Kennall Farm, Ponsanooth, Truro TR3 7HL (Stithians [0209] 860315).

Working farm. Kennall Farm is a 90-acre arable farm overlooking a valley of trees and the River Kennall. Within seven miles of many lovely sandy beaches. There are one family and two double rooms with washbasins, tea/coffee making facilities, accommodating six guests only at any one time. Bathroom, two toilets; TV lounge; diningroom with separate tables. Good farmhouse cooking. Children under 13 years at reduced prices. Sorry, no pets. Car necessary. Parking. Open May to end September. Electric blankets and central heating early and late in season. Bed and Breakfast or Bed, Breakfast and Evening Meal. Terms on request — SAE please.

TRURO. Mrs Ann Lutey, Cregan Gate Farm, Grampound Road, Truro TR2 4EL (St. Austell [0726] 882884). Working farm. At Cregan Gate our aim is to give

a restful holiday away from busy roads and noise. The house is comfortably furnished and there are carpets throughout. Meals consist of roast beef, lamb, pork, chicken, salads and good wholesome sweets. There are many interesting places to visit in Cornwall and we are central for them all — golfing, riding, surfing, roller skating, swimming, all within 10 miles. Very interesting museum in Truro for a wet day visit. Double, single and family rooms, three with washbasins; bathroom, toilet; sittingroom, diningroom. Children welcome. Cot, high chair and babysitting. Pets allowed. Open April to October. Car essential — parking. Evening Dinner, Bed and Breakfast or Bed and Breakfast only. Rates reduced for children.

TRURO. Mrs Janice E. Colwell, Higher Tregonjohn Farm, Creed, Grampound, Near Truro TR2 4SS (0726 882423). Working dairy farm with 30 cows, milking morning and evenings, approximately 20 calves are reared — help to feed our animals always welcome. Situated in mid-Cornwall, convenient for many beaches. We are just half a mile from the village of Grampound on A39 between St. Austell and Truro. There is one double and one family bedroom, both with washbasin and tea/coffee making facilities; separate toilet, bathroom; sittingroom with TV and video; diningroom. Children welcome, babysitting and reduced rates available. Open May to October. Terms from £8 to £11 per person per night; weekly terms available. Cornwall Tourist Board registered.

PLEASE SEND A STAMPED ADDRESSED ENVELOPE WITH ENQUIRIES

TRURO. Mrs Diane Dymond, Great Hewas Farm, Grampound Road, Truro TR2 4EP (St. Austell [0726] 882218). Working farm. This 160 acre working farm is situated in the centre of Cornwall. Ideal for touring or the safe sandy beaches, set in peaceful countryside it is excellent for just relaxing. All main bedrooms have extensive views. The farmhouse is tastefully furnished. Modern bathroom with shower and WC, also separate WC. Lounge with colour TV. Traditional English food is served in our spacious diningroom which has separate tables. Games room. Two family, one twin, two doubles and one single all with washbasins. Hand towels supplied. Tea-making facilities. Access/Visa accepted. Fire Certificate held. Car essential. Open June/early September. Bed and Breakfast or Bed, Breakfast and Evening Dinner. Terms on request.

Trevispian-Vean Farm

Trevispian-Vean is an attractive 300-year-old farmhouse nestling in the Cornish countryside. It has recently been extended to give increased lounge facilities; most bedrooms have en-suite facilities. Meals are prepared with great care by Bridget who provides a good variety of home cooking. Licensed. For the "active" – a fishing lake, a games room and participation in the feeding of the animals on this 300-acre mixed farm. With its location four miles from Truro, Trevispian-Vean is an ideal centre for touring the whole of Cornwall.

A warm welcome, good food and a friendly atmosphere guaranteed

Mrs B. Dymond, Trevispian-Vean Farm, St. Erme, Truro, Cornwall TR4 9BL. Truro (0872) 79514

HOLIDAY ACCOMMODATION
Classification Schemes in
England, Scotland and Wales

The National Tourist Boards for England, Scotland and Wales have agreed a common 'Crown Classification' scheme for **serviced (Board)** accommodation. All establishments are inspected regularly and are given a classification indicating their level of facilities and services.

There are six grades ranging from 'Listed' to 'Five Crowns ♛♛ ♛♛ ♛'. The higher the classification, the more facilities and services offered.

Crown classification is a measure of *facilities* not *quality*. A common quality grading scheme grades the quality of establishments as 'Approved', 'Commended' or 'Highly Commended' according to the accommodation, welcome and service they provide.

For **Self-Catering**, holiday homes in England are awarded 'Keys' after inspection and can also be 'Approved', 'Commended' or 'Highly Commended' according to the facilities available. In Scotland the Crown scheme includes self-catering accommodation and Wales also has a voluntary inspection scheme for self-catering grading from '1 (Standard)' to '5 (Excellent)'.

Caravan and Camping Parks can participate in the British Holiday Parks grading scheme from 'Approved (✓)' to 'Excellent (✓ ✓ ✓ ✓ ✓)'. In addition, each National Tourist Board has an annual award for high-quality caravan accommodation: in England – Rose Awards; in Scotland – Thistle Commendations; in Wales – Dragon Awards.

When advertisers supply us with the information, FHG Publications show Crowns and other awards or gradings, including AA, RAC, Egon Ronay etc. We also award a small number of Farm Holiday Guide Diplomas every year, based on readers' recommendations.

TRURO. Mrs A. Palmer, Trenestrall Farm, Ruan High Lanes, Truro TR2 5LX (Truro [0872] 501259).

TRENESTRALL FARM
Ruanhighlanes
Truro, Cornwall

A tastefully restored 200 year old barn, now a farmhouse offering comfortable accommodation on a 300 acre mixed farm. Situated on beautiful Roseland Peninsula, within easy reach of St. Mawes and Truro. Close to safe beaches and beautiful Fal estuary for sailing, bird watching etc. Accommodation consists of double or twin room with washbasins and tea/coffee facilities, own sittingroom with TV, bathroom and shower room. Amenities include private fishing lake and snooker room, table tennis and pony riding. Pride taken with presentation of food using home produce whenever possible. Children welcome, babysitting service. Truro Tourist Board registered. Phone or write for details of Bed and Breakfast with optional Evening Meal.

TRURO. Mrs J.C. Gartner, Laniley House, St. Clement, Near Trispen, Truro TR1 9AU (Truro [0872] 75201).

Laniley House, a Gentleman's Residence, built in 1830 and featured in "Homes and Gardens", stands in two acres of gardens amidst beautiful, unspoilt countryside, yet only two miles from the Cathedral City of Truro. Ideally situated for discovering Cornwall and close to major towns, beaches and National Trust properties, Laniley offers unequalled privacy and peace. Our aim is to make you feel at home, giving each person individual attention: only six guests at any one time. Accommodation consists of three large double bedrooms, two with washbasins, one with en-suite bathroom; separate breakfast room, lounge with colour television. All rooms with television, radio and Teasmade. Regret, unable to accommodate children under eighteen years, also no pets. Bed and Breakfast only. Terms on request with SAE, please. Highly recommended accommodation.

TRURO. Mrs Margaret Retallack, Treberrick Farm, Tregony, Truro TR2 5SP (087253 247). Working farm.

Treberrick is a 250 acre working farm situated on the edge of the Roseland Peninsula and two miles from unspoilt beaches at Carhays and Portholland and six miles from Mevagissey. Most parts of Cornwall reached by car within one hour. Guests are welcome to walk around the farm and also watch the cows and sheep being milked. Spacious house, bedrooms have washbasin and tea-making facilities. Diningroom with separate tables, lounge with TV always available. Guests can expect traditional home cooked food using own produce where possible. Member of the Cornish Tourist Board. Open from March to October. Maximum number of guests six. Sorry no smoking. Bed and Breakfast from £10; Evening Meal available. Telephone or SAE please for further details.

TRURO near. Mrs Marion Colwill, "Woodbury", Malpas, Truro TR1 1SQ (Truro [0872] 71466).

Attractive Victorian house in the picturesque village of Malpas one and a half miles from Truro. The house has spectacular views over the estuary and surrounding woodland. The old riverside inn, boat trips to Falmouth and scenic walks are just some of the attractions. Truro, with its Georgian streets, Cathedral and high class shops is an ideal centre for touring south Cornwall. The centrally heated accommodation offers two double and one single bedrooms all with river views, bathroom, toilets, elegant TV lounge and superb double-glazed conservatory for dining. Excellent home cooking, morning tea, English Breakfast, Evening Meal (optional). Sorry, no pets. Ample parking space. Open all year. Bed and Breakfast from £11.50.

WADEBRIDGE. Mr and Mrs G. Matthews, Higher Trevibban Farm, St. Ervan, Wadebridge (0841 540 392). Working farm. This 250-acre farm is used to raise beef cattle and sheep plus corn growing. The farmhouse stands surrounded by rolling countryside with sea views; several sandy beaches are within five miles as are horse riding, go-karting and golfing. Coarse fishing two miles. There are family and double bedrooms, each with washbasin and tea/coffee making facilities; a lounge with TV, books and games; diningroom where meals are served — traditional farmhouse fare. Open all year. No pets accepted. Bed, Breakfast and Evening Meal £90 per week. Reductions for children under 11 years. Cornwall Tourist Board Registered.

PLEASE SEND A STAMPED ADDRESSED ENVELOPE WITH ENQUIRIES

WADEBRIDGE. Mrs V.M. Davey, Carns Farm, Trewethern, Amble, Wadebridge PL27 6ER (Bodmin [0208] 880398). Working farm. A fully-modernised 15th Century farmhouse with its original oak beams and open fires, situated on a dairy farm. Guests are welcome to explore the farm and watch the milking. Only four miles from the safest beaches in North Cornwall, sailing, fishing, surfing and golf. Lovely walks nearby. Mrs Davey's aim is to give guests a restful holiday and real farmhouse fare, with home-produced eggs, cream, etc. One double, one single and two family bedrooms with washbasins; bathroom, two toilets; shower; own lounge and TV; diningroom, separate tables. Cot, high chair available, babysitting on request. Please enquire about pets. Car essential — parking. Open Easter to October. SAE, please, for terms for Evening Dinner/Meal, Bed and Breakfast or Bed and Breakfast only. Reductions for children.

WHITSAND BAY. Mrs V.J. Andrew, Trewrickle Farm, Crafthole, Torpoint PL11 3BL (St. Germans [0503] 30333). This 370-acre mixed farm is situated on the coast of Whitsand Bay — land runs down to Portwrinkle beach. Mid-way between Plymouth and Looe (about six miles). Good food and cleanliness guaranteed and a home from home atmosphere with freedom to come and go as you please. Two double and three family bedrooms, all with washbasins; one bath, shower room, two toilets; sitting/diningroom; TV. Children welcome at reduced rates, cot, high chair and babysitting available. Pets permitted. Open from April to December. Car essential — parking. Evening Dinner, Bed and Breakfast from £15 per night — £102 per week. Bed and Breakfast from £9.50 per night. Hot drinks and sandwiches at night if required. Fire Certificate. Also two fully furnished self-catering farmhouses available. Tourist Board Registered.

WHITSAND BAY. Mrs S.M. Hoskin, The Copse, St. Winnolls, Polbathic, Torpoint PL11 3DX (St. Germans [0503] 30205). The Copse is part of a mixed farm situated on the coast of Whitsand Bay, midway between Plymouth and Looe. The golf course of Whitsand Bay and the beaches of Downderry and Portwrinkle are two miles away. The bedrooms all have washbasins, shaver points, tea/coffee making facilities and TV. One room has en-suite facilities. There are two bath/shower rooms for guests' use and a comfortable lounge. Children over five years welcome. Sorry, no pets. Home produced food is served and every comfort for a quiet, restful holiday is assured. Bed and Breakfast from £9 per night; Evening Meal by arrangement. Please send SAE for brochure or telephone for details.

ZENNOR. Dr. E.G. Gynn, Boswednack Manor, Zennor, St. Ives TR26 3DD (0736 794183). An organic smallholding with free-range ducks, hens, geese, goats. Our granite farmhouse overlooks both sea and moorland with a quiet cove nearby and fine walks with much natural history and archaeological interest all around. Pub and church at Zennor, art galleries, restaurants, beaches at St. Ives (five miles) and Penzance (six miles). Two family, two double, two twin bedrooms; two bathrooms; lounge and diningroom. Open all year. Bed and full English Breakfast, vegetarian Evening Meal. No smoking. No pets. Bird watching, natural history and archaeology courses on selected weeks, and guided natural history walks available on a daily basis. SAE, please for further details.

CUMBRIA — English Lakeland

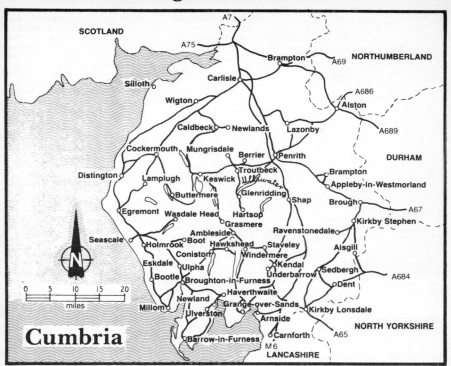

SCOTLAND

A7

A75

Silloth

Brampton   A69   NORTHUMBERLAND

Carlisle

Wigton

A686

Alston

Caldbeck   Newlands   Lazonby   A689

Cockermouth   Mungrisdale

Berrier   Penrith

Distington   Lamplugh   Keswick   Troutbeck   DURHAM

Buttermere   Ullswater   Brampton

Glenridding   Shap   Appleby-in-Westmorland

Egremont   Wasdale Head   Hartsop   Brough   A67

Grasmere   Ravenstonedale   Kirkby Stephen

Seascale   Ambleside   Boot

Holmrook   Hawkshead   Staveley   Aisgill

Coniston   Windermere

Eskdale   Ulpha   Kendal   Sedbergh

Bootle   Underbarrow   A684

Broughton-in-Furness   Dent

Haverthwaite

Newland   Grange-over-Sands

Millom   Ulverston   Kirkby Lonsdale

Arnside   NORTH YORKSHIRE

Barrow-in-Furness   Carnforth   A65

M6

LANCASHIRE

0 5 10 15 20
miles

Cumbria

ALSTON. Phil and Catherine Bradley, Shield Hill House, Garrigill, Alston CA9 3EX (Alston [0434]

381238). Set amidst the spectacular scenery of the North Pennines on the borders of Cumbria, Northumberland and Durham. Stone-built former farmhouse, in rural location with magnificent views. Ideally situated for walking — only 300 yards from the Pennine Way. Conveniently central for exploring further afield. Packed lunches, children's teas and Evening Dinners available. All bedrooms have private facilities. Guests' lounge, kitchenette, laundry facilities. No smoking throughout the house. Pets by arrangement. Open all year except Christmas. Bed and Breakfast from £15 per person; Evening Dinner £7.50 per person. Reductions for children and longer stays. Please send for brochure.

ALSTON. Mrs P.M. Dent, Middle Bayles Farm, Penrith Road, Alston CA9 3BS (Alston [0434]

381383). ❦ Working farm, join in. Family run hill farm with cattle and sheep in an area of outstanding natural beauty, described in David Bellamy's book "England's Last Wilderness". Ideal base for walking or touring, Lakes, borders, rural Northumbria or relaxing in the garden admiring the breathtaking views. Alston one mile with its cobbled streets, quaint cottages and narrow gauge railway. Accommodation — one double, one family room with central heating, washbasins, electric blankets, etc. Tea-making facilities. AA listed. Tourist Board approved. Member of Farm Holiday Bureau. Many visitors return to our warm welcome and good food. Bed and Breakfast from £11; Dinners £6. Reductions weekly and for children under 14 years. Non-smokers preferred. SAE, please for brochure.

PLEASE SEND A STAMPED ADDRESSED ENVELOPE WITH ENQUIRIES

AMBLESIDE. Mr and Mrs P. Hart, Bracken Fell, Outgate, Ambleside LA22 0HN (Hawkshead [09666] 289). Bracken Fell is situated in beautiful open countryside between Ambleside and Hawkshead, in the picturesque hamlet of Outgate. Ideally positioned for exploring the Lake District and within easy reach of Coniston, Windermere, Ambleside, Grasmere and Keswick. All major outdoor activities are catered for nearby including wind-surfing, sailing, fishing, pony trekking, etc. All six bedrooms have washbasins, complimentary tea/coffee and outstanding views. Four have en-suite facilities. There is central heating throughout, a comfortable lounge and diningroom, together with ample parking and two acres of gardens. Fire Certificate. Open all year. Bed and Breakfast from £13.50. Write or phone for brochure and tariff.

Bracken Fell

TARN HOWS
→ Country House Hotel ←

The Tarn Hows Hotel is situated about 10 minutes' walk from the Lake District's most famous beauty spot standing in 25 acres close to Beatrix Potter's house and with superb views of the surrounding countryside. This 3 star hotel has 23 bedrooms, all with private facilities.

Children and dogs are warmly welcomed. Prices from £38 per night Bed & Breakfast, free brochure on request.

The Tarn Hows Hotel, Hawkshead, Ambleside, LA22 0PR. Telephone: 09666 696

AMBLESIDE. Mrs S. Harryman, Fell Foot Farm, Little Langdale, Ambleside LA22 9PE (Langdale [096-67] 294). Working farm. Nestling at the foot of the famous Wrynose Pass Fell Foot, a 17th century farmhouse, once a coaching inn, welcomes visitors from March to November. Full of charm and character the house, owned by the National Trust, contains fine oak beams and panelling and a log fire blazes on chilly evenings. One mile from the village of Little Langdale, on a 431-acre sheep and beef farm, the house offers comfortable accommodation with beautiful views from all bedrooms and excellent home cooking. Three double bedrooms, all with washbasins; bathroom with shower, two toilets; sitting/diningroom. Tea/coffee making facilities all rooms. Sorry, no pets. Part central heating. Car essential, parking. Evening Dinner, Bed and Breakfast from £20 or Bed and Breakfast only from £13. Fishing in Blea Tarn and the coast is 20 miles away. Ideal base for walkers. SAE, please. Tourist Board registered.

AMBLESIDE. Jim and Joyce Ormesher, Rothay House, Rothay Road, Ambleside LA22 0EE (Ambleside [05394] 32434). Rothay House is an attractive modern detached Guest House, set in pleasant gardens with views of the surrounding fells. All bedrooms, most en-suite, are comfortable and well furnished with colour TV, tea and coffee trays. Our visitors are assured of warm and friendly service in attractive surroundings. The house is within easy walking distance of the village centre. Ambleside has a variety of interesting shops and restaurants and makes an ideal base for walking, touring or enjoying sailing, watersports and angling on Lake Windermere. Car not essential, but ample parking space in the grounds. Open all year. Children welcome. Sorry, no pets. Winter Weekend Breaks available.

AMBLESIDE. Mrs E. Peers, Fisherbeck Farmhouse, Old Lake Road, Ambleside LA22 0DH ([05394] 32523). 👐👐 The charming 16th-century old farmhouse/dairy (not a working farm) is situated in a quiet side lane at the foot of Wansfell to the south of the village. Warm, comfortable rooms, single, double, twin and family with hot and cold washbasins. Lounge with TV. Separate morning/breakfast room, tea/coffee making facilities. Parking no problem, either on own ground or free car park. Car is not essential however as village is only five minutes' level walk away; one minute walk to bus stop. SAE, please, for terms and details. Les Routiers recommended.

AMBLESIDE. Mr and Mrs John Morrisroe, Brantfell Guest House, Rothay Road, Ambleside LA22 0EE (05394-32239). 👐👐 Ambleside is the ideal resort for the Lake District holiday and Brantfell Guest House makes the perfect base. A tastefully converted Victorian house, it is convenient for all local amenities including tennis courts and bowling green. There are two double, two double/twin bedded with full ensuite facilities, one family and one single bedrooms, most of which have views over the fells. Tea/coffee making facilities and colour TVs in all rooms. Two shower rooms, three toilets; lounge and diningroom. Children welcome, cot available. Some private and public parking. Open from January to December, with terms for Bed and Breakfast from £11.50 per person. Optional Evening Meal £8.00.

AMBLESIDE. Helen and Chris Green, Lyndhurst Hotel, Wansfell Road, Ambleside LA22 0EG (Ambleside [05394] 32421). 🐾🐾 RAC Acclaimed, AA listed. Attractive Victorian Lakeland stone built, small family-run hotel with private car park, quietly situated in its own gardens. Good food, friendly service, lovely rooms all with private facilities. Beautiful Special Occasions room with four-poster bed. All with colour TV and tea/coffee trays. Full central heating for all-year comfort. Cosy bar. Winter and Spring breaks. A delightful base from which to explore the Lakes, either by car or as a walker. Evening Dinner, Bed and Breakfast or Bed and Breakfast. Phone or write for details.

AMBLESIDE. Mrs Bingham, Old Fisherbeck, Old Lake Road, Ambleside LA22 0DH (05394 33540). 15th-18th century house, with slate entrance hall, situated between village and lake. There are three bedrooms, one double, two twin and two bath/shower rooms with toilets. Centrally heated throughout with log fire and TV in sitting-room. Parking for three cars. Ideal base for walking and water sports. Bed and Breakfast from £14 with reductions for children over eight years. Spring Bargain Breaks. NO SMOKING. Open February to November. ETB registered.

AMBLESIDE. Ann, David and Liz Vatcher, Wanslea Guest House, Lake Road, Ambleside LA22 0DB (Ambleside [05394] 33884). 🐾🐾 Wanslea is a spacious Victorian house within easy walking distance of Ambleside village and the pier and lake shore at Waterhead. With fine views, it is readily accessible and walks begin at the door. Scenic beauty lies all around and the area offers outdoor pursuits of all kinds plus stately homes, literary associations, Roman remains and steam railways. Wanslea offers central heating, tea/coffee making facilities and washbasins in all rooms (some en-suite), a comfortable TV lounge and superb home and vegetarian cooking. Children welcome. Pets by arrangement. Bed and Breakfast from £15; Bed, Breakfast and Evening Meal from £23. Autumn, Winter and Spring Breaks at reduced rates. Brochure available. We look forward to welcoming you.

AMBLESIDE. Sally and Anthony Marsden, Betty Fold, Hawkshead Hill, Ambleside LA22 0PS (Hawkshead [096-66] 611). 🐾🐾🐾 Commended. Betty Fold is a large country house in its own spacious grounds with magnificent views and set in the heart of the Lake District National Park. The quaint village of Hawkshead is nearby and Coniston and Ambleside are within four miles. The beauty spot Tarn Hows is 20 minutes' walk away. The guest house is privately run by the resident owners and offers Bed, Breakfast, Evening Meals and Packed Lunches. All bedrooms are en suite. Children are welcome, cots are available and babysitting can be arranged. Parties are particularly welcome. We regret, no pets in the guest house. Open all year. Terms approximately £28.00 per night for Bed, Breakfast and Evening Dinner. See also advertisement in SELF CATERING section of the guide.

AMBLESIDE. Mrs E. Culbert, Kingswood, Old Lake Road, Ambleside LA22 0AE (05394 34081). Kingswood is ideally situated near the town centre, yet off the main road. Ample car parking. Well-equipped and comfortable bedrooms with washbasins and tea/coffee making facilities. Colour TV. Central heating. Single, double, twin and family rooms. Pets welcome. Open most of the year, with special bargain breaks off season. Evening Meal optional. Write or phone for rates and brochure.

AMBLESIDE near. Brian and Lisa Greasley, Inglewood, Chapel Stile, Great Langdale, Near Ambleside LA22 9JG (096-67 341). Inglewood, in the heart of the Lake District, is an 18th century traditional Lakeland stone cottage providing plenty of character and charm with its coal fires and beamed and hooked ceilings. The cottage has three letting rooms — a single, twin and double, all with pleasant views, easy chairs, tea/coffee making facilities. A cosy lounge provides plenty of reading material and TV. Guests can relax outside in the garden. The catering is all home-cooked with many choices of fruits and cereals and full English Breakfast. Evening Meal and packed lunches by arrangement. We aim to provide an informal homely atmosphere for our visitors to relax in. Families and dogs welcome. Bed and Breakfast £12.50-£13.50 per person.

AMBLESIDE. Mrs D. E. Wrathall, The Oaks, Loughrigg, Ambleside LA22 9HQ (Langdale [096-67] 632). Set in the secluded Loughrigg Valley in the heart of the Lake District, this 18th century farmhouse is the property of the National Trust. Fishing is available in nearby Loughrigg Tarn and this is also an ideal centre for many of the popular fell walks. Ambleside three miles, Grasmere two miles. Accommodation is offered in two family and one double bedrooms, with washbasins; bathroom, toilet; sittingroom, diningroom. Central heating in all bedrooms during winter months. Children welcome. Pets accepted. Open fires in lounge except July/September. Good farmhouse fare is served in a friendly atmosphere. Open February to November. Car essential, parking. Reductions for children under 10 years. Evening Dinner, Bed and Breakfast. SAE for prompt reply.

APPLEBY near. Mrs Ruth Tuer, Meaburn Hill Farm, Meaburn Hill, Maulds Meaburn, Penrith CA10 3HN (09315 205). Relax at our traditional 16th century Cumbrian Longhouse, overlooking tranquil river, valley and village green. We welcome guests to enjoy award-winning farm cookery, hearty breakfasts, splendid country suppers in a farmhouse which retains many original features of beams, panelling and fireplaces. Antique furnished rooms (two double with private facilities, and one twin) make a warm and comfortable base for touring Lakes and Dales or walking/cycling over our local quiet lanes and footpaths. Guests are welcome to explore our 200 acre suckler beef and sheep farm which offers outstanding views across the Pennines. Horses can be accommodated and shooting or fishing arranged. OS Ref NU625161. Bed and Breakfast from £12. One week Evening Meal, Bed and Breakfast £120.

APPLEBY-IN-WESTMORLAND. Mrs Edith Stockdale, Croft House, Bolton, Appleby-in-Westmorland CA16 6AW (Kirkby Thore [07683] 61264). Croft House is situated in Bolton, an unspoiled village of sandstone houses and inns on the banks of the River Eden, three miles north of Appleby off A66. This is an excellent base for exploring Eden Valley, Lake, Dales and Border Country or as a midway break from Scotland. The historic town of Appleby welcomes visitors to its ancient castles and churches and to the country's oldest Gypsy Fair, which is held annually in June. Local attractions include pony trekking, golf, fishing and swimming. The comfortable farmhouse offers traditional farmhouse breakfast and comprises sittingroom with colour TV; diningroom; one twin and two double bedrooms with washbasins. Separate bathroom and shower. Children welcome at reduced rates, cot, babysitting. Pets welcome by arrangement. Private fishing on River Eden available to our guests. Open all year (except Christmas). Rates from £10.50.

Terms quoted in this publication may be subject to increase if rises in costs necessitate

BOUTH. Mrs F. Cornthwaite, Old Hall Farm, Bouth, Near Ulverston LA12 8JA (Greenodd [022986] 1315). Working farm, join in. Farmhouse situated on the edge of the quiet picturesque village of Bouth, with children's playground, Post Office and public house. A working mixed farm within easy reach of Southern Lakes and West Coast, but own transport essential. Good home cooking, traditional English Breakfast and Evening Meal using own dairy products and locally grown fresh vegetables when available. Three family rooms; lounge with woodburning stove; diningroom. Children are very welcome. Babysitting, high chair, cot. A warm welcome with a friendly atmosphere. Cumbria Tourist Board registered. Bed and Breakfast from £12. Reduced rates for children and out of season bookings. Awarded FHG Diploma.

BOWNESS-ON-WINDERMERE. Langdale View Guest House, 114 Craig Walk (off Helm Road), Bowness-on-Windermere LA23 3AX (Windermere [09662] 4076). ♥♥♥ Langdale View Guest House is a family run, non smoking house, five minutes' walk from the lakeside yet in a quiet spot with views over the lake to the mountains. We offer Bed and Breakfast, dinner optional (with silver setting). There is a guests' lounge, central heating, fire certificate and ample private parking. All rooms have en-suite or private facilities. We will collect you from the bus/rail station. Our double, twin and single rooms cost from £15 per person per night with reduced rates for weekly bookings. For reservations or brochure please ring or write to **Mrs Marilyn Tordoff** and be assured of a warm welcome.

BRAMPTON. Mrs Ann Thompson, Low Rigg Farm, Walton, Brampton CA8 2DX (06977 3233). Working farm. Working dairy farm three miles from Brampton, nine miles from Carlisle. Ideal base for walking and touring; sailing and boating at Talkin Tarn; golfing, horse riding and swimming at Brampton and Carlisle; trout farm fishing. Historic Hadrian's Wall, stately homes, Lanercost Priory, castles, museums, garden centres. Ample facilities for eating out. Traditional farmhouse Breakfast, Dinner by arrangement. Free range eggs, fresh milk. Double/family room with washbasin; separate dining/sittingroom, colour TV; tea/coffee making facilities. Spacious garden. Ample parking. Children welcome at reduced rates, cot and high chair available. Bed and Breakfast from £10.50.

BRAMPTON. Mrs E. Ritson, Park Gate, Askerton, Brampton CA8 2BE (069-77 3607). Enjoy the natural beauty and peace of scenic surroundings. Our family home is situated on a 1300 acre hill farm, with easy access to Scotland and the Lakes. Visit Brampton's lovely Talkin Tarn for boating and windsurfing. Two miles from Roman Wall. Pets welcome. Large garden. Parking. Cot. Highchair, babysitting. Home cooking; vegetarians catered for. £8 Bed and Breakfast; Evening Meal £6. Reduced rates for children. Price includes light supper at bedtime and baths or shower. Open all year. Leave motorway at Junction 43; A69 to Brampton, Askerton six miles. SAE for further details.

BRAMPTON near. Mrs Annabel Forster, High Nook Farm, Low Row, Brampton CA8 2LU (06977 46273). Working farm, join in. Friendly farmhouse with relaxing atmosphere and good home cooking. Situated one mile from Low Row village and four miles from Brampton in peaceful Irthing Valley. Beef cattle, sheep, goats and poultry are kept and visitors are allowed to wander around the farm. Conveniently situated for touring Northumberland, Lake District and Scottish Borders and only a few miles from Roman Wall, Lanercost Priory and Talkin Tarn. Accommodation comprises one double and one family room, lounge, TV; diningroom. Bed and Breakfast from £8; Evening Meal from £5. Reductions for children under 12 years. Packed lunches available. Well controlled dogs accepted. Tourist Board listed.

CUMBRIA – LAKELAND SPLENDOUR!

The Lake District has for long been a popular tourist destination; however, the Fells and Pennine areas are also worth exploring. The many attractions of Cumbria include the Ennerdale Forest, St. Bees Head, Langdale Pikes, Bowness-on-Solway, the market town of Alston, Lanercost Priory, Scafell Pike – England's highest mountain – and the Wordsworth country around Ambleside, Grasmere and Cockermouth.

BRAMPTON. Mrs Margaret Mounsey, High Rigg Walton, Brampton CA8 2AZ (Brampton [06977] 2117). Working farm, join in. High Rigg Walton is situated on the road side four miles from Brampton and 10 miles from Carlisle. Excellent walking and touring centre, Roman Wall, riding school and nature conservation area within one-and-a-half miles. Near Birdoswald and Lanercost Priory. Family run dairy and sheep farm which provides genuine hospitality in a spacious, modernised listed farmhouse. Delicious home cooking. Large garden, patio and play area. Tea on arrival. One double, and one family room. Reductions for children. Pets by arrangement. Bed and Breakfast from £10; Evening Meal by arrangement.

BURTON-IN-KENDAL. Mrs A. Taylor, Russell Farm, Burton-in-Kendal, Carnforth, Lancs. LA6 1NN (Burton [0524] 781334). Working farm, join in. Why not spend a few days at Russell Farm? The proprietors pride themselves on giving guests an enjoyable holiday with good food, friendly atmosphere and relaxing surroundings away from the hustle and bustle. The 150 acre dairy farm is set in a quiet hamlet one mile from the village of Burton-in-Kendal, and five miles from the old market town of Kirkby Lonsdale. An ideal centre for touring Lakes and Yorkshire Dales, or going to the coast. Horse riding is available nearby. Two double, one single and one family bedrooms; bathroom, toilet; sittingroom and diningroom. Children welcome; cot, high chair and babysitting offered. Pets accepted, if well-behaved. Open from February to November (inclusive) for Evening Dinner, Bed and Breakfast or Bed and Breakfast. Reductions for children. Parking for essential car. SAE, please, for terms.

CALDBECK. Mr and Mrs A. Savage, Swaledale Watch, Whelpo, Caldbeck CA7 8HQ (Caldbeck [06998] 409). Working farm, join in. Ours is a mixed farm of 300 acres situated in beautiful countryside within the Lake District National Park. Easy reach of Scottish Borders, Roman Wall, Eden Valley. Primarily a sheep farm (everyone loves lambing time), with 60 dairy cattle. Visitors are welcome to see farm animals and activities. Many interesting walks nearby or roam the peaceful fells where John Peel hunted. Enjoyed by many Cumbrian Way walkers. Very comfortable accommodation with excellent home cooking. Central heating. Tea making facilities. Registered with the English Tourist board. We are a friendly Cumbrian farming family and make you very welcome. Bed and Breakfast £10.50; Evening Meal £6.

CARLISLE. Mr and Mrs Mike and Pat Armstrong, Skitby Farm, (Smithfield), Kirklinton, Carlisle CA6 6DL (Carlisle [0228] 75241). Working farm. Typical farmhouse built in 1791 with every modern amenity, situated six miles north of Carlisle in the village of Smithfield (shop, post office, garage and village inn), within easy reach of Scottish Borders, Lake District, Roman Wall, Solway Coast. Accommodation comprises one family, one double, one twin rooms, bathroom and toilets; two lounges (with colour TV); diningroom where fine food is a speciality using meat and vegetables produced on the farm. Dinner by prior arrangement, and packed lunches available on request. Children well catered for with reduced rates and babysitting provided. For sports enthusiasts fishing can be arranged, golf courses and swimming pools within easy reach. Sorry, no pets. Open Easter to October for Bed and Breakfast from £11. Car essential — parking.

CARLISLE. Mrs Jennifer Bainbridge, Beech House, Whitrigg, Kirkbride, Carlisle CA5 5AA (Kirkbride [06973] 51249). Beech House is situated on the Solway Firth and overlooks the Lake District Hills from the front, and the Scottish Hills from the rear. This is an ideal place for a quiet holiday and a bird watcher's paradise. Guests are assured of a friendly welcome at the house which is surrounded by lawns and flower gardens. Excellent home cooking using fresh garden produce, and Solway-caught salmon. Two family and one double rooms; two bathrooms, two toilets; lounge and diningroom. Children welcome and cot and babysitting available. Open all year except Christmas for Evening Dinner, Bed and Breakfast from £15 or Bed and Breakfast from £10. Welcome cup of tea at bedtime (inclusive). Reductions for children. Car essential — parking.

CARLISLE. Mrs Georgina Elwen, New Pallyards, Hethersgill, Carlisle CA6 6HZ (Nicholforest [022877] 308). 🏵🏵🏵 *Commended.* **Working farm, join in.** GOLD AWARD WINNER. Farmhouse filmed for BBC TV.

Relax and see beautiful North Cumbria and the Borders. A warm welcome awaits you in our country farmhouse tucked away in the Cumbrian countryside, yet easily accessible from M6 Junction 44. In addition to the surrounding attractions there is plenty to enjoy, including hill walking, peaceful forests and sea trout/salmon fishing or just nestle down and relax with nature. Two double en-suite, two family en-suite rooms and one twin/single bedroom, all with tea/coffee making equipment. Bowls, putting, etc. Bed and Breakfast from £14 to £18 per night; Bed, Breakfast and Evening Meal from £22.50 to £26.50. Half Board from £135 to £170. Menu choice. Self catering offered. Video available for small refundable deposit.

CARLISLE. Mrs Dorothy Nicholson, Gill Farm, Blackford, Carlisle (022875 326). In a delightful setting on a stock rearing farm this spacious farmhouse is only three miles from Junction 44 on the M6. Gill Farm offers a friendly welcome to all guests and is an ideal place for breaking a journey to or from Scotland or touring the Lake District. Roman Wall, golf, fishing, swimming all available nearby. Two double and one twin-bedded rooms; two bathrooms, toilet; lounge and diningroom. Open all year for Bed and Breakfast. Reductions for children. Cot and babysitting available. Central heating. Car essential — parking. Pets permitted. SAE please.

CARLISLE. Jean and Dennis Martin, The Hill Cottage, Blackford, Carlisle CA6 4DU (0228 74739). 🏵🏵 *Commended.* One minute from M6/A74 Junction 44, three miles north of Carlisle; 19th century cottage recently modernised and extended. Spacious, centrally heated rooms (most on ground floor), high standard of furnishings and decor. Enjoying a rural setting in farm country, an ideal base for Solway coasts, Lakes, Scottish Borders, Hadrian's Wall and historic Carlisle (expert historical advice) or for Scottish stopover. Golf, fishing and bird watching nearby. Accommodation in single, twin, double or family rooms with washbasins, shaver points, tea-making facilities and Yale locks. Bathroom/shower, two toilets; visitors' lounge with colour TV; diningroom. Excellent cuisine. Children welcome; cot, high chair, reduced rates. Sorry, no pets. Ample parking, car not essential, convenient public transport. Special weekly terms, out of season bookings, etc. Evening Dinner available

if booked in advance. Cumbria Tourist Board member. SAE for brochure.

CARLISLE. Mrs Elizabeth Woodmass, Howard House Farm, Gilsland, Carlisle CA6 7AN (Gilsland [069-72] 285). 🏵🏵 **Working farm.** A 250 acre mixed farm with a 19th century stone-built farmhouse situated in a rural area overlooking the Irthing Valley on the Cumbria-Northumbria border. Half a mile from Gilsland village and Roman Wall; Haltwhistle five miles and the M6 at Carlisle, 20 miles. Good base for touring — Roman Wall, Lakes and Scottish borders. Trout fishing on farm. Guests' lounge with colour TV where you can relax in comfort. Diningroom. One double room en-suite, one twin and one family room with washbasins, bath or shower. All bedrooms have tea/coffee making facilities. Bathroom with shower, toilet. Children welcome at reduced rates. Sorry, no pets. Car essential — parking. Open January to December for Bed and Breakfast with Evening Meal optional. SAE or telephone for further details.

See also Colour Display Advertisement **COCKERMOUTH via. Mr and Mrs John Richardson, The Fish Hotel, Buttermere, via Cockermouth CA13 9XA (Buttermere [07687] 70253).** 🏵🏵🏵 Peace and seclusion at The Fish Hotel. The Fish Hotel is personally run by the proprietors, Jean and John Richardson, who are on hand at all times to ensure that guests receive the warmest of welcomes and personal attention. The Hotel is ideally situated in one of Lakeland's most beautiful valleys between two lakes, Buttermere and Crummock Water (five minutes' walk from each). The delightful village of Buttermere lies at the foot of Honister Pass and Newlands Hause. There are 11 pleasant rooms all of which have their own private facilities and tea/coffee machine; direct dial telephone; radio alarms. Children are welcome and have a 30 per cent reduction if sharing a family room. A comfortable lounge is at residents' disposal and there is a separate residents' lounge bar. A delightful restaurant renowned for serving excellent food. The Hotel is fully centrally heated. Once the home of the famous Mary Robinson, the Beauty of Buttermere, whose life story has recently been made into a best selling novel. A Free House serving traditional and cask conditioned ales and cider. Members of British & English Lakes Tourist Board.

COCKERMOUTH. Mrs Alison Hewitson, High Stanger Farm, Cockermouth CA13 9TS (Cockermouth [0900] 823875). Working farm. Everyone is made to feel welcome here on this 17th century working farm, situated two miles from Cockermouth, the birthplace of Wordsworth. Keswick is 12 miles away and there are lovely views of the Lorton Valley as well as beautiful countryside close to Loweswater, Crummock and Buttermere Lakes. Accommodation is in two family bedrooms and one twin bedroom; bathroom, shower room; diningroom; lounge with colour TV. Ideal for children — cot, high chair and babysitting provided. Pets welcome. Bed and Breakfast from £13. Evening Meal available. Tea included in price.

COCKERMOUTH. Mrs Dorothy E. Richardson, Pardshaw Hall, Cockermouth CA13 0SP (Cockermouth [0900] 822607). Pardshaw Hall is pleasantly situated in a small village three-and-a-half miles from Cockermouth and is a listed building. Large garden at the rear where children can play safely. Pardshaw is ideally situated for touring the Lakes and there are some really lovely walks. Children delight in the Miniature Railway at Ravenglass. Good home cooking with succulent roast beef, roast lamb, roast chicken and home-made cheesecake and souffles. Accommodation in two double bedrooms, two single and one family rooms, one with washbasin; bathroom, two toilets; sittingroom, diningroom; open fires. Children are welcome and there is cot, high chair and babysitting. Sorry, no pets. Open all year. Car essential, parking. Evening Meal, Bed and Breakfast or Bed and Breakfast only. Rates reduced for children. SAE, please, for terms.

COCKERMOUTH near. Mr R. Sargent, Field End, Parsonby, Aspatria CA5 2DE (06973 21720). Small English Tourist Board listed guest house offering the best of home comforts in a quiet village location on the fringe of the National Park. Parsonby is seven miles north east of the ancient market town of Cockermouth, set in lovely countryside with panoramic views of the distant Scottish hills. Ideal location for the magnificent unspoilt Northern Lakes and within easy reach of the Solway coast. All three bedrooms are attractively furnished and have washbasins. Comfortable lounge with colour TV and open fire. Good home cooking and warm welcome assured. Open all year. Full central heating. Car essential. Brochure/tariff on request.

CRUACHAN

Cruachan is a modern detached house situated in a quiet cul-de-sac in the centre of Coniston village. All rooms are spacious and comfortable, some are en-suite. All bedrooms have TV and tea/coffee making facilities. Bed and Breakfast from £15.50 to £19.50. Special diets catered for. Car parking. Non smokers. No pets. Coniston is an attractive Lakeland village, renowned for its breathtaking views of the Fells and Coniston Water. It is a fine central base for visiting other parts of the Lake District.

Mrs Lilian Grant, Cruachan, Collingwood Close, Coniston, Cumbria LA22 8DZ. Telephone: 05394 41628.

CONISTON. Mrs B.E. Nelson, Townson Ground, Coniston LA21 8AA (Coniston [05394] 41272).

Townson Ground is a 400-year-old Lakeland Country House, located on the quiet eastern side of Coniston Water (approximately one mile from the village), tastefully converted into a quality family-run Guest House with a friendly atmosphere. The attached barn includes two luxury self-catering apartments and small cottage. The area is of outstanding natural beauty and there are numerous local walks as well as access to private jetty on the lake. It is an ideal location for touring and walking in the Lake District National Park. Four en-suite bedrooms and one single standard room, all with tea/coffee facilities. Large lounge which is traditionally furnished and has an open fire and woodburning stove. Television and reading area. Olde Worlde diningroom which offers quality, quantity and variety in home cooking with a complementary wine list. Children over three years very welcome. Fire Certificate. Payphone. Ample private parking. Central heating. Dogs by prior arrangement. Under the personal supervision of the proprietors Ken, Barbara and Richard Nelson.

CONISTON. Mrs M.C. Dutton, Knipe Ground, Coniston LA21 8AE (Coniston [05394] 41221). Working farm. Knipe Ground is a small agricultural holding situated on the hillside, two miles east of Coniston. Tucked away in its old-fashioned garden with commanding views of the Lake and mountains, the 16th century farmhouse provides a quiet, homely atmosphere with log fires which enhance the old oak timbers. Local produce is used in traditional and vegetarian fare. Two double and two single bedrooms. Bed and Breakfast from £11; Evening Meal £7. Full Board from £124 weekly. Sorry, no dogs in the house. No smoking. SAE for brochure.

CONISTON. Mrs Lee, Black Beck Cottage, East side of Lake, Coniston LA21 8AB (Coniston [05394] 41607). Magnificent lake and mountain views from your bedroom window. Double or twin-bedded rooms, some with en-suite bathrooms, all with washbasins, tea/coffee making facilities and firm divan beds. Comfortable lounge with TV. Central heating throughout. Large private car park. Sorry, no pets. Warm welcome and a good breakfast. We would prefer you not to smoke in the house. An ideal centre for walking, fishing, boating, etc. and touring all the Lakes. Our aim is to make your holiday enjoyable. Margaret and Doug Lee invite you to come and see.

DENT. Mrs E. Gardner, Bridge Cottage Guest House, Gawthrop, Dent, Near Sedbergh LA10 5TA (Dent [058-75] 240). Bridge Cottage is situated in beautiful Dentdale, which extends from Sedbergh to Newby Head. The old world village of Dent is half a mile away and still retains its cobbled streets and whitewashed stone houses. Birthplace of Adam Sedgewick (18th century geologist). Dentdale, with a remarkable variety of scenery, is one of the most picturesque and unspoilt Dales in the Yorkshire Dales National Park. Good centre for touring the Dales and the Lakes. Delicious food served including York ham and eggs. Local steak, home baking. Full central heating. Cosy TV lounge with coal fire to relax by in the evening and personal attention given to guests' comfort. One double and two family bedrooms with washbasins; bathroom, toilet; dining-room. Children welcome — babysitting and reduced rates. No pets. Open March to November. Car essential — parking.

Evening Dinner, Bed and Breakfast or Bed and Breakfast only. SAE for terms.

ENNERDALE. Mrs E. Loxham, Beckfoot Farm, Ennerdale, Cleator CA23 3AU (Lamplugh [0946] 861235). Beckfoot stands on the northern shore of Ennerdale Lake, two miles from Ennerdale village. Though not a working farm, we are situated in a mainly sheep farming community, in one of Lakeland's wildest and most spectacular valleys. Great for visitors wanting to spend a quiet, restful break away from the crowds. Ideally positioned for walking, climbing and touring, with fishing and trekking nearby. Two double and one twin rooms, all with washbasins, continental quilts and electric underblankets; guests' lounge with colour TV and tea-making facilities. Bedrooms have superb views of the Lake. Central heating. Delicious home cooking, with quality, variety and quantity being our aim. Open all year. Bed and four-course Breakfast from £11.50; three-course Evening Meal £7.50. For further details, please phone.

FAR SAWREY. Mr and Mrs J.B. Forbes, West Vale Country Guest House, Far Sawrey, Hawkshead, Ambleside LA22 0LQ (Windermere [09662] 2817). ❦ ❦ ❦ Superbly situated on the edge of the village of Far Sawrey, West Vale offers you personal service and home-cooked food in a warm, friendly atmosphere. We have full central heating, and log fire and TV in one lounge. Most bedrooms have private facilities en-suite, and all rooms have tea and coffee making facilities. Residential licence. Horse riding available locally, also free trout and coarse fishing. AA and RAC listed. Bed and Breakfast from £15; Half Board from £21 per day. For further details please send for brochure to Resident Proprietors — Irene and Brian Forbes.

FUN FOR ALL THE FAMILY IN CUMBRIA

Appleby Castle Conservation Centre, Appleby; *Brockhole National Park Visitor Centre*, near Ambleside; *Grizedale Forest Wildlife Centre*, Hawkshead; *Lowther Wildlife Adventure Park*, near Penrith; *Muncaster Castle*, Ravenglass; *Levens Hall*, near Kendal; *Ravenglass & Eskdale Railway*, Ravenglass; *Lakeside & Haverthwaite Railway*, Haverthwaite, near Newby Bridge; *Windermere Steamboat Museum*, Rayrigg Road, near Bowness-on-Windermere; *Fell Foot Park*, Newby Bridge, Lake Windermere.

GRANGE-OVER-SANDS. Mrs Jean Jackson, Templand Farm, Allithwaite, Grange-over-Sands LA11 7QX (Grange-over-Sands [05395] 33129). Working farm, join in. Though built in 1687, Templand offers comfortable and quiet accommodation with all modern conveniences. This 100 acre mixed farm is close to the Grange-over-Sands/Cartmel road and is within easy reach of the Lake District. Under two miles to the sea. Fishing and hill walking, swimming pool, golf and tennis at Grange. Superb 12th century Priory at Cartmel. Two double, one single amd one family bedrooms; bathroom, toilet; lounge and diningoom. Children welcome — cot, high chair and babysitting available. Car not essential but parking provided. Open 1st March to 31st October. SAE brings prompt reply. Terms for Evening Dinner/Meal, Bed and Breakfast from £14 or Bed and Breakfast from £8. Reductions for children. No pets.

GRANGE-OVER-SANDS. Mrs M.B. Legat, "Milton House", Grange Fell Road, Grange-over-Sands LA11 6DH (Grange-over-Sands [05395] 33398). Small, well-established guest house, comfortably furnished, central heating throughout. All bedrooms have a washbasin, fitted carpet and new divan beds. The meals are excellent. Bed and Breakfast £13.50 per day; £87.50 per week; Bed, Breakfast and Evening Dinner £19 per day; £126 per week. Reductions for children. We are open from February to November. Situated near woods and fells, within easy reach of Lakeland, the Cumbrian Coast and the Yorkshire Dales, this is an ideal holiday centre for tourists and hikers. The house commands beautiful and extensive views of Morecambe Bay. Two double and one family rooms; sitting/diningroom. Children welcome. Sorry, no pets. Available locally are a swimming pool, two golf courses, tennis and putting. A friendly welcome is assured here. Parking. Registered with the English Tourist Board.

GRANGE-OVER-SANDS near. Mrs B. Hodgson, Moss Howe Farm, Witherslack, Near Grange-over-Sands LA11 6SA (Witherslack [044852] 327). Moss Howe offers quiet and comfortable accommodation on 250 acre dairy and sheep farm, about five miles inland from Grange in the unspoilt Winster Valley. It is within easy access of the M6 motorway Junction 36 and the Lakes. The farmhouse is set in peaceful countryside with many local walks and a distant prospect of the Lake District Mountains. The accommodation consists of one twin-bedded room and one double room with TV, both with tea/coffee making facilities; bathroom/toilet with shaving point; lounge/diningroom with colour TV. Everyone made most welcome, with good home cooking. Bed and Breakfast. SAE, please or telephone for further details and terms.

GRASMERE. John & Stephanie Chapman, Woodland Crag, How Head Lane, Grasmere LA22 9SG (Grasmere [09665] 351). 👑👑 Charming Victorian Lakeland stone house in the heart of the Lake District. Situated on the edge of the village in secluded landscaped gardens and overlooking lake and Silver Howe. Many beautiful and scenic walks radiate from here. Accommodation is tastefully furnished with central heating throughout and comprises five double bedrooms with tea-making facilities, three of which are en-suite. Spacious lounge with log fire and colour TV. Bright, sunny diningroom where we serve hearty breakfasts. Packed lunches available. Sorry, no children under 12 years. Pets not accepted. Bed and Breakfast from £15. Peace and comfort assured.

HAWKSHEAD. Mr and Mrs P. Hart, Bracken Fell, Outgate, Ambleside LA22 0HN (Hawkshead [09666] 289). Bracken Fell is situated in beautiful open countryside between Ambleside and Hawkshead, in the picturesque hamlet of Outgate. Ideally positioned for exploring the Lake District and within easy reach of Coniston, Windermere, Ambleside, Grasmere and Keswick. All major outdoor activities are catered for nearby including wind-surfing, sailing, fishing, pony trekking etc. All six bedrooms have wash-basins, complimentary tea/coffee and outstanding views. Four have en suite facilities. There is central heating throughout, a comfortable lounge and dining room, together with ample private parking and two acres of gardens. Fire Certificate. Open all year. Bed and Breakfast from £13.50. Write or phone for brochure and tariff.

Bracken Fell

HAWKSHEAD. Linda and Alan Bleasdale, Borwick Lodge Country House, Outgate, Hawkshead, Ambleside LA22 0PU (Hawkshead [096-66] 332). A rather special 17th century country house with magnificent panoramic views of the Lakes and mountains yet quietly secluded in three acres of beautiful landscaped gardens and surrounded by fields and fells. Ideally placed in the heart of the Lakes and close to Hawkshead village with its good choice of restaurants and inns. Tastefully furnished en-suite bedrooms with colour TV, tea/coffee making facilities and outstanding views. "Special Occasion" four-poster room. Linda and Alan, with their warm, personal service, aim to make you feel welcome and relaxed and especially to make your stay enjoyable at Borwick Lodge, "a haven of peace and tranquillity" in this most beautiful corner of England. Ample parking. NON-SMOKING. Open all year, Bed and Breakfast from £15. Also self-catering cottage available. May we send our brochure?

HAWKSHEAD. Norrie and Michael Watson, Foxgloves, Hawkshead, Near Ambleside LA22 0NR (Hawkshead [09666] 352). Foxgloves is a non-smoking country guest house quietly situated on a rise on the edge of the picturesque vilage of Hawkshead. Magnificent views from all rooms. Ideally situated for walking and touring. Tastefully decorated and comfortably furnished, full central heating, guests' TV lounge. All bedrooms have washbasins, one en-suite. Delicious home cooking. Sorry, no pets. Open all year. Bed and Breakfast from £12.50 per person, optional Evening Meal £7.00. Vegetarian meals available. Minimum stay 2 nights.

HAWKSHEAD. Walter and Patsy Sommerville, Garth Country Guest House, Ambleside LA22 0JZ (Hawkshead [096-66] 373). ❦❦❦ Commended. AA "Selected", RAC "Acclaimed". THE GARTH is a beautiful Victorian Country House set in two acres of grounds overlooking Esthwaite Lake to the Coniston and Langdale mountains. Whilst retaining much of its Victorian charm The Garth offers up-to-date facilities to ensure the comfort of our guests. Central heating throughout. Washbasins in all seven bedrooms plus tea/coffee making facilities. Two en-suite rooms have four-poster beds. Log fired lounge. Delicious imaginative home cooking. High standards throughout. Table licence. Ample parking. Pets by prior arrangement. SAE for brochure and tariff.

GARTH GUEST HOUSE

HAWKSHEAD. Mrs Diane Rackham, Silverholme, Graythwaite, Hawkshead LA12 8AZ (Newby Bridge [05395] 31332). Set in an elevated position on the west side of Lake Windermere, this unique small Georgian mansion house set in its own grounds is furnished in traditional style and provides a special atmosphere for relaxation. All rooms are large, comfortable and have spectacular views over the lake. Enjoy a full English Breakfast in our beautiful sunny diningroom overlooking the colourful garden and see the first pleasure cruise passing down the lake. A beautiful lounge is available with log fire. Central heating throughout. We are open all year. Bed and Breakfast from £15 per person.

HAWKSHEAD. Mrs Nancy Penrice, Violet Bank Farmhouse, Hawkshead, Ambleside LA22 0PL

(Hawkshead [09666] 222). Violet Bank is a beautifully situated farmhouse of charm and character on a quiet country lane only half-a-mile from Hawkshead village and within walking distance of the famous Tarn Hows beauty spot. The owners keep rare breeds of pigs and poultry and have an interest in country bygones. Ideally situated for touring, walking and fishing. Two double rooms, one family room. Central heating. Sorry, no pets. Open all year. Bed and Breakfast from £13.50; reduced rates for children.

HAWKSHEAD, near Ambleside. Mrs S. Briggs, High Wray Farm, High Wray, Near Ambleside LA22 0JE (05394 32280). Working farm. A charming 17th century farmhouse once owned by Beatrix Potter. Friendly accommodation on this working sheep and beef farm in quiet, unspoilt location, ideal centre for touring and walking. Follow B5286 from Ambleside towards Hawkshead; turn left for Wray, follow road to High Wraye; the farm is on the right. A ramblers' paradise with a hearty breakfast to start the day. Families and children welcome. Pets also welcome. Terms from £12.

IVEGILL. Mrs J. Wilson, Streethead Farm, Ivegill, Carlisle CA4 0NG (06974 73327). Working farm.

A working farm in unspoilt countryside midway Penrith – Carlisle and only 10 minutes from junction 41 or 42 of the M6. Guests welcomed by tea and home baking. Comfort and cleanliness guaranteed. All food is homemade, much is fresh farm produce. Be tempted by creamy porridge, Borrowdale Teabread, Cumberland Rum Nicky. Large comfortable bedrooms either double or family. Views of garden and Lakeland hills. Guests' own lounge with colour TV; own bathroom. Heated throughout. Ideal for the Lakes, Carlisle, Roman Wall, Scotland. Bed and Breakfast from £11; Evening Meal £6. Child reductions. Unsuitable for children under seven years. No dogs. Separate brochure available. Tourist Board listed.

KENDAL. Mrs Sylvia Beaty, Garnett House Farm, Burneside, Kendal LA9 5SF (Kendal [0539]

724542). Working farm, join in. An AA and RAC listed and Tourist Board registered 15th century farmhouse on large dairy/sheep farm situated half a mile from A591 (Kendal/Windermere road). Two double, one twin, two family bedrooms with washbasins, shaver points and tea making facilities Bathroom, shower room, two toilets; 16th century panelling and four-foot-thick walls in colour TV lounge. Diningroom with separate tables for full English Breakfast and five-course Dinner using home produced beef and lamb; meringues, trifles, gateaux etc also served. Child reductions, cot, high chair, babysitting. Parking, but car not essential; walking distance to shops, inn, bus stops and railway station. Fire Certificate. Scrabble players welcome. Open all year for Bed and Breakfast from £11.50; Dinner from £5.50. Featured in "The Times" for excellent value. SAE for prompt reply and brochure.

KENDAL. Mrs A.E. Bell, Hill Fold Farm, Burneside, Kendal LA8 9AU (0539 722574). Working farm.

Situated three miles north of Kendal close to rolling hills of Potter Fell, with many quiet walks and within easy reach of lakes and sea. Genuine working farm over 350 acres; dairy and sheep. One double and two family rooms with washbasins, heaters and shaving points. Sittingroom; diningroom; bathroom, toilet. Cot and babysitting; reduced rates for under 12 years. Wholesome meals served. Car essential, parking. Open January to December. Sorry, no pets. Terms on request.

KENDAL. Mrs Jean Bindloss, Grayrigg Hall, Grayrigg, Near Kendal LA8 9BU (Kendal [0539 84] 689). Working farm. Comfortable, peaceful, 18th century farmhouse set in a beautiful country location, ideal for touring the Lakes and famous Yorkshire Dales. We run a beef and sheep farm only four and a half miles from Kendal and with easy access to M6 motorway, Junction 38. Guests are assured of the finest accommodation and a friendly welcome. One spacious family room and one double bedroom; tasteful lounge/diningroom with colour TV; bathroom. Children most welcome; cot, babysitting if required. Open March to November. Tourist Board Registered. Bed and Breakfast from £10 to £12 per person, with Evening Meal on request. Good home-made meals using local produce from £5. Further information gladly supplied.

KENDAL. Mrs Anne Knowles, Myers Farm, Docker, Grayrigg, Kendal LA8 0DF (053-984 610). Working farm. A 210 acre sheep and dairy farm. Children are welcome to see the working of the farm. The house is over 250 years old with oak beams and a beautiful partition in the lounge/dining room where the log fire burns. An excellent variety of good farmhouse meals served: roast beef, lamb, pork and poultry, with a good selection of sweets. Guests are made to feel at home with a friendly atmosphere. Two and a half miles from Junction 37 on the M6 motorway. Within easy reach of the Lakes, Yorkshire Dales and the seaside. Two family rooms with washbasins; bathroom, shower and toilet. Reduced rates for children under 10 years with cot, high chair and babysitting available. Central heating. Open from March to October for Evening Dinner, Bed and Breakfast or Bed and Breakfast only. Car essential, parking. SAE, please. Cumbria Tourist Board registered.

KENDAL near. Mrs Julia H. Thom, Riverbank House, Garnett Bridge, Near Kendal LA8 9AZ (Selside [0539-83] 254). ❦ ❦ Stone built country house situated in the quiet hamlet of Garnett Bridge at the foot of the beautiful unspoilt valley of Longsleddale four and a half miles north of Kendal just off the A6 and only eight miles from Windermere. Riverbank House stands at the head of 20 acres of pastureland bordered by three quarters of a mile of the River Sprint providing private fishing. Bedrooms have washbasins and tea/coffee facilities. Guests' sittingroom with TV and open fire, background central heating. Good parking area. Ideal location for walking or touring the Lakes and Dales. Bed and Breakfast from £11. Please telephone for details.

KENDAL. Mrs E. Robinson, Park End Farm, Brigsteer, Near Kendal LA8 8AS (Sedgwick [05395] 60641). Park End Farm is situated amidst beautiful surroundings in an elevated yet sheltered position overlooking the Kent Estuary and the Lythe Valley, famous for its damsons. Only two and a half miles from Junction 36 of the M6 motorway, an ideal base for touring the Lake District and the Yorkshire Dales. Within walking distance is Sizergh Castle, owned by the National Trust, and Levens Hall, the home of the Baggatt family. This charming 16th century farmhouse is one of the oldest in Westmorland, with oak beams and an attractive open fireplace in the diningroom. Guests return again and again to enjoy the comfortable, relaxed and friendly atmosphere. Lounge with open fire and colour TV; two double bedrooms and one twin-bedded room; bathroom with toilet. Ample parking. Open Easter to end October for Bed and Breakfast. Dinner by arrangement. Awarded FHG Diploma for providing holiday accommodation of the highest standard. Highly recommended. SAE brings prompt reply.

KENDAL. Mrs Catherine E. Packham, Docker Hall, Docker, Kendal LA8 0DB (Grayrigg [053-984] 216). Working farm. Docker Hall is a 358 acre dairy and sheep farm situated three-and-a-half miles from M6 (junction 37); three miles north-east of Kendal and Leisure Centre. Ideal base for touring the Lakes, Dales, Borders and Coast. The farmhouse is set in peaceful countryside with many local walks. Guests are assured of a warm welcome, with five-course breakfast. Accommodation consists of two double and one family bedrooms, all with washbasins and shaver points; bathroom with toilet, and second bathroom with shower plus extra toilet. Dining/sittingroom with tea making facilities. Colour TV. Central heating. Children welcome — cot, high chair and babysitting. Bed and Breakfast from £8 per night (from £50 weekly) with reduced rates for children under eight years. Parking. Open March to November. SAE, please, for further details.

KENDAL. Mrs Emma Ladds, Benson Hall Farm, Kendal (Kendal [0539] 721419). Working farm, join in. Old-world farmhouse, steeped in history, has been modernised for comfort with fitted carpets throughout. A Peel Tower, Priest Hole and a spiral stairway are just a few of the features of interest to visitors. Situated five miles from the M6 at Junction 37, Benson Hall is quiet and secluded with beautiful views of lakes and hills. Close to Yorkshire Dales, Kendal, Windermere and the seaside resort of Morecambe 20 miles. Warm welcome and good food assured. One double, two family and two single rooms; bathroom, two toilets; sittingroom, diningroom. Children welcome. Cot, high chair, babysitting and reduced rates for under 13's offered. Regret, no dogs. Open May to November. Bed and four-course Breakfast from £9, with reduction for weekly booking. Snack in the evening at no extra charge. Tea, flasks, etc. free; nothing spared in offering a comfortable, inexpensive holiday. Car preferable, ample parking.

WHEN MAKING ENQUIRIES PLEASE MENTION
FARM HOLIDAY GUIDES

KESWICK. Mrs H.A. Armstrong, Kiln Hill Barn, Bassenthwaite, Keswick CA12 4RG (Bassen-thwaite Lake [059-681] 454). Accommodation in Lakeland farmhouse, ideal for family holidays in relaxed informal surroundings. Delightful rural situation between Keswick and Cockermouth, just off A591 main road. Enjoying superb views to Skiddaw and Bassenthwaite Lake, the house has central heating and log fire. Games room and diningroom in converted barn. Open all year, the accommodation comprises one single, one twin and four family bedrooms, with washbasins; two bathrooms, three toilets; sittingroom; diningroom. Children welcome, cot provided. Sorry, no pets. Car not essential, the house is on good bus route, but there is ample parking. Walking, riding and fishing nearby. Evening Meal, Bed and Breakfast from £17.50; Bed and Breakfast from £12.75. Reductions for children.

KESWICK. Mr and Mrs R. Roper, "Grasslees", Portinscale, Keswick CA12 5RH (07687 71313). Luxurious Bed and Breakfast accommodation in delightful detached country house in the quiet village of Portinscale (very convenient for touring). Offering personal service and attention whilst respecting guests' privacy and freedom. Private parking and peacful garden with lovely views for guests' use. Very relaxing. Please write or telephone for full details.

KESWICK. I. and M. Atkinson, "Dancing Beck", Underskiddaw, Keswick CA12 4PY (07687 73800). Large Lakeland country house two and a half miles from Keswick just off A591 Carlisle road, signposted Millbeck. Situated in its own elevated, spacious grounds with summerhouse and swimming pool. Magnificent views of Derwent Valley and surrounding mountains. Walks onto Skiddaw Mountain are possible from the grounds of "Dancing Beck". All rooms are centrally heated. Bedrooms have washbasins and tea/coffee facilities. Children welcome. Car essential. Bed and Breakfast from £14 to £16. Weekly terms available. Open Spring to November. A pleasant welcome assured.

KESWICK. Mrs Sylvia Taylor, Hazelgrove Guest House, 4 Ratcliffe Place, Keswick CA12 4DZ (Keswick [07687] 73391). 🐾🐾 *Commended.* Keswick, situated at the head of one of Lakeland's most beautiful lakes, close to Borrowdale Valley with its many walks, ideal centre for touring the English Lakes — there is a regular bus service. The house is built of Lakeland slate and stands in a quiet street only a short level walk from town, Lake and parks. We have a reputation for excellent food and offer a hearty breakfast and a choice of menu for dinner. All rooms have central heating and tea/coffee making facilities. Very comfortable TV lounge. Children and pets welcome. All guests have own key for independent access to house at all times — a real home from home atmosphere. RAC recommended. Write or phone for further information.

KESWICK. Mr and Mrs G. Turnbull, Rickerby Grange, Portinscale, Keswick CA12 5RH (07687 72344).

 ❤❤❤ Quiet location in the pretty village of Portinscale — two minutes from A66, five minutes to Keswick. Ideal base for explorers of the Lakes by foot or car. Comfortable accommodation with first class facilities in friendly surroundings and real home cooked meals to satisfy the heartiest of appetites. Tea/coffee making facilities available throughout the day and night. TV lounge and Bar lounge for guests' use. Three ground floor rooms — two with separate patio door entrance. Private car park. AA Specially Recommended Award 1987, Selected Award 1988. Dinner, Bed and Breakfast from £21.50 per person. Colour brochure sent with pleasure. Contact **Gordon or Marion Turnbull.**

KESWICK. Mr and Mrs M. Felton, "Stoneycroft", Newlands, Keswick CA12 5TS (Braithwaite [07687] 82240).

Stoneycroft stands at the foot of Causey Pike in the Newlands Valley (one mile Braithwaite, three and a half miles Keswick). Magnificent views of Cat Bells, Skiddaw and Walla Crag. Comfortable accommodation comprising one double room with washbasin; two double rooms, one twin room and one family room, each with ensuite shower room. All with shaver points and tea making facilities. Large lounge; separate TV room; dining room. Full central heating. Residential licence. Full Fire Certificate. Open March till November inclusive for Bed, Breakfast and Evening Meal. Terms and brochure on request.

KESWICK. Sandra and John Williams, Avondale, 20 Southey Street, Keswick CA12 4EF (Keswick [07687] 72735). ❤❤ Commended. Avondale is a small, comfortable guesthouse close to the town centre, parks and Lake. A good centre for touring the Lake District be it by car or public transport. All our well appointed rooms are centrally heated with colour TV, tea/coffee making facilities; most are en-suite. Guests have own keys with access at all times. Good food and a friendly welcome are guaranteed. Guests' lounge with separate diningroom. Avondale has a full fire certificate and caters exclusively for non-smokers. Bed and Breakfast from £11; Dinner, Bed and Breakfast from £18.25. Turn off A591 at Cenotaph.

KESWICK. Mrs Margaret Harryman, Keskadale Farm, Newlands Valley, Keswick CA12 5TS (059682-544). Working farm, join in.

Bed and Breakfast at a traditional Lakeland working sheep and suckler farm, two miles from Buttermere, six miles from Keswick. Keskadale is best known for the "Yak's", one of the highest growing oak woods in England. The 17th century farmhouse with oak beams has a lounge with log fire and colour TV; diningroom; bathroom with shower and toilet; one double, one twin and one family bedrooms, all with washbasins and central heating. Look over surrounding fells, Robinson, Dalehead and Catbells. Bed and Breakfast from £11. Evening tea served with home made biscuits 10.00pm, inclusive in price. Children welcome, cot and high chair. Sorry, no pets. Also self-catering mobile home. SAE for terms. A66 four-and-a-half miles, Braithwaite to Buttermere road.

KESWICK. Mrs M.M. Beaty, Birkrigg Farm, Newlands, Keswick CA12 5TS (0596 82278 or 07687 78278). Working farm. Birkrigg is a dairy, cattle and sheep farm, pleasantly and peacefully situated in a valley surrounded by mountains. Ideal for walking and climbing. Five miles from Keswick and three miles from Buttermere — a mini bus service operates between the two, passing the farm several times daily. A car is essential if you wish to tour the many beauty spots. Parking space. Clean, comfortable accommodation comprises one single, two double, two twin-bedded rooms, one family room, all with washbasins and shaver points. Bathroom, toilets and shower room; sittingroom with colour TV; diningroom. Good meals assured. Children welcome at reduced rates. Bed and Breakfast; Evening Dinners available Mondays, Wednesdays and Fridays. Evening tea 10.00pm. Open late March to early November. Fire Certificate held. Tourist Board registered. Terms on request with SAE, please.

KESWICK. Mrs Christine Simpson, Skelgill Farm, Newlands, Keswick CA12 5UE (Braithwaite [059 682] 367). Working farm, join in. Traditional Lakeland sheep farm. Pleasant farmhouse situated at the foot of Catbells in the heart of Beatrix Potter country, an excellent area for touring and walking with lovely views. The farm is only 10 minutes' walk from Lake Derwentwater, four miles from Keswick, boating, fishing, golf and riding all relatively close. The comfortable farmhouse has one double room, one twin-bedded room and two family rooms, (all with washbasins), sittingroom, diningroom, bathroom and two toilets. Children welcome at reduced rates and a cot, high chair and babysitting are provided. Open Easter to October. Fire Certificate held. Ample parking space. Terms on request.

KESWICK. Mrs D. Mattinson, Bassenthwaite Hall Farm, Keswick CA12 4QP (Bassenthwaite Lake [059-681] 279). Working farm. A sheep and cattle farm in Bassenthwaite Village, with beautiful views of the Skiddaw Range on the front and the river rippling past at the rear. Flower garden and lawn. Ample parking. Open April to November, the four bedrooms all have washbasins. Bath/shower room, two toilets. Living/diningroom with colour TV. Coal/log fires when needed. Home cooking and hospitality. Children and pets welcome. Golf, riding and fishing nearby. Bed and Breakfast from £11; Bed, Breakfast and Evening Meal from £17. Cumbrian Tourist Board and AA listed.

KESWICK. Mrs Jean Tyson, Steps End Farm, Watendlath, Keswick CA12 5UW (Borrowdale [059-684] 245). Working farm. Farmhouse on sheep rearing farm offering holiday accommodation from March to October. One double bedroom and one family bedroom with washbasins; bathroom, toilet; sittingroom; diningroom. Children welcome, also pets free of charge. Central heating. Watendlath lies south of Derwentwater, in a picturesque valley, threaded by a beck adjoining the attractive Watendlath tarn, below Armboth Fell (1,588'). Sir Hugh Walpole used the village as a setting in his novel "Rogue Herries". A good touring area and a car is essential. Ample parking. Evening Dinner, Bed and Breakfast or Bed and Breakfast. SAE for terms.

KESWICK. Mrs Jean McNichol, "Glendene", 8 Southey Street, Keswick CA12 4EF (07687 73548).

A long established guesthouse with reputation for good good food and warm hospitality. Substantial English Breakfast and four course Evening Meal (optional). Private parking. Comfortable lounge; all bedrooms have washbasins, colour TV, electric blankets and tea/coffee making facilities. Central heating throughout. Bed and Breakfast from £12; Dinner, Bed and Breakfast from £16. Brochure on request. ETB member.

Glendene

KESWICK. Fred and Mary Lewis, Skiddaw Grove Hotel, Vicarage Hill, Keswick CA12 5QB (07687 73324).

🌑🌑 Skiddaw Grove is a licensed hotel with a very high standard of comfort and facilities, and enjoying magnificent views of the Lakeland fells. Quietly situated yet convenient for all local amenities. En-suite bedrooms, car park, outdoor swimming pool, TV lounge and bar lounge. Bed and Breakfast from £14 per person; weekly terms available. AA listed QQQ.

KESWICK (Lake District). Eileen and David Davenport, Greystones, Ambleside Road, Keswick CA12 4DP (Keswick [07687] 73108).

🌑🌑🌑 A quietly situated Hotel whose reputation is based on comfort and imaginatively cooked fresh food. Ideally situated for town, lake and fells. Rooms are en-suite with TV, radio and tea/coffee making facilities. Free golf is available to residents. AA. RAC Highly Acclaimed. Hunter Davies and Les Routiers recommended.

KESWICK. Mrs E.M. Richardson, Fold Head Farm, Watendlath, Borrowdale, Keswick CA12 5UW (Borrowdale [059-684] 255). Working farm. Fold Head Farmhouse is a white Lakeland farmhouse situated on the banks of Watendlath Tarn in this picturesque hamlet. It is a 3000 acre sheep farm and an ideal centre for touring, climbing, fell walking and fishing. Fly-fishing for Rainbow trout at Watendlath Tarn; permits available. Guests are accommodated in three double bedrooms and two family rooms, with washbasins; bathroom, two toilets; sittingroom; diningroom. Full central heating; separate TV lounge. Children are welcome at reduced rates, cot and babysitting available. Pets are allowed free. Open from February to December. Car essential; parking. Sir Hugh Walpole used this farmhouse in his book "Judith Paris" as the home of Judith Paris. Evening Dinner, Bed and Breakfast or Bed and Breakfast.

KESWICK. Mrs D. Cook, Swinside Farm, Newlands, Keswick CA12 5UE (Braithwaite [059-682] 363). Working farm. Swinside Farm is a small dairy and sheep farm with an old world farmhouse completely modernised. Ideally situated at the foot of the Catbells and Causey Pike, it sits on the roadside between Keswick and Newlands Pass, with beautiful views of the surrounding hills. Very good for walking and climbing. Braithwaite and Portinscale two miles; Cockermouth, with Wordsworth's birthplace and castle, 11 miles; Buttermere five miles and Borrowdale three miles; very close to Derwentwater. Two double bedrooms, one family room; dining/sittingroom; bathroom, toilet. Parking space for cars. Children welcome, and cot, babysitting and terms according to age. Bed and Breakfast, or Bed, Breakfast and Evening Meal. Open from March to November. Terms on request.

KESWICK near. Muriel Bond, Thornthwaite Hall, Thornthwaite, Near Keswick CA12 5SA (Braith-

waite [059682] 424 or [07687 82424). 👑👑👑 Thornthwaite Hall is a traditional 17th century farmhouse, modernised and converted into a very comfortable guesthouse. All rooms are en-suite with TV, tea/coffee making facilities. Catering includes good home cooking, residential license. The Hall lies in an acre of grounds complete with a lovely garden. Thornthwaite is a lovely quiet hamlet 3 miles west of Keswick. There are numerous walks from Thornthwaite, with a different feel to other parts of the Lake District. Climbing in pine forest locations on the numerous paths and forest trails, spectacular views rewarding those who climb to the tops of Barf, Lords Seat, Seat How. Dogs and children most welcome. Open all year, except Christmas. Send for brochure, please.

KESWICK near. Mrs Rosalind Hunter, Croft House, Applethwaite, Near Keswick CA12 4PN

(Keswick [07687] 73693). 👑👑 Beautifully situated house, enjoying magnificent views of Lakeland mountains, in a lovely quiet village at the foot of Skiddaw, one-and-a-half miles from Keswick. An excellent base for touring all parts of the Lake District, walking, pony trekking and all Lakeland pursuits. A warm welcome is assured and good home cooking a speciality. The comfortable accommodation in our non-smoking house comprises three double, two single and two family rooms en-suite, all with washbasins and showers. Lounge, diningroom. Children welcome. Well-behaved pets accepted. Ample private parking. SAE, please, or telephone for terms for Bed and Full English Breakfast, or Dinner, Bed and Breakfast. Open all year.

KESWICK (Borrowdale). Mrs J.C. Clarke, Brandlehow, Manesty Woods, Keswick CA12 5UG (Borrowdale [07687] 77292). Brandlehow is on the site of an old lead mine going back to Elizabethan times. The house is in a unique position on the shore of Derwentwater with lovely views of the lake and fells. It is very peaceful and is surrounded by National Trust land. Keswick is easily reached by car or launch. Ideal for walkers. Homely accommodation for up to four guests with en-suite twin/family room and two single rooms. Sitting room with colour TV. Access to house and garden at all times. No smoking. Open all year. Bed and Breakfast including evening drink £11 to £16. Advance booking only. ETB registered.

FHG DIPLOMA WINNERS 1990

Each year we award a small number of diplomas to holiday proprietors whose services have been specially commended by our readers and the following advertisers were pleased to receive the award in 1990.

ENGLAND

Tom and Pat Bagshaw, The Blacksmiths Arms, Talkin Village, Cumbria.
Mrs C. R. Faulkner, Mount Pleasant Farm, Near Longnor, Buxton, Derbyshire.
Mrs Mary MacKenzie, Staden Grange, Buxton, Derbyshire.
Mrs Ruth Gould, Bonehayne Farm, Colyton, Devon.
Mrs West-Taylor, Dalham House, Heslington, York, North Yorkshire.

SCOTLAND

Lt.Col. J. W. & Mrs Burnett, Portinnisherrich Farm, Loch Awe, By Dalmally, Argyll.
Mr and Mrs A. Cameron, Tulipan Lodge, Callander, Perthshire.
Peter and Barbara Rawlin, View Bank Guest House, Whiting Bay, Isle of Arran.

WALES

Mrs E. Jones, Hillcroft, Lampeter, Dyfed.
Mrs E. Wagstaff, Pinewood Towers, Conwy, Gwynedd.
Mrs Bronwen Prosser, Upper Genfford Guest House, Brecon, Powys.

KESWICK-ON-DERWENTWATER. John and Linda Lowrey, The Ravensworth, Station Street, Keswick-on-Derwentwater CA12 5HH (Keswick [07687] 72476). ♛♛ Built of local slate, the Ravensworth is situated only a short walk from the town centre, Parks and Lake with all their amenities. All rooms are tastefully furnished; bedrooms have tea/coffee trays and en-suite facilities, some with colour TV. Personally run by the Lowrey's for over six years the Ravensworth is now one of Keswick's superior small hotels. Our reputation has been built on our warm welcome, personal service and palate-tickling food caringly prepared. Enjoy our relaxing lounge with TV or have a chat in the Herdwick Bar. Car parking. AA listed. RAC Highly Acclaimed. We will be pleased to send you a brochure.

KIRKBY LONSDALE. Mrs Gillian Burrow, Garghyll Dyke, Cowan Bridge, Kirkby Lonsdale, Via Carnforth, Lancs. LA6 2HT (Kirkby Lonsdale [05242] 71446). ♛♛ **Working farm.** A friendly atmosphere with a cup of tea on arrival awaits you at this busy family run dairy farm set in the picturesque Lune Valley. Our ivy clad farmhouse provides every comfort in one double and one twin-bedded rooms with central heating, tea/coffee facilities, washbasins, and evening drink with biscuits. We are ideally situated to explore the beautiful countryside, Yorkshire Dales, coast and Lake District. Bed and Breakfast from £12. Weekly rates available, reductions for children. Pets welcome but under supervision. Members of the Farm Holiday Bureau.

KIRKBY STEPHEN. Mrs J. Atkinson, Augill House Farm, Brough, Kirkby Stephen CA17 4DX (Brough [093-04] 305). ♛♛ **Working farm.** Augill is a 40-acre dairy farm and is ideally situated for the Lakes, Yorkshire Dales, Tees Valley and Hadrian's Wall. The farmhouse is comfortably furnished and is AA Recommended. All bedrooms have washbasins, hot and cold water, soap and towels, spring interior mattresses, tea/coffee making facilities and TV. Diningroom, lounge. The house has full central heating — log fire when needed. The food is good and plentiful — beef, lamb, pork and fresh trout are served, and fresh cream desserts. Own milk, cream and eggs (butter and cheese when available); home-made bread. Bed and Breakfast or Bed, Breakfast and five-course Dinner is available. Pets welcome. Ample parking. Open all year except Christmas and New Year. Self-catering accommodation also available. Stamp for brochure.

KIRKBY STEPHEN. Mrs Wildman, Ellergill, Ravenstonedale, Kirkby Stephen CA17 4LL (Newbiggin-on-Lune [05873] 240). Working farm. This working farm is an ideal centre for walking and touring local places of interest. Enjoy the tranquillity of the quiet, peaceful surroundings! Accommodation consists of two double, one single, one family bedrooms. Lounge/diningroom. Colour TV. Hot/cold washbasins, tea making facilities in all rooms. Open fire in Lounge. Good English food. Special diets as requested. Children welcome. Animals housed outside only. AA Listed. Situated on main A683.

KIRKBY STEPHEN. Mrs C. M. Bainbridge, Bonnygate Farm, Soulby, Kirkby Stephen CA17 4PQ (Kirkby Stephen [07683] 71347). Bonnygate Farm is a comfortable and spacious old farmhouse set amidst lovely surroundings, near the River Eden. There is easy access from the A66 and M6 and the Lake District, Yorkshire Dales and the Pennines are all within easy reach. The area is excellent for walking and pony trekking, fishing and golf are also available. Accommodation comprises two double and one single bedrooms, all with washbasins, tea/coffee making facilities; bathroom, two toilets; sittingroom; dining room. Children welcome at reduced rates. Evening Meal, Bed and Breakfast offered all year round (Evening Meal optional). SAE, please, or telephone for further details and terms. Also **self catering holiday cottage** , with telephone, available on farm (sleeps five). Pets by arrangement.

PLEASE SEND A STAMPED ADDRESSED ENVELOPE WITH ENQUIRIES

LANGDALE VALLEY. Mrs Jean Rowand, Stool End Farm, Great Langdale, Ambleside LA22 9JU (Langdale [096 67] 615). Working farm. A warm welcome awaits all guests at Stool End Farm. Enjoy a welcome break in this 17th century farmhouse situated at the foot of Bowfell and Langdale Pikes. Ideal for walking or climbing; a good stopping off point for touring Ullswater, Coniston, Windermere and the rest of the Lake District. Ravenglass and Eskdale Railway only one hour away. Accommodation comprises one double and one family room, both with washbasins; dining/sitting room with wood-burning stove; bathroom with shower. Central heating all rooms. Bed and Breakfast; Bed and Breakfast with Evening Dinner. SAE, please for details.

LOWESWATER. Mrs A. Hayton, Brook Farm, Thackthwaite, Loweswater, Cockermouth CA13 0RP (Lorton [090-085] 606). ♥ Working farm. This 300-acre stockrearing hill farm is a good centre for walking and touring; Loweswater and Crummock Water two miles; boating, fishing and pony trekking nearby. Guests are assured of a quiet and comfortable holiday, with bedrooms having washbasins, razor points, tea making facilities and electric overblankets. Two double rooms, bathroom, shower and toilet; sittingroom. Homely atmosphere and good food. Children welcome at reduced rates. Sorry, no pets. Car essential — parking. Open from May to October for Evening Meal, Bed and Breakfast from £16; Bed and Breakfast from £11. Weekly terms Evening Meal, Bed and Breakfast from £112.

MILNTHORPE. Mr and Mrs P. Walters, Rigney Bank House, 17 The Square, Milnthorpe LA7 7QJ (05395 62236). ♥ ♥ Lovely old house (17th century) on picturesque village green, in traditional Cumbrian village. Bus stops in village. Ideal for walkers and bird watchers around beautiful Morecambe Bay area. Warm, friendly welcome and excellent cooking. Light, well maintained family, twin and single rooms, all with washbasins and tea/coffee making facilities. Two baths/showers/toilets per four rooms. Children welcome. Bed and Breakfast from £12 to £15 per person, per night. Ideal touring centre for Lakes, Yorkshire Dales and North Lancashire. Many interesting excursions within easy reach. Convenient for M6.

MOSEDALE. Colin and Lesley Smith, Mosedale House, Mosedale, Mungrisdale, Penrith CA11 0XQ

(07687 79371). ♥ ♥ ♥ Traditional 1862 built, lakeland farmhouse. Listed building. A smallholding with sheep, ducks and hens, it enjoys a magnificent position, nestling at the foot of Carrock Fell, overlooking open fields, the River Caldew and Bowscale Fell. Off the beaten track, yet only three-and-a-half miles to the A66 Keswick to Penrith road. Vegetarians welcome. Home-baked bread, farm produce — our own free-range eggs. Non-smokers preferred. Packed lunches. Central heating and cosy log fires. Open all year. Most bedrooms have en-suite facilities. Visitors' dining room and lounge. Two self-catering cottages in adjacent barns. SAE, please for brochure.

MUNGRISDALE. Mrs J. M. Tiffin, Wham-Head Farm, Hutton Roof, Mungrisdale, Penrith CA11 0XS

(Skelton [085-34] 289). Working farm. Hutton Roof is a peaceful hamlet, half an hour's ride from Lakes and 1,000 feet above sea level. Well-built farmhouse on 126 acre farm, carries Friesian cattle and Swaledale sheep. In John Peel country with easy access to Fells (of special interest to geologists). Golf, pony trekking, heated swimming pool in area. Very warm welcome assured to all guests; good home cooked farmhouse fare, mostly home produced. Children welcome — cot, high chair, babysitting, reduced rates. Pets allowed. Open March-October. Accommodation in two double and two family bedrooms, three with washbasins; bathroom, toilet; sittingroom. Car essential, ample parking. Wham-Head is within easy reach of Borders and Scotland. Evening Dinner, Bed and Breakfast from £15 daily, £100 weekly; Bed and Breakfast from £10 daily, £66.50 weekly.

MUNGRISDALE. Mrs O.M. Wilson, High Beckside, Mungrisdale, Penrith CA11 0XR (059-683 636). Working farm, join in. A true Cumbrian welcome awaits

you at High Beckside Farm, a dairy and hill farm set in the valley of Mungrisdale by the River Glendermackin. eight miles from Keswick and 10 miles from Penrith. It is ideally situated for touring the Lakes or for a walk in the hills. There is a well furnished, comfortable farmhouse where good farmhouse food and home baking is served. One double and one family room with washbasin and tea/coffee making facilities; bathroom, toilet; sittingroom; diningroom. Children over four years welcome. Sorry, no pets. Car essential, parking. Open from May to November with central heating. Bed and Breakfast from £11 daily, £75 weekly; Evening Meal available. Reductions for children. Cumbria and English Tourist Board listed. SAE, please, for prompt reply.

Terms quoted in this publication may be subject to increase if rises in costs necessitate

NEAR SAWREY. Ms. Gillian Fletcher, High Green Gate Guest House, Near Sawrey, Ambleside LA22 0LF (Hawkshead [09666] 296). ♥♥ The Guest House is a converted 17th-century farmhouse in the quiet hamlet where Beatrix Potter lived and wrote. Her house, owned by the National Trust is close to and open to the public. The area abounds with pleasant easy walks and is a good centre for the Southern Lakes. Open from March to October. Good food and service under the personal attention of the owner. Spacious diningroom, lounge and separate TV lounge. All bedrooms have hot and cold water and individual heating in addition to central heating. Rooms with private facilities available. Reduced rates for children sharing with parents. Cot and highchair are available and babysitting can be arranged. Dogs welcome. A car is desirable and there is parking for seven cars. AA listed, RAC acclaimed. Bed and Breakfast from £13.50 per night; Bed, Breakfast and Evening Meal from £21 per night (£135 weekly).

NETHER WASDALE. Mrs Ruth Knight, Church Stile Farm, Nether Wasdale, Near Gosforth CA20 1ET (09406 252). Set in the charming village of Nether Wasdale amid superb Lakeland views, this interesting farmhouse of mixed periods is tastefully decorated and offers visitors a friendly welcome. It is an excellent base for fell walking and climbing, and is also ideal for those who just want to enjoy the beautiful surroundings. Amenities for guests include central heating, hair dryers, tea/coffee makers and ironing facilities in all rooms, B/W TV, and comfortable seating areas. Family and double room with bathrooms, single room with washbasin; towels provided on request. Home cooking; evening meals and packed lunches also provided.

NEWBY BRIDGE. Mr and Mrs F. Cervetti, Lightwood Farmhouse, Cartmel Fell LA11 6NP (Newby Bridge [05395] 31454). Lightwood is a 17th century farmhouse situated half way up a fell side with extensive views of unspoiled natural beauty. Built around 1650 retaining the charm of all the original oak beams, staircase and inglenook fireplaces, whilst having all modern amenities. It stands in one and a half acres of lovely garden with streams running through. Only two miles from the southern end of Lake Windermere, just off the A592 Newby Bridge — Bowness road at fell foot near Bowland Bridge. Lightwood offers four double and two twin-bedded rooms, two en-suite, all with washbasins, tea making facilities and central heating. Charming oak beamed diningroom facing the early morning sun. Guests' own cosy sittingroom with log fire and colour TV. We offer Dinner, Bed and Breakfast from £22; Bed and Breakfast from £14. Serving a good variety of home cooking using fresh produce wherever possible. Assuring you of our personal attention at all times.

NEWLANDS. Mrs M.A. Relph, Littletown Farm, Newlands, Keswick CA12 5TU (Braithwaite [059-682] 353). Working farm. Littletown is a working beef cattle and sheep farm, situated in a peaceful part of the beautiful Newlands Valley, with surrounding hills providing excellent walking and climbing. Market towns of Keswick and Cockermouth, Lakes, Derwentwater and Bassenthwaite all within easy distance. Farmhouse, though fully modernised, still retains a traditional character with comfortable lounge, diningroom, and cosy licensed bar. Some bedrooms en-suite, all with tea-making facilities, heating and washbasins. Traditional four-course dinner (roast beef, lamb etc) served six nights a week; full English Breakfast every morning. Littletown Farm is featured in Beatrix Potter's "Mrs Tiggy Winkle". Ample parking. Terms on request, SAE please.

Littletown farm

CUMBRIA – LAKELAND SPLENDOUR!

The Lake District has for long been a popular tourist destination; however, the Fells and Pennine areas are also worth exploring. The many attractions of Cumbria include the Ennerdale Forest, St. Bees Head, Langdale Pikes, Bowness-on-Solway, the market town of Alston, Lanercost Priory, Scafell Pike – England's highest mountain – and the Wordsworth country around Ambleside, Grasmere and Cockermouth.

PATTERDALE. Mrs A.M. Knight, Fellside, Hartsop, Patterdale, Near Penrith CA11 0NZ (07684 82532). Fellside is a 17th century Cumbrian farmhouse built of local slate, situated in a quiet and picturesque little village, away from the main roads, in a beautiful Lake District valley at the foot of Kirkstone Pass. It is surrounded by magnificent scenery and has panoramic views overlooking Brotherswater. Perfect for fellwalkers, also artists are welcome. There is boating on Ullswater, fishing in smaller lakes and tarns, pony trekking in Patterdale. Open most of the year. One twin, one double and one single bedrooms. Bed and Breakfast, tea making facilities, drying facilities, parking space available. Dogs accepted. Children welcome, cot and high chair available on request. Central heating and log fire when cold. SAE for brochure and terms. ETB approved.

FELLSIDE
HARTSOP, PATTERDALE,
Nr. PENRITH, CUMBRIA CA11 0NZ

GALE HALL · MELMERBY · PENRITH
Telephone: Langwathby (076 881) 254

Mrs Ann Toppin welcomes guests to her home on a working beef/sheep farm ten miles east of Penrith and the M6, a mile and a half from the peaceful village of Melmerby. Beautiful setting at the foot of the Pennines and with extensive views of the Lakeland Fells. Ideal for fell walking, convenient for the Lake District. Double and family rooms available; cot and babysitting.
Bed and Breakfast from £11.
Reductions for children under 12 years. Write or phone for details.

PENRITH. Mrs M.R. Taylor, Tymparon Hall, Newbiggin, Stainton, Penrith CA11 0HS (Greystoke [07684] 83236). Working farm. Relax in this charming character farmhouse standing in half-acre of garden on 160-acre mixed farm, combining comfort, home cooking and personal service for an enjoyable holiday. Within easy reach are pony trekking, fell walking, swimming and golf. Situated close to M6, Lake Ullswater also Lowther Wild Life Park. Accommodation for guests in two double, one family en-suite and one single bedrooms, three with washbasins; two bathrooms, two toilets; sittingroom with colour television; diningroom. Open April/October. Car essential. Evening Dinner, Bed and Breakfast from £15; or Bed and Breakfast only from £10. Reduced rates for children. Tourist Board registered.

PENRITH. Mrs Bellas, Bedland Gate, Newby, Penrith CA10 3EF (09316 226). We are offering comfortable accommodation to our guests in three bedrooms: one double, one family and one twin-bedded. Good base — handy for the M6. As we are situated near to the Lake District visitors can enjoy the scenic views of the Lakes and surrounding countryside. Why not take this opportunity to explore the Eden Valley which is located close by! Terms: Bed and Breakfast from £9.50; Evening Meal available if required. Further details on request.

See also Colour Display Advertisement PENRITH. Anne and Chris Broadbent, The White House, Clifton, Penrith CA10 2EL (0768 65115). Would you like the opportunity to be thoroughly spoiled in our comfortable and attractive 17th century converted farmhouse? Our home and gardens are situated in a fascinating rural area close to Ullswater and Haweswater? We give you the holiday you deserve — your children too are particularly welcome. Bed and Breakfast from £12; Evening Meal £8.50. Special reductions for children. To find out more about us please do not hesitate to contact us.

PENRITH. Mrs Brenda Preston, Pallet Hill Farm, Penrith CA11 0BY (Greystoke [08533] 247). Pallet Hill Farm is pleasantly situated two miles from Penrith on the Penrith-Greystoke-Keswick road (B5288). It is four miles from Ullswater and has easy access to the Lake District, Scottish Borders and Yorkshire Dales. There are various sports facilities in the area — golf club, swimming pool, pony trekking; places to visit such as Lowther Leisure Park and the Miniature Railway at Ravenglass. Good farmhouse food and hospitality with personal attention. Double, single, family rooms; diningroom and sittingroom. Children welcome — cot, high chair available. Sorry, no pets. Car essential, parking. Open Easter to November. Bed and Breakfast from £8 (reduced rates for children and weekly stays). Excellent bar meals available locally.

SHAP. Mr and Mrs D.L. and M. Brunskill, Brookfield, Shap, Penrith CA10 3PZ (Shap [093-16] 397).

Situated one mile from M6 motorway (turn off at Shap interchange No.39), first accommodation off motorway. Excellent position for touring Lakeland, or overnight accommodation for travelling north or south. Central heating throughout, renowned for good food, comfort and personal attention. All bedrooms are well appointed. Diningroom where delicious home cooking is a speciality. Well stocked bar. Residents' lounge (colour TV). Sorry, no pets. Open from February to December. Terms sent on request. Car essential, ample parking. Tourist Board registered. AA listed. Fire Certificate granted.

TROUTBECK. Mary and Tony Bew, Lane Head Farm, Troutbeck, Penrith CA11 0SY (0768 779 220).

♣ ♣ ♣ **Working farm.** Charming 17th century farmhouse, set in beautiful gardens overlooking undisturbed views of Lakeland Fells. Midway between Keswick and Penrith. The house has been tastefully decorated throughout with many rooms featuring beams. Five rooms with en-suite, and all have washbasins, colour TV. Residential licence. We will be happy to supply further details on receipt of SAE. AA Specially Recommended, Ashley Courtenay recommended.

TROUTBECK. Mrs M. Whittam, Netherdene Guest House, Troutbeck, Penrith CA11 0SJ (Grey-stoke [08533] 475).

♣ ♣ Delightful country house situated in peaceful garden, with extensive mountain views. Midway between Keswick and Penrith, just off the A66 road on the A5091 road to Ullswater. Ideal for touring Lake District. Delicious home cooking with personal supervision. Two double and two family rooms, all with washbasins, colour TV, tea and coffee making facilities, bedside lights. Bathroom, shower room, two toilets. Separate diningroom and lounge with colour TV. Car essential, ample parking. Sorry, no pets. Fire certificate. Open March to November. Evening Dinner, Bed and Breakfast or Bed and Breakfast only. SAE, please, for terms. English Tourist Board registered.

ULLSWATER. Mrs S. Hunter, Grove Foot Farm, Watermillock, Penrith CA11 0NA (07684 86416). Working farm. Grove Foot is a 90 acre dairy farm just off the A66 and two miles from Lake Ullswater. The house, built around 1650, has oak beams and open fires and sleeps six guests. Close by are historic houses and gardens, fishing, swimming pools, golf and pony trekking. Open March to October. Children welcome. Sorry, no pets. Bed and Breakfast from £10; Evening Meal (optional) £6.

ULVERSTON near. Mrs M. Irving, Riddingside Farm, Colton, Greenodd, Near Ulverston LA12 8HF (0229 861336). Working farm. Riddingside Farm is pleasantly situated in the Rusland Valley only five miles from the sea. It is a 110-acre mixed dairy farm with Friesian cows and sheep. Ideally situated for touring the Lakes, being six miles from Windermere and seven from Coniston. Your every comfort is assured in the farmhouse which has three double and one family bedrooms; bathroom and toilet; dining and sittingroom. Colour TV. Children welcome; cot, high chair, babysitting. Sorry, no pets. Open Easter to October. Car essential, parking. Ulverston swimming pool four miles. Plentiful food. Evening Dinner, Bed and Breakfast or Bed and Breakfast only. SAE, please, for terms. Reductions for children under 14.

UNDERBARROW. Mrs D.M. Swindlehurst, Tranthwaite Hall, Underbarrow, Near Kendal LA8 8HG (Crosthwaite [044 88] 285).

This magnificent old world farmhouse is said to date back to 1186 and is known to be one of the oldest in the district with fantastic oak beams and original Black Iron fire grate and many other interesting features. Excellent Bed and Breakfast is offered in clean, comfortable surroundings and furnishings. This farm and farmhouse have an idyllic setting, being half a mile up an unspoilt country lane where deer and other wildlife can be seen. Kendal three miles; Windermere five miles. There are many good country pubs and inns within easy reach. Accommodation comprises one double, one twin and one family room; bathroom and shower; lounge and dining room. Bed and Breakfast from £11 to £13. ETB Listed. AA "Highly Recommended".

WARTON. Kiln Croft, 15 Main Street, Warton, Carnforth LA5 9NR (0524 735788).  Kiln Croft is a detached Edwardian house where guests are free to relax in their own lounge or enjoy our tranquil garden from where, according to season, they can see our few hens, sheep, pigs and calves. We are in the quiet historic village of Warton yet only five minutes from Junction 35 off M6. Our field backs onto beautiful Warton Crag Nature Reserve which adjoins Leighton Moss RSPB. Easy touring for Lakes and Dales. Ample private parking. Log fire and central heating, colour TV, kettles, etc, in bedrooms. We serve our organically grown meats and vegetables when available. Bed and Breakfast from £12. Dinner by prior arrangement.

Mrs Dorothy Studholme, Newlands Grange, Hesket Newmarket, Caldbeck Wigton, Cumbria CA7 8HP. Telephone Caldbeck (069-98) 676.

This 70-acre mixed farm with sheep, cows, calves, hens and ducks, looks on to the Fells of Caldbeck. A truly warm welcome awaits all guests from March to October – good home cooking with own milk, eggs and some meats. One double, two family, one single bedrooms (three have washbasin); bathroom, toilet; sittingroom; diningroom. Central heating. Cot, babysitting and reduced rates for children. Pets accepted. Car essential – Parking. EVENING DINNER, BED AND BREAKFAST OR BED AND BREAKFAST.

Also six-berth caravan for hire.

Terms and further details on request.
* FISHING RIGHTS ON RIVER CALDEW *
* TOURING – JOHN PEEL COUNTRY – LAKES & SCOTTISH BORDERS – ROMAN WALL *

WINDERMERE. Miss Betty Holmes, Acton House, 41 Craig Walk, Windermere LA23 2HB (Windermere [096-62] 5340). ♥♥ *Approved.*

Acton House is situated in a quiet street off the main road from Windermere to Bowness Bay. Ideal for access to the rest of the Lake District. Traditionally-built house of stone and slate with modern plumbing. Three double rooms (one has twin beds), all with washbasins, two with private facilities, all with tea-making facilties. No restrictions on access to house or use of sittingroom (colour TV); central heating throughout. Emphasis on comfort and good home cooked food. Packed lunches on request. Children over 10 welcome. Open March to November for Evening Dinner, Bed and Breakfast, mid-season from £99 per week; reductions for OAP's. No pets please. THIS IS A NO SMOKING ESTABLISHMENT.

HILTON HOUSE HOTEL

New Road, Windermere, Cumbria LA23 2EE
Telephone: 09662 3934

Within easy reach of everything the Lake District has to offer.
Hilton House is a charming detached residence. Several rooms en-suite; all have TV and tea/coffee making facilities. Spacious car park. Well-mannered dogs are welcome. Residential Licence. Bed and Breakfast; Guests' TV Lounge. Non-smoking rooms. Children welcome and family room is available.

Telephone for terms. Mr & Mrs A. Barnicott. ETB ♥♥♥

HOLLY LODGE · A Lakeland Guest House

Holly Lodge is one of the oldest houses in Windermere and is run by the resident proprietors who give a personal and friendly service. A full English breakfast is provided and an evening meal if required. There is central heating, a comfortable lounge and a pleasant dining room. Each bedroom has hot and cold water, tea and coffee making facilities, and colour TV. No pets except guide dogs. Children welcome; up to 12 years at reduced rates. Open all year. Bed and Breakfast from £14. Evening Meal from £8.

Tony and Lindy Priestley, Holly Lodge, 6 College Road, Windermere LA23 1BX Telephone: (09662) 3873

AA Listed   Licensed   ♥♥ Approved   Parking

WINDERMERE. Mr and Mrs L. Ripa, Hollythwaite Guest House, Holly Road, Windermere LA23 2AF (Windermere [09662] 2219). Comfortable family-run guest house situated in a quiet area of Windermere away from the main road but within easy walking distance of bus and train. All parts of the National Park are easily accessible. The accommodation comprises seven bedrooms: single, twin, double and family; all have tea/coffee making facilities. Lounge with colour TV; separate diningroom. Reductions for children, sharing parents' room. Cot available. Sorry, no pets. Open March to November. Bed and Breakfast, optional Evening Meal. Terms from £11. Low season mini-breaks available. Cumbria Tourist Board listed. SAE, please, for brochure.

WHEN MAKING ENQUIRIES PLEASE MENTION
FARM HOLIDAY GUIDES

KIRKWOOD

Prince's Road, Windermere, Cumbria LA23 2DD

Telephone: 09662 3907

Kirkwood occupies a quiet, corner position betwixt Windermere and Bowness. We are proud of our reputation for home cooking, plus a warm and friendly atmosphere with individual and personal service. All rooms have colour TV, tea/coffee making facilities. Some rooms have shower en-suite. Guests collected from train/bus station if they phone on arrival at Windermere. We will be happy to arrange sightseeing tours on request, making your holiday one to remember.

B&B from £12.50 to £18.00.

WINDERMERE. John and June Curme, Orrest Close, 3 The Terrace, Windermere LA23 1AJ (Windermere [096-62] 3325). Orrest Close is a Listed Building built about 1847 and believed to be the work of Augustus Pugin, well known for his work on the Houses of Parliament. Situated in a private tree lined drive but only 100 yards from train and bus station and close to many restaurants and tourist information centre. Car is not essential but private parking is available. We can offer well appointed rooms to include tea/coffee making facilities, colour TV and some en-suite. Accommodation includes two double bedrooms, one single, one twin and three family rooms. Children welcome, cot, high chair and babysitting. Pets allowed. Reduced rates for children and special rates for three night breaks. Open all year.

SANDOWN

Lake Road

Windermere

Cumbria LA23 2JF

Tel: 09-662 5275

Superb Bed and Breakfast accommodation. All rooms en suite with colour TV and tea/coffee making facilities. Situated two minutes from Lake Windermere, shops and cafes. Many lovely walks. Open all year. Residential licence. Special out of season rates, also two-day Saturday/Sunday Breaks. From £16 to £19.50 per person. Well behaved dogs welcome. Each room has own safe private car parking. SAE or telephone for further details.

Proprietors – Irene & George Eastwood.

WINDERMERE. Mr and Mrs J.N. Fowles, Rockside Guest House, Ambleside Road, Windermere LA23 1AQ (09662 5343). Rockside is a family run Guest House, 100 yards from Windermere village, bus stop and railway station. If any help is needed to plan a day's outing the proprietors, Neville and Mavis Fowles, will book trips, loan maps, car routes and plan walks. Single, twin, double and family rooms are all centrally heated and have colour TV, clock radio and telephone; most rooms en-suite with tea/coffee making facilities. A car park at the rear holds 12 cars. Open all year — as every season has its own magic and beauty. RAC acclaimed. Bed and Breakfast from £13.50 to £20.50 per person. Visa, Mastercard and Access accepted.

DERBYSHIRE

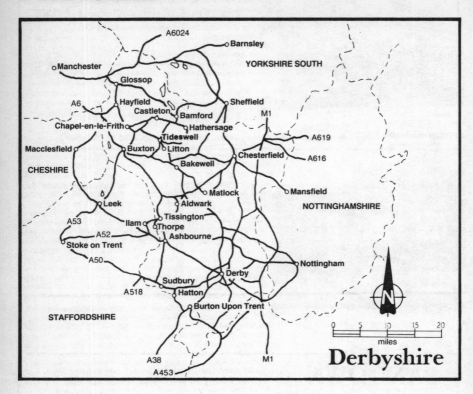

Derbyshire

ALKMONTON, near Ashbourne. Mr and

Mrs A. & D. Harris, Dairy House Farm, Alkmonton, Longford, Derby DE6 3DG (Great Cubley [0335] 330359 or Fax (0335) 330359). ♛♛♛ *Commended.* **Working farm.** This is a working dairy farm with accommodation for guests in one twin, one double and two single rooms and also one double, one twin and one family room en-suite. Tea/coffee making facilities. Two lounges, diningroom and colour TV. Open all year with central heating and log fires in inglenook fireplace. Warm welcome and hospitality guaranteed in a comfortable, homely atmosphere with good food and residential licence. Car essential, parking. AA. RAC acclaimed. FHB member. Les Routiers approved. Bed and Breakfast from £14 (£17 en-suite); Evening Meal £8.50.

ASHBOURNE. Mrs C. Akers, New Park Farm, Moorend, Bradley, Ashbourne DE6 1LQ (Ashbourne

[0335] 43425). ♛♛ A tastefully furnished comfortable farmhouse with log fires, in quiet position with open views of surrounding countryside two and a half miles from Ashbourne. We offer en-suite rooms, two with washbasins, and ground floor en-suite. Guests' own diningroom with separate tables; two sittingrooms with colour TV, tea/coffee making facilities. Good home cooking with Evening Meal by arrangement. Special diets catered for. Children welcome. Play area. Ample parking. Terms on request.

ASHBOURNE. Mrs M.A. Griffin, Coldwall Farm, Okeover, Ashbourne DE6 2BS (Thorpe Cloud

[033-529] 249). ✿✿ Working farm. The farmhouse is set in a secluded spot overlooking Dovedale. The comfortable stone-built house is 200 years old and ideally situated for touring the Peak District and visiting Alton Towers. It has an attractive garden. Guests are welcome to watch farm activities; milking cows, calves, sheep and lambs and a Shire horse are kept. Most of the food is home produced. Lovely walks through woods and by the river on the farm. Two family bedrooms, with washbasins; bathroom, toilet; sittingroom; diningroom. Children welcome, cot, high chair available. Sorry, no pets. Car essential, ample parking. Open from March to October for Evening Dinner, Bed and Breakfast or Bed and Breakfast. Bed and Breakfast from £10.50. SAE, please. Reductions for children.

ASHBOURNE. Mrs E.J. Harrison, Little Park Farm, Mappleton, Ashbourne DE6 2BR (Thorpe Cloud

[033-529] 341). ✿ *Commended.* **Working farm.** This 125 acre family-run dairy farm is in the peaceful Dove Valley and is ideally situated for the Derbyshire Dales and Alton Towers; three miles from Ashbourne. Plenty of wildlife and beautiful walks — ideal for a get-away-from-it-all holiday. Good wholesome farmhouse cooking. An oak-beamed listed farmhouse over 300 years old. Colour TV lounge. One double, one twin and one family size bedrooms, all with washbasins; bathroom, toilet; diningroom. Sorry, no pets. Car essential, parking. Open Easter to end October. Bed and Breakfast from £10; Evening Meal £7. AA listed. Cycle hire nearby.

ASHBOURNE near. Mrs S.R. Foster, Shirley Hall Farm, Shirley, Brailsford, Near Ashbourne DE6

3AS (Ashbourne [0335] 60346). ✿✿ *Commended.* **Working farm.** Come and stay at Shirley Hall Farm, a 17th century manor house with exposed beams in the large comfortable bedrooms. Quietly situated on a 200-acre farm, there is free still water fishing, and nearby woodland walks. A good base for visiting Chatsworth, Kedleston and Sudbury; also for Alton Towers, the caves and Lead Mining Museum at Matlock. Guest facilities include diningroom with separate tables and sittingroom with colour TV. One en suite bedroom, two with washbasins, guests' bathroom and WC. Two further bedrooms with own bathroom in annexe. All rooms have tea/coffee making facilities. Bed and Breakfast from £11 per person. Quality Evening Meals served locally in traditional village pubs, Sunday included.

ASHBOURNE near. Mr and Mrs P.J. Watson, Weaver Farm, Waterhouses, Near Ashbourne ST10 3HE (Oakamoor [0538] 702271; Car telephone number [0831] 386190). ✿✿ Working farm. Situated off A52 on the Weaver Hills close to Ashbourne, Dovedale and Alton Towers. Stone farmhouse with central heating and open fires offering family, twin and double bedrooms with washbasins. Cot. Bathroom with shower and WC. Guest diningroom and lounge with TV. Children welcome. Home produced fresh farmhouse cooking is served. The 320 acre farm with dairy cows, calves, sheep and lambs provides many activities which guests are welcome to watch and they can also enjoy extensive walks and views. Car essential; ample parking. No pets. SAE or ring for terms. A warm welcome awaits you.

ASHBOURNE near. Mrs H. Leason, Overdale, Lode Lane, Alstonefield, Near Ashbourne DE6 2FZ

(Alstonefield [033 527] 206 or 275). Overdale is a beautiful, spacious house situated in one and a half acres of landscaped gardens, including shaded walks, orchard, lily pond and tennis court. Alstonefield is a quiet, extremely pretty village adjacent to Dovedale, the spa towns of Buxton and Matlock, Chatsworth House and Haddon Hall. The guest house has full central heating, two family and five double bedrooms, all equipped with washbasins; three toilets, bathroom. A charming sittingroom and pleasant diningroom complete this perfect holiday home in its exclusive setting. Bed and Breakfast including evening drink £12. Open all year.

ASHOVER. Mrs D. Wootton, Old School Farm, Uppertown Lane, Uppertown, Ashover, Near Chesterfield S45 0JF (Chesterfield [0246] 590813). Working farm, join in. This working farm in a small hamlet on the edge of the Peak District enjoys unspoilt views. Ashover is three miles away and mentioned in the Domesday Book; Chatsworth House, Haddon Hall, Hardwick Hall, Matlock Bath and Bakewell all within seven miles. Accommodation comprises two family, one double, one single rooms. Guests have their own bathroom; washbasins in three of the large rooms. Plenty of hot water; fitted carpets; large livingroom/diningroom with colour TV. Car essential. NO PETS. Disabled guests welcome. Children welcome. Open from April to October. Bed and Breakfast or Bed, Breakfast and Evening Meal (reductions for children). Take the B5057 Darley Dale Road off the A632 Chesterfield to Matlock main road. Take second left. Keep on this road for approximately one mile. Old School Farm is on left opposite the stone water trough. AA and RAC listed.

BAKEWELL. Mrs Sheila Gilbert, Castle Cliffe Private Hotel, Monsal Head, Bakewell DE4 1NL

(Great Longstone [062-987] 258). 👑👑 Monsal Head is a popular beauty spot in the heart of the Derbyshire Dales. There are superb views from all the bedrooms in Castle Cliffe Hotel, some overlooking Monsal Dale and the famous viaduct. It is an ideal centre for visiting the dales, caverns and historic houses. Some of the hotel's three double, two family and four twin rooms have en-suite shower/WC, all have tea making facilities. Centrally heated plus open fires in the lounge and bar. Food is home cooked with the emphasis on British dishes from old traditional recipes. Special diets are catered for and packed lunches are available. Drying facilities for wet clothes and boots. Children welcome. Sorry, no pets. Bed and Breakfast from £16.50.

BAKEWELL. Mrs Ann Lindsay, Gritstone House, Greaves Lane, Ashford in the Water, Bakewell

DE4 1QH (Bakewell [0629] 813563). 👑👑 Be assured of a warm welcome at this charming Georgian house located in Peak National Park on B6465 leading to Monsal Dale and in picturesque village on the Wye, one and a half miles north-west of Bakewell off A6. Lounge with TV, tea/coffee making facilities; two double and one twin bedded rooms all with washbasins and shaver points. Luxury bathroom with shower, two toilets. Full central heating. A perfect location for visiting the Stately Homes and Dales of Derbyshire. Bed and Breakfast from £13, reduced for weekly stays. Sorry, no pets.

BELPER. Mr and Mrs C. Postles, Chevin Green Farm, Chevin Road, Belper DE5 2UN (Belper

[077382] 2328). 👑👑👑 Comfort, a warm welcome and good food are the criteria of our Three Crown establishment which is situated in the peaceful Derbyshire countryside overlooking the beautiful Derwent Valley. The spacious, centrally heated accommodation provides single, twin, double and family rooms, all en-suite; lounge with colour TV; diningroom with separate tables. Enjoy generous breakfasts with our own free range eggs. Tea/coffee making facilities at no extra charge. Arrangements made for riding, golf and fishing. Being on the Gritstone Way, walkers are catered for. Only 30 minutes from the Dales, Alton Towers, American Adventure, Chatsworth etc. Bed and Breakfast from £12 to £16. Reductions for children and weekly bookings.

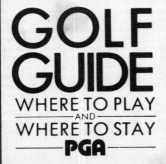

· STADEN GRANGE FARM ·

At Staden Grange we strive to offer a high standard of accommodation, food and service with a warm welcome, made possible by our small size and personal service. Our visitors book will confirm this! **Bedrooms are en suite** and centrally heated. Residents lounge with colour TV and we are **Licensed**. Informal dining room serves home cooking. Children are welcome. No parking problems. **Nordic Sauna and Spa Pool. Horse Riding**. An ideal country residence in a beautiful area. Also available are **Self Catering Apartments**.

Mrs Mary MacKenzie, Staden Grange Farm, Staden, Buxton SK17 9RZ. Telephone: Buxton (0298) 24965.

BUXTON. Mrs Lorraine Naden, Barms Farm, Fairfield, Buxton SK17 7HW (0298 77723). Working farm, join in. Modern dairy farm situated in heart of Peak District offering high class accommodation in recently refurbished farmhouse. Guests have own spacious diningroom, oak beamed lounge with colour TV, central heating and garden. All bedrooms beautifully decorated and offering delightful views over surrounding countryside. Less than one mile from spa town of Buxton and bordering the edge of the local 18 hole golf course. Barms Farm is the ideal base for exploring the Peak District. Good home cooking and a warm welcome awaits. Regrettably no pets. Bed and Breakfast from £12.50 per person. Contact **Lorraine Naden** for further details.

BUXTON. Mrs C. Holland, Shallow Grange, Chelmorton SK17 9SG (0298 23578). Working farm, join in. Shallow Grange is a family run farm with dairy and mixed enterprises. Situated in the heart of the Peak National Park and surrounded by superb rolling countryside, it is the perfect setting for a peaceful and relaxing holiday any time of the year. Within easy reach of Buxton, Bakewell, Castleton, Chatsworth Stately Home and just 30 minutes' drive from Alton Towers. The 18th century farmhouse has been totally renovated. Fully carpeted, centrally heated, double glazed and equipped to a very high standard yet still retaining its character. Rooms are en-suite with colour TV and tea/coffee facilities. From £15 Bed and Breakfast; Evening Meal £10.

BUXTON. Mrs Lynne P. Fearns, Heath Farm, Smalldale, Buxton SK17 8EB (0298 24431). Farm in Peak District with walking, caving, parks, gardens, caverns, pony trekking, historic houses, hang gliding, riding stables and rock climbing all within reasonable driving distance. Four and a half miles from Buxton (A6), two miles from Peak Forest (A623). One double and one family bedroom; bathroom, two toilets; sittingroom and diningroom. Cot and babysitting available. Pets welcome. Open all year except Christmas, mid-week bookings accepted. Car essential, parking. Bed and Breakfast from £11.50 per night; reductions for children and weekly stays. Registered with East Midland Tourist Board.

BUXTON. Mr Rys Edge, Lakenham, 11 Burlington Road, Buxton SK17 9AL (Buxton [0298] 79209).

👑👑👑 *Commended.* Kathryn and Rys invite you to LAKENHAM, their beautifully appointed Victorian Guest House in residential area, set on a broad tree-lined avenue overlooking the Pavilion Gardens. The bedrooms are spacious and furnished with your comfort in mind. All have en-suite bathrooms, hospitality trays and colour TVs. Decorated throughout in a Victorian manner, our elegantly furnished lounge and diningroom overlook our own peaceful and private gardens. Close to all amenities, Lakenham is the perfect base for exploring the Peak District. Private parking. We hope to give a personal service in a friendly, relaxed atmosphere and plenty of good home cooked food. For colour brochure contact **Rys Edge.**

Fernydale Farm

Earl Sterndale,
Buxton SK17 0BS
(Longnor [029-883] 236)

A warm welcome awaits you at Fernydale, a 220 acre dairy farm. A luxury farmhouse situated on the B5053 by the village of Earl Sterndale approx 5 miles from Buxton, in the heart of the Peak District National Park amidst superb scenery, we are ideal for walking or touring in the Park. Both our double bedrooms are ensuite and comfortably furnished to a high standard having tea/coffee making facilities and colour TV's. Terms for B&B from £15. Evening Meal £10. SAE or telephone **Joan Nadin** for brochure.

BUXTON. Mrs S. Fosker, Brunswick Guest House, 31 St. John's Road, Buxton SK17 6XG (Buxton [0298] 71727). 👑👑 Brunswick House, a quietly situated home from home family guest house. Ideally located, only two minutes' walk from Buxton's Pavilion Gardens, Shopping Centre and overlooking the beautiful Serpentine walks. All bedrooms are en suite with TV. Tea and coffee making facilities in all rooms. Centrally heated throughout. Relaxing television lounge. Private car parking facilities. Pets welcome. Good home cooking and a warm welcome from your hosts. Bed and Breakfast from £16 per person. Further details on request.

BUXTON near. Mrs A. Barnsley, Dale House Farm, Litton, Near Buxton SK17 8QL (Tideswell [0298] 871309). Working farm. Bed and Breakfast and good farmhouse food is provided on this friendly farm in clean, comfortable, spacious accommodation with fine open views, on the outskirts of a pleasant picturesque village with its unique village greens. Within easy walking distance of many well-known beauty spots, centrally situated in the heart of the Peak District National Park. Two double and one family bedrooms; bathroom, toilet; sittingroom; diningroom. Sorry, no pets. Plenty of parking space. Open all year. AA listed. Bed and Breakfast from £11. Guests assured of a friendly welcome.

BUXTON near. Mrs Mary Preston-Cox, Glebe House Farm, Heathcote, Hartington, Near Buxton SK17 0AY (Buxton [0298] 84313). This cosy old house is in a quiet position on the edge of a small country village in the heart of the Peak District. Ideal touring centre for the Dales and caverns of Derbyshire, stately homes of Chatsworth, Haddon Hall, Hardwick Hall, etc. The Spa of Buxton with its many attractions, 10 miles. The house commands excellent views of the surrounding countryside. Accommodation comprises two double, one single and one family bedrooms (washbasin in family room); bathroom and toilet; sittingroom; diningroom with own tables. Car essential — parking. Open March to October. Bed and Breakfast from £12 per night. Reductions for children under 12.

Terms quoted in this publication may be subject to increase if rises in costs necessitate

BUXTON near. Mrs C.R. Faulkner, Mount Pleasant Farm, Elkstone, Longnor, Near Buxton SK17 0LU (Blackshaw [053-834] 380).

🌷🌷 FHG Diploma Winner. This BTA Commended Farmhouse is set on a two acre smallholding surrounded by lovely countryside, peaceful and relaxing with beautiful open views. It makes a comfortable centre for touring the Peak District; a car is essential to get the most out of your holiday. Plenty of parking space. Three double bedrooms with washbasins, tea/coffee making facilities, bathroom, two toilets, guest lounge, diningroom, table tennis room. Full central heating. Children over six years welcome. Pets by arrangement only. Open March to November inclusive for Bed and Breakfast. Evening Meal by arrangement. Liz Faulkner used to demonstrate cookery for the Gas Board and serves traditional English fare using fresh local produce wherever possible. Terms on receipt of SAE, please, or telephone for personal attention and full particulars.

CASTLETON. Mrs B. Johnson, Myrtle Cottage, Market Place, Castleton, Near Sheffield S30 2WQ (Hope Valley [0433] 20787). Myrtle Cottage is pleasantly situated near the village green in the picturesque village of Castleton, famous for its castle and caverns. It is an ideal base for walking, caving, hang gliding or touring the Peak District and Derbyshire Dales. Buxton, Bakewell, Chatsworth House and the plague village of Eyam are within 20 minutes' drive. Registered with the English Tourist Board. The guest accommodation comprises family, twin and double bedrooms all with private shower/toilet and tea/coffee making facilities; sittingroom with TV and diningroom. Central heating. Fire Certificate. Parking. Regret no pets. Open all year (except Christmas) for Bed and Breakfast only.

DERBY. Mr and Mrs J. Richardson, Rangemoor Hotel, 67 Macklin Street, Derby DE1 1LF (Derby [0332] 47252).

🌷 The Rangemoor Hotel is situated in Derby City Centre, an ideal location for hikers, ramblers and tourists who prefer city night life — restaurants, cinemas, theatres, night clubs and shopping precincts nearby. The hotel has single, double and a few family rooms, all with central heating, washbasins, tea/coffee making facilities and colour TV. Shared bathroom, toilets and showers. Separate colour TV lounge and diningroom. Own key. Large car park. Derbyshire's Dales, stately homes and leisure parks, and delightful countryside are within a few miles of the City. AA and RAC listed. Member of the English Tourist Board.

HELP IMPROVE BRITISH TOURIST STANDARDS

You are choosing holiday accommodation from our very popular FHG Publications. Whether it be a hotel, guest house, farmhouse or self-catering accommodation, we think you will find it hospitable, comfortable and clean, and your host and hostess friendly and helpful. Why not write and tell us about it?

As a recognition of the generally well-run and excellent holiday accommodation reviewed in our publications, we at FHG Publications Ltd. present a diploma to proprietors who receive the highest recommendation from their guests who are also readers of our Guides. If you care to write to us praising the holiday you have booked through FHG Publications Ltd. – whether this be board, self-catering accommodation, a sporting or a caravan holiday, what you say will be evaluated and the proprietors who reach our final list will be contacted.

The winning proprietor will receive an attractive framed diploma to display on his premises as recognition of a high standard of comfort, amenity and hospitality. FHG Publications Ltd. offer this diploma as a contribution towards the improvement of standards in tourist accommodation in Britain. Help your excellent host or hostess to win it!

FHG DIPLOMA

We nominate ....

....

Because

Name ....

Address ....

.... Telephone No. ....

DOVEDALE. Mrs Julia Brookfield, Green Gables, Thorpe, Near Ashbourne DE6 2AW (Thorpe Cloud [033-529] 386). ☙ This old farmhouse has been renovated to offer comfortable accommodation for its guests. Two double rooms and one twin-bedded room. Two bathrooms and shower. Diningroom with oak beams; lounge with colour TV (log fire in winter). Full central heating. Tea and coffee making facilities. Children and pets welcome. Ample parking space. Open Easter week-end to November. Bed and Breakfast £14; Evening Meal £6.50. Singles £16.

DOVEDALE (near Ashbourne). Mrs F.M. Gould, St. Leonard's Cottage, Thorpe, Ashbourne DE6 2AW (Thorpe Cloud [033-529] 224). One of the oldest cottages in the village, St. Leonard's stands in its own grounds of one third of an acre overlooking the village green, near to the entrance to Dovedale. Thorpe Cloud rises in the background. Many historic houses easily reached, walking in Manifold Valley and Tissington Trail. Fully modernised but retaining the original oak beams, the house has one double and one single bedrooms with washbasins, near to the bathroom. Three bedrooms have bathroom en-suite. Diningroom and sittingroom, colour TV. A new extension has provided space and comfort for the guests. Open to visitors all day. Open all year except Christmas. Full central heating. Sorry, no pets in the house. Ample parking. Fire Certificate held. Terms for Bed and Breakfast from £13.50 to £15.50 per night. Evening Dinner £6.50 (optional). Weekly terms. Licensed. Tea/coffee facilities.

DOVEDALE. Mrs Joan Wain, Air Cottage Farm, Ilam, Ashbourne DE6 2BD (Thorpe Cloud [033-529] 475). Working farm, join in. Holidaymakers to the Peak District will enjoy staying at Air Cottage Farm situated at the edge of Dovedale with picturesque views of Thorpe Cloud and Dovedale Valley. The famous Stepping Stones are just 10 minutes away and it is an ideal base for touring the Peak District National Park, stately homes and many other places of local historic interest. Unlimited walks in the Manifold Valley and the Tissington Nature Trail and scenic routes for motorists. Within easy reach of Alton Towers and Matlock's "Gulliver's Kingdom". Sports available include swimming, squash and horse riding, all within easy reach. Two double bedrooms and one single (sleeping two); bathroom, two toilets; sittingroom; diningroom. Cot and high chair provided for children. Open March to November. A car is essential — parking. Terms and further details on request.

DERBYSHIRE – PEAK DISTRICT AND DALES!

The undulating dales set against the gritstone edges of the Pennine moors give Derbyshire its scenic wealth. In the tourists' itinerary should be the prehistoric monument at Arbor Low, the canal port of Shardlow, the country parks at Elvaston and Shipley, the limestone caves at Creswell Crags and Castleton and the market towns of Ashbourne and Bakewell. For walkers this area provides many excellent opportunities.

GEE CROSS, near Manchester. Mrs Charlotte R. Walsh, Needhams Farm, Uplands Road, Werneth Low, Gee Cross, Near Hyde SK14 3AQ (061 368 4610).

Working farm. A cosy 16th century farmhouse set in peaceful, picturesque surroundings by Werneth Low Country Park and the Etherow Valley, which lie between Glossop and Manchester. The farm is ideally situated for holidaymakers and businessmen, especially those who enjoy peace and quiet, walking and rambling, golfing and riding, as these activities are all close by. At Needhams Farm everyone, including children and pets, receives a warm welcome. Good wholesome meals available in the evenings. Residential Licence and Fire Certificate held. Open all year. Single Bed and Breakfast from £16, Evening Meal from £6.75. AA listed. RAC acclaimed.

HATHERSAGE. Mrs Jill Salisbury, Lane End Farm, Abney, Hathersage, Via Sheffield S30 1AA (Hope Valley [0433] 50371). Working farm, join in.

Come and relax in our lovely Derbyshire farmhouse. We are a working dairy and sheep farm in the Peak District National Park. Lane End, having panoramic views, is situated in the small hamlet of Abney midway between Hathersage and Tideswell. The area is ideal for most outdoor pursuits and for visiting all local places of interest. We offer a high standard of accommodation — one family room, one double room and one twin room, all with washbasins and tea/coffee making facilities. Car recommended. Farm trail. Own horse welcome. Self Catering six berth caravan available. Bed and Breakfast from £13. Reductions for children. Open all year. East Midlands Tourist Board member, listed and commended.

HATHERSAGE. Mrs Carolann B. Colley, Sladen, Jaggers Lane, Hathersage, The Peak District, Derbyshire S30 1AZ (Hope Valley [0433] 50706). A large comfortable family house situated in lovely grounds in the heart of the Peak District, in one of the old traditional Derbyshire villages. Steeped in history including the legends of Robin Hood. Within easy reach of Chatsworth House, Haddon Hall, the Caves of Castleton, with lovely walks and climbs. "Sladen" is within two minutes' walk of the centre of Hathersage. It has spacious rooms, most overlooking the beautiful view of the valley and hills. Private guests' bathroom. A warm welcome for all, including children and pets.

HOPE. Mrs Barbara Singleton, Underleigh, off Edale Road, Hope, Near Sheffield S30 2RD (0433 21372). Underleigh is a private home welcoming guests who appreciate good food in good surroundings. Situated approximately one and a half miles from village centre in the glorious Peak District National Park. Ideal for visiting stately homes, the Blue John Mines of Castleton and the Edale Centre. Pony trekking, beautiful walks, bird watching, golf and fishing available in the area. Majority of rooms en-suite. Dinners are "en-famille". Hearty and Continental Breakfasts available. Children over 10 years welcome. Dogs allowed but are restricted. Tariff and brochure available.

MATLOCK near. Ray and Pauline Sanders, Sycamore Guest House, Town Head, Bonsall, Near Matlock DE4 2AA (Wirksworth [0629] 823903). ♛ ♛ A

lovely 18th century family guest house in the village of Bonsall, nestling high on Masson Hill on the edge of the Peak District National Park. Easy access to Matlock Bath (for cable cars), Chatsworth House, Haddon Hall, Dovedale, Alton Towers, etc. All bedrooms with washbasins and tea/coffee making facilities. Two bathrooms, two showers, three toilets. Lounge with TV. Diningroom with open fire. Full central heating. Residential licence. Ample car parking. AA Listed. Bed and Breakfast from £14; Evening Meal from £8. Open all year including special Christmas Break. SAE for brochure.

SHEFFIELD near. Mrs Janet Biggin, Cordwell Farm, Cordwell Valley, Holmesfield, Near Sheffield S18 5WH (0742 890303). A 16th century listed farmhouse

set on working dairy and poultry farm. This beautiful old house nestles in the charming Cordwell Valley, within easy reach of Chatsworth House (seat of the Duke of Devonshire), Haddon Hall and the historic market town of Bakewell. On fringe of Peak Park yet only five miles from Chesterfield and Sheffield. Two double rooms, one family room. Children and pets welcome. Bed and Breakfast from £12.50. Open March to October.

WESTON UNDERWOOD. Mrs Linda Adams, Parkview Farm, Weston Underwood, Derby DE6 4PA (Ashbourne [0335] 60352). ♛ ♛ *Commended.* **Working**

farm. Enjoy country house hospitality in our elegant farmhouse, set in a large garden overlooking our 370 acre farm and Kedleston Hall and Park. Or enjoy the peace and tranquillity of the Derbyshire countryside in one of our two lovely farm cottages. The bedrooms at Parkview are beautifully furnished and decorated and have washbasins and tea/coffee facilities. The double bedrooms have antique four-poster beds. Guests' own bathrooms. Sittingroom with colour TV and delightful diningroom. Visit Dovedale, the Peak District, Alton Towers and the market town of Ashbourne. Country pubs and restaurants close by. Bed and Breakfast from £16 to £18. Brochure on request.

WIRKSWORTH. Mrs B.M. Corbett, Sycamore Farm, Hopton, Wirksworth DE4 4DF (062 982 2466).

This unique round-fronted brick and stone farm house was originally an Elizabethan Coaching Inn. It is situated on a 230 acre mixed farm with all the amenities of modern-day living but still retaining its historic charm and the peace associated with the countryside. It is an ideal situation for walking, touring, close to the Peak District, Chatsworth, Haddon Hall, Bakewell and Ashbourne. Comfortable visitors' lounge with colour TV. Two double bedrooms with an extra bed if required. Terms for Bed and Breakfast from £12. SAE for brochure.

**If you've found
FARM HOLIDAY GUIDES
of service please tell your friends**

DEVON

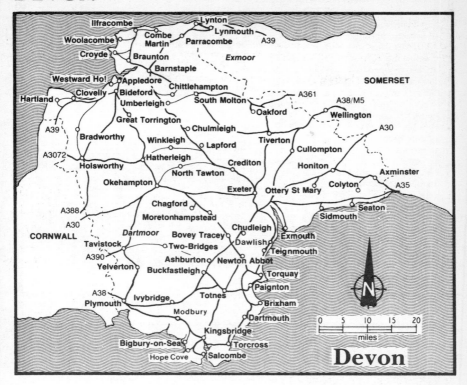

ASHBURTON. Mrs D.E. Harvey, Higher Brownswell Farm, Ashburton, Newton Abbot TQ13 7EZ (Ashburton [0364] 52309). Working farm. Working farm in Dartmoor National Park. Turn into Roborough Lane opposite Golden Lion, Ashburton, one-and-a-half miles straight ahead and ours is the first farm on the left. Golf course, riding stables, leisure and sports centre all within six mile radius, sea twelve miles. All rooms with hot/cold washbasin, and open country views. Shower room, bathroom with toilet, separate toilet. TV lounge with tea/coffee making facilities. Children welcome — half price under 12 years. Bed and Breakfast only. Good inns and restaurants in Ashburton and surrounding area. Car essential. Ample parking. West Country Tourist Board Registered, Dartmoor Tourist Association Member.

ASHBURTON. Mrs D.M. Dent, Adams Hele Farm, Ashburton TQ13 7NW (Ashburton [0364] 52525). Working farm. This 16th century farmhouse

nestles on the south facing hill overlooking the Dart Valley and the Moors. The farm consists of 90 acres stocked with cattle, sheep and ponies on pleasant grassland. It is an ideal base for exploring the unspoilt scenery of Dartmoor. The accommodation consists of double bedrooms, all with washbasins; two bathrooms, three toilets; sittingroom; two diningrooms. Children are welcome: cot, high chair, babysitting, special mealtimes and reduced rates. Pets by arrangement. Open March to October. Car essential, parking. The South Devon beaches are only 15 miles; Plymouth and Exeter within an hour's drive. Excellent fishing, beautiful walks, moorland pony rides and many golf courses within easy reach. A warm welcome to all guests.

ASHBURTON (Dartmoor). Mrs Anne Haycraft, Middle Leat, Holne, Near Ashburton, Newton Abbot TQ13 7SJ (Poundsgate [03643] 413). A warm welcome awaits you at Middle Leat, a comfortable smallholding with wonderful views, on the edge of Dartmoor. The picturesque village of Holne lies three and a half miles west of Ashburton. The River Dart Country Park is nearby and there are many other places of interest nearby. Attractions include horses, pony to ride, free range hens and ducks. Children usually like to join in, collecting eggs, feeding the ducks etc. Three ground floor bedrooms, one twin, one double and one family, private bathroom available. All have TV, radio and tea-making facilities. Full English Breakfast, plenty of good home cooking, home grown vegetables and clotted cream. Vegetarians made welcome. Bed and Breakfast, optional Evening Meal. Sorry, no smoking in house. Please send SAE for details, or telephone.

PLEASE ENCLOSE A STAMPED ADDRESSED ENVELOPE WITH ENQUIRIES

BAMPTON. Mrs Lindy Head, Harton Farm, Oakford, Tiverton EX16 9HH (Oakford [039-85] 209). Working farm, join in. Lovely 17th century farmhouse with original fireplaces and witches' window on 53-acre mixed farm that is virtually self-supporting with own friendly cows, pigs, chickens, sheep, goats, home spun wool, etc. Secluded, but accessible, it is an ideal touring centre for Exmoor, the Exe Valley and Devon. Comfortable accommodation in three double bedrooms with washbasins and tea-making facilities; bathroom; diningroom serving real country cooking with farm-produced organic vegetables, meat, eggs, butter; home baking a speciality; guests' lounge with colour TV. Children over four welcome. Pets accepted. Car essential — parking. Open for Evening Meal, Bed and Breakfast from £14; Bed and Breakfast from £9. Reductions for children. Farm walks. Fishing, shooting, riding can be arranged. Vegetarian meals available on request. ETB listed.

BARNSTAPLE. Mrs M. Lethaby, Home Park Farm, Lower Blakewell, Muddiford, Barnstaple EX31 4ET (0271 42955). Working farm. Home Park Farm has approximately 70 acres and is mainly a sheep farm with a few beef cattle. Ideal for peace and relaxation, we make every effort to ensure that our guests have a comfortable and happy stay. There is a children's play area outside with Wendy house, slide and swings. The farmhouse has a sittingroom with colour TV; en-suite bedrooms with tea trays and TVs. We take only one or two families in the farmhouse at a time. Also available, a four-berth caravan that is let either on a self-catering basis or with meals in the farmhouse. Numerous beauty spots and beaches nearby. SAE for brochure. AA QQQ listed; Tourist Board inspection applied for.

BARNSTAPLE. Mrs L.P.A. Joslin, Stone Farm, Brayford, Barnstaple EX32 7PJ (0271 830473).

Charming old character farmhouse on 180 acres working farm. Seven acres woods, well situated in peaceful countryside. Six miles between the market town of Barnstaple and Exmoor. Ideal touring centre for moors and North Devon's sandy beaches. Spacious and comfortable accommodation offered in three family/double bedrooms with washbasins, tea/coffee facilities and heaters, two rooms have TV points; two bathrooms; diningroom; two lounges with TV and toys for children. Plentiful fresh food of the highest quality provided for Full English Breakfast and excellent four course Dinner. A friendly, relaxed holiday with no restrictions. Bed and Breakfast from £12; Bed, Breakfast and Evening Meal £18. No pets. Write or telephone for brochure.

BARNSTAPLE. Mrs Andrea Cook, Higher Churchill Farm, East Down, Near Barnstaple EX31 4LT (0271 850543). Working farm. Friendly farming family welcome you to our 300 year old farmhouse, situated on a National Trust Estate. Comfortable accommodation with "real" farmhouse cooking using our own or fresh local produce. The farm has a dairy herd and sheep, plus many other animals. Ideal for quiet breaks early and late in the season. Children welcome. Tea/coffee making facilities. Central for beaches and Exmoor. Farm Holiday Bureau member. Tourist Board listed.

BARNSTAPLE. Mrs Elizabeth Smyth, Higher Clifton Farm, East Down, Barnstaple EX31 4LX (Shirwell [0271] 850372). 🌸 *Approved.* A warm welcome awaits you on our 340 acre, family-run working farm with beef cattle, sheep and lambs, dogs, cats and a Jersey cow who provides the milk and clotted cream! Comfortable 17th century farmhouse with lovely views in a very peaceful setting not far from Exmoor beaches, fishing, golf and horse riding. Only a few minutes' walk to the village pub. Accommodation consists of one family, one double and one twin bedrooms with washbasins, plus cot; bathroom with toilet, also a separate toilet. Lounge/diningroom with tea/coffee facilities. Good farmhouse food, using our own produce when possible. Children welcome, babysitting by arrangement. Sorry, no pets. Car essential. Tourist Board inspected annually. Bed, Breakfast and Evening Meal.

DEVON – ENDLESS CHOICES!

People never tire of visiting Devon. There's so much to do, like visiting Alscott Farm Museum, Berry Head Country Park, Bickleigh Mill Farm, Farway Countryside Park, Haytor Granite Railway, Kent's Cavern, Dartmoor National Park and of course Plymouth and its Hoe.

BARNSTAPLE. Mrs Hazel Kingdon, Waytown Farm, Shirwell, Barnstaple EX31 4JN (Shirwell [0271] 850396). 🐦🐦 *Commended.* **Working farm.**

Waytown is a beef and sheep farm on the A39 three miles from Barnstaple which has a Leisure Centre. Our attractive 17th century farmhouse is set in pleasant countryside. Dartmoor can be seen in the distance; within easy reach of Exmoor National Park and sandy beaches. Fishing nearby. Guests made welcome with home cooking — own vegetables, cream, eggs. Accommodation consists of two double and one family bedrooms — shaver points, washbasins, heating and tea/coffee making facilities in each; bathroom, two toilets; lounge with TV. All children welcome. Babysitting. Cot, high chair. Ample parking. Sorry no pets. Open all year. Bed and Breakfast from £12; Bed, Breakfast and Evening Meal from £17. Reductions for children under 12 years. SAE, please, for prompt reply.

BARNSTAPLE near. Ms Angela Sexon, Castle Hill Barton, Filleigh, Near Barnstaple EX32 0RX (05986 242). 🐦🐦 Family run 330 acre dairy and beef farm set in picturesque Fortescue Estate countryside. Four course evening dinner of traditional farmhouse cooking with fresh garden produce and home made clotted cream. Two family and one twin bedrooms, all with washbasins. Three toilets; bathroom and separate shower room. Large lounge and separate diningroom. Children love to ride the family pony. Ideal touring centre for Exmoor and the coast. Pets welcome. Open Easter to October. Bed and Breakfast from £12; Evening Meal from £6.

BEAFORD. Miss H. Tucker, Hall Farm, Beaford EX19 8NS (08053 426). Situated close to the moors and near Torrington where the Dartington Glass comes from. Only half an hour's drive to beaches (Westward Ho!) and to the market town of Barnstaple. Within easy reach of family attractions for all types of weather. Five large bedrooms, all with washbasin and tea/coffee making facilities. Spacious lounge with log fire. Full size snooker room. Large garden. Plenty of parking. Good farmhouse cooking. Bed, Breakfast and Evening Meal from £95 per week; Bed and Breakfast also available.

BEAFORD. Mrs R. Hookway, "East Villavin Farm", Roborough, Near Winkleigh (08053 272). Working farm. Guests are made welcome at "East Villavin" and they return year after year. This mixed farm has cows, sheep, tame lambs, chickens, cats, free donkey rides. Entrance situated on a good road, B3217. Golf course and fishing nearby. Excellent touring centre Dartmoor, Exmoor and within easy reach of the beautiful North Devon beaches. Farmhouse tastefully decorated; diningroom; lounge, colour TV; bedrooms have washbasins and tea-making facilities. We serve good food, varied each day. Sweets served with cream made on the farm. A warm welcome awaits you. Bed and Breakfast. Evening Meal optional.

BERRYNARBOR. Ken and Jenny Holley, Langleigh House, The Village, Berrynarbor, Near Ilfracombe EX34 9SG (Combe Martin [0271] 883410). 🐦🐦 *Approved.* Langleigh House is situated in the middle of the beautiful unspoilt village of Berrynarbor, approximately three miles from Ilfracombe and one mile from Combe Martin. It is ideally placed for exploring Exmoor and the whole of North Devon, with its sandy beaches such as Woolacombe and Croyde, and the more dramatic coast from Lynton to Ilfracombe. The House has its own car park located well off the road. All rooms have washbasins and tea-making facilities. Two rooms have en-suite shower rooms and toilets. Central heating. Access at all times. Children and pets welcome. Open all year. Bed and Breakfast from £12 per night.

BIDEFORD. Mrs C.M. Tremeer, Garnacott Farm, Alverdiscott, Torrington EX38 7HG (Newton Tracey [027-185] 282). Working farm. Situated amidst quiet and peaceful countryside with delightful scenery, mixed working farm of 85 acres carrying cows, sheep, calves and poultry, where visitors are welcome to participate in farm activities. Homely, comfortable accommodation with plenty of good farmhouse cooking using own produce — milk, eggs, cream and vegetables. Within easy reach of North Devon and Cornish beaches and moors. Bideford, Torrington four miles, Barnstaple seven miles and lovely sandy beaches only five miles. Two family bedrooms, one single (two with washbasins); bathroom, toilet. Sitting/diningroom with wood-burning stove and colour TV. Children welcome; babysitting arranged. Sorry, no pets. Car essential — parking. Evening Dinner, Bed and Breakfast from £90 weekly (from £15 daily); Bed and Breakfast from £11 daily. Reductions for children under 10 years. Open March to November. Also one modern six-berth caravan for self-catering.

BIDEFORD. Mrs Betty Willes, Raddy Farm, Instow, Bideford EX39 4LW (Instow [0271] 860433).

Working farm. Set in quiet countryside typical of North Devon, Raddy Farmhouse, a south-facing farmhouse, old but modernised, with lawn at front. Sandy beach at Instow only three-quarters of a mile away; market towns of Bideford and Barnstaple three and six miles away respectively. Very central for touring the beautiful beaches of North Devon and the much-loved Exmoor and Dartmoor area nearby. Cooking is traditional with most of the food home produced (home produced Farmhouse Cheddar available). Colour TV for visitors; babysitting. Double, single and family bedrooms, all with washbasins; bathroom, two toilets; two sittingrooms and diningroom. Sorry, no pets. Car essential, parking. Children welcome at reduced rates. Evening Dinner, Bed and Breakfast or Bed and Breakfast only. Terms on request. Tourist Board member.

BIDEFORD. Mrs C. Colwill, Welsford Farm, Hartland EX39 6EQ (0237 441296). Working farm, join in. Relax, enjoy the peaceful countryside yet be within easy reach of towns, interesting places and picturesque beaches with miles of scenic cliff walks. This 360-acre dairy farm is situated two miles from Hartland Village; four miles from cobble-stoned Clovelly and the rugged Hartland coastline. Comfortably furnished farmhouse with colour TV lounge and washbasins in bedrooms. Children welcome at reduced rates. Wander around the farm and "pets' corner". Babysitting always available. Good country food using home grown produce. Car essential. Bed, Breakfast and four course Evening Meal from £84 weekly. Warm welcome. Regret no pets. Open April to October.

BIDEFORD. Nikki Mason, Little Burrough, Churchill Way, Northam, Bideford (0237 476007). Nikki Mason invites you for a carefree holiday in her Georgian house; her aim is for you to enjoy your stay. Good food, well prepared and served at a time to suit. TV and tea making facilities in rooms. TV lounge, separate diningroom and tables. Car parking. Full Fire Certificate held. The house is centrally heated and is open at Christmas — want a country Christmas? Rates and reductions on special breaks and for children. Pets welcome. SAE for brochure.

BIDEFORD near. Mr and Mrs J. Ridd, Bakers Farm, Torrington EX38 7ES (0805 23260). This is a

farm of just over 100 acres with attached 16th century farmhouse. A warm welcome awaits all visitors, who are free to come and go as they please. The food and accommodation is highly recommended by previous guests, and visitors are assured of delicious meals prepared from fresh produce only, including meat, vegetables, milk, eggs, cream and cheese. Accommodation consists of one family, two double and one twin-bedded rooms; two toilets, one shower room, one bathroom. Comfortable lounge with colour TV which visitors may use at any time. Full Fire Certificate. Local amenities in Torrington include indoor swimming pool, golf, tennis and fishing (coarse fishing available within the farm), as well as the famous Dartington Glass Factory. We are within easy reach of the coast, Exmoor, Dartmoor and many other places of interest, and are just under a mile from Torrington. Guests are welcome to walk around the farm and see our various animals. Reasonable rates for Evening Meal, Bed and Breakfast (from £14) or Bed and Breakfast only. Reductions for children. Please send SAE for full particulars.

BIDEFORD near. Mrs B.A. Ford, Webbery Barton, Near Bideford EX39 4PU (Newton Tracey [0271-85] 395). Working farm, join in. Webbery Barton is a 400 acre mixed farm with a large 18th century farmhouse. Situated three miles from Bideford, five miles from the nearest beach, eight miles from Barnstaple with its Leisure Centre. Ideal for touring all North Devon's many beaches and beauty spots. We take only one family at a time and provide a relaxed friendly atmosphere with plenty of good home cooking and personal attention at all times. Reduced rates for children, babysitting offered. Open May to September. Sorry no pets. Car essential, parking. Bed, Breakfast and Evening Meal from £15 per day. SAE, please for weekly terms or telephone.

BIDEFORD near. Mrs Yvonne Heard, West Titchberry Farm, Hartland, Near Bideford EX39 6AU (0237 441 287). Working farm, join in. Spacious, completely renovated 17th century farmhouse, carpeted and well appointed throughout. One family room with washbasin, one double room with washbasin, and one twin room; bathroom and two toilets. Downstairs lounge with colour TV; toilet; diningroom where excellent home cooking is served using fresh farm produce. A games room and sheltered walled garden are available for guests' use. The coastal footpath winds its way around this 150 acre mixed farm situated between Hartland Lighthouse and the National Trust beauty spot of Shipload Bay (sand at low tide). Hartland three miles, Clovelly six miles, Bideford and Westward Ho! 15 miles, Bude 18 miles. Children welcome at reduced rates; cot, high chair, babysitting available. Open all year except Christmas. Tourist Board registered. Terms on application for Evening Dinner/Meal, Bed and Breakfast. Also self catering cottage available.

BIGBURY. Mrs Julie Widger, Lower Cumery, Bigbury, Kingsbridge TQ7 4NN (Modbury [0548]

830160). Farmhouse set in a very secluded position with fine country views. One double, one twin and one family room each with vanity unit (hot and cold water). All beds have duvets. Two bathrooms. Large diningroom and spacious lounge with colour TV and well stocked library. Excellent food with a good variety of home grown fruit and vegetables and free-range eggs. Large gardens and play area extending to two acres altogether. Open all year. Sorry, no pets. Lovely sandy beaches nearby. Ideal walking country, fishing, riding, golf and many places of interest and local beauty spots within easy reach. Car essential — parking. Bed and Breakfast £11; Evening Meal (optional) £5.50. Reduced rates for children and for weekly stays.

BRATTON FLEMING. Mr and Mrs M.J. Dyer, Lower Stowford Farm, Bratton Fleming, Barnstaple

EX31 4SG (Parracombe [05983] 219). Our 300-year-old homely, centrally heated farmhouse is set in two acres of peaceful countryside. Just six miles from the sea and close to Exmoor, it is ideally situated for most holiday activities. Three double bedrooms, two en suite; one twin room; one guest bathroom; lounge with TV. Log fires lit early and late season. Good fresh food with free range chickens and duck eggs; four course dinners. Sorry, no pets. Ample parking. German spoken. For terms please send SAE, or telephone.

Lower Stowford Farm

HOLIDAY ACCOMMODATION
Classification Schemes in
England, Scotland and Wales

The National Tourist Boards for England, Scotland and Wales have agreed a common 'Crown Classification' scheme for **serviced (Board)** accommodation. All establishments are inspected regularly and are given a classification indicating their level of facilities and services.

There are six grades ranging from 'Listed' to 'Five Crowns 👑👑👑👑👑'. The higher the classification, the more facilities and services offered.

Crown classification is a measure of *facilities* not *quality*. A common quality grading scheme grades the quality of establishments as 'Approved', 'Commended' or 'Highly Commended' according to the accommodation, welcome and service they provide.

For **Self-Catering**, holiday homes in England are awarded 'Keys' after inspection and can also be 'Approved', 'Commended' or 'Highly Commended' according to the facilities available. In Scotland the Crown scheme includes self-catering accommodation and Wales also has a voluntary inspection scheme for self-catering grading from '1 (Standard)' to '5 (Excellent)'.

Caravan and Camping Parks can participate in the British Holiday Parks grading scheme from 'Approved (✓)' to 'Excellent (✓ ✓ ✓ ✓ ✓)'. In addition, each National Tourist Board has an annual award for high-quality caravan accommodation: in England – Rose Awards; in Scotland – Thistle Commendations; in Wales – Dragon Awards.

When advertisers supply us with the information, FHG Publications show Crowns and other awards or gradings, including AA, RAC, Egon Ronay etc. We also award a small number of Farm Holiday Guide Diplomas every year, based on readers' recommendations.

The Edgemoor
Lowerdown Cross, Bovey Tracey, South Devon TQ13 9LE

Beautifully refurbished family-run Country House Hotel on edge of Dartmoor one mile west of BOVEY TRACEY. Ideal walking and touring centre. Exeter, Torbay, Dartmouth, Plymouth and nine National Trust properties within 35 miles. Local produce, ample choice of food and wine. 15 rooms with private bath. Bargain breaks available "all year", excluding Christmas – New Year. Resident Proprietors: Mr & Mrs J. R. Day.

Telephone: Bovey Tracey (0626) 832466.

BRAUNTON. Mrs Jean M. Barnes, Denham Farm, North Buckland, Braunton EX23 1HY (Croyde [0271] 890297). ❦❦❦ *Commended.* **Working farm, join in.** This is a 160 acre beef farm where guests are allowed to roam around and join in with the farming activities. We provide everything for a relaxing holiday. Peace and quiet, countryside, good food, friendly atmosphere and super, comfortable accommodation. All the food is personally prepared by Mrs Barnes to ensure a high standard, desserts are a speciality. The rooms are of an equally high standard, all are en-suite and have own colour TV, radio alarm and tea/coffee making facilities; TV lounge; bar lounge; large diningroom; reading room; laundry facilities. Games room outside and small pets for children are kept. A short drive to long sandy beaches, rolling surf, cliff walks and rugged moorland. Nearby you will find golf, riding, sailing, windsurfing and miles of country walks. This 17th century farmhouse has been tastefully decorated to offer you the best. AA and RAC listed. Telephone now and book your break. Open all year. Bed and Breakfast, Evening Dinner optional. Sorry, no pets.

BRIXHAM. Roger and Laurian Snowden, Richmond House Hotel, Higher Manor Road, Brixham TQ5 8HA (Brixham [0803] 882391). ❦❦ Detached Victorian house of character, decorated in the "Laura Ashley" style, with a relaxed and friendly atmosphere owned by young family. Quiet location (first left after "Golden Lion" on New Road) central to shops and historic harbour. Licensed restaurant 100 yards. An excellent base for touring South Hams and Dartmoor. Three-quarters of an hour from M5. Ideal sea-fishing, diving, painting, walking holiday. Coastal golf course nearby. With access to the house at all times, there is a cosy TV lounge, central heating, tea making facilities, extensive library and games. The eight clean, spacious bedrooms have vanity units and pleasant views. En suite available. Child reductions: cot, high chair, toys available. Terraced gardens. Courtesy car from Stations. Car park. VISA and ACCESS credit cards accepted. Bed and four course varied Breakfast from **£13** per person per night. Mid-week bookings welcome.

BRIXHAM. Graham and Yvonne Glass, Raddicombe Lodge, 102 Kingswear Road, Brixham TQ5 0EX (Brixham [0803] 882125). 🌸🌸 The Lodge lies midway between the picturesque coastal towns of Brixham and Dartmouth, overlooking sea and country, with National Trust land between us and the sea. The house has charm and character, with pitched ceilings and lattice windows. Scrumptious traditional English Breakfast, with locally baked crusty bread. Colour TV, tea/coffee making in all bedrooms. Central heating. Come and go as you please, make The Lodge your home from home. Ample parking. AA, RAC listed, Les Routiers recommended. Offering room and Breakfast only from £15.70 to £23.40 for one or two night stay. En-suite rooms £3 per night extra. Access/Visa cards accepted.

ROYAL OAK GUEST HOUSE
LICENSED
59 Jordan Street, Buckfastleigh, Devon TQ11 0AX
Tel: Buckfastleigh (0364) 43611
Prop: Mrs Margaret Richardson

The Royal Oak is a small family-run guest house situated in Buckfastleigh, the "Gateway to Dartmoor" and ideal for touring and walking. All bedrooms are spacious and have washbasins, central heating, razor points and tea trays. Some en-suite rooms. Terms and brochure on request.

CHILDREN AND PETS WELCOME · PRIVATE CAR PARKING · PAY TELEPHONE AVAILABLE

BUCKFASTLEIGH. Mrs Rosemarie Palmer, Wellpark Farm Bungalow, Dean Prior, Buckfastleigh TQ11 0LY (0364 43775). Welcome to Wellpark and a family atmosphere. We are a family-run dairy/arable farm, set on the edge of the Dartmoor National Park, with fantastic views of the moor. Near Buckfast Abbey and Steam Railway. Close to Torquay, half an hours' drive from Plymouth and Exeter. Traditional English farmhouse Breakfasts with homemade preserves. Afternoon teas and packed lunches available. Children very welcome. Local amenities include Leisure Centre, tennis, swimming, golf, bowling, sailing, fishing and trips on River Dart. Accommodation comprises one double room, one family room. Cot available. Large lounge with colour TV. Central heating. Wood burning fires early/late season. Please send SAE for brochure. ETB listed and commended.

BUDLEIGH SALTERTON near. Mrs E.J. Earl, Ropers Cottage, Ropers Lane, Otterton, Near Budleigh Salterton EX9 7JF (Colaton Raleigh [0395] 68826).

🌸🌸 Situated in the delightful small village of Otterton (just off the A376), Ropers Cottage, previously a farm, is a 350 year old, centrally heated and comfortably modernised home. Accommodation comprises diningroom with separate tables; beamed lounge with inglenook fireplace; two twin bedded and one en suite double room, all with washbasins and shaver points; modern bathroom with WC and separate WC downstairs. An excellent touring centre, the Cottage is well situated for either the beach or for country walks. Exeter 13 miles, Exmouth six miles, Budleigh Salterton three miles. Dartmoor is roughly one hour's drive. Children are welcome. Bed and Breakfast from £10.50. All home cooking. Brochure on request.

CHUDLEIGH. Jill Shears, Glen Cottage, Rock Road, Chudleigh TQ13 0JJ (0626 852209). 🌸🌸 Just off the A38 at Chudleigh, Glen Cottage is set in 10 acres of gardens with small lake and waterfall adjoining Chudleigh rocks and caves, providing a natural amphitheatre to this haven of wildlife. Kingfishers, buzzards and herons are a common sight. Swim in the outdoor swimming pool or mess about on boats on the lake. 20 minutes from Dartmoor and coast. Residents' lounge, TV, tea-making facilities. Bed and Breakfast from £10 to £11.

PLEASE SEND A STAMPED ADDRESSED ENVELOPE WITH ENQUIRIES

CHULMLEIGH. Mrs Marcia Govier, Cadbury Barton, Chulmleigh (0769 80217). A warm and friendly welcome at Cadbury Barton for farmhouse bed and breakfast accommodation. Our stone built farmhouse is surrounded by 330 acres of mixed farming. Spacious bedrooms with family room available. Tea/coffee making facilities with full English Breakfast. Diningroom and colour TV lounge. Two miles from the delightful town of Chulmleigh. Evening Meals available locally. Excellent touring centre for many areas — Exmoor, Dartmoor and within easy reach of north and south beaches.

COLDRIDGE. Ms V. Quick. Birch Farm, East Leigh, Coldridge, Crediton EX17 6BG (0363 83216). Georgian stone built farmhouse in the centre of a large family-run beef, sheep and arable farm. Situated in the peaceful countryside of mid-Devon with easy access to Dartmoor, Exmoor, North Devon coast and the historic city of Exeter. Comfortable accommodation includes sittingroom with colour TV and log fire; diningroom. Family and double bedrooms with washbasins and tea/coffee making facilities. Good home cooking, own produce. Full English Breakfast. Children welcome, babysitting. Ample parking. Bed and Breakfast from £10 per person; Bed, Breakfast and Evening Meal from £15 per person. SAE or phone for brochure.

COLYTON. Mrs Sally Gould, "Hayne", Colyton (0297 53777). A warm friendly welcome and homely hospitality greets one and all who visit "Hayne" situated two miles from the historic little town of Colyton and four and a half miles from the sea at Seaton. Amidst beautiful farmland where the River Coly flows through the fields offering good trout fishing. South facing and warm with really lovely views and walks in all directions. "Hayne" offers one family, one double and one twin-bedded children's room. Bathroom and shower. Lounge with colour TV. Log fires and central heating when required. Plenty of good traditional farmhouse food including desserts with Devonshire clotted cream. Children welcome. Small pets allowed. Plenty of parking space. The market towns of Axminster and Honiton (four and a half miles) and Lyme Regis and Sidmouth all within eight miles. Pony trekking, tennis and golf close by. Bed and Breakfast, with Evening Meal alternate nights on request.

COLYTON. Mrs Sandra Gould, Bonehayne Farm, Colyton EX13 6SG (040487 416). Located in the heart of the beautiful Coly Valley, Bonehayne nestles on the banks of the River Coly on a 250 acre working farm. This attractive farmhouse offers spacious accommodation with washbasins in most rooms. Lounge with colour TV, log fire. Breakfast and meals are served in the conservatory overlooking a large garden. Good traditional home cooking using farm produce where possible. Trout fishing, shooting and woodland walks are freely available. Ideal for exploring all East Devon coastal resorts and many places of historic and scenic interest. Bed and Breakfast with alternative Evening Meals or just Bed and Breakfast. Terms on request.

FUN FOR ALL THE FAMILY IN DEVON

Babbacombe Model Village, Torquay; *Beer Modelrama*, Beer, near Seaton; *Dart Valley Steam Railway*, Buckfastleigh; *Torbay & Dartmouth Steam Railway*, Paignton; *Bicton Gardens*, East Budleigh, near Budleigh Salterton; *Grand Western Horseboat Trips*, Tiverton; *The Shire Horse Centre*, Dunstone, Yealmpton, near Plymouth; *Farway Countryside Park*, near Honiton; *Dartmoor Wildlife Park*, Sparkwell, near Plymouth; *Paignton Zoo*, Totnes Road, Paignton; *Plymouth Aquarium*, Plymouth Hoe, Plymouth; *Exeter Maritime Museum*, The Quay, Exeter; *Torbay Aircraft Museum*, Higher Blagdon, near Paignton; *Exmoor Brass Rubbing Centre*, The Smuggler's Den, Queen Street, Lynton; *Dartington Glass*, Linden Close, off School Lane, Torrington; *Yelverton Paperweight Centre*, Leg O'Mutton Corner, Yelverton; *Kents Cavern*, Ilsham Road, Wellswood, Torquay.

COLYTON. Mrs Ruth Gould, Bonehayne Farm, Colyton EX13 6SG (Farway [040-487] 396).

Working farm. Bonehayne Farm, situated in beautiful Coly Valley, set amidst 250 acres dairy farmland on banks of River Coly, where daffodils are a feature in springtime, and Mallard duck and Kingfishers are a common sight. Trout fishing freely available. Woodlands to explore. Visitors welcome to participate in farm activities and make friends with the animals. One family, one double bedroom, with washbasins; bathroom, toilet. Spacious, homely lounge with inglenook fireplace, TV. Varied menu includes roast beef, Yorkshire pudding, sherry trifle, Devonshire cream etc. Reduced rates, cot, high chair, babysitting for children. Small pets accepted. Parking. Farway Country Park, two riding schools, Honiton Golf Course, weekly cattle market, sea at Seaton, all within four-and-a-half miles. Open April to October. Bed and Breakfast; Evening Meals alternative evenings. Terms on request.

COLYTON. Mrs Maggie Todd, Smallicombe Farm, Northleigh, Colyton EX13 6BU (Wilmington [040483] 310). ♛♛ Working farm, join in. Small

working farm set in an area of outstanding natural beauty between Colyton and Honiton. Conveniently situated for all East Devon coastal resorts and an ideal base for touring. Children are encouraged to make friends with the wide variety of farm animals including three Jersey cows, calves, pigs, sheep, goats and numerous poultry. Sit in the large garden enjoying glorious views while the children use the play area. Excellent home cooking using fresh farm produce. Self-contained family suite on first floor comprising large double bedroom with colour TV (plus single bed and cot if required), adjoining bedroom with bunk beds and en-suite bathroom. Twin-bedded room on ground floor with its own bathroom. Automatic teamaker, your own sitting/dining-room with colour TV. Cot, high chair and babysitting available. Night storage heaters. Bed, Breakfast and optional Evening Meal. Special rates for children. Regret no pets.

COMBE MARTIN. Mrs Lesley Nicholas, Girt Down Farm, Combe Martin EX34 0PG (Combe Martin [0271] 882323). Working farm, join in. Join us on our working family farm, situated within the Exmoor National Park. Outstanding views over the Bay of Combe Martin and surrounding countryside. Ideal for walkers being only 500 yards from the Coastal Footpath, and as a family base is perfect — only three-quarters of a mile from Combe Martin, nine miles to Woolacombe, 10 miles to Lynton. Nearby shooting, fishing, golf course and horse riding. Comfortable centrally heated accommodation consisting of three doubles (two en-suite), separate toilet and bathroom. Large lounge with open fire. Children welcome, babysitting service available. Good home cooking. Bed and Breakfast from £10.

COMBE MARTIN. Mrs V. Plesner, The Old Coach House, Leigh Road, Combe Martin EX34 0NE (Combe Martin [0271] 882242).

Small, quiet yet friendly guest house open all year, situated on the outskirts of the village, one and a half miles from the sea. Comfortably furnished with accommodation in three spacious double bedrooms and one family room, all with washbasins and shaver points. Diningroom with separate tables; lounge with colour TV. Homely atmosphere and a selection of delicious food with generous portions to satisfy those holiday appetites. Children welcome, cot available. Pets permitted. Car essential, parking. Visitors can be assured of comfortable accommodation combined with a superb location and a friendly atmosphere. Terms and further details on application.

COMBE MARTIN. Mrs Mary Peacock, Longlands Farm, Combe Martin, Ilfracombe EX34 0PD (Combe Martin [027-188] 3522). "Longlands" is situated

on the edge of the Exmoor National Park, in a beautiful and peaceful valley. The House stands on a plateau, above its own Lake, enjoying panoramic views. Within easy reach of all well-known North Devon beauty spots, the resorts of Ilfracombe and Lynton and the sandy beaches of Woolacombe. The market town of Barnstaple is about 10 miles. The house has four double and two family rooms, all with washbasins and shaver points; some rooms with showers en-suite; one bathroom and three WCs. Lounge, TV lounge and sun lounge. Diningroom with separate tables. Residential licence. Children welcome — cot, high chair and babysitting provided. Reduced rates for children. Dogs by arrangement. Devon Fire Certificate held. Car essential — plenty of parking. SAE, please for brochure and terms for Bed and Breakfast or Bed, Breakfast and Evening Meal. Free fishing for residents.

COMBE MARTIN. Colin and Shirley Willoughby, North Patchole Farmhouse, Kentisbury Ford, Barnstaple EX31 4NB (Combe Martin [0271] 882029).

A traditional 250 year old Devon Longhouse set in a six acre smallholding. Sea at Combe Martin three miles, market town of Barnstaple nine miles. The house is centrally heated and has a choice of double, twin, family and single bedrooms all with vanity basins and TV. One has en-suite shower and toilet. Diningroom with separate tables. Lounge and diningroom have woodburning stoves. Sun lounge and attractive garden. We offer interesting and varied four-course meals using home produce, and our aim is to give you a holiday to remember.

CREALY BARTON. Mrs M. Prouse, Crealy Barton, Clyst St. Mary, Exeter EX5 1DR (0395-32567).

♥♥♥ A delightful farmhouse offering three en-suite bedrooms — family, double and twin; colour TV; tea/coffee trays. Spacious lounge and diningroom overlooking peaceful garden, patio and barbecue area. Access at all times. Ideally situated two miles from the M5 Junction 30 making Devon's moors and coasts within easy reach. Walk to Crealy Adventure Park (on the farm, reduced admission for guests) with its attractive shop, restaurant, animals, adventure playground. Feed the ducks on the lake. Short or long stay, a warm welcome awaits throughout the year.

CREDITON. Mrs Watson, Higher Perry Farm, Cheriton Fitzpaine, Crediton EX17 4BQ (03636 573).

Higher Perry is a pretty, thatched 16th century farmhouse set midway between Exmoor and Dartmoor, nine miles from Exeter and 40 minutes from the coast. Just 25 minutes from M5, only 30 minutes from all the attractions of Torbay. Situated in beautiful, peaceful countryside, there is a lovely garden and a heated swimming pool. Accommodation is in two double bedrooms with bathroom en-suite. The atmosphere is happy and relaxed and guests are welcome to make use of the family drawing room. Log fires. Good home cooking served. Use of stables if required for your own horse. Car essential — parking available. Double room from £15 per person; Evening Meal on request. Tourist Board listed.

CREDITON. Mrs S.M. Bowden, Woodview, Stoneshill, Sandford, Crediton EX17 4EF (03632 2001). Working farm. Mrs Bowden, having catered for the public

for some years and renowned for good food and friendly atmosphere, now welcomes guests to this new, spacious bungalow on the 112 acre mixed farm. One mile from the village of Sandford on the outer edge of the old market town of Crediton. Cathedral city of Exeter, which now has a new leisure centre, nine miles. Beautiful country walks, tennis and golf nearby. Overlooking scenic valley and wood. Only small numbers catered for. One family (or twin-bedded) room and one double, both with washbasins, shaver points and tea-making facilities. Luxuriously furnished lounge/diner with colour TV. Full central heating. Bed and Breakfast; occasional Evening Meals. Children welcome. Sorry, no pets. Terms on request.

See also Colour Display Advertisement **CROYDE. Mrs G.M. Adams, Combas Farm, Croyde EX33 1PH (Croyde [0271] 890398). Working farm.** Combas Farm (140 acres) is three-quarters of a mile from the sea, a 17th century farmhouse with attractive garden and orchard where children can play. Set in unspoilt valley close to excellent beaches sand, surf, rock pools. National Trust coastline. Own dairy produce, vegetables, fruit and herbs. Care is given to presentation and variety of menu. Tennis one mile, golf three. Access at all times. Tea/coffee available on request. Sorry, no pets. Children welcome, cot, high chair and babysitting. There are two double bedrooms, two family rooms, one twin-bedded and one single room, all with washbasins; bathroom, three toilets; sittingroom; diningroom. Evening Dinner, Bed and Breakfast. Rates reduced for children under 12 years, and for Senior Citizens early and late season. Tourist Board listed and Commended.

CULLOMPTON. Mrs R.M. Parish, Weir Mill Farm, Jaycroft, Willand, Near Cullompton, Tiverton

EX15 2RE (Tiverton [0884] 820803). ✿✿ *Commended.* Recently modernised farmhouse on an 80-acre beef and sheep farm. Very peaceful and relaxing setting with a large enclosed lawn for guests' enjoyment. Excellent touring centre for both north and south coast resorts, also Dartmoor and Exmoor, with many places of interest locally. Ideal stopover for Cornwall being only two miles M5 Motorway (Junction 27). Very comfortable accommodation with one family room, two double rooms. Bathroom. Diningroom; sittingroom with colour TV. Cot, high chair and babysitting available. Central heating. Car advisable, ample parking. Bed and Breakfast from £12; Evening Meal by arrangement. Reductions for children.

CULLOMPTON. Mrs Diane Pring, Lower Ford Farm, Cullompton EX15 1LX (Tiverton [0884]

252354). ✿✿ Working farm, join in. A warm and friendly welcome awaits you at Lower Ford Farm where guests can enjoy a relaxed and memorable family holiday. Lower Ford is a 120 acre beef and sheep farm set in a peaceful unspoilt valley, beside a small stream, three miles from Cullompton and M5, ideal base for touring moors and coast. Traditional 15th century farmhouse has original oak beams and panelling, inglenook fireplace with bread ovens. Large lounge with colour TV; diningroom where guests enjoy good home cooking with fresh farm produce. Family, double and twin rooms, all with washbasins, tea/coffee facilities; two bathrooms. Games rooms and laundry room. Children welcome, cot and high chair available. Car essential. Open all year except Christmas. Bed and Breakfast £10.50; Bed, Breakfast and Evening Meal £16.50 daily, £105 weekly.

CULLOMPTON. Mrs Sylvia Baker, Wishay Farm, Trinity, Cullompton EX15 1PE (Cullompton

[0884] 33223). Working farm. Wishay Farm is a 200-acre working farm with a recently modernised Grade II listed farmhouse with some interesting features. It is situated in a quiet and peaceful area with scenic views, yet is central for touring the many attractions Devon has to offer. Comfortable and spacious accommodation offering two family rooms, one with en-suite bathroom and one with washbasin and adjacent guests' bathroom; both rooms have tea/coffee making facilities. Central heating. Children welcome with ample toys and games provided. Cot and high chair available. Bed and Breakfast from £12. Evening Meal by arrangement. Reduced rates for children.

CULLOMPTON. Mrs B. Hill, Sunnyside Farm, Butterleigh, Cullompton EX15 1PP (08845 322). Working farm. Here at Sunnyside Farm everything is done

to give guests a happy holiday. Conveniently situated three and a half miles from M5 it makes an excellent overnight stop and is three miles from the lovely village of Bickleigh, a great tourist attraction, with a craft centre, etc. Guests are free to wander round the 150 acre farm and there is a spacious garden for children to play on the lawn and a pony for them to ride. Trout fishing nearby and many places of interest. Comfortable accommodation in two double, one single and two family bedrooms with washbasins; bathroom, shower, two toilets. Sittingroom has log fire and colour TV; diningroom with separate tables and a sun lounge with panoramic views. Cot, high chair, babysitting and reduced rates for children. Pets allowed. Car essential, parking. Open all year except Christmas. Evening Meal, Bed and Breakfast from £13; Bed and Breakfast from £8.50; weekly rates from £84 for Bed, Breakfast and Evening Meal. Tourist Board registered. Fire Certificate held.

CULLOMPTON. Mrs Hazel Selway, Moorland Farm, Bradninch, Exeter EX5 4NA (0392 881385). Working farm, join in. Moorland Farm is an 80 acre dairy farm four-and-a-half miles from junction 28 on the M5, and eight miles from the cathedral city of Exeter. Ideally situated for visits to the coast or rambles on the moors, with local National Trust properties and attractions in plenty. The large Georgian-style house is open from March until October. Accommodation comprises one double, one family and one twin bedded room, all with washbasins and shaver points. Children welcome; swing and slide for their enjoyment. Cot and babysitting available. Separate sitting and diningrooms. Terms: Evening Meal, Bed and Breakfast from £15 per night, £100 per week. Bed and Breakfast only from £10. Nightly reductions for children.

DARTMOOR. Mrs Sue Hutchinson, Sloutts Farmhouse, Slapton, Kingsbridge TQ7 2PR (Kingsbridge [0548] 580872). Sloutts is a delightful Georgian farmhouse in the attractive village of Slapton. Only half-a-mile from beach, coastal footpath and Slapton Ley Nature Reserve. Midway between Dartmouth and Kingsbridge. Bedrooms have lovely open views of village and rolling South Devon countryside. Wholesome home made food using fresh local produce. Log fires and central heating. Reductions for weekly reservations and for children sharing parents' accommodation. En suite available. Well behaved dogs welcome. Open all year for Bed, Breakfast and Evening Meal (optional). Non-smokers preferred. Brochure and tariff on request. Self catering accommodation also available.

DARTMOOR. Miss P. Neal, Middle Stoke Farm, Holne, Near Ashburton, Newton Abbot TQ13 7SS (Poundsgate [036 43] 444). Middle Stoke Farm stands in 43 acres of beautiful, peaceful countryside on Holne Moor, Dartmoor. We have racehorses, mares, foals, a pony and sheep, and visitors are welcome to take an interest. Your own horses are welcome. Every room enjoys extensive views over farmland or the valley of the River Dart. Ideal centre for walking, riding, touring, birdwatching etc. Car not absolutely essential as walks can start from the farm, but preferable. Ample parking. Dartmoor National Park has an extensive programme of guided walks; Buckfast Abbey, Dart Valley Railway and Butterfly Farm, Shire Horse Centre are examples of places to visit in wet or dry weather. Beaches at Torbay approximately 15 miles. Warm welcome in a relaxed atmosphere with plenty of good food will, we hope, make you want to return again and again. Six bedrooms including family,

double, twin and single with washbasins; bathroom, two toilets; sittingroom; diningroom. Children welcome at reduced rates, cot. Pets £7 per week. Evening Dinner, Bed and Breakfast from £15 to £18; Bed and Breakfast from £10.86 to £12.50. No VAT. SAE, please, or telephone Miss Neal.

DARTMOUTH. Mr Nigel Peter Jestico, The Captain's House, 18 Clarence Street, Dartmouth TQ6 9NW (Dartmouth [080383] 2133). ❦ ❦ ❦ The Captain's House is a small Georgian listed house built about 1760 and is only a few minutes' level walk from the shops and 50 yards or so from the River Dart promenade. Attractions include historic Dartmouth itself, nearby beaches, sailing, fishing and coastal walks. The house is centrally heated and all bedrooms have private facilities, colour TV, radio and alarm clock, tea and coffee making equipment, and hairdryer, etc. Access to your room at all times. Open January to December. AA listed and "Specially Selected" award. Bed and Breakfast from £14.

See also Colour Display Advertisement **DAWLISH. Mr and Mrs T.C. Crump, MHCI, Radfords Country Hotel, Dawlish EX7 0QN (Dawlish [0626] 863322).** Come and relax at Radfords in one of our lounges, comfortable bar, our lovely garden or alternatively enjoy an action-packed holiday — many activities and sports available here and in the locality. We have family bedrooms or two family suites available, all with private bathroom; accommodation for about 30 families. The children will love their special heated indoor swimming pool, the outdoor playground, the freedom of our large gardens and the assorted ponies and dogs there are to talk to. In the evening they can look forward to a swimming gala, live entertainment, a party and their own cartoon show, etc. Playroom now available. The adults can look forward to superb food lovingly cooked and served and the various entertainments we arrange for them from skittles tournaments to a feature film. We also have a fully equipped

launderette and an evening babysitter to help make your holiday as relaxing as possible. Mothers can bring babies and small children here with every confidence. Member West Country Tourist Board. Featured on TV by Judith Chalmers. Farm Holiday Guide Diploma winner. Please telephone or send for illustrated brochure.

DAWLISH. Mrs Alison Thomson, Lidwell Farm, Dawlish EX7 0PS (0626 773001). Lidwell Farm is situated at the head of the Aller Valley, two and a half miles from Dawlish town centre and beaches, 30 minutes' drive to Dartmoor. Come and see calves and lambs in the spring. Explore the ruins of Lidwell Chapel or relax in the garden where on a summer evening we are able to produce a barbecue and an optional Evening Meal. Plenty of space for children to run, safely. We offer one double, one family bedrooms and children's bunkroom. All with hot drinks facilities. Bed and Breakfast from £10 to £12; Evening Meal £7. ETB listed.

DAWLISH. Mr and Mrs C.J. Sanford, Mimosa Guest House, 11 Barton Terrace, Dawlish EX7 9QH

(Dawlish [0626] 863283). This family guest house is AA and RAC listed and lies in a quiet part of town opposite the Manor Gardens, only a few minutes' walk from the sea and shops. Dawlish has a good train, bus and coach service for touring this lovely part of Devon. The town nestles at the foot of Haldon Moor between Exeter and Torquay. Miles of safe sandy beaches, good sports facilities, golf and tennis, bowling, fishing, etc. Three double, one en-suite, four family, two single bedrooms with washbasins, shaver points, bedlights, cotton sheets; five toilets; bathroom and shower; lounge; diningroom with separate tables. Licensed. Central heating. Children over five welcome. Car not essential. Open all year. Tourist Board registered.

DUNSFORD. Mrs Jean May, Copplestone Farm, Dunsford, Exeter EX6 7HQ (Christow [0647]

52784). Situated just within the Dartmoor National Park, Copplestone is a small farm enjoying stunning views across the Teign Valley, convenient for both moors and sea. In ideal walking country, with varied wildlife and lovely hedgerows, we are one and a half miles from Dunsford and eight from Exeter. The non-smoking accommodation comprises double and twin rooms, both with washbasins and tea/coffee facilities; lounge with log fire; diningroom and large garden. Enjoy good home cooking from our own fresh produce, vegetarians catered for by arrangement. Bed and Breakfast from £11; Evening Meal (most nights) £6.50. We regret that we cannot accommodate dogs or children. There is also a small self-catering cottage sleeping four/five maximum, please ask for separate details.

EXETER. Mrs Maureen Pring, Ford Farm, Woodbury, Exeter EX5 1NJ (0395 32355). For an overnight

stop or longer stay, a friendly family awaits you on this working farm near Woodbury Common. Easy to find from M5 Junction 30, and ideal centre for exploring the coast and countryside of East Devon and the city of Exeter. Children are always welcome. Baby equipment available. Hot drinks facilities in rooms. Lounge with TV. Garden. Good meals available at local inns and restaurant. Open February to November. Bed and Breakfast from £10.

EXETER. Mr & Mrs G. Stevens, Venn Farm, Bridford, Exeter EX6 7LF (Christow [0647] 52328). Working farm, join in. Gilbert and Mabel Stevens invite you for a holiday on their small 50-acre stock farm with homely and friendly accommodation in the beautiful surroundings of the Teign Valley. Situated between Exeter (eight miles) and the Moors, it is an ideal position for touring, within easy reach of Torbay, the South, as well as the many beauty spots and walks on Dartmoor. Fishing on the River Teign by permit. Bed and Breakfast, with optional Evening Meal, at reasonable prices. Open all year round with a varied menu of good home cooking. Children welcome. Pets accepted. Arrive as guests, depart as friends. Car essential — parking. For further information please write or phone the above.

EXETER. Mrs Sally Glanville, Rydon Farm, Woodbury, Exeter EX5 1LB (Woodbury [0395] 32341).

🐄🐄 **Working farm, join in.** Come, relax and enjoy yourself in our lovely 16th century Devon longhouse. We offer a warm and friendly family welcome at this peaceful dairy farm. Three miles from M5 junction 30 on B3179. Ideally situated for exploring the coast, moors and the historic city of Exeter. Only 10 minutes' drive from the coast. Inglenook fireplace and oak beams. All bedrooms have heating, washbasins and tea/coffee making facilities. The family room has en-suite bathroom. A traditional farmhouse breakfast is served with our own free range eggs and there are several excellent pubs and restaurants close by. Pets by arrangement. Farm Holiday Bureau member. Open all year. Bed and Breakfast from £13.

EXETER. Mrs Mary Brown, Cottles Farm, Woodbury, Exeter EX5 1ED (Woodbury [0395] 32547). Working farm. A charming thatched farmhouse with comfortable accommodation and good home cooking. Our dairy farm is situated in 200 acres of peaceful countryside with wonderful views as far as Dartmoor. Only four miles to Exmouth and the nearest sandy beach, and seven from Exeter where there are many interesting places to visit. Dartmoor and Exmoor are within easy driving distance. Two double bedrooms and one family room with washbasins; bathroom, toilet; lounge/diner. Children welcome; cot and high chair provided; babysitting offered. Bed and Breakfast from £11 per night. Open July, August, September. Reductions for children aged 11 and under.

EXETER near. Mrs Cathie Cottey, Middle Cobden Farm, Whimple, Near Exeter EX5 2PZ (Whimple

[0404] 822276). Working farm. Ideally positioned for all local beaches, moorland and inland attractions, a warm, friendly, homely welcome awaits you at this 200-year-old farmhouse (with 16th-century fireplace). The 65-acre family run dairy farm is in secluded surroundings half-a-mile from A30, seven miles east of Exeter. Lounge with colour TV, separate diningroom where traditional cooking is served using fresh produce whenever possible. One bedroom with en-suite facilities, others with washbasins and shaver points, all with hot drinks facilities. Guests' bathroom. Children at reduced rates — cot, high chair and babysitting; washing/ironing facilities. Central heating. Sorry, no pets. Bed and Breakfast from £10; Evening Meal from £6. Reduced rates for weekly bookings. ETB listed. Brochure.

EXETER near. Mr and Mrs R.H. Cornall, Taylors Farm, Brampford Speke, Near Exeter EX5 5HN (Exeter [0392] 841255). Working farm. Taylors Farm is situated in one of Devon's most peaceful villages in the Exe Valley, only two minutes' walk from river and five miles from Exeter. The house is 16th century, thatched and of historical interest. Although modernised, it still retains open beams and fireplace in lounge. Peaceful, restful and homely holidays, with wholesome food personally prepared. Highly recommended. Two double, two single, one family bedrooms; bathroom, three toilets; sittingroom; diningroom. Children at reduced rates. No pets, please. Open March to October. Plenty of parking. Evening Meal, Bed and Breakfast or Bed and Breakfast terms on application. Tourist Board registered. SAE, please, for early reply.

EXETER near. Mrs B. Lacey, Whitemoor Farm, Doddiscombsleigh, Near Exeter EX6 7PU (0647

52423). Working farm, join in. Listed 16th century thatched farmhouse set in the seclusion of 284 acres of farmland within easy reach of Exeter, coast, Dartmoor and forest walks. The cobb house has exposed oak beams and doors. Accommodation in one twin, one double and two single bedrooms all with washbasins and tea/coffee making facilities; bathroom. Home produce. Bed and Breakfast from £12; Evening Meals available at local inn. Reductions for children. Pets welcome.

DEVON – ENDLESS CHOICES!

People never tire of visiting Devon. There's so much to do, like visiting Alscott Farm Museum, Berry Head Country Park, Bickleigh Mill Farm, Farway Countryside Park, Haytor Granite Railway, Kent's Cavern, Dartmoor National Park and of course Plymouth and its Hoe.

EXMOOR. Mr and Mrs P. Carr, Greenhills Farm, Yeo Mill, West Anstey, South Molton EX36 3NU

(Anstey Mills [03984] 300). Gillian and Philip invite you to relax with your family and friends on their dairy and sheep farm, set in the beautiful Devon countryside on the edge of the Exmoor National Park. This lovely farmhouse set in the Yeo Valley has two prettily furnished bedrooms, one family and one twin-bedded, with tea making facilities, etc. Guests' lounge is comfortable with oak beamed ceiling, inglenook fireplace and colour TV. Separate diningroom. Bathroom with shower. Cot, high chair and babysitting available. Fresh home grown produce used to complement traditional cooking to a high standard. Watch the cows being milked, see the Shire horse at work, watch the resident Farrier shoeing. Children love Robin the family pony — the list of interests on the farm is endless. Horse riding, golf, swimming within easy distance. Bed and Breakfast from £11 per person, with Evening Meal from £15. Reductions for children under 14 years and weekly stays. Farm Holiday Bureau Member. English Tourist Board listed.

EXMOOR. Mrs Farthing, Brendon House Hotel, Brendon, Lynton EX35 6PS (05987 206). ♛ ♛

Small friendly 18th century country hotel situated in the beautiful River Lyn Valley — Lorne Doone country. Comfortable accommodation, some en-suite bedrooms. Good home cooking. Licensed — interesting wine list. Wonderful walking and touring areas. Riding, fishing available locally. Permits sold for fishing on River Lyn (salmon, sea trout and brown trout). Children and dogs welcome. Open all year except Christmas. Bed, Breakfast and Evening Meal from £22; Bed and Breakfast from £13.50. Reduced rates for children. Weekly terms for Bed, Breakfast and Evening Meal from £147. Parking in grounds. AA listed.

EXMOUTH. Mrs J. Hallett, Gulliford Farm, Lympstone, Near Exmouth EX8 5AQ (Topsham [0392] 873067). ♛ ♛

You are assured of a warm welcome to this 16th century farmhouse with its spacious rooms and beautiful garden with sun terrace, lawns, tennis court and swimming pool. This working farm stands in the beautiful Exe Valley only a short distance from the many beaches. One family suite, two double or family rooms, one single room, most with washbasin and tea-making facilities. Lounge with colour TV and inglenook fireplace, diningroom with separate tables, ample parking. There is access to rooms at all times. A full English breakfast is served and there are many delightful inns and restaurants to provide your evening meal. Terms for Bed and Breakfast are from £14 per person per night. We also have two delightful self catering cottages.

PLEASE ENCLOSE A STAMPED ADDRESSED
ENVELOPE WITH ENQUIRIES

HARTLAND. Mrs E.D. Underhill, Fosfelle Country House Hotel, Hartland, Bideford EX39 6EF (0237

441273). 17th century manor house set in six acres of grounds in peaceful surroundings with large ornamental gardens and lawns. Fosfelle offers a friendly atmosphere with excellent food, licensed bar, TV lounge with log fires on chilly evenings. Games room for children. Comfortable bedrooms, some en-suite, all with washbasin and tea-making facilities. Family room and cots available. Within easy reach of local beaches and ideal base for touring Devon and Cornwall. Fishing available at the hotel. Riding anf golf also nearby. Open all year. Reductions for children. Dogs welcome. Details on request.

HATHERLEIGH. Tony and Angela Jones, Hartleigh Barton, Petrockstowe, Okehampton EX20 3QJ (Black Torrington [040-923] 344). Working farm, join in. Relax in the peace of one of Devon's oldest farmhouses set on 230 acres on a mixed farm overlooking Dartmoor. Ideal location for fishing, shooting, riding, walking and golf. Watersports, beaches and Dartmoor within half-an-hour's drive. Guests can look forward to beautifully furnished rooms, two double en-suite and one twin, in a house of great character with every comfort. Huge breakfasts with home made produce and memorable "Devon Fare" dinners. Children welcome at reduced rates, babysitting offered, baby equipment available; safe gardens and orchard. Children under three years FREE. A holiday where we assure you of quality and a warm welcome. Bed and Breakfast from £12.50, Evening Meal £6.50.

HIGHAMPTON. Mrs G.M. Bowden, Higher Odham, Highampton, Beaworthy EX21 5LX (Black

Torrington [040923] 324). Working farm. Red and white bricked house, on a 124 acre dairy, beef and sheep farm one mile from the village with its public house, shop and trout fish farm. Between two market towns and central for touring moors and sea, lovely walks on farm and adjoining moor. A happy atmosphere prevails. Two double or family rooms with shower and washbasins, single room; bathroom, two toilets; sittingroom, diningroom, playroom. Cot, high chair and babysitting available. Car essential, parking. Swing, slide, seesaw and sandpit on the lawns for children. Bed and Breakfast from £10 daily (£65 weekly). There are local inns and restaurants which provide meals at reasonable prices. Reduced rates for children. SAE please.

HOLSWORTHY. Mrs Catherine Smale, Bason Farm, Bradford, Holsworthy EX22 7AW (Shebbear

[040-928] 277). Working farm. Beautiful five-bedroomed farmhouse set in spacious lawns on a 230-acre beef and sheep farm. Enjoy the peace and relaxation of unspoilt countryside. Fishing and shooting rights; interesting walks; golf and horse riding facilities nearby. Family pony. Well positioned for touring Dartmoor and Exmoor and the beautiful North Devon and Cornwall coastline. Good home cooking. Three double rooms with bathroom. Tea making facilities. Diningroom/lounge with colour TV. Children welcome — cot, babysitting available. Adult Bed and Breakfast from £10, with Evening Meal £16.

HOLSWORTHY near. Mrs Elizabeth Bellew, Court Barton, Abbots Bickington, Near Holsworthy EX22 7LQ (Milton Damerel [040-926] 214). Working farm. Court Barton, a mixed farm of 648 acres, is situated on the River Torridge in a very beautiful, peaceful position, centrally placed for touring all North Devon and North Cornwall coasts and beauty spots. Fishing and rough shooting on the farm at no extra cost. Excellent accommodation is assured in a friendly and homely atmosphere. Two family bedrooms with washbasins, two single bedrooms. Children over four years welcome. Sorry, no pets. Generous servings of good food are always served based mainly on our own farm produce — eggs, poultry, beef, lamb, cream etc. No extra charge is made for the welcome cup of tea on arrival and hot drinks and biscuits at bedtime. Open Whitsun to October. Bed, Breakfast and Evening Dinner or Bed and Breakfast. AA Recommended. SAE, please, for terms and brochure which will be gladly sent on request.

If you've found
FARM HOLIDAY GUIDES
of service please tell your friends

HOLSWORTHY. Mrs Beryl Holdcroft, Ley Farm, Milton Damerel, Holsworthy EX22 7NY (040-926

259). Situated in a secluded position 250 yards from the A388 Bideford to Holsworthy road, within easy reach of Dartmoor and numerous sandy beaches. The house is spacious and dates from the 15th century and possesses a wealth of character and old world charm. Guests are welcome to wander around the 100 acre dairy farm. Comfortable family atmosphere. Colour TV. Early morning tea and late night snack included. Two family bedrooms (one with vanity unit); bathroom, two toilets; sittingroom; diningroom; kitchenette. Children welcome. Cot, high chair, babysitting available. Also self contained unit for two adults. Sorry, no pets. Open from April to October. Car essential, parking. Bed and Breakfast from £10; Evening Meal optional. Tea/coffee facilities. Reduced rates for children. Brochure on request.

HOLSWORTHY. Mrs K.P. Hockridge, "Blakes", Bulkworthy, Holsworthy EX22 7UP (Milton

Damerel [040-926] 249). Blakes Farmhouse is well recommended accommodation midway between Bideford and Holsworthy, ideal for touring North and South Devon, Cornwall, Exmoor, local beaches — all easily reached for day trips. Guests enjoy walks in unspoilt countryside or along banks of River Torridge, which runs through the farm. Many guests return each year to enjoy the relaxed informal atmosphere and excellent Devon Farmhouse Fare. Personal attention. High standard of cleanliness. Warm welcome awaits all guests. Large lounge with stone fireplace beams; colour TV, electric organ and piano for guests. Cool diningroom. One double, one family bedrooms, with washbasins, shaver points, divan beds, wall lights. Teenage children only. Sorry no pets. Car essential, parking. Bed and Breakfast. SAE, please, for prompt reply. Many sporting activities locally.

HOLSWORTHY. Mrs Barbara Morris, Chasty House, Chasty, Holsworthy EX22 6NA (Holsworthy

[0409] 253511). Warm welcome assured at Chasty House. We grow our own fruit and vegetables and our free range hens keep us well supplied with eggs. Home cooking for the largest appetite! Early morning tea/late night snack included. Chasty House has lovely views across open country to Bodmin and Dartmoor yet is only three-quarters of a mile from the town of Holsworthy. Just 15 minutes' drive to sandy beaches at Bude and many other unspoilt spots along the rugged coastline of North Devon and Cornwall. Children especially welcome at reduced rates; babysitting available. Sorry, no pets. Bed and Breakfast £10; plus Evening Meal £14.

HONITON near. Mrs Sylvia J. Retter, Higher Northcote Farm, Monkton, Near Honiton EX14 9QQ (Honiton [0404] 42986). Working farm, join in. Guests are made welcome from May to October on this very old modernised farmhouse lying in pleasant surroundings of 246 acres of grassland for the 180 milking cows; guests have all the benefits of the country and we are only eight miles from the sea. Accommodation in one double, one single, two family rooms, all with washbasins; bathroom, two toilets; sittingroom, diningroom. Children welcome, cot, high chair and babysitting provided. Pets are allowed. Car essential and there is parking. Evening Dinner, Bed and Breakfast or Bed and Breakfast only. Rates are reduced for children. Terms on request.

HONITON. Mrs Elizabeth Tucker, Lower Luxton Farm, Upottery, Honiton EX14 9PB (Churchstanton [082-360] 269). Working farm, join in. Get away

from the toil of everyday life and come to Lower Luxton Farm where a warm welcome awaits you. Set overlooking peaceful Otter Valley facing south, this olde worlde farmhouse fully modernised, but retaining its charm, is on 120 acres of farmland keeping usual animals and pets to make it a real farm. Guests are welcome to watch the activities. Peaceful walks. Trout fishing on farm. Ideal base for touring. Several places of interest in area. Coast 14 miles; village inn one mile. Good home cooking assured using fresh farm produce (four-course breakfasts and dinners) — including sweets topped with Devon cream — Evening Tea and biscuits included in terms. Family, double, twin rooms available with washbasins and razor points. Children welcome at reduced rates; children's play area. Snooker table available for guests. Mid-week bookings and reductions early and late in season. Pets welcome. Terms from £80 per week — Dinner, Bed and Breakfast. SAE for brochure and terms. Open all year.

HORWOOD. Mrs Kathy Clements, Church Farm, Horwood, Near Bideford EX39 4PB (Newton Tracey [027-185] 254). ♥♥ Working farm, join in. A

small working farm in the hamlet of Horwood, situated midway between Bideford and Barnstaple. Long sandy beaches nearby and facilities for golf, horse riding, sailing, etc. Ideal for touring North Devon, Exmoor and Dartmoor. A homely atmosphere with log fires, central heating, TV lounge for guests only, diningroom with separate tables. One en-suite bedroom (shower), two double bedrooms, one with sole use of bathroom; all with TV and tea/coffee making facilities. Good home cooking with produce from the farm. All diets catered for. Pets welcome. Regret, no children under 12. Ample parking. SAE, please, for terms or telephone.

ILFRACOMBE. J. and E. Park, Sunnymeade Country House Hotel, Dean Cross, West Down, Ilfracombe EX34 8NT (0271 863668). ♥♥♥ A charm-

ing country house hotel in its own large gardens set in the rolling Devonshire countryside. AA. Every effort is made to ensure that guests feel welcome and relaxed from the moment they arrive, a feeling which is enhanced by the standard of food and accommodation. Most of the 10 pretty bedrooms are en-suite and all have tea-making facilities and colour TV. Fresh local ingredients are used in the home cooked food presented in the spacious diningroom. Sunnymeade is close to Woolacombe, Exmoor and Ilfracombe. Access and Visa. Dinner, Bed and Breakfast from £130 weekly.

ILFRACOMBE near. Mrs Olga M. Basten, Daymer Cottage, Lee, Near Ilfracombe EX34 8LR (Ilfracombe [0271] 863769). Situated on the cliffs overlooking the sea on the outskirts of the unspoilt village of Lee. Only ships pass the front of the house — the road is at the back. Ilfracombe three miles. Plenty of rock pools at Lee Bay to keep children happy. A car is essential to tour the many beauty spots in the area. Ample parking. This is a very happy household where children and pets are welcome. Three-course Breakfast, four-course Evening Meal. Early morning tea for Mums and Dads and tea and biscuits around 10pm included in the very reasonable terms. Cot, high chair and babysitting provided. Reductions for children. Open March to October. Terms on request.

IVYBRIDGE. Pat Stephens, Venn Farm, Ugborough, Ivybridge PL21 0PE (0364 73240). Venn Farm is

situated in a peaceful position in the South Hams. We are a busy working farm and have always encouraged our guests to help on the farm — this is especially popular with children. We are near Dartmoor and many sandy beaches. Carve your own roast is a favourite here and many come back for more! Gardens are expansive, we are bordered by streams and a wild garden has been added recently. One family room, another family room en-suite and a two bedroomed cottage also en-suite available. Send for brochure for more details.

PLEASE SEND A STAMPED ADDRESSED ENVELOPE WITH ENQUIRIES

IVYBRIDGE near. Mrs Susan Winzer, "The Bungalow", Marridge Farm, Ugborough, Near Ivybridge PL21 0HR (Gara Bridge [054-882] 560). Working farm.

Marridge Farm is a traditional family run dairy farm with its own drive completely off the main road, and is situated in the heart of the peaceful South Hams countryside. Near Dartmoor and local unspoilt sandy beaches. A new bungalow, built in the old orchard setting with beautiful garden and meadow views. One double and one twin rooms, both with washbasins. Good home cooked food, cream and fresh home grown vegetables. Children welcome — cot, high chair and babysitting available. Bed and Breakfast from £10 daily; optional Evening Meal extra. Open all year. A379 turnoff from the main A38 Exeter to Plymouth road.

IVYBRIDGE. Mr and Mrs D. Johns, Hillhead Farm, Ugborough, Ivybridge PL21 0HQ (0752 892674). Working farm, join in. Comfortable accommodation and good home-produced food. Busy farm with plenty to see. Beautiful views of the rolling Devonshire countryside within walking distance of Dartmoor. Choice of beaches within 10 miles. Near towns of interest including Plymouth (15 miles approximately) with its new Theatre Royal, Totnes, Kingsbridge and Salcombe. Pony trekking, golf available nearby. Bed and Breakfast — £8.50 per night; Bed, Breakfast and Evening Meal £13 per night. Reduced rates for over two nights and children — cot, baby equipment available. Double and twin bedrooms with washbasins. Open all year. From A38 at Wrangaton Cross, turn left to Ermington B3210, turn right at first crossroads (signposted Ugborough), across next crossroads, continue three quarters of a mile to Hillhead Cross, turn left — farm 75 yards on left.

KENTON. Mrs K. Williams, Chiverstone Farm, Kenton, Near Exeter EX6 8NL (Starcross [0626] 890268). Working farm. This is a working farm of 120 acres, half a mile from the village of Kenton, which lies on the A379 coastal road between Exeter and Dawlish. Just four miles to a sandy beach, six miles to Exeter; Dartmoor is within easy reach, making it an ideal base for touring the beautiful countryside. Good walking area. Riding, golf, birdwatching, racing etc. all nearby. Accommodation comprises twin, family and double rooms; two bathrooms; comfortable lounge with woodburning fire and colour TV. Cot available. Ample parking space. Bed and Breakfast or Bed, Breakfast and Evening Meal available. Reductions for children. For further information or brochure please write or telephone.

KINGSBRIDGE. Mrs I. Dodds, Ayrmer House, Ringmore, Kingsbridge TQ7 4HL (Bigbury-on-Sea [0548] 810391). Ayrmer House is a luxury farmhouse

situated in a picturesque village, near Bigbury-on-Sea and Burgh Island. Within easy reach of sandy beaches, National Shire Horse Centre, towns of Totnes, Kingsbridge and Salcombe. Half mile from secluded beach. Accommodation consists of a family room and two twin-bedded rooms with balconies giving superb views of valley and sea; all have washbasins, colour TV and tea/coffee making facilities. Bathroom, separate toilet. We also have a suite consisting of a twin-bedded room adjoining double room with bathroom en-suite. Delicious home cooking, fresh vegetables, home made bread. Children welcome. No smoking. No pets. Ample parking. Terms on request.

KINGSBRIDGE. Yvonne Helps, Hillside, Ashford, Kingsbridge TQ7 4NB (Kingsbridge [0548] 550752). 🐾 🐾 Character house set in acre of orchard

garden surrounded by lovely countryside, in a quiet hamlet just off the A379 Plymouth to Kingsbridge road. Superb beaches and sandy coves nearby. Dartmoor 20 minutes' drive. Very comfortable accommodation with washbasins, shaver points, tea/coffee making facilities in all bedrooms. Colour TV in lounge. Diningroom with separate tables. Car parking. Visitors find a friendly, relaxed atmosphere with own keys. Full central heating. Bed and full English Breakfast from £10; Evening Meal optional. Open all year. Booking any day of the week. Write or phone for brochure.

KINGSBRIDGE. Mr and Mrs J. and M. Taylor, Ashleigh House, Ashleigh Road, Kingsbridge TQ7 1HB (Kingsbridge [0548] 2893). 🐾 🐾 Elegant Victorian licensed Guest House. Colour co-ordinated airy bedrooms with tea/coffee making facilities. All first floor rooms have private facilities. TV lounge, sun lounge. On edge of town, ideal centre for touring and beaches. Parking. No smoking is requested in the house but there is a garden room available for smokers. Nice views over rolling countryside. Close to coastal paths and Dartmoor. Excellent home cooking, and friendly atmosphere prevails in this happy house run by Jenny and Mike Taylor. Terms on request. AA, Les Routiers recommended.

See also Colour Display Advertisement **KINGSBRIDGE near. Mrs Felicity Moody, Cotmore Farm, Chillington, Near Kingsbridge TQ7 2LR (Kingsbridge [0548] 580374).** Comfortable accommodation in a delightful period farmhouse set in 15 acres. Well appointed bedrooms with washbasins, tea/coffee making facilities. Family suite with private bathroom. Guests' sittingroom and sun lounge. Excellent home cooking. Friendly atmosphere. Magnificent views, spectacular coastal and country walks. Many recreations readily available. Ample parking for cars/boats. Pets welcome. Bed and Breakfast from £80 per week; Evening Meals optional. Reductions for children. Send for a brochure. Also a self-catering cottage available.

Heron House Hotel

ASHLEY COURTENAY RECOMMENDED

Surrounded by sea and rolling countryside, 50 yards off uncommercialised sandy beach. On National Trust Coastal Path. Friendly, family run, modern hotel. All bedrooms have colour TV, tea/coffee making facilities. Large outdoor heated swimming pool in own grounds. Fully licensed. Open all year.

SPECIAL CHRISTMAS AND NEW YEAR CELEBRATIONS

For brochure send to Mrs Rowland, Heron House Hotel, Thurlestone Sands, Near Salcombe, Kingsbridge, South Devon. Telephone: (0548) 561308.

KINGSBRIDGE near. Mrs M. Newsham, Marsh Mills, Aveton Gifford, Near Kingsbridge TQ7 4JW (Kingsbridge [0548] 550549). Formerly a Mill House, overlooking the River Avon, set in four and a half acres of gardens and pastures with orchard and duck pond, and now a smallholding. Peaceful and quiet, just off the A379, four miles from Kingsbridge. Beautiful sandy beaches at nearby Bigbury Bay, Bantham and Thurlestone. Salcombe seven miles, Plymouth 17 miles. Walk or ride on Dartmoor, only eight miles away, or enjoy the unspoilt beauty of the Avon Estuary, just a short walk from the house. This is a family run guest house, and a warm welcome is extended to all guests, who have access to the house at all times. Bedrooms have washbasins and tea/coffee making facilities. Bathroom, separate WC. Diningroom and lounge, colour TV. Car essential; parking. Evening Meals optional, packed lunches available. English Tourist Board registered. Brochure and prices on request.

See also Colour Display Advertisement KINGSBRIDGE near. Mr Kenneth Small, The Cove Guest House, Torcross, Near Kingsbridge TQ7 2TH (Kingsbridge [0548] 580448). Torcross, a small seaside village, and The Cove House are a combination which can serve to be one of the most relaxing holidays you have ever had. The Cove House is situated in three and a half acres of its own coastline and is an ideal place from which to enjoy fishing, swimming or just strolling along the beach. Dartmouth, Torquay, Paignton, Plymouth or Dartmoor within one hour's drive. Excellent food is served in the diningroom which immediately overlooks the sea. Attractive licensed bar, and all bedrooms have TV and basins with hot and cold water. Some have private showers. Car desirable but not essential. Ample parking. Children under eight years and pets not catered for. Open from March 1st to November 30th for Dinner, Bed and Breakfast.

KINGSBRIDGE. Mrs C. Lloyd, Lower Norton, East Allington TQ9 7RL (East Allington [054-852] 246). Lower Norton is a stone built farmhouse now run as a guest house within a one acre smallholding, providing vegetables, eggs and milk. The house is surrounded by farmland situated approximately five miles from Kingsbridge and eight miles from Dartmouth; the nearest beach is Slapton. Torbay, Plymouth and Dartmoor are all within 25 miles. One double and three family bedrooms; two bathrooms with toilets; separate lounge and diningroom; utility room and tea making facilities. Children welcome. Cot, high chair and babysitting available. Fire Certificate held. Car essential, parking. Open April to October for Evening Meal, Bed and Breakfast from £84 weekly. Reductions for children. Non-smokers preferred. Stamp only please for brochure.

KINGSBRIDGE. Mrs M.E. Lonsdale, Fern Lodge, Hope Cove, Kingsbridge TQ7 3HF (Kingsbridge [0548] 561326). ♥♥ "Fern Lodge" is a detached guest house with colourful garden, flanked by palm trees. It is delightfully situated in Hope Cove, an uncommercialised fishing village with safe, sandy beaches, surrounded by National Trust land, offering beautiful cliff and country walks. The scenery is truly magnificent and totally unspoilt. Dartmoor is nearby, Totnes 19 miles, Dartmouth 21, Torbay 25 and Plymouth 23 miles. The eight bedrooms, most en-suite, have either a sea or landscape view (sea approximately 250 yards). Full central heating. Two lounges, one with colour TV. Separate tables in the dining room. Car parking. Children and pets welcome. AA listed (Merit Award).

KINGSBRIDGE. Mrs B. Kelly, Blackwell Park, Loddiswell, Kingsbridge TQ7 4EA (Gara Bridge [054-882] 230). ♥♥ Blackwell Park is a 17th century farmhouse situated five miles from Kingsbridge and two miles from Loddiswell. Many beaches within easy reach, also Dartmoor, Plymouth, Torbay and Dartmouth. Seven bedrooms for guests, all with washbasins, some en suite. Separate tables in diningroom; lounge with colour TV. Large games room with darts, snooker, skittles etc. Garden with plenty of grass for games, and large car parking area. Ample food with choice of menu; home grown produce. Help yourself to tea and coffee at any time. Fire Certificate. Children and pets especially welcome. Babysitting. Open all year round for Bed, Breakfast and Evening Meal. Reduced rates out of season.

KINGSBRIDGE. David and Anne Rossiter, Burton Farm, Galmpton, Kingsbridge TQ7 3EY (Kingsbridge [0548] 561210). Working farm in South Huish Valley, one mile from the fishing village of Hope Cove, three miles from famous sailing haunt of Salcombe. Walking, beaches, sailing, windsurfing, bathing, diving, fishing, horse-riding — facilities for all in this area. We have a dairy herd and three flocks of pedigree sheep. Guests are welcome to take part in farm activities when appropriate. Traditional farmhouse cooking and home produce. Four course dinner, Bed and Breakfast. Access to rooms at all times. Tea/coffee making facilities in rooms, all of which have private facilities, some en-suite. Games room. No smoking. Open all year, except Christmas. Warm welcome assured. Self-catering also available. Tourist Board registered. Dogs by arrangement. Details and terms on request.

KINGSBRIDGE. Mrs P. Venables, Hopedene, Grand View Road, Hope Cove, Kingsbridge TQ7 3HF (Kingsbridge [0548] 561602). This registered Guest House is situated away from the main road in Hope Cove with magnificent views of National Trust headland, cliffs and sea. Just five minutes' walk along the safe footpath from the garden brings you to the village and beaches. All five bedrooms have washbasins, beverage facilities, etc. Separate dining tables; residents' lounge; verandah. Excellent traditional cooking, set Dinner, choice of Breakfast. Residential licence. Large car park and garden. Accommodation for children over eight; small dogs only strictly by arrangement. Terms from £12 for Bed and Breakfast; from £18 for Bed, Breakfast and Evening Dinner.

See also Colour Display Advertisement KINGSBRIDGE near. Mr and Mrs C.M. Davies, Maelcombe House, East Prawle, Near Kingsbridge TQ7 2DA (Chivelstone [054-851] 300). Working farm. This small coastal working farm nestles beneath wooded cliffs overlooking Lannacombe Bay. The beach is one minute from the comfortable farmhouse which is nearly the most southerly in Devon. Guests have a choice of family, double or single rooms. Food is excellent — much being produced on the farm, and freshly caught seafood is a speciality. There is much to do — fishing, bathing, spectacular walking, exploring, climbing, boating, tennis or just relaxing in the gardens. Prices from £79.50 per week for Bed and Breakfast or £123.50 for Bed, Breakfast and Evening Meal, with special reductions for children. There is also a self-catering flat to sleep six, and limited camping facilities are provided. Telephone or write for colour brochure.

KINGSBRIDGE near. Mrs L.M. Smith, Yeo Farm, Topsham Bridge, Woodleigh, Near Kingsbridge TQ7 4DR (Kingsbridge [0548] 550586). Working farm. ETB registered. Beautiful farmhouse tastefully renovated to high standard of comfort, nestling in Avon Valley, bounded by river with one mile of salmon and sea trout single bank fishing lying within property boundary. Behind and to the north of the house are woods rich in bird and animal life. Ideal situation for bird watching and walking; beaches and Dartmoor within 15 minutes. Accommodation comprises two double, one family bedrooms; two bathrooms, three toilets. Sittingroom, large colour TV, diningroom. Central heating and log fires. Children welcome at reduced rates, babysitting available. Pets accepted at small charge. Car essential — parking. Bed and Breakfast; Dinner optional. Prices on request.

LAPFORD. Mrs L. Hindley, Nymet Bridge Country Guest House, Lapford EX17 6QX (0363 83334).

♛ ♛ Peaceful 14th century country house offering comfortable accommodation with old world charm and a reputation for good food. Set by the River Yeo, close to Eggesford Forest and Two Moors Way, in "Tarka" country where abundant wildlife delights nature lovers. Golf, fishing, riding and tennis available locally with many places of interest within easy travelling distance. Charming lounge with inglenook, oak beams throughout. Home cooked meals served in separate diningroom. Residential licence. All bedrooms have adjustable central heating and washbasins, en-suite available. Regret no children or pets. Bed and Breakfast from £12; optional Dinner £6. BTA Commendation.

LEE near Ilfracombe. Mrs M. Cowell. Lower Campscott Farm, Lee, Near Ilfracombe EX34 8LS (Ilfracombe [0271] 63479). Working farm. Lower Camp-

scott Farm is situated at the head of the locally known "Fuchsia Valley" of Lee. Our main enterprise is a herd of Friesian cows for milk production but there are other animals — ponies, goats, cats and hens etc. The sea is only a 15 minute walk away through the farmland. Accommodation comprises two double rooms (one with washbasin) and one twin-bedded room. Bathroom with shower and toilet. Lounge with TV; diningroom. Ideal base for touring the various beauty spots in the area; delightful walking country.

LYNMOUTH. Mr P.R. Green, Seaview, Summerhouse Path, Lynmouth EX35 6ES (0598 53460).
SEAVIEW is one of the oldest family houses in Lynmouth. Situated in a quiet area of the village on the Two Moors Way — ideal for walkers. Completely refurbished this year to provide very comfortable accommodation in one double room with en-suite facilities, two twin rooms with washbasins and adjoining bathroom. All with hot drinks equipment and beautiful sea views. Residents' lounge with TV. Central heating. Open all year. Bed and Breakfast from £12 per night. Two Star commended.

LYNMOUTH. Mr and Mrs Bilney, The Heatherville, Tors Park, Lynmouth EX35 6NB (Lynton [0598]

52327). Beautiful House situated in Sunny, Quiet, Secluded Position. *Overlooking the River Lyn. *Excellent Home Cooking of Traditional English Food, plus Vegetarian Menu. *Full Central Heating. *Comfortable Colour TV Lounge. *Separate Charming Bar Lounge. *Four Minutes from Village and Harbour. *Private Car Park Adjacent to Hotel. *Some Rooms with Private Shower/Toilet. *All Rooms with Tea/Coffee making Facilities. *AA Listed. *RAC Acclaimed. *Guestaccom Member. *Brochure, Sample Menu and Tariff on Request.

LYNTON. Mr and Mrs J.E. Travis, Gordon House Hotel, Lynton EX35 6BS (Lynton [0598] 53203).

♛ ♛ ♛ *Commended.* A very special hotel, with a "Highly Acclaimed" award from the RAC. Family run, with a warm welcoming atmosphere, this gracious Victorian house has many charming period features, together with modern luxury amenities. Each pretty bedroom has en suite facilities, colour television and beverage making equipment. Two attractive lounges for relaxation after roaming Exmoor and exploring the spectacular coastline. Dine by candlelight in the elegant diningroom and enjoy delicious home cooking and good wines. Full central heating. Parking. Open March to November. Bed and Breakfast from £18 nightly, £120 weekly; Dinner, Bed and Breakfast from £26 nightly, £176 weekly. Please send for free colour brochure and local information.

LYNTON. Joanne and Michael Walker, Mayfair Hotel, Lynway, Lynton EX35 6AY (Lynton [0598] 53227). ♛ ♛ In quiet surroundings, five minutes' walk from the village centre and Cliff Railway, the Mayfair has lovely views of the magnificent Exmoor coastline and countryside, the Bristol Channel and the famous Watersmeet Valley. Our pretty bedrooms have tea/coffee facilities, colour TV, central heating and most have en-suite bathroom. Our residents' bar is comfy and welcoming, our quiet lounge ideal for relaxing. Try some tasty home cooking, local dishes and traditional English puddings. We are open all year, Christmas included; we also offer Spring/Autumn Breaks and welcome pets. Private car park. Terms per person — Bed and Breakfast from £18 daily (£115 weekly). Dinner, Bed and Breakfast from £25.50 daily (£162 weekly).

LYNTON. Dennis and Jean Gay, The Denes, Longmead, Lynton EX35 6DQ (Lynton [0598] 53573). Our guest house has a friendly atmosphere and is situated at the entrance to the Valley of Rocks. It is ideal for walking and exploring Exmoor with its magnificent views over sea, woodland and moor. Convenient for buses, shops, tennis courts, putting and bowling greens and cliff railway to Lynmouth. Lynton is within easy reach of Combe Martin, Ilfracombe, Doone Valley and many more places of interest. One mile from the sea. The house has eight bedroooms, three toilets, two bathrooms, diningroom and lounge with colour TV. Own car park. Open all year for Bed and Breakfast. Evening Meal optional. Licensed. Lunches and packed lunches on request. Send for free brochure. ETB registered. NO SMOKING. Booking recommended.

LYNTON. Mrs R. Pile, Coombe Farm, Countisbury, Lynton EX35 6NF (Brendon [059-87] 236). ♨♨

Working farm. Coombe Farm, set amid 370 acres of beautiful hill farming country, dates back to the 17th century. Ideal holiday base from which to visit lovely Doone Valley and Exmoor countryside. Two double rooms with en-suite shower rooms; one twin and two family rooms with washbasins, and all with hot drink facilities. Bathroom, shower, two toilets; lounge; diningroom. Central heating. Children welcome, cot, high chair and occasional babysitting. Dogs by arrangement. Car essential, parking space. Guests enjoy watching farm animals, including Devon cattle, Exmoor Horn sheep and horses. Pony trekking, tennis, fishing, golf nearby. Open mid-April to October. Fire Certificate held. Excellent country fare served. Evening Dinner, Bed and Breakfast from £150 per week; Bed and Breakfast from £12.75 per night. Reductions for children 11 years and under sharing family room. Stamp, please, for brochure. Residential licence.

LYNTON. Mr and Mrs B. Peacock, Seawood Hotel, North Walk, Lynton EX35 6HJ (Lynton [0598] 52272). ♨♨♨

Seawood Hotel is set in its own grounds overlooking the sea with breathtaking views of Lynmouth Bay and Exmoor. The Peacock family makes guests very welcome in their charming old-world house, which is now an AA/RAC one star hotel. Five course dinners with imaginative home cooking, for which great praise is received. Both lounges, diningroom and all bedrooms enjoy sea views. The latter all have en-suite bathroom and/or shower/WC, colour TV and tea/coffee making facilities. Four-posters are also available. Full central heating. Residential licence. Pets welcome. Terms from £27 daily; £180 weekly. Colour brochure on request. Open March to November.

MORETONHAMPSTEAD. Mary Cuming, Wooston Farm, Moretonhampstead, Newton Abbot TQ13 8QA (0647 40367). ♨♨

Quietly situated above the Teign Valley in the Dartmoor National Park, once part of the Manor House estate owned by Lord Hambledon. With views over Mardon Down, the farmhouse is surrounded by a delightful garden with grass play area. There are plenty of walks nearby with the open moor and wooded Teign Valley right on the doorstep. Children and pets welcome. Open March to October for Bed and Breakfast from £11 to £13; Bed, Breakfast and Evening Meal from £17.50 to £19.50.

MORETONHAMPSTEAD. Mrs T.M. Merchant, Great Sloncombe Farm, Moretonhampstead TQ13 8QF (Moretonhampstead [0647] 40595). ♨♨ **Working**

farm. A warm welcome and friendly uncommercial atmosphere awaits you at Great Sloncombe Farm, a lovely listed farmhouse dating from the 13th century. Situated in a peaceful wooded valley within Dartmoor National Park. A traditionally run 170 acre dairy farm, guests are welcome to watch and walk the farm which is rich in wildlife. Central for touring, walking, riding, fishing, golf or just relaxing. Comfortable double, twin or family rooms all with washbasins, tea/coffee making facilities, electric blankets and heating. Two bath/shower rooms. Sittingroom with colour TV; diningroom. Generous helpings of delicious home produced farmhouse food. Open all year.

DEVON – ENDLESS CHOICES!

People never tire of visiting Devon. There's so much to do, like visiting Alscott Farm Museum, Berry Head Country Park, Bickleigh Mill Farm, Farway Countryside Park, Haytor Granite Railway, Kent's Cavern, Dartmoor National Park and of course Plymouth and its Hoe.

MORTEHOE. Roger and Dena Sells, Lundy House Hotel, Mortehoe EX34 7DZ (Woolacombe [0271] 870372). 🏵🏵🏵 Small friendly Private Hotel midway between Mortehoe and Woolacombe, with gardens adjoining the rugged coastal path, access to a secluded beach and spectacular sea-views over Morte Bay to Lundy Island. Traditional home cooking is served, with vegetarian and special diets catered for by prior arrangement. The Hotel benefits from complete double glazing and has central heating, a very comfortable licensed bar lounge and a separate guests' lounge. Rooms have en-suite bath or shower and there is ample car parking. National Trust land surrounds the Hotel providing an ideal base for walking, rambling, or visiting many local beauty spots. Open from February to October. Les Routiers Commended. Pets welcome free of charge. Please write or telephone for colour brochure, tariff and details of Bargain Breaks, special discount weeks and reductions for Senior Citizens.

NEWTON ABBOT. Mrs V. Smith, Coombe Hatch, Combeinteignhead, Newton Abbot TQ12 4RG (Shaldon (0626) 873433). A 19th century friendly family run guest house situated in the picturesque unspoilt village of Combeinteignhead — an area of outstanding natural beauty. Coombe Hatch caters for all the family with double, twin and a delightful family room, all tastefully furnished and centrally heated throughout. Newton Abbot is a bustling market town (three miles) with a main line station. Shaldon with its sandy beaches is only a short drive and Torquay is five miles. The tidal Teign Estuary is a 10 minute walk away and here all watersport facilities are offered — windsurfing, sailing and fishing. Coombe Hatch is ideal for all holidays; a quiet break exploring the magnificent countryside, walking, birdwatching or playing golf at nearby courses. Centrally based for touring: Dartmoor with its dramatic scenery is just 10 miles away. Open all year. Parking. Bed and Breakfast from £14.

NEWTON ABBOT. Mrs Susan Stafford, Newhouse Barton, Ipplepen, Newton Abbot TQ12 5UN (0803 812539). 🏵🏵🏵 As featured on ITV's "Wish You Were Here". A lovely old farmhouse set in 115 acres of Devon's rolling countryside yet only a short drive to the coast or Dartmoor. All bedrooms have private bathroom, tea/coffee making facilities and colour TV. Oak-beamed lounge with stone fireplace. Diningroom with separate tables — plenty of good food. A delightful place in the country with a friendly atmosphere. Also two newly converted, three bedroomed self-catering cottages available. Bed and Breakfast from £14 to £17; Evening Meal from £8 to £9.

NEWTON ABBOT. David and Frances Pike, Kellinch Farm, Bickington, Newton Abbot TQ12 6PB (0626 821252). Welcome to South Devon. Kellinch is a 17th century working livestock farm set in a beautiful Devonshire valley with lovely views across the rolling hills, and boasts a secluded and truly rural position. Within easy reach of Dartmoor, coast and many places of interest. David and Frances extend a warm welcome and offer good farmhouse cooking from their own produce when available. TV lounge; separate diningroom; children's play area; laundry room. Many tame animals, help to feed always appreciated! Double or twin en-suite £12.50, double with washbasin £10; Evening Meal £7.50. Reductions for children.

NEWTON ABBOT. Mrs G.A. Stone, Milton Farm, East Ogwell, Newton Abbot TQ12 6AT (Newton Abbot [0626] 54988). Homely accommodation in farm bungalow in pleasant village with good view of Dartmoor, two miles west of Newton Abbot. Village lies equal distance from Torbay, Teignmouth and Dartmoor National Park, all about eight miles. Golf, riding, sailing and fishing all within easy reach. Dairy farm with cows and calves. Five minutes' walk from bus; railway two miles. Parking. One double room with H & C, one twin bedded room. Bathroom with shower, separate WC. Sitting/diningroom. Sorry, no pets. Mostly fresh produce served. Bed and Breakfast from £8.50. Evening Meal optional. Reduced rates for children. Closed November to mid-April. Details with SAE. Mid-week bookings if required.

Terms quoted in this publication may be subject to increase if rises in costs necessitate

NEWTON ABBOT. Mrs M.R. Chitty, Bittons Guest House, Ipplepen, Newton Abbot TQ12 5TW (Ipplepen [0803] 812489). Delightfully situated Guest House offering every comfort, good food and personal attention. Ideal touring centre within easy reach of both sea and moorland. We offer all that you would expect to ensure a pleasant and happy holiday base. Guest accommodation in three double, one family bedrooms, all with washbasins. Bathroom, two toilets. Guests' lounge and separate diningroom. Central heating in all rooms. Children welcome, cot, high chair available. Also reduced rates. Car essential — parking. Open all year for Bed and Breakfast from £12. Please write or telephone for further details.

NEWTON ABBOT near. Mrs Heather Young, Bremridge Farm, Woodland, Ashburton, Near Newton Abbot TQ13 7JX (Ashburton [0364] 52426). Working farm. In the heart of South Devon, 10 miles from sea and close to Dartmoor, this small working farm stands in eight acres amidst peaceful Devon countryside. Part of the house dates back to the 16th century yet it has been fully modernised, offering every comfort with fitted carpets and woodburning central heating. The accommodation includes two family rooms and two adjoining rooms with washbasins; lounge with TV; diningroom; bathroom and toilets. Children welcome, cot, high chair and babysitting available. Plenty of farm produce and vegetables. Large garden; ample parking. Car essential. Open all year for Dinner, Bed and Breakfast from £90 weekly. Reduced rates for children. AA listed. West Country Tourist Board registered. SAE or phone for illustrated brochure.

OAKFORD. Mrs Anne Boldry and Mrs Lillian Barnikel, Newhouse Farm, Oakford, Tiverton EX16 9JE (Oakford [039-85] 347). ✿✿ Working farm. 16th century Devon Longhouse situated in a quiet valley on southern fringe of Exmoor National Park, featuring heavy oak beams and inglenook fireplace with original bread oven. All bedrooms have washbasins, central heating and tea trays. We offer a high standard of country cooking using many original and traditional recipes. Much of the food is home produced and all the bread is home made — as are 13 varieties of marmalade! Newhouse Farm is an ideal centre for touring Devon and Exmoor. Entrance on B3227 (formerly A361), five miles west of Bampton. We aim to provide the welcome and comfort you always hoped for. AA listed. Bed and Breakfast £12; Bed, Breakfast and Evening Meal £19 (10 per cent discount for five days or more). En-suite £2.50 extra. Please send for brochure.

OKEHAMPTON. Margaret Hockridge, Week Farm, Bridestowe, Okehampton EX20 4HZ (083-786 221). ✿✿ Commended. A warm welcome awaits you at this 17th century farmhouse set in peaceful surroundings, three quarters of a mile from the main A30 road. Ideal touring centre for both North and South coasts and Dartmoor with its beautiful walks and scenery. Good home cooking assured, diningroom with separate tables; lounge with colour TV and log fires; tea/coffee facilities, washbasins, shaver points and heating in all bedrooms, three with TV, en-suites available and ground en-suite also available. Fire Certificate. AA listed. Terms and brochure available on request.

OKEHAMPTON near. Miss Una Cornthwaite, Hayne Mill, Lewdown, Near Okehampton EX20 4DD (Lewdown [056-683] 342). Hayne Mill, the home of the Braddabrook Bearded Collies and Cavaliers, is an attractive old Mill House lying beside the River Thrushel and sheltered by woodland. The house is situated midway between the north and south coasts between Dartmoor and Bodmin Moor and is very central for hiking, touring and pony trekking. Several good beaches within one hour's drive. Miss Cornthwaite owns the fishing rights (brown trout, sea trout and salmon) and guests may avail themselves of this facility. Delicious home cooking is served including organically grown fruit and vegetables from the garden. Vegetarian and special diets catered for. One single, two double bedrooms, with washbasins; two bathrooms, three toilets; sittingroom, diningroom. Central heating and log fire. Children welcome, cot, high chair, babysitting and reduced rates under 10 years. Pets by prior arrangement at £2.50 (including food). Car essential — ample parking. Full Board from £17; Evening Dinner, Bed and Breakfast from £14.50; Bed and Breakfast from £9. Open all year. Special Winter Breaks at reduced rates.

OKEHAMPTON. Mrs J.A. King, Higher Cadham Farm, Jacobstowe, Okehampton EX20 3RB (Exbourne [083-785] 647). ♛♛ *Commended.* **Working farm, join in.** Higher Cadham is a 139 acre beef and sheep

farm just off the A3072 Holiday Route, five miles from Dartmoor. It is a 16th century modernised farmhouse with accommodation for guests in two double, one single and one family bedrooms all with washbasins and shaver points; bathroom, toilet; sittingroom with colour TV, and games room with plenty to amuse the children. There are free tea-making facilities; free fishing and shooting. Plenty of home produced food. Residential licence. Children over three are welcome. Open from April to November. Car is essential and there is ample parking. Sorry, no pets. Excellent holiday for all the family. Fire Certificate held and AA listed. There are no extra charges. Bed and Breakfast from £10.50; Dinner £6. Weekly terms £100 per person. Reductions for children. Brochure on request.

OTTERY ST. MARY. Mrs Doreen Turl, Home Farm, Escot, Ottery St. Mary EX11 1LU (Honiton [0404] 850241). ♛ Working farm. Situated in beautiful

parkland within easy reach of the City of Exeter, coast and moors. 16th century home farm is a 300 acre mixed farm approximately half a mile A30, eight miles M5. Many places of architectural interest and pleasure facilities nearby. Plenty of local pubs and restaurants which provide excellent meals. Peaceful rural walks for nature watching. Guests are welcomed to this family home with its oak beams and comfortable accommodation. Double and family rooms with washbasins, tea/coffee making facilities; bathroom, shower room, toilets; guests' lounge with colour TV. Attractive diningroom, where full English breakfast is served. Sorry, no pets. Car essential, parking. SAE, please, for terms and quick reply.

OTTERY ST. MARY. Mrs E.A. Forth, Fluxton Farm, Ottery St. Mary EX11 1RJ (0404 812818).

♛♛♛ Lovely 16th century farmhouse in beautiful Otter Valley, with two acre gardens including stream, trout pond and garden railway. Only four miles from beach at Sidmouth. Beamed candlelit dining room; two lounges with colour TV, one non-smoking. Log fires, central heating; "Teasmade" in all rooms, all double rooms en-suite. Large garden room, lily pond. Good home cooking our speciality, using all local fresh produce. Children and pets welcome. Parking. Licensed. Open at Christmas. AA listed; Ashley Courtenay recommended. Terms from £170 per person per week.

OTTERY ST. MARY near. Claypitts Farm, East Hill, Ottery St. Mary EX11 1QD (0404 814599). ♛♛

Have a relaxing holiday on our farm situated in the beautiful Otter Valley, one mile off the B3176 at Tipton St. John. Enjoy walks through woods and wonderful views, also many tourist attractions nearby. Sidmouth with its pebble and sand beaches only four and a half miles away. Excellent accommodation is offered in double rooms en-suite, also double and twin rooms with washbasins; guests' own bathroom and toilets. Tea/coffee facilities in all rooms. Beamed ceilings and central heating throughout. Massive lounge with log burner, colour TV; large diningroom serving good farmhouse cooking. Spacious garden to relax in, children's play area, many small animals and birds. Regret no pets or children under three years. Bed and Breakfast from £13; Evening Meal from £7.

FUN FOR ALL THE FAMILY IN DEVON

Babbacombe Model Village, Torquay; *Beer Modelrama*, Beer, near Seaton; *Dart Valley Steam Railway*, Buckfastleigh; *Torbay & Dartmouth Steam Railway*, Paignton; *Bicton Gardens*, East Budleigh, near Budleigh Salterton; *Grand Western Horseboat Trips*, Tiverton; *The Shire Horse Centre*, Dunstone, Yealmpton, near Plymouth; *Farway Countryside Park*, near Honiton; *Dartmoor Wildlife Park*, Sparkwell, near Plymouth; *Paignton Zoo*, Totnes Road, Paignton; *Plymouth Aquarium*, Plymouth Hoe, Plymouth; *Exeter Maritime Museum*, The Quay, Exeter; *Torbay Aircraft Museum*, Higher Blagdon, near Paignton; *Exmoor Brass Rubbing Centre*, The Smuggler's Den, Queen Street, Lynton; *Dartington Glass*, Linden Close, off School Lane, Torrington; *Yelverton Paperweight Centre*, Leg O'Mutton Corner, Yelverton; *Kents Cavern*, Ilsham Road, Wellswood, Torquay.

Venn Ottery Barton COUNTRY HOTEL

Venn Ottery, Nr. Ottery St. Mary, Devon EX11 1RZ

ETB ♛♛♛

AA and RAC Acclaimed

Ashley Courtenay Recommended

Telephone: Ottery St. Mary (0404) 812733

Three miles from Ottery St. Mary and only five from the seafront at Sidmouth, this delightful 16th Century Licensed Country Hotel offers the charm of old oak beams and log fires combined with all modern comforts. Tucked away amid farmlands, only six miles from M5, Exit 30, 'Venn Ottery Barton' is family run to high standards and is close to many well-known beaches and picturesque seaside towns including Beer, Branscombe, Exmouth and Charmouth. Exeter 11 miles. Diningroom, lounge with colour TV, separate well-stocked bar (residential licence). Large games room.

There are eleven double or twin-bedded rooms, two single and three family, eleven with en-suite bath or shower and toilet, all with washbasins and full central heating. All bedrooms are on ground or first floor and all have tea/coffee making facilities (no charge). Terms daily or weekly; reductions for children sharing parents' room. Small dogs by arrangement. Open all year. AA and RAC Acclaimed. Bargain breaks. Brochure on request.

PAIGNTON. Mr and Mrs White, Newbarn Farm, Totnes Road, Paignton TQ4 7PT (Paignton [0803] 553602). ♛ Working farm. Newbarn Farm is set in 64 acres of beautiful countryside and has panoramic views which include Dartmoor. Half a mile off A385 Paignton/Totnes road. Two miles from Paignton and sea, four from Totnes, 12 from Dartmoor. Trout fishing and coarse fishing available at our Angling Centre. House has three double bedrooms, two of which can be used as family rooms, and the third (twin-bedded) can be used as a single (£2 supplement). All rooms have washbasins. Central heating throughout. Two bathrooms, three toilets. Sittingroom with TV; diningroom. Games room. Home produce. Dogs and children over five years welcome (half price for those under 11 years). Car essential; ample parking. Bed and Breakfast from £7 daily (£40 per week) low season and from £9 daily (£54 per week) high season. SAE for brochure.

PAIGNTON (Torbay). Mrs B.J. Tooze, Elberry Farm, Broadsands, Paignton TQ4 6HJ (Churston [0803] 842939). Working farm, join in. Elberry Farm is situated in the middle of a popular holiday area. Guests have access to the house at all times, facilities for making light refreshments, washing, etc available. Dartmoor and Plymouth within one hour's journey. Pitch and putt outside farm; Broadsands safe beach for children and Elberry Cove is very popular for water ski-ing, both are about 400 yards away. All cooking is done by Mrs Tooze and vegetables are home grown. Three family and one double bedrooms (three with washbasins). Lounge, diningroom and all modern conveniences. Children welcome. Two cots, two high chairs and babysitting available. The 60 acre farm is open from Easter to October. No pets please. Reductions for children up to 12 years old. ETB registered. Featured on BBC2 Holiday Travel 1986, gained full marks. Evening Dinner, Bed and Breakfast or Bed and Breakfast only. Terms on request with SAE, please.

PLEASE SEND A STAMPED ADDRESSED ENVELOPE WITH ENQUIRIES

PARRACOMBE. Lower Dean Farm and Riding Stables, Trentishoe, Parracombe EX31 4PJ (Parracombe [05983] 215). ♥ ♥ Charming 18th century licensed farmhouse within the Exmoor National Park offers all the peace of the countryside plus the glorious beaches of North Devon, a short drive away. All ten bedrooms have bathroom or shower en-suite. Spacious lounge, colour TV, diningroom and bar. Leisure activities. Horses for hire. Clay pigeon shooting and archery. Games room, snooker, pool, table tennis. Golf course five miles. Sea two-and-a-half miles. First class home cooked food. Ideal for family holidays. No pets. Open February to December. Car essential. Dinner, Bed and Breakfast or Bed and Breakfast. Reductions for children sharing parents' room. AA listed. SAE please.

PLYMOUTH. Mrs Margaret MacBean, Gabber Farm, Down Thomas, Plymouth PL9 0AW (Plymouth [0752] 862269). Working farm. This 120-acre dairy farm is situated one mile from the Wembury and Bovisand beaches. Ideally located for touring — the lovely historic town of Plymouth, Dartmoor and the beaches of Bigbury, Bantham, etc. within easy reach. Many beautiful coastal walks in the area; golf course and riding nearby. Open Easter to November. One family, two double, one twin-bedded rooms and one children's room, all with washbasins; bathroom, and separate toilet; sitting and diningrooms. Good home cooking using own farm produce when available with a varied menu so that visitors will not be served the same meal over a two-week period. Children welcome at reduced rates — cot, high chair, babysitting available. Sorry, no pets. Car essential, parking. Colour TV. Evening Meal, Bed and Breakfast. SAE, please, or telephone for terms and further details.

PLYMOUTH. Mrs Suzanne MacBean, Coombe Farm, Wembury Road, Plymstock, Plymouth PL9 0DE (Plymouth [0752] 401730). Working farm, join in. A warm welcome awaits you at Coombe. This working Dairy Farm dates back to the 14th century and is situated in a quiet valley on the outskirts of Plymouth. It is within easy reach of Plymouth City Centre, good safe beaches and Dartmoor National Park. It is an ideal touring centre with many places of interest within half an hour's drive. The farmhouse offers peaceful homely accommodation with plenty of good farm produce and home cooking. Lounge, colour TV; bedrooms have washbasins and tea/coffee making facilities. Riding, country walks. Children welcome, cot and babysitting. Sorry, no pets. Car is essential and there is parking space. Open Easter to end of November. Evening Meal, Bed and Breakfast or Bed and Breakfast only. Reduced rates for children. Plymouth Marketing Bureau member. SAE, please, or telephone for further details or terms.

SALCOMBE. Mrs Sally Rossiter, Cholwells Farm, Woolston, Kingsbridge TQ7 3BH (Kingsbridge [0548] 560127). Working farm. Cholwell Farm, a working family farm, is ideally situated midway between Salcombe and Kingsbridge in the hamlet of Woolston. The lovely beaches, sailing, riding, coastal walks and golf just 10 minutes away, Dartmoor 30 minutes. This lovely old 16th century farmhouse with exposed beams offers excellent homely accommodation with good food and a warm welcome. There is a double and two twin bedrooms; bathroom, two showers and two toilets. Non smokers preferred. Children over five years welcome — reduced rates for under 12's, babysitting available. Bed and Breakfast from £12 per person. Weekly terms available.

See also Colour Display Advertisement **SALCOMBE. Mrs C. Jeyes, Beadon Farmhouse, Beadon Road, Salcombe TQ8 8LX (0548 843020).** Victorian farmhouse set in three and a half acres in a quiet position overlooking a peaceful valley. Accommodation comprises one double en-suite bedroom and two twin-bedded rooms with washbasins. Diningroom with separate tables. Sittingroom with colour TV. Central heating. Cot and high chair available if required. Children's evening meals and babysitting by arrangement. Ample parking. Terms from £12 per night; £80 per week.

The information in the entries in this guide is presented by the publishers in good faith and after the signed acceptance by advertisers that they will uphold the high standards associated with FHG PUBLICATIONS LIMITED. The publishers do not accept responsibility for any inaccuracies or omissions or any results thereof. Before making final holiday arrangements readers should confirm the prices and facilities directly with advertisers.

SALCOMBE. Tom and Elaine Stidston-Nott, Bolberry House Farm, Bolberry, Malborough, Kings-

bridge TQ7 3DY (0548 560926). Bolberry House Farm is a 300 acre working coastal farm situated in the delightful hamlet of Bolberry, which lies between Salcombe and Hope Cove. To our guests we offer every comfort in the friendly atmosphere of our home. Large lounge with colour TV; two family bedrooms, both with washbasin and tea/coffee making facilities. Traditional English breakfast. Own keys. Reduction for children under 12 years, if sharing; babysitting available. This area provides good beaches, excellent watersports and sailing facilities, also many popular inns with carveries, restaurants, cafes, etc. Our land adjoins Bolberry Downs with lovely walks, magnificent scenery. Dartmoor National Park, Torquay and Plymouth all within one hour's drive. Terms on request.

SALCOMBE. Mrs Madge Bullock, Pine Cottage, Froude Road, South Sands, Salcombe TQ8 8LH

(Salcombe [054-884] 2170). A comfortable detached cottage in wooded surroundings with beautiful sea views from all bedrooms; lounge, diningroom and sun terrace. Car preferable, but not essential — parking space provided. Log fires out of season — bedrooms with heaters. Safe, sandy beach within 100 yards for swimming, sailing, windsurfing, diving and fishing. Ideal countryside for walkers and visitors appreciative of wild life, with magnificent views of the estuary and English Channel. Other beaches and coves nearby. Children over three years welcome at reduced rates if sharing parents' room. Substantial cooked breakfast, pot of tea with biscuits early morning and afternoon from £12 inclusive — no extra charge. Bed and Breakfast only. Open from January to December. Reductions for senior citizens November to March. SAE, please.

SALCOMBE (Kingsbridge). Richard and Jill Berrill, Holbeche House, Inner Hope Road, Hope Cove, Salcombe TQ7 3HH (Kingsbridge [0548] 561809). This is a modern guest house in a beautiful, unspoilt village, with many delightful walks, two good sandy beaches three minutes' walk away. We offer you a peaceful holiday in a comfortable friendly atmosphere, together with the very best of home cooking prepared from fresh local produce. Family, double and single rooms, most en-suite, all with tea-making facilities. Central heating. Large car park. Children welcome at reduced rates. Free babysitting. Two good pubs within walking distance. Bed and Breakfast from £11.50, with Evening Meal £17.50; Bed, Breakfast and Evening Meal from £110 weekly per adult. Open all year (except Christmas).

SEATON. Mr and Mrs P. Millard, Beach End, 8 Trevelyan Road, Seaton EX12 2NL (Seaton [0297]

23388). ♛♛ *Commended.* This attractive 60-year-old house situated on the Esplanade at Seaton is the nearest guest house to the beach. There is a good range of shops with golf club and harbour close by. Ideal centre for exploring the beauty spots of Devon, Dorset and Somerset. Four double, two single and one family bedrooms, all with washbasins and sea views; two bathrooms; three toilets; sittingroom; diningroom. Cot, high chair, babysitting and reduced rates for children. Sorry, no pets. Open February to October, mid-week bookings accepted. Parking. Traditional British cooking our speciality and terms include early morning tea and late evening beverage. Residential licence. SAE for brochure and tariff.

SIDMOUTH. Mrs Elizabeth Tancock, Lower Pinn Farm, Peak Hill, Sidmouth EX10 0NN (Sidmouth

[0395] 513733). ♛♛ **Working farm.** Set amidst unrivalled East Devon countryside, two miles west of the unspoilt coastal resort of Sidmouth, and one mile to the east of the pretty village of Otterton. A working farm extending to over 220 acres offering a relaxed and friendly atmosphere. Comfortable bedrooms (two ensuite) all with colour TV, hot drink facilities, electric blankets, shaver points and fan heaters. Guests have their own keys and may return at all times throughout the day. Ample parking. English Breakfast served, local inns and restaurants nearby provide excellent Evening Meals. Children and pets welcome.

SIDMOUTH. Mr and Mrs H. Tillotson, Seniors Farm, Exeter Road, Newton Poppleford, Sidmouth EX10 0BH (0395 68807). A 16th century thatched farmhouse on the A3052 Exeter to Sidmouth road. We are situated in the lovely Otter Valley four miles from Sidmouth and Budleigh Salterton; Bicton Gardens approximately two miles. Accommodation comprises two double/family and one twin rooms, all with washbasins; bathroom, shower, toilet; diningroom; large lounge with inglenook fireplace and colour TV. Dogs welcome. Parking space. Bed and Breakfast from £11; Bed, Breakfast and Evening Meal from £16.50. Reductions for children under 12 years; no extras. Open all year spend Christmas with us.

SIDMOUTH. Mrs S.A. Rabjohns, Wiscombe Linhaye, Southleigh, Colyton EX13 6JF (Farway [040 487] 342). 🐾 **Working farm.** Wiscombe Linhaye Farm is in the quiet countryside but only 10 minutes from Branscombe and Sidmouth beach. On the B3174 just one mile off A3052. The farm is small but fully operational and stocked with sheep, cattle, ducks and geese. Children welcome. Good home cooking with full English breakfast. One double room with private bathroom downstairs, also one twin room and one family room, both with washbasins. Terms from £10 – £15.

Orchardside Hotel

This delightful small country hotel and restaurant stands in an acre of lovely gardens, with panoramic views of the countryside. It is situated on the edge of the lovely unspoilt village of Sidmouth, only two and a half miles from the sea. This is ideal walking country, with opportunities too for golf, fishing and horse riding. All the well furnished bedrooms have tea/coffee making facilities, colour TV and central heating, and most have showers en suite. The restaurant offers a good choice of menu and a full bar. Large car park.

Resident Proprietors:
Ken & Barbara Harper

Dinner, Bed and Breakfast from £25.00 per person per night.
Bed and Breakfast from £15.00 per person.
Open all year. Cotford Road, Sidbury, near Sidmouth, Devon EX10 0SQ. Tel: 03957 351.

SIDMOUTH. Mrs Betty F. Sage, Pinn Barton, Peak Hill, Sidmouth EX10 0NN (Sidmouth [0395] 514004). 🐾🐾 **Working farm.** Pinn Barton is a farm of 330 acres situated on the coast, two miles from Sidmouth, where there is a good choice of eating places. There are many safe bathing beaches nearby and lovely walks along the cliffs around the farm. It is very peaceful, being just off the coast road, between Sidmouth and the village of Otterton. Pinn Barton has been highly recommended and you will be given a friendly welcome in comfortable surroundings, and a good farmhouse breakfast. Some bedrooms have en-suite facilities and all have colour TV, central heating, washbasins, tea/coffee making facilities, razor plugs and electric blankets for chilly nights. There is a diningroom and separate sittingroom for guests (with colour TV and a fire). There is also a bathroom/shower and separate toilet. Children are very welcome and there is a cot, high chair, swings, etc. Baby-sitting by arrangement. Bed and Breakfast including bedtime drink from £12. Reductions for children sharing parents' room. Own keys provided. Stamp, please.

SIDMOUTH. Mrs B.I. Tucker, Goosemoor Farm, Newton Poppleford, Sidmouth EX10 0BL (0395 68279). Goosemoor Farmhouse is an old Devon Long House with bread oven in diningroom. The 25 acre mixed farm is on the Exeter/Lyme Regis bus route about four miles from the sea and has streams running through its meadows. There are many delightful walks in country lanes or over Woodberry and Alsbeare Commons. Guests may wander freely on the farmland. There are four double and one family rooms, all with washbasins; two bathrooms, three toilets; sittingroom; diningroom. Children over 10 years welcome. Sorry, no pets. Open all year with log fires. Central heating throughout. Car not essential but there is parking. Evening Meal, Bed and Breakfast from £8. Cream teas also available.

SIDMOUTH. Mrs Lorna F. Lever, Canterbury House, Salcombe Road, Sidmouth EX10 8PR (0395 513373). 🐾🐾 This charming small Georgian residence overlooking the River Sid offers comfortable accommodation and some free parking. Set in this quaint and interesting town it is only a third of a mile from the seafront with level walk to nearby shops, etc. Double, twin and family bedrooms, some ground floor and seven with en-suite facilities. Washbasins, shaver sockets, bedside lamps, colour TV and tea-making facilities in all bedrooms. Partial central heating. Colour TV lounge. Full English breakfast and varied dinner menu. AA and RAC listed, Hotels and Caterers Association. Weekly terms from £145 including VAT.

SIDMOUTH. Mrs Kerstin Farmer, Higher Coombe Farm, Tipton St. John, Sidmouth EX10 0AX

(Ottery St. Mary [0404] 813385). 🐄🐄 **Working farm, join in.** Comfortable farmhouse accommodation, peacefully situated in the beautiful Otter Valley only four miles from Sidmouth seafront and the surrounding National Trust and Devon Heritage Coast. Half a mile off B3176. It is within easy reach of many beaches, ideal for touring all of East Devon, but also Exeter, Dartmoor and Exmoor. Enjoy the good, mainly home produced, farmhouse food, full English Breakfast and friendly relaxed atmosphere. Family, twin, single/bunk-bedded rooms, all with washbasins, tea-making facilities and electric blankets. Guests' bathroom, toilet; dining-room and lounge with colour TV. Children very welcome with cot, high chair and babysitting available. Terms from £77 weekly for Bed and Breakfast to £119 weekly for Bed, Breakfast and Evening Meal.

SOUTH MOLTON near. Messrs H.J. Milton, Partridge Arms Farm, Yeo Mill, West Anstey, Near South Molton EX36 3NU (Anstey Mills [039-84] 217).

🐄🐄 **Working farm, join in.** "Partridge Arms" Farm was, until 1909, a country inn, off the A361, four miles west of Dulverton on the Devon/Somerset border. Ideal for touring Exmoor National Park or the North Devon and West Somerset coastal resorts. Riding, trekking and fishing available. Guests enjoy the atmosphere of a one-time country inn now a guest house and family farm of over 200 acres. Two ponies on the farm for children's amusement. Open all year, guests can enjoy excellent and varied menu — no dish repeated in any one week. Original four-poster bedroom, single, double and twin-bedded rooms, some of which have en-suite facilities; two sittingrooms and three diningrooms. Children welcome with reduced rates according to age; cot. Full Fire Certificate. Residential licence. Pets by arrangement. Car essential, ample parking. Farm Holiday Guide Diploma Winner. Relais Routiers. Evening Dinner, Bed and Breakfast from £122.50 inc VAT weekly; Bed and Breakfast from £84 inc VAT weekly.

TAWSTOCK. Mrs C.H. Thorne, Higher Uppacott Farm, Tawstock, Barnstaple EX31 3LA (Newton Tracey [0271-85] 393). Working farm, join in. Situated in lovely countryside not far from beaches and moors, we are a working farm with assorted animals, including a pony to ride. Accommodation downstairs comprises lounge and diningroom, both with colour TV, one with video; toilet. Upstairs are a bathroom with toilet and shower, two family rooms, (one en-suite), a double room and a children's room. All rooms have washbasins. Central heating. Babysitting provided. No pets. Play area, garden and parking. Plenty of home cooking and a warm welcome will be given to everyone. Bed and Breakfast from £12; Evening Meal £5. Reduced rates for weekly stay and for children. Open May to September.

TEIGN VALLEY. S. and G. Harrison-Crawford, Silver Birches, Teign Valley, Trusham, Newton Abbot TQ13 0NJ (Chudleigh [0626] 852172).

A warm welcome awaits you at Silver Birches, a comfortable bungalow at the edge of Dartmoor. A secluded, relaxing spot with two acre garden running down to river. Only two miles from A38 on B3193. Exeter 14 miles, sea 12 miles. Car advisable. Ample parking. Excellent pubs and restaurants nearby. Good centre for fishing, bird watching, forest walks, golf, riding; 70 yards salmon/trout fishing free to residents. Centrally heated guest accommodation with separate entrance. Two double bedded rooms, one twin bedded room, all with own bath/shower, toilet. Guest lounge with colour TV. Diningroom, sun lounge overlooking river. Sorry, no children under eight. Terms including tea on arrival, full English Breakfast from £16 nightly, £112 weekly. Evening Meal optional. Open all year. ETB Registered.

TIVERTON. Mrs Barbara Pugsley, "Hornhill", Exeter Hill, Tiverton EX16 4PL (0884 253352). 🐾 🐾

Commended. "Hornhill" is a comfortable country house surrounded by farmland, yet only five minutes from Tiverton and ten minutes from M5 Junction 27. The double and twin-bedded rooms (one with four poster) have private bathrooms, heating, colour TV and tea/coffee-making equipment; one ground floor double room has en-suite shower room. Guests have the use of the large garden, drawing room and dining room. Local attractions include riding, swimming, golf and tennis. Exmoor, Dartmoor, the north and south coasts, National Trust properties and Exeter are all within easy reach. No smoking please. Children over eight years welcome. Bed and Breakfast from £14. Dinner by arrangement.

TIVERTON. Mrs H. Seez, Cove Cottage, Cove, Tiverton EX16 7RU (Bampton [0398] 31430).

Country house with friendly atmosphere in a peaceful, unspoilt valley, yet only 15 miles from M5. Enjoy the beautiful, quiet surroundings and the plentiful wildlife. Four miles north of Tiverton, three miles south of Bampton — an ideal centre for touring Exmoor and the coastline. Pleasant comfortable accomodation includes lounge and diningroom with log fires; three double rooms (one twin/family, as preferred) all with hot/cold washbasins and tea/coffee making facilities. Outdoor swimming pool and large garden. Open all year. Bed and Breakfast £12.50. Evening Meal, by arrangement, £8.00. Reductions for children under 12 years.

TIVERTON. Mrs Sylvia Hann, Great Bradley Farm, Withleigh Cross, Tiverton EX16 8JL (Tiverton [0884] 256946). 🐾 🐾 **Working farm.** With its lovely 16th

century farmhouse, Great Bradley is a perfect place to relax. We can assure you of good reliable accommodation, a comfortable bed, a delicious breakfast and true rural hospitality to make your holiday complete. We offer pretty bedrooms with central heating, washbasins, tea/coffee facilities and private bathrooms, together with a delightful lounge overlooking the garden and the beautiful view beyond. Within easy driving distance of Exmoor, Dartmoor and many good beaches. Sorry, no pets. NON-SMOKERS ONLY PLEASE. Bed and Breakfast from £12.50 to £15.

TIVERTON. Mr and Mrs R.C. Pratt, Moor Barton, Nomansland, Tiverton EX16 8NN (Tiverton [0884] 860325). Working farm. Full Fire Certificate. Set in glorious countryside where guests are free to roam the 200-acre mixed dairy farm. Economically situated for touring all Devon. Visit Tiverton market, heated swimming pool, enjoy horse riding, canal trips. Equidistant North and South coasts, Exmoor, Dartmoor. Guests return annually to enjoy the free family atmosphere given by Colin, Rita and family and the excellent fresh home cooking including full English Breakfast of bacon and eggs. Dinners of home produced beef, lamb, pork, chicken, pies, cream, etc served. All bedrooms have washbasins (one ground floor). Bathrooms and ample toilet facilities. Central heating. Lounge with colour TV and open log fire. Children welcome at reduced rates, high chair. Evening Dinner, Bed and Breakfast from £17.50 per night, £105 weekly; Bed and Breakfast from £12.50 per night. House suitable for disabled guests. Open all year.

TIVERTON near. Mrs F. A. Luxton, Thorne Farm, Stoodleigh, Near Tiverton EX16 9QG (Rackenford [088-488] 232). Working farm, join in. Thorne Farm is quietly situated in Devon's rolling hills, overlooking wooded valleys with marvellous views. There is a suckler herd and sheep, and visitors are welcome to take an interest in the various jobs on the farm and walk on the 120 acres of farmland. Within easy reach of the Exmoor National Park and many local beauty spots. Food is a speciality, with fresh vegetables, milk, cream, meat and home-made bread. Two double, one family bedrooms; bathroom, two toilets; sittingroom. Central heating. Reduced rates, cot and occasional babysitting. Sorry, no pets. Open March to November. Car essential; ample parking. Evening Meal, Bed and Breakfast from £105 (weekly); Bed and Breakfast from £10. Reduced rates for children under fourteen years. SAE, please.

DEVON – ENDLESS CHOICES!

People never tire of visiting Devon. There's so much to do, like visiting Alscott Farm Museum, Berry Head Country Park, Bickleigh Mill Farm, Farway Countryside Park, Haytor Granite Railway, Kent's Cavern, Dartmoor National Park and of course Plymouth and its Hoe.

TIVERTON. Mrs J. Babbage, Palfreys Barton, Cove, Tiverton EX16 7RZ (0398 331456). Palfreys

Barton is a working farm with a 17th century farmhouse set in its 290 acres of glorious countryside with marvellous views. Within easy reach of the North and South coasts, Exmoor and Dartmoor. 10 miles from the M5 Sampford Peverell interchange, Junction 27. Numerous attractions nearby. Food is a speciality — fresh from the garden. Friendly atmosphere. Three double rooms with washbasin and one single bedroom; two bathrooms and two toilets; diningroom and lounge with colour TV. Car essential. Evening Dinner, Bed and Breakfast. Reduced rates for children under 12. SAE or phone for further details and terms.

TORBAY. Mrs J. Ireland, Holt, 7 Greenhill Road, Kingskerswell, Near Newton Abbot TQ12 5DT

(0803-87 2336). Welcome to our gracious country guesthouse. Relaxed atmosphere, super food, comfortably furnished, tastefully decorated for six/eight guests in family, double and single bedrooms, all having vanitory units, washbasins, tea-making facilities and lovely views. Bathroom, two toilets; lounge with colour TV; separate diningroom. We have our own fields, horses, dogs, cats, their babies and three goldfish won at the fair. The charming village of Kingskerswell with its old church, stream, thatched restaurant and several shops is only three miles between Torquay and Newton Abbot. Many excellent local pubs with atmosphere, food and rooms for children. Bed and Breakfast from £10; optional Evening Meal.

Ke'thla House

Situated in the main hotel road in Torquay, Ke'thla House is five minutes' walk from the sea front and town centre of this beautiful seaside resort, and only 100 yards from the new sports and conference centre. Accommodation is restricted to the ground and first floors only and all rooms have colour TV with satellite channel, radio/alarms and tea making facilities; some rooms with own shower or en-suite rooms. Own keys are available and there are full fire precautions. Bed and special English Breakfast from £10 to £18. Snack meal available in the evening at very competitive prices. Children welcome at reduced rates, cot/high chair available. Sorry, no pets. Please send stamped addressed envelope for brochure. Open all year.

**Mr and Mrs T. Wilson, Ke'thla House, Belgrave Road, Torquay TQ2 5HX
Telephone: Torquay (0803) 294995**

TORQUAY. Bowden Close Hotel, Teignmouth Road (A379), Maidencombe, Torquay TQ1 4TJ (Torquay [0803] 328029). ♥ ♥ ♥ Delightful elevated Victorian country house hotel midway between Torquay and Teignmouth with panoramic sea and coastal views. Friendly, informal atmosphere with emphasis on comfort, courtesy and good food. Ideal for walking, touring or just relaxing. Close to Torbay attractions without the hustle and bustle. There are 19 bedrooms, mostly en-suite, all with colour TV and tea making facilities. Central heating. Ample parking. Open all year. Just 600 yards from sheltered beach. Bed, Breakfast and Evening Meal from £150.50 per week, including VAT. We also offer special spring and autumn breaks. Well behaved pets only by arrangement only. AA/RAC 2 star. Write or phone for brochure.

TORQUAY. Mrs N. Edwards, Kingsway Lodge, 95 Avenue Road, Torquay TQ2 5LH (0803 295 288). This clean, comfortable guest house comes well recommended for good home cooked meals as well as for its situation — just 15 minutes' level walk from beach, shops, Abbey Gardens. Central for touring beauty spots in the area. Personal attention at all times. There are four double, one single and one family bedrooms with central heating, spring interior divans and washbasins. Ground floor en suite. Carpeted throughout. Colour TV lounge; diningroom; bathroom, two toilets. Children are welcome at reduced rates. Sorry, no pets. Free parking though car not essential. Open all year. ETB registered. Bed and Breakfast £8.50 daily. Bed, Breakfast and Evening Meal from £12.50 daily (£84 weekly).

Torcroft Hotel

CROFT ROAD, TORQUAY TQ2 5UE

Telephone TORQUAY (0803) 298292

AA & RAC Listed

Licensed

This comfortable and friendly 22-bedroom Hotel is situated on a quiet tree-lined road, only 400 yards from Abbey Sands. We offer good food, a restful atmosphere, combined with easy access to the town centre, Abbey Gardens and Holiday entertainment. Colour Brochure with pleasure from Resident Proprietor:

MRS W. COOPER

We offer: ○ *Ample free parking in grounds for all cars* ○ *Four-course Dinner with choice of menu* ○ *Full English breakfast* ○ *Charming dining room with separate tables* ○ *Spacious lounge bar* ○ *Colour TV lounge* ○ *All rooms washbasins, shaver sockets, tea/coffee making facilities, bedside lights* ○ *Most rooms en suite* ○ *Bedroom TV available* ○ *Some ground floor rooms* ○ *Fire certificate* ○ *Evening refreshment service*
Evening Dinner, Bed & Breakfast. Terms on request.

FOR THE MUTUAL GUIDANCE OF GUEST AND HOST

Every year literally thousands of holidays, short-breaks and overnight stops are arranged through our guides, the vast majority without any problems at all. In a handful of cases, however, difficulties do arise about bookings, which often could have been prevented from the outset.

It is important to remember that when accommodation has been booked, both parties — guests and hosts — have entered into a form of contract. We hope that the following points will provide helpful guidance.

GUESTS: When enquiring about accommodation, be as precise as possible. Give exact dates, numbers in your party and the ages of any children. State the number and type of rooms wanted and also what catering you require — bed and breakfast, full board, etc. Make sure that the position about evening meals is clear — and about pets, reductions for children or any other special points.

Read our reviews carefully to ensure that the proprietors you are going to contact can supply what you want. Ask for a letter confirming all arrangements, if possible.

If you have to cancel, do so as soon as possible. Proprietors do have the right to retain deposits and under certain circumstances to charge for cancelled holidays if adequate notice is not given and they cannot re-let the accommodation.

HOSTS: Give details about your facilities and about any special conditions. Explain your deposit system clearly and arrangements for cancellations, charges, etc, and whether or not your terms include VAT.

If for any reason you are unable to fulfil an agreed booking without adequate notice, you may be under an obligation to arrange alternative suitable accommodation or to make some form of compensation.

While every effort is made to ensure accuracy, we regret that FHG Publications cannot accept responsibility for errors, omissions or misrepresentation in our entries or any consequences thereof. Prices in particular should be checked because we go to press early. We will follow up complaints but cannot act as arbiters or agents for either party.

COURTHOUSE

MAIDENCOMBE, TORQUAY, S. DEVON TQ1 4SU
Telephone: [0803] 328335

Originally a 12th Century Manor Court House, mentioned in Domesday, now a family-run Country House Hotel. Steeped in history yet offering guests the best of English fare and present day comforts, including en suite facilities and teasmades, licensed bar, own car park. Set in rural surroundings in the unspoilt hamlet of Maidencombe, 300 yards from the beach, yet only four miles from Torquay. An ideal centre for touring glorious South Devon.

★ Open April to October
★ Midweek or Saturday-Sunday bookings accepted
★ Children very welcome at reduced rates
★ Reduced terms for Spring and Late Summer

RAC Listed
♛♛
Member of
West Country Tourist Board

To find out more about us, please write, enclosing stamp, for colour brochure to the Resident Proprietors Sheila and Godfrey Walker.

TORQUAY. Mr and Mrs G. and B. Hurren, Treander Guest House, 10 Morgan Avenue, Torquay TQ2 5RS (Torquay [0803] 296906). Come and enjoy a first class informal holiday at our clean, comfortable establishment, which is in a superb position for beaches and amenities. Some rooms have a sea view. Tea making facilities and colour TV in each room. Car park. Own key, with access at all times. Full central heating. Children welcome. Bed and Breakfast with optional Evening Meal. WCTB listed. Hotel Association "Highly Recommended".

TORQUAY. Mr and Mrs D.E. Anning, Craig Court Hotel, 10 Ash Hill Road, Torquay TQ1 3HZ (Torquay [0803] 294400). ♛♛ Resident proprietors

Joyce and David Anning supervise this Grade II listed building beautifully situated facing south in one of the most convenient positions in Torquay, although away from the main road, within easy walking distance of beaches, amusements and shops. Pleasant TV lounge and separate bar overlook a secluded garden in which there is a model railway. Diningroom has separate tables and there is a choice of menu at all meals. The hotel has six double bedrooms (three en-suite), two family rooms (one en-suite) and two single rooms, all with hand basins; three bathrooms and toilets. Children are welcome. Parking on the premises. AA and RAC listed. Bed and Breakfast from £15 per person, Dinner, Bed and Breakfast from approximately £140 per week. Reduced rates for children sharing parents' room. SAE for colour brochure.

TORRINGTON. Mrs R. Wood, Lake Farm, Langtree, Torrington EX38 8NX (08055 320). Lake Farm is a dairy farm with cows, calves, sheep, ducks and free range hens. The farmhouse overlooks large lawns with beautiful views beyond. Within easy reach of Torrington with the famous Dartington glass factory and the R.H.S. Garden at Rosemoor, Clovelly and the market towns. Fishing is available on the farm. Accommodation comprises double and twin-bedded rooms, one with washbasin; diningroom; sittingroom. TV, Rayburn and open fire. Pets by arrangement. Car essential. Bed and Breakfast or Bed, Breakfast and Evening Meal. Children welcome. SAE, please, or telephone for terms and further information.

Terms quoted in this publication may be subject to increase if rises in costs necessitate

TOTNES. Mrs Trant, Chittlesford Mill Farm, Halwell, Near Totnes TQ9 7HZ (080423 674). Enjoy a

friendly relaxed atmosphere combined with high standard of comfort, where children are welcome at reduced rates and babysitting service is available. Our charming spacious farmhouse has large lounge/diningroom with beams, large stone fireplace and colour TV/video. Family, double and twin bedrooms. Two bathrooms. Guests are more than welcome to take part in the farm activities which are sheep and horses (of great interest to children) or just relax in the gardens. A car is essential with plenty of parking available. We are ideally situated for touring Dartmoor with its outstanding natural beauty and wild ponies. Plymouth, Exeter, Torquay with their big shopping centres close by. Beautiful sandy beaches at nearby Bantham, Bigbury Bay, Salcombe and Thurlstone. Plenty of things to see and do. We are open all year. Bed and Breakfast from £9. Please phone for more details.

TOTNES. Mrs Jan Finch, Island Farm, Moreleigh, Totnes TQ9 7SH (Gara Bridge [054 882] 441).

Working farm, join in. This working sheep/arable farm is ideally situated in the South Hams, enjoying a panoramic view extending to Torquay. Seven miles between Totnes/ Kingsbridge/Dartmouth. Within easy reach of coast with windsurfing beaches and Dartmoor with many walks. There is a trout farm nearby and many old pubs. Open all year. A car is essential. Visitors may use lounge with TV. Children are welcome and a cot and high chair are provided. One double bedded room, two twin bedded rooms. Guests' own bathroom and toilet. Bed and Breakfast from £9. Children and OAP's at reduced rates.

TOTNES. Mrs Susan Freeth, Wonton Farm, Diptford, Totnes TQ9 7LS (South Brent [036-47] 2210).

Working farm. Dating back to the 16th century, Wonton Farm is situated in one of the loveliest parts of Devon, two miles from the A38 dual carriageway, three miles from the historic town of Totnes and within easy reach of Dartmoor and the coast. Guests are welcomed to this dairy farm and Pony Stud from February to November, and enjoy comfortable accommodation, excellent farmhouse cooking, central heating, large sittingroom with colour TV (available at all times) and a large pleasant garden. Three double, one family bedrooms; two bathrooms, three toilets. Children welcome at reduced rates; babysitting available. Pets accepted. Central base for visiting the Dart Valley Railway (steam trains), the Shire Horse Centre, Paignton Zoo, River Dart, Boat Trips and many National Trust properties. There are a number of good public houses in the immediate vicinity. Bed and Breakfast. Evening Meal by arrangement.

TOTNES. Jeannie and Peter Allnutt, The Old Forge at Totnes, Seymour Place, Totnes TQ9 5AY (Totnes [0803] 862174). 🌸🌸🌸 *Commended.* A charm-

ing 600 year old stone building, recently converted from blacksmith and wheelwright workshops and coach houses. Meet Peter Allnutt working in his traditional forge, complete with blacksmith's prison cell. Although fronting an interesting historic church there is no sound of bells! Very close to the River Dart steamer quay, shops and station (also steam train rides). Ideally situated for touring most of Devon — including Dartmoor and Torbay coasts. A day trip from Exeter, Plymouth and Cornwall, May to September — Elizabethan costume worn Tuesdays. Double, twin and family rooms with some en-suite/ground floor. All rooms have colour TV, teamakers, colour co-ordinated Continental bedding, central heating. Licensed lounge and patio. No smoking indoors. Parking, walled gardens. Excellent choice of breakfast menu. Children welcome but sorry, no pets. AA Merit Award. Cottage also available for two or four.

TOTNES near. Mrs Sheree Palmer, Hatchlands Farm, Bluepost, Avonwick, Near Totnes TQ9 7LR (South Brent [0364] 72224). A warm welcome awaits you at Hatchlands, a beautiful farmhouse in panoramic countryside close to beaches, Dartmoor, Torbay, Plymouth, Exeter. Riding, fishing, sailing, walking, golf, dry slope ski-ing all nearby. Furnished to a high standard, bedrooms have tea-making facilities; sun lounge to relax in; large sittingroom with wood-burning fire and colour TV. Every comfort provided with caring personal attention and plenty of mouth-watering farm-produced food. Children take delight in the calves, pony, dogs and ducks. Bed and Breakfast from £10; Evening Meal from £6. Reductions for children and weekly bookings. No smoking in farmhouse. Please telephone for brochure.

TOTNES. Mrs Susan Baker, Higher Torr Farm, East Allington, Totnes TQ9 7QH (0548 52278).

Spend your holiday on our family-run mixed farm set in a beautifully secluded position with pleasant garden and glorious views. Lovely walks in splendid isolation. Centrally situated within easy reach of beautiful beaches, the moors and many interesting places, including Dartmoor and Salcombe. Comfortable accommodation, homely atmosphere, good home cooking using our own and local produce. Personal attention, access to rooms at all times. Family room, en-suite facilities. Twin room with washbasin, single room; guest bathroom. Tea/coffee making facilities. Lounge with colour TV. Mid-week bookings accepted. Tourist Board listed. Special weekly half board rates. Bed and Breakfast from £11.50; Dinner by arrangement. Reductions for children.

TOTNES. Mrs Anne Barons, Charford Farm, Avonwick, Totnes TQ9 7LT (South Brent [03647] 3263). Working farm, join in. A warm and friendly welcome awaits you at this lovely old farmhouse on a 250 acre dairy, sheep and arable farm where visitors are free to roam.

Central for coast, Dartmoor, Plymouth and Torbay; within easy reach of many tourist attractions. Family, double and twin-bedded rooms all with washbasins and tea-making facilities. Bathroom and separate toilet; diningroom and lounge with colour TV. Home from home comfort in a relaxed, informal atmosphere. Children are very welcome at reduced rates. Cot, high chair and babysitting available, also children's ponies. Open Easter to October for Evening Meal, Bed and Breakfast or Bed and Breakfast only. Please telephone or write for terms and brochure.

TOTNES/KINGSBRIDGE/DARTMOUTH. Mrs H. Reeve, Stanborough Farm, Halwell, Totnes TQ9 7JG (Gara Bridge [054 882] 306). Working farm, join in.

DARTMOUTH

Stanborough Farm is a 140-acre dairy farm ideally situated for the above towns (6 miles to each), beaches, Dartmoor, National Trust properties, other tourist attractions plus rolling countryside. The farmhouse has two rooms that can be double, twin-bedded or family. Each has washbasin and tea/coffee making facilities. Guest bathroom, lounge with colour TV. Garden area, parking facilities. Children welcome, pets outdoors. Two country pubs quarter of a mile either side of farm, serving good food. Come rain or shine you will find something enjoyable to do. Find us on the map! Dinner, Bed and Breakfast or just Bed and Breakfast. Good home cooking and baking. Please ring or write for details.

WINKLEIGH. June Western, Middlecott Farm, Broad Woodkelly, Winkleigh EX19 8DZ (0837 83381). 🐾🐾 The real farmhouse accommodation offered at Middlecott Farm, in the heart of rural Devon, will guarantee you a relaxing holiday away from the hurly-burly of everyday life. To see Devon at its best come and sample the delights of the unspoilt countryside, walk on Dartmoor, visit nearby fishery and cider factory, enjoy our delicious food. Children welcome. Dogs by arrangement. Open all year excluding Christmas and New Year. Bed and Breakfast from £12; Bed, Breakfast and Evening Meal from £18. Weekly terms: Bed, Breakfast and Evening Meal £99.

WOOLACOMBE. Mr David Ellis, Crossways Hotel, The Seafront, Woolacombe EX34 7DJ (Woolacombe [0271] 870395). ♥ ♥ ♥ Homely, family-run, licensed hotel, beautifully situated, overlooking Combesgate beach and the pretty Combesgate Valley, and surrounded by National Trust land. Bathing and surfing from the hotel. Well situated for golf courses, horse riding and many beautiful walks. All bedrooms recently completely refurbished to a very high standard, many en-suite, or with showers; all with colour TV and tea/coffee making facilities. Centrally heated. Menu choice for evening dinner and breakfast, and a varied choice of bar snacks available at lunchtime. Children and pets welcome. Many of our guests return year after year. Why not come and see for yourself? Free on-site parking. Children half price or FREE. AA/RAC one star.

WOOLACOMBE. William and Ruby Seymour, Gull Rock, Mortehoe, Woolacombe EX34 7EA (Woolacombe [0271] 870534). ♥ ♥ Gull Rock is a delightful detached Edwardian house quietly set amidst National Trust land, with gardens adjoining some of the most spectacular coastal and inland walks, including the 550 mile coastal path. Direct access can be gained to the sandy beaches of Barricane and Woolacombe. Delightful views of Baggy Point, Hartland Lighthouse and Lundy Island can be enjoyed from the sun terrace. Five en-suite family/double rooms with sea and country views. Excellent food. Tea/coffee making facilities in all rooms. Large bar, separate guest lounge (non-smoking) both having superb sea views. Dogs by arrangement. Central heating. Private car parking. Fire Certificate. Open all year. Bed and Breakfast from £16.50–£17.50; Dinner, Bed and Breakfast from £19–£20. Weekly terms from £125–£130, depending on season.

WOOLACOMBE. John and Jose Rolfe, Combe Ridge Hotel, The Esplanade, Woolacombe EX34 7DJ (Woolacombe [0271] 870321). ♥ ♥ You are assured of a warm welcome and a happy stay at this friendly caring hotel. Beautifully situated with superb views of the bay and picturesque coastline. Beach and spectacular coastal walks start at the front gate. You can relax in cosy rooms, many en-suite, all with colour TV and tea/coffee making facilities. We prepare quality traditional food. Intimate diningroom and lounge enjoy beautiful sea views. Relax, unwind, we do everything possible to make your holiday especially happy. AA listed. RAC acclaimed. Special offer for pensioners early and late season. Write or telephone for brochure and tariff.

HELP IMPROVE BRITISH TOURIST STANDARDS

You are choosing holiday accommodation from our very popular FHG Publications. Whether it be a hotel, guest house, farmhouse or self-catering accommodation, we think you will find it hospitable, comfortable and clean, and your host and hostess friendly and helpful. Why not write and tell us about it?

As a recognition of the generally well-run and excellent holiday accommodation reviewed in our publications, we at FHG Publications Ltd. present a diploma to proprietors who receive the highest recommendation from their guests who are also readers of our Guides. If you care to write to us praising the holiday you have booked through FHG Publications Ltd. – whether this be board, self-catering accommodation, a sporting or a caravan holiday, what you say will be evaluated and the proprietors who reach our final list will be contacted.

The winning proprietor will receive an attractive framed diploma to display on his premises as recognition of a high standard of comfort, amenity and hospitality. FHG Publications Ltd. offer this diploma as a contribution towards the improvement of standards in tourist accommodation in Britain. Help your excellent host or hostess to win it!

FHG DIPLOMA

We nominate ....

....

Because ....

Name ....

Address ....

.... Telephone No. ....

WOOLACOMBE. Tom and Win Cooper, Seawards, Beach Road, Woolacombe EX34 7AD (Woolacombe [0271] 870249).

Well-appointed guest house, hillside situation, facing south and west. Magnificent views across fields and valley to the beach, three-quarters of a mile away. Here you will find friendly informality, combined with high standard of totally home-cooked food, well presented. Full English Breakfast and four-course Evening Dinner. Residential Licence. Moderate charges (from £118) reflect the fact that Seawards is family-run and attracts no VAT. Children five to ten are welcome, at half-price; 11 to 15 years 75 per cent. Three miles sand and Atlantic breakers for surf-riding. Lovely villages and beautiful countryside, including Exmoor, within reach. Plenty of walking for the energetic.

WOOLACOMBE. Mr and Mrs E.W. and R.G. Adey, "Caertref," Beach Road, Woolacombe EX34 7BT (Woolacombe [0271] 870361).

👑👑👑 "Caertref" is two minutes from Woolacombe's glorious beach, one of the most beautiful in North Devon, surrounded by unspoilt National Trust protected landscape. The main aim of the proprietors is to give each guest an enjoyable holiday, in relaxed friendly atmosphere. Accommodation comprises large, comfortable lounge, colour TV; cosy bar, residential licence; hot and cold, shaver points and tea/coffee facilities in all bedrooms, seven double (three en-suite), two twin (one en-suite), one single and three family (three en-suite); bathroom plus two toilets; one shower room; sitting and diningroom. Full central heating. Cot, high chair and reduced rates for children. Pets taken by arrangement. Parking. Fire certificate held. Bed and Breakfast (Evening Meal optional). Open all year. SAE please for terms. RAC listed — acclaimed award.

WORLINGTON. Derek and Rosemary Webber, Hensley Farm, Worlington, Crediton EX17 4TG (Tiverton [0884] 860346). Working farm, join in.

A friendly farming family offers accommodation in their thatched farmhouse near a picturesque country village overlooking one of the prettiest valleys in Devon. A 180 acre dairy and sheep farm which extends to the river where there are superb walks. Ideal centre for Exmoor, Dartmoor and North Coast beaches. Large lawns, pony for children. Large bedrooms with washbasins, colour TV. Diningroom; lounge. Delicious food using local and home grown produce. Send for details.

YELVERTON. Mrs Esme Wills, Callisham Farm, Meavy PL20 6PS (0822 853901). Working farm, join in. Nestled in the valley of Meavy in the south west corner of the Dartmoor National Park is a family-run mixed hill farm. Lovaton Brook and Meavy River run through the wooded farmland reaching to the wild yet beautiful moor. This charming old farmhouse, once owned by Sir Francis Drake, with open fireplaces, oak beams and an abundance of original stripped pine offers guest lounge, colour TV, comfortable bedrooms with washbasins, heating, shaver points and electric blankets. Generous servings of home cooked food, morning tea, evening beverages. Evening Meal by arrangement. The historic city of Plymouth with its busy ferry port is 10 miles away. Activities nearby. Please telephone for enquiries. ETB registered.

DORSET

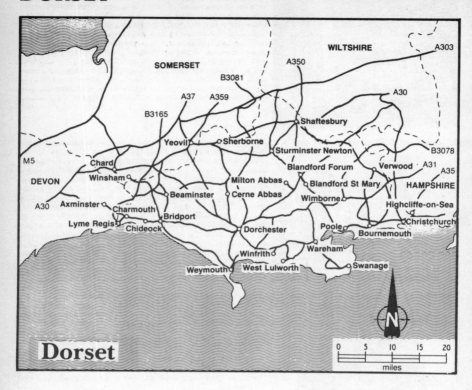

Dorset

BEAMINSTER. Mrs Jackie Spooncer, Lewesdon Farm, Stoke Abbott, Beaminster DT8 3JZ (Broadwindsor [0308] 68270). ♛ ♛ Lewesdon Farm is situated in an area of outstanding natural beauty, five miles from Bridport, off a private road off the B3162. We offer warm comfortable accommodation in double or twin-bedded rooms with washbasins and shower, tea-making equipment and colour TV. This is a superb location for walking, bird watching or just relaxing with an abundance of wildlife and extensive conservation lakes. Good home-cooked food served in pleasant dining room. Open all year. Bed and Breakfast from £14, Bed, Breakfast and Evening Meal from £18. Reduced rates for children. Non-smokers please. Also luxury self-catering barn conversion sleeping six, designed with the disabled in mind.

BEAMINSTER. Mrs Barbara Hedditch, Silverhay Farm, Netherhay, Drimpton, Beaminster DT8 3RH (Broadwindsor [0308] 68423). Working farm. Our comfortable farmhouse is on the edge of a quiet village. Family, double and twin bedded rooms. Large lounge/diningroom with colour TV. Central heating. Good farmhouse cooking using own produce when possible. Children welcome at reduced rates. Large garden, beautiful views. Places of interest include Cricket St. Thomas Wildlife Park, Parnham House and Abbotsbury Swannery and Gardens. Horse riding, golf and fishing within easy reach. Numerous beaches. Bed and Breakfast with Evening Meal or Bed and Breakfast only. Sorry, no pets. Car essential. A warm friendly welcome is given to everyone. SAE for details or phone.

BLANDFORD. Patricia and John Benjafield, Farnham Farm House, Farnham, Blandford DT11 8DG

(0725 516254). Working farm. Set in three-quarters of an acre of garden, with swimming pool, is this 19th century farmhouse, part of a 350-acre cereal farm situated in the heart of Cranborne Chase. Ideal touring centre, being within easy reach of the coast and many other places of interest. Bed and Breakfast only is provided all year round, but numerous inns in the surrounding area all serve excellent food. Guests are accommodated in two double and one family bedrooms (all with washbasins); bathroom, two toilets; sittingroom-cum-diningroom. Cosy log fires provided in winter months. Children welcome, cot, high chair and babysitting available. Pets accepted free of charge. Car essential — unlimited parking. English Tourist Board listed. Bed and Breakfast from £15 with reductions for children under 12 years.

BLANDFORD FORUM. Mr and Mrs D.N. Cross, Rivermead Farm, Childe Okeford, Blandford DT11

8HB (0258 860293). ♥♥ Working farm, join in. 60 acres grass and horticulture in beautiful North Dorset countryside. Explore Hardy's country, National Trust houses and the Purbeck coast. Family and twin rooms, both with washbasins, razor points, TV and tea/coffee making facilities; separate bathroom and shower; comfortable sittingrooms with log fires. Non-smokers preferred. Breeding Shires, DIY livery, safe good hacking, own ponies welcome for long or short stays; coarse fishing; organic horticulture, harvesting help welcomed. Farmhouse offers Bed and Breakfast for long or short stays in friendly family atmosphere, no Evening Meal (sorry), but good inns within walking distance. Terms from £12 per night. Ample parking.

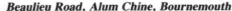

BOURNEMOUTH. Mrs Annie Habgood, Northover Hotel, 10 Earle Road, Alum Chine, Bournemouth

BH4 8JQ (Bournemouth [0202] 767349). ♥♥♥ *Commended.* OLD-FASHIONED COURTESY AWAITS YOU AT THE NORTHOVER HOTEL situated facing Alum Chine, 400 yards from sea and sandy beaches and only 20 minutes' walk from Bournemouth Pier. Near bus routes for town centre where there is superb shopping and all types of entertainment. The New Forest, Purbeck Hills and lovely Dorset and Hampshire countryside within easy reach. Choice of double, single or family rooms with double or twin beds, fitted carpets, hot and cold water and shaver points; tea/coffee making facilities FREE; most rooms with en-suite facilities. Attractive lounge, colour TV; spacious diningroom serving varied and excellent food. Residential licence. Central heating. Under personal supervision of proprietors, the hotel is open Easter to October for Bed and Breakfast from £16, Dinner, Bed and Breakfast from £22. Weekly from £120. Mid-week bookings accepted. Special rates for Senior Citizens early and late season. Children and pets welcome. Ample parking. Off season bargain breaks. Our aim is to make you want to return. AA/RAC listed. AWARDED FHG DIPLOMA 1988/89 — ONLY FIVE AWARDED TO HOTELS IN ENGLAND!

FARM GUEST HOUSE

This farm/guest house, built in Victorian times, set in ten acres of pastures and woods, bordered by streams, lies in beautiful peaceful surroundings, only five miles from Charmouth's unspoilt beach with its store of fossils. The house has a

comfortable, relaxed and informal atmosphere and really good food is a speciality, including home made bread, jams, farm butter etc. The gardens provide fresh fruit and vegetables. Swimming pool in walled garden. Car essential. Ample parking space provided. Four double and six family rooms, most en-suite. Five bathrooms. Colour TV in all bedrooms. Comfortable lounge. Cots, high chairs and babysitting provided. Children can play safely in fields and large indoor games room. Part of house suitable for disabled guests. Central heating, log fires. Evening Dinner, Bed and Breakfast. Tea/coffee making facilities in all rooms. Reductions for children. Pets welcomed. Riding nearby. Open all year. Special "off season" rates.

TERRY & TRICIA SHAKESHAFT, MARSHWOOD MANOR
Bridport, Dorset DT6 5NS

TOURIST BOARD ♥♥♥
Tel: Broadwindsor (0308) 68442 and 68825
AA LISTED

See also Colour Display Advertisement **BRIDPORT. Terry and Tricia Shakeshaft, Marshwood Manor, Bridport DT6 5NS (Broadwindsor [0308] 68442 and 68825).** ♥♥♥ Farm/guest house built in Victorian times, set in 10 acres of pasture and woods and bordered by streams. It lies in beautiful surroundings only five miles from Charmouth's unspoilt beach. Comfortable, relaxed, informal atmosphere with good food a speciality. Car essential, ample parking. Four double, six family rooms, most en-suite; colour TV in all bedrooms. Comfortable lounge. Cots, high chairs, babysitting provided. Large indoor games room. Central heating, log fires. Part of house suitable for disabled guests. Pets welcome. Open all year. Special off season rates. AA Listed.

BRIDPORT. Mrs L.M. Hutchings, Dunster Farm, Broadoak, Bridport DT6 5NR (Bridport [0308] 24626). Working farm, join in. 17th century thatched farmhouse amidst beautiful, peaceful surroundings in the Marshwood Vale. Ideal touring centre for Lyme Regis, Charmouth and West Bay. Swimming, fishing, horse riding etc, five miles. The farm consists of dairy cows, calves, beef, pigs, sheep and chickens. Guests are welcome to join in farm activities. One double and one family room; bathroom, toilet; sittingroom with TV, diningroom. Hot/cold in all rooms. Open wood fire. Cot, high chair, babysitting. Car essential. Sorry, no pets. Open Easter to October. Evening Dinner, Bed and Breakfast or Bed and Breakfast only. Food mostly home produced including own meat and fresh garden vegetables. SAE, please for terms. Prompt reply. Reductions for children.

DORSET – RURAL SPLENDOUR!

Absorbing old towns like Dorchester and Shaftesbury, surrounded by panoramic vales, undulating chalklands and peaceful villages contribute to Dorset's great appeal. Included in any tourist's itinerary should be, Abbotsbury Village and Swannery, Ackling Dyke Roman road, Brownsea Island, Lulworth Cove and, of course, the many locations that constitute Hardy's Dorset.

BRIDPORT. Mrs D. Batten, Northay Farm, Wootton Fitzpaine, Bridport DT6 6NL (Charmouth [0297] 60481). Working farm. Northay Farm is a working farm situated in lovely peaceful countryside, away from it all but within easy motoring distance of the seaside. Charmouth three and a half miles, Lyme Regis six miles. A family farm with cows and sheep, and guests are able to wander around and see the animals. There is a homely atmosphere, farmhouse fare is served, own milk, cream, eggs and vegetables in season. There are two family rooms both with washbasins; bathroom, two toilets; sitting/diningroom. Evening Meal, Bed and Breakfast with reduced rates for children according to age (cot, high chair and babysitting also). Open May to September. Also six-berth self- catering caravan, fully equipped. Please send SAE for terms.

CERNE ABBAS. Mrs V.I. Willis, "Lampert's Cottage", Sydling St. Nicholas, Cerne Abbas DT2 9NU (Cerne Abbas [0300] 341659). Bed and Breakfast in unique 16th century thatched cottage in unspoilt village. The cottage has fields around and is bounded, front and back, by chalk streams. Accommodation consists of three prettily furnished, double bedrooms with dormer windows, set under the eaves, and breakfast is served in the diningroom which has an enormous inglenook fireplace and original beams. The village, situated in countryside made famous by Thomas Hardy in his novels, is an excellent touring centre and beaches are 30 minutes' drive. West Dorset is ideal walking country with footpaths over chalk hills and through hidden valleys and is perfect for those wishing peace and quiet. Open all year. Terms on request.

CHARMOUTH. Mrs K.M. Baker, Dodpen Farm, Wootton Fitzpaine, Charmouth DT6 6NW (Hawkchurch [029-77] 372). Working farm, join in. This is a 70 acre farm situated on the southern slope of Dodpen Hill with tree plantations on all boundaries. The 16th century house is approached by a quarter of a mile farm road. Within easy distance of all resorts on the Dorset Coast including Charmouth (three miles) and Lyme Regis (six miles). Lovely walks; birdwatching, forest and coastal walks not far away. Deer, foxes, badgers, etc abound in this unspoilt area. Good farmhouse food is assured and log fires are blazing when needed. Radiators in all rooms, also electric kettles for drinks, flasks, etc. Three double bedrooms, two with washbasins; bathroom and toilet; dining/sittingroom. Colour TV. Car essential, parking. Open April to October for Evening Dinner, Bed and Breakfast. SAE for terms.

CORFE CASTLE near. Mrs Gillian Hole, Bradle Farmhouse, Bradle, Corfe Castle, Wareham BH20 5NU (Corfe Castle [0929] 480712). Working farm. The

farmhouse, built in 1862, is situated in the Purbeck Hills and lies in a valley between the villages of Kimmeridge and Church Knowle. The coast is two miles away with safe bathing and windsurfing on a selection of beaches, whilst the surrounding hills and cliffs offer spectacular views and walks. There is local pony trekking and evening entertainment in Bournemouth, Swanage and Wareham. A warm friendly atmosphere with good farmhouse cooking is assured and families are especially welcome on this 500-acre farm. Family/double twin rooms with two bathrooms; lounge with colour TV, diningroom with tea/coffee facilities. Open all year for Bed and Breakfast from £12, reductions for children. Evening Meals by arrangement with the local inn, with special weekly rate/children welcome. ETB Commended. Apply for brochure.

DORCHESTER. Mr and Mrs M.J. Deller, Churchview Guest House, Winterbourne Abbas, Dorchester DT2 9LS (Martinstown [0305] 889296). 🏵 🏵 🏵 This

300 year old guesthouse noted for its warm, friendly hospitality is set in a small village five miles west of Dorchester, in an ideal touring area. All bedrooms have tea-making facilities and full central heating. There are two lounges, one non-smoking; an attractive diningroom and well stocked bar. AA listed. Evening Meal, Bed and Breakfast from £21; Bed and Breakfast only from £14. Write or telephone for further details.

See also Colour Display Advertisement **DORCHESTER. Mrs C. Walford, Rectory House, Fore Street, Evershot, Dorchester DT2 0JW (Evershot [093-583] 273).** 🏵 🏵 🏵 *Commended.* Lovely 18th-century Rectory situated in the picturesque village of Evershot in the heart of Thomas Hardy countryside. Evershot has its own bakery, shops and village pub and is an ideal centre for visiting many places of interest and seaside resorts. Many beautiful walks can be taken and wonderful scenic views abound. Fishing, riding and sailing facilities are nearby. Rectory House offers the utmost comfort, with lovely centrally heated bedrooms both in the main house and in the recently converted stables, each with en-suite bathroom, tea/coffee making facilities and colour TV. In the guests' diningroom, the emphasis is on superb home cooking of fresh local produce to add to the enjoyment of your holiday. There is a separate lounge with log fire during the winter months. Open all year (except Christmas and New Year). Car not essential but there is parking. Bed and Breakfast from £150 weekly; Evening Dinner, Bed and Breakfast from £195 weekly. AA. Les Routiers.

DORCHESTER near. Mrs V. Fry, Foxholes Farm, Littlebredy, Dorchester DT2 9HJ (Longbredy [0308] 482395). A working farm set in a secluded valley along a farm track. Foxholes has a large milking herd plus chickens, sheep and pigs. Ideal for family holidays, with children especially welcome. Lovely walking country, five miles from the sea, through the beautiful Bride Valley. Central for Dorchester, Weymouth and Bridport. The farmhouse has five bedrooms with washbasins; guests' lounge; diningroom; bathroom and shower room. Coffee/tea making facilities in all bedrooms. Full central heating. Bed and Breakfast from £13 per night. Reduced rates for children. Evening Meal by arrangement. Pets welcome.

LULWORTH COVE. Mrs M. Hoblyn, Graybank Guest House, West Lulworth, Wareham BH20 5RL (West Lulworth [092941] 256). ♥♥ Period Guest House situated in beautiful country surroundings, five minutes from the sea at Lulworth Cove. Comfortably furnished bedrooms with washbasins, heating and tea/coffee making facilities. Lulworth is an ideal base for exploring the magnificent cliff scenery and delightful coves and bays. There are many famous beauty spots within easy reach. The coastal path is close by giving many walks over unspoilt countryside. Graybank Guest House offers every comfort with excellent food. There is a lounge and car park. Sorry, no children under four years. Bed and full English Breakfast from £13. Evening Meal (optional) £5.

LULWORTH COVE. Mr and Mrs J. Else, The Old Barn, West Lulworth, Wareham BH20 5RL (092-941) 305). The Old Barn is situated in a superb position with a glorious view of the rolling Dorset hills, yet only a few hundred yards from the famous beauty spot of Lulworth Cove. Choice of Bed and Breakfast and/or "Please Yourself" rooms (fully equipped for self-catering). Central heating. Fire Certificate. Large garden. Parking. Shops and sea nearby and wide choice of restaurants offering local specialities. Entertainment at Bournemouth (22 miles) and Weymouth (15 miles). Southern Tourist Board listed. Terms from £15. Details on request with SAE.

LYME REGIS. Mrs S.G. Taylor, Buckland Farm, Raymonds Hill, Near Axminster EX13 5SZ (0297 33222). Smallholding of five acres, three miles from Lyme Regis and Charmouth. Children, Senior Citizens all welcome. Bed and Full English Breakfast. Accommodation on ground floor. We are situated back off the A35 in quiet and unspoilt surroundings, ideal for guests to relax or stroll. Three family bedrooms, one double, all with TV, washbasin and tea/coffee making facilities. Lounge with colour TV and log fire if needed. Diningroom with separate tables. Bathroom, shower in bath, WC, plus separate WC. Plenty of good food with free range eggs. Cot and high chair available. Guests welcome to stay in if wet. Full English Breakfast served. Friendly pub within two minutes' walk for evening meals. Also Caravan available, sleeping six — all mains facilities, Calor gas cooker and water. Send SAE for details and terms.

OSMINGTON. Mrs Joyce Norman, Dingle Dell, Osmington, Near Weymouth DT3 6EW (Preston (Dorset) [0305] 832378). Not a farm, but situated down a lane on the fringe of the picturesque village of Osmington, in the centre of farming country, with safe bridle-ways and footpaths right by the gate a beautiful rural setting with the coast only one and a half miles away. This family home of mellow local stone is set in a large garden full of roses and apple trees. The two spacious, attractively furnished bedrooms, with washbasins and tea-making facilities, have views over garden and fields and the famous "White Horse" on the nearby hill. Regret, no pets. This is a quiet corner of Hardy's Wessex, a peaceful and friendly base for exploring the beautiful Dorset countryside whether by car, on foot or on horseback. Open March to October. Bed and Breakfast from £12.50. Car essential, parking. ETB Listed.

SHERBORNE near. Mrs Ann Osmond, Sunnyside Farm, Holnest, Hermitage, Near Sherborne DT9 6HA (Holnest [096-321] 276). Working farm. A 50-acre dairy farm with various farm pets to interest children. The cosy farmhouse welcomes guests all year round. Good farmhouse cooking served in the dining room with separate tables. Good riding school and fresh water fishing nearby. The historic town of Sherborne with its Abbey and Castle, and the pretty village of Cerne Abbas within easy reach. All guests are assured of a warm welcome in this homely atmosphere. Log fires on chilly evenings. Outdoor amusements for the children in the large garden with spacious lawns. Accommodation consists of one double (twin-bedded), one single, one family bedrooms all with washbasins and shaving points; bathroom, toilet; sitting room with TV. Children welcome at reduced rates. Babysitting arranged. Sorry, no pets. Car essential, parking. Bed and Breakfast. Evening meal by arrangement. Also 32-foot modern mobile home available. Terms on request. SAE, please.

FUN FOR ALL THE FAMILY IN DORSET

Brownsea Island, Poole Harbour; *Abbotsbury Swannery & Gardens*, near Dorchester; *Merley Tropical Bird Gardens*, near Poole; *Worldwide Butterflies*, Compton House, near Sherborne; *Poole Park*, Poole; *Tuckton Leisure Park*, Stour Road, Christchurch; *Wimborne Model Town*, West Row, Wimborne Minster; *The Model Village*, Corfe Castle; *The Tank Museum*, Bovington Camp, near Wareham; *Barney's Fossil & Country Life Exhibition*, Charmouth, near Bridport.

SHERBORNE. Mrs J. Mayo, Almshouse Farm, Hermitage, Sherborne DT9 6HA (Holnest [096-321]

296). Working farm, join in. ♥♥ Relax and get away from it all on this friendly family-run dairy farm. The attractive stone-built house, overlooking the unspoilt countryside of the Blackmore Vale, was restored from a monastery in 1849. Six miles from Sherborne, with its interesting castle and abbey, one mile off the A352. Good English food and personal attention offered. Open from March to October. Accommodation comprises three double bedrooms, all with washbasins; bathroom and toilet, shower and toilet; diningroom with separate tables and large inglenook fireplace; comfortable lounge with TV and log fires. Some central heating also. Car advisable, parking. Sorry, no dogs. AA Listed. Bed and Breakfast. SAE please for terms.

STALBRIDGE. Mrs A. Wallis, Spire Hill Farm, Stalbridge, Sturminster Newton DT10 2SG (0963 62136). Spire Hill is set in the beautiful Blackmore Vale, just over the Dorset/Somerset border. Surrounded by many interesting and historic towns including Sherborne and Shaftesbury. We offer comfortable accommodation for either a family or couple; bathroom; diningroom. Hot/cold washbasins, colour TV. Cot, high chair and babysitting available. Central heating. Ample parking. Easy to find on A357 between the villages of Stalbridge and Lydlinch. Open 99 days per year, phone for availability. Bed and Breakfast from £12.50. Reductions for children. WCTB listed.

STURMINSTER NEWTON. Mrs Sheila Martin, Moorcourt Farm, Moorside, Marnhull, Sturminster

Newton DT10 1HH (Marnhull [0258] 820271). Working farm. Marnhull is situated four miles from Sturminster Newton, five from Shaftesbury. New Forest and coast within 28 miles. This is a modern dairy farm of 100 acres lying in the Blackmore Vale in Hardy country. Visitors are welcome to watch the farm activities and laze in the large garden. There is a friendly atmosphere created "down on the farm". Accommodation comprises one large room with double bed; two double bedrooms (one with twin beds, one with double bed), with washbasins; shower room with sink and toilet; bathroom, toilet. Sittingroom with colour TV; diningroom. Children over 10 only. Sorry, no pets. Car essential, ample parking. Some Evening Meals provided. Bed and Breakfast £12 to £13. Weekly lets only in peak season. Open April to October. Further details on request.

STURMINSTER NEWTON. Mrs Thea Pond-Jones, Old Post Office, Hinton St. Mary, Sturminster

Newton DT10 1NG (Sturminster Newton [0258] 72366). The Old Post Office is a cosy and comfortable guest house near the interesting market town of Sturminster Newton. Situated in the beautiful Blackmore Vale, it is an ideal centre for exploring the many picturesque villages and seaside towns that Dorset has to offer. We appreciate the importance of holidays and make every effort to ensure you have a really enjoyable stay. Facilities for hot drinks in all bedrooms, access at all times, good home cooking. One family, two double rooms, with washbasins; guests' lounge with colour TV. Bed and Breakfast from £11.50; Evening Meals (optional) £6.50. Reductions for weekly bookings. Southern Tourist Board listed — commended.

SWANAGE. Mrs Justine Pike, Downshay Farm, Haycrafts Lane, Harmans Cross, Swanage BH19 3EB (0929 480316). Downshay Farm is a working dairy farm on beautiful Isle of Purbeck, situated midway between Corfe Castle and Swanage, half a mile from A351. Ideal for walking coastal path. Sandy beaches nearby at Studland and Swanage. Within walking distance of station on Isle of Purbeck steam railway. One family room with TV and one double room, both with washbasins. Shower room and bathroom. Sittingroom with TV and diningroom with tea/coffee making facilities. Ample car parking. Large garden for guests' use. Bed and Breakfast only. Children are welcome, cot provided on request. Babysitting service available.

WAREHAM. Mr and Mrs D.H. Gegg, "Glen Ness", 1 The Merrows, Off St Helens Road, Sandford, Wareham BH20 7AX (0929 552313). A warm welcome is guaranteed at "Glen Ness", a small friendly guest house. The cedar/stone bungalow is set in secluded surroundings and guests are greeted with a cup of tea. Iris and Doug appreciate the importance of holidays and make every effort to ensure you have a really enjoyable stay. All bedrooms have fitted washbasins, razor points and interior sprung mattresses. Bathroom with separate shower, two toilets. Morning tea, evening beverages can be provided on request. Safe off-road parking. It makes an ideal central base for exploring Dorset and there is a bus service to Rockley Sands, Poole, Bournemouth, Southampton, Dorchester, Weymouth, Corfe Castle, Studland Bay and Swanage. Colour TV in dining/sitting room. Access at all times. Tourist Board registered. Bed and full traditional Breakfast. Choice of several local inns and restaurants for varied evening meals close by.

Terms quoted in this publication may be subject to increase if rises in costs necessitate

WEST BAY. Mr and Mrs G.M. Rice and Mr and Mrs D.R. Haddon, Durbeyfield Guest House, West Bay, Bridport DT6 4EL (Bridport [0308] 23307).

"Durbeyfield", a Georgian guest house situated near the small harbour of West Bay and the famous Chesil Beach, is surrounded by beautiful scenery, coastal and old world villages. At West Bay there are fishing trips, bathing, fishing from piers and an 18-hole golf course situated on the cliff top. The proprietors pride themselves on hospitality and good home cooking. Four double, two single and two family bedrooms, all with washbasins; bathroom, shower, two toilets; sittingroom and diningroom. Colour TV. Fire Certificate held. Pets allowed. Children welcome, cot, high chair and babysitting; reduced rates. Open all year for Evening Meal, Bed and Breakfast or Bed and Breakfast only. Reductions for Senior Citizens — low season.

WEST LULWORTH. Mr and Mrs T.H. Williams, Shirley Hotel, West Lulworth, Wareham BH20 5RL (West Lulworth [092-941] 358). ♔♔♔ Comfortable,

small, friendly hotel of 19 bedrooms, all en-suite, with colour TV, radio, bedside lights, tea-making facilities and direct-dial telephones. Situated in a Conservation Area, in the village of West Lulworth, half a mile from the famous Lulworth Cove, with spectacular scenery and cliff walks, pleasure and fishing trips, proximity to Bournemouth (shopping; entertainment); sandy beaches (16 miles); local shingle beaches; many places of interest. Light, airy diningroom with bar; excellent cuisine, varied menu prepared by hosts and served by friendly staff. Lounge with card tables, pool table and reading area. Coin-op laundry. Car park. Lovely swimming pool and patio; lunchtime snacks on large lawn adjacent. Children welcome, cot, high chair, baby listening by arrangement, reduced rates. Pets allowed. Brochure available on request giving full details of this licensed, family-run hotel. Member of Southern Tourist Board. RAC/AA one star. Les Routiers. Open March to November. Terms approximately £157 to £192 per person (half board) per week.

WEYMOUTH. Mrs S. Foot, West Shilvinghampton Farm, Portesham, Weymouth DT3 4HL (Abbotsbury [0305] 871493). An old manor house set in picturesque and unspoiled Waddon Vale. A family run farm of arable land and beef cattle, amid peaceful countryside, yet within five miles of scenic coastline and sandy beaches, plus plenty of historic places to visit. Mr and Mrs Foot aim to provide a comfortable, homely atmosphere with emphasis on home cooking. Two double and two family rooms all with washbasins; bathroom and toilet; sittingroom with colour TV. Cot, high chair and babysitting available. Open Easter to end of September. Bed and Breakfast/Evening Meal. Regret no pets. Car essential. SAE, please, for further details.

WIMBORNE. Mrs D. Gent, Homeacres, Homelands Farm, Three Legged Cross, Wimborne BH21 6QZ (Verwood [0202] 822422). ♔♔ Working farm, join in. Homeacres is ideally situated for visiting the many

local attractions. There are miles of sandy beaches, water sports and boat trips. The local market towns where a variety of animals change hands are of great interest, and there is a wealth of eating places to tempt the most discerning palate. There are also many historic places and lovely gardens to explore, and walks through the forests for country lovers. Homeacres offers large family rooms, with central heating, hot and cold water, shaver points and tea/coffee making facilities, and a TV lounge for visitors' exclusive use. Open all year. Dogs allowed with certain restrictions. Terms: En-suite rooms from £15 per night, £98 per week; rooms with shared bathroom from £12 per night, £77 per week; one night supplement £1.50. Reductions for children. AA Listed. SAE please for brochure.

DURHAM

BARNARD CASTLE. Mrs R.M. Lowson, "West Roods", West Roods Farm, Boldron, Barnard Castle DL12 9SW (Teesdale [0833] 690116). ♛♛♛ Working farm, join in. A warm welcome awaits you in the Land of the Prince Bishops in Teesdale. Over 100 years old, West Roods nestles in the Pennine Hills. Dairy Farm (no bull) blending tourism with farm life. Water Dowsing and Art Activity Holidays available (as reported in "Tit Bits", May 1988 and "Northern Life", Tyne Tees TV, also in "Home and Freezer Digest" 1989). One single, one double and family room both with en-suites. All bedrooms with washbasins and tea-making facilities, hairdryer. Bathroom with shower, three toilets. Laundry facilities on request. AA/RAC listed. Weekly terms from £80 for Bed and Breakfast. Child reductions. Touring caravan/camping site with facilities. Solar/electric shower. Travel west on A66, third farm on right (north) from Boldron T junction, two and a half miles east of Bowes. SAE for further details.

BURNOPFIELD. Mrs Maureen Tulip, Lintz Hall Farm, Burnopfield, Newcastle-upon-Tyne NE16 6AS (0207 70233). Working farm. Lintz Hall Farm offers quality accommodation at affordable prices. Situated in the picturesque Derwent Valley, peacocks with their spectacular courtship displays roam the grounds freely. Enjoy the beauty of the countryside, yet be only minutes from the historic cities of Durham and Newcastle. The Metro Centre, Europe's largest shopping and leisure complex, and Beamish Museum are close by. Northumbrian coast within easy reach. Several local inns provide excellent food. Golf, horse riding and country walks also nearby. Our spacious rooms are tastefully decorated; all have colour TV, heating, tea/coffee making and washbasins. Bed and Breakfast from £15. Reduced child rate available. Member of Northumbria Tourist Board.

WHEN MAKING ENQUIRIES PLEASE MENTION
FARM HOLIDAY GUIDES

CONSETT. Mrs L. Lawson, Bee Cottage Farm, Castleside, Consett DH8 9HW (0207 508224). A working farm in lovely surroundings with unspoilt views, situated one and a half miles west A68 between Tow Law and Castleside. Visitors are invited to participate in all farm activities — feeding calves, milking goats, bottle feeding lambs, etc. Quiet country walks. Fire Certificate. Ideally located for Beamish Museum, Metro Centre, Durham Cathedral or a break on a journey between England and Scotland. Bed and Breakfast from £14 to £20; Evening Meal from £8.50. Self catering also available.

MIDDLETON IN TEESDALE. Mrs Mary Body, Greengates, Lunedale, Middleton in Teesdale DL12 0NV (Teesdale [0833] 40447). Greengates, a stone built farmhouse on the B6276 road to Brough and the Lake District, has a commanding view over the lower dale and Grassholm Reservoir. The area is ideal for walkers with fishing, sailing and pony trekking facilities available nearby. Accommodation comprises two double and one twin bedrooms, all with washbasins and tea-making facilities. Guest lounge with colour TV and open fire, separate diningroom. Emphasis is placed upon comfort with good plain cooking using the best local produce and free range eggs. Open all year. Ample car parking facilities. Northumbria Tourist Board listed. Bed and Breakfast from £11; Bed, Breakfast and Evening Meal from £17. Reductions for children.

MIDDLETON-IN-TEESDALE. Mrs S.E. Parmley, Snaisgill Farm, Middleton-in-Teesdale, Barnard Castle DL12 0RP (0833 40343). Working farm, join in. Our smallholding is situated in beautiful scenic and peaceful countryside, one mile from Middleton-in-Teesdale. Ideal base for walking or touring the Dales. Accommodation is offered in two double bedrooms. Large comfortable lounge/diner with colour TV. Tea and coffee on request. Call in and enjoy our relaxed atmosphere, personal attention and farmhouse fare. Sorry, no pets. Bed and Breakfast from £10.50. Tourist Board listed.

MIDDLETON-IN-TEESDALE. Mrs A.M. Sayer, Grassholme Farm, Lunedale, Middleton-in-Teesdale, Barnard Castle DL12 0PR (Teesdale [0833] 40494). Working farm. A warm welcome awaits you at our family run farm, with beef cattle and Swaledale sheep. Set in Lunedale, three miles from Middleton-in-Teesdale off the B6276 Brough road. The farm overlooks Grassholme reservoir which is stocked with Rainbow trout. Grassholme is part of the Earl of Strathmore's estate and has the Pennine Way route crossing the farm yard. This makes Grassholme an ideal base for walking. There is also horse riding nearby. Accommodation is in one double and one twin room. Children are welcome. Good plain farmhouse cooking and baking is offered. Evening Meal with home produced beef and lamb, full English breakfast with free range eggs. Open Easter to October. Bed and Breakfast from £10; Evening Meal £4.75.

MIDDLETON-IN-TEESDALE. Mrs June Dent, Wythes Hill Farm, Lunedale, Middleton-in-Teesdale,

Barnard Castle DL12 0NX (Teesdale [0833] 40349). Working farm, join in. Friendliness and comfort are assured at Wythes Hill, a 500 acre hill farm with sheep and suckler herd of beef cattle. Situated right on the Pennine Way route it has commanding views of the surrounding hills and valley of reservoirs. Trout fishing and sailing available. Pony trekking nearby. An area abounding in history with Hadrian's Wall, many castles and the Bowes Museum to visit and only an hour's drive to the Lake District. Guests will enjoy good plain cooking including free range eggs and home produced meat. Accommodation in one double room, one twin room with washbasin and one family room with washbasin, all rooms with tea/coffee making facilities; bathroom, shower room, two toilets; diningroom; sittingroom with colour TV. Children welcome, cot, high chair, babysitting provided. Car essential — parking. Evening Meal, Bed and Breakfast from £18; Bed and Breakfast from £12; Evening Meal from £6. Reductions for children. Open Easter to October. ETB Listed.

DURHAM – MOORS, VALLEYS AND INDUSTRY!

At its western extent Durham embraces the moors and valleys of the Pennines but otherwise this is an industrial county, with a strong coal mining tradition. Places worth a visit include Barnard Castle, the Upper Teesdale Valley, the gothic church at Brancepeth and the farm and industrial museum at Beamish.

ESSEX

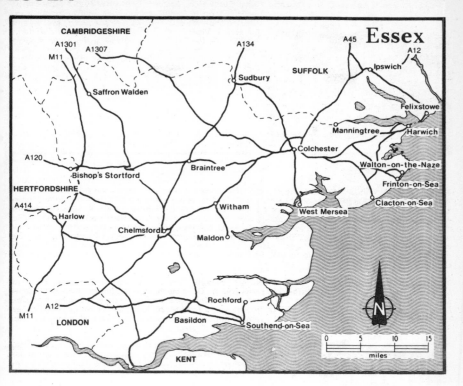

COLCHESTER. Mrs Jean Freeman, May's Barn Farm, May's Lane, Off Long Road West, Dedham, Colchester CO7 6EW (0206 323191). ♛♛ May's Barn Farm is situated in the heart of Constable country, a quarter of a mile off the road, with outstanding views of beautiful Dedham Vale. You can be sure of peace and tranquillity in the comfortable farmhouse and the sittingroom with log fire is for the use of guests. The large, well appointed bedrooms each have television and tea/coffee making facilities and en-suite or private bathrooms. All day access. Ideal touring centre for East Anglia. Substantial well cooked breakfast. Children over 10 years welcome. No pets. Open all year except Christmas. Bed and Breakfast from £15 per person.

COLCHESTER. Mrs A.G. Daniels, Morants, Colchester Road, Great Bromley, Colchester CO7 7TN (Colchester [0206] 230240). ♛♛ Within easy reach of England's first recorded town of Colchester (four miles), steeped in history, Constable Country and famous village of Dedham (four miles), the popular and famous seaside resorts of Walton, Clacton and Frinton (12 miles). Morants is a former farmhouse and part of it is 15th-century, set back from the road in 11 acres of parkland. There is a hard tennis court. Golf, sailing and riding facilities all close by. Central heating. Open Easter to October. Bed and Breakfast from £14 per person.

COLCHESTER. Mrs Jill Todd, Seven Arches Farm, Chitts Hill, Lexden, Colchester CO3 5SX (Colchester [0206] 574896). Working farm. Georgian

farmhouse set in large garden close to the ancient town of Colchester. The farm extends to 100 acres and supports both arable crops and cattle. Private fishing rights on the River Colne, which runs past the farmhouse. This is a good location for visits to North Essex, Dedham and the Stour Valley which are famous for having been immortalised in the works of John Constable, the landscape painter. Children welcome. Pets welcome. Open all year. Bed and Breakfast from £16; Evening Meal from £5. Twin room £30.

MARGARET RODING. Mrs Joyce Matthews, Greys, Ongar Road, Margaret Roding, Near Great Dunmow CM6 1QR (024531 509). Comfortable country

Bed and Breakfast. Formerly two cottages "Greys" is pleasantly situated on family farm — arable and sheep — at a little distance from main buildings. Just off the A1060 Bishops Stortford/Chelmsford road; by telephone box in village. Easy journeying London, Cambridge, coast etc. Ideal for quiet breaks and exploring. Beamed throughout and with large garden. Good breakfasts, tea and coffee always available. Children over 10 years. No smoking. Two double rooms and one with twin beds. From £13 per person. Listed by the AA and Tourist Board. Open most of the year.

ONGAR. Mrs Joyce Withey, "Bumbles", Moreton Road, Ongar CM5 0EZ (0277 362695). Working farm. A warm welcome awaits you at "Bumbles". This large

cottage, built in 1700s, has inglenook and oak beams, and is now run as a smallholding. Very comfortable with guests' lounge, TV, guest bathroom plus additional shower room. Tea/coffee always available. Well placed for touring with easy access to M11 and M25, East Anglia and London. Open all year. Children over 12 years welcome. Sorry, no pets. Non-smokers preferred. Bed and Breakfast from £13 – £16. ETB listed.

SAFFRON WALDEN. Mrs Lily Vernon, Thistley Hall, Widdington, Saffron Walden CB11 3ST (Saffron Walden [0799] 40388). This lovely red and blue

brick period farmhouse stands in 30 acres, surrounded by peaceful, relaxing, unspoilt countryside and gardens. One mile from charming village with Tythe Barn, Wildlife Park and 15th century inn, where good food is served at reasonable prices. Two miles from B1383, with easy access to M11 and Stansted Airport. On the borders of three counties, central for touring and sightseeing. Accommodation comprises one double and one twin-bedded rooms, with washbasins, shaver points, tea facilities; central heating all rooms when necessary. Bathroom, shower room, three toilets; large lounge/diningroom with colour TV for guests only. Homely atmosphere and personal attention. Choice of menu. AA listed. Bed and Breakfast only from £14 per person.

WIX. Mrs H.P. Mitchell, New Farm House, Spinnell's Lane, Wix, Manningtree CO11 2UJ (Clacton [0255] 870365). ☙ ☙ ☙ Working farm. A comfortable,

centrally heated modern farmhouse ideally situated for touring the famous Constable countryside, local seaside resorts, historic Colchester and other towns. Convenient for Harwich (Parkeston Quay) Car Ferry to Holland, Denmark, Germany and Sweden. Seven bedrooms with en-suite facilities, TV etc; all other bedrooms have washbasins, tea/coffee making facilities and optional colour TV. Guests' lounge with colour TV, second quiet lounge with kitchenette available for making snacks. Children welcome at reduced prices, cot, high chair and babysitting provided. Large play area with swings, etc. Good farmhouse cooking. Open all year. AA listed and RAC commended. Bed, Breakfast and Evening Meal. SAE for brochure.

GLOUCESTERSHIRE

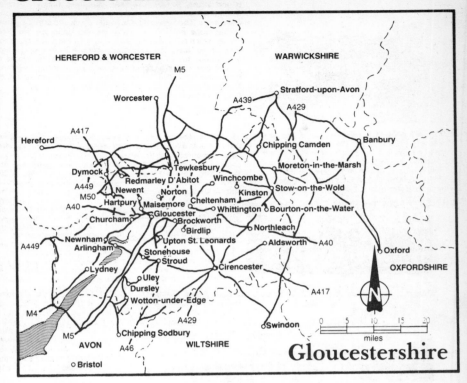

Gloucestershire

ARLINGHAM. Mrs D. Turrell, Horseshoe View, Overton Lane, Arlingham, Gloucester GL2 7JJ (Gloucester [0452] 740293). Guests are given a friendly welcome, all year round, in this comfortable private house enjoying beautiful views of River Severn and Forest of Dean. Within easy reach of A38 and M5, and excellent base for touring the Cotswolds, Bath, Slimbridge Wildfowl Trust, Berkeley Castle and many other places of interest. Dry ski slope, Gloucester Leisure Centre and Three Choirs Festival attract many visitors. Accommodation in two double bedrooms (one en suite), one twin-bedded and one single room, with usual amenities. Children over eight years welcome. Sorry, no pets. Car essential — ample parking. Bed and Breakfast (Evening Meal by arrangement). Reductions for children and senior citizens. SAE, please, for terms. HETB registered.

BIRDLIP. Mrs P.M. Carter, Beechmount, Birdlip GL4 8JH (Gloucester [0452] 862262). 👻👻 Good

central base for touring Cotswolds, conveniently situated for many interesting places and picturesque views with lovely walks. "Beechmount" is in centre of Birdlip Village, convenient for garage, post office/village store and public house. Prices include morning tea and choice of menu for breakfast. Front door key is provided so that guests may come and go freely. All bedrooms with washbasins, some with en-suite facilities; bathroom, separate shower, shaver point; toilet. Children welcome at reduced rates, cot, high chair provided. Pets allowed by arrangement. Home produce when available. Competitive rates. Small family-run guest house, highly recommended.

PLEASE ENCLOSE A STAMPED ADDRESSED ENVELOPE WITH ENQUIRIES

BISHOP'S NORTON. Mrs Denise Blanchard, Hill Farm, Bishop's Norton GL2 9LN (Gloucester [0452] 730351). 👑 👑 👑 Working farm. A warm welcome

awaits you at this picturesque 14th century thatched, oak-timbered farmhouse offering comfortable, homely atmosphere and good home cooking. Situated in quiet village in the Severn Valley, within easy reach of the M4 and M5/6 it is ideal for touring the Cotswolds, Malverns, Forest of Dean and the Wye Valley, Berkeley and Sudeley Castles, Prinknash Abbey and Wild Fowl Trust. Riding, golfing, boating nearby — fishing within walking distance. Scenic walks. Colour TV. All rooms have tea/coffee facilities. Licensed. Terms for Bed and Breakfast plus four course evening meal from £21.45. Stamp only for brochure.

BREDONS NORTON. Michael and Pippa Cluer, Lampitt House, Lampitt Lane, Bredons Norton, Tewkesbury GL20 7HB (0684 72295). 👑 👑 Lampitt House is situated in a large informal garden on the edge of a quiet village at the foot of Bredon Hill. Splendid views across to the Malverns. Ideal for visiting the Cotswolds, Stratford, Worcester, Cheltenham, Gloucester and the Forest of Dean. All rooms are furnished to a high standard and have private bathrooms, central heating, colour TV and tea/coffee making facilities. Children are welcome. Ample parking. Open all year. Hill and riverside walks. Arrangements can be made for windsurfing and riding. Terms from £14 to £16 per night for Bed and Breakfast.

CHELTENHAM. Mrs Sheila Chick, Old Vineyards, Timberscombe Lane (Off Cirencester Road), Charlton Kings, Cheltenham GL53 8EE (Cheltenham [0242] 582893). 👑 👑 Grade Two listed farmhouse situated

in an area of outstanding natural beauty with panoramic views. Just a few minutes from Cheltenham, cultural centre of the Cotswolds, and within easy reach of Stratford-upon-Avon, Bath and Bristol. Beautiful scenic walks including the "Cotswold Way" with an abundance of birds and flowers. Accommodation comprises five bedrooms, each with wash-basin, shaver point, tea/coffee making facilities. Comfortable lounge with colour TV; diningroom with separate tables. Central heating throughout. Packed lunches by arrangement. Children welcome. Non-smokers preferred. Bed and Breakfast £15.50 per person per night. Special two-day breaks available. RAC listed.

HOLIDAY ACCOMMODATION
Classification Schemes in England, Scotland and Wales

The National Tourist Boards for England, Scotland and Wales have agreed a common 'Crown Classification' scheme for **serviced (Board)** accommodation. All establishments are inspected regularly and are given a classification indicating their level of facilities and services.

There are six grades ranging from 'Listed' to 'Five Crowns 👑👑👑👑👑'. The higher the classification, the more facilities and services offered.

Crown classification is a measure of *facilities* not *quality*. A common quality grading scheme grades the quality of establishments as 'Approved', 'Commended' or 'Highly Commended' according to the accommodation, welcome and service they provide.

For **Self-Catering**, holiday homes in England are awarded 'Keys' after inspection and can also be 'Approved', 'Commended' or 'Highly Commended' according to the facilities available. In Scotland the Crown scheme includes self-catering accommodation and Wales also has a voluntary inspection scheme for self-catering grading from '1 (Standard)' to '5 (Excellent)'.

Caravan and Camping Parks can participate in the British Holiday Parks grading scheme from 'Approved (✓)' to 'Excellent (✓ ✓ ✓ ✓ ✓)'. In addition, each National Tourist Board has an annual award for high-quality caravan accommodation: in England – Rose Awards; in Scotland – Thistle Commendations; in Wales – Dragon Awards.

When advertisers supply us with the information, FHG Publications show Crowns and other awards or gradings, including AA, RAC, Egon Ronay etc. We also award a small number of Farm Holiday Guide Diplomas every year, based on readers' recommendations.

CHELTENHAM. Mrs Patricia Linsdell, Blind Lane Cottage, Kineton, Guiting Power, Cheltenham GL54 5UG (0451 850616). Blind Lane Cottage is 18th century and set in an old world cottage garden overlooking open countryside. Kineton is a farming area in North Cotswolds. Nearby public houses serve evening meals. The

following places are within easy reach; Stratford-upon-Avon, Oxford, Stow-on-the-Wold, Burford, Tewkesbury, Bourton-on-the Water, Winchcombe, Chipping Campden and Moreton-in-Marsh. Many well-known historic places of interest to be found in any published guide. Leisure activities include riding, swimming, golf and walking. The immediate area has many public footpaths giving access to some of the most beautiful countryside in England. The Cotswold Way passes the outskirts of Winchcombe. Nearest motorway access Cheltenham, junction 10, M5. Double and twin bedded rooms, with washbasins; children welcome. Open all year with central heating. Car essential, parking. Full Board; Evening Dinner, Bed and Breakfast or Bed and Breakfast only. Reduced rates for under 12's. Further details on application.

CHELTENHAM near. (Cotswolds). Mrs D. Trott, "Cosy Cottage", The Avenue, Bourton-on-the-Water, Near Cheltenham GL54 2BB (Cotswold [0451] 21748). ❦ ❦ Quietly situated in the heart of the Cotswolds,

four minutes' walk from the village centre of Bourton-on-the-Water, surrounded by many beautiful and historic places of interest "Cosy Cottage", a family home, offers clean, comfortable accommodation in a friendly atmosphere. Twin and double bedrooms with washbasins, tea/coffee making facilities. Bathroom, two toilets. TV lounge, diningroom. Central heating. Good home cooking using fresh vegetables in season. Car preferable to enjoy the delightful Cotswolds countryside. Parking. Full English Breakfast. Bed and Breakfast or Bed, Breakfast and Evening Meal. SAE or phone for terms and further details.

CHELTENHAM. Mrs P.L. Butler, New Barn Farmhouse, Temple Guiting, Cheltenham GL54 5RW (Guiting Power [04515] 367). Working farm. New Barn Farmhouse is situated in an unspoilt Cotswold village, one

mile off the B4077 road between Stow-on-the-Wold and Tewkesbury. The farmhouse has one double and two twin-bedded rooms, a TV room and a drawingroom, all with central heating. It is a lovely peaceful place in good walking country. There are many places of natural beauty and historic interest nearby. Within seven miles of Broadway, Chipping Campden, Moreton-in-the-Marsh and Bourton-on-the-Water. Children over 10 years welcome, but sorry, no pets. Many places to eat locally. Terms from £13.50 to £15 per person per night.

CHELTENHAM. Mr and Mrs Farley, Rooftrees, Rissington Road, Bourton-on-the-Water GL54 2EB (0451 21943). ❦ ❦ Warmth, comfort and hospitality are offered in the relaxed atmosphere of this detached Cotswold stone guest house, situated on the edge of the famous village of Bourton-on-the-Water which is eight minutes' level walking distance from the centre of the village. Bourton is central to all the main Cotswold attractions. Rooftrees offered four bedrooms, three en-suite, two on the ground floor. The two en-suite have four-poster beds, TV and tea-making facilities. A payphone is available. Traditional English home cooked dinners provided using fresh local produce. An enjoyable stay is assured here while visiting the Cotswolds. No smoking in bedrooms.

GLOUCESTERSHIRE – THE IDYLLIC COTSWOLDS COUNTY!

A combination of the Cotswolds and The Vale of Severn, Gloucestershire is a popular tourist destination. Visit Chipping Campden, Cirencester, The Cotswolds Farm Park, The Forest of Dean, Keynes Park and Tewkesbury and you will not be disappointed. If you are around at the right time, the Severn Bore can also be quite a spectacle.

See also Colour Display Advertisement **CHELTENHAM. Mr and Mrs A.E. Hughes, Ham Hill Farm, Whittington, Cheltenham GL54 4EZ (Cheltenham [0242] 584415).** All visitors will be made welcome and everything will be done to make their stay enjoyable at this new farmhouse on a 160-acre farm. Leisure activities nearby include riding, golf, walking on the Cotswold Way. All bedrooms with washbasins, TV and Teasmade, three rooms with full en-suite facilities. Central heating. Open all year. Bed and Breakfast from £12.50. No smoking. Children over seven years welcome.

CIRENCESTER. Miss Braidwood, "Wits' End", 50 Ashcroft Road, Cirencester GL7 1QX (0285

658926). "Wits' End" is a small and extremely friendly guest house where everyone is made to feel very welcome. Situated an easy two minutes' walk from the centre of the old Cotswold market town and hunting centre of Cirencester with its many attractions, it is an ideal base from which to tour the beautiful Cotswolds. The accommodation is comfortable and centrally heated. There is an open fire during the winter months. All rooms have colour TV. Tea/coffee making facilities are available for guests' use. Bed and Breakfast from £12–£15; Evening Meal £6.50. Packed lunches if desired. For further details contact the proprietress, **Miss Braidwood.**

COTSWOLDS. Mrs V. Keyte, The Limes, Tewkesbury Road, Stow-on-the-Wold GL54 1EN (0451 30034). 👑 👑 Over the last 14 years this RAC and AA listed guesthouse has established a reputation for its homely and friendly atmosphere. It is just four minutes' walk from the town centre; central for visiting Stratford-upon-Avon, Burford, Bourton-on-the Water, Cirencester, Cheltenham, etc. The Limes overlooks fields and has an attractive large garden with ornamental pool and waterfall. Single, double, twin and family rooms with washbasins. Two rooms en-suite, one four poster and two twin bedrooms; two public showers, four toilets. Central heating. TV lounge. Diningroom. Children welcome, cot. Open all year. Log fires in winter. Pets welcome. Car park. Fire Certificate held. Bed and full English Breakfast from £12 per person. Reductions for children. Vegetarians catered for.

DURSLEY. Mrs E. Williams, Claremont House, 66 Kingshill Road, Dursley GL11 4EG (0453

542018). Claremont, a large Victorian house with fine views of the Cotswold Escarpment overlooking the Cam Valley, offers most comfortable accommodation and a warm welcome to all visitors. It is ideally situated for touring the Severn Vale and many Cotswold beauty spots; convenient for visits to Berkeley Castle, Slimbridge Wildfowl Trust, Cirencester, Wye Valley, Cheltenham and Severn Bridge. Fresh farm produce always available. Double, family and twin bedded rooms available, all with either hot and cold or en-suite facilities. Tea/coffee making facilities. Ample parking. Bed and Breakfast; Evening Meals by arrangement.

DURSLEY. Mrs Catherine Cobham, 61a The Street, Uley, Dursley DL11 5SL (0453 860313). Large bungalow with pleasant garden situated on B4066, within easy reach of the Cotswold Way, Berkeley Castle, Slimbridge Wild Fowl Trust, Tetbury, Cheltenham, Cirencester and many other places of interest. This is very suitable for the disabled. Two double bedrooms with washbasins; guests' bathroom with toilet. Spacious sitting/diningroom with colour TV. Pets accepted, if kept under strict control, at a small charge. Central heating. Ample parking. Bed and Breakfast £12.50 for one night. Reduction for longer stays. Open all week, all year round.

DURSLEY near. Gerald and Norma Kent, Hill House, Crawley Hill, Uley, Near Dursley GL11 5BH

(Dursley [0453] 860267). Cotswold stone house situated on top of a hill with beautiful views of the surrounding countryside, near the very pretty village of Uley. Ideal spot for exploring the various walks in the area including the Cotswold Way and there are many places of interest within reasonable driving distance of Uley. Bed and Breakfast offered though Evening Meals are normally available on request. Choice of bedrooms with or without en-suite facilities, all with washbasins, central heating, shaver points, tea/coffee making facilities. Guest lounge with colour TV. Your hosts' aim is to make your stay in the Cotswolds an enjoyable and memorable one, with comfort and hospitality of prime importance. Please phone or write for brochure.

Hill House

PLEASE ENCLOSE A STAMPED ADDRESSED ENVELOPE WITH ENQUIRIES

BURROWS COURT HOTEL

RAC *AA*

♛♛♛
NIBLEY GREEN, NORTH NIBLEY,
DURSLEY GL11 6AZ
Tel: Dursley (0453) 546230

This 18th century mill is idyllically set in an acre of garden surrounded by open country with beautiful views of the Cotswolds. Decorated and furnished in the country style, the house has eight bedrooms, all with private shower room or bathroom, colour TV, beverage facilities and radio. A choice of dishes is offered at dinner with a range of wines. Other facilities include two lounges, one with residents' bar, central heating. Log fires in winter, outside swimming pool and croquet lawn. Children over 5 years. AA Listed, RAC Highly Acclaimed. Dinner, Bed and Breakfast from £175 weekly, two days from £54.

ELTON. Mrs G. Tucker, Upper Hall, Elton, Newnham-on-Severn GL14 1JJ (0452 76 243). Upper Hall is a 17th century stone built country house set in its own grounds nestled between the Royal Forest of Dean and the River Severn. The old elm beamed rooms have private bathrooms, radio alarms and facilities for making tea/coffee and hot chocolate. Breakfasts are generous and include local butcher's home cured bacon and sausages, fresh fruit, home baked bread and our own preserves and honey. Comfortable sittingroom with inglenook fireplace, TV and books. Bed and Breakfast from £15 per person per night. Single room supplement. Reductions for stays of seven nights or more. Self catering cottage also available.

GLOUCESTER near. S.J. Barnfield, "Kilmorie Guest House", Gloucester Road, Corse, Staunton, Near Gloucester GL19 3RQ (Gloucester [0452] 840224). Built in 1848 by the Chartists, Kilmorie is Grade 2 listed in a conservation area, and is a smallholding keeping farm livestock and fruit in a lovely part of Gloucestershire. Good home cooking with own produce and eggs when available. Large garden. Children are welcome to "help" with the animals if they wish, and a child's pony is also kept. There are many places of both historic and natural interest to visit, and river trips can be enjoyed from Tewkesbury and Upton-on-Severn. Kilmorie is situated close to the borders of Herefordshire and Worcestershire and the Forest of Dean, the Cotswolds, Malvern Hills, the Wye Valley and four castles are all within easy reach. Four double, one twin, one single and one family bedrooms; two bathrooms and two additional toilets, shower. Tea-making facilities. Lounge with colour TV; diningroom. Central heating. Fire Certificate. Children over five years welcome. Pets accepted. Ample parking. Three course Dinner, Bed and Breakfast from £14; Bed and Breakfast from £9. Reduced rates for children. Open all year.

LECHLADE-ON-THAMES. Mrs Anne Amor, Manor Farm, Kelmscott, Lechlade-on-Thames GL7 3HJ (Faringdon [0367] 52620). ⚘⚘ Working farm. Manor Farm, a working dairy farm in the quiet Cotswold village of Kelmscott, nestles in the foothills on the banks of the River Thames. Famous for the William Morris Manor, Kelmscott is ideally situated for touring, fishing, golfing, walking and cycling, with many historic places to visit nearby. Within easy reach of Swindon, Oxford, Burford, Bourton-on-the-Water and Stow-on-the-Wold; 10 miles from M4 Motorway Exit 15.

This 17th century Cotswold stone house, owned by the National Trust, has large comfortable rooms, all with washbasins, tea and coffee making facilities and shaving points. The house is fully centrally heated and has a log fire in the winter. Terms from £14 per person; reduced rates for children sharing with parents. Family rooms available. AA listed. Open all year.

MINCHINHAMPTON. Mrs Margaret Helm, Hunters Lodge (formerly Two Trees Corner), Dr Brown's Road, Minchinhampton Common GL6 9BT (0453 883588). Hunters Lodge is a beautiful stone-built Cotswold country house set in an acre of secluded garden adjoining 600 acres of National Trust commonland at Minchinhampton. Accommodation available — one family room and two double rooms, all with washbasins, tea/coffee making facilities, full central heating, private bathroom. All rooms furnished and decorated to a high standard. Large lounge with TV and a delightful conservatory. Car essential, ample parking space. Ideal centre for touring the Cotswolds, Stroud, Bath, Cheltenham, Cirencester with many delightful pubs and hotels around for meals. You are sure of a warm welcome, comfort and help in planning excursions to local places of interest. Bed and Breakfast from £14. Non smokers preferred. SAE, please, for further details or telephone.

MORETON-IN-MARSH near. Mrs P.A. Allen, Lines Farm, Chastleton Road, Little Compton, Near Moreton-in-Marsh GL56 0SL (Barton on the Heath [060874] 343). ⚘⚘ Beautiful Cotswold stone house with lovely views situated on the edge of pretty village midway between Moreton-in-Marsh and Chipping Norton. Ideal for touring Cotswolds, Stratford-upon-Avon, Oxford, etc. Centrally heated rooms with guests' TV lounge; diningroom; one en-suite family bedroom; one double and one twin, both with washbasins; all with tea/coffee making facilities. Pets and children welcome. Prices from £12 to £14 per person per night. Discounts for three or more nights. Horses and cattle kept.

NORTHLEACH. Mrs Patricia Powell, Cotteswold House, Market Place, Northleach GL54 3EG (Cotswold [0451] 60493). This is a listed building of considerable charm and character, and is renovated to a high standard, showing a fine blend of old stone and oak beams. It is situated in the heart of the Cotswolds, ideal for touring this beautiful area: Oxford, Sudeley Castle, Stratford-upon-Avon and many more places of interest. Visitors are welcome all year round for Bed and Breakfast from £14 per person per night. Individual room controlled central heating. Accommodation in double, twin and family rooms. Two well fitted and well appointed bathrooms. Car parking space in Square. Further details on request.

NORTHLEACH. Theresa and Mike Eastman, Market House, The Square, Northleach GL54 3EJ (Cotswold [0451] 60557). ⚘⚘ A 400 year old Cotswold stone cottage guesthouse of Olde Worlde charm characterised by exposed beams, inglenook fireplace and flagstone floors. Located in the centre of a quiet, unspoilt Cotswold town amongst a variety of shops, inns and restaurants. Cosy bedrooms, single, double and twin with washbasins, tea facilities and touring guides, ensure a good night's rest. Central heating throughout makes for a comfortable stay. A choice of farmhouse breakfasts will sustain you for the day's tour in the Cotswolds, Stratford or Bath. Just £13 to £16 per night.

FHG PUBLICATIONS LIMITED publish a large range of well-known accommodation guides. We will be happy to send you details or you can use the order form at the back of this book.

NORTHLEACH near. Mrs E. Powell, Saltway Farm, Northleach GL54 3QB (Fossebridge [0285] 720387). Working farm, join in. Small 18th century Cotswold Stone Farmhouse with original stone barn. Delightful cottage garden. Peaceful. Set in 10 acres, overlooking The Saltway in the heart of the Cotswolds — Shetland sheep kept — spinning — fleeces and sheepskins usually available. Conifer tree garden with a collection of over 400 varieties. One double room with washbasin and one twin. Bathroom. TV. No smokers. No pets. Children welcome. Cot. Babysitters. On road from Northleach to Bibury — both within three miles (Cirencester and Bourton-on-the-Water 10 miles). Bed and Breakfast £15. Tourist Board Registered.

STONEHOUSE. Mrs D.A. Hodge, Welches Farm, Standish, Stonehouse GL10 3BX (Stonehouse [045382] 2018). Working farm. Welches Farm is about three miles from Stroudwater Interchange on the M5, standing near Standish Hospital on the outskirts of Stonehouse. It is a very old Cotswold farmhouse with exposed beams, also an old wood-panelled staircase (Listed Building). It is reputed that Oliver Cromwell stayed at Welches before the siege of Gloucester. Ideal for visits to the Forest of Dean; also National Trust park and woods and many beautiful Cotswold villages. A short distance from the Cotswold Way. In guest bedrooms only cotton and linen sheets are used. Large sittingroom, spacious bedrooms. Good food, guaranteed satisfaction. Children welcome, cot and babysitting. Pets by prior arrangement. Car essential — parking. Bed and Breakfast from £11. Reduced rates for children. No smoking. Tourist Board registered.

STOW-ON-THE-WOLD. Mrs S. Davis, Fairview Farmhouse, Bledington Road, Stow-on-the-Wold, Cheltenham GL54 1AN (Cotswold [0451] 30279). ♥♥♥ You are invited to a warm welcome at Fairview Farmhouse situated one mile from Stow-on-the-Wold on a quiet B road with outstanding panoramic views of the surrounding Cotswold Hills. Ideal base for touring the pretty villages of Bourton-on-the-Water, The Slaughters, Broadway, Chipping Campden, Stratford etc. The cosy bedrooms are furnished to a high standard and all are en-suite with colour TV and tea/coffee making equipment. Lounge and additional lounge area with books, maps, etc. Central heating. Ample parking. Open all year. Evening Meals by arrangement.

Fairview **FARMHOUSE**
Telephone Cotswold (0451) 30279
Bledington Road, Stow-on-the-Wold, Cheltenham, Glos. GL54 1AN

STOW-ON-THE-WOLD. Shaun & Gaye Kenneally, South Hill Farm House, Fosseway, Stow-on-the-Wold GL54 1JY (Cotswold [0451] 31219). ♥♥ Enjoy a visit to our Victorian Farmhouse and explore the area at your leisure. Stratford-on-Avon 18 miles, Oxford 30 miles, Cheltenham 20 miles, Gloucester 30 miles — an ideal base. The house is constructed of the honey coloured Cotswold stone, set along an avenue of beech trees on the outskirts of Stow. High standard of accommodation, all rooms furnished traditionally, but with all modern facilities and most with full en-suite bathrooms. Hot/cold washbasins in all rooms. Fully centrally heated. En-suites available. Spacious lounge with log fire, TV. Our farmhouse Breakfast is served in the dining-room, featuring oak beams and a large inglenook fireplace. Laundry service offered. Ample parking. Weekly terms, competitive off-season rates. Write or phone for brochure.

STOW-ON-THE-WOLD. Mrs F.J. Adams, Banks Farm, Upper Oddington, Moreton-in-Marsh GL56 0XG (Cotswold [0451] 30475). The Cotswold stone farmhouse is situated in an elevated position in the centre of the village of Oddington, three miles from Stow-on-the-Wold. All rooms enjoy lovely views over fields to the 11th century church. It is centrally situated for all the Cotswold villages, while Blenheim Palace, Oxford, Stratford-upon-Avon, Cheltenham, Cirencester and Gloucester are within easy reach. Accommodation comprises a double and a twin-bedded room, both with washbasins, tea-making facilities and electric blankets. Dining/sittingroom with TV available for guests' use in the evening. Guests, and children over 10 years, are welcomed to our home March to November. Car essential — ample parking. Sorry, no pets. Bed and good English Breakfast, bedtime drink from £13.50. Packed lunches available. ETB listed. SAE with enquiries please.

Banks Farm

STOW-ON-THE-WOLD. Robert and Dawn Smith, Corsham Field Farmhouse, Bledington Road, Stow-on-the-Wold GL54 1JH (Cotswold [0451] 31750). Homely farmhouse with traditional features and breathtaking views, one mile from Stow-on-the-Wold. Ideally situated for exploring all the picturesque Cotswold villages such as Broadway, Bourton-on-the-Water, Upper and Lower Slaughter, Chipping Campden, Snowshill etc. Also central point for places of interest such as Blenheim Palace, Cotswold Wildlife Park, Stratford and many stately homes and castles in the area. Twin, double and family rooms available, one with en-suite bathroom. All rooms have washbasins, TV and tea/coffee making facilities. Pets and children welcome. AA and Tourist Board listed. Bed and Full English Breakfast from £10 per person.

STROUD near. Mrs B.J. Clarke, Furners Farm, Elcombe, Slad, Near Stroud GL6 7LA (Painswick [0452] 813674). Working farm, join in.

Furners Farm, with its 17th century farmhouse, is a small mixed farm of 10 acres set in the Slad valley, an area of unspoilt beauty three miles north of Stroud. Cheltenham and Gloucester are 10 miles away. There is a nature reserve and riding stables nearby. Ideal centre for walking and touring. The comfortable farmhouse has a homely atmosphere, with lovely views from the sunny rooms. Lounge with colour TV, oak beams and stone fireplace (log fire). Central heating; washbasins and teamaking facilities in rooms. Home grown produce and home baking. Reductions for children; cot, high chair, babysitting. Registered with local and Heart of England Tourist Boards. SAE, please, for terms for Evening Dinner, Bed and Breakfast or Bed and Breakfast only. Weekly rates available.

STROUD near. Miss E.M. MacSwiney, New Inn House, The Camp, Near Stroud GL6 7HL (028-582 336). New Inn House, built in 1694 as a posting-inn, is a Grade Two listed building. It stands in half an acre of grounds in a small Cotswold hamlet 820 feet above sea level amidst unspoilt countryside. Excellent touring centre for Cotswolds and Wye Valley, Bath, Stratford-upon-Avon. Gloucester 10 miles, Cheltenham nine miles and Cirencester 10 miles. Nearby are the Cotswold Way and Prinknash Abbey; three golf courses within easy reach and riding stables in the village. The Severn Wild Fowl Trust approximately 15 miles. Both bedrooms (one twin-bedded and one single with extra folding bed) have washbasins, tea-making facilities. Central heating. Three course Evening Dinner available at weekends. Own produce served where possible. Full English Breakfast. Large garden. TV. Guests have own sittingroom. Access at all times. Dogs by prior arrangement. Children over 10 welcome. Car essential. Bed and Breakfast from £11. Weekly terms available. SAE, please.

TEWKESBURY. Mrs A. Meadows, Home Farm, Bredons Norton, Tewkesbury GL20 7HA (0684 72322). ✿ ✿ *Commended.* Mixed 150 acre family run farm

with sheep, cattle and poultry. Situated in an extremely quiet, unspoilt little valley nestling under Bredon Hill. Superb position for touring or relaxing. The 18th century farmhouse is very comfortably furnished. All bedrooms have en-suite bathrooms. Gas central heating. Good home cooking. Evening meals by arrangement. Lounge, TV. Children and pets welcome. Bed and Breakfast from £14 to £16; Evening Meal £9.

TEWKESBURY. Mrs Bernadette Williams, Abbots Court, Church End, Twyning, Tewkesbury GL20 6DA (Tewkesbury [0684] 292515). ✿ ✿ ✿ **Working farm.**

A large, quiet farmhouse set in 350 acres, built on the site of monastery between the Malverns and Cotswolds, half a mile M5-M50 junction. Large bedrooms, five en-suite, fully carpeted, with washbasins, tea making facilities and colour TV. Centrally heated. Open all year. Large lounge with open fire and colour TV. Spacious diningroom. Licensed bar. Good home cooked food in large quantities. Home produced where possible. Children's own TV room, games room and playroom. Tennis lawn. Play area and lawn, pony to ride. Cot, high chair and babysitting available. Laundry facilities. Ideally situated for touring with numerous places to visit. Swimming, tennis, sauna, golf within three miles. Coarse fishing available on the farm. Bed and Breakfast from £12.50. Reduced rates for children and Senior Citizens.

WINCHCOMBE. Mrs B. Scudamore, Sudeley Hill Farm, Winchcombe GL54 5JB (0242 602344).

🏵️ 🏵️ Delightfully situated above Sudeley Castle with panoramic views across surrounding valley, this is a 15th century listed farmhouse with a large garden on a working mixed farm of 800 acres. Ideal centre for touring the Cotswolds. Family unit en-suite, one double, one twin and one single bedrooms. Comfortable lounge with TV and log fires. Separate diningroom. Sorry, no dogs. Bed and Breakfast from £14.

WOTTON-UNDER-EDGE. Paul Cory, The Thatched Cottage, Wortley, Near Wotton-under-Edge

(0453 842776). Situated in a charming and peaceful little hamlet on the edge of the Cotswolds, surrounded by farmland and wooded hillsides. Walkers' paradise. Easy distance to Gloucester, Cirencester, Bath and Bristol with numerous smaller market towns and villages well worth visiting. The Thatched Cottage dates from the 14th century and sits on land where the remains of a Roman Villa are at present being excavated by Keele University. Accommodation comprises two twin-bedded rooms with washbasins. Bathroom with shower available. Bed and Breakfast (good English) from £12 per night, weekly reductions.

WOTTON-UNDER-EDGE. Mrs Sylvia Scolding, Varley Farm, Talbots End, Cromhall, Near Wotton-under-Edge GL12 8AJ (Chipping Sodbury [0454] 294292). Working farm. This dairy farm of 75 acres is

situated near the edge of the Cotswolds. An ideal centre for visiting Wales, Cheddar, Bristol, Bath and Wildfowl Trust. The grey stone farmhouse, recently modernised, has washbasins in all bedrooms — four double or four family rooms. Two bathrooms, three toilets. Lounge with colour TV; diningroom with separate tables. Central heating. Fire Certificate granted. Children welcome, highchair and babysitting available. Sorry, no pets. Car essential, parking. Good English Breakfast. Open Easter to September. Visitors are welcome to walk round the farm and watch the farm activities. Bed and Breakfast, or Bed, Breakfast and Evening Meal. Reductions for children. AA and RAC listed. SAE please for early reply.

WOTTON-UNDER-EDGE. Mrs K.P. Forster, Under-the-Hill-House, Adey's Lane, Wotton-under-Edge

UNDER-THE-HILL-HOUSE

GL12 7LY (Dursley [0453] 842557) Open from April to October, accommodation is provided in this wing of a fine Queen Anne listed house on the edge of the ancient wool town of Wotton-under-Edge. Bounded on the east by National Trust land which is let to the owners who run a breeding herd of cattle, the house is only a few minutes' walk from the town centre, and there are beautiful walks with views of the Severn Vale and river. Ideally situated for Bath, Berkeley Castle, Wildfowl Trust and the Cotswolds. The guest wing has four bedrooms with washbasins and tea/coffee making facilities. One bedroom with en suite toilet and shower (£4 per night extra). Dining room and comfortable lounge. Night storage heaters in public rooms, convector heaters in bedrooms. Sorry, no pets. Shared garden for guests' use. Bed and Breakfast £12 per night for three or more nights; £14 per night for one or two nights. Two-thirds for children 12 years and under.

If you've found
FARM HOLIDAY GUIDES
of service please tell your friends

HAMPSHIRE

CADNAM (New Forest). Mrs A.M. Dawe, Budd's Farm, Winsor Road, Winsor, Cadnam, Southampton SO4 2HN (Southampton [0703] 812381). 🐦🐦 Working farm. The farm is a 200-acre dairy/beef holding, quietly situated, yet close to a variety of tourist attractions — cathedrals, stately homes, Beaulieu, Broadlands, Breamore, Wilton Country Park, Butterfly Farm, wagon rides and many more. Also close to pubs etc. The thatched farmhouse has been tastefully restored and modernised to a high standard. Accommodation is in one family/double room and one twin/double room, both with washbasins and a shared bathroom. There is a lounge with colour TV, and a lovely English garden to relax in. Terms from £12–£13 per person. AA listed.

COPYTHORNE. Copythorne Lodge, Romsey Road, Copythorne, Cadnam, Near Southampton SO4 2PB (Southampton [0703] 812127/813945). Large country house set in its own grounds on the A31 road, one mile from the New Forest, a beautiful 93,000 acre forest with ponies, deer, wildlife and of great historic interest. A paradise for walkers and riders. Friendly, homely atmosphere. The house is conveniently situated for the cathedral towns of Winchester and Salisbury, also Southampton and Bournemouth. Part of a small farm, a good farmhouse breakfast is served. Single, double, twin and family rooms available, most en-suite. All rooms have radio, colour TV and tea/coffee making facilities. Open all year round. DIY facilities if you wish to bring your own horse. Bed and Breakfast from £20. Minimum stay two nights. Special offer — stay seven nights, pay for only six. Car essential — parking. Telephone for further details.

LYMINGTON (New Forest). Mrs Hamilton-Silvester, 'Carters Farmhouse', Norleywood, Lymington SO41 5RR (East End [059-065] 630). The Farmhouse is

situated on the edge of the New Forest, off the B3054 Lymington-Beaulieu route, overlooking pasture land to the Isle of Wight. There's always plenty to do and a wealth of places to explore. Visit the towns of Salisbury, Winchester, Portsmouth and Bournemouth; Lymington Old Town with its 18th century houses, quaint cobbled Quay Mill and magnificent yachting marina; Beaulieu Abbey and the popular Motor Museum. Open all year, 'Carters Farmhouse' offers guest accommodation in two double bedrooms with electric heating. No pets. Bed and Breakfast; Evening Meal optional. Terms on application. SAE please.

MILFORD-ON-SEA. Mr and Mrs D. Emberson, Compton Hotel, 59/61 Keyhaven Road, Milford-on-Sea SO4 0QX (Lymington [0590] 643117). 🐦🐦 Small,

friendly, family hotel. Most rooms en-suite; with colour TV, radio, baby listening and tea-making facilities. Central heating. Mainly English-style cuisine, varied menu. The friendly bar, with dance floor and seating, provides nice social evenings. Separate lounge with video. Games room with table tennis, pool and darts. Heated swimming pool set in a natural sun trap. Ample parking. Pets welcome. No service charge. Half Board or Bed and Breakfast. Children under 14 years half price. Special OAP's rates May/June/September. Half Board £140 inclusive. Open all year. SAE.

MINSTEAD. Mrs A. Saunders, Orchard Gate, Minstead, Near Lyndhurst SO4 7FX (Southampton [0703] 813584). Orchard Gate is a large country house set

in the picturesque village of Minstead. Facilities for riding and fishing are only a short distance away, in an area noted for fascinating New Forest walks. All the family are welcome, and we offer friendly accommodation at reasonable prices, good food and comfortable beds. The popular village of Lyndhurst is only three miles down the road, with excellent shopping and above-average catering establishments. Bed and Breakfast from £13.50 (children seven to 12 years £7.50, young children negotiable); Evening Dinner from £5. Disabled guests welcome with downstairs en-suite room available. Further information on application.

HAMPSHIRE – VARIED ATTRACTIONS!

Coastal resorts like Southsea, river valleys like that of the Itchen, The New Forest and the nautical centres of Southampton and Portsmouth combine to give Hampshire its reputation as a holiday destination. Also of interest in this large county are places like Avington, Breamore Countryside Museum, Butser Ancient Farm and Wellington Parkland and Dairy Museum.

Built about 1800, overlooking Otterbourne Common, near the entrance to Cranbury Park Estate; standing in ¾ acre of mature woodland garden. Within easy reach of Winchester, New Forest and Southampton. Ferries to Isle of Wight from Portsmouth are 30 minutes' drive away. Our accommodation is of the highest standard, each twin bedded room having its own bathroom, air conditioning, tea/coffee facilities, colour TV; independent access, including a ground floor en suite. Open all year. Enclosed parking. Regret no animals and no smoking. We pride ourselves on having a homely and welcoming atmosphere. Terms from £17.50 per person. For reservations please contact: **Vera and Peter Walford, Lilac Cottage, Otterbourne Hill, Otterbourne, Hampshire SO21 2HJ. Tel: (0703) 267070.**

Lilac Cottage Otterbourne

PETERSFIELD. Mrs G.W. Baigent, Trotton Farm, Trotton, Rogate, Petersfield GU31 5EN (0730 813618). ♛♛ We offer twin bedded ensuite rooms (showers) with guests' own lounge/games room looking over our own farmland in this beautiful part of West Sussex. We are easily to be found on the A272 between Petersfield and Midhurst. Ideally situated for visiting many local, historic and sporting attractions and within one hour of major airports. Children welcome but regret no pets. Terms: single from £15 to £25, double from £35 to £40.

PETERSFIELD. Mrs Mary Bray, Nursted Farm, Buriton, Petersfield GU31 5RW (Petersfield [0730] 64278). Working farm. This late 17th century farmhouse, with its large garden, is open to guests throughout most of the year. Located quarter-of-a-mile west of the B2146 Petersfield to Chichester road, one and a half miles south of Petersfield, the house makes an ideal base for touring the scenic Hampshire and West Sussex countryside. Queen Elizabeth Country Park two miles adjoining the picturesque village of Buriton at the western end of South Downs Way. Accommodation consists of three twin bedded rooms (one with washbasin), two guests' bathrooms/toilets, plus additional toilet and washbasin; sittingroom/breakfast room. Children welcome, cot provided. Sorry, no pets. Car essential — ample parking adjoining the house. Terms on application with SAE, please, for Bed and Breakfast only. Reductions for children under 12. ETB registered.

RINGWOOD. New Forest. Mrs M.E. Burt, Fraser House, Salisbury Road, Blashford, Ringwood BH24 3PB (Ringwood [0425] 473958). Fraser House is situated one mile from the market town of Ringwood, overlooking the Avon Valley. This comfortable family house is on the edge of the New Forest, famous for its ponies, deer and pleasant walks. It is ten miles from Bournemouth and the south coast, and is convenient for visiting Southampton, Stonehenge and the Cathedral city of Salisbury. All rooms have central heating, hot and cold water, shaver points, comfortable beds, colour TV, tea/coffee making facilities. Some en-suite rooms available at extra charge. Children welcome, cot and high chair available, reduced rates if sharing parents' room. Ample parking space. Open all year. Bed and Breakfast from £12.50 per night. Please send SAE for brochure.

ROMSEY (New Forest). Mrs J. Hayter, "Woodlands", Bunny Lane, Sherfield English, Romsey SO51 6FT (Whiteparish [0794] 884840). ♛♛♛ Small family guest house situated close to New Forest. Places of interest nearby include Romsey, Broadlands, Beaulieu, Salisbury Cathedral and Isle of Wight Ferry. Ideal for relaxing holiday, large garden with country views, lovely walks. Friendly family accommodation with family/double/twin bedrooms, with washbasins (one bedroom with toilet), also coffee/tea making facilities in all rooms. Lounge with colour TV. Bathroom/shower. Diningroom with separate tables. All good home cooking. Bed and Breakfast from £9.50 (£65 weekly); Bed, Breakfast and three course Evening Meal from £85 weekly. Reduced rates for children and Senior Citizens. Sorry, no pets. Open January to November.

HEREFORD & WORCESTER

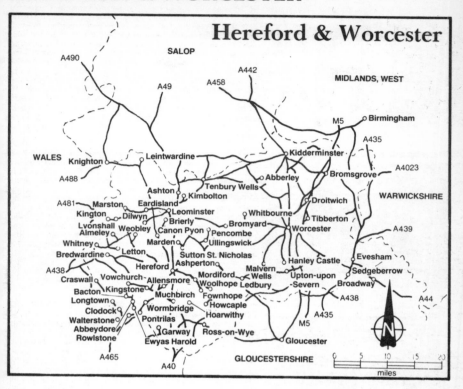

Hereford & Worcester

SALOP

MIDLANDS, WEST

A490

A442

A458

A49

M5   Birmingham

A435

WALES   Knighton   Leintwardine   Kidderminster   A4023

A488   Abberley   Bromsgrove

Ashton   Tenbury Wells   WARWICKSHIRE

A481   Marston   Eardisland   Kimbolton   Droitwich

Kington   Dilwyn   Leominster   Whitbourne   Tibberton

Lyonshall   Brierly   Bromyard   Worcester   A439

Almeley   Weobley   Canon Pyon   Pencombe

Whitney   Marden   Ullingswick

Bredwardine   Letton   Sutton St. Nicholas   Hanley Castle   Evesham

A438   Hereford   Ashperton   Malvern   Sedgeberrow

Craswall   Vowchurch   Allensmore   Mordiford   Wells   Upton-upon-   Broadway

Bacton   Kingstone   Muchbirch   Woolhope   Ledbury   Severn   A44

Longtown   Fownhope   A438

Clodock   Wormbridge   Howcaple   A435

Walterstone   Pontrilas   Hoarwithy   M5

Abbeydore   Garway   Ross-on-Wye

Rowlstone   Ewyas Harold   Gloucester

A465   GLOUCESTERSHIRE

A40

N

0   5   10   15   20
miles

BACTON. Mrs Herdman, Fair Oak Farm, Bacton, Hereford HR2 0AT (0981 240033). Fair Oak Farm is a working stock farm set in beautiful countryside in the Golden Valley within easy reach of the Black Mountains and Brecon Beacons, Hay-on-Wye (famous for its book shops) and the market towns of Hereford and Abergavenny. Accommodation comprises one double, one twin and one single bedroom, all with central heating and tea/coffee making facilities. Open from February to October. Car essential. SAE, please, for brochure.

BEWDLEY near. Margaret Nott, Bullockhurst Farm, Rock, Near Bewdley DY14 9SE (029922 305). ♣ Come and savour the peace and tranquillity of our Georgian farmhouse set in large gardens and beautiful undulating countryside, off the A456 or B4202. Well situated for exploring the Wyre Forest, Bewdley with its Severn Railway and enjoying the panoramic views over the Worcestershire and Shropshire countryside. Excellent meals available in village pub (walking distance). Children welcome. Open Easter to October. Bed and Breakfast from £12.

PLEASE SEND A STAMPED ADDRESSED ENVELOPE WITH ENQUIRIES

BROADWAY. Mr Andrew Riley, "Olive Branch" Guest House, 78 High Street, Broadway WR12 7AJ (Broadway [0386] 853440). ♛ ♛ ♛ The attractive village of Broadway is one of the loveliest places in the Cotswolds and has remained completely unspoiled. This guest house, dating back to the 16th century, is conveniently situated, close to the centre of the village which is well provided with places to eat out, ranging from tea rooms to a four star hotel. Combining modern amenities with old world charm, the house has five double/twin, (five en-suite), two family and two single bedrooms, all with washbasins; diningroom, separate lounge; TV; showers, toilets. Parking for eight cars. Cot available. Fire Certificate held. Six miles to Evesham, 10 to Bourton-on-the-Water, 15 to Stratford-upon-Avon, 16 to Cheltenham. Open all year except Christmas. Owners' adjacent antique shop is available to browse around, in or out of shop hours. AA, RAC recommended. SAE, please, for terms for Bed and Breakfast.

BROADWAY. Mr Andrew Scott, Crown and Trumpet Inn, Church Street, Broadway WR12 7AE (Broadway [0386] 853202). ♛ ♛ 16th century country inn situated in the picturesque village of Broadway, just behind the village green. Log fires and oak beams throughout the pub. Horse riding can be arranged and there is pub sing-along music on Saturday nights. An ideal centre for touring the Cotswolds. The Crown and Trumpet specialises in home cooking, supplemented by an extensive menu of traditional English dishes. Accommodation comprises three double rooms, all with colour TV, tea/coffee making facilities, some with original brass beds. Electric blankets in the winter months. Full central heating throughout. Heart of England and English Tourist Board registered. 1985/1986/1987/1988/ 1989 Good Beer Guide. Special winter rates and offers for two nights or more. Please telephone or write for details.

BROMYARD near. Mrs J. Keenan, Paunceford Court, Much Cowarne, Near Bromyard HR7 4JQ (Hereford [0432] 820208). Paunceford Court is a large country house situated in pleasant gardens. The house dates back to the 11th century and was the home of De Pauncefort, one of William the Conqueror's knights. Situated beside the lovely 13th century church of St. Mary's, with its listed Norman Bell Tower, Paunceford Court makes an ideal centre for travelling to Ledbury, Bromyard, Hereford, Worcester and the Malvern Hills, while Gloucester, Ludlow, Hay etc are all within easy reach. Children's paradise: cot, high chair, baby-sitting, games room and reduced rates. Regret no pets. Open all year. Comfortable bedrooms; bathroom, two toilets; sittingroom; diningroom. Car essential, ample parking. Evening Meal, Bed and Breakfast from £18.50 daily, £126 weekly; Bed and Breakfast from £12 daily, £80.50 weekly. Heart of England Tourist Board registered.

COTHERIDGE. Mrs A. Rogers, Little Lightwood Farm, Lightwood Lane, Cotheridge, Near Worcester WR6 5LT (090566 236). ♛ ♛ Come and enjoy the peace and tranquillity at Little Lightwood Farm where a warm welcome awaits you. Farmhouse breakfast is served, evening meals by prior arrangement. The house is very tastefully decorated and furnished for your comfort. Dairy farm situated three miles west of Worcester off the A44 towards Leominster. Bed and Breakfast from £12. Also self catering accommodation available.

HEREFORD & WORCESTERSHIRE – THE HEART OF ENGLAND!
A beautiful county which includes The Vale of Evesham and the rugged – if petite – Malvern Hills. It has been designated an "Area of Outstanding Beauty". Places of interest include The Avoncroft Museum of Buildings, Brockhampton, Ross-on-Wye, The Teme Valley and The Hereford & Worcester County Museum.

DROITWICH. Mrs G. Jackson, Wessex House Farm, Trench Lane, Oddingley, Droitwich WR9 7NB

(0905 772826 or 090569 234). Our modern farmhouse in pleasant surroundings on stock and arable farm is three miles from Droitwich, four miles from Junctions 5 and 6 of M5, convenient for Worcester and Cotswolds. Double and family rooms with washbasins, tea/coffee making facilities. Children welcome, cot and high chair available. Guests are assured every comfort and good farmhouse food. Evening Meals by arrangement. Excellent food also available locally. Bed and Breakfast from £12; Evening Meal from £5 to £6. Farm Holiday Bureau member.

DROITWICH. Mrs P. Chilman, Old House Farm, Tibberton, Droitwich WR9 7NP (090565 247). ❀ ❀

Family run 100 acre dairy farm set off B4084 in peaceful village of Tibberton, only one mile from M5 Junction 6. The farmhouse is tastefully furnished for comfort and relaxation with large garden and splendid views of Malvern Hills. Accommodation is in family, twin and single bedrooms with shower and washbasins en-suite. Central for all the Heart of England including Worcestershire, Herefordshire, Warwickshire, Gloucestershire and the Cotswolds. Excellent local pub for snacks or restaurant for evening meals. Children and pets welcome. Open Easter to October.

DROITWICH. Mrs Tricia Havard, Phepson Farm, Himbleton, Droitwich WR9 7JZ (Himbleton

[090-569] 205). ❀ ❀ **Working farm.** We offer a warm welcome and a comfortable and relaxed atmosphere in our 17th century farmhouse with oak beamed lounge and dining-room. Situated on peaceful stock farm just outside the unspoilt village of Himbleton where visitors may see farm animals and walk on Wychavon Way. Home cooking. Full English Breakfast. Double and twin rooms with en-suite bathroom and colour TV. Tea/coffee making facilities available. Convenient for M5 and M42 and two miles from B4090, it is central for touring many places of interest in the Heart of England. Children welcome. Bed and Breakfast from £13.50. Evening Meal by arrangement. AA listed, featured on "Wish Your Were Here", 1987. Self catering flat also available.

DROITWICH near. Mrs Joyce Ulyet, Valley Farm, Hanbury, Near Bromsgrove B60 4HJ (Hanbury

[052-784] 678). ❀ ❀ **Working farm.** A warm welcome and comfortable accommodation in our lovely old farm-house, sympathetically restored, with a wealth of old beams and a superb inglenook. Well situated, only 10 minutes from the M5 and M42, and an ideal centre for Stratford, Warwick, Worcester, the Cotswolds and Malverns. Two double bedded rooms (one with bath en-suite) and one twin-bedded room. All rooms have colour TV, tea-makers, washbasins. Bed and Breakfast from £12. Also four self-catering cottages, colour TV, fully equipped with linen, electricity, gas etc. Washing machine and telephone at extra charge. Open all year.

HEREFORD. Mrs Catherine B. Smith, Tremorithic, Bacton, Hereford HR2 0AU (Golden Valley [0981] 240291). Working farm. Have a peaceful away-from-it-all holiday in a 17th century farmhouse offering good home cooking and comfortable accommodation. The house enjoys panoramic views of the Black Mountains and provides easy access to the Brecon Beacons, Wales and the many beauty spots of the Wye Valley. Open from April to October there are two double and one single bedrooms; bathroom, toilet; sittingroom, diningroom. Children welcome; cot, high chair and babysitting provided. Pets by arrangement. Car essential — parking. Bed and Breakfast from £10 per person per night, including bedtime drinks. Evening Meal available. Reduced rates for children by arrangement. Send SAE for brochure.

HEREFORD. Mrs Helen Jones, Sink Green Farm, Rotherwas, Hereford HR2 6LE (0432-870 223). Working farm, join in. Warm and friendly atmosphere awaits your arrival at this 16th century farmhouse, on the banks of the River Wye. Three miles south of the cathedral city of Hereford, with Ross-on-Wye, Leominster, Ledbury, Malvern and the Black Mountains within easy reach. All rooms have ensuite or private bathroom, tea/coffee making facilities and colour TV. One room with four-poster, family room by arrangement. Guests' own lounge. Babysitting if required. Pets by arrangement. Bed and Breakfast from £14 per person, Evening Meal optional.

HEREFORD. Mrs J. Layton, Grafton Villa Farm, Grafton, Hereford HR2 8ED (0432 268689). ♥♥ A farmhouse of great character and warmth set in an acre of lawns with panoramic views of our beautiful countryside. We offer our guests a relaxing holiday enjoying an excellent varied menu to Cordon Bleu standard using local produce with farmhouse proportions! Charmingly furnished bedrooms with vanity unit, TV and drinks facilities. Guests' own bathrooms, separate log-fired lounge and diningroom. Twin and double bedrooms. Children and pets welcome. Closed Christmas. Bed and Breakfast from £12; Evening Meal from £8.50. Herefordshire Hamper.

HEREFORD. Mrs L.M. Powell, Parsonage Farm, Walterstone, Hereford (Crucorney [0873] 890341). Working farm. Parsonage Farm is situated in the heart of the country with some glorious views, and many rambles down country lanes to enjoy. Many of the activities on the farm should both educate and amuse adults and children alike. Pony trekking and mountain climbing close at hand. Excellent country food, with four-course Evening Meal. One family and three double bedrooms (two with washbasins); bathroom, toilets; sitting/dining room with separate tables. Cot, high chair and babysitting available, plus ponies for children to ride. Pets allowed. Open all year except Christmas and New Year. Suitable for the disabled. Car essential. Evening Dinner, Bed and Breakfast, or Bed and Breakfast only. Reductions for children and Senior Citizens. SAE, please.

HEREFORD. Mrs R.T. Andrews, Webton Court, Kingstone, Hereford HR2 9NF (0981 250220). ♛♛

Working farm. Webton Court is a Georgian Black and White Farmhouse situated in open country in the heart of beautiful Wye Valley amidst green fields. This is ideal touring country at any time of the year. It would be difficult to find lovelier scenery than that around Symonds Yat, Forest of Dean, Chepstow and the Severn Bridge or, to the west, the rugged grandeur of the Welsh Mountains. Malvern and Stratford-upon-Avon also offer peace and tranquillity. There is accommodation in three double, one single and two family bedrooms, all with washbasins; two bathrooms, five toilets; sittingroom; diningroom. Children are welcome, cot, high chair and babysitting. Pets welcome. Open all year with electric heating. Plain home cooking using fresh garden and farm produce. Roasts of all meats are enjoyed. Early morning tea. Children under 12 and Senior Citizens are welcome at 10 per cent reductions. Horse riding available in local woods and countryside. Riding lessons, etc. Full Board, Evening Dinner, Bed and Breakfast or Bed and Breakfast only. Fire Certificate granted. Terms: Bed and Breakfast (one week stay) £10 per person per night; Evening Meal £6.50. One night only £12. Two-five nights £11 per night.

APPLE TREE COTTAGE – Near HEREFORD

**Enquiries to MONICA BARKER,
Apple Tree Cottage, Mansel Lacy,
Near Hereford HR4 7HH.
Tel: (098 122) 688 – 24 hrs.**

15th-century Cruck-construction cottage set in beautiful Hereford countryside – quiet, peaceful and friendly. Ideal for walkers and birdwatchers. Within easy reach of Cotswolds, North and South Wales, Black Mountains and many historic sites. One twin-bedded room with en-suite facilities, one double (single) and one twin-bedded room with shared bathroom; extra WC; lounge with TV for evening use. BED AND BREAKFAST FROM £15 (en-suite) and £12. Evening Meal and Packed Lunch by arrangement. SPECIAL BREAKS throughout the Winter, including CHRISTMAS. Car essential. Situated in the small hamlet of Mansel Lacy, seven miles N.W. of HEREFORD CITY, off the A480.

KIMBOLTON. Mrs Jean Franks, The Fieldhouse Farm, Kimbolton, Near Leominster HR6 0EP (0568-4789). Working farm.

A warm friendly welcome awaits you on our working family farm three miles from the attractive market town of Leominster, and eleven miles from the historic town of Ludlow. We offer excellent accommodation in peaceful surroundings, with truly magnificent views. The comfortable and spacious bedrooms have tea-making facilities. There is an attractive guests' sitting/diningroom, with oak beams and inglenook fireplace. Home cooking is a speciality and delicious breakfasts are served by Mrs Franks, a former Home Economics teacher; Evening Meals on request. Personal attention and high standards are assured. Bed and Breakfast from £11. Tourist Board registered.

KINGTON. Mrs E.E. Protheroe, Bucks Head House, School Farm, Hergest, Kington HR5 3EW (Kington [0544] 231063). Working farm.

Newly modernised farmhouse on 290-acre mixed farm which has been worked by the Protheroe family since 1940 and carries cattle, sheep and crops. Wye Valley, Black Mountains, Elan Valley, Ludlow, Hereford Cathedral, Black and White villages all within easy reach. Pony riding available at extra charge. Two double, two single, two family bedrooms, with washbasins; two bathrooms, two showers, four toilets; two sitting rooms; tea/coffee making facilities in all rooms; diningroom. Snooker room with full size table. Cot, high chair and reduced rates for children; babysitting by arrangement. Pets free of charge, by arrangement only. Car essential, parking. Central heating. Peaceful walks around the farm and its sheep walk "Hergest Ridge". Evening Dinner/Meal, Bed and Breakfast or Bed and Breakfast only. Eight-berth mobile home also available. ETB registered.

KINGTON. Mrs Pat Griffiths, The Beacon, Bradnor Hill, Kington HR5 3RE (Kington [0544] 230182).

The Beacon, set in picturesque countryside of the Herefordshire/Welsh border, is situated high above the little market town of Kington with wonderful views of surrounding hills — Malverns to the East, Black Mountains to the south. Excellent walks; ideal for naturalists; surrounded by National Trust land; 50 yards from the clubhouse of Kington's 18-hole golf course, highest in England and Wales. Spacious, comfortable lounge with colour TV. Bedrooms (double, twin-bedded, family, single) all with washbasins; own toilet and showers. Bed and Breakfast £16 per night; Dinner £8.95. Stay for seven nights, we charge for six giving one night free per person. A wide and varied menu provided, home cooking prepared to highest standard. Licensed. Car park. Send or 'phone for brochure. Open all year. Tourist Board registered.

LEDBURY. Mrs Anne Brazier, Munsley Acre Country Guest House, Ledbury HR8 2SH (0531 670568).

Munsley Acre is situated in its own grounds, down a quiet lane in open countryside with splendid views in all directions. Ideal centre for the Malverns, Forest of Dean, Wye Valley, Welsh Borders, and the cathedral cities of Hereford, Worcester and Gloucester. Excellent walking and cycling country. Single, double and twin rooms with washbasins; two bath/shower rooms, three WCs. Central heating with open fire in lounge; colour TV. Good home cooking using own produce; Table Licence; morning tea and other beverages available. Fire Certificate. Ample parking. Sorry, no pets. Non-smokers preferred. Bed and Breakfast £13.50 daily; Bed, Breakfast and Dinner £19 daily. Three-day rates available. Discounts for parties of five or more adults. Send for free brochure and details — SAE appreciated.

LEDBURY. Mrs Jane West, Church Farm, Coddington, Ledbury HR8 1JJ (053186 271). Working farm.

A Black and White 16th century listed farmhouse on a working farm, close to the Malvern Hills. Ideal for touring. Warm hospitality assured. There ia accommodation in two double and one single bedrooms; bathroom, toilet; sitting-room; diningroom. Children are welcome (reduced rates under 10 years), cot and babysitting provided. Plenty of good English fare, everything home made wherever possible. Log fires, TV, pets allowed. Open all year. Bed and Breakfast from £11. Bedtime drink included. Car essential — parking. Situated midway between Ross-on-Wye, Hereford, Gloucester and Worcester. Tourist Board listed. SAE, please, for further details.

LEDBURY near. Mrs Elizabeth Godsall, Moor Court Farm, Stretton Grandison, Near Ledbury HR8 2TR (053183 408).

Relax and enjoy our beautiful 15th century timber-framed farmhouse with adjoining Oast-house whose location will ensure a peaceful break. We are a traditional working Herefordshire hop and livestock farm situated in scenic countryside. Central to the major market towns, easy access to the Malverns, Wye Valley and Welsh Borders. Spacious bedrooms, en-suite or private bathroom, tea/coffee making facilities; oak-beamed lounge and dining-room. Walks through surrounding farmland and woods. Bed and Breakfast from £12; En-suite £16.

LEOMINSTER. Mrs Mary O. Carter, Kimbolton Court, Kimbolton, Leominster HR6 0HH (Leysters [0568-87] 259). ✿ ✿ Situated at the end of a peaceful lane half a mile from A4112, which is off the A49, is Kimbolton Court where guests are always assured of a very warm welcome in friendly relaxing surroundings. Set amidst grazing land, it is a small stone farmhouse which offers two en-suite bedrooms either double or twin. Tea/coffee facilities and clock/radio. Superb Cordon Bleu meals are served in garden room which overlooks patio and lawn. Large TV lounge, woodburner and small library. Open all year except Christmas and New Year. Bed and Breakfast from £13.50; Dinner optional at varied prices from £6.50 to £12. Natural spring water supply.

WELCOME TO RATEFIELD FARM

A traditional livestock farm set amidst glorious National Trust parkland laid out by Capability Brown. Secluded and peaceful yet only three miles from the antiques town of Leominster. Nature trail; lots of animals, including pony. Guests welcome to watch and join in farm chores. Riding and fishing nearby. Rooms have washbasins and tea making facilities. Two bathrooms, sitting room with colour TV, diningroom. Children welcome; pets by arrangement. Award winning food, including vegetarian. Bed and Breakfast £12.50 per night, dinner £7.00. Inspected and Listed by the English Tourist Board.

Mrs Evelyn Mears, Ratefield Farm, Kimbolton, Leominster, Hereford and Worcester HR6 0JB (Leominster [0568] 2507)

LEOMINSTER. Mrs Pauline Edwards, Stocklow Manor Farm, Staunton-on-Arrow, Pembridge, Leominster HR6 9HT (Pembridge [054-47] 436). Working farm. Delightful countryside surrounds this 350 acre mixed farm (cattle, sheep and arable crops, pet Jacob sheep) which is worked by the Edwards family. Farmhouse has panoramic views; in an ideal area for walking and bird watching. Situated near the Welsh borders it is a perfect base for touring the many places of interest. Pembridge with its historic inns three miles, Leominster 11 miles and Hereford 17 miles. Elan Valley, Ludlow, Black Mountains, Hereford Cathedral all within easy reach. Staunton-on-Arrow village one mile away. Overlooking a pretty garden with lawns, shrubs, rose borders and beyond to a large pool with wildfowl, the accommodation consists of one family, one double and one twin-bedded rooms (all with washbasins); bathroom, separate shower, toilet; sittingroom, diningroom; TV; shaver points. Tea and coffee making facilities in all bedrooms. Sorry, no pets. Children welcome at reduced rates. Cot available. Jacko, the donkey, will amuse the young guests. Coarse fishing on the farm. Car essential — ample parking. Evening Dinner, Bed and Breakfast or Bed and Breakfast only. Fresh eggs from free range hens. SAE, please, for brochure and terms. Registered with English Tourist Board.

LONGTOWN. Mrs I. Pritchard, Olchon Cottage Farm, Longtown, Hereford HR2 0NS (Longtown Castle [087-387] 233). Working farm. An ideal location for a peaceful holiday in lovely walking country close to Offa's Dyke Path and Welsh Border. A smallholding of 32 acres, mostly sheep and cattle. The farmhouse is noted for its good, wholesome home-produced food, and many guests return to enjoy the homely, relaxing atmosphere. Magnificent views and many places of interest to visit. Accommodation comprises two family bedrooms with washbasins, electric blankets and tea/coffee making facilities; bathroom, toilet; sittingroom and diningroom with separate tables. Towels and soap provided. Reductions for children under 10 with cot, high chair and babysitting provided. Pets accommodated. Open all year round except Christmas for Evening Meal, Bed and Breakfast or Bed and Breakfast. Car essential — parking provided. ETB and WTB registered. Terms on application with stamp for brochure, please.

MALVERN. Jean and John Mobbs, Rock House, 144 West Malvern Road, Malvern WR14 4NJ (0684 574536). ♛♛ *Commended.* Attractive family-run early Victorian guest house situated high on hills. in peaceful atmosphere with superb views of over 40 miles. Ideal for rambling on hills or open country. 11 comfortable bedrooms, all with washbasins, most overlooking our splendid view. TV lounge, separate quiet room. Licensed to enhance excellent cuisine. Groups welcome. Parking on premises. Bed and Breakfast from £13.50. Stamp only, please, for brochure.

MALVERN WELLS. Mrs D.J. Knight, "The Dell House", Green Lane, Malvern Wells WR14 4HU (Malvern [0684] 564448). ♛♛ A former rectory in a peaceful village location, yet only two miles from Great Malvern, this elegant Regency period home lies in a glorious setting on the slopes of the magnificent Malvern Hills. Central heating, showers and tea/coffee facilities; TV lounge. Enjoy full English or Continental Breakfast in the beautiful morning room with breathtaking views across the Severn Vale to the Cotswolds beyond. Ample private parking. Golf, horse riding and Three Counties Showground nearby. Convenient for Stratford, Cotswolds, Wye Valley. Double or twin rooms. Bed and Breakfast from £16 per person. **Self catering apartments for two/three and four/six persons also available.** Open all year.

MALVERN WELLS. Mrs J.L. Morris, Brickbarns Farm, Hanley Road, Malvern Wells WR14 4HY (Malvern [068-45] 61775). Working farm. Brickbarns, a 200-acre mixed farm, is situated two miles from Great Malvern at the foot of the Malvern Hills, 300 yards from the bus service and one-and-a half miles from the train. The house which is 300 years old, commands excellent views of the Malvern Hills and guests are accommodated in one double, one single and one family bedrooms with washbasins; two bathrooms, shower room, two toilets; sittingroom and diningroom. Children welcome and cot and babysitting offered. Central heating. Car essential, parking. Open Easter to October for Bed and Breakfast from £11 nightly per person (£10.50 for longer stays). Reductions for children and Senior Citizens. Birmingham 40 miles, Hereford 20, Gloucester 17, Stratford 35 and the Wye Valley is just 30 miles.

HEREFORD & WORCESTERSHIRE – THE HEART OF ENGLAND!

A beautiful county which includes The Vale of Evesham and the rugged – if petite – Malvern Hills. It has been designated an "Area of Outstanding Beauty". Places of interest include The Avoncroft Museum of Buildings, Brockhampton, Ross-on-Wye, The Teme Valley and The Hereford & Worcester County Museum.

PERSHORE. Mrs P. Schermuly, The Old House, Naunton Beauchamp, Pershore WR10 2LQ (Bishampton [038682] 635). 👑👑 The Old House was originally built in the 17th century, with later additions. Four miles north of Pershore, off B4082, it is situated deep in the heart of the Midlands. The house is well away from crowds, yet it provides an excellent centre for seeing Stratford-upon-Avon, Worcester, Hereford and Gloucester with their Cathedrals; glass making in Stourbridge. Within reach of the Cotswolds, Wye Valley and Warwick. A car is essential. The centrally heated accommodation comprises one twin bedded room, one twin bedded room with en-suite bathroom, one double room. Lounge available with colour TV during the evenings; coal fire. Children welcome; cot available. Spacious garden. Bed and Breakfast, with Evening Meal, if required. Vegetarians catered for. Tourist Board registered. Brochure and terms on request.

ROSS-ON-WYE. Mrs Rice, Craig Farm, Coughton, Ross-on-Wye HR9 5SF (0989 65449). Craig Farm stands in 12-and-a-half acres of wooded grounds some two-and-a-half miles south of Ross-on-Wye off the B4228. The converted farmhouse, beautifully furnished and in a secluded setting, has three double letting bedrooms which enjoy a view across the swimming pool and lawns to the Chase Woods in a northerly direction. A covered patio with changing room and sauna stands alongside the pool where guests can enjoy the benefits of a relaxing few hours in the sun. Bed and Breakfast is available all year round from £17.

ROSS-ON-WYE. Mrs M.E. Drzymalska, Thatch Close, Llangrove, Ross-on-Wye HR9 6EL (Llangarron [098-984] 300). 👑👑 **Working farm, join in.** Secluded Georgian farmhouse set in large colourful gardens in 13 acres of pasture situated in the beautiful Wye Valley between Ross and Monmouth. Thatch Close offers a comfortable, homely atmosphere where guests are welcome to help feed the sheep, cows, calves, pigs and chickens or just relax and enjoy this traditionally run farm. Places of scenic beauty and historic attractions nearby include Forest of Dean, Black Mountains, Cathedral Cities, old castles and buildings. Guests have their own lounge/diningroom with colour TV. Twin bedroom, one double room with bathrooms en-suite, one double room with private bathroom; bathroom with shower. Breakfast and optional Evening Meal are prepared using mainly home grown produce. Vegetarian and diabetic meals arranged. Daily and weekly rates. Reduced rates for children. SAE for further details.

THE ARCHES

ROSS-ON-WYE. Jean and James Jones, The Arches Country House Hotel, Walford Road, Ross-on-Wye HR9 5PT (Ross-on-Wye [0989] 63348). 👑👑👑 The Arches Country House is an attractive Georgian-style building set in half-an-acre of lawns. Ideally situated, only ten minutes' walk from the town centre. All bedrooms are furnished and decorated to a high standard and have views of the lawned gardens. Tea making facilities are available in bedrooms also optional colour TV. Attractive residents' lounge with colour TV. Excellent home cooking, using fresh produce whenever possible. Licensed. Full central heating. Ample parking. A warm friendly atmosphere with personal service. Children at reduced rates sharing. Pets by arrangement. Open all year except Christmas. Bed and Breakfast from £14. Evening Meal optional. Weekly reductions. Single, double, twin, and family rooms, also one with en-suite facilities. AA listed. RAC Acclaimed. Les Routiers Award. SAE please.

ROSS-ON-WYE. Mr and Mrs L.M. Baker, Walnut Tree Cottage, Symonds Yat West, Ross-on-Wye HR9 6BN (Symonds Yat West [0600] 890828). 👑👑👑 This is a charming 19th century Cottage Hotel with a friendly atmosphere. All rooms have central heating, washbasins and en-suite facilities. Log fires, colour TV; bar; lounge and diningroom. Full English Breakfast served with good homely cooking and personal attention. Situated in a panoramic Alpine-style setting on the banks of the River Wye, home of the nesting peregrine falcons. Symonds Yat provides beautiful river and woodland walks. Ideal touring base for upper and lower Wye Valley areas and Forest of Dean. Children welcome. Sorry, no pets. Car essential — parking. Open January to December. Bed and Breakfast from £18; Evening Meal (optional) £9.50. Licensed. Send stamp, or telephone for details. Registered with WTB, Wye Dean Tourist Board Commendation Award.

ROSS-ON-WYE. Mrs Susan Dick, Merrivale Place, The Avenue, Ross-on-Wye HR9 5AW (Ross-on-Wye [0989] 64929).

🐾🐾 Merrivale Place is a lovely big Victorian house set in half an acre of gardens in a splendid tree-lined avenue. Peaceful surroundings overlooking trees and hills, yet close to the old market place centre of Ross, and near the River Wye. Guest accommodation in three spacious, comfortable bedrooms (double, twin and family) with wash-basins and shaver points. Three bathrooms, three toilets. TV lounge and separate diningroom. Full central heating. Good home cooking with garden produce. A very warm welcome extended to all guests. Sorry, no pets. Ample parking space inside grounds. Open April to October. Bed and Breakfast from £13 (Dinners available). Weekly terms. Come and see the lovely Wye Valley, Malverns, Brecon Beacons and the Golden Valley.

ROSS-ON-WYE. Mrs Marian Morris, Fairfields, Bromsash, Ross-on-Wye HR9 7PJ (Lea [098-981] 378).

Smallholding on the outskirts of Ross-on-Wye with a small herd of pedigree beef cattle. An 18th century farm-house with large gardens, tastefully renovated to retain character, and enjoying panoramic views of the Forest of Dean, the Black Mountains and lovely undulating country-side. One downstairs twin-bedded room (ideal for the dis-abled); two upstairs double bedrooms, all with washbasins. Bathroom, shower room, three toilets. Excellent home cooking with own or local produce. Early morning tea/coffee. Bed and Breakfast from £11; Evening Dinner optional. Short Breaks or weekly terms available. Registered with Wyedean and Heart of England Tourist Board.

ROSS-ON-WYE. Geoffrey and Josephine Baker, Brookfield House, Ledbury Road, Ross-on-Wye HR9 7AT (0989 62188).

🐾🐾 Geoffrey and Josephine Baker extend a warm welcome to guests and their pets. Early 18th century listed building five minutes' walk from town centre. Licensed. Garden and car park. Close to A40 and M50. TV and tea-making facilities in all rooms. Ideal centre for golfers and walkers. RAC/AA listed.

STOKE PRIOR. Mrs Shirley Bemand, Great House Farm, Stoke Prior, Near Leominster HR6 0LG (Steensbridge [056882] 663).

Nestled in the quiet pic-turesque village of Stoke Prior you can stay at Great House Farm, a large homely 17th century farmhouse set in pleasant gardens with lawn tennis and outdoor swimming pool, also many quiet country walks on the 800 acres of farmland. Guests' own TV lounge; diningroom; bathroom; two double, one twin-bedded rooms available with tea-making facilities. Babysitting by arrangement. Friendly service and good home cooking await you, to ensure that your stay is a pleasant one. A delightful Bed and Breakfast stop in a delightful part of North Herefordshire. Bed and Breakfast from £11; Evening Meal £7. HETB listed.

SYMONDS YAT WEST. Mr and Mrs Tony and Val Blunt, Woodlea Hotel, Symonds Yat West HR9 6BL (Symonds Yat [0600] 890206).

🐾🐾🐾 Friendly family run licensed Victorian hotel, set in secluded woodland valley overlooking famous Wye Rapids. Ideal holiday centre, just a mile away from A40, between nearby Monmouth and Ross-on-Wye, and numerous local attractions. Double, twin, single and family rooms, all with washbasins, razor points, central heating, radio/intercom, tea/coffee making equip-ment; most have en-suite facilities. Colour TV lounge, reading lounge, separate well-stocked bar and wine list, spacious diningroom — imaginative and distinctive home-cooked menu. Swimming pool. Dogs by arrangement. AA listed, RAC acclaimed. Bed and Breakfast from £19 per person. Party booking welcome. Brochure and tariff on request.

TARRINGTON. Mrs Jean Philips, Wilton Oaks, Tarrington, Hereford HR1 4ET (Tarrington [043-279] 212). 💜💜 *Commended.* Enjoy a farm holiday at

Wilton Oaks set in beautiful gardens surrounded by 30 acres of grounds. It has magnificent views over the majestic Malvern Hills and is a short drive away from the historic City of Hereford and the picturesque town of Ledbury. The house is comfortably furnished and has full central heating. There are two double rooms available and one twin bedded room, all with tea and coffee making facilities. The bedrooms also have their own vanity units. There is a guest bathroom and toilet available. Additionally there is a diningroom and separate lounge with colour TV. Bed and Breakfast from £12; Evening Meal from £6. Fresh produce. Ample car parking space available. Sorry, no pets. Open all year. ETB Registered. Write or telephone for further details.

TENBURY WELLS. Chris and Jane Keel, Hunthouse Farm, Frith Common, Between Tenbury Wells and Bewdley WR15 8JY (Clows Top [029922] 277 changing to 0299 892277). 💜💜 *Commended.* **Working**

farm. Relax and enjoy the comfort, peace and hospitality of our 16th century timber-framed farmhouse. In a tranquil location, elevated amidst a 180 acre arable/sheep farm, the house commands breathtaking views. The three comfortable bedrooms are en-suite (one with a private bathroom) all having tea/coffee making facilities. The house is a listed building and boasts oak beams and open fireplaces with full central heating and colour TV in the guest sittingroom where visitors are welcomed with tea and homemade cake. Excellent local facilities for meals. Convenient for Worcester, Shropshire, Hereford, NEC, Ironbridge and Wales. AA listed. Children over eight years welcome. Sorry, no pets. Bed and Breakfast from £14.

Cordon bleu dinners by candlelight in 17th century Country House.

"The Steppes"

💜💜💜

B.T.A. Commendation Award, Ashley Courtenay, Farm Holiday Guide Readers Diploma, A.A. Selected, Relais Routiers. Recommended by leading travel writers, Member of English Tourist Board and Heart of England Tourist Board. Featured on Central Television, January 1983.

Special 3-day Christmas and New Year house parties.

"The Steppes" is a delightful old country house set in 1½ acres of grounds and situated in the glorious Wye Valley. This characterful house retains its historic features, including exposed beams throughout and a grand inglenook fireplace in the dining room, yet it has been sympathetically modernised to provide for all year round comfort, including full central heating. Log fires are lit during the colder months. Cobbled and flagged farmhouse cellars have been restored to provide an intriguing bar in which to enjoy a relaxing drink. All bedrooms are furnished to a high standard, including en suite facilities, clock/radio, colour television and tea & coffee making facilities, telephone, personal drinks fridge.

Unsolicited praise from previous guests has established "The Steppes" as a gourmet's paradise, with the emphasis on originality of menu and interesting English and Continental dishes. "The Steppes" is licensed and a full range of aperitifs and fine wines is always available. Older children are welcome. Prices including Breakfast, Dinner and en-suite room from £34 per person per night. "The Steppes" is open all year round and we are pleased to offer "Winter Bargain Break" terms.

The area offers the quiet timelessness of the English countryside at its finest and is ideal for the walker being within easy reach of the Malvern Hills and Black Mountains. Here too are grand old houses and castles, picturesque Tudor villages, markets and antique shops.

For colour brochure SAE or telephone: **Mrs Tricia Howland, "The Steppes," Ullingswick, Herefordshire. Tel. Hereford (0432) 820424**

Terms quoted in this publication may be subject to increase if rises in costs necessitate

VOWCHURCH. Mr & Mrs Alan Watkins, Upper Gilvach Farm, St. Margarets, Vowchurch, Hereford HR2 0QY (Michaelchurch [098-123] 618). Working farm, join in. Enjoy a peaceful holiday on this family run dairy farm in the depths of West Herefordshire. Upper Gilvach is between the Black Mountains and Golden Valley, unspoiled country steeped in history, St. Margarets church having its own Rood Screen. A warm welcome awaits guests: Jenny the donkey will amuse the younger visitors. Double and family rooms are available, all with washbasins, some en-suite. Tea/coffee making facilities. Sittingroom, lounge with colour TV. Separate diningroom where tasty farmhouse cooking is served. Central heating throughout. Large attractive garden. SAE, for terms.

VOWCHURCH. Mrs Joan Powell, Little Green Farm, Newton, Vowchurch, Hereford HR2 0QJ

Little Green Farm

(Michaelchurch [098-123] 205). Working farm. Little Green Farm has 50 acres with cattle and sheep, modernised farmhouse facing south, peacefully situated between the Golden Valley and Black Mountains. Hereford 15 miles. Many places of historic interest and natural beauty within easy distance. Literature provided to help guests. Two family, one double bedrooms (all with washbasins, shaving points and electric heating); electric blankets on all beds. One bathroom, two toilets. Separate tables in diningroom. Colour TV in lounge. A warm welcome assured, with good farmhouse fare, mainly home grown. Bed, Breakfast and Evening Dinner. Bedtime drink and biscuits included. Open all year except Christmas. Ample parking. AA listed. ETB registered. SAE please.

Tudor Guest House

Broad Street, Weobley, Herefordshire

Tel: (0544) 318201 RAC Listed

Quietly situated at the centre of this picturesque village, a small friendly Grade II Listed Guest House which offers two double and two single rooms, all beautifully decorated with Laura Ashley soft furnishings and vanity units; tea and coffee making facilities; luxury guests' bathroom and separate WC. Cosy TV lounge with log fires, tourist information, books and magazines. Full central heating. Licensed oak-beamed dining room serving good fresh food. Delightful cottage garden with patio sun-trap. Beautiful unspoilt countryside on the English/Welsh border. Very high standards. RAC Listed. Bed and Breakfast from £15.00; Evening Meal from £10. Reductions for stays of 3 days or longer.

WEOBLEY. Tony and Una Williams, "The Gables Guest House", Broad Street, Weobley, Hereford

HR4 8SA (Weobley [0544] 318228). Beautiful old 14th century Tudor house situated in the centre of one of England's prettiest villages. Open from January to November, "The Gables" is renowned for its hearty English Breakfasts. Several small cafes, restaurants and hotels in the village. An area of great natural beauty with the Malvern Hills and the Welsh Mountains easily accessible, it is also an antique and art lovers' paradise. "The Gables", set in one acre of lovely gardens, offers a choice of double, single and family bedrooms, all with washbasins, shaver points, tea/coffee making facilities; three rooms en-suite. All rooms are beautifully and comfortably furnished. Guests' lounge with colour TV. Three garden rooms. Two rooms available in Coach House, with shower/toilet. Pets accepted. Car not essential, but there is ample parking. Several golf courses nearby. Teas, coffees, snacks served all day. Registered with Heart of England and Promotion of Herefordshire Tourist Boards. Bed and Breakfast from £12.50.

HEREFORD & WORCESTERSHIRE – THE HEART OF ENGLAND!

A beautiful county which includes The Vale of Evesham and the rugged – if petite – Malvern Hills. It has been designated an "Area of Outstanding Beauty". Places of interest include The Avoncroft Museum of Buildings, Brockhampton, Ross-on-Wye, The Teme Valley and The Hereford & Worcester County Museum.

WORCESTER near. Mrs Sally Stewart, Leigh Court, Near Worcester WR6 5LB (Leigh Sinton [0886] 32275). ♛ ♛ *Approved.* **Working farm.** One mile off A4103 four miles west of Worcester and four miles north of the Malverns, follow Tithe Barn signs. This mellowed Teme Valley farmhouse offers you a warm welcome, a relaxed atmosphere and spacious, comfortable accommodation. Double or twin, H&C or en-suite, hot drinks facilities. Lounge with colour TV, diningroom with separate tables, billiards room. Guests may explore the 270 acre farm. The great 14th century tithe barn has been restored by English Heritage. River fishing. Open Easter to October. Bed and Breakfast from £14, Dinner by prior arrangement. Brochure available.

WORCESTER near. Sylvia and Brian Wynn, The Old Smithy, Pirton, Worcester WR8 9EJ (Worcester [0905] 820482). A 17th century half-timbered country house set in peaceful countryside with many interesting walks. Centrally situated, within easy reach of Cheltenham, Gloucester, Malvern and Bredon Hills and Cotswolds, Worcester Cathedral and Royal Worcester Porcelain. Four and a half miles from the motorway M5 junction 7. Relaxed homely atmosphere. Lounge with inglenook log fire and colour TV. Two/three double bedrooms (one twin-bedded), bathroom and toilet. Private facilities also available. Central heating. Gardens and Paddock. Ample parking. Bed and farmhouse Breakfast from £12; Evening Meal optional extra. Sorry, no pets or children under 10 years. Heart of England Tourist Board listed — commended. Craft Workshop — Harris Tweed, woollens, pottery etc.

WORCESTER near. Miss Jo Morris, Knowle Farm, Suckley, Near Worcester WR6 5DJ (0886 884347). Part-timbered 17th century farmhouse with 25 acres grassland, used mainly for horses. Adjacent to a small, quiet country inn, the house is in an elevated position with unrivalled views of the Malvern Hills and offers accommodation all year round. Large colourful garden. The quaint market towns of Bromyard, Ledbury and Hereford are nearby, and Knowle Farm is in the heart of a fruit-growing area where visitors enjoy the magnificent spring blossoms. Superb walking country. One double and two single bedrooms (one with washbasin); bathroom, toilet. Sittingroom with woodburner fire, diningroom. Central heating keeps the house comfortable throughout the year. Car essential — parking. Traditional hearty English Breakfast. Fresh farm eggs. Bed and Breakfast from £12 (bedtime drink). This is a non-smoking establishment.

KENT

ASHFORD. Mrs E. Ashby, Bevenden House, Spicers Hill, Great Chart, Ashford TN26 1JP (Bethersden [023382] 226). A warm welcome awaits you in this superior 17th century country residence with an elevated position and beautiful views set in 10 acres. Ideally situated for touring south-east England. On A28 Ashford to Tenterden road: four miles Ashford, eight miles Tenterden, 18 miles Maidstone, 48 miles from London. Full central heating. Diningroom; sittingroom with TV; one twin-bedded room and one double room with en-suite showers and washbasins and a further double room with own guests' bathroom. All with tea/coffee making facilities. Heated outdoor swimming pool. Bed and Breakfast from £15; Evening Meals by arrangement. Children over eight years welcome. Tourist Board registered.

WHEN MAKING ENQUIRIES PLEASE MENTION
FARM HOLIDAY GUIDES

AYLESFORD. Mrs Diane Tucker, Court Farm, Aylesford ME20 7AZ (Maidstone [0622] 717293).

Court Farm, which is situated at the end of the old village of Aylesford, near the North Downs, is easily accessible from the M2 and M20. London is only 33 miles away and the coast 29. Carmelite Priory, castles, ancient bridge and leisure facilities are all nearby. Spacious bedrooms with electric radiators, colour TV, tea/coffee making facilities; bathroom, two toilets. Ample parking. Miniature ponies, dog, ducks, etc. Renowned for friendly relaxed atmosphere.

BIRCHINGTON near. Mrs Liz Goodwin, Woodchurch Farmhouse, Woodchurch, Near Birchington

CT7 0HE (Thanet [0843] 32468). This attractive Elizabethan/Georgian farmhouse is situated in a quiet rural area yet only two minutes from long stretches of sandy beach. Within easy reach of Canterbury, Sandwich, Rye, Chilham and the cross-Channel ferries. There is ample parking and a car is essential. Very comfortable bedrooms with tea/coffee making facilities. Sittingroom with TV. Bathroom and shower for guests' use only. Separate beamed diningroom. A warm welcome and a comfortable stay assured at Woodchurch. Four course Evening Meal by arrangement. Bed and Breakfast from £11.50. Please write or telephone for further details.

CANTERBURY. Mr and Mrs R. Linch, Upper Ansdore, Duckpit Lane, Petham, Canterbury CT4 5QB

(Petham [022 770] 672). Working farm. Beautiful secluded listed Tudor farmhouse with various livestock, situated in an elevated position with far-reaching views of the wooded countryside of the North Downs. The property overlooks a Kent Trust Nature Reserve. It is five miles south of the cathedral city of Canterbury and only 30 minutes' drive to the ports of Dover and Folkestone. The accommodation comprises three double and one twin bedded rooms. All have shower, WC en-suite and tea/coffee making facilities. Dining/sitting room, heavily beamed and with large inglenook. Open all year, excluding Christmas. Car essential. Bed and Full English Breakfast from £14 per person. South East Tourist Board Listed.

CANTERBURY. Mrs Lisa Dellaway, Anns House, 63 London Road, Canterbury CT2 8JZ (0227 768767). A large Victorian guest house situated close the the city centre. Take first turning on the left from A2 motorway. 19 bedrooms, all with washbasin, TV and tea/coffee making facilities, some with en-suite and four-poster beds. Terms from £15 per person per night. Large private car park. Tourist Board listed.

The Woodpeckers Country Hotel Ltd

R.A.C.; ETB Bedroom 👑👑👑

Womenswold, Near Canterbury, Kent
Tel: Canterbury [0227] 831319

A charming Victorian hotel, just six miles from Canterbury and nine miles from the coast. The garden comprises 2½ acres including lawns, flower beds and vegetable garden. Children will love their play area which has a sandpit and a swing, while all the family can have fun in the heated swimming pool with its water slide and diving board. There are 16 comfortable rooms all with H/C water and tea and coffee making facilities.

Four poster Georgian brass bedstead, bridal bedrooms all en suite with colour TV. Warm air central heating. Woodpeckers is highly recommended for traditional country home baking as reported in 'The Daily Express', 'The Guardian', the 'Dover Express' and 'The Telegraph'. Horse riding, fishing, golf and tennis nearby. There are a wealth of historical places to visit just a short car ride away. Licensed; new luxury bar. Farm Holiday Guide Diploma winner for accommodation and food 1979-80-81.

CANTERBURY. Mrs A. Hunt, Bower Farmhouse, Stelling Minnis, Near Canterbury CT4 6BB (Stelling Minnis [022787] 430). Anne & Nick Hunt welcome you to Bower Farm House, a traditional 17th-century Kentish farmhouse situated in the midst of Stelling Minnis, a medieval common of 125 acres of unspoilt trees, shrubs and open grassland; seven miles south of the cathedral city of Canterbury and nine miles from the coast. The countryside abounds in beauty spots and nature reserves. The house is heavily beamed and maintains its original charm. The accommodation comprises a double room with en-suite shower and handbasin and a twin-bedded room; guests' own bathroom. Full traditional English breakfast is served with home-made bread, marmalade and fresh free-range eggs. Children welcome; pets by prior arrangement. Open all year (except Christmas). Car essential. Excellent pub food five minutes away. Bed and Breakfast from £13.50 per person. Tourist Board listed.

CANTERBURY near. Mrs Sheila Wilton, Walnut Tree Farm, Lynsore Bottom, Upper Hardres, Near Canterbury CT4 6EG (Stelling Minnis [022-787] 375). Walnut Tree Farm, a 14th century thatched cottage situated in a peaceful valley, completely unspoilt with no new development, in one of the most attractive corners of Kent, is an ideal place for those "wishing to get away from it all" or "en route" to the Continent. Canterbury six miles, Folkestone and Dover 12 miles. The farm is a smallholding of six acres offering good Farmhouse Breakfast, home-made bread, marmalade, preserves and fresh eggs. Accommodation in a period annexe adjacent to the cottage offers excellent family accommodation, one double room, one twin-bedded room, all tastefully furnished with pine furniture. Guests' own shower and toilet. Annexe can be let as self-catering cottage if desired. Also dormer bedroom in cottage with en-suite shower room. Reductions for children under 13. Regret no pets. Open all year except Christmas. Car essential, parking. Bed and Breakfast from £15 per person per night. SAE for brochure. Excellent pub food five minutes' drive away.

Terms quoted in this publication may be subject to increase if rises in costs necessitate

DEAL. Mr and Mrs P.S.F. Jailler, "Blencathra Country Hotel", Kingsdown Hill, Kingsdown, Deal

CT14 8EA (0304 373725). ♛ ♛ Blencathra is a friendly, well appointed family run hotel in the unspoilt village of Kingsdown. Situated in a private road it has panoramic views of the Channel and golf course. Only five miles from ferries for Continental travellers or ideal base for exploring this historic area. Close to beach, cliff and country walks. Most rooms have showers or en-suite facilities, TV and tea/coffee making facilities. Pleasant garden, croquet lawn and ample off-road parking. Bed and Breakfast from £15. SAE, please, for brochure.

HAWKHURST. Mrs R. Piper, Conghurst Farm, Hawkhurst TN18 4RW (Hawkhurst [0580] 753331).

♛ ♛ *Commended.* **Working farm.** Conghurst is a sheep and arable farm situated on the Weald of Kent. This is an excellent centre for holidaymaking, Cranbrook, Tenterden and Rye are all nearby. Tunbridge Wells, 16 miles away, is the nearest largest town. The coast is 14 miles away. There are many National Trust and private houses and gardens in the area. The Georgian farmhouse is comfortable and has three double bedrooms, all with private bathrooms. Guests' TV room. Evening Meals by arrangement. Unheated swimming pool. Children welcome, but sorry no pets. Car essential. Bed and Breakfast from £14 per person per night.

MARGATE. Mr and Mrs A. Hendry, Ivydene Guest House, 54 Grosvenor Place, Margate CT9 1UV (0843 223152). A stone terraced guest house situated in a high position overlooking the well-known Dreamland Amusement Park. Within five minutes' walk of town centre, sandy beaches and all amusements. Ramsgate five miles, Canterbury 14. Many places of interest within easy reach. Four double and four family bedrooms, all with washbasins; bathroom and two toilets; sittingroom; diningroom. Cot, high chair, reduced rates for children. Pets permitted. Open all year. Coin phone. Parking nearby. Packed lunches by arrangement. Senior Citizens very welcome. Reduced rates May or September. SAE, please for terms.

FOR THE MUTUAL GUIDANCE
OF GUEST AND HOST

Every year literally thousands of holidays, short-breaks and overnight stops are arranged through our guides, the vast majority without any problems at all. In a handful of cases, however, difficulties do arise about bookings, which often could have been prevented from the outset.

It is important to remember that when accommodation has been booked, both parties — guests and hosts — have entered into a form of contract. We hope that the following points will provide helpful guidance.

GUESTS: When enquiring about accommodation, be as precise as possible. Give exact dates, numbers in your party and the ages of any children. State the number and type of rooms wanted and also what catering you require — bed and breakfast, full board, etc. Make sure that the position about evening meals is clear — and about pets, reductions for children or any other special points.

Read our reviews carefully to ensure that the proprietors you are going to contact can supply what you want. Ask for a letter confirming all arrangements, if possible.

If you have to cancel, do so as soon as possible. Proprietors do have the right to retain deposits and under certain circumstances to charge for cancelled holidays if adequate notice is not given and they cannot re-let the accommodation.

HOSTS: Give details about your facilities and about any special conditions. Explain your deposit system clearly and arrangements for cancellations, charges, etc, and whether or not your terms include VAT.

If for any reason you are unable to fulfil an agreed booking without adequate notice, you may be under an obligation to arrange alternative suitable accommodation or to make some form of compensation.

While every effort is made to ensure accuracy, we regret that FHG Publications cannot accept responsibility for errors, omissions or misrepresentation in our entries or any consequences thereof. Prices in particular should be checked because we go to press early. We will follow up complaints but cannot act as arbiters or agents for either party.

MARGATE (Cliftonville). The Malvern Private Hotel, Eastern Esplanade, Cliftonville, Margate CT9 2HL (Thanet [0843] 290192). 👑👑👑 Credit Cards; Access, Visa, Amex, Diners. A small seafront licensed hotel, overlooking the promenade and lawns, with panoramic sea views. Close to indoor/outdoor bowling greens, Margate Winter Gardens, amusements, etc. The Channel ferry ports of Ramsgate, Dover and Folkestone are within easy reach for day trips to France, Belgium and Holland. Historic Canterbury Cathedral and zoo 16 miles. Central heating. *En-suite shower and toilet in most rooms. *Colour TV and tea/coffee making facilities. Bed and Breakfast from £15 per night. Telephone bookings accepted from Access and Visa cardholders.

ROLVENDEN. Mrs B.J. Hilder, Little Halden Farm, Rolvenden, Cranbrook TN17 4JL (0580 241254). The farmhouse on a working hop and livestock farm is situated in an area of outstanding natural beauty. The picturesque town of Tenterden with its steam railway and leisure centre is only two miles away. Visit the old Cinque Port town of Rye, Canterbury Cathedral, Dover Castle and many other places of interest in the area. There are two double rooms and one twin, each furnished to a high standard and having washbasins, colour TVs and tea/coffee making facilities. Separate shower and bathroom for guests' use. All rooms are centrally heated. Bed and Breakfast from £12.50 per person. Non-smoking.

SEVENOAKS. Mrs Amanda Webb, Pond Cottage, Eggpie Lane, Weald, Sevenoaks TN14 6NP (Sevenoaks [0732] 463773). Beautiful Grade II listed 16th century farmhouse with inglenook fireplace and oak beams. Set in three and a half acres of ground with tennis court and a large, safely fenced pond with fish, kingfishers and wild duck. This is beautiful countryside and yet only 30 minutes by train to London; one hour to the coast at Dover, Eastbourne and Brighton. Sir Winston Churchill's Chartwell, Penshurst, Knole and some excellent and historic pubs nearby. Accommodation in one family room/double room (own bathroom, toilet and shower), one single room. Mrs Webb provides lovely cooked Breakfasts plus fruit juice, cereal and home made bread. Colour TV in sittingroom. Children welcome at reduced rates; babysitting. Pets by prior arrangement. Open all year. Registered with English Tourist Board. Please telephone for reservation or more information.

TENTERDEN. Mrs M.R. O'Connor, The Old Post House, Stone-in-Oxney, Tenterden TN30 7JN (Appledore [023 383] 258). Experience the peace and tranquillity of rural England at its best. This guest house overlooks the historic expanse of Romney Marsh and nestles against the hill of the Isle-in-Oxney in the heart of Kentish farmland. Only about ten minutes' drive to the delightful market towns of Rye and Tenterden, where excellent meals can be enjoyed. All rooms are equipped with central heating, washbasins, razor points, tea/coffee making facilities. One room with en-suite facilities. Bathroom and shower room. Open all year round. Children over eight years welcome. Pets must be left in car. Bed and traditional English Breakfast from £15 – £17 per person; delicious food can also be had in the village. Car essential, ample parking.

WHITSTABLE. Mrs N. Fitchie, Windyridge, Wraik Hill, Whitstable CT5 3BY (0227 263506). 👑👑👑 Windyridge is situated in a quiet country lane, 10 minutes away from the M2 motorway, mainline stations and the historic city of Canterbury with its magnificent cathedral and interesting buildings. This charming house has splendid views over the Thames Estuary with a wealth of old world charm. Large comfortable lounge with colour TV, spacious garden and sun lounge for relaxation. Two double rooms en-suite, one double with shower, one family room en-suite and three singles with washbasins; all have colour TV, radio alarm clock, hair dryer and tea/coffee making facilities. Bathroom with shower, three toilets. Two sittingrooms; diningroom. Licensed. Ample parking. Sorry, no pets. Children over nine years welcome. Whitstable, two miles away, is noted for its sailing, water ski-ing and golfing. Approximately 20 miles away lie Ramsgate, Pegwell Bay and Dover. Evening Meal, Bed and Breakfast or Bed and Breakfast only. Weekly and daily terms on request. Fire Certificate. ETB registered.

LANCASHIRE

BLACKPOOL near. Mrs H.J. Smith, Swarbrick Hall Farm, Weeton, Near Blackpool PR4 3JJ (0253 836 465). ☙☙ Working farm. A warm welcome awaits you at this Georgian farmhouse on a 200 acre working farm. Situated in the rural area of Fylde, Swarbrick Hall is within easy reach of the hustle and bustle of the seaside resort of Blackpool and also the quieter resort of Lytham St Annes. The location is also ideal for access to the Lake District, Trough of Bowland and the Yorkshire Dales. Comfortable and spacious accommodation is offered comprising one twin/family bedroom with en-suite bathroom, central heating, colour TV and tea/coffee making facilities. Children welcome, but regret no pets. Terms from £15. Car essential. Open January to December. Also available is one self contained cottage which sleeps four/five. Terms available on request.

CARNFORTH. Mrs Gill Close, Cotestones Farm, Sand Lane, Warton, Carnforth LA5 9NH (0524 732418). Situated on the North Lancashire coast near to the M6 Junction 35. This is a family-run dairy farm which adjoins Leighton Moss RSBP Reserve, also very near to Steamtown Railway Museum. Situated between Lancaster/Morecambe and the Lake District, it is an ideal base for touring the area. Tea/coffee facilities and washbasins in all rooms. Open all year except Christmas. Bed and Breakfast from £10. Reductions for children. Pets welcome. OS Ref: SD487715.

CHIPPING. Doreen and David Ingram, Hough Clough Farmhouse, Houghclough Lane, Chipping PR3 2NT (0995 61272). ☙☙ Commended. Stonebuilt Victorian farmhouse in a delightful hillside setting in the Ribble Valley close to Bleasdale Moors and Trough of Bowland. Superb views to the south overlooking the valley to Longridge Fells, Pendle Hill, Winter Hill and beyond. Easy access from M6/M55 in ideal walking country or as a base for touring inland to the Lakes and Yorkshire Dales, and to the coast with Blackpool just 40 minutes away. Two family and one double bedrooms, all with colour TV, tea/coffee making and en-suite/private facilities. Comfortable lounge, lovely separate diningroom. Children welcome, babysitting service. Under personal supervision of resident proprietors. Licensed. Bed and Breakfast £14.50 (maximum) per person.

CLITHEROE. Mrs Frances Oliver, Wytha Farm, Rimington, Clitheroe BB7 4EQ (0200 445295). Working farm. Farmhouse accommodation on dairy farm in Ribble Valley with extensive views. Within walking distance of Pendle Hill. Ideal touring centre for Lake District, Yorkshire Dales, Bronte Country, interesting and historic Clitheroe. Children welcome. Babysitting service. Beautiful picnic area. Packed lunches available. Farm produce when possible, and home cooking. Accommodation comprises family and double rooms; TV lounge; central heating. Ample car parking. Pets by prior arrangement (£1 per day). Bed and Breakfast from £12.50; Evening Meal £7. Reduced rates for children under 11 years. Open all year.

CLITHEROE. Mrs M.A. Berry, Lower Standen Farm, Whalley Road, Clitheroe BB7 1PP (Clitheroe [0200] 24176). ☙☙ Working farm, join in. Comfortable farmhouse accommodation with Bed and Breakfast all year round except Christmas, for holidaymakers planning to tour the Lake District and the scenic west coast. Blackpool is an hour's drive away; also convenient for touring the Yorkshire Dales; one mile from A59. Visitors can participate in the activities of this 40 acre farm by arrangement. Golf club and swimming pool nearby. Two double bedrooms, each with shower and additional single bed if required; one twin bedded room. All have washbasins, shaver points, TVs and tea/coffee making facilities. Bathroom, toilet; sittingroom; diningroom. Children welcome; cot, high chair, babysitting and reduced rates for under 12's. Pets welcome. Car essential — parking; public transport half a mile. Open all year except Christmas and New Year. Further details on request.

PLEASE SEND A STAMPED ADDRESSED ENVELOPE WITH ENQUIRIES

GARSTANG near. Mrs D.J. Hodge, Lower House Farm, Bilsborrow Lane, Bilsborrow, Near Garstang PR3 0RQ (Brock [0995] 40581). Working farm. Relax deep in the heart of the Lancashire countryside on a working dairy farm. Peaceful surroundings yet only 10 miles from Preston and 15 miles from Lancaster. Ideal situation for the seaside, the Lakes and the Ribble Valley. Excellent walks in the area but car essential. Stay in the recently renovated luxurious farmhouse. One double bedded room and one twin bedded room with adjoining shower room. Own dining/sittingroom, hospitality tray in bedrooms. Terms from £10.50 onwards for Bed and Breakfast. Reductions for children. Sorry, no pets. SAE for details.

KIRKHAM. Mrs Joan Colligan, High Moor Farm, Weeton, Kirkham PR4 3JJ (Blackpool [0253] 836273). 👑👑 High Moor Farm is situated six miles from Blackpool and is within easy reach of Lancaster, Lytham St. Annes, Morecambe, the Lake District and the Dales of Yorkshire. Local attractions include sea fishing, golfing, sand yachting, riding schools, Isle of Man Ferry (July/August) Fleetwood. Bed and Breakfast accommodation in one double, one family, one twin and one single rooms. Family and double have central heating, colour TV and tea making facilities. Full English or Continental Breakfast. Reductions for children under 12. Bed and Breakfast from £10 per night. Also available is a caravan site which is on level ground and all pitches are hard standing. On site shop, showers, launderette. Dogs must be kept on lead. AA listed. Terms: Car, Caravan and four people from £4.50 per night. Frame tent, caravanette £4.50 per night. SAE for further information.

PRESTON. Mrs Beryl Richardson, Bell Farm, Bradshaw Lane, Pilling, Preston PR3 6SN (Pilling [0253] 790324). Our Farmhouse is 200 years old with the original oak beams in every room. It is situated in North Fylde, a good central base for touring the Lake District, Yorkshire Dales, the historic city of Lancaster and Blackpool. For the horse lover, enjoy our quiet lanes and tracks. Stables available for your own horse and trap. Carriage rides can be arranged. Accommodation comprises two double and one single bedrooms, bathroom, parlour with open fire and TV, and dining room. Children welcome. Bed and Breakfast from £11.

Bell Farm

SOUTHPORT. Mrs Wendy E. Core, Sandy Brook Farm, 52 Wyke Cop Road, Scarisbrick, Southport PR8 5LR (Scarisbrick [0704] 880337). 👑👑 Bill and Wendy Core offer a homely, friendly atmosphere at Sandy Brook, a small working farm situated three and a half miles from the seaside resort of Southport and five miles from the historic town of Ormskirk. Motorways are easily accessible, and the Lake District, Trough of Bowland, Blackpool and North Wales are within easy reach. New barn conversions enable us to offer guests six en-suite bedrooms with colour TV and tea/coffee making facilities. Central heating throughout. Sittingroom with colour TV; diningroom. High chair, cots and babysitting available. Open all year round. Member of North West Tourist Board. Bed and Breakfast from £13; reductions for children. Weekly terms on request.

WYCOLLER. Mrs Pat Hodgson, Parson Lee Farm, Wycoller, Colne BB8 8SU (Colne [0282] 864747). 👑 **Working farm, join in.** Parson Lee is a 250-year-old farmhouse situated just outside Wycoller on both the "Bronte Way" to Haworth and the new 45-mile "Pendle Way". There are magnificent views and a relaxed, friendly atmosphere with plenty of good farmhouse food. One hundred and ten acres are farmed and guests are welcome to look round the stock or participate in farm activities. The two very comfortable bedrooms both have en suite shower rooms and can sleep up to six people. The Yorkshire Dales, Pendleside and the Fylde Coast are easily accessible and the proprietors are happy to plan outings. Children and well behaved pets welcome. Terms are from £11 to £14. Please ring for further details.

LANCASHIRE – A COMBINATION OF COAST AND COUNTRY!

The choice is yours! A day on the beach or a trip to the moors – and don't forget Blackpool and Morecambe. In between all this the discerning tourist would also do well to visit the Roman fort and museum at Ribchester, the country park at Wycoller, the nature reserve at Lytham St. Annes, the Royal Empire Exhibition at Leyland and the Steamtown Railway Museum at Carnforth.

LEICESTERSHIRE

LUTTERWORTH. Mrs A.T. Hutchinson and Mrs A.M. Knight, Knaptoft House Farm and The Greenway, Bruntingthorpe Road, Near Shearsby, Lutterworth LE17 6PR (0533 478388). ✿✿ *Commended.* Convenient for M1 (exit 1). A50 nine miles south of Leicester, Bruntingthorpe-Saddington crossroads. Peacefully situated on 145 acre mixed farm with superb views . Warmth, comfort and good farmhouse breakfast — wholefoods. Twin/double, single and family rooms available, some ground floor. All beautifully appointed, some with en-suite showers. All rooms have washbasins, central heating, electric blankets, tea/coffee facilities. Sunny dining and sittingrooms, with wood burners and colour TVs. Excellent food at local pubs. AA. English Tourist Board. Bed and Breakfast from £13. Phone for leaflet.

LUTTERWORTH. Mrs Sue Timms, Wheathill Farm, Church Lane, Shearsby, Lutterworth LE17 6PG (Peatling Magna [0533] 478663). ✿✿ **Working farm.** This 130-acre dairy farm with attractive old house, beamed ceilings and inglenook fireplaces, is situated in a tiny village that dates back to the Saxons. The area is steeped in history and offers many stately houses and castles within easy reach. Sporting needs catered for locally with fishing, golf and gliding within nine miles. Leicester contains much of interest including Roman ruins and modern theatres. A warm welcome and good home produced food is assured to all, including children. Five miles M1 Exit 20, M6 Exit 1. Easy distance N.E.C., N.A.C. One family room on the ground floor, one double, one single, one twin on first floor. Two guests' bathrooms and toilets. Central heating. Bed and Breakfast. Babysitting by arrangement. For full details and prices an SAE would be appreciated.

MELTON MOWBRAY. Mrs Valerie Anderson, Home Farm, Church Lane, Old Dalby, Melton Mowbray LE14 3LB (Melton Mowbray [0664] 822622). 18th/19th century Farmhouse; quiet lane on edge of village in lovely Vale of Belvoir. Home Farm and garden are ideal for overnight stop, or base for more leisurely explorers; Belvoir Castle, Burghley and Belton Houses nearby; Lincoln and Coventry Cathedrals, Chatsworth and Peaks are comfortable day trips. Stables in heart of world-famous Quorn Hunt country offer liveries in winter. Long distance riders stop over in summer. Easy access from motorways (M1, M69, M42 and main routes A1, A6, A46, A47). Seven miles north-west Melton (A606). Open January to December (not Christmas). Twin and family rooms (all with washbasins). Full central heating. Guests' own sittingroom and diningroom, double glazed, log fires in season. Children welcome, babysitting. Quiet dogs kennelled (not in house). Car, horse or bicycle essential. Bed and Breakfast from £12.

LINCOLNSHIRE

BENNIWORTH. Mrs Olivant, Skirbeck Farm, Panton Road, Benniworth LN3 6JN (050781 682; from February 1991 0507 313682). ✿✿ Enjoy a stay on a working farm, whilst visiting the beautiful Lincolnshire Wolds. This peaceful location is surrounded by good walking country including the Viking Way. It is 16 miles east of the Cathedral city of Lincoln and only a few miles from the interesting market towns of Louth, Horncastle and Market Rasen. The east coast and South Yorkshire (via the Humber Bridge) all within easy touring distance. Fishing is available by arrangement. The farmhouse is comfortably furnished, has central heating and log fires. All bedrooms have colour TV and teasmade, with bathrooms adjacent. Sun lounge overlooking secluded garden. Children welcome. Non-smokers only please. Country cottage also available.

LINCOLNSHIRE – OUTSTANDING NATURAL BEAUTY!

The Lincolnshire Wolds are indeed worthy of their designation as an "Area of Outstanding Natural Beauty". Anybody visiting this county should explore The Wolds and visit such places as Bourne, Grantham, Honington, the woodland at Kesteven and the Museum of Lincolnshire Life in Lincoln itself.

GRANTHAM. Mrs Freda Mival, Woodlands, West Willoughby, Near Ancaster, Grantham NG32 3SH

(Loveden [0400] 30340). This quiet farmhouse accommodation is set on a 12 acre smallholding on the A153 coast road, with Grantham and Sleaford seven miles, Lincoln 20 miles. Within easy reach of Robin Hood country, and Belton House is four miles away. A car is essential and there is ample parking. We are open Easter to October. There is a double room, single room and a family room, tea/coffee making facilities available; bathroom and toilet. Evening Meal provided by arrangement using mainly home produced food. Children are welcome and there is a cot, high chair and babysitting. Tourist Board registered. AA listed. Bed and Breakfast from £11. Rates are reduced for children.

HALFWAY FARM MOTEL & GUEST HOUSE

Ideally situated for Lincoln and Newark this Georgian House and converted Farmstead offers 11 en-suite plus 8 other bedrooms furnished and equipped to a high standard of cleanliness and comfort. All rooms have welcome trays and heating under guests' control. Facilities for guests include public telephone, lounge with coal fire and beamed ceilings, unlimited parking, and pub with restaurant within walking distance. Tourist Board Registered, AA listed, Routiers Recommended. Payment by Access or Visa if desired, excellent value from £14 per person for Bed and Full Breakfast. Open all year. Prior inspection welcomed.

Mr R.D. Underwood, Halfway Farm Motel & Guest House, Swinderby, Lincoln LN6 9HN

Telephone Swinderby (052286) 749

🏵🏵🏵   AA Listed   Les Routiers

LANGTON-BY-WRAGBY. Miss Jessie Skellern, Lea Holme, Langton-by-Wragby LN3 5PZ (Wragby [0673] 858339). Comfortable, chalet-type house set in own half-acre peaceful garden. All amenities. Central for touring Wold, coast, fen, historic Lincoln etc. So much to discover in this county with wonderful skies and room to breathe. Attractive market towns, Louth, Horncastle, Boston, Spilsby, Alford, Woodhall Spa. Two double bedrooms on ground floor (can be let as single), with washbasins; bathroom, toilet; sittingroom; diningroom. Children welcome at reduced rates; some babysitting may be available. Pets welcome. Car almost essential, parking. ETB registered. Basically Room and Breakfast, but Evening Meals can be had by arrangement. Bed and Breakfast from £12 per person; Evening Meal from £6. Open all year.

MAXEY. Mrs Fitton, Abbey House, West End Road, Maxey PE6 9EJ (Market Deeping [0778] 344642).

🏵🏵 Comfortably furnished guest house in one acre of mature gardens. Dating in part from 1190, it belonged to Thorney Abbey and Peterborough Minster before serving as a vicarage and possesses several features of historical interest. Full central heating. All bedrooms are well appointed, offering refreshment facilities and colour TV. The locality abounds in attractive stone built villages, stately homes and castles. Stamford (five miles), Crowland Abbey, Rutland Water, Peakirk Wildfowl Trust and Peterborough Cathedral are close at hand, whilst Ely and Cambridge are reached within one hour. Private Carp Lake. SAE, please, or telephone for details.

STAMFORD near. Mrs Liebich, Spa House, Braceborough, Near Stamford PE9 4NS (Greatford [077836] 310). Nearest roads A1, A15 and A16. A very

pleasant house offering comfortable and quiet accommodation and a friendly welcome to visitors. Spa House is about a mile from Braceborough Village and seven miles from Stamford which is an interesting town with some very old buildings. The countryside is unspoilt and has many historic houses. Superbly situated in a secluded setting amidst undulating and wooded countryside, the house and garden are surrounded by a spa, once famous for its healing waters, where King George III bathed, around 1788. Accommodation comprises three double and one single bedrooms; shower, two toilets; large oak-panelled drawing room with open fireplace, where good food is served. Open all year with central heating. Bed and Breakfast from £12; Evening Dinner available on request. 25 per cent reduction for children. Cot and babysitting available. Pets permitted.

WEST MIDLANDS

BIRMINGHAM. Acocks Green Hotel, 24 Yardley Road, Birmingham B27 6ED and Western House Hotel, 14 Yardley Road, Birmingham (021-7060738/7070974/7066359/7072419). Friendly family-run guest houses. Convenient for National Exhibition Centre; Airport; City and Warwickshire countryside; rail, bus and motorway links nearby. Car hire service available to guests at discount rates. All our bedrooms have tea/coffee making facilities, colour TVs, vanity units; en-suite rooms available. Centrally heated. Also pleasant gardens for guests' use.

HENLEY-IN-ARDEN. Pamela Shaw, Irelands Farm, Irelands Lane, Henley-in-Arden, Solihull B95 5SA (0564 792476). ✿✿ Working farm. A warm wel-

come awaits you at this elegant, spacious and friendly family farmhouse, tucked away down a quiet country lane in peaceful surroundings. Only a stone's throw from NEC, Stratford, Warwick and the Cotswolds. Our late Georgian house offers one double and two twin-bedded rooms with en suite bath/shower, TV, tea/coffee facilities, electric blankets, central heating. Pets welcome by prior arrangement. Terms from £12.50 – £20. Self catering cottages also available — terms from £145 to £250.

SOLIHULL. Mrs Janet Haimes, Yew Tree Farm, Wootton Wawen, Solihull B95 6BY (05642 2701).

✿✿✿ A fine Georgian farmhouse conveniently situated on the A3400 in the village of Wootton Wawen, two miles south of Henley-in-Arden, six miles north of Stratford-upon-Avon and within easy reach of Warwick Castle, Royal Showground, NEC and the Cotswolds. A 700 acre dairy/arable farm with lake and woodland walks. Three large centrally heated double bedrooms, one en-suite, adjoining bathrooms, tea/coffee making facilities. Cot available. Comfortable visitors' lounge with colour TV. Excellent pubs and restaurants nearby. Two self catering houses set in the parklands of Edstone Hall also available.

NORFOLK

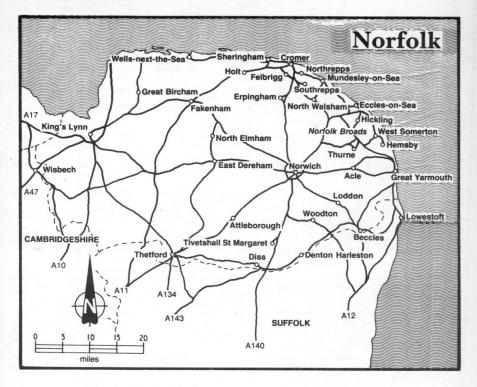

BECCLES near. Mrs R. M. Clarke, Shrublands Farm, Burgh St. Peter, Near Beccles, Suffolk NR34 0BB (Aldeby [050-277] 241). ✿✿ *Commended.* This attractive homely farmhouse which is pleasantly situated in the Waveney Valley on the Suffolk border, is surrounded by one acre of garden and lawns. The River Waveney flows through the 480 acres of mixed working farmland; opportunities for bird-watching. Ideal base for touring Norfolk and Suffolk; Beccles, Lowestoft, Great Yarmouth and Norwich are all within easy reach. The house has two double rooms and one family room, with washbasins; two toilets, shower room, bathroom; sittingroom, diningroom, separate lounge with colour TV and tea/coffee making facilities. Games room for snooker and darts. Tennis court available; swimming pool and food at River Centre nearby. Children welcome. Car essential, parking. Open all year. Bed and Breakfast from £12.50. No pets. Reductions for children. SAE, please.

BUNGAY. Mrs Bobbie Watchorn, Park Farm, Harlston Road, Earsham, Bungay, Suffolk NR35 2AQ (0986 892180). Come and enjoy rural luxury in our beautiful Victorian farmhouse with wonderful views. The large, newly refurbished rooms have colour TV, beverage facilities and en-suite shower rooms. Meals, taken in the sunny diningroom, include our own eggs, vegetables and local bacon. Our 600 acre working farm has thriving wildlife. Guests are welcome to help with the animals or just enjoy the large gardens. Norwich and the coast are about half a mile away. The Otter Trust and many other attractions are nearby. Children welcome. Sorry, no pets or smoking. Farm Holiday Bureau Member. Bed and Breakfast from £15. Tourist Board grading and classification applied for.

CROMER. Mr J. R. Graveling, The Grove, Overstrand Road, Cromer NR27 0DJ (Cromer [0263] 512412).

 ❦❦ The Grove is an 18th-century holiday home magnificently set in its own three-acre grounds of fields, gardens and trees. There are walks through the fields and woods to cliffs, golf courses and beach. The small fishing town of Cromer is within walking distance, with its pier, lifeboat, fine church, museum, shops and eating places. We have a lounge, games room, venture-type playground for children, and we grow our own vegetables. Ideal holiday for young or old. Six double, two single, three family bedrooms with washbasins; four rooms have showers; six with en-suite bathrooms; four toilets. Diningroom. Cot, high chair, reduced rates for children. Sorry, no pets. Open April to October for Evening Meal, Bed and Breakfast from £132 per week; Bed and Breakfast from £88 per week.

CROMER. Mrs A. Youngman, Shrublands Farm, Northrepps, Cromer NR27 0LN (026378 297).

 ❦❦ Shrublands Farm is a working arable farm in the village of Northrepps, two miles south east of Cromer. Ideally situated for exploring the north Norfolk coast. Within easy reach of National Trust properties of Blickling and Felbrigg Halls. Norwich is 30 minutes by car where one can visit the cathedral, castle, museum and medieval heart of the city. Accommodation comprises one twin room, one double room, both with washbasins and tea/coffee making facilities, shared bathroom; and one twin room with private bathroom. Sittingroom and diningroom. Central heating. Own keys. Parking space. Sorry, no pets or children. Bed and Breakfast, Evening Meal available. Terms on request.

DEREHAM near. Jenny and John Davies, Pound Green Hotel, Pound Green Lane, Shipdham IP25 7LS (0362 820165). ❦❦❦ An attractive, quietly located, private family run hotel offering the best in comfort and hospitality. Set in one acre of secluded gardens with a heated, open-air swimming pool, Pound Green really is a perfect retreat for urban dwellers. Offers 14 bedrooms (many en-suite), licensed bar, a cosy restaurant serving à la carte meals and barbecues in the summer by the pool. Centrally located within easy distance of Norwich, King's Lynn, the coast and the Broads. Children welcome — cot and high chair provided. Dogs welcome. Nearby leisure facilities include golf, fishing, walking and water sports. Ample parking. Bed and Breakfast from £22.50 per person. AA and RAC one star.

DISS. Mrs Susan Chubbock, Rookery Farm, Aslacton, Norwich NR15 2ER (037977 250). Working farm. You are assured of a warm welcome at Rookery Farmhouse, our timbered 17th century Listed home, on arable/livestock farm; three and a half miles from A140 Norwich to Ipswich road, eight miles from historic town of Diss, 14 miles Norwich. Well equipped sports centre four miles. We have pigs, cattle, chickens, rabbits and horses, and are situated in peaceful countryside ideal for walking and horse riding. Excellent livery facilities — bring your horse! Accommodation — one family/double room with washbasin and colour TV. Separate toilet; diningroom. Children welcome at reduced rates, climbing frame, slide and cot. Long stay reductions. Central heating. Kennel available for well mannered dogs. Tourist Board registered. Bed and Breakfast from £10.

DISS. Mrs Helen Gowing, Shimpling Hall Farm, Diss IP21 4UF (Diss [0379] 741233). 🐾 Working

family farm with spacious Georgian farmhouse set in peaceful surroundings in south Norfolk, one and a half miles from main A140 Norwich/Ipswich road. Excellent base for touring Norfolk and Suffolk. Many local attractions include Bressingham Steam Museum and Gardens, historic Norwich and Suffolk Heritage Coastline. Our comfortable rooms with unspoilt views across farmland all have washbasins and tea/coffee facilities. Residents' lounge with log fire. Many good pubs and restaurants locally.

DISS. Mrs Cynthia Huggins, Malting Farm, Blo' Norton Road, South Lopham, Diss IP22 2HT

(037988 201). 🐾🐾 **Working farm, join in.** Malting Farm is situated on the Norfolk/Suffolk border amid picturesque open countryside. As a working dairy farm it's possible to see the cows being milked and mix with the farmyard pets. An Elizabethan timber-framed farmhouse, with inglenook fireplaces and four poster beds. Within easy reach of Norwich, Cambridge, local museums and gardens. Cynthia is a keen craftswoman in quilting, embroidery, spinning and weaving. TV and guest lounge available. Bed and Breakfast from £13. No pets and no smoking.

DISS near. Mrs Brenda Webb, Strenneth Farmhouse, Old Airfield Road, Fersfield, Near Diss IP22

2BP (Bressingham [037988] 8182). 🐾🐾🐾 *Commended.* Brenda Webb invites you to her former 16th century farmhouse for Bed and Breakfast from £16 and an excellent three-course Evening Meal for £10.50. Enjoy a superb holiday or break in quiet countryside, close to many holiday attractions. Comfortable accommodation, most bedrooms with en-suite facilities, all with washbasins and tea/coffee making facilities. Wine, beer and spirits licence. Children catered for at reduced rates, babysitting available. Non-smokers' lounge. Log fires and full central heating. Open Christmas and New Year. Ample parking. Chauffeured Anglian Discovery Tours arranged. Pets welcome. Situated off A1066 near South Lopham. Colour brochure available.

EAST DEREHAM. Mrs Jane Faircloth, Moat Farm, Mattishall, East Dereham NR2 3NL (Dereham

[0362] 850288). Working farm. Situated in the centre of the village, 11 miles from Norwich, a fine city with cathedral, many interesting buildings and museums, theatre and cinemas. Within easy reach of Sandringham and the Coast. Offering Bed and Breakfast and Evening Meal with traditional farmhouse meals using home grown fare. Family room and twin-bedded room with washbasins; separate bathroom and WC. Lounge with log fire and TV. Sorry, no pets. Cot not provided. Open May to October. AA recommended. Please send SAE for terms.

FAKENHAM. Mrs Maureen Walpole, "Hardlands", East Raynham, Fakenham, Norfolk NR21 7EQ

(Fakenham [0328] 862567). A friendly welcome and relaxing atmosphere await you at "Hardlands". Peaceful countryside surrounds the house and its pleasant one acre gardens. Furnished to high standards the comfortable five-bedroomed house is four miles from Fakenham on A1065, ideally situated for visiting Royal Sandringham, historic King's Lynn, North Norfolk coast, Bird Sanctuaries, Pensthorpe Waterfowl Trust, National Trust properties, Norwich and the Broads. Top quality three course Evening Dinner usually available by arrangement. Double and twin bedrooms with tea/coffee making facilities. Guests' TV lounge/dining room. Evening Dinner from £7.50; Bed and full English Breakfast from £12.50. Weekly terms available. Open all year for weekly or short breaks. Log fires and central heating. English Tourist Board Commended and Listed.

FAKENHAM near. Mrs Ann Green, Old Coach House, Thursford, Near Fakenham NR21 0BD

(Thursford [0328 878] 273). Working farm. This peaceful Norfolk farmhouse, converted from 17th century coach house, affords modern comforts but retains its charm. Entered from the main King's Lynn to Cromer road (A148), by a straight drive curving into a sheltered sunny courtyard. Norfolk offers miles of sandy beaches, golf, sailing, fishing and riding also stately homes, museums, bird sanctuary and wildlife park to visit. Main bedroom has four poster bed, washbasin, shaver point and kettle; second bedroom with twin beds and washbasin; third bedroom with twin beds and en-suite bathroom and WC; guests' bathroom and WC. All bedrooms have tea/coffee making facilities. Farmhouse kitchen/diningroom. Sittingroom with sun lounge and access to garden. Good country cooking and personal attention. Children welcome and pets by arrangement. Bed and Breakfast from £13 per night (from £85 per week); optional Evening Meal £5 (six nights per week). Reduced rates for children. Open all year. Also self-catering accommodation available.

GREAT YARMOUTH. Mrs Margaret Bowles, Gables Farmhouse, Scratby Road, Scratby, Great

Yarmouth NR29 3NL (0493 732107). A pleasantly situated farmhouse, tastefully restored to preserve all its natural charm, including exposed beams and inglenook fireplaces. Conveniently situated for Great Yarmouth, Norwich, Broads, beach and north Norfolk coast. The house stands in over two acres of pleasant gardens with pond-side walk. An ideal holiday area with facilities for sailing, golf, bird watching, medieval churches, fishing (sea and freshwater), walking, riding and swimming. Guesthouse accommodation in three double and one twin-bedded rooms each with en-suite facilities and tea/coffee making equipment; sittingroom with TV and separate diningroom. Good country cooking using produce from kitchen garden. Ample parking. Sorry, no pets.

GREAT YARMOUTH near. Mrs Margaret Adnitt, The Cannons, West Caister, Near Great Yarmouth

NR30 5SS (Great Yarmouth [0493] 728557). This is a Georgian country house in two acres of lovely grounds with ample parking. Two miles from beaches, Norfolk Broads and Great Yarmouth, yet in peaceful, rural surroundings. Close to golf course, race course and riding stables. Caister Castle Motor Museum half a mile. Offering guesthouse accommodation in one family room and one double room with washbasins; also two double rooms with en-suite bathrooms. Children over four years welcome. Sorry, no pets. Open all year, including Christmas. Electric blankets. Home grown and local produce, choice of food. Evening Dinner, Bed and Breakfast from £15 per day; Bed and Breakfast from £10 per day. Car essential. Member of ETB and EATB. Also available, two holiday flats within house.

NORFOLK – NOT JUST THE BROADS!

There's more to do in Norfolk than messing about in boats – pleasurable though that may be. Other places of interest include the gardens and steam museum at Bressingham, the Broadland Conservation Centre, the flint mines at Grimes Graves, The Norfolk Rural Life Museum, Sandringham – which is often open to the public, and of course Norwich itself.

GREAT YARMOUTH near. Mrs Winifred Youngs, Street Farm, Horsey, Near Great Yarmouth NR29 4AD (Winterton-on-Sea [0493-393] 212). Working farm.  A detached flintstone farmhouse situated in the centre of the picturesque village of Horsey. Delightful views of Horsey Mill and the clean, sandy beach which stretches for two miles, is only a 20 minute stroll away. It is a birdwatchers' paradise, within easy reach of the Norfolk Broads from which there are organised trips. There are many good eating places in the area with a typical local pub just two minutes from the farmhouse. Double, single and family bedrooms, some with washbasins. Shower/bathroom. Tea/coffee facilities available. Bed and home cooked Breakfast a speciality, from £12. No smoking household. Car essential.

HAPPISBURGH. Mrs Jill Morris and Miss Diana Wrightson, Cliff House Guest House and Teashop, Beach Road, Happisburgh, Norwich NR12 0PP (Walcott [0692] 650775). Commanding views of sea and lighthouse, Cliff House is situated in an attractive, unspoilt and friendly village, six miles east of North Walsham. Happisburgh's wide sandy beach — safe for bathing — is rated as one of the cleanest Norfolk beaches so it is a favourite family resort. Visitors can enjoy the Broads, craft centres, windmills, stately homes and interesting small market towns. Accommodation comprises one twin/family room, one double and one single room — all with washbasins and tea/coffee making facilities; two bathrooms and a residents' lounge with TV. We offer a warm welcome, excellent home cooking, fresh vegetables and home-made bread. Diets catered for. Bed and Breakfast £12.50; Bed, Breakfast and Dinner £19.50. Special prices for children and senior citizens. Budget Breaks.

HARLESTON. Mrs K. Pointer, Paynes Hill Farm, Denton, Harleston IP20 0AW (098686 628). This is an old beamed farmhouse in peaceful countryside. Central for Norwich, Lowestoft or Yarmouth. Near Waveney for fishing. Otter Trust at Earsham, wildlife park at Kessingland. Steam trains and gardens at Bressingham. One single, one family room, also twin room, all with washbasins; bathroom, two toilets; sitting/diningroom. Children welcome, cot, high chair. Sorry, no pets. Electric or open fires. Good home grown food and well cooked meals. Personal attention from Mrs Pointer. Parking — car essential. Open May to September. Also available two caravans, each sleeping four. SAE for terms please.

HEMSBY. Mrs Margaret Lake, Old Station House, North Road, Hemsby, Near Great Yarmouth NR29 4EZ (0493 732022).  This large country house, set in the village of Hemsby, is only half a mile from golden beaches and is ideally situated for touring the Norfolk Broads and National Trust properties. This lovely accommodation comprises guest lounge/diningroom with colour TV; three double bedrooms and one family room, all with vanitory units and washbasins. Separate toilet and bathroom. Free tea-making facilities. Full central heating. No smoking. Bed and Breakfast from £12 adult, £8 per child. Open all year except Christmas. Telephone or send SAE for further details.

KING'S LYNN, Central Norfolk. Mr G.J. Davidson, Holmdene Farm, Beeston, King's Lynn PE32 2NJ (Fakenham [0328] 710284). Holmdene Farm is a mixed farm situated in central Norfolk within easy reach of the coast and Broads. Horse riding, golf and fishing are available locally, and the village pub is only quarter of a mile away. The 17th century farmhouse is comfortable and welcoming with log fires and beams. Two double rooms, one en-suite, both with tea/coffee trays. Pets including horses welcome. Bed and Breakfast from £10 per person; Evening Meal from £10. Weekly terms available. Also fully equipped six-berth mobile home available, self catering or meals provided.

MUNDESLEY. Mrs Bridget Fryer, The Grange, High Street, Mundesley NR11 8JL (0263 721556).  Beautiful well furnished house in attractive half-acre garden. Guest TV lounge and conservatory. Two double rooms, one family and one twin, all with own washbasins. Two bathrooms. Good car parking facilities. Children welcome, aged 11 and under half price. "The Grange" is a ten minute stroll from some outstanding sandy beaches, with an excellent golf course nearby. Ideally situated for birdwatching, walking and fishing enthusiasts. The Norfolk Broads and historic Norwich are within easy reach. Good eating establishments within walking distance. Bed and Breakfast only. Sorry, no pets.

PLEASE SEND A STAMPED ADDRESSED ENVELOPE WITH ENQUIRIES

NEATISHEAD (Norfolk Broads). Alan and Sue Wrigley, Regency Guest House, Neatishead Post Office Stores, Neatishead, Near Norwich NR12 8AD (Horning [0692] 630233).

An 18th century guest house in picturesque, unspoilt village in heart of Broadlands. Personal service top priority. Long established name for very substantial English Breakfasts. Only 20 minutes from interesting old city of Norwich and six miles from coast. Ideal location for touring East Anglia, all boating activities, sailing, hiring, cruising, sightseeing. Haven for fishermen. Easy access to wild life and bird watching grounds. Guesthouse, holder of "Good Care" Award for high quality services, has five tastefully Laura Ashley decorated rooms (including king-size double with en-suite bathroom). Colour TV, tea/coffee making facilities in all rooms. Two main bathrooms. Separate tables in beamed-ceiling breakfast room. Cot, babysitting, reduced rates for children and three night stays. Pets welcome. Parking. Open all year. Fire Certificate held.

NORTH WALSHAM. Ernest and Jenny Townsend, Beechwood Hotel, 20 Cromer Road, North Walsham NR28 0HD (North Walsham [0692] 403231).

Commended. Within three minutes' walk of interesting market town shopping centre and yet secluded in lovely grounds, Beechwood is ideally situated for sandy beaches, the Broads, Norwich and many other interesting places. Open all year, except Christmas. There are four family rooms, six double/twin and one single, all with washbasins, fitted carpets, shaver points and comfortable beds; most have private bathroom/WC. Two lounges, diningroom (separate tables) and games room. Licensed. Central heating. Ample parking space. AA listed. Ashley Courtenay recommended. Friendly personal service. Write or telephone for brochure. See outside back cover for display advert.

NORWICH. Mrs Karen Finch, Hall Farmhouse, High Common, Hardingham, Norwich NR9 4AE (0953 851113).

Commended. Experience the friendly atmosphere of Hall Farmhouse, a delightfully spacious Regency farmhouse set in the peaceful mid-Norfolk countryside. Ideally sited to visit many historic towns including the City of Norwich, the beautiful North Norfolk coast and several stately homes. Three double/family bedrooms, all with washbasin and central heating. Two guest bathrooms. Evening Meals available six days a week. Reductions for children. Bed and Breakfast from £15; Evening Meal from £9. Open all year. Farm Holiday Bureau member.

NORWICH. Mrs M.A. Hemmant, Poplar Farm, Sisland, Loddon, Norwich NR14 6EF (Loddon [0508] 20706). Working farm, join in.

This 400-acre mixed farm is situated one mile off the A146, approximately nine miles south east of Norwich. An ideal spot for the Broads and the delightful and varied Norfolk coast. We have a Charolais X herd of cows, with calves born March-June. The River Chet runs through the farm. Accommodation comprises double, twin and family rooms, bathroom, TV sittingroom/diningroom. Central heating. Tennis court; children's trampoline. Children very welcome. A peaceful, rural setting. Car essential. Open all year for Bed and Breakfast. Terms from £12 per person per night.

FUN FOR ALL THE FAMILY IN NORFOLK

Banham Zoo & Monkey Sanctuary, The Grove, Banham; *Kilverstone Wildlife Park*, Thetford; *Thrigby Hall Wildlife Gardens*, near Filby; *The Otter Trust*, Earsham, near Bungay; *Wildfowl Trust*, Welney; *Kelling Park Hotel & Aviaries*, near Holt; *Cromer Zoo*, Cromer; *Caister Castle Motor Museum*, near Great Yarmouth; *Banham International Motor Museum*, The Grove, Banham; *Bressingham Gardens & Live Steam Museum*, near Diss; *North Norfolk Railway*, Sheringham Station, Sheringham; *Maritime Museum for East Anglia*, Marine Parade, Great Yarmouth; *Iceni Village*, Reconstructed, Cockley Cley, near Swaffham; *Colman's Mustard Museum*, The Mustard Shop, 3 Bridewell Akkey, Norwich.

NORWICH. Mrs Carolyn Holl, Hillside Farm, Brooke, Norwich NR15 1AU (0508 50260). Working

farm. Brooke is seven miles south of Norwich (B145 Bungay to Norwich road), three-quarter hour drive to excellent beaches. Hillside Farm, built 1600's, is timber-framed and thatched and has been recently restored. Full central heating. Two family/double rooms with tea-making faciliites; one has en-suite loo, bidet, washbasin and TV; also one single room; two bathrooms; large diningroom with inglenook fireplace, sitting area. Car essential, ample parking. Children welcome, cot, high chair and babysitting. Fishing in two secluded private lakes; games room with snooker, pool and table tennis; large garden. Laundry room. Tennis and swimming available nearby. Sorry, no pets. Reduced rates for children. Bed and Breakfast, some light suppers. Terms on request. Registered with East Anglia Tourist Board.

NORWICH. The Old Pump House, Penfold Street, Aylsham, Norwich NR11 6BY (0263 733789).

Comfortable detached period house set in the centre of small market town of Aylsham overlooking the old town pump. Accommodation offered in three bedrooms with washbasin, TV and tea-making facilities. Drawing room with log fire. Secluded gardens. Short distance form National Trust houses, north coast and Broads and the Bure Valley Steam Railway. Historic city of Norwich is nine miles away. Bed and Breakfast from £15, reductions for children. Plenty of pubs in the area serving good food, and we can particularly recommend a restaurant in the market place. Special diets catered for; non-smokers welcome. Brochure available.

NORWICH. Mr and Mrs R. M. and B. M. Harrold, Salamanca Farm, Stoke Holy Cross, Norwich NR14

8QJ (Framingham Earl [050-86] 2322). ♛♛ **Working farm.** At Stoke Holy Cross, Colmans first produced their famous mustard — the original Mill still stands on the River Tas, the Harrolds' cows graze nearby. Salamanca Farm, a short walk from the river, was named by a former owner who fought with Wellington in the battle of Salamanca. Norwich, a Cathedral city, is only four miles away. The Harrolds will give you a warm, personal welcome and have an extensive knowledge of the attractions of the area. Guests are accommodated in four bedrooms; three bathrooms; spacious diningroom; guests' sittingroom with colour TV. Central heating. Large colourful garden. Bed and Breakfast from £13. AA listed.

NORWICH. Mrs J. Pilgrim, Manor Farm, Quidenham, Norwich NR16 2NY (095387 540). Working

farm. Large farmhouse in delightful secluded setting on 950 acre working arable farm. Large informal garden, games room, log fires on cold nights and good home cooking, own meat, poultry, game, eggs and vegetables used. Large rooms, guests' own bathroom and lounge. A real friendly Norfolk welcome awaits you. Children over five years only accepted but sorry, no dogs. OS ref TM025888. Open all year except Christmas and New Year. Bed and Breakfast from £13; Evening Meal from £7. Tourist Board listed.

NORWICH near (Cawston). Mrs R. Snaith, Grey Gables, Norwich Road, Cawston, Near Norwich

NR10 4EY (Norwich [0603] 871259). ♛♛♛ Former rectory in wooded grounds offering excellent food and wine. Lounge with log fire. Elegant candle-lit diningroom where traditionally prepared food is served using fresh fruit and vegetables from our own kitchen garden. Lawn tennis court and bicycles available. All bedrooms have en suite bathrooms, tea/coffee making facilities, radio, colour TV and telephone. Children under 10 sharing parents' room accommodated free of charge. Bed and Breakfast from £20 to £28 per person per night; Dinner from £14. Discount Breaks — two or more nights Dinner, Bed and Breakfast £58. East Anglia Tourist Board registered. Egon Ronay recommended Hotel and Restaurant.

NORWICH. Mrs Joanna Douglas, Greenacres Farm, Woodgreen, Long Stratton, Norwich NR15 2RR (0508 30261). A 17th century period farmhouse with a warm friendly atmosphere — wealth of character, exposed beams and inglenook fireplace. Farm is situated in an idyllic, rural situation — yet only one and a half miles from Long Stratton (A140) with a variety of shops, public houses, sports centre — golfing, fishing, riding, swimming facilities nearby. The beautiful historic city of Norwich is 12 miles away as are other character market towns. Central location provides easy access to Norfolk Broads, coast and the Suffolk Constable country. Car essential. Accommodation comprises one double with en-suite shower, one twin with washbasin; bathroom; sittingroom with TV. Children welcome, cot, high chair, babysitting available. Games room. Tennis court. Open all year. Bed and Breakfast from £14; Evening Meal £6.50. Reductions for week-long stays. ETB listed and approved.

NORWICH near. Mrs G. Vivian-Neal, Welbeck House, Brooke, Near Norwich NR15 1AT (Brooke [0508] 50292). Come and enjoy our Georgian country house with interesting flower arranger's garden in a woodland setting at the edge of the village and near a bus route. Ideal centre for visiting historic Norwich with its excellent shops and theatres, Otter Trust, nature reserves and good specialist gardeners' nurseries. Attractive twin, double and two single bedrooms available. Bed and Breakfast from £12. Given notice we cater for special diets. Well behaved dogs and children over 12 are welcome.

NORWICH. Mrs Margaret Smith, "Flitcham Cottage", Fir Covert Road, Felthorpe, Norwich NR10 4DT (Norwich [0603] 867493). Flitcham Cottage is pleasantly situated on Marriot Walk in typically Norfolk countryside, overlooking farmland bordered by woods. Within easy reach of city, Broads and coast. Guests can relax in large lounge, conservatory or garden and enjoy a peaceful holiday all year except Christmas and New Year. Full central heating with log fire in the oak beamed lounge. Two double bedrooms and one family room, all with washbasin; bathroom with shower, two toilets; sittingroom, diningroom. Cot provided and babysitting by arrangement. Pets also by arrangement. Bus stop one mile away. Ample parking. Great Witchingham Wild Life Park four miles away. Bed and excellent full English Breakfast from £11.50. Reduced rates for children. East Anglia Tourist Board Listed.

NORWICH. Mrs S. Clarke, The Poplars, Ipswich Road, Long Stratton, Norwich NR15 2TJ (Long Stratton [0508] 30502). Delightful early 18th century timber-framed farmhouse standing well back on A140 in one and a half acres of lawns and orchard. Guests can enjoy year-round hospitality in a friendly atmosphere where log fires glow on chilly evenings. Excellent home cooking and varied menu. Accommodation comprises twin-bedded room with own separate bathroom; double bedroom with bathroom en suite; sittingroom, diningroom. Children welcome, cot, high chair and babysitting offered. Sorry, no pets. Car is not essential, public transport 400 yards, but there is parking. New South Norfolk Sports Centre in village and fishing, horse riding and golf available locally. The scenic Norfolk Broads for cruising and sailing 20 miles; the coast 28 miles. Bed and Breakfast from £13. Reductions for children under 10. Mid-week bookings accepted. Closed Christmas.

NORWICH near. Garden House Hotel, Salhouse Road, Rackheath, Norwich NR13 6AA (0603 720007). 👑 👑 👑 *Approved.* Superb food, comfortable accommodation, relaxed, informal atmosphere and lovely surroundings — the Garden House recipe for a really enjoyable holiday. Ideally situated for Norwich City, the Norfolk Broads and coast with adequate parking, the hotel boasts a restaurant renowned in the area for its classical English cooking, specialising in beautifully prepared fresh local vegetables, game and shellfish when in season. All rooms have telephones, colour TVs and beverage making facilities and are mostly en-suite. There is a large lounge with bar and two diningrooms, one of which overlooks our lovely garden. Two nights Dinner, Bed and Breakfast from £60 per person.

SOUTHREPPS. Mrs C. Codling, Church Farm Guest House, 20 Church Street, Southrepps NR11 8NP (Southrepps [026379] 248). Church Farm Guest

House is set on a smallholding in lovely Norfolk countryside, three miles from the coast at Mundesley and Cromer with safe sandy beaches. There is one twin and one family bedrooms and one family room, all with washbasins; bathroom, three toilets; sittingroom and diningroom. Tea and coffee making facilities in bedrooms. There is a play area for children; pets allowed. A car is not essential, but there is parking. 10 miles from the Norfolk Broads with fishing nearby. Home cooking with fresh garden produce a speciality. Railway station one mile; collection by arrangement. Open January to November. Full central heating. Evening Dinner, Bed and Breakfast or Bed and Breakfast only. Winter Breaks available. Caravan and camping site also available; and luxury holiday cottages sleeping six/10, with central heating and open fires, fitted kitchens including washing machines and colour TV.

WALSINGHAM near. Mr and Mrs R.L. Hunt, Birds Farm, Walsingham Road, Hindringham NR21 0BT (Walsingham [0328] 820209). Peacefully situated, ideal

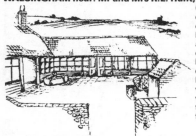

centre for enjoying most of the North Norfolk coast and countryside with secluded bathing beaches, lovely walks, bird reserves, stables, good fishing, golf courses. Cycle hire available. Near to the famous medieval Walsingham village complete with its shrines, and Thursford Organs, Sheringham Steam Railway. Large beamed lounge, log fire, tea/coffee making facilities available. Full English Breakfast. Restricted smoking. Regret, no young children or pets. Caravan available for those guests with older children. Open all year. Excellent pub meals locally, try our own old world style tea-room for home baking, snacks etc. Bed and Breakfast from £13. Reduced weekly rates.

WELLS-NEXT-THE-SEA. Mrs J.M. Court, Eastdene, Northfield Lane, Wells-next-the-Sea NR23 1LH (Fakenham [0328] 710381). ✿ ✿ A homely guest house offering a warm welcome. Bed and Breakfast and optional Evening Meal. Traditional cooking with own garden produce. Close to marshes, lovely coast walks. Central for Cley and Titchwell bird reserve and historic places such as Holkham Hall Estate and Walsingham Shrine. Heritage Coastal Walk nearby. Central heating; TV lounge with coffee and tea making facilities. Three double bedrooms and one single, all en-suite. Own front door key. Private car park. Pets welcome. Terms on application. Holder of Farm Holiday Guide Diploma. Les Routiers recommended.

WELLS-NEXT-THE-SEA. Sylvia and Andrew Strong, The Cobblers Guest House, Standard Road, Wells-Next-The-Sea NR23 1JU (0328 710155/711092).

The Cobblers is a friendly eight bedroomed guesthouse (four double, one twin, one family and two single rooms); centrally heated and doubled glazed with full Fire Certificate. There is a large diningroom and two guest lounges (one overlooking the attractive, secluded garden). All bedrooms have washbasins, TV and tea/coffee facilities. Ample car parking. Personal keys provided for free access at all times. Bed and Breakfast from £12.50; Dinner £7.50. Come and discover the glorious North Norfolk Coast.

WOODTON. Mrs J. Read, George's House, Woodton, Near Bungay NR35 2LZ (Woodton [050-844] 214). This is a charming late 17th century cottage with

four-acre market garden. It is situated in the centre of the village, just off the main Norwich to Bungay road. Wonderful holiday area, ideal for touring Norfolk and Suffolk. Historic Norwich, with its castle, cathedral, theatre and good shops is only nine-and-a-half miles and everyone should find something there to suit them. Sea 18 miles. Guest accommodation comprises three double bedrooms, with washbasins. There is a bathroom and toilet. Diningroom and TV lounge. A car is essential to make the most of your holiday and there is ample parking. The house is open to guests for Evening Meal, Bed and Breakfast. SAE, please, for terms.

WYMONDHAM. Mrs J. Durrant, Rose Farm, Suton, Wymondham NR18 9JN (0953 603512). Working farm, join in. Rose Farm is situated between Attleborough and the charming market town of Wymondham. We are a poultry farm with ducks, geese and chickens. Norwich, Norfolk Broads and the coastal resorts are all within easy reach. Private fishing available. All bedrooms are on the ground floor. Bed and Breakfast from £16; Evening Meal available. Half price for children under 10 years. Pets welcome. ETB listed.

NORTHUMBERLAND

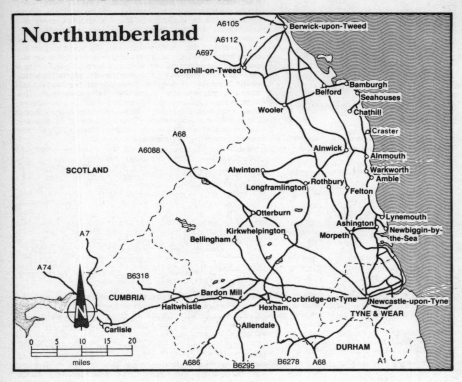

Northumberland

SCOTLAND

CUMBRIA

DURHAM

TYNE & WEAR

Berwick-upon-Tweed
A6105
A6112
A697
Cornhill-on-Tweed
Bamburgh
Belford
Seahouses
Wooler
Chathill
Craster
A68
A6088
Alnwick
Alnmouth
Alwinton
Warkworth
Rothbury
Amble
Longframlington
Felton
Otterburn
Lynemouth
A7
Kirkwhelpington
Ashington
Newbiggin-by-the-Sea
Bellingham
Morpeth
A74
B6318
Bardon Mill
Corbridge-on-Tyne
Newcastle-upon-Tyne
Haltwhistle
Hexham
Carlisle
Allendale
A686
B6295
B6278
A68
A1

0 5 10 15 20
miles

ALLENDALE. John and Isabel Wentzel, Crowberry Hall, Allendale, Hexham NE47 9SR (Allendale [0434] 683392). Allendale is ideally situated for visiting the Roman Wall, Scottish Borders and Lake District as well as the majestic North Pennines. Crowberry Hall lies one and a half miles off the B6295 between Allendale and Nenthead, along the minor road signposted Acton. Crowberry Hall offers comfortable accommodation in two twin-bedded and one family rooms, all with washbasins. Children over five and dogs welcome. No smoking in house, please. Self-guided walks, pony treking and golf can be enjoyed locally with swimming, windsurfing and other activities nearby. Open all year. Traditional English cooking plus vegetarian menu available. Bed and Breakfast from £9.50. Evening Meal if pre-booked.

ALNMOUTH. Glendower Guest House, Argyle Street, Alnmouth NE66 2SB (0665 830262). Our

Guest House is personal and cosy, and each guest is treated as a friend. We welcome single people and families and will offer you whatever domestic facilities you require to make your stay happy and anxiety-free. Situated very near the river, Glendower affords easy access to the beach and sea. Diningroom is licensed and serves quality food. Special Package Deals, Seasonal Breaks and Specialist Weekends are available — send for our brochure for full details. Terms from £16 per night.

ALNMOUTH. Mrs M.I. Cleghorn, St. Julian's, 21 Argyle Street, Alnmouth NE66 2SB (Alnmouth [0665] 830486). This guest house is situated four miles east of Alnwick, off the A1. It is 70 yards from the beach in a small seaside village. Nearby there are numerous beautiful beaches, golf courses, National Trust areas and properties plus places of historic interest. Good walking country. Fishing and riding available in the area. Accommodation in family, twin and single rooms, some with washbasins. Two bathrooms; two toilets. Sittingroom and diningroom. Children are welcome and provided for. Pets welcome. A car is not essential but is advantageous. Parking. Visitors' lounge with TV. Open May to October. Mid-week bookings accepted. Bed and Breakfast from £14. Non-smokers only.

ALNMOUTH. Janice and Norman Edwards, Westlea, 29 Riverside Road, Alnmouth NE66 2SD

(Alnmouth [0665] 830730). ♛♛♛ We invite you to relax in the warm friendly atmosphere of Westlea situated at the side of the Aln Estuary. We have an established reputation for providing a high standard of care and hospitality. Guests start the day with a hearty breakfast of numerous choices and in the evening a varied and appetising four-course traditional meal is prepared using local produce. All bedrooms are bright and comfortable with colour TVs, hot drink facilities, washbasins, shaver points, central heating, electric blankets, while some have private facilities. Large visitors' lounge and diningroom overlooking the estuary. The house is suitable for disabled guests. Babysitting and reductions for children available. Ideal for exploring castles, Farne Islands, Holy Island, Hadrian's Wall. Fishing, golf, pony trekking, etc within easy reach. Bed and Breakfast from £15; Bed, Breakfast and Evening Meal from £22. English Tourist Board and Northumberland Tourist Board registered. Alnwick District Council Hospitality Award 1989.

ALNMOUTH. Sheila and Gordon Inkster, Marine House Private Hotel, 1 Marine Road, Alnmouth

NE66 2RW (Alnwick [0665] 830349). ♛♛ This 200 year old stone house, once a granary, is situated on the edge of the village golf links overlooking beautiful beaches. It has been recently modernised, but retains its original charm. There are 10 comfortable bedrooms, all en-suite, and a cocktail bar, games room and spacious TV lounge with log fire. Local leisure activities include fishing, sea angling, pony trekking and golf (venues can be booked). Alnmouth is ideally situated for exploring the magnificent Northumberland coastline. Dinner, Bed and Breakfast from £29 per person daily. Short Breaks £57 per person — two nights Dinner, Bed and Breakfast. Extra nights pro rata. 1st February to 30th April 1991. Children and pets welcome.

ALNMOUTH. Mrs A. Stanton, Mount Pleasant Farm, Alnmouth, Alnwick NE66 3BY (0665

830215). Alnmouth's only working farm, traditional stone farmhouse with magnificent views of surrounding country and seaside village. House is warm and comfortable; both family room and double have colour TV, washbasin and tea making facilities. Safe play area with swing, etc. Guests' bathroom with shower and toilet. Ample parking. Pets by arrangement. Children over five years welcome. As well as wonderful beach and nearby golf courses, Mount Pleasant is a nature lover's paradise with the River Aln meandering along its boundary, a feeding place for herons and other water birds. Bed and Breakfast from £12.50.

ALNWICK. Mrs Hilary Harcourt-Brown, New Moor House, Edlingham, Alnwick NE66 2BT (066574

638). ♛♛ This charming stone coaching house built around 1800 set in the midst of spectacular countryside on A697/B6341 Junction. Alnwick seven miles, Rothbury four and the sea 10 miles. Excellent centre for exploring Northumberland, walking and sporting activities. Three double/family rooms and one single, all with washbasins, shaver points, electric blankets, tea/coffee making equipment. Good farmhouse style cooking. Children and pets welcome. Bed and Breakfast with or without Evening Meal. On the smallholding the family keep a kennel of top show dogs, horses and other animals. Full Fire Certificate. Bed and Breakfast from £13.50; with Evening Meal from £21. Reduced terms for longer stays.

NORTHUMBERLAND – BORDER COUNTRY!

You cannot go any further north and remain in England! There is much outstanding scenery, both inland and on the coast, and a host of interesting places to visit. Border Forest Park has everything you would expect, plus many interesting Roman remains. There are also remains at Housesteads and other places of interest include Lindisfarne, the "conserved" village of Blanchland, Hexham, Heatherslaw Mill and Craster.

ALNWICK. Mrs L. Edridge, Norfolk, 41 Blakelaw Road, Alnwick NE66 1BA (0665-602892). ⬬⬬ *Commended.* A private house where cleanliness and comfort are guaranteed. Good home cooking with garden produce. Refreshments at 9 pm. One double room (or family room) and one twin room, both with washbasins. Tea making facilities. Central heating. Double glazing. Bathroom/shower, two toilets. TV lounge. Situated in a peaceful area of this market town, ideal for open countryside and quiet roads. Forestry walks six miles. Northumbrian coastline four miles. Historic houses and castles are plentiful. Bed, Breakfast and Evening Meal from £19.50. Non-smokers welcome.

ALNWICK. Mrs Anne Davison, Alndyke Farm, Alnwick NE66 3PB (Alnwick [0665] 602193). ⬬⬬

Commended. **Working farm.** Beautiful Georgian farmhouse standing in its own grounds, commanding excellent views of the lovely countryside, only one mile from Alnwick near to A1068 and three miles to lovely sandy beaches. An ideal base for touring Northumberland with the Cheviot Hills, castles, country homes, fishing, golf, riding and swimming nearby. The farmhouse offers spacious accommodation to high standard with double and twin rooms superbly furnished having vanity units, clock/radio, hair dryers and hot drinks facilities. Guests have own sittingroom with TV, diningroom, bathroom with toilet and shower, also separate toilet room. Excellent home cooking at Alndyke. The farm land runs to the River Aln with disused railway line and right-of-way with lots of wildlife and lovely walks. Uninterrupted views. Children welcome from 10 years old. Sorry, no pets. Car essential, ample parking. Fire Certificate. FHB member. Bed and Breakfast, optional Evening Meal. SAE for brochure and terms.

BERWICK-ON-TWEED. Mrs J. Gray, Middle Ord Manor House Farm, Berwick-on-Tweed TD15 2XQ

(0289 306323). ⬬⬬ *Commended.* **Working farm.** An attractive Georgian residence, built 1783, with a Victorian extension, on mixed cattle, sheep, arable farm, set in unspoilt position surrounded by woodland and walled gardens. Period lounge and diningroom overlook the garden. Colour TV. Tea/coffee making facilities. Two twin, one double with washbasins (one en-suite room with four-poster bed). Central heating. Car essential parking. Three miles from coast. Bed and Breakfast from £14. Many places of interest to visit and sporting activities are within easy reach. Also available, Middle Ord Farmhouse, for self-catering holidays all year round an 18th century farmhouse, completely detached, to accommodate nine people, plus cot for small baby if required. Three double, one twin-bedded room; bathroom; sittingroom; diningroom; kitchen. Fully equipped except linen. Pets accepted. Weekly terms £90-£220. ETB listed and inspected.

CORBRIDGE. Mr and Mrs F.H.G. Matthews, The Hayes, Newcastle Road, Corbridge NE45 5PL (Corbridge [0434] 632010). ⬬⬬ The Hayes, spacious, attractive stone-built guest house, set in seven acres of gardens, lawns, pasture and woodland. Notable centre set on the River Tyne for exploring glorious countryside. Fishing, golf, riding, swimming in nearby areas. Double, single and family bedrooms; bathrooms, toilets; spacious lounge and diningroom. Children welcome, cot, highchair. Small pets only by arrangement. Open all year except Christmas/New Year. Parking. Evening Meal by arrangement. Bed and Breakfast £13 per person; Bed, Breakfast and Dinner £19.50, including VAT. Reductions for children under 14 and for Senior Citizens in low season. Awarded the Farm Holiday Guide Diploma and ETB registered. Full Fire Certificate. Also available, self catering cottages, flat and caravan. All properties, except flat, suitable for disabled. Write with SAE (ref FHG), or phone for details.

CORBRIDGE. Mrs Sue Jones, Low Barns, Thornbrough, Corbridge NE45 5LX (0434 632408).

Lovely stone built 18th century farmhouse set in open countryside one mile east of Corbridge on the B6530. Recently renovated to a very high standard with exposed beams and stone walls. All three double rooms have private bathrooms, central heating, tea/coffee facilities, colour TV, radio/alarm clock, electric blankets and hair dryers. Evening Meals are available using home grown produce, and there is ample parking. A washing machine and drying room are available. Terms from £16.25 per person; £32.50 for two in a double room with private bathroom. All prices include full English Breakfast.

The information in the entries in this guide is presented by the publishers in good faith and after the signed acceptance by advertisers that they will uphold the high standards associated with FHG PUBLICATIONS LIMITED. The publishers do not accept responsibility for any inaccuracies or omissions or any results thereof.
Before making final holiday arrangements readers should confirm the prices and facilities directly with advertisers.

CORNHILL-ON-TWEED. Mrs V. Watson, Flodden Edge Farm, Mindrum, Cornhill-on-Tweed TD12

4QG (06686 287). Large country house set in own grounds in quiet rural area, one-and-a-half miles from A697 Newcastle to Edinburgh road. Central for hills and coast. Within half hour's drive of Lindisfarne and Bamburgh Castle, also Border Abbeys. Edinburgh one and a quarter hour's drive. Four miles from Scottish border and one and a half miles from Flodden Field. Ideal for children. Dogs welcome. Homely atmosphere and no restrictions. Bedrooms have washbasins, tea/coffee facilities and TV. Bathroom with shower. Residents' lounge with TV. Separate diningroom. Ideal for fishing, walking and exploring the National Park. Gliding and horse riding nearby, also miniature steam railway. Open all year. Reduced rates for children and for Senior Citizens early and late season.

See also Colour Display Advertisement **GREENHEAD. Mrs Pauline Staff, Holmhead Farm Licensed Guest House, Hadrian's Wall, Greenhead, Via Carlisle CA6 7HY (Gilsland [06977] 47402).** ♥♥ ♥♥♥
If you are visiting Hadrian's Wall, or en route to the Lakes or Scotland, come and stay with us and enjoy the longest breakfast menu in the world! Our modernised and converted farmhouse actually sits on the line of the Wall and is only 15 minutes' walk from the highest remaining parts and the Roman Army Museum; two miles Birdoswald Fort; six miles Vindolanda and Housesteads. Discount tickets for guests staying more than two days and special inclusive tour. Helicopter flights over the Wall. Holmhead is approached by driving over a picturesque ford and half a mile private drive from Greenhead Village which is on A69 three miles west of Haltwhistle, Exit 43 from M6 then 14 miles east. All bedrooms have shower/toilet, lovely views. Upstairs residents' lounge has colour TV, tea/coffee making facilities. For children — garden, games room. Sorry, no pets. Diets catered for. Guests may choose own breakfast times. Home cooking all freshly prepared. Guests dine together (dinner party style) round large oak candlelit table. Full central heating. Bed and Breakfast from £17.50; Evening Meal £10. Residential/restaurant licence. Open all year. Well equipped self-catering flat also available, 3 Keys Awarded.

HALTWHISTLE. Mrs Mary Dawson, Park Burnfoot Farm, Featherstone Park, Haltwhistle NE49 0JP (0434 320378). Working farm. When visiting the Roman Wall area for an overnight stop or a longer visit, you can be sure of a friendly welcome at this 18th century farmhouse on a 200-acre working farm. Park Burnfoot, with the waterfalls to the front of the house and the River South Tyne at the back, makes an ideal setting. Woodland walk 100 yards away. Two miles from Haltwhistle, one mile from Featherstone Castle and about four miles from the best parts of the Roman Wall, the farm is an ideal touring centre; Ullswater and the Scottish Borders within easy motoring distance. One double and one family bedrooms, with washbasins, soap and towels, colour TV and tea maker; bathroom with shower, separate toilet; large, warm visitors' lounge. Terms for accommodation and good English Breakfast from £10.50, late drink included. Evening Meal available. Self-catering cottage also available from £75 per week. Registered with English Tourist Board.

HALTWHISTLE. Mrs D.M. Laidlow, White Craig, Shield Hill, Haltwhistle NE49 9NW (Haltwhistle [0434] 320565). ♥♥ ♥♥ ♥♥ Quality en-suite Bed and Breakfast on a croft-style 17th century farmhouse on working livestock farm (also some rare breeds). Overlooks South Tyne Valley, one mile from Hadrian's Wall, half a mile A69 'twixt Northumberland National Park and North Pennines. Area of outstanding natural beauty. Wonderful area for touring on quiet roads, birdwatching, walking, Roman history or just enjoying the peace. Nearby inn provides excellent meals. SAE for brochure.

HEXHAM. Mrs Doreen Cole, Hillcrest House, Barrasford, Hexham NE48 4BY (Humshaugh [0434]

681426). ♥♥ ♥♥ ♥♥ *Commended.* Hillcrest House has been specifically extended to provide a high standard of accommodation, with a homely, comfortable atmosphere. One family, one double, one twin, one single rooms, all with ensuite shower rooms, colour TV, tea/coffee facilities. Evening meal optional; packed lunches on request. Comfortable lounge, separate tables in diningroom. Residential licence. Situated seven miles from historic Hexham in beautiful North Tyne Valley. Ideal for touring Hadrian's Wall and within easy distance of Kielder, the Borders, Newcastle and Gateshead Metro Centre. Car essential. Bed and Breakfast £16 single, £28 double.

HEXHAM near. Mrs M.I. Lee, Manor House Farm, Ninebanks, Whitfield, Hexham NE47 8DA (0434

345236). A 500 acre working farm situated amidst the beautiful scenery of the West Allen Valley on the edge of Northumberland, close to the Durham and Cumbria borders. Ideally situated for visiting the North Pennines, Hadrian's Wall, English Lakes, Beamish Museum, Metro Centre and an ideal overnight stop between England and Scotland. Tea-making facilities, washbasins, two bathrooms, central heating plus an excellent farmhouse Breakfast all add to an enjoyable holiday.

HEXHAM. Mrs M.G. Carter, East Wood House, Fallowfield Road, Acomb, Hexham NE46 4RN (Hexham [0434] 603188). 👑👑 *Commended.*

A small, comfortable, well-appointed country house in a peaceful rural setting with gardens and three and a half acres of land, south-facing with extensive views over the Tyne Valley. Ideal centre for visiting the Roman Wall, the magnificent Northumberland countryside and many places of historic interest. The attractive old market town of Hexham is three miles away. The house is centrally heated. One double, one twin, one single bedroom, all with washbasins. Adjacent guests' bathroom (including shower). Separate guests' diningroom and sittingroom (colour TV). Good food. Bed and Breakfast from £12 (£13 for one night stay). Dinner from £5.50. Dogs welcome by prior arrangement. ETB registered. Open April to October. SAE for brochure.

The Old Vicarage

Relax in the tranquil beauty of Northumberland and enjoy the old world charm of this historic Georgian house, originally a 13th-century Pele Tower with the house built around it in 1760. The present owners have sympathetically restored the old house to its former elegance without losing modern comfort and convenience. There is an acre of walled garden, with sweeping lawns.

Children and pets welcome. Cot/baby sitting available. Some bedrooms en-suite. All have tea/coffee facilities. Full central heating. TV lounge. Sunny diningroom. Dinners on request. Kirkwhelpington is just off the A696 Newcastle/Edinburgh road and is two miles from Wallington Hall. Ample private car parking. Brochure on request. ETB registered. PAINTING HOLIDAYS A SPECIALITY.

Mrs A.H. Wells, The Old Vicarage, Kirkwhelpington, Northumberland NE19 2RT
Telephone: Otterburn (0830) 40319

HOLIDAY ACCOMMODATION
Classification Schemes in
England, Scotland and Wales

The National Tourist Boards for England, Scotland and Wales have agreed a common 'Crown Classification' scheme for **serviced (Board)** accommodation. All establishments are inspected regularly and are given a classification indicating their level of facilities and services.

There are six grades ranging from 'Listed' to 'Five Crowns 👑👑👑👑👑'. The higher the classification, the more facilities and services offered.

Crown classification is a measure of *facilities* not *quality*. A common quality grading scheme grades the quality of establishments as 'Approved', 'Commended' or 'Highly Commended' according to the accommodation, welcome and service they provide.

For **Self-Catering**, holiday homes in England are awarded 'Keys' after inspection and can also be 'Approved', 'Commended' or 'Highly Commended' according to the facilities available. In Scotland the Crown scheme includes self-catering accommodation and Wales also has a voluntary inspection scheme for self-catering grading from '1 (Standard)' to '5 (Excellent)'.

Caravan and Camping Parks can participate in the British Holiday Parks grading scheme from 'Approved (✓)' to 'Excellent (✓ ✓ ✓ ✓ ✓)'. In addition, each National Tourist Board has an annual award for high-quality caravan accommodation: in England – Rose Awards; in Scotland – Thistle Commendations; in Wales – Dragon Awards.

When advertisers supply us with the information, FHG Publications show Crowns and other awards or gradings, including AA, RAC, Egon Ronay etc. We also award a small number of Farm Holiday Guide Diplomas every year, based on readers' recommendations.

LOWICK. Janet and John Dunn, The Old Manse Guest House, 5 Cheviot View, Lowick, Berwick upon Tweed TD15 2TY (Berwick upon Tweed [0289] 88264).

The Old Manse Guest House, situated in the quiet farming village of Lowick, is a Georgian Grade II listed former church manse of considerable character. The adjoining church (circa 1821), which is still used every Sunday, was the first Scottish church to be built in England. The house, which overlooks the village common, offers comfortable accommodation which comprises double and twin-bedded rooms with en-suite bathrooms, a family room, and a further double-bedded room. Bed and Breakfast from £12 per person; Evening Meal which is four course with choice of menu, is £6.50.

ROTHBURY. Mrs Alison Giles, Thropton Demesne Farmhouse, Thropton, Morpeth NE65 7LT (Rothbury [0669] 20196). 🌑🌑 Comfortable farm-

house with a friendly atmosphere lying in the beautiful Coquet Valley overlooking the river and the Simonside Hills. Privately situated on the edge of a quiet village, two miles from Rothbury where there is golf, riding, tennis, fishing and swimming. Superb walking country within easy reach of the coast and Cheviots. The farmhouse has full central heating. There is one double/family room with en-suite bathroom, one double and one twin-bedded room; each with washbasin and sharing a guest bathroom. Comfortable guest lounge; diningroom/lounge (non-smoking). Cot etc available and also babysitting if required. Colour TV in every bedroom. Bed and Breakfast from £13.50; Evening Meal £8. Reductions for children. Packed lunches available. Open all year.

SLALEY, near Hexham. Mrs Elizabeth Courage, Rye Hill Farm, Slaley, Near Hexham NE47 0AH (Hexham [0434] 673259). 🌑🌑🌑 Rye Hill Farm is a 300

year old Northumbrian stone farmhouse, set in its own 30 acres of rural Tynedale. Guests have the unique opportunity to see life on a small working farm, while the self-contained accommodation in the converted farm buildings offers all the comforts of good farm hospitality. We provide full English Breakfast and optional three course Evening Meal. Table licence held. All bedrooms are centrally heated with colour TV and tea/coffee making facilities; half the rooms have bathrooms en-suite. Northumberland Moors, Kielder Forest, Kielder Water nearby. Visit the historic city of Durham, or the market town of Hexham which is only five minutes away. Bed and Breakfast from £13 to £16; Evening Meal £9.

WARKWORTH. Mrs S.C. Lillico, Aulden, 9 Watershaugh Road, Warkworth, Morpeth NE65 0TT (Alnwick [0665] 711583). 🌑 *Commended.* A friendly family home on the outskirts of this historic village, with beautiful riverside walk to its Norman church, castle and hermitage. Also near long unspoilt sandy beaches. With a car you are close to Cheviot Hills, forest walks, Farne Islands, historic castles, Roman Wall and bird reserves. Twin, double bedrooms with washbasins, shaver points and tea/coffee making facilities. Residents' lounge; colour TV. Tastefully decorated throughout. Bed and Breakfast from £12.50 nightly; Bed, Breakfast and three course Dinner from £21. Sorry, no pets. SAE for brochure.

NOTTINGHAMSHIRE

COTGRAVE. Mrs S. Herrick, Jerico Farm, Cotgrave NG12 3HG (Kinoulton [0949] 81733). 🐦🐦

Commended. Jerico Farm is situated off the Fosse Way (A46) between Newark and Leicester, eight miles from both Nottingham and Melton Mowbray. Accommodation in the friendly farmhouse comprises twin/double bedded rooms each with washbasin, shaver point, tea/coffee making facilities and heating. Guests have their own comfortable sitting/dining room with colour TV and cosy woodburner. Good farmhouse breakfast. Jerico overlooks the Nottinghamshire Wolds and is on the edge of the Vale of Belvoir, within easy reach of Belvoir and Nottingham castles, Sherwood Forest and Holme Pierrepont National Water Sports centre. Non-smoking household. Open all year for Bed and Breakfast from £12. Please ring for further details.

MANSFIELD. Mrs L. Palmer, Boon Hills Farm, Nether Langwith, Mansfield NG20 9JQ (Mansfield [0623] 743862). Working farm.

Farmhouse accommodation in stone-built farmhouse standing in 155 acres of mixed farmland, 300 yards back from A632 on edge of the village. Comfortably furnished with fitted carpets throughout, the house has electric heating, open fire. Large sitting/diningroom with colour TV. One family room, one double room and another room with twin beds. Children welcome and there are many pets for them on the farm. Babysitting arranged. Pets accepted. Situated on edge of Sherwood Forest, six miles from Visitors' Centre; eight miles M1; 10 miles A1. Places of interest include Hardwick Hall, Thoresby Hall, Chatsworth House, Newstead Abbey. Pleasant half-mile walk to picturesque village inn serving evening meals. Car essential, ample parking. Tourist Board Commended. Bed and Breakfast only from £10 per night. Non-smokers only. Reductions for children. Open March to October inclusive.

NORTON (Sherwood Forest). Mrs J. Palmer, Norton Grange Farm, Norton, Cuckney, Near Mansfield NG20 9LP (Mansfield [0623] 842666). 🐦🐦

Working farm, join in. Norton Grange Farm is a listed Georgian-type stone farmhouse and is situated on the edge of Sherwood Forest overlooking peaceful open countryside, away from the traffic. The 172 acre mixed arable farm carries beef cattle, poultry and arable crops, also many domestic farm animals. A car is advantageous for visiting the many places of local interest — ample parking. Accommodation comprises family room, double and twin-bedded rooms with washbasins. All rooms have tea/coffee making facilities. Fitted bathroom with shower, separate toilet. Sittingroom, diningroom. Bed and full English Breakfast, from £12, is provided all year except Christmas. Flasks filled on request. Reductions for children sharing family room. Sorry, no pets.

NOTTINGHAM. Mrs M. Watchorn, The Dairies, 22 The Green, Barkestone-le-Vale, Nottingham NG13 0HH (0949 42495).

Farmhouse in the middle of small village with quiet country lanes for walking. On Leicestershire, Nottinghamshire and Lincolnshire border, it is an ideal location for exploring the East Midlands, convenient for Robin Hood country, Byron and D.H. Lawrence and the Dukeries. Central for several market towns — Melton Mowbray, Newark-on-Trent, Nottingham. Eight miles from A1 (Grantham), two miles Belvoir Castle. Central heating. One double en-suite from £11 each Bed and Breakfas, one twin and single from £10 each Bed and Breakfast. Family room available. Reductions for children sharing. Evening meal by arrangement. TV, tea/coffee facilities in all rooms. Bathroom plus separate shower, three toilets.

REDMILE. Mrs M. Need, Peacock Farm, Redmile, Nottingham NG13 0GQ (0949 42475). 🐦🐦 Ideal for a family holiday. 18th century farmhouse set in open countryside with views of nearby Belvoir Castle and the Vale of Belvoir. Marjorie, Peter, and Nicky Need welcome house guests with first-class service and old-fashioned hospitality. Facilities include covered pool, bikes, table tennis, pet animals, sunbed, play areas inside and out, gardens etc. Good area for walking and exploring. Our cheery bar and restaurant ensure families enjoy the best of both worlds. Favourable quotations for family holidays. Some self catering available.

OXFORDSHIRE

ABINGDON. Mrs Maureen Lay, Manor Farm, Fyfield, Near Abingdon OX13 5LR (Frilford Heath [0865] 390485). Working farm. This large Queen Anne style farmhouse is situated in the heart of a historic and attractive village on a working farm (750 acres) with sheep, beef cattle and corn. The proprietors have a young family between the ages of eight and eighteen, so facilities for children and reduced rates are available. Ideally situated for Oxford, Abingdon and the Cotswolds. One double and one family bedroom with washbasins, one single; bathroom, two toilets; sittingroom and diningroom. TV. Pets permitted. Parking. Thames and Chilterns Tourist Board member. Open from January to December for Bed and Breakfast from £12 single, and £22 double.

BANBURY near. Mrs Rebecca Trace, Rectory Farm, Sulgrave, Near Banbury OX17 2SG (Sulgrave [029 576] 261). Working farm, join in. Delightful 350-year-old thatched farmhouse, set in five acres overlooking Sulgrave Manor, ancestral home of George Washington. This working farm keeps sheep, ducks, chickens and ponies. Convenient for Oxford, Stratford, Cotswolds and canals. House retains many original features: flagstone floors, exposed beams, open fireplaces, bread oven. Excellent home produced food served in friendly, homely atmosphere. Two double, one twin, two family rooms, all with washbasins; two bathrooms, two toilets; sittingroom, diningroom. Children welcome, cot, high chair and babysitting available. Central heating. Car essential, ample parking. Open all year except Christmas. Bed and Breakfast from £13; optional Dinner (weekdays only) from £7. Rates reduced for children and weekly bookings. Licensed. Tourist Board registered.

BANBURY near. Mrs E.J. Lee, The Mill Barn, Lower Tadmarton, Near Banbury OX15 5SU (Swalcliffe [0295-78] 349). Tadmarton is a small village, three miles south-west of Banbury. The Mill, no longer working, was originally water powered and the stream lies adjacent to the house. The Mill Barn has been tastefully converted, retaining many traditional features such as beams and exposed stone walls, yet it still has all the amenities a modern house offers. Two spacious en-suite bedrooms, one downstairs, are available to guests in this comfortable family home. Base yourself here and visit Stratford, historic Oxford, Woodstock and the beautiful Cotswolds, knowing you are never further than an hour's drive away. Open all year for Bed and Breakfast from £15, reductions for children. Weekly terms available.

BRAILES. Mrs R. Cripps, Agdon Farm, Brailes, Banbury OX15 5JJ (060-885 226). Working farm. A working farm with a traditional stone farmhouse in beautiful countryside on the Compton Wynyates Estate, surrounded by wheat fields, farm animals and wild life. Ideal for touring the Midlands, Stratford-upon-Avon, Warwick, Oxford, Cotswolds and Blenheim Palace. Bed and Breakfast, TV room. Children welcome. Bed and Breakfast from £10.

SUPERIOR
FARM ACCOMMODATION
Around Oxford . . . Along the Thames

1 Anne Amor   0367 52620
2 Pat Hoddinott   0367 240175
3 Mary Pike   0235 868204
4 Della Barnard   0367 240229
5 Janet Rouse   0993 850162
6 Katherine Brown   0993 703120
7 Angela Widdows   0608 810314
8 Stella Pickering   0865 300211
9 Vanessa Maundrell   0993 882097
10 Hilary Warburton   086732 8406
11 Jean Bowden   0734 713166
12 Audrey Dunkley   08677 2248

14 Binnie Pickford   0844 237360
15 Joan Bury   0844 201103
16 Bridget Silsoe   0491 680258
17 Anita Cooper   0844 238276
18 Frances Emmett   0494 881600
19 Marjorie Aitken   084421 2496
20 Mary-Joyce Hooper   0844 291650
21 Jackie Cook   0296 748660
22 Christine Abbey   029672 275
23 Rosemary Nunneley   029588 512
24 Jane Kimber   0494 21082

All farms are inspected annually by the English Tourist Board

**For special help and guidance to find the farm most suitable for your needs,
telephone Margaret Palmer on 0993 850162.**

DEDDINGTON. Mrs Audrey Fuller, Earls Farm, Deddington, Oxford OX5 4TH (Deddington [0869] 38243). ♛ ♛ Working farm. Delightfully situated on edge of village 200 yards from main Banbury to Oxford road, this farm covers 230 acres of cropping fields. Open all year, it has two double, one family bedrooms, all with washbasins; two bathrooms, two toilets; sittingroom, diningroom. Central heating. Children very welcome and facilities for them include cot, high chair, babysitting and reduced rates; also swing and slide. Fishing available on River Swere. Trout fishing on local lake by arrangement. Golf five miles away, tennis two. Banbury six miles. This is an ideal touring base. Pets accepted. Car essential, parking. Bed and Breakfast from £15 single; £28 double. Also new self-catering accommodation available. SAE, please, for further details.

FARINGDON. Mrs Pat Hoddinott, Ashen Copse Farm, Coleshill, Faringdon SN6 7PU (0367 240175). ♛ ♛ Working farm. Perfect spot to tour or relax.

Our 850 acre National Trust farm is set in peaceful countryside on borders of Oxfordshire, Wiltshire and Gloucestershire. The large stone and brick farmhouse has two family bedrooms for guests: a) double bed, two single beds, ensuite; b) three single beds, washbasin. Cot available. Large garden, farm animals, lovely views, small swimming pool. So much to see and do — tourist information available. Facilities locally for fishing, riding, golfing, swimming, boating and walking. Good choice of places to eat out. Open all year. Bed and Breakfast from £14 to £16 (reductions for children 10 years and under sharing).

FARINGDON. Mr D. Barnard, Bowling Green Farm, Stanford Road, Faringdon, Oxfordshire SN7 8EZ (0367 240229 Fax: 0367 242568). ♛ ♛ Attractive

18th century farmhouse offering 20th century comfort. Situated in the Vale of White Horse, just one mile south of Faringdon on the A417. Easy access to M4 Exit 15 for Heathrow Airport. An ideal place to stay for a day or longer. A working farm of cattle, horse breeding, poultry and ducks. Large twin-bedded/family room on ground floor, en-suite. All bedrooms have colour TV, tea/coffee making facilities and full central heating throughout. Perfect area for riding, golf, fishing and walking the Ridgeway. Interesting places to visit include Oxford, Bath, Windsor, Burford, Henley, Blenheim Palace and the Cotswolds. Open all year. Registered with the Thames and Chilterns Tourist Board. Member of the Farm Holiday Bureau.

HENLEY-ON-THAMES. The Old Bakery, Skirmett, Near Henley-on-Thames RG9 6TD (Turville Heath [049-163] 309). This welcoming family house is

situated on the site of an old bakery, seven miles from Henley-on-Thames and Marlow; half an hour from Heathrow and Oxford; one hour from London. It is in the Hambleden Valley in the beautiful Chilterns, with many excellent pubs selling good food within walking distance. Riding school nearby; beautiful walking country. Two double rooms with TV, one twin-bedded and two single rooms; two bathrooms. Tea/coffee facilities. Central heating throughout. Open all year. Parking for five cars (car essential). Pets and children welcome. Bed and Breakfast from £15 to £18 single; £30 to £40 double. Registered with English and Chilterns Tourist Boards.

OXFORD. Mr and Mrs L.S. Price, Portland House, 338 Banbury Road, Oxford OX2 7PR (Oxford [0865] 52076 or 53796). ♛ ♛ Large attractive Edwardian guest house, family run, with pleasant friendly atmosphere. It is set in one of the best parts of Oxford and is an excellent base for touring — Woodstock, Stratford, London, Cotswolds etc. can all be visited for the day from here. Close to city centre, shops and restaurants. Fire Certificate. Portland House is comfortably furnished, all rooms having H&C, tea/coffee making facilities, TV, and some have showers. Double, single, family rooms, three bathrooms, three toilets; diningroom. Children welcome. Open all year round. Centrally heated. Launderette facilities. Bus stop outside. Parks, river, beautiful walks close by. Swimming pool, tennis courts five minutes' walk. River sports. Bed and Breakfast from £15. "Les Routiers", RAC.

OXFORDSHIRE – CHILTERNS, COTSWOLDS AND COLLEGES!

Many fine days can be spent studying Oxford's architecture – both old and new. Other interesting pastimes might include trips to Banbury and Europe's biggest cattle market, the Cotswold Wildlife Park near Burford, the Rollright Stones near Chipping Norton and the Vale of the White Horse at Uffington.

OXFORD. Mrs B.B. Taphouse, "Wrestler's Mead", 35 Wroslyn Road, Freeland, Oxford OX7 2HJ (0993 882003).

A warm welcome awaits you at the home of the Taphouses. We are conveniently located for Blenheim Palace (10 minutes), Oxford (20 minutes) and the Cotswolds (25 minutes). Accommodation comprises one double and one single room both with washbasins and at ground level. Our first floor family room has its own en-suite shower room with washbasin and toilet. The double and the family room each have a colour TV; a black and white portable is available for the single room, if required. Cot, high chair and baby-sitting service available. Pets by arrangement. No hidden extras. Bed and Breakfast from £13.

OXFORD. Mrs E. Neville, Ascot Guest House, 283 Iffley Road, Oxford OX4 4AQ (Oxford [0865] 240259/727669). This pleasant Victorian guest house, situated one mile from the city centre, offers six most charming and comfortable rooms with modern furnishings, TV and tea/coffee making facilities. En-suite available. Cots also provided upon request. One four-poster bed. Mrs Neville makes all her guests very welcome and will help plan tours. A good base for visiting the city of "Dreaming Spires". A short drive takes you to Blenheim Palace, the Cotswolds, Stratford-upon-Avon and within a day's drive is Windsor Castle. A vegetarian Breakfast is provided if required. Terms from approximately £13 to £22 per person. Thames and Chiltern Tourist Board Registered.

STANTON HARCOURT. Mr S.S. Clifton, Staddle Stones, Linch Hill, Stanton Harcourt OX8 1BB (0865 882256). Set in its own delightful grounds of five acres, complete with carp pool, Staddle Stones offers very comfortable accommodation and exceptionally good food, bread freshly baked; special diets catered for; packed lunches provided for fishermen; our full English Breakfast will satisfy the keenest of appetites. Disabled guests are very welcome, as are children and pets. Fishing (trout and coarse) is available close at hand, while Oxford and the Cotswolds are readily accessible. Margaret and Spencer Clifton offer a very warm, friendly welcome. Bed and Breakfast from £13. Tourist Board listed.

UFFINGTON. Mrs Carol Wadsworth, The Craven, Uffington SN7 7RD (Uffington [036-782] 449).

The Craven, an attractive 17th century thatched and beamed farmhouse, mentioned in 'Tom Brown's Schooldays ', is situated on the outskirts of Uffington. The unspoilt country-side, in the picturesque Vale of the White Horse, provides a lovely walking area, including the famous Ridgeway Path. Ideally situated for visiting Oxford, the Avebury Circle, the City of Bath and the Cotswolds. Three golf courses in the area. Children welcome and babysitting offered. Pets by arrangement. Guests welcome all year round to enjoy the friendly atmosphere and good country home cooking. There is central heating and log fires in winter. Tourist Board registered. Bed and Breakfast from £14 to £24. SAE for further details and terms.

WANTAGE near. Mrs M.E. Pike, Manor Farm, Lyford, Wantage OX12 0EG (West Hanney [0235] 868204). ♛♛ **Working farm.**

Our stone manor house built in the 15th century is tucked away in the peaceful hamlet of Lyford, five minutes north west of Wantage in the Thames Valley. Well situated for enjoying some of England's finest countryside — Oxford 20 minutes' drive, London one and a quarter hours. Four well appointed bedrooms, two on ground floor, all with private bath/shower rooms. Tea/coffee making facilities in rooms. Guests' sittingroom with open fire and TV. No smoking in the house. Breakfast is served in conservatory overlooking large, well stocked garden where guests can sit and relax. Open all year, children welcome. Car essential, plenty of parking space.

WOODSTOCK. Gorselands, Near Long Hanborough, Near Woodstock, Oxford OX8 6PU (0993 881202).

Situated in an idyllic peaceful location in the Oxfordshire countryside, Gorselands has its own grounds of one acre. This Cotswold stone farmhouse has exposed beams, flagstone floors, billiards room (full size table), guest lounge, dining conservatory and satellite TV. We have one large family room with washbasin, one double room with washbasin and an en-suite twin-bedded room. Large main bathroom with bath and shower. Tea/coffee making facilities available. Near to Oxford, Blenheim Palace, East End Roman Villa, Cotswold Villages. Children welcome. Bed and Breakfast from £10 per person; four course Evening Meal £8.50.

SHROPSHIRE

BISHOPS CASTLE. Mrs M. Beddoes, Pentrehyling Farm, Churchstoke, Montgomery, Powys SY15 6HU (05885 249 or 0588 620249). ❀ ❀ Working farm, join in.

Pentrehyling Farm offers you a friendly family atmosphere in a listed 17th century Border farmhouse, with a wealth of oak beams and log fires in season. Excellent home cooking, vegetarian menu available. Centrally situated in the historic Marches, you can easily explore unspoilt rural Shropshire or beautiful Mid Wales. Ideal for walking with Offa's Dyke just half a mile away. Pony trekking, fishing, golf, hang gliding all within easy reach. Large comfortable lounge with TV, spacious diningroom. One family, one double/twin, one single, all with washbasin, shaver point and hot drinks facility. Guests' bathroom, separate toilet. Central heating. Children welcome. Ample car parking space. Please write or phone for brochure.

BRIDGNORTH. Mr and Mrs Roberts, Dinney Farm, Chelmarsh, Bridgnorth WV16 6AU (0746 861070). ❀ ❀

A working farm of 150 acres for sheep and cattle occupying an outstanding, elevated position overlooking some of Shropshire's most beautiful scenery. Bedrooms command panoramic views of the countryside and have central heating and en-suite bathrooms. Tea/coffee making facilities are available. You are assured of a warm welcome and Dinney Farm makes an ideal base from which to visit many interesting places. Dogs welcome. Brochure available.

BRIDGNORTH. Mrs G.W. Green, Charlcotte Farm, Cleobury North, Bridgnorth WV16 6RR (074-633 238). ❀ ❀

Charlcotte is a dairy, sheep and arable family farm nestled amidst undulating countryside at the foot of the Brown Clee Hill, renowned for its woodland walks and panoramic views. Close to the medieval market towns of Ludlow and Shrewsbury. Local attractions include the historic Ironbridge Gorge and the Severn Valley Steam Railway. Guests are invited to enjoy the large country garden and comfortable drawing room which are available for their use at all times. There are two family rooms (one en-suite), one twin-bedded room; tea-making facilities, shaver points.

BUCKNELL. Mrs Christine Price, The Hall, Bucknell SY7 0AA (Bucknell [05474] 249). ❀ ❀

Commended. You are assured of a warm welcome at The Hall, which is a Georgian farmhouse with spacious accommodation. The house and gardens are set in a secluded part of a small South Shropshire village, an ideal area for touring the Welsh Borderland. Offa's Dyke is on the doorstep and the historic towns of Shrewsbury, Hereford, Ludlow and Ironbridge are within easy reach as are the Church Stretton Hills and Wenlock Edge. Three bedrooms — one twin en-suite, 2 doubles (with washbasins). Guest lounge, colour TV, bedtime drinks, morning hospitality trays. Guest lounge, colour TV. Bedtime drinks and morning hospitality trays. Bed and Breakfast from £12; Dinner £7. Heart of England Tourist Board approved. SAE, please for details.

CHURCH STRETTON. Mrs Mary Jones, Acton Scott Farm, Church Stretton SY6 6QN (Marshbrook [069-46] 260). Working farm.

Acton Scott Farm is a 320 acre working farm in the heart of South Shropshire's beautiful hill country, an area of outstanding natural beauty. The lovely old 17th century farmhouse is full of old world character. The comfortable and spacious bedrooms have storage radiators and there is often a cheery log fire in the lounge, colour TV. Separate diningroom. Children welcome. Pets by arrangement. The farm is easy to find and centrally situated for touring; Shrewsbury, Ludlow and Ironbridge can all be reached within half an hour. Visitor information available. Bed and full English Breakfast from £10 per person. Open all year excluding December and New Year. English Tourist Board Approved. A49 at Marshbrook, Acton Scott turning.

CHURCH STRETTON. Mrs Joanna Brereton, Woolston Farm, Church Stretton SY6 6QD (06946 201). Woolston Farm lies within the tiny hamlet of Woolston above the village of Wistonstowe, with lovely views of Wenlock Edge. Convenient for the A49 from Craven Arms to Church Stretton, making it ideal for sightseeing with Ludlow and Ironbridge within easy reach. Offa's Dyke and Long Mynd offer good walking facilities. Golf and horse riding nearby. Woolston Farmhouse is Victorian, brick built, with lovely garden and peaceful atmosphere. Children very welcome. Cot, high chair and babysitting available. Lounge with colour TV. Bed and Breakfast from £11; Evening Meal optional. Reductions for children under 12 years.

♛♛♛ Commended

Mrs J. A. Davies, Rectory Farm,
Woolstaston, Church Stretton, Shropshire SY6 6NN
Tel. Leebotwood (069-45) 306

Half-timbered farmhouse built in the early 1600's situated on the edge of the National Trust Long Mynd Hills. Guest accommodation comprises two twin-bedded rooms and one double bedroom, all with private bathrooms and extensive views of Shropshire. No small children. Oil central heating. The house which is open from March to November provides Bed & Breakfast only from £15 per person. A car is essential and there is ample parking space. There are many attractive places for evening meals locally. English and Heart of England Tourist Board registered.

AA SELECTED
Worldwide Bed and Breakfast Association winner
Cotswolds and Marches 1987.

CHURCH STRETTON. Mrs C.J. Hotchkiss, Olde Hall Farm, Wall-Under-Heywood, Church Stretton SY6 7DU (Longville [06943] 253). Working farm. A warm welcome awaits you from the Hotchkiss family at Olde Hall Farm, a modern 275 acre dairy farm. Delightful Elizabethan farmhouse with central heating offers accommodation in twin or double-bedded rooms (extra child's bed) with washbasins, colour TV, tea/coffee making facilities and clean towels daily. A single room is also available and there is a well appointed bathroom. Comfortably furnished guests' lounge with TV and a selection of books is accessible at all times. In the separate diningroom with inglenook fireplace, good wholesome English Breakfast is provided or alternatives to suit your requirements, with home produced fare where possible. Lovely walking area and within easy reach of Ironbridge Gorge, Ludlow, Bridgnorth or Shrewsbury. No pets. Car essential, parking. Bed and Breakfast from £13.50. AA listed.

CHURCH STRETTON. Mrs J. Tory, "Jinlye", Castle Hill, All Stretton, Church Stretton SY6 6JP (Church Stretton [0694] 723243). "Jinlye" is situated 1,400 ft. above sea level in the lovely Stretton Hills, immediately adjoining 6,000 acres of National Trust land. An area of outstanding natural beauty, delightful valleys, mountain streams. "Jinlye" is a newly built 16th century-style house with magnificent views, a large garden with unusual plants and a friendly, homely atmosphere. Very peaceful. Excellent food. A smallholding with mainly racehorses, it is situated 13 miles from Shrewsbury and 15 miles from Ludlow. We are ideally situated for touring Wales and Midlands. Church Stretton has the highest 18 hole golf course in England. Heart of England Tourist Board listed. Bed and Breakfast from £14; weekly from £150. Brochure free.

Terms quoted in this publication may be subject to increase if rises in costs necessitate

Malt House Farm

Lower Wood, Church Stretton,
Shropshire SY6 6LF
Prop. Mrs Lyn Bloor
Tel: Leebotwood (06945) 379
TOURIST BOARD LISTED

Comfortable accommodation in our olde worlde farmhouse situated amidst stunning scenery on the lower slopes of the Long Mynd Hills. We are a working farm producing beef cattle and sheep. There are two double bedrooms and one twin bedded room, all with washbasins. Guest bathroom; sittingroom with colour TV. Breakfast is served in the diningroom which has a lovely Inglenook fireplace. Sorry, no children or pets.
BED AND BREAKFAST FROM £11 PER PERSON

CHURCH STRETTON. Mrs Maureen Hind, Cwm Head House, Marshbrook, Church Stretton SY6 6PX (Marshbrook [06946] 279). Cwm Head House is a Victorian Farmhouse, set in nearly two acres of secluded gardens offering peace and tranquillity amid the beautiful Shropshire Hills. Extensive views of the Long Mynd which is easily reached for walking. Guests are accommodated in one family room with double and single beds, and one twin-bedded room, and have their own bathroom, toilet and lounge with colour TV. Tea/coffee making facilities are provided in bedrooms. Sorry, no pets. Children over eight years welcome. Open all year except Christmas. Bed and Breakfast from £10.50 per person. Evening Meal by arrangement. Full English or Continental breakfast. Vegetarians catered for.

CHURCH STRETTON. Mrs Barbara Norris, Court Farm, Gretton, Church Stretton SY6 7HU (Longville [069-43] 219). ♥♥ Working farm. Stone Tudor farmhouse in a very quiet and peaceful area of outstanding natural beauty, ideally situated for visiting Ironbridge, Bridgnorth, Ludlow and Shrewsbury. This is excellent walking country and, round about, there is much to interest the visitor or simply enjoy relaxation at Court Farm. Riding and trout fishing can be arranged. Three double rooms, one en-suite and two with washbasins, all with tea/coffee making facilities. Colour TV; central heating. High quality cuisine served, and the house is open from February to the beginning of November. Car preferable, ample parking. Sorry, no pets. Non-smoking household. Bed and Breakfast from £15; Dinner from £7.50. Further details may be obtained from Mrs Norris. Tourist Board registered. Our guests return year after year — why not join them.

CHURCH STRETTON near. Mrs Margaret Robinson, Blakemoor, Marshbrook, Church Stretton SY6 6QA (Marshbrook [069-46] 345). Charming old farmhouse with rare breed poultry where a friendly homely welcome awaits all guests. Panoramic views of glorious peaceful countryside. Excellent touring, cycling and walking centre, two miles from A49. Close to Long Mynd, Wenlock Edge and Welsh border towns. Historic town of Ludlow approximately 10 miles, Church Stretton four miles, Shrewsbury, Ironbridge and many tourist attractions within easy reach. Two comfortable double rooms with guests' bathroom and central heating. Heart of England Tourist Board registered. Regret, no children under eight, no pets. Full English Breakfast (free range eggs) from £11 per person. Ample parking.

CLUN. Mrs Jennifer Grand, The Elms Farm, Churchbank, Clun SY7 8LP (Clun [05884] 665). A Welsh border longhouse said to date back to the 17th century, three-quarters of a mile out of the historic town of Clun. A small hill farm with panoramic views, four miles from the Welsh border, close to Offa's Dyke. One double, one twin/family rooms with superb views, sittingroom with colour TV and log fire; own diningroom. Hot drinks available at all times, afternoon tea on arrival. Excellent varied home cooked food, home baked bread, home grown vegetables, our own spring water. Transport to and from Offa's Dyke walks between Knighton and Lower Spoad. Packed lunch on request. HETB member. Phone for terms.

CLUN. Mrs Miriam Ellison, New House Farm, Clun, Craven Arms SY7 8NJ (Bishops Castle [0588]

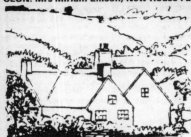

638314). 🐾 🐾 Isolated 18th century farmhouse set high in the Shropshire Hills. Off the beaten track (A488 Clun to Bishops Castle, left at crossroads to Colebatch, then on to Cefneinion, over crossroads, right at next crossroads, farm first on left) but with easy access. Working farm of approximately 325 acres situated in an environmentally sensitive area. Enjoy peaceful and quiet walks on the farm along Offa's Dyke Path and nearby Welsh borderland. Traditionally furnished farmhouse, spacious and comfortable bedrooms with scenic views, tea/coffee making facilities. Guests are assured of a warm welcome plus home cooking. One family/double room, one twin — both with washbasins; one single. Children welcome. Pets by arrangement. Bed and Breakfast from £12; Evening Meal £7. OS Ref: 50275863.

CLUN. Bob and Margaret Wall, Woodside Farm House, Woodside, Clun SY7 0JB (Clun [058-84]

695). 🐾 🐾 A warm welcome is extended to all guests, seeking peace and quiet in idyllic surroundings, at this 300-year-old farmhouse situated about one mile from Clun, on the sheltered side of Soudley Hill. Offa's Dyke is only three miles away and the surrounding countryside, for many miles, affords delight to ramblers — combined with the historic interests of the many castles and towns of the Border Country making this an ideal holiday location for people of all ages. Accommodation comprises one double and one (twin) family bedrooms, with washbasins; bathroom, toilet; sitting-room; diningroom. Central heating. Car not essential, but an advantage to make the most of touring this picturesque and historic part of England. Parking. Cot, high chair, babysitting, reduced rates for children. Pets welcome. Open March to October for Bed and Breakfast from £11. Evening Meal by arrangement from £6.50.

CLUN. Mrs M. Jones, Llanhedric, Clun, Craven Arms SY7 8NG (Clun [05884] 203). Working farm.

A mixed farm just two miles off the A488 road, overlooking the picturesque Clun Valley, near the Welsh border and Offa's Dyke. Ideal for walking or exploring the many places of historic interest including Ludlow and Shrewsbury. Attractive old stone house with lawns and garden, spacious accommodation, friendly atmosphere and good food. One double and one family bedroom, both with washbasins and tea/coffee making facilities; bathroom, toilet; lounge; separate diningroom. Sorry no dogs. Open Easter to October. Bed and Breakfast from £10; Bed, Breakfast and Evening Meal from £16. Reductions for children. HETB member.

CLUNBURY. Mrs Veronica M. Oates, Hillside, Twitchen, Clunbury, Craven Arms SY7 0HN (Little

Brampton [058-87] 485). 🐾 🐾 South west facing 200 year old stone cottage standing in own three acre grounds in quiet hamlet in area of outstanding natural beauty. Offa's Dyke nine miles and many places rich in historic interest within easy reach. Drive leads to ample car park. Large private sittingroom for guests with inglenook log fire. Separate diningroom with individual tables. Accommodation for adults only in one double and two twin-bedded rooms all with washbasins and tea/coffee making facilities. Two toilets. No objections to pets if kept under control. House open all day. Packed lunches available. Guests assured of a high standard of food and comfort. Fishing, golf, etc are available within reasonable distance. Open April to November. Transport available. HETB registered. Terms on request for Evening Dinner, Bed and Breakfast or Bed and Breakfast.

SHROPSHIRE – HISTORIC BORDER COUNTY!

The lonely Shropshire Hills – an "Area of Outstanding Natural Beauty" – are much favoured by walkers. Those seeking more traditional tourist activities would do well to visit the Acton Scott Working Museum, Ironbridge, Offa's Dyke or the market town of Bridgnorth.

CRAVEN ARMS near. Mrs Caroline Morgan, Strefford Hall, Strefford, Near Craven Arms SY7 8DE (Craven Arms [0588] 672383). ✿✿ Working farm.

Guests are assured of a warm welcome at this spacious Victorian farmhouse, with outstanding views of the Wenlock Edge and Long Mynd Hills. The Hall stands in a large garden where guests are welcome to relax. A working farm keeping cattle, sheep and growing corn, we are situated approximately 250 yards off the A49 just five miles south of Church Stretton. Accommodation in one double, one family and one twin bedroom, all with washbasin, shaver point and tea/coffee making facilities. Guest bathroom, two toilets. Comfortable lounge has log burner for cooler evenings and colour TV; separate diningroom with individual tables. Non-smokers preferred. AA listed. Bed and Breakfast from £12.50; Evening Meal £7.50. Less 10 per cent for three nights or more.

CRAVEN ARMS. Mrs S.J. Williams, Hurst Mill Farm, Clunton, Craven Arms SY7 0JA (Clun [058-84] 224). ✿✿ Working farm.

"Hurst Mill Farm" is situated in the prettiest part of the Clun Valley, renowned as a completely unspoilt part of England. One mile from the small town of Clun, which has a Saxon church and a Norman castle. Legend says one is wiser after crossing Clun Bridge. Within easy reach are Ludlow, Newtown, Elan Valley, Ironbridge and Long-Mynd Hills. Through the fields runs the River Clun where one can bathe. Woods and hills provide wonderful walks, which can be organised. Fishing and pony trekking locally. The farm has cattle, sheep, quiet riding ponies. Three double, one single bedrooms, all with washbasins and tea/coffee making facilities; lounge, diningroom. Parking. Children and pets welcome; cot and babysitting. Good food, pretty garden. Dinner, Bed and Breakfast from £16. Bed and Breakfast £11. Lunches. Open all year. AA listed.

IRONBRIDGE. Mrs Melanie Palmer, Sutton Hill Farm, Sutton Maddock, Shifnal, Near Ironbridge TF11 9NL (0952-71 217). ✿✿ Working farm, join in.

A 130 acre dairy farm situated 3 miles east of Ironbridge. Spacious farmhouse comprising 3 large bedrooms (one en-suite) with washbasins, hot drink-making facilities; sittingroom, colour TV; games and a dining/reading room with adjoining patio. Guests welcome to relax in the house and gardens during the day. Open all year. Car essential — ample parking. Children and pets welcome. Bed and Breakfast from £12.50 per person, Evening Meal by arrangement.

IRONBRIDGE. Mrs Virginia I. Evans, Church Farm, Rowton, Wellington, Near Telford TF6 6QY (Telford [0952] 770381). ✿✿ Working farm, join in.

Guests are welcome to join in the farming way of life at this listed 300-year-old farmhouse which is ideal for a friendly, family holiday. A real working farm with dairy cows, sheep, pigs and free range hens. Peacefully situated in a quiet village, yet near the historic towns of Shrewsbury, Chester, Ironbridge, Ludlow. Visit Potteries, Alton Towers, Weston Park, Cosford Aerospace Museum, Hawkstone Golf, Hodnet Gardens. Guest TV lounge, diningroom, shower-room, bathroom. All bedrooms have washbasins, tea/coffee making facilities and towels provided. Twin-bedded rooms, family room and four-poster bedroom with en-suite facilities. Home produced fresh food. Have a fresh egg with your large country breakfast. Children welcome. Day or weekly terms — Bed and Breakfast from £11.50 per person; Evening Meal (optional) £6. Reductions for children. Discounts for Spring/Autumn breaks. AA listed.

IRONBRIDGE. Mrs P. Williamson, Lower Huntington Farm, Little Wenlock, Telford TF6 5AP (0952

505804). ✿✿ Working dairy farm set in peaceful Shropshire countryside. Listed 17th century black and white farmhouse, beamed, exposed wattle and daub walls and centrally heated throughout. Large comfortable bedrooms — double, twin, family or single, with private bathroom, one ground floor with en-suite shower room. Each room has colour TV and tea-making facilities. 10 acres unspoilt woodland, fishing in farm pools, walkers' paradise. Ideally situated for Ironbridge, World Heritage Museums, Cosford Aerospace Museum, medieval Shrewsbury, Steam Railway, National Trust properties, Telford New Town with ice rink and 10-screen cinema. Three and a half miles from M54 Junction 7. Self catering caravans also available for hire.

IRONBRIDGE/TELFORD. Mrs Julia Thomas, Stoke Manor, Stoke-on-Tern, Market Drayton TF9 2DU

(063084 222). ✿✿ Commended. A warm welcome awaits you at Stoke Manor, which has a large garden and is situated on a working farm. Three charming bedrooms, each with bathroom, colour TV, tea/coffee making facilities. Unusual features include a particularly welcoming cellar bar, an 18th century bread oven, collection of vintage tractors, cast iron seats, artefacts from an archaeological dig on the farm's castle site, and farm trails. Central to Ironbridge, Wedgwood Pottery and Cosford Aerospace Museum, Shrewsbury, Chester and North Wales. An abundance of good eating places nearby. Residents' licence. Terms from £19 per person. AA listed.

LEINTWARDINE. Hildegard and Graham Cutler, Lower House, Adforton, Leintwardine, Craven

Arms SY7 0NF (Wigmore [056-886] 223). ✿✿ LOWER HOUSE is a delightful 17th century guesthouse, set amidst the peaceful and beautiful surroundings of the English/Welsh border country. Explore Ludlow, Knighton, Hereford, Leominster, Ironbridge and Shrewsbury, all within easy driving distance, whilst the nearby Offa's Dyke and Longmynd provide visitors with an opportunity to enjoy the magnificent scenery. Guests are assured of every comfort here — excellent food and large gardens, whilst all bedrooms are very comfortably furnished and equipped with washbasins, shaver points and facilities for making tea and coffee. Two en-suite bedrooms are also available. Our visitors can also enjoy their own separate inglenook diningroom and lounge with colour TV. Regret, no pets. Please write or phone for brochure to **Mrs Cutler.**

LUDLOW. Mrs R.M. Edwards, Haynall Villa, Little Hereford, Ludlow SY8 4BD (Brimfield [058472]

589). ✿✿ Approved. **Working farm, join in.** A warm welcome awaits you at Haynall Villa, our early 19th century farmhouse situated in the beautiful countryside of the Teme Valley on the Shropshire/Hereford border. We have easy access by leaving the A456 at Little Hereford (near River Teme bridge) towards LEYSTERS. The house is three-quarters of a mile along the lane. The spacious bedrooms, one en-suite, all have vanity units, tea/coffee making facilities, central heating. Guests' bathroom, separate shower and toilet. Diningroom and lounge with TV and log fires. Large attractive garden. We serve freshly prepared Evening Meals using home grown and Herefordshire produce. Award winner. Special diets catered for. Ideally situated for touring the Welsh Marches, historic Ludlow, National Trust properties and gardens, etc. One hour to Ironbridge, three-quarters of an hour to the Severn Valley Railway. Appealing places to walk. Nearby is a superb stretch of fishing on the River Teme, also pool fishing for carp, let only to our guests. Children welcome, high chair, etc available. National Trust Breaks.

PLEASE SEND A STAMPED ADDRESSED ENVELOPE WITH ENQUIRIES

LUDLOW. Mrs V.M. Humphreys, Seifton Court, Culmington, Ludlow SY8 2DG (Seifton [0584-73]

214). Situated on the Welsh Borders, set in the heart of The Corvedale Valley. Surrounded by peaceful and beautiful countryside, six miles from the historic town of Ludlow and 16 miles to Ironbridge. Racecourse, golf course and horse riding stables nearby and ideal for walking and visiting the Long Mynd at Church Stretton. We offer friendly and comfortable accommodation in four bedrooms including one en-suite, one double, one single and one twin; bathroom and toilet. Good home cooking served in separate diningroom. Residents' lounge with colour TV and open fire. Residential and restaurant licence. Bed and Breakfast from £13.50 nightly; Evening Meal £7. Tourist Board registered.

LUDLOW. Clare and David Currant, Corndene, Coreley, Ludlow SY8 3AW (Ludlow [0584] 890324).

🌻🌻 This spacious 18th century country home stands in two acres of attractive grounds in the beautiful South Shropshire hills, 20 minutes' drive from Ludlow. Convenient for exploring Shropshire, Herefordshire and the Welsh Border. Ground floor rooms (twin and family) with en-suite modern bathrooms; single room with private bathroom; guests' own diningroom and sittingroom with TV and open fire. Central heating throughout. Ideally suited for disabled visitors. Good home cooking; packed lunches, special diets by arrangement. Children welcome, cot, highchair. Own transport essential. Regret, no dogs. Bed, Breakfast and Evening Meal from £21 per day or from £132 per week. Reduced rates for children under 12 years. Brochure on request. No smoking please.

LUDLOW. Mrs J.S. Bowen, Arran House, 42 Gravel Hill, Ludlow SY8 1QR (Ludlow [0584] 873764).

🌻 Arran House is ideally situated for exploring Shropshire's beautiful countryside and the medieval town of Ludlow with its fine castle in the heart of the Welsh Marches. This small friendly Guest House is only five minutes from Ludlow town centre and station. Guests are welcome all year round and are comfortably accommodated in two double and one twin-bedded rooms with shower, washbasins and shaver points. Bathroom, shower, toilet. TV lounge; diningroom. Plenty of good home cooking is provided. Pets accepted. Ample private car parking. Terms: Bed and Breakfast £9.50; Evening Meal £4.50. Weekly: Bed, Breakfast and Evening Meal £75. HETB registered.

LYDBURY NORTH. Mr and Mrs R. Evans, Brunslow, Lydbury North SY7 8AD (Lydbury North

[058-88] 244). Working farm, join in. "Brunslow" is a beautiful Georgian style farmhouse, centrally heated throughout, ideal for walking and those who enjoy the peace and quiet of unspoiled countryside. The house is set in large gardens with lovely views in all directions and the farm mainly produces milk; pigs, poultry and calves are reared and "feeding time" is very popular with younger guests. The cellar has been converted into a games room with billiards, darts and other games. One double, one single and two family rooms, all having washbasins. Bathroom, toilets; separate sittingroom and diningroom; colour TV, high chair and babysitting available. Open all year, except Christmas, for Bed and Breakfast. Evening Dinner if required. SAE, please, for terms. Packed lunches available. Car essential, parking.

If you've found
FARM HOLIDAY GUIDES
of service please tell your friends

MARKET DRAYTON. Mrs L. Jane Crewe, Norton Farm, Norton-in-Hales, Market Drayton TF9 4AT (Market Drayton [0630] 3003). Norton Farm is an ivy-clad 300 year old oak-beamed farmhouse set in an acre of gardens. The farm is a 200 acre arable and livestock farm set on the edge of Shropshire's Best Kept Village of Norton-in-Hales. Ideal for touring unspoiled North Shropshire, Chester, Ironbridge and the five Pottery towns. Close to Hawkestone Park Golf Club and two and a half miles from Market Drayton. Ample parking. Separate lounge and diningroom. Central heating throughout. Meals in the evening by arrangement. One family room with en-suite shower, one double room. Terms from £10 per person per night.

NEWCASTLE-ON-CLUN. Mrs T.L. Davies, Lower Duffryn, Newcastle-on-Clun, Craven Arms SY7 8PQ (Clun [058-84] 239). Working farm. Enjoy the quiet rural surroundings and lovely views of this farm which is situated five miles west of Clun on the right hand side of the B4368. The area is suitable for walking or touring. On the farm there are Clun Forest sheep, and calves are reared. Guests are welcome to watch them being fed. There are two double and one family bedrooms, each with washbasin, tea/coffee making facilities (one has own toilet). Soap and towels supplied. Bathroom with toilet. Sittingroom and diningroom. Ample parking. Open from Easter to October. ETB registered. Bed and Breakfast or Bed, Breakfast and Evening Meal. Terms on request.

NEWPORT. Mrs Judy Palmer, Oulton House Farm, Norbury, Stafford ST20 0PG (Woodseaves [0785] 284264). 🐝 🐝 Working farm. Oulton House Farm is a 230 acre dairy farm situated on the Staffordshire/Shropshire border. Our large Victorian farmhouse offers warm, comfortable and well appointed bedrooms, all en-suite and with tea trays. Within easy driving distance there are many interesting places to visit, ranging from the historic county towns of Stafford and Shrewsbury, the famous Ironbridge Gorge Museum, Wedgwood, the Potteries and many stately homes to the modern splendours of Alton Towers and the National Sports Centre. For dinner we have many excellent local pubs and restaurants to choose from. Bed and Breakfast from £15.

SHAWBURY. Mrs Sue Clarkson, Longley Farm, Stanton Heath, Shawbury SY4 4HE (Shawbury [0939] 250289). Working farm. Longley Farm is a small farm comprising sheep and arable. It is the ideal venue for a family holiday, guests being welcome to participate in farming activities. The farmhouse is situated in picturesque countryside with many good local walks. One of our guests' favourite evening strolls is to our popular local pub "The Tiddly", only 200 yards away. We are situated within easy access of the Iron Gorge Museum and the historic town of Shrewsbury. Also within easy reach of the City of Chester. Double and family bedrooms; bathroom/toilet; sittingroom; diningroom. Children welcome, cot, high chair, babysitting available. Central heating. The house, open all year except Christmas, is suitable for disabled persons. English Tourist Board registered. Bed and Breakfast from £12 daily. Evening Meal from £6. Weekly terms on request. Reductions for children under 12.

SHREWSBURY. Mrs Janet Jones, Grove Farm, Preston Brockhurst, Shrewsbury SY4 5QA (093928 223). 🐝 🐝 A warm and friendly welcome, excellent home cooking and comfortable rooms await guests in our 17th century farmhouse set in mixed farmland in small village on A49. Central heating and log fires. All bedrooms have tea/coffee making facilities. One large double/family room with shower en-suite, one twin and one single with washbasins. Easy access to Shrewsbury, Ironbridge, Chester and Wales. Bed and Breakfast from £13. AA listed.

SHREWSBURY. Mrs J.M. Lowe, Yeaton Peverey Farm, Bomere Heath, Shrewsbury SY4 3AT (Shrewsbury [0743] 850454). Working farm. This modern mixed dairy farm is situated in park-like surroundings, half-mile up a private tarmac road. It is only six miles from Shrewsbury which has a castle and lies in the loop of the river Severn, a tributary of which runs through the centre of the farm which affords views of the South Shropshire and Welsh Hills. These are easily accessible as are several golf courses, riding stables, Ellesmere lakes, Llangollen Canal and even Ironbridge with its museums. The guests have a private entrance through a sun lounge which adjoins a heated swimming pool. Two double rooms; two bathrooms; three toilets; two sittingrooms; diningroom. Car essential; parking. Bed and Breakfast only from £12.50.

SHREWSBURY (Telford). Mrs G. C. Evans, New Farm, Muckleton, Near Shawbury, Telford TF6 6RJ (Shawbury [0939] 250358). Working farm. 🐾🐾

Commended. New Farm is a modernised farmhouse on a 70 acre farm set amidst the beautiful, peaceful surroundings of the Shropshire/Welsh border country, one mile off A53. The attractive and historic towns of Shrewsbury, Chester, Ludlow, Bridgnorth, Ironbridge and also the Potteries are within easy reach. Guests are assured of every comfort with good farmhouse food. Most bedrooms with shower en-suite and all bedrooms have colour TV and tea/coffee making facilities. Comfortable guest lounge with colour TV; spacious diningroom. Central heating and electric fires. Children welcome, babysitting available. Sorry, no pets. Car essential, parking. Open all year. Bed and Breakfast from £13.50. Evening Meal by arrangement Friday, Saturday and Sunday only. Reduced rates for children. Please send for tariff and further details. AA, RAC.

TELFORD. Mrs A.J. Savage, Church Farm, Wrockwardine, Wellington, Telford TF6 5DG (Telford [0952] 244917). 🐾🐾🐾 *Commended.* Enjoy a warm welcome in our large 200 year old farmhouse with oak beams, log fires and spacious gardens in the centre of a pleasant

peaceful village. The attractive and prettily furnished bedrooms have washbasins, tea trays and colour TV. Some with en-suite facilities. High standards of accommodation. One mile from A5 and M54 giving easy access to Ironbridge Gorge Museum, Cosford Aerospace Museum, Alton Towers, Shrewsbury, Ludlow, South Shropshire Hills, the heart of England and Wales. Farmhouse Evening Meals by arrangement, cooked with fresh produce, served in diningroom overlooking garden and floodlit church. Bed and Breakfast from £18. AA QQQ.

WEM. Mrs Elizabeth A. Jones, Lowe Hall Farm, Wem SY4 5UE (Wem [0939] 32236). 🐾🐾 **Working**

farm. Historically famous 16th century listed farmhouse, once country residence of Judge Jeffreys 1648-1689. Situated one mile north of Wem and convenient to Shrewsbury, Ironbridge, Chester and Llangollen. Two golf courses within seven miles and only one mile to Welsh Border. Ideal touring centre. Ample parking space. Inside is a splendid Jacobean staircase and Charles II fireplace. Fully centrally heated. Accommodation comprising family, double and twin rooms all with handbasins, colour TV and tea/coffee making facilities. Bathroom with bath and shower. Excellent full farmhouse breakfast with choice of menu. All guests have separate tables. Bed and Breakfast £13. Reductions for children. The highest standard of food, decor and accommodation is guaranteed. SAE for terms or telephone.

WHITCHURCH. Miss J. Gregory, Ash Hall, Ash Magnor, Whitchurch SY13 4DL (Whitchurch [0948] 3151). Working farm. An early 18th century house set in

large garden with ample room for children to play, on a medium-sized farm with pedigree Friesians. Situated in the small North Shropshire village of Ash, approximately one and a half miles from A41. Within easy reach of Chester and Shrewsbury (about 20 miles); Crewe 15 miles. Interesting features of this house are two oak-panelled reception rooms and an oak staircase; one of the two guest bedrooms is also panelled. One bedroom has en-suite facilities. Bathroom, toilet; sittingroom; diningroom. Table tennis room. Children welcome, cot, high chair and reduced rates available. Open April to October. Evening Meal, Bed and Breakfast from £15; Bed and Breakfast from £11.50. Sporting facilities in the area include swimming, golf, fishing, squash, etc. Car is desirable, but not essential. Mid-week bookings accepted. Tourist Board registered.

SOMERSET

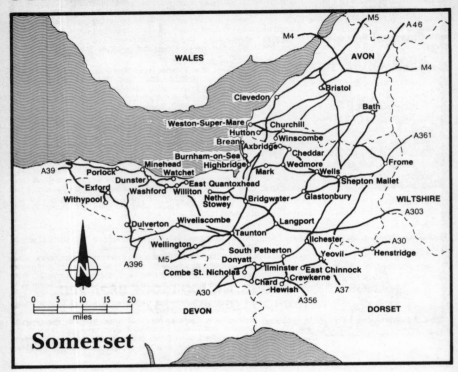

Somerset

ASHBRITTLE. Mrs M.A. Heard, Westcott Farm, Ashbrittle, Wellington TA21 0HZ (Clayhanger [039-86] 258). ᭦ ᭦ Working farm, join in. Westcott

Farmhouse is a 17th century house with delightful views, six miles from A38 and within easy reach M5 (Junction 26). Set on the Devon/Somerset border the farm is 215 acres mixed, with numerous animals. Ideal for touring the West Country, Exmoor, Quantock Hills, National Trust properties and Wimbleball Reservoir with fishing. Two en-suite family bedrooms; lounge/diningroom with TV; bathroom. Children welcome, cot available. No pets. Car essential. Home produced food served whenever possible. Open April to October. Evening Meal, Bed and Breakfast from £100 weekly, £15.50 daily. Bed and Breakfast from £11. Reductions for children. SAE with enquiries, please.

BRENT KNOLL. Mr and Mrs Gibson, Woodlands Hotel, Hill Lane, Brent Knoll TA9 4DF (Brent Knoll [0278] 760232). Woodlands Hotel nestles into its own wooded grounds and looks towards the Quantock Hills. An idyllic setting, suitable for a restful, relaxing holiday. Family, double and single rooms, most with private shower and toilet. Two sittingrooms; diningroom; cocktail bar. Children welcome. Woodlands pride themselves on their real home cooking and varied menus. Special diets catered for by prior arrangement. Meals served at separate tables in diningroom. Separate television room. Heated swimming pool. Perfectly situated for visiting places of historic interest and scenic beauty, the Woodlands is within easy reach of Bath, Glastonbury Abbey, Wells Cathedral, Longleat House and many stately homes. Horse riding arranged. Golfing, sea fishing, sailing, bowls and tennis nearby at Weston-super-Mare and Burnham-on-Sea. Free holidays offered to those organising parties. Also bargain breaks and special hunting weekends. Livery arranged. Terms on application.

BRIDGWATER. Mrs O.M. Duckett, Elm Tree Farm, Stawell, Bridgwater TA7 9AD (Chilton Polden [0278] 722612). Working farm. Conveniently situated for Junction 23 of M5, one mile off A39 Bridgwater to Glastonbury road and in a quiet rural village, this year Elm Tree Farm is offering Bed and Breakfast only. All rooms with washbasins, shaver points and tea/coffee making facilities. Bathroom with shower. Lounge with TV. Evening Meals are available within walking distance or, for greater choice, five miles by car. Pub with carvery and also restaurant. For further details please write or telephone.

AA Listed

Central for sightseeing
Super for Cider drinkers

The farmhouse lies on a mixed
working farm extending to 250 acres.
It is an excellent position for touring
and sightseeing in the Mendips and
there is a wide variety of sporting facilities in this area. For guests interested in the past this
is a house with an atmosphere, that of a by-gone age when it was a coaching inn no less
than 400 years ago. It has six double bedrooms and two family rooms, both of which have
washbasins; and all have tea/coffee making facilities. Bathroom; shower and two toilets;
colour TV lounge and diningroom. Children are made welcome and, besides supplying cot
and highchair, Manor Farm is willing to make arrangements for babysitting. Pets are
accepted. A car is not considered necessary for your holiday enjoyment but there is ample
parking space for those who need it. The beach is nine miles away.

A feature of the hospitality offered at Manor Farm is the Somerset cider served free of
charge with evening meals.

Open all year for Evening Meal, Bed and Breakfast or for Bed and Breakfast only. Rates
are reduced for children. Terms on request with SAE, please.

MANOR FARM, CROSS, Nr. AXBRIDGE BS26 2ED.
(AXBRIDGE [0934] 732577)

BRIDGWATER. Mrs E. Brown, Parrett Cottage, Stathe, Bridgwater TA7 0JJ (082369 468). A

beautiful riverside location in central Sedgemoor, Parrett
Cottage is a fully modernised 17th century base for your
holiday in Somerset. Set in two acres of gardens, orchard
and smallholding our varied menus include fresh fruit and
vegetables grown on the premises. Our guests enjoy their
meals in a separate diningroom and there is a comfortable
lounge with many facilities. We offer a choice of single,
double and twin-bedded rooms. We are 15 minutes from the
M5, 30 minutes from Glastonbury, Yeovil, Taunton and
Bridgwater with easy access to West Somerset and the South
Devon Coast. Many local facilities and interesting places to
explore. Open all year for Bed and Breakfast £8 from per
night. Weekly rates from £50; Evening Meal optional. Bed,
Breakfast and Evening Meal from £80 per week.

HOLIDAY ACCOMMODATION
Classification Schemes in
England, Scotland and Wales

The National Tourist Boards for England, Scotland and Wales have agreed a common 'Crown Classification' scheme for **serviced (Board)**
accommodation. All establishments are inspected regularly and are given a classification indicating their level of facilities and services.
There are six grades ranging from 'Listed' to 'Five Crowns ♛♛♛♛♛'. The higher the classification, the more facilities and services offered.
Crown classification is a measure of *facilities* not quality. A common quality grading scheme grades the quality of establishments as 'Approved',
'Commended' or 'Highly Commended' according to the accommodation, welcome and service they provide.
For **Self-Catering**, holiday homes in England are awarded 'Keys' after inspection and can also be 'Approved', 'Commended' or 'Highly
Commended' according to the facilities available. In Scotland the Crown scheme includes self-catering accommodation and Wales also has a
voluntary inspection scheme for self-catering grading from '1 (Standard)' to '5 (Excellent)'.
Caravan and Camping Parks can participate in the British Holiday Parks grading scheme from 'Approved (✓)' to 'Excellent
(✓ ✓ ✓ ✓ ✓)'. In addition, each National Tourist Board has an annual award for high-quality caravan accommodation: in England – Rose
Awards; in Scotland – Thistle Commendations; in Wales – Dragon Awards.
*When advertisers supply us with the information, FHG Publications show Crowns and other awards or gradings, including AA, RAC, Egon Ronay
etc. We also award a small number of Farm Holiday Guide Diplomas every year, based on readers' recommendations.*

BURNHAM-ON-SEA near. Mrs Carolyn Young, Lower Wick Farm, Wick Lane, Lympsham BS24 0HG (0278 751333). 🐾 🐾 A warm welcome awaits you at our

delightful old farmhouse, pleasantly situated in peaceful countryside within easy reach of Somerset attractions such as Cheddar Gorge, Wells and Glastonbury. All bedrooms have toilet, shower and washbasin en-suite and views over surrounding countryside. In addition to diningroom, the large inglenook guests' lounge with colour TV offers quiet relaxation. We serve a full English Breakfast using dairy products from our Jersey cow and eggs from our free range hens. An Evening Meal can be arranged. Lovely garden and spacious lawns for just sitting or sunbathing. Regret unable to accommodate young children. Bed and Breakfast from £12 daily; £80 weekly. SAE, please, for brochure.

CHARD. Mrs Sue Eames, Wambrook Farm, Wambrook, Chard TA20 3DF (0460 62371). Our farm is

in a pretty rural village two miles from Chard in the Blackdown Hills. It has an attractive farmhouse and buildings which are listed. On our 350 acre farm we have beef cattle, breeding sheep, corn and koi carp in several ponds, with an abundance of wild life all around. We are half an hour from the Devon/Dorset coast. One double with single and one twin-bedded room. Bed and Breakfast from £11.50. Children welcome, reduced rates, cot and babysitting available. Open up to 99 days a year, please telephone for availability.

CHARD. Mrs J. Wright, Yew Tree Cottage, Hornsbury Hill, Chard TA20 3DB (Chard [0460] 64735).

Attractive cottage, tastefully modernised throughout, situated in lovely countryside with an acre garden. One mile from Chard on A358 between Chard and Ilminster, 15 miles from the coast, it makes an ideal base for touring Devon, Dorset and Somerset. Nearby are many historic houses, beautiful gardens, Wildlife Park, and golf and squash facilities. Comfortable, friendly accommodation consisting of twin/single and double rooms, all with H&C. Two WC's and shower room. Lounge/dining room with colour TV. Parking. Children welcome. Cot free. Pets by arrangement. Good home cooking. English Tourist Board registered. Bed and Breakfast £11.50 per night; optional Evening Meal £7. Reductions for weekly bookings. SAE please, for further details.

CHEDDAR. Mr & Mrs F. Barker, Gordon's Hotel, Cliff Street, Cheddar (0934 742497). 🐾 🐾 🐾

Gordon's Hotel, once a farmhouse, is set at the foot of the beautiful Cheddar Gorge in glorious Somerset and is within walking distance of the Caves, Marineland, Cheese Factory and shops, only 10 miles from the sea. The Hotel is well established and recommended for its high standard of comfort and happy informal atmosphere, privately run to ensure a homely holiday. Gordon's has a TV lounge, licensed bar and superb Old World Restaurant. Outside there is parking and a heated swimming pool. All 15 bedrooms have TV and teasmades, some have private showers and some private bathrooms en suite. Children welcome, cots and high chair; horse riding arranged. Closed January. Bed and Breakfast from £14.50. Child reductions. Weekly rates on application. SAE for brochure. AA and RAC One Star.

See also Colour Display Advertisement **CHEDDAR near. Mrs C. Ladd, Tor Farm, Nyland, Cheddar BS27 3UD (Cheddar [0934] 743710). Working farm.** Set in 33 acres, this working mixed farm is situated on the quiet Somerset Levels. Ideal base for exploring Cheddar Gorge/caves; Roman Bath; Wells and mystic Glastonbury; beach 20 minutes. The farmhouse offers one family room, two twin bedrooms and five double rooms, some en-suite; lounge with colour TV; separate diningroom. Full central heating and log fires on cooler evenings. Open views from every window. Large lawn and ample car parking. Private fishing. Tea/coffee on arrival. Children welcome. Sorry, no pets in house. Bed and Breakfast £10 to £16. Evening Meal bookable. Home produced meat and vegetables always used. Weekly reductions.

CHEWTON. Mrs B. Clothier, Franklyns Farm, Chewton Mendip, Near Bath BA3 4NB (Chewton Mendip [076121] 372). Working farm. Franklyns Farm is

situated just off the main A39 road on the B3114, amongst the peaceful setting of the Mendip Hills. It is a 250 acre mixed farm with cows and corn. Plenty of interesting places to visit: Bath being only 12 miles away, Cheddar and the Chew Valley Lake eight miles, the city of Wells five miles and the West Coast only 20. First class comfortable farmhouse Bed and Breakfast accommodation, with excellent eating out places all at hand. Lounge/diningroom; bathroom. TVs and tea/coffee making facilities in all bedrooms. Pets permitted if kept under control. Bed and Breakfast from £12 per night.

CREWKERNE/DORSET BORDER. Mrs G. Swann, Broadview, East Street, Crewkerne TA18 7AG

(0460 73424). ＷＷＷ *Commended.* GOOD ROOM AWARD. Secluded, really comfortable Colonial bungalow traditionally furnished with a wonderfully relaxing atmosphere. Set in an acre of feature gardens including fish ponds and many interesting shrubs and trees. Three carefully furnished and decorated en-suite rooms, each with easy chairs, remote control colour TV, tea/coffee making facilities and luxury bath/shower, basin and toilet. Fully controllable central heating. Situated in an area of outstanding natural beauty. So much to see and do. List provided of over 50 places to visit. Substantial quality home cooked Dinner £8.50; Bed and full English Breakfast £14.50. Open all year.

DULVERTON. Mrs Strong, Lower Chilcott Farm, Dulverton TA22 9QQ (0398 23439). Lower Chilcott

Farm, which is reputed to date from the 13th century, provides an excellent base for an Exmoor holiday. It lies in its own secluded valley, almost on the edge of the Exmoor National Park yet only two miles from picturesque Dulverton. If you wish to stay put we have 25 acres of woods and fields to roam in, and for the fishermen a trout pond. Traditional yet imaginative cooking — with own thick clotted cream. Children, pets and horses (stabling available) and mother-in-laws welcome. Log fires. Garden with children's play area. Happy family atmosphere. Tea and coffee making facilities in all rooms. Two rooms with en-suite facilities, other rooms have washbasins. Bed and Breakfast from £12; Dinner, Bed and Breakfast from £18. Weekly terms from £115. Children aged one to 12 years 50 per cent reduction. Also self-catering cottage available, sleeps six/seven.

DULVERTON. Mrs A.M. Spencer, Dassels, Dulverton TA22 9RZ (Anstey Mills [039-84] 203).

Dassels is a superb Georgian style Country Guest House, magnificently situated on the edge of Exmoor, three miles west of Dulverton on the outskirts of East Anstey, set in nine and a half acres of tranquil grounds with panoramic views. A spacious house, large diningroom, separate lounge, TV and log fires. 10 bedrooms, all en-suite. A high standard of comfort is maintained and Dassels is noted for its excellent home cooked food, farm produce, delicious sweets served with clotted cream, fresh bread and rolls baked locally. A beautiful area near the Exmoor National Park where horse riding, walking, fishing and nature study are available. Many beauty spots within easy reach, also places of archaeological and historic interest with easy access to North Devon and West Somerset coastal resorts. Residential licence, ample parking, Fire Certificate, stabling. Open all year. Children welcome. Dinner, Bed and Breakfast from £20.

WHEN MAKING ENQUIRIES PLEASE MENTION
FARM HOLIDAY GUIDES

DULVERTON. Mrs P.J. Vellacott, Springfield Farm, Dulverton TA22 9QD (Dulverton [0398] 23722). Working farm. Springfield is a working farm of 270 acres peacefully situated overlooking the River Barle with magnificent moorland and woodland views. Within the Exmoor National Park, between Dulverton and Tarr Steps. Good walking country and within easy reach of the many Exmoor attractions, North Devon and Somerset coastal resorts. Hunting in season. Riding and fishing nearby. All bedrooms (one double with washbasin, one twin-bedded, one single), diningroom and sittingroom with TV face south. Guests' bathroom and separate toilet upstairs. Cot, highchair, babysitting. Pets by arrangement. A warm welcome and plentiful good home cooked food. Bed and Breakfast from £11 nightly; Evening Meal £6. ETB Listed – Approved.

DUNSTER. Mr & Mrs W.A. Greenfield, Burnells Farm, Knowle Lane, Dunster TA24 6UU (Dunster (0643) 821841). Working farm. Comfortable and friendly farmhouse accommodation, one mile from Dunster, two miles from sea, with glorious views of Exmoor. Ideal walking or touring centre for the National Park. Accommodation comprises one double, one family and one single bedroom, all with washbasins; one public bathroom and one shower room, toilet upstairs and down; lounge with TV and diningroom. Ample parking. Packed lunches on request. Open all year. Reduced rates for children under 12. Bed and Breakfast £12. Evening Meal, Bed and Breakfast £16. Weekly £112.

EXMOOR. Jean and Ian Hamilton, Fern Cottage, Allerford, Near Porlock TA24 8HN (Porlock [0643] 862215). ✿✿ The forgotten part of the West. Never crowded, this is the place to find peace and solitude within the 260 square miles of the National Park's dramatic, beautiful scenery. The soft, warm climate nurtures the wonderful wooded coombes and furze-mantled hills. Forest paths are adorned with wild flowers; here wild red deer browse whilst buzzards soar the rising thermals. The heron's loping flight follows the river, falcons and ravens enjoy the sea cliff vistas. The villages of this, Exmoor's most spectacular vale, reflect a bygone way of life. Our large 17th century cottage has all the expected comforts of a country home, log fires, central heating. We are now noted for classic cooking. Comprehensive wine list. Private parking. Open all year. Bed and Breakfast £15.65; Dinner, Bed and Breakfast £24.15; weekly £152 inclusive of VAT. No other charges. Non-smoking establishment.

SOMERSET – THE CREAM AND CIDER COUNTY!

Wookey Hole, the great cave near Wells, is the first known home of man in Great Britain. Other places of interest in this green and hilly county include The Mendips, Exmoor National Park, Cheddar Gorge, Meare Lake Village and The Somerset Rural Life Museum. The villages and wildlife of the Quantocks, Poldens and Brendons should not be missed.

EXMOOR. (Wheddon Cross). Barry and Caroline Westin, Raleigh Manor Country House Hotel, Wheddon Cross, Near Dunster TA24 7BB (Timberscombe [0643] 841484). Raleigh Manor is an elegant 19th-century Manor House standing within the Exmoor National Park. From wooded grounds of over an acre, the hotel enjoys superb views across Exmoor, Snowdrop Valley, and the Bristol Channel. A bridle path leads from the hotel grounds to Dunkery Beacon. The hotel is furnished with antiques and has two comfortable lounges with log fires. All seven bedrooms are en-suite and have tea/coffee making facilities and colour television. The Squire's Bedroom features a magnificent half-tester bed. The hotel restaurant serves traditional home-cooked fare and a selection of quality wines. Well-behaved dogs welcome. Recommended by Michelin Guide, AA Two Stars.

FROME. Mrs E.M. White, Brookover Farm, Orchardleigh, Frome BA11 2PH (Frome [0373] 62806). Brookover Farm is a 1670 farmhouse in a quiet position off the road (signposted, on the Frome to Radstock road A362). Two double and one family rooms, bathroom, shower, TV lounge for guests. Trout fishing and horse riding available on farm. Brookover Farm is close to Bath, Wells, Salisbury, Cheddar and Longleat, all places of great interest. Very good pubs, restaurants and bar meals available close by, within one-and-a-half miles. Open all year round. Bed and Breakfast only.

FROME. Mrs Mandy Hulme, Highcroft Farmhouse, West Woodlands, Frome BA11 5EQ (Frome

[0373] 61941). Comfortable old stone farmhouse, formerly part of Longleat estate, in scenic country setting, two miles south of Frome, one mile from Longleat House. Easy access to Stourhead, Bath, Wells, Glastonbury, with many other local attractions. Large, pleasant rooms, with rural views, centrally heated throughout. Double, twin-bedded and family rooms available with or without shower/washbasin. Children welcome. Pets by arrangement. Guests' lounge with television. Full English Breakfast. Lovely mature gardens available to guests. Ample secure car parking. ETB Listed. Daily rates from £10 Bed and Breakfast. Weekly rates available. Open all year.

FROME near. Mrs J. Down, Gloucester Farm, Lullington, Near Frome BA11 2PQ (Frome [0373]

830293). ☙ Working farm. Approximately 10 miles from Bath and three miles from Frome, Gloucester Farm is an arable and stock farm of 166 acres situated in a very quiet, unspoilt village of "old world charm" attached to a beautiful park. Ideal base for touring being within easy reach of Longleat, Stourhead, Cheddar, the cathedral cities of Wells, Exeter and Salisbury, the New Forest and seaside resorts of the Bristol Channel. Sports facilities in Frome. Riding, fishing, golf available in the area. Lounge with colour TV; family rooms available with hot and cold water. Sorry, no pets. Bed and Breakfast £9.50, children under 10 years £7.50. Evening Meal by arrangement using home grown produce — £6.50. Many interesting country pubs in the locality.

GLASTONBURY. Mrs J.M. Gillam, The Dower House Farm, Butleigh, Glastonbury BA6 8TG (Baltonsborough [0458] 50354). Quiet farmhouse, over 200 years old, not isolated, where every attention is given to guests. Within easy reach of all local beauty spots, beautiful Vale of Avalon and historic houses; the nearest coast only 20 miles. Good food served using fresh vegetables from secluded garden and local butter, cheese and free-range eggs on the menu. Open from February to November, there are three double and one family bedrooms, with washbasins (one bedroom is ground-floor with en-suite facilities); bathroom, one shower room, three toilets. Attractive sittingroom and diningroom. Cot and babysitting offered for children, who are welcome, also reduced rates. Many attractions locally for children including Butterfly Farm, aeroplane museum, rural museum, cheese-making and steam engines (Cranmore). No objection to pets but not in bedrooms. Car essential, parking. Evening Dinner/Meal, Bed and Breakfast from £17.50 or Bed and Breakfast only from £11. An ideal touring centre. SAE for prompt reply.

HIGHBRIDGE. Mrs V.M. Loud, Alstone Court Farm, Alstone Lane, Highbridge TA9 3DS (Burnham-on-Sea [0278] 789417). Working farm. 17th century

farmhouse, situated on outskirts of town, two miles from M5 Edithmead inter-change, on a mixed farm of 200 acres. The land adjoins Bridgwater Bay, ideal as touring centre for Somerset. Within easy reach of Burnham-on-Sea, Weston-Super-Mare, Wells, Cheddar Gorge, Wookey Hole and the Mendips. Ideal for sea and coarse fishing. Horse-riding on the farm — qualified instructor. Spacious comfortable bedrooms — two family, two double, two twin-bedded rooms. Lounge with colour TV, large diningroom. Central heating. Home produce when available. Children welcome. Ample parking space. Evening Meal, Bed and Breakfast. Terms on request with SAE, please.

ILMINSTER. Mrs Grace Bond, Graden, Peasmarsh, Near Donyatt, Ilminster TA19 0SG (Ilminster [0460] 52371). Spacious comfortable accommodation, log fire in TV lounge/diner. Situated just off the A358 Ilminster/Chard road, within easy reach M5 Junction 25, close to Devon, Dorset borders; nearest beach Lyme Regis. Many local interests including Cricket St. Thomas. Selection of bedrooms, eg four family, two double, one twin, all with washbasins and tea-making facilities. Bathroom with toilet and shower upstairs. Separate shower and toilet downstairs. Cot and high chair available. Bed and Breakfast from £10, reductions for children. Evening Meal optional. Good home cooking assured. Happy to furnish further details.

LANGPORT near. Mr and Mrs T.W. Jones, Highfields, Hambridge Road, Curry Rivel, Langport TA10 0BP (Langport [0458] 251342). Highfields is a 200-year-

old house, a Gentleman's Residence, set in an acre of gardens in peaceful surroundings with panoramic views from all rooms. Half a mile from Hambridge, five miles from Langport, 10 miles to Taunton. Ideal for walking, fishing and touring holidays. Within easy reach of both north and south coasts as well as Exmoor and Dartmoor. There are three spacious double/family bedrooms with washbasins and tea/coffee facilities; bathroom with shower; lounge/diningroom with separate tables, colour TV and central heating. Bed and Breakfast from £11, children half price. Evening Meal optional.

MINEHEAD. Mrs A. Kendal, Chidgley Farm, Watchet, Minehead TA23 0LS (Washford [0984] 40378). Working farm. Chidgley Farm is a 90-acre sheep

farm situated in a small hamlet in the Exmoor National Park. Magnificent views over extensive green pastures to the coastline. The house is 17th century with oak beams and inglenook fireplace. Three double bedrooms, all with washbasins; bathroom, two toilets; sittingroom, diningroom. Central heating. Children over 10 years of age only. Ideal touring centre for North and South coast; wonderful walking area. Farmhouse fare includes succulent roast beef, lamb and pork. Minehead 10 miles, Taunton 17 and Dunster five miles distant. Car is essential and there is ample parking. Bed and Breakfast from £12; Dinner, Bed and Breakfast from £18. Reduced terms for weekly stays. Open for up to 99 days a year. Phone for availability.

See also Colour Display Advertisement **MINEHEAD. Mrs A.R. Brown, Emmetts Grange, Simonsbath, Minehead TA24 7LD (Minehead [064-383] 282). ❀ ❀ ❀** *Commended.* The farmhouse is in a quiet situation with lovely views, on a large stock farm of 1200 acres. Comfortably furnished. Centrally heated. Attractive sittingroom with log fire. We are renowned for our delicious country cooked food with home-made butter and cream. Table licence. Four course Dinners and large English Breakfasts. Marvellous riding and trekking country; stabling available. Well behaved dogs welcome. Beautiful moorland and coastal walks nearby. Close to North Devon and Somerset coast. Also self-catering cottages available for hire. Farmhouse open March to October, cottages available from March to November. Apply for detailed brochure, stating which property required, with SAE please.

MINEHEAD. Mr and Mrs G. Collop, Alcombe Cote Guest House, 19 Manor Road, Alcombe, Minehead TA24 6EH (Minehead [0643] 703309).

Alcombe Cote is a charming 19th century residence situated at the entrance to Alcombe Coombe and within a short distance of Exmoor. Ideal base for exploring the coast and countryside by foot, car or coach. Castles, manor houses, churches, ancient monuments and historic villages abound, also many famous beauty spots and the West Somerset Steam Railway in Minehead. Two double, one single, one family, two twin bedrooms all with washbasins; two bathrooms, two toilets, diningroom. Central heating plus log fire in lounge. Children over five years welcome — reduced rates. Sorry, no pets. Open March to November. Parking. ETB and WCTB registered. Evening Meal, Bed and Breakfast from £14 daily (£89 weekly); Bed and Breakfast from £10 daily.

MINEHEAD near. Mrs Gillian Lambie, Edgcott House, Exford, Near Minehead TA24 7QG (064383 495).

Country house of great charm and character amidst beautiful countryside in the heart of Exmoor National Park, quarter of a mile from village of Exford. Peaceful and quiet. All bedrooms have washbasins, private bathroom available. Excellent home cooking using fresh local produce is served in the elegant "longroom" with its unique murals. Large garden, stabling available. Comfortable, friendly centre for relaxing, walking, riding and fishing. Children and pets welcome. Open all year for Bed and Breakfast or Bed, Breakfast and Evening Meal. Terms available on request.

ROADWATER. Mrs Sheena White, Glasses Farm, Roadwater, Watchet TA23 0QH (0984 40552).

GLASSES FARM

Working farm. Thatched 16th century farmhouse situated in a beautiful rural setting on the edge of the Brendon Hills, within the Exmoor National Park. Ideal for touring and walking around the picturesque countryside. Also available riding, hunting (stabling if needed), clay pigeon shooting and water sports. The farm consists of 220 acres, arable and dairy. Three bedrooms all with washbasins, tea/coffee making facilities and central heating. Bathroom and shower room. Ample parking, car essential. Open all year round except Christmas. Terms available on request. Please send SAE.

SHEPTON MALLET. Mrs M. White, Barrow Farm, North Wootton, Shepton Mallet (Pilton [074-989] 245). Working farm. This farm accommodation is AA listed and registered with the English Tourist Board. Barrow is a dairy farm of 146 acres. The house is 15th century and of much character, situated quietly between Wells, Glastonbury and Shepton Mallet. It makes an excellent touring centre for visiting Somerset's beauty spots and historic places, for example, Cheddar, Bath, Wookey Hole and Longleat. Guest accommodation consists of two double rooms, one family room, one single and one twin bedded room, each having hot and cold and tea/coffee making facilities. Bathroom, two toilets; two lounges, one with colour TV; diningroom with separate tables. Guests can enjoy farmhouse fare in generous variety, home baking a speciality. Home made bread. Bed and Breakfast, with optional four-course Dinner available. Car essential; ample parking. Children welcome; cot and babysitting facilities. Open March to November; sorry no pets. Terms on application.

SOMERTON near. Mrs D.J. Maunder, Home Farm, Kingweston, Near Somerton TA11 6BD (045822 3268). Home Farm, 500 acres arable and beef cattel, is situated in very peaceful surrounding with a large lawn and garden in which stands an ancient pigeon loft. We also make cider with a press and mill which is 300 years old. The Farmhouse was built in 1763. We are within easy reach of north and south coasts and just six miles from Glastonbury, 10 miles from Wells, 30 miles from Bath and 40 miles from Stonehenge. Children and pets welcome. Bed and Breakfast from £12.50.

STOGUMBER. Christine Hayes, Hall Farm Guest House, Stogumber, Taunton, Somerset TA4 3TQ (0984 56321). Working farm, join in. Hall Farm is the centre of the picturesque village of Stogumber situated between the Brendon and Quantock Hills. Two miles from Exmoor National Park and four miles from the sea. This 15th century farmhouse is comprised of seven bedrooms, two of which have en-suite facilities. Excellent reputation for farmhouse cooking, also open to non-residents. For terms and details send for current brochure, please.

STOKE-ST.-GREGORY. Mrs Peggy House, Parsonage Farm, Stoke-St.-Gregory, Taunton TA3 6ET (Burrowbridge [082-369] 205). Working farm. A friendly welcome awaits you at our Georgian farmhouse which is situated on a ridge overlooking the Somerset Levels with the Quantock and Mendip hills in the background. Ten miles from the county town of Taunton and an excellent centre for touring both the south and the Channel Coasts. Good fresh water fishing within half a mile. The accommodation comprises lounge with TV; one double, one single, one family, two twin-bedded rooms. Bed and Breakfast only from £12 to £14 per person per night; reduced rates for children. Very good meals can be obtained in the village. ETB listed. Located on ordnance survey map Landranger 193.

TAUNTON. Chris and Elaine Wrighton, Hunters Lodge, Churchingford, Taunton TA3 7DW (Churchstanton [082-360] 253). Working farm, join in. A homely old farmhouse on a 30-acre farm with cattle, sheep and horses. Situated on the Somerset/Devon borders in the beautiful countryside and forest area of the Blackdown Hills. Ideal for ramblers, ornithologists, fishing enthusiasts and riders. Trout lake one mile, golf courses and driving ranges about eight miles, north and south coasts and beaches approximately 35 minutes' drive, lots of National Trust Houses and Gardens and children's activities within a 15 miles' radius. Guests are welcome to join in with the general farm work. Riding Holidays available. Single and family rooms with washbasins. Pets can be accommodated. Guests can be met at either Taunton or Honiton station if required, a car is not essential. Open all year. Special activity weeks available and Christmas House Party. Bed and Breakfast from £10; Evening Meal £6. Reductions for children, cot available.

TAUNTON. Mrs Dianne Besley, Prockters Farm, West Monkton, Taunton TA2 8QN (West Monkton [0823] 412269). ♛ ♛ Working farm, join in. Prockters is a large 17th century oak beamed farmhouse with an open fireplace. It is situated only two miles from Taunton and five minutes from the M5, just off the A38 and A361. A cup of tea and a cake welcomes you on arrival at our family farmhouse at the foot of the Quantock Hills. All the bedrooms have washbasins and tea-making facilities. Also ground floor en-suite bedroom suitable for disabled guests. We are ideally situated for a farmhouse holiday. Lovely walks, wildlife parks and historic houses to see. Bed and Breakfast from £14 — £18. To reach Prockters Farm turn left off A361 or A38 marked West Monkton.

PLEASE SEND A STAMPED ADDRESSED ENVELOPE WITH ENQUIRIES

YEW TREE COUNTRY HOUSE

Sand, Wedmore, Somerset.
Tel: Wedmore (0934) 712520

👑👑👑 **Commended**
RAC Commended

'Yew Tree Country House' is a delightful 18th century house set in 2 acres of grounds in the hamlet of Sand just outside the lovely Georgian village of Wedmore and an ideal centre from which to visit the charming little City of Wells, the dramatic Cheddar Gorge, the caves of Wookey Hole, Glastonbury and Weston-Super-Mare. Ideal area for country and field sports.

The house whilst retaining its historic features has been sympathetically modernised and provides year-round comfort with central heating and log fires. All rooms are furnished to a high standard with en suite bathrooms, colour television and tea/coffee making facilities.

Yew Tree is licensed with a good range of Aperitifs and Wines available. We have earned a reputation for excellent food and offer a variety of English and Continental dishes.

Prices include Breakfast, Dinner and en-suite room from £32 per person per night. Weekly terms available. Also Winter Breaks.

Visa and Access cards accepted. 💳 💳

Tastefully furnished self-catering accommodation also available.

For brochure SAE or telephone: Mrs Elaine Corbett, Yew Tree Country House, Sand, Wedmore, Somerset. Tel: Wedmore (0934) 712520.

WEDMORE. Mrs Sarah Willcox, Townsend Farm, Sand, Near Wedmore BS28 4XH (0934 712342).

Townsend Farm is delightfully situated in peaceful countryside with extensive views of the Mendip Hills. Set on the outskirts of the picturesque Georgian village of Wedmore with easy access to many places of natural and historic interest, such as the famous Cheddar Gorge, Wells Cathedral, Glastonbury Tor and Abbey ruins, and only six miles from the M5 motorway, junction 22 (one night stops welcome). We offer Bed and Breakfast with optional Evening Meal. All bedrooms have tea/coffee making facilities and some have portable TVs. Guests can be assured of a warm and pleasant atmosphere. Bed and Breakfast from £12 per person; ensuite from £15; Evening Meal from £7. Open for up to 99 days a year. Phone for availability.

WELLS near. Mrs H.J. Millard, Double-Gate Farm, Godney, Near Wells BA5 1RZ (Glastonbury [0458] 32217) 👑 👑 **Working farm.**

Located in the heart of beautiful Somerset, Double-Gate nestles on the banks of the River Sheppey, on a dairy farm. This charming Georgian farmhouse (now listed) is tastefully renovated to include comfortable guest lounge with colour TV; spacious bedrooms with washbasins; luxury bath and shower room. Children most welcome. Delicious and generous home-cooked meals with morning teas and evening beverages available. No restrictions on access. Ideal for touring: six miles from the magnificent city of Wells, three miles from Glastonbury — legendary home of King Arthur and central for most attractions — Bath, Cheddar Gorge, Wookey Hole Caves, Weston-super-Mare. Car essential, free parking. Sorry, no pets except guide dogs. Country Rover Farm Holidays. T.H.A Approved accommodation. Bed and Breakfast from £11, with Evening Meal from £16. Reduced terms children/weekly stays.

WELLS. Mrs Jennie Clements, Eastwater Cottage, Wells Road, Priddy, Wells BA5 3AZ (0749 76252). Situated two miles from A39 Bath/Bristol road and three miles north of Wells in the centre of the Mendip Hills, this comfortable 250 year old farmhouse-type cottage offers all amenities. Flagstone floors, woodburner, central heating and tea/coffee making facilities. Within walking distance of Forestry Commission land and National Trust Ebbor Gorge Nature Reserve. Peaceful and rural setting close to Wells, Cheddar Gorge, Wookey Hole and Glastonbury; half an hour to Longleat, Bath, Bristol, Weston-super-Mare, Burnham-on-Sea. Golf, pot holing, horse riding and coarse fishing nearby. Children and pets welcome. Bed and Breakfast from £12. Reduced rates for children.

WELLS. Mrs Janet Gould, Manor Farm, Old Bristol Road, Upper Milton, Wells BA5 3AH (Wells [0749] 73394). ☙ Working farm. Manor Farm is a Grade 2 star listed Elizabethan Manor House superbly situated on southern slopes of Mendip Hills one mile north from Wells. It is a beef farm of 130 acres. Three large rooms for visitors with hot and cold water, electric heating and tea/coffee facilities. Full English Breakfast with choice of menu served at separate tables in panelled diningroom. Colour TV. Large peaceful garden with lovely view towards the sea. Ideal for walking on the Mendip Hills and exploring local places of historic interest. Access to house at all times. Fire Certificate held. AA listed. Open January to December for Bed and Breakfast from £12 per person. Reductions for children and week-long stays. Brochure on request.

WELLS near. Mrs Alcock, Cross Farm, Yarley, Near Wells BA5 1PA (0749 78925). A 17th century Elizabethan longhouse, formerly a farm. Tastefully modernised and furnished offering one family, one double and one twin-bedded rooms, all with washbasins and shaver points. Comfortable residents' lounge and separate breakfast room, centrally heated throughout. The location enables easy access to Wells, Bath, Glastonbury, Cheddar and Wookey Hole with nearby pubs offering an excellent selection of evening meals. Bed and full English Breakfast from £12.

`See also Colour Display Advertisement` **WESTON-SUPER-MARE. Margaret & David Holt, Moorlands, Hutton, Near Weston-Super-Mare BS24 9QH (Bleadon [0934] 812283). ☙☙** *Approved.* Late Georgian house with large landscaped gardens in an attractive village nestling below the slopes of the western Mendips, with good walking on the hills giving views down the Bristol Channel. An excellent centre; masses of interesting places for day outings and broad sandy beaches nearby. A happy, friendly atmosphere prevails at Moorlands and families with children are especially welcome. Ample facilities and reduced terms for children; pony rides can be arranged for them in the paddock adjoining the gardens. Good wholesome food generously varied, using fresh fruit and vegetables from the garden when possible; home baking a speciality. Some rooms en-suite; ground floor room suitable for the less mobile is available. All cotton or cotton blend bed linen is used. Full central heating and open fire in lounge on chilly days. Open early February to early November for family holidays. Residential licence. No pets allowed.

`See also Colour Display Advertisement` **WESTON-SUPER-MARE near. Mr and Mrs D.J. Brown, Batch Farm Country Hotel, Lympsham, Near Weston-super-Mare BS24 0EX (0934 750371). Working farm.** Batch Farm Country Hotel is licensed and AA/RAC two star, Ashley Courtenay recommended. It is a charming spot in a lovely part of England. Modern accommodation with old world charm. Ideal centre for touring; acres of freedom for the children; fishing, riding, swimming, tennis, golf locally. Guests made welcome all year except Christmas. Double, single and family bedrooms all with washbasins, shaver points, teasmaid and all with bathrooms en-suite and colour TV. All rooms have panoramic views of hills and countryside. Fully licensed lounge bar, also three lounges, one with colour TV; large diningroom with separate tables. Traditional home cooking. Personal attention by resident proprietors and their family and staff, whose ambition is to make your holiday a happy one. Sorry no pets. Brochure and terms on request.

FUN FOR ALL THE FAMILY IN SOMERSET

Cheddar Caves, Cheddar Gorge; *Madame Tussaud's,* Wookey Hole, near Wells; *Cricket Wildlife Park,* near Chard; *Ambleside Water Gardens & Aviaries,* near Weston-Super-Mare; *Tropical Bird Gardens,* Rode; *Brean Down Bird Garden,* Brean Down, near Weston-Super-Mare; *Marineland,* Cheddar; *Minehead Model Town & Pleasure Gardens,* Minehead; *East Somerset Railway,* Cranmore Station, near Shepton Mallet; *West Somerset Railway,* Minehead Station, Minehead; *Cheddar Motor Museum,* near Cheddar Caves; *The Fleet Air Arm Museum,* Royal Naval Air Station, Yeovilton, near Ilchester.

Set in the heart of Exmoor, one of the last truly unspoilt areas of the country, Cutthorne, – a working farm with lots of animals and poultry – is beautifully secluded and dates from the 14th century. The house is spacious and comfortable with log fires and central heating. All rooms have lovely views of the countryside. Four bedrooms, two of which have luxury en suite bathrooms; the master bedroom has a four-poster bed. Candlelit dinners, high teas for children. Bed and Breakfast from £13.50, Dinner £9.50. For extra privacy there are the superbly appointed barn conversions located at the side of the house, overlooking pond and cobbled courtyard with patio and sunbathing area. Baby listening. Horses and dogs welcome. ETB ♜♜.

**Ann and Phillip Durbin,
Cutthorne Farm, Luckwell Bridge,
Wheddon Cross TA24 7EW.**
☎ Exford (064-383) 255

Cutthorne

WILLITON. Mrs S.J. Watts, Rowdon Farm, Williton TA4 4JD (0984 56280). Farmhouse Bed and

Breakfast. All bedrooms have washbasins, electric blankets and central heating. TV. Scenic views of the Quantock Hills. Within easy reach of coast and Exmoor. Fishing and clay shooting on the farm if booked. Good bar meals in local villages. Also self-catering accommodation in front wing of Manor house with garden available. Bed and Breakfast from £10. SAE, please, for further details.

YEOVILTON near. Mrs Susie Crang, Cary Fitzpaine Farmhouse, Cary Fitzpaine, Yeovil BA22 8JB

(Charlton Mackrell [045822] 3250). A gracious Georgian Manor Farmhouse set in two acres of gardens on a 600 acre working farm — arable, sheep, beef and horses. Peaceful and friendly atmosphere. Close to a wealth of historic buildings, gardens, towns and an aircraft museum. Plenty to suit all tastes. Bedrooms are beautifully furnished and luxurious; one with en-suite bathroom, others have washbasins. TV in rooms on request. Tea/coffee making facilities in all rooms. Packed lunches available. Pets at our discretion. Open March to October. Terms from £13 per person.

STAFFORDSHIRE

ASHBOURNE near. Will and Carolyn Appleby, Monks Clownholme Farm, Rocester, Near Uttoxeter

ST14 5BP (Rocester [0889] 590347). ♜♜ **Working farm.** A 16th century farmhouse in peaceful surroundings, offering beautiful views overlooking River Dove and Valley: 89 acres of grassland for working dairy farm. Small play area in garden. Guests welcome around farm or they can enjoy walks across our fields. Dogs by arrangement. Barbecue facilities available. Accommodation includes one large family room and one double room which features a romantic four-poster bed. Both have washbasins and tea/coffee making facilities. Guests have separate toilet, bathroom with shower; comfortable sittingroom with colour TV and a large oak-floored diningroom. Ideal for Alton Towers (four miles), and the Peak District. Car essential. Terms on request.

BALTERLEY. Mrs D. Edwards, Balterley Hall Farm, Balterley, Crewe CW2 5QG (Crewe [0270] 820206).

👑👑 Balterley Hall is a 17th century farm house situated on the Cheshire/Staffordshire border, three miles from M6 motorway, Exit 16. Municipal Golf Course nearby. Many places of interest within easy reach; Wedgwood and Doulton potteries, Stoke-on-Trent, Alton Towers and also the historic towns of Nantwich and Chester. One family room, one twin en-suite and one single, all with washbasin, TV and tea/coffee making facilities. Fully fitted bathroom with bath and shower; sitting/diningroom. Member of the Heart of England Tourist Board. Bed and Breakfast from £11.50 per night with reductions for children under 12 years.

CODSALL. Mrs Denise E. Moreton, Moors Farm and Country Restaurant, Chillington Lane, Codsall, Near Wolverhampton WV8 1QH (Codsall [090-74] 2330). 👑👑👑 **Working farm.** Moors Farm is a livestock farm with its own farmhouse restaurant, situated in a pleasant rural valley. It lies one mile from Codsall Village, which has shops, pubs, churches and its own railway station with links to Shropshire, Wales and the Birmingham National Exhibition Centre. The farm has a variety of animals including cows, pigs, sheep and poultry. The kitchen uses home-produced meat, dairy products and garden vegetables; we also cater for vegans and vegetarians. Fishing, riding, tennis, golf and swimming within easy reach. Ideal situation for touring. Accommodation comprises three double and three family rooms — two rooms with en-suite facilities. All bedrooms have washbasins and tea/coffee making equipment. Two bathrooms; sittingroom; diningroom; "Oak Room" Licensed Bar with log fires. Open all year. Fire Certificate held. Bed and Breakfast or Evening Dinner, Bed and Breakfast. AA listed; RAC acclaimed; British Routiers approved; Member of Staffordshire Vale of Trent Farm Group.

LEEK near. Mrs E. Lowe, Fairboroughs Farm, Rudyard, Near Leek ST13 8PR (Rushton Spencer [0260] 226341). 👑👑 **Working farm.**

This is a working beef/sheep farm of 150 acres. The house is 17th century with oak beams and log fires when necessary. All the large rooms have panoramic views and central heating. The bedrooms have washbasins and shaver points. Separate lounge with colour TV, dining room for visitors' use. Situated in Staffordshire Moorlands within easy reach of Peak Park, Alton Towers, Potteries and Cheshire. Fishing at Rudyard and Tittesworth Reservoirs. Children welcome at reduced rates. We endeavour to make your stay comfortable and happy. Open 99 days — phone for availability. Bed and Breakfast from £12 single, £22 double. CC/CL.

LEEK near. Stan and Elizabeth Winterton, Brook House Farm, Cheddleton, Leek ST13 7DF (Churnet Side [0538] 360296). 👑👑👑 **Working farm, join in.**

Brook House is a 180-acre dairy farm situated in a picturesque valley with scenic views and pleasant walks, half a mile from the A520 and near to Cheddleton Village with its Brindley Mill Railway Museums, Cauldon Canal and beautiful Churnet Valley. Convenient for the Peak District, the Pottery Museum and Alton Towers. Two family rooms in a tastefully converted cowshed with patio doors; two rooms in the farmhouse; all with en-suite facilities, central heating and tea/coffee makers. Attractive lounge has colour TV and patio doors. A warm welcome and good food a speciality. Reduced rates for children. Bed and Breakfast from £12 to £15; optional Evening Meal £7. Farm Holiday Bureau member.

BACK LANE FARM · WINKHILL · NEAR LEEK
Telephone: 0538 308273
Farmhouse Bed and Breakfast
STAFFORDSHIRE MOORLANDS

🏵🏵🏵 Commended

Tranquilly set in the beautiful rolling hills of the Staffordshire Moorlands, this 18th century farmhouse offers you the best in Bed and Breakfast. In close proximity to such places as modern-day Alton Towers and the Potteries and to picturesque Dovedale, Manifold Valley, Chatsworth House, Haddon Hall, Bakewell and much more. Enjoy the delights of home cooked meals from your qualified hostess. The accommodation includes 2 lounges with colour TVs and open fires; dining room; four bedrooms – one double, one single, two twin – all en suite or with private facilities.

Bed and Breakfast from £15. Reduction for longer stays.
Evening Meal £9 – by arrangement.

RIBDEN, near Oakamoor. Mrs J. Miller, Tenement Farm, Ribden, Near Oakamoor, Stoke-on-Trent ST10 3BW (0538 702333). Tenement Farm is situated in Staffordshire moorlands and on the outskirts of the Derbyshire Dales. A 10-minute drive to Dovedale, Manifold Valley and three miles from Alton Towers Leisure Complex. Tenement Farm is a traditional working farm specialising in pedigree Charolais cattle. It has a homely atmosphere; TV lounge; private bathrooms. One double bedroom and one family room with tea/coffee facilities. Parking. Bed and Breakfast available. Terms from £12.50 to £15.00.

Tenement Farm
Ribden

STOKE-ON-TRENT. Mrs Barbara White, Micklea Farm, Micklea Lane, Longsdon, Near Leek, Stoke-on-Trent ST9 9QA (Leek [0538] 385006). Quietly situated off A53 yet ideally located for touring the area, this delightful old stone house, boasting a warm friendly atmosphere and comfortable accommodation, is the perfect base for a family holiday. Open all year; guest lounge with TV; large garden; ample parking. Children welcome. Visitors will enjoy pleasant canal and country park walks, fishing, golf, gliding and hang gliding. Alton Towers and the beautiful Peak District and Potteries are near at hand. Tourist Board Listed. Bed and Breakfast from £8.50; Evening Meal optional. Further details on request.

WHEN MAKING ENQUIRIES PLEASE MENTION
FARM HOLIDAY GUIDES

STOKE-ON-TRENT. Mrs Anne Hodgson, The Hollies, Clay Lake, Endon, Stoke-on-Trent ST9 9DD (Stoke-on-Trent [0782] 503252).

Delightful Victorian house quietly situated off the B5051, convenient for the M6, Alton Towers, Staffordshire Moorlands and the Potteries (Royal Doulton, Wedgwood and Spode etc). Spacious bedrooms, including three en-suite, have central heating and tea/coffee making facilities. The lounge with colour TV and the diningroom overlook a large secluded garden where there is ample parking. Dogs by prior arrangement. No smoking, please. Bed and Breakfast from £12. Guests are assured of a friendly welcome.

SUFFOLK

BUNGAY/BECCLES. Mrs Sarah Cook, Butterley House, Leet Hill Farm, Yarmouth Road, Kirby Cane, Bungay NR35 2HJ (050845 301). Working farm.

A warm welcome awaits at this dairy/arable farm set in the heart of the Waveney Valley, with excellent rural views, situated between the historic towns of Beccles and Bungay, 15 miles from Norwich, 20 minutes' drive from Norfolk/Suffolk coasts, and nearby the famous Otter Trust. Accommodation comprises one double/family room with en-suite, one double room with washbasin and one twin room; bathroom, two toilets. Guests have their own sittingroom with TV, separate diningroom. Full English Breakfast. Evening Meal by arrangement. Farm produce used whenever possible. Car essential. No pets please. Reductions for children. Terms on request. Tourist Board registered.

BURY ST. EDMUNDS. Mrs Elizabeth Nicholson, The Grange Farmhouse, Beyton, Bury St. Edmunds IP30 9AG (Beyton [0359] 70184).

The Grange is a very attractive, traditional Suffolk farmhouse standing in six acres with a large secluded garden. Situated in the picturesque village of Beyton, five miles east of the historic market town of Bury St. Edmunds, just off A45. Within easy reach of Cambridge, Newmarket, Ely Cathedral, medieval wool town of Lavenham, Constable country; an ideal stop-over point for travellers to and from the European Ferries at Felixstowe and Harwich. Local amenities include golf, riding, swimming and tennis. Two National Trust properties nearby and Theatre Royal in Bury. Choice of comfortable bedrooms, two en-suite, all with washbasins; bathroom, two toilets. Central heating, plus log fires in winter evenings. Excellent home cooking for Bed and Breakfast (Evening Meal optional). Colour TV in guests' lounge. Reduced rates for under 10's. Sorry, no pets. Car essential — parking. Open all year. AA Listed. Please ring for brochure. We look forward to hearing from you.

BURY ST. EDMUNDS. Mrs N.B. Less, Broad Acre, 10 Parklands Green, Fornham St. Genevieve, Bury St. Edmunds IP28 6UH (Bury St. Edmunds [0284] 769340).

A large attractive house in a quiet location offering excellent accommodation and cooking, and set in delightful partly wooded grounds of one and a half acres. The village of Fornham St. Genevieve is two miles north of the historic market town of Bury St. Edmunds. Cambridge, Newmarket, Thetford and medieval wool towns such as Lavenham are within easy reach. The house has double, twin and single bedrooms with washbasin; shower room, bathroom, diningroom/lounge with TV are for guests' exclusive use. Children are welcome from threee years old and there is a reduced rate up to age 10. Sorry, no pets. Open year-round for Bed and Breakfast; Evening Meals available. Write or phone for bookings or full details.

BURY ST. EDMUNDS. Mr and Mrs J.O. Truin, Brighthouse Farm, Melford Road, Lawshall, Bury St. Edmunds IP29 4PX (Bury St. Edmunds [0284] 830385).

🐂 🐂 **Working farm, join in.** Set in beautiful surroundings of the Suffolk countryside "Brighthouse Farm" is a timbered farmhouse dating back to the 18th century. Offering homely accommodation consisting of two double (one en-suite), one twin and one single (with shower) bedrooms. Two bathrooms and all modern conveniences. Can also provide for the camping/caravan enthusiasts who seek the tranquillity of surrounding Constable countryside. Large games room, TV and central heating. Numerous pubs and restaurants nearby for good food, plus shops. Open January to December. Bed and Breakfast from £12.

COLCHESTER. Mrs C.A. Somerville, Rosebank, Lower Street, Stratford St. Mary, Colchester, Essex CO7 6JS (Colchester [0206] 322259). Attractive 14th-century part Manor House, with river frontage and fishing rights, in peaceful village in the Dedham Vale, which is renowned for its period architecture and old inns. Our boathouse is reputed to have featured in Constable's paintings. Guests are accommodated in three double and one family bedrooms, all with washbasins; two bathrooms and three toilets. Diningroom. Central heating. Rooms are comfortable and attractive with television plus tea and coffee making facilities. Family bedroom has toilet en-suite. Delightful chalet set in the grounds, twin-bedded with bathroom en-suite. English Breakfast of your choice — good cooking. Tourist Board registered. Terms £14 to £16 for Bed and Breakfast. Open all year except Christmas week.

FELIXSTOWE. Mrs N. Matthews, Redhouse, Levington, Ipswich IP10 0LZ (047-388-670). Victorian

farmhouse in heart of countryside with views over the Orwell Estuary in AONB. Ideal for walkers, riders, artists, sailors or anyone wanting a quiet place 'away from it all', yet only six minutes from Felixstowe. Many walks and bridleways — riding holidays arranged. Visit 'Constable' country or explore the unspoilt coastline. The Continent is closer than you think. You can have a great day out to Belgium for as little as £12 adult return, half for children. No passport needed if you are British. Bed and Breakfast from £13. Evening Meal £9 by arrangement. Home cooking, fresh produce and eggs. Special diets catered for. Reductions for children. No pets.

FRAMLINGHAM. Mrs Ann Proctor, Grove Farm, Laxfield, Framlingham, Woodbridge IP13 8EY (Ubbeston [098683] 235). Working farm. This is a Georgian farmhouse standing in a 30 acre mixed farm with pigs and sheep, ponies and pedigree breeding dogs. Beautiful view of village and only 12 miles from the coast. Within easy reach of Norwich, Norfolk Broads, historic houses with quaint unspoilt villages. The accommodation is in two double and two family bedrooms (with washbasins); diningroom; lounge with colour television; bathroom, three toilets; full central heating. Children welcome, cot, high chair and babysitting. Sorry, no pets. Open March to November. The emphasis is on a friendly atmosphere with good home cooking, meat, vegetables, honey, etc., mainly produced on farm. Car essential, ample parking. Bed and Breakfast or Bed, Breakfast and Evening Meal; children under 12 years reduced rates. Please phone or send SAE for terms.

FRAMLINGHAM. Mrs Jennie Mann, Fiddlers Hall, Cransford, Near Framlingham, Woodbridge IP13 9PQ (Rendham [072878] 729). Working farm, join in.

Signposted on B1119. Fiddlers Hall is a 14th century, moated, oak-beamed farmhouse set in a beautiful and secluded position. It is two miles from Framlingham Castle, 20 minutes' drive from Aldeburgh, Snape Maltings, Woodbridge and Southwold. A Grade II Listed building, it has lots of history and character. The bedrooms are spacious; one has en-suite shower room, the other has a private bathroom. Use of lounge and colour TV. Plenty of parking space. Lots of farm animals kept. Traditional farmhouse cooking. Bed and Breakfast terms from £15. Tourist Board registered.

SUFFOLK – CONSTABLE COUNTRY!

To be precise Dedham Vale is Constable Country and it is only one of Suffolk's attractions. The others include the country parks at Brandon and Clare Castle, Debenham, Lavenham, Newmarket, The Museum of East Anglian Life and the river port of Woodbridge.

FRAMLINGHAM. Mrs C. Jones, Bantry, Chapel Road, Saxtead, Woodbridge IP13 9RB (Earl Soham [072-882] 578). ✿✿✿ Bantry is set in half an acre of gardens overlooking open countryside in the picturesque village of Saxtead, which is close to the historic castle town of Framlingham. Best known for its working windmill beside the village green, Saxtead is a good central base from which to discover East Anglia. Accommodation is offered in self-contained apartments (one ground floor), each comprising its own private diningroom/TV lounge and bathroom for secluded comfort. Good home cooking from home grown produce. Terms: Bed and Breakfast from £14.50 per night. Non Smoking.

FRAMLINGHAM. Mrs Katherine Cook, Boundary Farm, off Saxmundham Road, Woodbridge, Framlingham 1P13 9NU (0728 723401). A 17th century Grade II Listed farmhouse set in one and a half acres of gardens amidst open countryside, one and a half miles north of Framlingham. Two double rooms, one with en-suite toilet; one twin bedroom with wash-hand basin; guests' lounge with colour TV and log fires in winter. Breakfast served in guests' dining room; Evening Meals by arrangement if required. All rooms have central heating and double glazing. Tea/coffee facilities available. A warm and friendly atmosphere and a pleasant stay is assured. Leaflet available on request.

FRAMLINGHAM near. Mrs J.R. Graham, Woodlands Farm, Brundish, Near Woodbridge IP13 8BP (Stradbroke [037-984] 444 or 520). ✿✿ Woodlands Farm has a cottage-type farmhouse set in quiet Suffolk countryside. Near historic town of Framlingham, with its castle, and within easy reach of coast, wildlife parks, Otter Trust, Easton Farm Park and Snape Maltings for music lovers. Ideally suited for family holidays. Open all year. Family room with private shower, washbasin and WC. Two double bedrooms with bathroom en-suite. Diningroom and sittingroom with inglenook fireplaces for guests. Good home cooked food assured. Full central heating. Car essential, good parking. Cot and babysitting. Sorry, no pets. Bed and Breakfast from £12.50; Evening Meal £8. Reduced rates for children under 10. SAE, or telephone.

FRESSINGFIELD, near Eye. Mrs S.M. Webster, Elm Lodge Farm, Fressingfield, Eye IP21 5SL (Fressingfield [037-986] 249). ✿✿ **Working farm.** Elm Lodge is a spacious Victorian farmhouse with 112 acres, mainly arable, overlooking a large common where animals graze in summer. Within easy reach of coast, Southwold 18 miles, and many places of interest including historic castles, churches, stately homes and towns such as Framlingham. Equidistant Norwich, Bury St. Edmunds and Ipswich 30 miles approximately. Open Easter to October. Two double and one twin-bedded rooms (all with washbasins); bathroom, toilet; diningroom; sittingroom with colour TV; convector heating and/or log fires. Reductions for children. Cot, high chair, babysitting. Car essential parking. Home cooking. Bed and Breakfast from £13; Evening Meal from £7. Farm Holiday Bureau member.

FRESSINGFIELD, near EYE. Mrs Rose Tomson, Hillview Farm, Fressingfield IP21 5PY (Fressingfield [037 986] 443). ✿✿ *Commended.* **Working farm.** Enjoy a break away from the stresses of city life in our warm, comfortable farmhouse set in peaceful surroundings, yet central for touring East Anglia. We offer excellent food, friendliness and a relaxed atmosphere. Two double and one twin-bedded rooms with washbasins, sharing separate bathroom. Tea/coffee making facilities in bedrooms. Separate diningroom and lounge with log fire for the cooler evenings. Pleasant garden with summerhouse. Car essential. Dogs by arrangement. Member of Farm Holiday Bureau. Bed and Breakfast from £13; Evening Meal from £7.

HALESWORTH. Mrs Eileen Webb, "Saskiavill", Chediston, Halesworth IP19 0AR (Halesworth [0986] 873067). ♥♥♥

"Saskiavill" is set back from the road and stands in one-and-a-half acres of garden. The spacious bungalow offers holidaymakers an ideal touring base for the fine City of Norwich, the coast and nearby Minsmere Bird Sanctuary. The village has many thatched cottages and an old church and is only two miles from the market town of Halesworth. Convenient for golf courses, nature reserves, museums, trust house, gardens, etc. Two double, one family, one twin bedrooms, with washbasins; two bathrooms, two toilets; one room adapted for disabled visitors. TV lounge, sittingroom, diningroom. Children welcome at reduced rates, babysitting available. Sorry, no pets. Car essential — parking. Open all year for Evening Dinner/ Meal, Bed and Breakfast or Bed and Breakfast. Varied menus with good home cooking including home made pastries, bread and preserves. Telephone or SAE for terms. Reductions for Senior Citizens out of season. EATB member.

HITCHAM. Mrs Philippa McLardy, Hill Farmhouse, Bury Road, Hitcham IP7 7PT (Bildeston [0449] 740651). ♥♥

Hill Farmhouse has lovely views and is set in its own grounds of three acres. It is an ideal touring centre, close to Lavenham, Constable and Gainsborough country. The coast, Cambridge, Norwich, Ipswich and Colchester are within an hour's drive. Restaurant and three pubs serving food all within two miles. Accommodation is in the main farmhouse and adjoining oak timbered Tudor cottage. Twin, double and family suites all have private or en-suite bathrooms, colour TVs, tea/coffee making facilities. Pets by arrangement. Special diets catered for. Bed and Breakfast from £12 to £14. Reductions for children. Dinner (choice of menu) available at £7.50.

HITCHAM. Mrs Mollie Loftus, Little Causeway Farmhouse, Hitcham IP7 7NE (Bildeston [0449] 740521).

This 16th century Tudor farmhouse is situated in the heart of the beautiful Suffolk countryside, near to Lavenham, Constable country and many other places of interest. Guests are welcome all the year round to enjoy the comforts at this most attractive farmhouse, the accommodation being two double bedrooms (one twin); lounge, diningroom; bathroom. Central heating. Car is essential and there is ample parking. Regret, no pets allowed. This is a lovely part of Suffolk and well worth seeing. Bed and Breakfast, with tea and coffee-making facilities offered in bedrooms. Within strolling distance of local village pub.

HITCHAM. Mrs Brenda Elsden, Wetherden Hall, Hitcham, Ipswich IP7 7PZ (Bildeston [0449] 740412 & 740574). Working farm.

Wetherden Hall is a farm of 250 acres mostly arable, but also carries pigs, cattle, chickens and geese. Private trout fishing available. In a quiet position on the edge of a picturesque village; close to Lavenham, Bury St. Edmunds, Ipswich, Cambridge and in Constable country. Good touring centre. Car essential. Ample parking. Delightful farmhouse with full central heating. Large attractive bedrooms; one double, one single and one family room. Bathroom; toilet. Large sitting/diningroom. Children over 12 years welcome. Sorry, no pets. Bed and full traditional Breakfast. Choice of several local inns and restaurants for varied evening meals. SAE please for terms. AA listed.

IPSWICH. Mrs P. Redman, Mount Pleasant Farm, Offton, Ipswich IP8 4RP (Offton [047-333] 8896 changing to (0473-658896) mid 1991). ☙☙☙ **Working farm, join in.** Secluded 16th century farmhouse situated on a working farm with many different animals. Genuinely secluded, yet sea only 30 minutes away, Water Park only five minutes. Sports centres with varied activities 15 minutes. Many local beauty spots to visit and enjoy. Evening Meals a speciality, by arrangement. Bed and Breakfast — single rates from £12, double £22. Evening Meal £7. Children welcome.

SAXMUNDHAM. Mrs Margaret Gray, Park Farm, Sibton, Saxmundham IP17 2LZ (Yoxford [072 877] 324). ☙☙☙ **Working farm.** Accommodation in a friendly farmhouse in gentle Suffolk countryside, six miles from our coast which is a bird-watcher's paradise; and 25 miles from Ipswich and Norwich. Mrs Gray enjoys looking after guests, who are treated as members of the family. Individual tastes catered for, and mostly local and garden produce is used in cooking. One double and two twin bedrooms, both with hot and cold water; bathroom, toilet; dining room. Cot, high chair, babysitting and reduced rates for children. Sorry, no pets. Open from March to November. Mid-week bookings accepted. Car essential, parking. Evening Dinner/Meal, Bed and Breakfast from £16; Bed and Breakfast from £11. Mrs Gray aims to give guests an enjoyable holiday, so that they go home feeling refreshed and relaxed.

WOODBRIDGE. Mrs R.J. Newnham, Priory Cottage, Low Corner, Butley, Woodbridge IP12 3QD (0394 450382). Not so remote that it's difficult to find us, but tucked away down a "no through lane" adjoining the Heritage Coastal Path. Ideal for those who enjoy quietness and solitude. Bring your dog and enjoy miles of heath and forest walks or maybe wander down to the creek for a spot of bird watching. We will be pleased to arrange fishing, riding, shooting, golf, bird watching, sailing, all of which are close at hand. Sample the warmth and hospitality of our comfortable beamed cottage, good English cooking; vegetarians and those with dietary problems catered for. Non-smoking house. Brochure/tariff on request. ETB Listed.

SURREY

LINGFIELD. Miss Vanessa Hornsby, Stantons Hall Farm, Eastbourne Road, Blindley Heath, Lingfield RG7 6LG (Lingfield [0342] 832401). Stantons Hall Farm is an 18th century farmhouse set amidst 18 acres of farmland and adjacent to Blindley Heath Common. Family, double and single rooms, most with toilet, shower and washbasins en-suite. Separate bathroom. All rooms have colour TV, tea/coffee facilities and are centrally heated. There are plenty of parking spaces. We are conveniently situated within easy reach of M25 (London Orbital), Gatwick Airport and Lingfield Park Racecourse. Enjoy a traditional English Breakfast in our large farmhouse kitchen. Bed and Breakfast from £15 per person, reductions for children sharing. Cot and high chair available. Well behaved dogs welcome by prior arrangement.

LINGFIELD. Mrs Vivienne Bundy, Oaklands, Felcourt, Lingfield RH7 6NF (Lingfield [0342] 834705). Oaklands is a spacious country house of considerable charm dating from the 17th century. It is set in its own grounds of one acre and is about one mile from the small town of Lingfield and three miles from East Grinstead, both with rail connections to London. It is convenient to Gatwick Airport and is ideal as a "stop-over" or as a base to visit many places of interest in south east England. Dover and the Channel Ports are two hours' drive away whilst the major towns of London and Brighton are about one hour distant. One family, one double and one single bedrooms, one with washbasin; three bathrooms, two toilets; sittingroom; diningroom. Cot, high chair, babysitting and reduced rates for children. Gas central heating. Open all year. Parking. Bed and Breakfast from £14. Evening Meal by arrangement.

OXSHOTT. Mrs Crowhurst, Apple Tree Cottage, Oakshade Road, Oxshott KT22 0LF (0372-842087). This charming cottage originally built for village servants now offers comfortable central heated accommodation in prettily appointed rooms, modernised to a high standard. Breakfast is available from 7.00am and a welcome tray of tea awaits all guests returning after a busy day. The cottage is conveniently located for Hampton Court Palace, numerous National Trust properties, RMS Gardens, Wisley, south coast channel ports and historic towns of Chichester, Winchester and Guildford. London is 30 minutes away. The M25 is easily accessible so Gatwick and Heathrow are also within reach. For those seeking peace and quiet the cottage is quietly located with woods and heathland five minutes' walk away. Open all year for Bed and Breakfast. BTA Listed.

APPLETREE COTTAGE

HELP IMPROVE BRITISH TOURIST STANDARDS

You are choosing holiday accommodation from our very popular FHG Publications. Whether it be a hotel, guest house, farmhouse or self-catering accommodation, we think you will find it hospitable, comfortable and clean, and your host and hostess friendly and helpful. Why not write and tell us about it?

As a recognition of the generally well-run and excellent holiday accommodation reviewed in our publications, we at FHG Publications Ltd. present a diploma to proprietors who receive the highest recommendation from their guests who are also readers of our Guides. If you care to write to us praising the holiday you have booked through FHG Publications Ltd. – whether this be board, self-catering accommodation, a sporting or a caravan holiday, what you say will be evaluated and the proprietors who reach our final list will be contacted.

The winning proprietor will receive an attractive framed diploma to display on his premises as recognition of a high standard of comfort, amenity and hospitality. FHG Publications Ltd. offer this diploma as a contribution towards the improvement of standards in tourist accommodation in Britain. Help your excellent host or hostess to win it!

FHG DIPLOMA

We nominate ....

....

Because

....

Name ....

Address ....

.... Telephone No. ....

SUSSEX

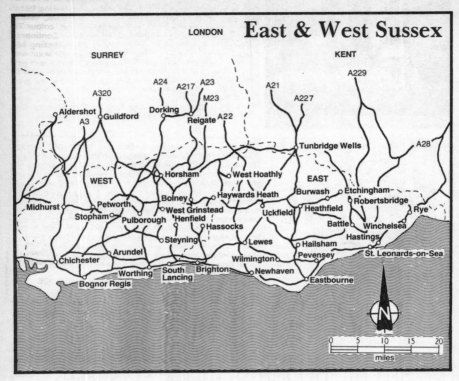

EAST SUSSEX

BRIGHTON. Amblecliff Hotel, 35 Upper Rock Gardens, Brighton BN2 1QF (0273 681161). 🌸🌸🌸

An elegant Victorian hotel recently refurbished to very high standards. Recommended on Breakfast and South Today TV programmes, and in The Sunday Times. *Highly recommended for its cleanliness, comfort and hospitality. *Close to the sea, shops, all entertainment and the conference centre. *Attractively decorated rooms with colour TV, hospitality tray, central heating, telephones, hair dryers, majority with en-suite toilet. *Four-poster beds and non-smoking rooms. *Access at all times. *A choice of English Breakfast in the dining room or continental in bed. Supplements for en-suites and one night stays. Special low season rates. Weekly rate: seven nights for the price of six. Bed and Breakfast from £16. AA, RAC acclaimed.

FUN FOR ALL THE FAMILY IN SUSSEX

Bodiam Castle, near Hawkhurst; *Battle Abbey*, Battle; *The Warnham War Museum*, near Horsham; *Royal Greenwich Observatory*, Herstmonceux Castle, near Hailsham; *Polegate Windmill*, near Eastbourne; *Burton Water Mill*, near Petworth; *St. Clement's Caves*, West Hill, Hastings; *Bentley Wildfowl*, Halland, near Lewes; *National Butterfly Museum & St. Mary's*, Bramber, near Shoreham; *Aquarium & Dolphinarium*, Marine Parade, Brighton; *Drusilla's Zoo Park*, near Eastbourne; *Woods Mill Countryside Exhibition*, near Henfield; *Tilgate Park*, Crawley; *Brooklands Pleasure Park*, East Worthing; *Children's Playpark*, The Stade, Old Town, Hastings; *Hastings Model Village*, White Rock Gardens, Hastings; *Rainbow's End*, Hotham Park, Bognor Regis, West Sussex; *Bluebell Railway*, Sheffield Park Station, near Uckfield.

BRIGHTON. Kempton House Hotel, 33/34 Marine Parade, Brighton BN2 1TR (0273 570248). ♛ ♛ ♛ AA/RAC Highly Acclaimed. We are a private seafront hotel offering a relaxed and friendly holiday or short break. Rooms available with magnificent views overlooking beach and pier, all with full en-suite shower and toilet, central heating, tea/coffee facilities, self dial telephones, colour TV, radio, hair dryer. Full English Breakfast served or Continental Breakfast in bed. Four-poster bed available overlooking sea. Residents' bar and sea-facing patio garden for your use. Ideally situated for business or pleasure. Children and pets always welcome. Please telephone for details. From only £20 per person per night Bed and Breakfast. Dinner by prior arrangement. Open all year.

Sea Breeze

GUESTS ARE VERY IMPORTANT TO US.
"ARRIVE AS A GUEST LEAVE AS A FRIEND".

Your home from home, only 2 minutes' from the sea and 5 from the best Brighton has to offer. Conference Centre, Shops, Royal Pavilion, Theatres, Lanes and the Marina close by. Every room completely refurbished to a very high standard and ♛ ♛ ♛ have been awarded by Brighton Tourist Board. Full en-suites available and a Four Poster Suite, colour television and two video satellite channels, tea and coffee and access at all times. Breakfast highly recommended. All major credit cards accepted. Pets by request. Prices from £15 per person.

12a UPPER ROCK GARDENS, BRIGHTON, E. SUSSEX BN2 1QE
Telephone: 0273 602608

BURWASH. Mrs E. Sirrell, Woodlands Farm, Burwash, Etchingham TN19 7LA (Burwash [0435] 882794). Working farm, join in. Woodlands Farm stands one third of a mile off the road surrounded by fields and woods. This peaceful and beautifully modernised 16th century farmhouse offers comfortable and friendly accommodation. Sitting/dining room; two bathrooms, one en suite, double or twin bedded rooms (one has four poster bed) together with excellent farm fresh food. This is a farm of 55 acres with mixed animals, and is situated within easy reach of 20 or more places of interest to visit and half an hour from the coast. Open Easter to October. Central heating. Literature provided to help guests. Children welcome. Dogs allowed if sleeping in owner's car. Parking. Evening Meal optional. Bed and Breakfast from £12. ETB registered. AA listed. Telephone or SAE, please.

ETCHINGHAM. Norma Hawke, Little Grandturzel, Fontridge Lane, Etchingham TN19 7DE (0435 882279) Fax (0435 883618). ♛ Peace and quiet guaranteed at Little Grandturzel, situated in a beautiful spot right in the heart of "Kipling Country". There are many walks and historic places of interest to visit. It is an excellent touring base for the many charming villages and towns in Kent and Sussex. Within easy reach of channel ports and for day trips to London. Children welcome. Bed and Breakfast from £14; Evening Meal from £8.

PLEASE ENCLOSE A STAMPED ADDRESSED
ENVELOPE WITH ENQUIRIES

HAILSHAM. Mr and Mrs R.E. Gentry, The Stud Farm, Bodle Street Green, Near Hailsham BN27 4RJ (Herstmonceux [0323] 833201). Working farm. 🐦🐦

Commended. The Stud Farm keeps mainly cattle and sheep. It is peacefully situated between A271 and B2096 amidst beautiful undulating countryside. Ideal for walking and touring lovely East Sussex, being within easy reach of Eastbourne (12 miles), Bexhill (10 miles) and Hastings (15 miles). There are many places of historic interest in the vicinity and the coast is only eight miles away at Pevensey. Upstairs there is a family unit (only let to one set of guests — either two, three or four persons — at a time), consisting of one twin-bedded room and one double-bedded room both with handbasins and shaver points and their own bathroom with toilet. There is also downstairs one twin-bedded room with shower, handbasin and toilet en-suite. Guests have their own sittingroom with TV and diningroom and sunroom. Sorry, no pets. Open all year. Central heating in winter. Car essential, parking available. Bed and Breakfast from £14. Evening Meal £8 (by arrangement). SAE, please. AA listed.

HASTINGS. Mr and Mrs S. York, Westwood, Stonestile Lane, Hastings TN35 4PG (0424 751038). Large bungalow on small farm off quiet rural lane away from traffic, with outstanding views over open countryside. Half a mile off B2093, yet only two miles from seafront and town centre. Central position for visiting places of interest to suit all ages. The accommodation comprises one double, one family and one twin bedrooms, all with washbasin, shaver point and central heating. Two bedrooms on the ground floor. Children welcome. We keep pet sheep, chickens, etc. Parking. Bed and Breakfast from £12 per person. Reduced rates for weekly bookings.

HASTINGS. Mrs B.M. Beck, Lower Lidham Hill Farm, Guestling, Near Hastings TN35 4LX (Hastings [0424] 814225). Working farm. Lovely, fully beamed 18th century farmhouse situated on 100-acre farm, just off the A259 Hastings — Rye road, turn off between Guestling and Icklesham. Ideal for touring with Battle seven miles, Hastings five miles and Rye six miles; sea just five miles away. Two family rooms sleep seven. Bathroom/toilet; sitting/diningroom. Children welcome — cot, high chair and babysitting provided. Well behaved pets accepted. Open all year for Bed and Breakfast. No Smoking. Car essential — parking. SAE for terms please.

NINFIELD (Battle). Mrs June B. Ive, Moonshill Farm, The Green, Ninfield, Battle TN33 9LH (0424 892645). 🐦🐦 In the heart of the "1066 country" in the centre of Ninfield opposite pub. Farmhouse in 10 acres of garden, orchard, stables. Enjoy beautiful walks, golf and riding arranged. Comfortable rooms, three en-suite. Central heating and electric fired, hospitality trays. TV lounge. Parking and garage. Babysitting service. Every comfort in our safe, quiet and peaceful home. Children over five years and pets welcome. Reduced rates for weekly bookings.

ROBERTSBRIDGE. Mrs M. Hoad, Parsonage Farm, Salehurst, Robertsbridge TN32 5PJ (Robertsbridge [0580] 880446). Working farm. A warm welcome awaits anyone visiting this 15th century farmhouse which has oak beams and panelling and lies in a quiet unspoiled hamlet half-a-mile from the main A21. It is within easy reach of many of the popular South Coast resorts and, inland, many places of historic interest and natural beauty. Plenty of country walks and there is fishing. A genuine working farm with calves and beef cattle. Good plain cooking of mostly home produced food. Colour TV. Bedtime drinks available if required. There are one single, one double and one family rooms; bathroom, toilet; sittingroom, diningroom. Central heating. Children welcome at reduced rates. Sorry, no pets. Open from November to August (except Christmas week). A car is an advantage here and there is ample parking. Bed and Breakfast £12 per person. Evening Meal £6.50. ETB registered.

ROBERTSBRIDGE. Sedlescombe Vineyard, Robertsbridge TN32 5SA (Staplecross [058083] 715).

A warm welcoming atmosphere awaits you at the self-built farmhouse, set in England's first organic vineyard, surrounded by beautiful countryside. Delightful rooms with modern amenities: full central heating, tea/coffee makers, washbasins, TV, wine/cold drinks cooler, telephone available. Child sleeping spaces. Parking. Ideal base for exploring 1066 country, the coast, Bodiam Castle, the numerous local vineyards, Eastbourne and Brighton. Cross-country walks in all directions, golfing and horse riding possible. Excellent pub/restaurant five minutes' walk away. Wholefood organic breakfast option available on request. English and German spoken. Children welcome. Open all year for Bed and Breakfast from £10.50 per person.

RYE. Pat and Jeff Sullivin, Cliff Farm, Iden Lock, Rye (Iden [079 78] 331, long ring please).

Working farm. Our farmhouse is peacefully set in a quiet elevated position with extensive views over Romney Marsh. Cliff Farm is a working smallholding with sheep, goats, chickens, ducks and pets. The ancient seaport town of Rye with its narrow cobbled street is two miles away. We are an ideal touring base although the town and immediate district have much to offer — golden beaches, quaint villages, castles, gardens etc. Comfortable guest bedrooms with washbasins and tea/coffee making facilities; two toilets; own shower; diningroom and sittingroom. Home produce. Open March to October for Bed and Breakfast from £12. Reduced weekly rates. AA and RAC listed.

WEST SUSSEX

BILLINGHURST. Mrs B. Sims, Lannards, Okehurst Lane, Billinghurst RH14 9HR (040378 2692).

Comfortable bungalow with view and walks in Sussex Weald. Surrounded by fields, dairy herd quarter of a mile. Attached is a Fine Art Gallery. Sotheby's Auction Rooms half a mile, Petworth and its antique shops and galleries seven miles. Within easy reach of London, M25 half an hour, Gatwick 20 minutes, Chichester, Arundel, Goodwood and Brighton readily accessible. There are many historic gardens and theatres to visit, and golf courses, riding schools and racing are all within easy reach. Open all year except Christmas and New Year. Bed and Breakfast from £12.50. ETB Listed.

BOGNOR REGIS. Mr and Mrs G.E. Soothill, Black Mill House, Princess Avenue, Bognor Regis PO21 2QU (Bognor Regis [0243] 821945). ❀ ❀ ❀ A family-run

Hotel in Aldwick, the quieter west side of Bognor Regis, only 300 yards from the sea and Marine Gardens. The Hotel faces south and has all the characteristics of a large private house, surrounded by attractive enclosed gardens. The Hotel is centrally heated throughout. 26 bedrooms (18 with private bathroom/shower and toilet) including 11 twin or double, six family and nine single. All have radio, telephone, colour TV and tea/coffee making facilities. There is an attractive Cocktail Bar and Restaurant, fully licensed. Two lounges, one non-smoking, large games room with table tennis, darts, small snooker table and model railway "O" gauge. Bed and Breakfast; Dinner, Bed and Breakfast or Full Board terms on request. Afternoon teas available; special diets catered for. Children special offers: babies under two years FREE; with two children sharing parents' room, younger child under 10 years free. "Listening Service", washing and drying facilities. Out of season Mini-Breaks, two days from October-May £52 to £60 Dinner, Bed and Breakfast. Also Spring and Summer Short Breaks. Open all year including Christmas. Dogs welcome. Own car park. Illustrated brochure. An excellent centre for touring in the south. AA/RAC one star, Ashley Courtenay recommended. Member South East England Tourist Board.

BOGNOR REGIS. Mrs B.M. Hashfield, Taplow Cottage, 81 Nyewood Lane, Bognor Regis PO21 2UE

(Bognor Regis [0243] 821398). The Cottage lies in a residential part, west of the town centre, 600 yards from the sea and shops. Proximity to many beaches and contrasting towns and countryside make for an ideal touring centre. Chichester, Goodwood Racecourse, Arundel Castle, Brighton, Portsmouth and Southsea are but a few of the places of interest within easy reach. Accommodation comprises one double, one twin-bedded and one family bedroom, all with vanity units, also tea and coffee making facilities. Lounge, diningroom; central heating throughout. The cottage is well appointed and the area is served by public transport. Parking space available. Bed and Breakfast from £12. Dogs by prior arrangement. SAE, please. Arun Tourist registered.

"TAPLOW COTTAGE"

HENFIELD. Mrs J. Forbes, Little Oreham Farm, Near Woodsmill, Henfield BN5 9SB (Henfield [0273]

492931). Delightful old Sussex farmhouse situated in rural position down lane, adjacent to footpaths and nature reserve. One mile from Henfield village, eight miles from Brighton, convenient for Gatwick and Hickstead. Excellent base for visiting many gardens and places of interest in the area. The farmhouse is a listed building of great character; oak-beamed sittingroom with inglenook fireplace (log fires), and a pretty diningroom. Two comfortable attractive bedrooms with en-suite shower/bath; WC; colour TV; tea-making facilities. Central heating throughout. Lovely garden with views of the Downs. Winner of Kellog's award: "Best Bed and Breakfast" in the South East. You will enjoy a friendly welcome and pleasant holiday. Sorry, no children under 10. Bed and Breakfast from £15 per person. Evening Meals by arrangement. Open all year. ETB registered.

HENFIELD. Mrs M. Wilkin, Great Wapses Farm, Henfield BN5 9BJ (Henfield [0273] 492544).

Working farm. The Tudor/Georgian Farmhouse is set in rural surroundings, ten miles north of Brighton, off the B2116 Albourne/Henfield road. Hickstead is nearby. There are horses, calves, etc. The three comfortable rooms (one with four-poster bed) all have their own bathroom, shower en-suite, TV and tea/coffee making facilities. Children and well behaved dogs are welcome. Hard tennis court. Open all year round for Bed and Breakfast from £16 per person. Snacks usually available by arrangement. There is also an attractive self-contained comfortable cottage sleeps two/three. Let on weekly basis from £110 including electricity, TV etc. Tourist Board registered.

HORSHAM. Mrs E.C. Sawyer, Swallows Farm, Dial Post, Horsham RH13 8NN (Partridge Green

[0403] 710385). Working farm. Swallows Farm is a 200-acre mixed farm, including Shire horses, and is situated in mid-west Sussex; it has been farmed by the family for over 50 years. The farmhouse is Grade II listed, and is situated half a mile from the busy A24 which goes from London to the coast, 40 minutes from Gatwick Airport. Many places of historic interest such as Arundel Castle, Petworth House, the South Downs, and many well-known gardens are all within 20 miles. All rooms have washbasins, tea/coffee making facilities and colour TV. Guests' lounge with colour TV. Open March — October. Bed and Breakfast from £14.50 to £17.50; Evening Meal, optional, from £7. SAE for brochure, or phone please.

WEST SUSSEX – COASTAL RESORTS AND DOWNS!

Although dominated perhaps by Bognor Regis, West Sussex does have much to offer. Places like Marden-Stoughton Forest, Midhurst, and its historic inn, the open-air museum at Singleton and the National Butterfly Museum at Bramber are worth a visit.

HORSHAM. Mr J.F.V. Christian, Brookfield Farm Hotel, Winterpit Lane, Plummers Plain, Horsham RH13 6LU (0403 891 568). ♛♛♛ Working farm. Brookfield is a modern farmhouse hotel with full central heating. It is situated adjoining a golf course in beautiful countryside, with its own lake for boating, fishing and swimming. Golf driving range. Accommodation comprises 23 bedrooms (21 with all facilities), including honeymoon suite. Large lounge with a log fire and colour TV. Licensed bars and restaurant. Sauna. Children welcome, cot, high chair and babysitting. Children's play park with swings, slides, boats and animals. Pets welcome. There is ample parking space. Persons travelling abroad may leave their cars safely with us. A car service to and from Gatwick Airport is maintained. Hire Cars available by arrangement. Single room, Bed and Breakfast from £25 per person per night plus VAT; double room, Bed and Breakfast from £35 per night per couple plus VAT. Reductions for children and a children's play area in the hotel. AA listed.

PETWORTH near. Mrs Diana Caplin, Little Selham, Near Petworth GU28 0PS (Lodsworth [07985] 402). Little Selham is a country house built of local stone situated well away from main roads. It has a large secluded garden with swimming pool and is very close to the South Downs in excellent walking country. Ideal centre for touring West Sussex with Chichester, Worthing, Brighton, Arundel, Portsmouth, Petworth and Midhurst within easy driving distance. Many historic places of interest in the area. Approximately 16 miles from the sea. Accommodation in two double bedrooms with washbasins; bathroom; diningroom, drawing room. Central heating. Parking available for six cars. Open February 1st to October 31st. Premises suitable for disabled guests. Children over 10 years welcome. Sorry, no pets. Bed and Breakfast from £16.

PULBOROUGH. Mrs E. West, Sparright Farm, Rackham, Pulborough RH20 2EY (07982 2132). Stay in a 17th century farmhouse in beautiful countryside. One family room, one double room. Tea/coffee making facilities in bedrooms. Ideal centre for exploring the Avon Valley. Visit Arundel Castle, home of the Duke and Duchess of Norfolk, the Arundel Wildfowl Reserve, Amberley Chalkpits Industrial Museum or Elizabethan Parham House and Gardens, all within easy reach. Walk the South Downs Way or drive to the coast. Bognor, Worthing and Brighton are about 30 minutes or less away. Bed and Breakfast from £12 per person.

PULBOROUGH near. Mrs A. Steele, New House Farm, Broadford Bridge Road, West Chiltington, Near Pulborough RH20 2LA (0798 812215). ♛♛♛ Listed 15th century farmhouse with oak beams and inglenook fireplace, in the centre of the village, close to local inns which provide good food. A new 18-hole golf course, open to non-members, is only quarter of a mile away. Many places of historic interest in the area including Goodwood House, Petworth House, Parham House, Arundel Castle. Gatwick 40 minutes. En-suite facilities and colour TV in bedrooms. Children over 10 years welcome. Open all year except December.

WEST HOATHLY. Mrs R. Blackman, Duckyls Farm, Selfield Road, West Hoathly (Sharpthorne [0342] 810429). Duckyls Farm 16th century 120-acre hill farm, situated in area of outstanding beauty. Built around 1537, has historic background and features in Peter Brandon's book "The Sussex Landscape" as "typical of the area". Beautiful views, delightful bedrooms with bath en-suite. Cordon Bleu cooking. Within easy reach of many places of interest. Only 30 minutes' drive to Brighton, Haywards Heath, East Grinstead, Gatwick. Two double, two single, two family bedrooms; two bathrooms, three toilets; sittingroom, diningroom. Children welcome, cot, high chair, babysitting. Pets permitted. Car essential parking. Full Board; Evening Meal/Dinner, Bed and Breakfast or Bed and Breakfast; reduced rates for children. SAE, please, for terms.

WORTHING. Mrs E. Greenyer, Greenacres Farm, Washington Road, Storrington, Worthing RH20 4AF (0903 742538). Set in a valley at the foot of the Sussex Downs surrounded by trees. Walks or horse riding with direct access to the Downs. Five minutes from the lovely village of Storrington, with Steyning, Findon and Washington villages just 10 minutes away. Worthing and the beach eight miles, also easy access for touring London and the south. All rooms have central heating, tea-making facilities, colour TV and hair dryers. One standard room en-suite. Plenty of parking. Swimming pool. Bed and Breakfast from £16 to £20 per person.

WARWICKSHIRE

ALCESTER. Mrs Sylvia Williams, Sunnyside House, Exhall, Alcester B49 6EA (0789 772265). Working farm, join in. Sunnyside is situated on the edge of the peaceful hamlet of Exhall, in a conservation area, ideally situated for walking, sightseeing Shakespeare countryside (Stratford-upon-Avon 10 minutes' drive) or just relaxing. This Victorian farmhouse has recently been extended and improved to give very comfortable en suite accommodation whilst keeping its charm and character. The grounds extend to over four acres with a small selection of farm animals and birds. Evening Meals are available by arrangement, home cooking using local fresh produce. There is always a warm welcome, tea and biscuits and in cooler months a log fire awaiting you on your arrival at Sunnyside. Regret, no children or pets. Bed and Breakfast from £15 per person. Open all year except December. Weekly terms available.

Warwickshire Farm Holidays

Warwickshire farming families welcome guests into their homes to enjoy the comforts of a traditional English farmhouse and discover the peace of the English countryside. Each home listed has it own unique character and differs in size, style, and price, but all offer a high standard of accommodation, good food, a warm welcome and excellent value for money to holidaymakers and business travellers. All owners are members of the Farm Holiday Bureau, all properties are inspected and classified by the English Tourist Board, some also participate in the ETB grading scheme. Warwickshire, in the heart of England, provides the perfect setting for the perfect holiday. Mile upon mile of rolling countryside, picturesque villages and meandering waterways. There are castles, stately homes, theatres, country gardens and some of the prettiest villages to be found.

Places to visit within easy reach include Stratford-upon-Avon, Warwick, Royal Leamington Spa, The Cotswolds, Oxford, Coventry, National Exhibition Centre and National Agricultural Centre.

FARM HOLIDAY BUREAU

For further details about Bed & Breakfast or Self-catering cottages, please write or telephone for a free brochure to: Warwickshire Farm Holidays (FHG), Crandon House, Avon Dassett, Leamington Spa CV33 0AA. Telephone: (029577) 652.

COVENTRY near. Mrs Sandra Evans, Camp Farm, Hob Lane, Balsall Common, Near Coventry CV7 7GX (Berkswell [0676] 33804). Camp Farm is a farmhouse 150 to 200 years old. It is modernised but still retains its old world character. Nestling in the heart of England in Shakespeare country, within easy reach of Stratford-upon-Avon, Warwick, Kenilworth, Coventry with its famous Cathedral, and the National Exhibition Centre, Camp Farm offers a warm, homely atmosphere and good English food, service and comfortable beds. The house is carpeted throughout. Diningroom and sun lounge with colour TV. Bedrooms — five double, three family rooms and five single, all with washbasins. Part of the house is suitable for disabled guests. Children welcome. Cot and high chair, babysitting on request. Fire Certificate granted 1974. All terms quoted by letter or telephone.

LEAMINGTON SPA. Miss Deborah Lea, Crandon House, Avon Dassett, Leamington Spa CV33 0AA (029577 652). ✿✿ Working farm. Guests receive a specially warm welcome at our comfortable farmhouse offering an exceptionally high standard of accommodation. Set in 20 acres, with beautiful views over unspoilt countryside, the small working farm with Jersey cows, calves, sheep and poultry provides produce used in our excellent meals. Three attractive bedrooms with private facilities, tea/coffee making equipment and colour TV. Guests' diningroom and sittingrooms, one with colour TV. Full central heating and log fire in chilly weather. Electric blankets available. Car essential. Ample parking. Pets by arrangement. Peaceful and quiet yet offers easy access for touring the Heart of England, Warwick, Stratford-upon-Avon, the Cotswolds. Open all year. Bed and Breakfast from £14; Dinner, Bed and Breakfast from £21. Write or ring for further details.

LEAMINGTON SPA. Mrs R. Gibbs, Hill Farm, Lewis Road, Radford Semele, Leamington Spa CV31 1UX (0926 337571). ✿✿ Working farm. Guests are welcome all year to this friendly, comfortable farmhouse on 350 acre mixed farm, ideally situated for Warwick, Stratford-upon-Avon, Leamington, Coventry, Royal Showground, Birmingham and N.E.C. and the Cotswolds. Children welcome; reductions for under 12's. Cot and high chair. Large garden with swing. Babysitting. Excellent farmhouse fare using home produce. Central heating. Log fires in chilly weather. Four double bedrooms and two twin rooms, some with en-suite facilities. Guests' sittingroom, colour TV and diningroom. Car preferable; ample parking. Supper drinks available. Evening Meal optional on request. Spacious five van site available. AA recommended. Farm Holiday Bureau member. FHG Diploma. Bed and Breakfast from approximately £15 single; £22 double.

Terms quoted in this publication may be subject to increase if rises in costs necessitate

LONG COMPTON. Mrs J.R. Haines, Ascott House Farm, Ascott, Whichford, Near Long Compton, Shipston-on-Stour CV36 5PP (0608 84655). ♥♥

Working farm. Cotswold stone farmhouse with peaceful surroundings in designated area of natural beauty on edge of the Cotswolds. A 500 acre arable/sheep farm, lovely views, attractive garden, outdoor swimming pool, snooker room and interesting walks. Ascott House Farm is ideal for relaxing, as well as being very well situated for exploring Cotswolds, Oxford, Stratford-upon-Avon and Warwick. Three miles off A34 from Long Compton. One double room ensuite, one family room and one twin room with vanity units, tea/coffee making facilities, central heating; TV lounge; traditional diningroom. Riding two miles, golf five miles. Children welcome, dogs by arrangement. Bed and Breakfast from £13 per person. Closed Christmas. Farm Holiday Bureau member.

ROYAL LEAMINGTON SPA near. Rudi Hancock, Snowford Hall, Hunningham, Near Royal Leamington Spa CV33 9ES (0926 632297). ♥♥♥ We offer a warm welcome and peaceful surroundings in our 18th century farmhouse on a 300 acre mixed working farm set in rolling countryside. Near the Roman Fosse Way, ideally suited for visiting Stratford, Warwick, Leamington, Cotswolds, NAC and NEC. Accommodation in one twin bedded room, one twin/family room, both with shower/washbasin and toilet and one double room with washbasin; singles extra. Also offered is a two-bedroomed self catering cottage (ETB approved) sleeping four/six people. Children welcome. Terms and further details on request.

RUGBY near. Mrs Helen Sharpe, Manor Farm, Willey, Near Rugby CV23 0SH (0455 553143). ♥♥

Commended. Quiet yet convenient, comfortable yet affordable — on the borders of Warwickshire, Leicestershire and Northamptonshire, Willey is the perfect place to re-charge your batteries when travelling north/south or as a super country holiday retreat. A warm welcome within peaceful surroundings awaits the weary traveller or businessman. Here you can experience true farmhouse hospitality. Our 93 acre stock farm is located five miles from the modern motorway network and central for all destinations. Within easy reach of the N.A.C., N.E.C., Bosworth Battlefield, Warwick Castle plus lots more. Phone anytime; you won't be disappointed. Balloonists welcome. Sorry, no smokers.

STRATFORD-UPON-AVON. Mrs N. Smyth, "Bramdean", 60 Evesham Road, Stratford-upon-Avon CV37 9BA (0789 298640). ♥♥ Just minutes from Ann

Hathaway's Cottage, Shakespeare's birthplace, the famous theatre and town centre. This restored spacious English cottage-style house offers a delightful interior of tastefully arranged antique furniture, pictures, collectables and unusual Victorian bedsteads thrown in for flavour. Lovely olde worlde garden in which to take afternoon tea or just relax. Two doubles and one family room all with washbasins, shaving points and radios; two with ensuite showers and one with semi private facilities. Two toilets, plus ground floor washroom. Parking. Free range eggs and only fresh farm produce used for our breakfasts. Pets welcome, reduced rates for children.

STRATFORD-UPON-AVON. Mr John H. Monk, Hunters Moon Guest House, 150 Alcester Road, Stratford-upon-Avon CV37 9DR (Reservations: 0789 29288; Guests: 0789 204101). ♛♛ Hunters Moon has been operated by the same family for over 30 years and has recently been completely modernised and refurbished. We can now offer hotel-type accommodation at Guest House prices. Single, double, twin and family rooms are available, majority with private facilities, fitted hair dryers and colour TV. Orthopaedic beds available. There are tea/coffee making facilities in all rooms. TV lounge, free parking for cars and coaches. Arrangements can be made for coach parties at reduced rates. AA listed. Recommended by Arthur Frommer. Visa, Access, American Express and J.C.B. Cards accepted. Single night bookings accepted.

STRATFORD-UPON-AVON. Mrs Marion J. Walters, Church Farm, Dorsington, Stratford-upon-Avon CV37 8AX (Stratford-upon-Avon [0789] 720471). ♛♛ **Working farm.** A warm and friendly welcome awaits you all year at our 127-acre mixed farm with woodlands and stream which you may explore. We offer good farmhouse cooking at our Georgian Farmhouse, situated on the edge of an extremely pretty village. Stratford-upon-Avon, Warwick, NEC, Royal Showground, Cotswolds, Evesham and Worcester all within easy driving distance. Family, twin and double bedrooms, all with tea/coffee facilities, some en-suite with TVs in converted stable block. Cot and high chair available. Central heating. Gliding, fishing, boating and horse riding nearby. Full Fire Certificate held. AA listed. Bed and Breakfast from £11. Write or phone for further details.

STRATFORD-UPON-AVON. Mrs A. Millington, Larkstoke Cottage, Ilmington, Shipston-on-Stour CV36 4JH (060882 220). Luxury en-suite accommodation and a warm welcome await you in this lovely Cotswold-stone country house with its stone-tiled roof, beamed ceilings and elegant furniture. Standing in beautiful half acre garden in an area of outstanding natural beauty at the foot of Larkstoke Hill, it is the perfect base for visiting Stratford-upon-Avon, Warwick Castle, the Cotswold villages or simply relaxing in the peace and tranquillity of the glorious surroundings. Family, double or twin rooms are spacious, bright and tastefully decorated, each has remote control colour TV and tea/coffee making facilities. Bed and Breakfast from £14 per person. Book early to avoid disappointment.

LARKSTOKE COTTAGE.

LUXURY ACCOMMODATION

WHEN MAKING ENQUIRIES PLEASE MENTION
FARM HOLIDAY GUIDES

Sun Patio Beer Garden

White Horse Inn

E.T.B.

Banbury Road, Ettington, Near Stratford-upon-Avon
Proprietors: Roy & Valerie Blower   Tel: 0789 740641

We extend a warm welcome to our traditional oak-beamed pub where guests are assured of personal service. We offer Bed and Breakfast at reasonable prices and have a restaurant where good food is always served, also real ale.
All our bedrooms are tastefully furnished and have radiators, TV, tea and coffee facilities and hand basins. En-suite also available.
Set in the heart of Shakespeare country, The White Horse Inn is ideal for Stratford-upon-Avon and the Cotswolds, and close to NEC Birmingham, Royal Show Ground at Stoneleigh and also Warwick Castle.

STRATFORD-UPON-AVON. Mrs M. Turney, Cadle Pool Farm, The Ridgway, Stratford-upon-Avon CV37 9RE (Stratford-upon-Avon [0789] 292494). Working farm. Situated in picturesque grounds, this charming oak-panelled and beamed family house is part of 450 acre mixed farm. It is conveniently situated two miles from Stratford-upon-Avon town, between Anne Hathaway's Cottage and Mary Arden's House, also only eight minutes from The Royal Shakespeare Theatre. Ideal touring centre for Warwick, Kenilworth, Oxford, the Cotswolds and Malvern Hills. Accommodation comprises one twin-bedded room and family room, both with private bathrooms and central heating. There is an antique oak diningroom, and lounge with colour TV. The gardens and ornamental pool are particularly attractive, with peacocks and ducks roaming freely. Children welcome at reduced rates; cot, high chair, babysitting. Sorry, no pets. Open all year.

STRATFORD-UPON-AVON. Mrs J. Wakeham, Whitfield Farm, Ettington, Stratford-upon-Avon CV37 7PN (Stratford-upon-Avon [0789] 740260). Working farm. Situated down its own private drive, off the A429, this 220-acre mixed farm (wheat, cows, sheep, geese, ponies, hens) is ideal for a quiet and relaxing holiday. Convenient for visiting the Cotswolds, Warwick, Coventry, Stratford, Worcester. Fully modernised centrally heated house with separate lounge and colour TV; two double and one family bedrooms with washbasins, tea/coffee making facilities; bathroom/shower, two toilets; diningroom. Sorry, no pets. Reduced rates for children, cot, high chair and babysitting by arrangement. Car essential, parking. Open all year (except Christmas) for Bed and Breakfast from £11 per night. Home produced food served. Full English Breakfast. Heart of England Tourist Board registered. SAE, please.

PLEASE SEND A STAMPED ADDRESSED ENVELOPE WITH ENQUIRIES

COTSWOLDS. Major and Mrs P.B. Hartland, 2 Cove House, Ashton Keynes SN6 6NS (Cirencester [0285] 861221). ♥♥♥ A 17th century manor house,

steeped in history and set in a secluded garden, Cove House is five miles south of Cirencester and within easy reach of Bath, Oxford, Avebury and the charming Cotswold countryside. It is close to the Cotswold Water Park where you may observe the wild fowl or windsurf, water ski, sail or fish. Accommodation is in spacious rooms (three with private bath/shower). There is an information and TV room, large sitting and dining rooms with antiques and interesting paintings throughout. A car is essential. Children welcome. Pets by prior arrangement. Bed and Breakfast from £13–£28 per person. Dinner by arrangement. Send SAE for brochure. Regional Winners of Kelloggs Award for Excellence.

DEVIZES. Mr and Mrs C. Fletcher, Lower Foxhangers Farm, Rowde, Devizes SN10 1SS (0380 828254). Working farm. Lying in a secluded hollow by the

Kennet and Avon Canal, two and a half miles west of Devizes on the A361, Lower Foxhangers is nicely placed for touring Wiltshire, rich in places of historic, scenic and recreational interest. Heated swimming pool and tennis courts within three miles; horse riding and public golf seven miles. The canal provides boating, fishing in season and excellent walking along the towpath as an alternative to the open Downs or woodland walks nearby. The spacious 18th century farmhouse provides double and twin bedrooms with washbasins; two bathrooms, three toilets; lounge with colour TV; separate diningroom. Cot and high chair available. Pets welcome. Open Easter to October. Bed and Breakfast from £23 per night (double); weekly from £150 (double). Leaflet by return.

DEVIZES near. Mrs Pam Hampton, Longwater, Lower Road, Erlestoke, Near Devizes SN10 5UE (0380 830095). ♥♥♥ *Commended.* A peaceful retreat

overlooking our own lakes and parkland with two and a half acre waterbird area. Longwater offers the comfort of a young house with the atmosphere of a family home. Family suite, double/twin rooms all en-suite, TV and tea making facilities. Central heating. Two ground floor bedrooms. Guests' lounge with lovely views. Our menu is traditional farmhouse fare using local produce. Special diets by arrangement. Coarse fishing included. Bed and Breakfast from £16; Evening Meal from £10. Weekly terms from £180. Also caravan and camping facility. Farm Holiday Guide Award. Farm Holiday Bureau Member. AA listed, WI Member.

GASTARD. Mrs D. Robinson, Boyds Farm, Gastard, Gorsham SN13 9PT (0249 713146). ♥♥ A

warm welcome awaits you at our cosy 16th century listed farmhouse, situated in the peaceful rural setting of Gastard, with magnificent views of the rolling Wiltshire hills. We offer you peace and comfort in our home, characteristic of its period. Easy access to Bath, the M4 (Junction 17), Castle Combe, Lacock, Bowood House, Bradford-on-Avon, Avebury and many other places of interest. Accommodation comprises one family room, one double room, one twin-bedded room. Full central heating; tea/coffee making facilities. Guests' own lounge with colour TV. Open all year. Children welcome; reductions available. Bed and Breakfast from £12.50 per person.

MALMESBURY. Mrs C.M. Parfitt, Angrove Farm, Rodbourne, Malmesbury SN16 0ET (Malmesbury [0666] 822982). ♥♥ Working farm. Peacefully secluded

working beef farm, homely atmosphere, ideal for a quiet relaxing holiday. Junction 17, M4 only five miles away. Angrove Wood lies behind the farmhouse, and River Avon bounds the farm, where trout and coarse fishing is available. Centrally situated for the Cotswolds, Bath, Lacock and Castle Combe. TV lounge. Diningroom with separate tables. Washbasins in all rooms; free drink making facilities. Warm welcome and personal attention assured. Access at all times. Sorry, no dogs. Open May to September. Bed and Breakfast only from £11 to £16. Choice of Breakfast menu. Brochure on request.

MALMESBURY. John and Edna Edwards, Stonehill Farm, Charlton, Malmesbury SN16 9DY (0666 823310). Working farm.

Stonehill Farm is a 15th century farmhouse situated three and a half miles from Malmesbury, England's oldest borough. This working dairy and sheep farm is ideally situated for days out at Bath, the Cotswolds, Berkeley Castle, Salisbury and Stonehenge. Horse riding is available nearby and there are Water Parks six miles away with fishing, boating and windsurfing. Eight miles from M8. Guests can see bottle-fed lambs in spring. A warm welcome is assured at this traditional farmhouse where full English Breakfast is served. Three bedrooms, one with en-suite facilities. Ample parking. Children and dogs welcome. Terms from £13.

MALMESBURY. Mrs D. Freeth, Vancelettes Farm, Tetbury Road, Sherston, Malmesbury SN16 0LU (Malmesbury [0666] 840253). ☞ Working farm.

70-acre mixed farm, situated at side of quiet country road, one-third-of-a-mile from the Cotswold type village, one-and-a-half miles from Westonbirt Arboretum. Convenient for Tetbury, Cheltenham, Cirencester, Bath, Slimbridge, Castle Combe. Ideal touring centre. Varied menu, home-produced vegetables. Two double, one twin bedrooms, with washbasins; bathroom, toilet; sitting/diningroom. Children welcome, reduced rates — cot, high chair. Pets permitted. Car essential — parking. Full central heating. Open all year round, except Christmas. Mid-week bookings. Evening Dinner, Bed and Breakfast or Bed and Breakfast. SAE, please, for terms.

MELKSHAM. Mrs J. Podger, Seend Bridge Farm, Seend, Melksham SN12 6RY (Devizes [0380] 828534).

Bed and Breakfast in 18th century Wiltshire Farmhouse. Secluded, yet only three miles from Bath/Devizes road. First-class centre for visiting places of historic and scenic interest. Bath, Longleat, Stonehenge, Avebury, Stourhead, the Mendip Hills and Caves, Salisbury Plain, the Cotswolds and many more places within an hour's travel. Recommended by Egon Ronay, Daily Telegraph and Les Routiers. Evening Meal on request. Bed and Breakfast from £12.50.

MERE. Mr and Mrs C. Ross, Chetcombe House Hotel, Chetcombe Road, Mere BA12 6AZ (Mere [0747] 860219). ☞ ☞ ☞ Commended.

This Country House Hotel, set in one acre of lovely gardens, is situated just off the A303 on the eastern approach road to the picturesque little town of Mere. Ideal as a stopover en route to the West Country or as a centre to explore the delights of Wiltshire. Close to Stourhead and Longleat, with Stonehenge, Salisbury, Wilton and Shaftesbury all within 20 mile radius. All bedrooms have private bath/shower rooms, colour TV and tea/coffee making facilities. The hotel has a residential licence and is open all year. Write or phone for brochure and terms. Off Season two or three day breaks available. AA listed.

SALISBURY. Mrs S. Barker, Vale View Farm, Slab Lane, Woodfalls, Salisbury SP5 2NE (0725 22116). ☞ ☞

A warm and friendly welcome awaits you at Vale View Farm, situated on the Hampshire/Wiltshire border, seven miles south of Salisbury and two miles from the New Forest. This area offers many scenic walks through woods, country lanes and footpaths. Horse riding in village. Well suited for touring and exploring the South. Good food readily available in village. Many interesting museums and historic places to visit. Bed and Breakfast from £13 to £16 per person.

PLEASE SEND A STAMPED ADDRESSED ENVELOPE WITH ENQUIRIES

SALISBURY. Mrs P.A. Helyer, Little Langford Farm, Little Langford, Salisbury SP3 4NR (Salisbury [0722] 790205). Working farm, join in. Little Langford

Farm is a dairy and arable farm situated in the beautiful rolling Wiltshire Downs just eight miles north west of the lovely Cathedral City of Salisbury. Guests have freedom of the farm and delightful marked walks. The beautiful Victorian farmhouse stands in its own grounds with large pleasant garden and countryside views. It has spacious, tastefully furnished rooms, double/family and two twin bedded with tea/coffee making facilities. Two guests' bathrooms. Separate diningroom and lounge with colour TV. Three-quarter size billiard table. Excellent touring area. ETB registered. Near Stonehenge, Wilton House, Stourhead, Longleat, New Forest. Quaint village pubs nearby. Open all year. Bed and Breakfast from £15 per person per night. A warm, friendly atmosphere awaits you.

LITTLE LANGFORD FARMHOUSE

SALISBURY. Mrs Pam Hibbs, Newton Farm, Southampton Road, Whiteparish, Salisbury SP5 2QL (Whiteparish [0794] 884416). 🏵🏵🏵 Newton Farm —

16th/17th century — part of the original Trafalgar Estate bequeathed to Lord Nelson. It is in fields bordering the New Forest, which is perfect for nature walks. We have two acres of garden with a swimming pool. Diningroom with original flagstone floors, oak beams and huge open fireplace. We have tastefully modernised the farmhouse with en-suite facilities and have one de luxe master bedroom with bath/shower/dressing room. Large family rooms plus double and twin rooms, all colour co-ordinated. Colour TV in all rooms. Reductions for children. Pets welcome. Light snacks and hot and cold drinks available. Perfect location for Stonehenge, Salisbury, Wilton House, Broadlands, Breamore, Beaulieu, Paultons Park, Winchester, Southampton and Bournemouth area. Ample parking. Central heating. Registered with English Tourist Board. A warm welcome and personal attention awaits all guests. Bed and Breakfast from £15.

HOLIDAY ACCOMMODATION
Classification Schemes in
England, Scotland and Wales

The National Tourist Boards for England, Scotland and Wales have agreed a common 'Crown Classification' scheme for **serviced (Board)** accommodation. All establishments are inspected regularly and are given a classification indicating their level of facilities and services.

There are six grades ranging from 'Listed' to 'Five Crowns 🏵🏵🏵🏵🏵'. The higher the classification, the more facilities and services offered.

Crown classification is a measure of *facilities* not *quality*. A common quality grading scheme grades the quality of establishments as 'Approved', 'Commended' or 'Highly Commended' according to the accommodation, welcome and service they provide.

For **Self-Catering**, holiday homes in England are awarded 'Keys' after inspection and can also be 'Approved', 'Commended' or 'Highly Commended' according to the facilities available. In Scotland the Crown scheme includes self-catering accommodation and Wales also has a voluntary inspection scheme for self-catering grading from '1 (Standard)' to '5 (Excellent)'.

Caravan and Camping Parks can participate in the British Holiday Parks grading scheme from 'Approved (√)' to 'Excellent (√ √ √ √ √)'. In addition, each National Tourist Board has an annual award for high-quality caravan accommodation: in England – Rose Awards; in Scotland – Thistle Commendations; in Wales – Dragon Awards.

When advertisers supply us with the information, FHG Publications show Crowns and other awards or gradings, including AA, RAC, Egon Ronay etc. We also award a small number of Farm Holiday Guide Diplomas every year, based on readers' recommendations.

SWINDON. Mrs D. Freeston, Smiths Farm, Bushton, Swindon SN4 7PX (0793 731285). Uneven floors, old latch doors, beams in and out, history throughout. A garden to browse, fields for to roam — most important of all, Smiths Farm is our home. Welcome to our dairy and beef farm, to cosy double and family rooms with private bathroom. Excellent pub food five minutes' walk, easy drive to M4, Bath, Marlborough, Swindon. Children and pets welcome. Open all year except Christmas. Bed and Breakfast from £12 – £13.

TROWBRIDGE near. Mrs J. Awdry, Spiers Piece Farm, Steeple Ashton, Near Trowbridge BA14 6HG (0380 870266). ❤❤ *Commended.* A warm welcome awaits visitors to our Georgian Farmhouse in the peace and quiet of Wiltshire's beautiful countryside with its fantastic views of rolling hills. A family run arable/mixed farm within easy reach of many tourist attractions. Follow the treasure trail and find us approximately two miles from the A350 Melksham, Westbury-Warminster road. Follow the Keevil Airfield signs and find us half a mile down Spiers Piece Lane on the left. Double, twin and single rooms with washbasins, tea/coffee making facilities. Guests' own bathroom; lounge with colour TV and diningroom. Central heating. Large garden to enjoy. Bed and Breakfast from £12.50. Open February to November.

WARMINSTER. Mrs Jean Crossman, Stalls Farm, Longleat, Warminster BA12 7NE (Maiden Bradley [098-53] 323). Working farm. Stalls Farm is a 350 acre dairy farm on Wiltshire/Somerset border, situated at Longleat on road from Longleat House to Safari Park. Pleasant garden with terrace, lawns and pond, games room. Lovely walks. Ideally situated for visiting Longleat, Stourhead, Bath, Cheddar, Wells, Salisbury, Stonehenge, Avebury, Castle Combe, Rode Bird Gardens, Claverton Manor, Westbury White Horse etc. A car is essential. All bedrooms with comfortable divans, fitted carpets and washbasins. Children welcome, cot and high chair. Access to house at all times. Open all year for Bed and Breakfast. SAE or telephone for terms. Full central heating. AA listed. Tourist Board registered.

WESTBURY. Mrs M. Hoskins, Spinney Farmhouse, Chapmanslade, Westbury BA13 4AQ (Chapmanslade [037-388] 412). ❤❤❤ **Working farm.** Off A36, three miles west of Warminster; 16 miles from historic city of Bath. Close to Longleat, Cheddar and Stourhead. Reasonable driving distance to Bristol, Stonehenge, Glastonbury and the cathedral cities of Wells and Salisbury. Golf, pony trekking and fishing available locally. Washbasins, tea/coffee-making facilities and shaver points in all rooms. Family room available. Guests' lounge with colour TV. Central heating. Children and pets welcome. Ample parking. Open all year. Bed and Breakfast from £11. Reduction after two nights. Evening Meal £7. Farm fresh food in a warm friendly family atmosphere.

WOOTTON BASSETT. Mary Richards, Little Cotmarsh Farm, Broad Town, Wootton Bassett, Swindon SN4 7RA (0793 731322). Listed 17th century farmhouse situated in the quiet hamlet of Cotmarsh. (From Wootton Bassett take Broad Hinton road for two miles, turn left for Cotmarsh). Comfortable, attractive bedrooms with washbasins, one with toilet and shower en-suite, all with tea/coffee making facilities and electric heating. Colour TV on request. Beams throughout, flagstone diningroom with inglenook fireplace and woodburning stove. Lounge for guests' use. Close to Avebury, Marlborough, Oxford and the Cotswolds. Bath 26 miles. M4 Junction 16 four miles. Good local pub food within 2/3 miles. No smoking.

Terms quoted in this publication may be subject to increase if rises in costs necessitate

YORKSHIRE

DURHAM

A1 A19 A172 A171

Ruswarp Whitby
Grosmont Robin Hood's Bay
CUMBRIA Fylingthorpe
Ravenscar
Richmond Goathland
NORTH YORKSHIRE Rosedale Abbey
Low Mill Scarborough
Sedbergh Hardraw Askrigg Leyburn Kirkbymoorside Pickering
A683 Hawes Bain- Aysgarth Bedale Thirsk Helmsley Thornton Dale Filey
Hardraw bridge Masham Coxwold
A65 Ingleton Starbotton
Burton-in-Lonsdale Kettlewell Ripon Easingwold Malton Rudston
High Bentham Pateley Bridge Huby Bridlington
Austwick Malham Knaresborough Gt. Driffield
Settle Airton Harrogate
Gargrave York
A59 Skipton Ilkley Acaster Malbis **HUMBERSIDE**
Lothersdale
LANCASHIRE A6068 Keighley Yeadon Cawood
Stanbury Haworth Bingley Leeds Selby Kingston-upon-Hull
Wilsden Bradford
Hebden Bridge **WEST YORKSHIRE** Brough
Halifax Wakefield
Huddersfield Grimsby
0 5 10 15 20
miles Denby Dale Barnsley Doncaster
A62
SOUTH YORKSHIRE
Yorkshire & Rotherham **LINCOLNSHIRE**
Humberside Sheffield A1

EAST YORKSHIRE (Humberside)

BRIDLINGTON. Mrs Joy Miller, Wold Farm, Flamborough, Bridlington YO15 1AT (0262 850536). If

it's peace and quiet you are looking for, somewhere to relax and unwind, somewhere with comfortable spacious rooms, open fires and country cooking for hearty appetites sharpened by the fresh air, then Wold Farm is the place to be. A short walk across the fields brings you to the spectacular chalk cliffs of Flamborough's Heritage Coast and the Bempton R.S.P.B. Reserve, where myriads of seabirds nest. The old farmhouse is nearly half a mile from the road with panoramic views across farmland and out to sea. Two miles from Flamborough and five from Bridlington, so a car is essential. Bed and Breakfast from £9.50; Evening Meal by arrangement.

BRIDLINGTON. Mrs J.M. Thompson, The Grange, Bempton Lane, Flamborough, Bridlington YO15 1AS (Bridlington [0262] 850207). Working farm. This

attractive 150-year-old house is situated on 475 acres of dairy and arable land, half-a-mile from Flamborough Village on the B1229, 100 yards off the road with tarmac drive and ample parking space. It has a large garden with tennis court, children's play area, swings and slides. Within easy reach of sandy beaches at Bridlington or Filey, also Yorkshire moors and Wolds. Golf at Flamborough, Puffin and Gannet colonies at Bempton. Guests welcome all year except Christmas and New Year, and can look around the farm. One double, one single and one family bedrooms, all with tea-making facilities; two bathrooms and toilets; sittingroom and diningroom. Children welcome at reduced rates. Cot, high chair, babysitting available (free of charge). Pets permitted. Car advisable — ample parking. Terms on request for Bed and Breakfast only. Evening Meals in Flamborough or Bridlington four miles away. Tourist Board listed.

DRIFFIELD. Mrs Tiffy Hopper, Kellythorpe, Great Driffield YO25 9DW (0377 42297). Working farm. Imagine peacocks strutting, ducks swimming and trout rising. Enjoy a cup of tea on the sun terrace overlooking a crystal clear shallow river. The friendly atmosphere of our lovely Georgian farmhouse with its mellow antique furniture, pretty chintz and new bathrooms, one en-suite, is sure to captivate you. Delicious traditional country cooking. Children are very welcome, they enjoy playing in our large garden with swings and playcastle. Ideally placed for touring on the A163. Bed and Breakfast from £11; optional Evening Meal from £8 by prior arrangement. 10 per cent discount for seven nights or more. Reductions for children under 12 years. Tourist Board listed.

LUND. Mrs G. Lamb, Clematis House, Lund, Driffield YO25 9TQ (0377 81204). Clematis House is a 389 acre arable and livestock farm, situated on the east side of the village of Lund. There are two large bedrooms, both en-suite, with tea/coffee making facilities, etc. The lounge/diningroom has colour TV and overlooks the south-facing walled garden. The pretty village, several times winner of the National Britain in Bloom Competition, is found just off the B1248, seven miles north of Beverley. The Wellington Inn does evening meals as do many other local pubs. Central for Hull, Beverley, York, Malton, North Yorks Moors, Scarborough, Bridlington and Hornsea. En-suite rooms from £15 per person sharing double room; £18 for single person. Further details on request.

POCKLINGTON near. Mrs A. Pearson, Meltonby Hall Farm, Meltonby, Near Pocklington YO4 2PW (Pocklington [0759] 303214). Working farm, join in. Meltonby Hall Farm is in a small village at the foot of the Yorkshire Wolds, offering a relaxed and homely atmosphere. It provides a good base for historic York 13 miles, coast 30 miles, as well as the beautiful North Yorkshire Moors with their forest drives, also for Stately Homes. Pocklington, with its magnificent water lilies, is two and a half miles away. Gliding Club nearby. Double and twin rooms, cot and high chair if required; guests' own bathroom, dining room/lounge. Own and local produce used. Central heating and open fire. Car essential, parking. Children welcome. Open Easter to October. Bed and Breakfast from £10; Dinner from £6. Reduced rates for children under 12. Registered ETB; AA listed.

YORK. Mr and Mrs Peter Scott, The Mohair Farm, York Road, Barmby Moor, York YO4 5HU (Wilberfoss [07595] 308). Working farm, join in. The Mohair Farm is on the main A1079 between the villages of Wilberfoss and Barmby Moor. Situated on the main route between York and the Humber Bridge, an ideal centre to explore York and district, coast within easy reach. The farm is a highly productive small-holding with a variety of animals, including rare Angora Goats; the house is set well back from the main road and surrounded by conifers. One double, one twin-bedded, one family bedrooms, all with washbasins, tea-making facilities and TVs. Spa Bath. Reduced rates, babysitting for children. Pets welcome. Full central heating. Car essential — parking. Guests welcome to participate in farm activities which may be of interest to people who wish to derive an income from a small acreage. Bed and Breakfast £10 per person. Tourist Board registered.

NORTH YORKSHIRE

AMPLEFORTH. Mrs Anna Taylor, Carr House, Ampleforth, Near Helmsley YO6 4ED (Coxwold [03476] 526). 🌸🌸 **Working farm.** Carr House — 16th century farmhouse in peaceful, beautiful 'Herriot' country-side, half an hour from York. Recommended by Sunday Observer "a fresh-air fiend's dream — good food, good walking and a warm welcome". Tour the Moors, Dales, National Parks, York coast, nearby famous Abbeys, Castles and Stately Homes. Carr House — HOME OF AMPLEFORTH SPRING WATER — provides a comfortable, relaxing homely base. Romantics will love the four-poster double bedrooms, both en-suite. Central heating, log fires. Enjoy a full Yorkshire farmhouse Breakfast with home-made preserves, free-range eggs, own produce used whenever possible. Bed and Breakfast from £11, Evening Meal £7.50 — weekly rates available. Sorry, no pets or children under seven. No smoking indoors. Open all year; closed Christmas. SAE, please, for brochure. Farm Holiday Bureau Member.

ASKRIGG. Mrs B. Percival, Milton House, Askrigg, Leyburn DL8 3HJ (Wensleydale [0969] 50217). Askrigg is situated in the heart of Wensleydale and is within easy reach of many interesting places — Aysgarth Falls, Hardraw Falls, Bolton Castle. This is an ideal area for walking. Milton House is a spacious house with all modern amenities. There are two double bedrooms and one family room, two with private facilities. All have washbasins and tea making facilities. Bathroom with shower, two toilets; visitors' lounge with TV; diningroom with separate tables. Children are welcome (at reduced rates). Central heating. It is open all year and Askrigg is one of the loveliest villages in the Dales. You are sure of good home cooking, a friendly welcome and a homely atmosphere. Car essential, parking space. Pets are allowed. Evening Meal, Bed and Breakfast or Bed and Breakfast only. Terms on application with SAE, please. ETB listed.

BAINBRIDGE. Mrs A. Harrison, Riverdale House, Bainbridge, Leyburn DL8 3EW (Wensleydale [0969] 50311). 🌸🌸🌸 Riverdale House overlooks village green and stocks in centre of a lovely village in Upper Wensleydale, the famous "James Herriot Country". Good touring centre for the Dales and other places of interest — Aysgarth Falls, Hardraw Scar, Richmond and Bolton Castles, Ingleton Falls and Caves are but a few. Excellent walking over hills and moors. Good food a speciality, all fresh produce, traditional roasts, home made soups, delicious puddings, plus a carefully chosen wine list. Most bedrooms with private facilities and all expected comforts, colour TV. Fire Certificate granted. Leyburn 11 miles. Bargain breaks March or November. SAE for brochure or telephone from November to 31st March **(0969 663381)** — thereafter as above.

BEDALE. Mrs Patricia Knox, Mill Close Farm, Patrick Brompton, Bedale DL8 1JY (0677 50257). Mill Close is a working dairy farm surrounded by beautiful rolling countryside at the foothills of the Yorkshire Dales and Herriot country. Rooms are spacious and furnished to a very high standard. One double or family room, one twin-bedded room. Guests' own sittingroom with colour TV. Relaxing, peaceful atmosphere with large garden, open fires and central heating. Children welcome, cot available. Pets housed by arrangement. Enjoy wholesome farmhouse cooking using local produce, freshly prepared. Open all year. Bed and Breakfast from £12. Evening Meal from £8.

BEDALE. Mrs Sheila Dean, Hyperion House, 88 South End, Bedale DL8 2DS (Bedale [0677] 22334). 🌸🌸 An attractive, warm, friendly house situated at the south end of the market town of Bedale, only five minutes from the A1. An ideal base for touring the Dales, Moors, Teesdale or en route to other destinations. Excellent varied breakfast with home baked bread and preserves (vegetarians catered for). All rooms with washbasins, plus large guests' bathroom and shower. Further toilet on ground floor. Guests' lounge and diningroom. Hospitality trolley. Heat controlled radiators all rooms. Separate guests' entrance, own keys. No access restrictions. Private parking. **Non-smoking establishment.** Bed and Breakfast from £11.50 – £13; Evening Meal from £5 – £8. Open throughout the year except Christmas and New Year.

BENTHAM. Mrs Betty Clapham, Lane House Farm, Bentham, Near Lancaster LA2 7DJ (Bentham [05242] 61479). ✿✿ *Commended*. Working farm. Lane

House Farm is a family run farm on the Yorkshire/Lancashire border. The 17th century beamed farmhouse overlooks the market town of High Bentham (one mile away) and has beautiful views of the Yorkshire Dales. Ideal base for walking or touring. On the edge of the Trough of Bowland and within easy reach of Yorkshire Dales, Lake District or coastal beauty spots. Bedrooms have washbasins, shaver points and tea-making facilities. Guests' lounge has colour TV. Separate diningroom. Farm Holiday Bureau member. Bed and Breakfast from £12. Phone or SAE for details.

BENTHAM. Mrs Shirley Metcalfe, Fowgill Park Farm, High Bentham, Near Lancaster LA2 7AH (05242 61630). ✿✿ *Commended*. Working farm, join

in. Fowgill is a 200 acre stock rearing farm, situated in an elevated position having magnificent views of the Dales and Fells. Only 20 minutes from M6 Junction 34. A good centre for touring the Dales, Lakes, coast and Forest of Bowland. Visit Ingleton with its waterfalls and caves only three miles away. Golf, fishing and horse riding nearby. Bedrooms have washbasins, shaver points and tea-making facilities, one bedroom en-suite. Comfortable beamed visitors' lounge to relax in with colour TV. Separate diningroom. Reductions for children. Bedtime drink included. Brochure available.

CARLTON-IN-COVERDALE. Mrs Anne Dinsdale, Town Foot Farm, Carlton-in-Coverdale, Leyburn DL8 4BA (Wensleydale [0969] 40651). Working farm.

Run by Dales people. Situated in Coverdale, one of the lesser known Yorkshire Dales. Accommodation comprises two double and one twin bedrooms, all with own shower/toilet/ H&C and heated towel rails. Towels provided; poly-cotton sheets used. Spacious "guests' only" lounge, with TV. Guests' kitchen is available for making sandwiches and ingredients provided for a selection of hot drinks. Home-cooked meals are served in our oak-beamed dining room. Free range eggs used. Open Easter to October inclusive for Bed, Breakfast and Evening Dinner. Private parking. Sorry, no pets. SAE for terms on request, please.

COVERDALE. Mrs Eileen Allinson, Middleham House, Carlton-in-Coverdale, Leyburn DL8 4BB (0969 40645). Coverdale, although in the heart of Herriot country, is a quieter dale. Ideal for walking and touring. Comfortable and friendly accommodation with washbasins in all bedrooms. Lounge for guests with colour TV. There are tea making facilities and a private car park. We have lovely open views of The Dale and are within easy reach of neighbouring Dales such as Wensleydale, Wharfedale and Swaledale. Full English Breakfast and four course Dinner. Good home cooking. Open from Easter to end of September.

COVERDALE (Leyburn). Mrs Gillian M. Smith, "Abbots Thorn", Carlton-in-Coverdale, Leyburn DL8 4AY (Wensleydale [0969] 40620). "Abbots Thorn" is an old farmhouse of character, still surrounded by a working farm, which has been modernised to offer every comfort to guests, with sealed unit double glazing, central heating and coal fires in cool weather. It lies amidst unspoilt countryside in the heart of Herriot country in the Yorkshire Dales National Park, with Wensleydale, Wharfedale and Swaledale nearby. Good walking and several interesting historical places in the area. One double, one twin and one family bedroom, all with lovely views across the Dale and with shaver points, electric blankets, washbasins, and tea-making facilities. Guests' bathroom with shower and toilet; also lounge with colour TV; guests' dining room. Visitors can sit by an inglenook fireplace, and for their comfort we use only poly-cotton sheets and supply towels. Children welcome. Pets permitted. Car essential, parking. Full English Breakfast and four-course Evening Dinner — good home cooking and free range eggs. Open from approximately Palm Sunday. Tourist Board registered.

Terms quoted in this publication may be subject to increase if rises in costs necessitate

COXWOLD. John and Jean Richardson, School House, Coxwold YO6 4AD (03476 356). Under the

personal supervision of the owners, this charming 17th century cottage offers you accommodation of the highest standard and delicious home cooking. The lovely village of Coxwold lies in the heart of beautiful dales 18 miles north of York and east of the A19 between Easingwold and Thirsk. For visitors it makes an ideal base for exploring the market towns, castles, great houses and other places of interest which are nearby. Accommodation consists of four double bedrooms, each with TV and tea/coffee making facilities; two bathrooms with showers. Bed and Breakfast from £13 per night, from £80 weekly; Bed, Breakfast and Evening Meal from £19 per night, from £119 weekly. Also delightful garden cottage. Apply to owners for details.

DALTON, near Thirsk. Mrs Barbara Ramshay, Garth House, Dalton, Near Thirsk YO7 3HY (0845

577310). Working farm, join in. Garth House is situated in Herriot country amidst beautiful scenery. Near to York, Harrogate and many historic buildings this is an ideal area for touring with its many attractions. Guest accommodation is in one family room with washbasin and one twin room, both with tea/coffee making facilities; TV in lounge; central heating. Large gardens and lawns, children's pets and toys. Access to badminton court and other sporting facilities. Bed and Breakfast from £10. Easy access from A1 turn off onto A168 and follow signposts for Dalton. Brochure on request.

DANBY. Mrs B. Tindall, Rowantree Farm, Danby, Whitby YO21 2LE (Castleton [0287] 660396). Working farm, join in. Rowantree is situated in the heart of the North Yorkshire Moors and has panoramic moorland views. Ideal walking area and quiet location just outside the village of Danby. Accommodation comprises one double room, one twin-bedded room and one family room all with full oil-fired central heating. Residents' lounge with colour TV. Children welcome — cot provided if required. Babysitting available. Pets accepted. Good home cooking. Bed and Breakfast from £9; Evening Meals provided by request £5 each. Ample car parking space. Tourist Board registered.

DARLINGTON. Mr and Mrs Armstrong, Clow-Beck House, Monk-End Farm, Croft-on-Tees,

Darlington DL2 2SW (Darlington [0325] 721075). 🐦🐦 *Commended.* **Working farm.** Clow-Beck House stands on the very northern edge of Yorkshire and overlooks the River Tees. This is a modern, luxuriously appointed house on a working farm and offers individual and extra-special accommodation for just a few guests. The rooms are spacious, centrally heated and are all furnished with taste and charm. One bedroom has en-suite shower facilities whilst another has a tented ceiling and Laura Ashley decor. All bedrooms are furnished to the highest possible standards with every amenity that guests could require. The diningroom features hand-made furniture. We are both from local farming families and enjoy sharing our home and farm with our guests. We offer true Yorkshire hospitality together with a substantial breakfast to start the day! Our guests are very welcome to visit the farm and fish on the River Tees. Bed and Breakfast rates start from £14 per person. Further details on request.

EASINGWOLD. Mrs Rachel Ritchie, The Old Rectory, Thormanby, Easingwold, York YO6 3WN (0845 401417). 🐦🐦 A warm welcome awaits you at this interesting Georgian rectory built in 1737 furnished with many antiques including a four-poster bed. Three comfortable and very spacious bedrooms with washbasins; charming lounge with colour TV and open fire. Separate diningroom. Large mature garden. An excellent base for touring the Moors, Dales and York. This is the centre of "James Herriot" country with many historic houses and abbeys to visit in the area. Thormanby is a small village between Easingwold and Thirsk. York is 17 miles. Many delightful inns and restaurants serving good food locally. Bed and Breakfast from £12 — reductions for children under 12 years and reduced weekly rates. Ample parking. Open all year. SAE for brochure or telephone.

GLAISDALE (Whitby). Mrs S.E. Burtt, York House, Glaisdale, Whitby YO21 2PZ (0947 87357). Working farm. Stone built coaching house with oak beams and log fires, dating back to 1780. Situated in North Yorkshire Moors National Park. Now a 185 acre dairy and sheep farm, pleasantly situated in beautiful peaceful Dale of Glaisdale 'twixt moors and sea. Only 20 minutes by car from Whitby. Good home cooking with generous helpings of farm produce; free range eggs, cream, milk, meat and vegetables. One double, one twin and one family bedrooms with washbasins, tea/coffee making facilities. Bathroom and two toilets. Lounge with beams and colour TV. Diningroom with separate tables. Full central heating. Children over five welcome, babysitting offered. Children's play area. Boating, golfing, fishing, riding nearby. Car essential. Sorry, no pets in house, kennels in area. SAE or telephone for terms with reductions for children. No VAT.

GOATHLAND. Mrs V.A. MacCaig, Prudom House, Goathland, Whitby YO22 5AN (0947 86368). ❧ ❧ Situated nine miles from the coast, Goathland offers some of the finest walking countryside and is an ideal touring centre. An added attraction is the North Yorkshire Moors Historic Railway Trust running through the village. Delightful scenery. Prudom House is situated in attractive well-maintained gardens in the centre of the village. Careful restoration of the farmhouse has provided guests with modern amenities whilst retaining its character. Open beams a feature and cosy log fires. All bedrooms provided with razor points and washbasins. Comfortable accommodation and good food. Children are welcome; cot, high chair, babysitting and reduced rates. Dogs allowed. Tea room and craft shop. Open all year except Christmas and New Year. Please phone or send SAE for brochure.

GOATHLAND. Mr J.A. Lusher, Whitfield House Hotel, Darnholm, Goathland, Whitby YO22 5LA (Whitby [0947] 86215). ❧ ❧ ❧ On the fringe of Goathland in the beautiful North York Moors, this residentially licensed, family run hotel has 10 bedrooms, all with en-suite bathrooms. All bedrooms have tea/coffee making facilities and radio. Central heating throughout. It offers a friendly atmosphere with colour TV Lounge, cosy Bar Lounge and excellent food. Ideally situated for walking or touring the National Park, the North York Moors Railway is close by, and Whitby and the coast just nine miles away. Children three years and over welcome (reductions when sharing parents' room). Open February to November. AA*; Guestaccom member. Les Routiers recommended. Write or phone for brochure and tariff.

GOATHLAND. Mrs Christine Chippindale, Barnet House Guest House, Goathland, Whitby YO22 5NG (Whitby [0947] 86201). ❧ ❧ Situated in large garden just outside the delightful village of Goathland, an ideal centre for walking and touring the North Yorkshire Moors, Dales and coast. Warm, comfortable accommodation, friendly atmosphere, excellent food. Lounge with colour TV; three double, three twin-bedded, one family room all with washbasins, razor points, heating, tea/coffee making facilities and magnificent views over surrounding moorland. Bathroom, shower room, three toilets. Reductions for children 11 years and under (minimum six years) sharing parents' room. Sorry no pets. Parking. Open from March to November for Bed and Breakfast from £13; Evening Meal, Bed and Breakfast from £19.50. Les Routiers recommended. Brochure on request.

GROSMONT. Mrs S. Counsell, Eskdale, Grosmont, Whitby YO22 5PT (Whitby [0947] 85385). Eskdale is a Georgian detached house set in large attractive gardens. The house overlooks the Esk Valley with views to the North Yorkshire Moors. Good walking area and convenient for coast and steam railway. Two double rooms and two single. Families can also be catered for. Separate lounge for guests' use. Ample parking is available. Children welcome with babysitting offered. Pets also welcome. Full English Breakfast. SAE, please, for terms or telephone. Tourist Board Listed.

GROSMONT. Mrs D. Hodgson, Fairhead Farm, Grosmont, Whitby YO22 5PN (0947 85238). Working farm, join in. Grosmont is a beautiful Eskdale village with steam railway. The modernised farmhouse which is on a 172 acre dairy/sheep farm is pleasantly situated in a quiet area, with superb views, half a mile from Grosmont village. Accommodation offered in one double and one twin-bedded rooms for Bed and Breakfast; Evening Meal if required. No pets. Ideal touring base for the moors and coast. SAE, please, for terms. Open all year.

HARROGATE. Anne and Bob Joyner, Roan Guest House, 90 King's Road, Harrogate HG1 5JX (Harrogate [0423] 503087). AA — RAC listed. "Excellent!", "Exceptional value!", "Good food!", "Quiet!", "Never had it so good!" — just a few testimonials visitors have written in our book on leaving. Situated in a tree-lined avenue in a central position close to all amenities. Conference and Exhibition Centre two minutes' walk. Valley Gardens, town and local swimming baths close by. Our house is centrally heated, with tea/coffee making facilities in all rooms, hot and cold throughout. Some rooms en suite. Home cooking. Bed and Breakfast from £14; en-suite from £16.50; Four-course Dinner, plus tea or coffee on request, £8.50. Ideal centre for touring Dales/Herriot country. Yorkshire and Humberside and English Tourist Board members.

HARROGATE. Mrs A. Wood, Field House, Clint, Near Harrogate HG3 3DS (0423 770638). Field House is situated five miles from Harrogate and a mile above the attractive village of Hampsthwaite, commanding beautiful views over the Nidd Valley. Ideal for exploring the Dales and Moors with ancient abbeys, castles and country houses. The market towns of Skipton, Ripon and Knaresborough and the historic city of York are all within easy reach. Accommodation is in one twin and one double room with private bathroom. Private sittingroom with TV, etc. Open all year. Car essential — private parking. Bed and Breakfast from £11 with Evening Meals readily available. A warm welcome guaranteed in a peaceful friendly atmosphere. Telephone or SAE, please, for further details.

HARROGATE. Mrs Janice Kellett, Moorfield House, Bishop Thornton, Ripley, Near Harrogate HG3 3LE (Sawley [0765] 620680). An old but modernised house of great character and charm, Moorfield House with its own beautiful garden and set in open farmland offers peace and tranquillity. Only two miles from Fountains Abbey, ideally positioned to explore the beautiful Dales and nearby Pateley Bridge, Ripon, Knaresborough and Harrogate. The centrally heated accommodation consists of one double, one twin and one family room, each with washbasin and tea/coffee making facilities. Bathroom and toilet. A comfortable lounge with gleaming brasses, log fire and colour TV. The diningroom has separate tables. Children at reduced rates if sharing parents' room. Car essential. Parking provided. Open Easter to October. Evening Dinner, Bed and Breakfast. SAE, please, for terms. Highly recommended with guests returning annually.

HARROGATE. Mrs N. Iveson, Newton Hall, Ripley, Harrogate HG3 3DZ (Harrogate [0423] 770166). Working farm, join in. Newton Hall is a 17th century farmhouse where guests receive a warm welcome. A farm with cattle, sheep and crops, quietly situated away from the noise of the traffic, with lovely views across open countryside. Ideal for touring the Yorkshire Dales, being four miles from Harrogate and half a mile from the charming village of Ripley with its beautiful castle. Family, twin and double rooms, all with washbasins; bathroom, shower room; lounge with colour TV; diningroom. Full English Breakfast with home-made preserves and free range eggs. Open all year. Bed and Breakfast only — there are a number of places nearby where evening meals may be obtained. ETB registered. Write or phone for terms.

HARROGATE near. Mrs B. Sowray, Bowes Green Farm, Bishop Thornton, Near Harrogate HG3 3JX (Harrogate [0423] 770114). Working farm. TWICE AWARDED FARM HOLIDAY GUIDE DIPLOMA FOR ACCOMMODATION OF THE HIGHEST STANDARD. Those planning a holiday amidst the beautiful Yorkshire Dales should consider staying at this 17th century farmhouse set on a 300 acre mixed farm within easy reach of many beauty spots and places of historic interest. Fountains Abbey, Ripley Castle and the market towns of Knaresborough and Ripley are easily reached. The accommodation is in two twin bedded rooms with vanity units and two double bedrooms with washbasins; bathroom, toilet, shower; lounge with colour TV. Central heating. There are separate tables in the diningroom where the best of farm produce is served. Children from 14 years welcome. Regret, no dogs. SAE, please for terms for Evening Dinner, Bed and Breakfast or Bed and Breakfast only.

HARROGATE near. Mrs Jo Austin, Hookstone House Farm, Low Lane, Darley, Near Harrogate HG3 2QN (Harrogate [0423] 780572). A 300-year-old-cottage farmhouse, 10 miles west of Harrogate, in the picturesque Nidderdale Valley. Ideally situated for touring the many local attractions; Herriot countryside to the north and Bronte country to the south; golf, walking or fishing on local reservoir. A traditional Yorkshire welcome, comfortable bedrooms (one with en-suite facilities); separate guests' sittingroom with colour TV; central heating and log fires await all our guests. Fresh farm and local produce used in home-cooked fare; special diets can be arranged. Open all year. Bed and Breakfast from £12; Dinner, Bed and Breakfast from £18. Special weekly rates available. Tourist Board registered. Please send for further details.

NORTH YORKSHIRE – RICH IN TOURIST ATTRACTIONS!

Dales, moors, castles, abbeys, cathedrals – you name it and you're almost sure to find it in North Yorkshire. Leading attractions include Castle Howard, the moorlands walks at Goathland, the Waterfalls at Falling Foss, Skipton, Richmond, Wensleydale, Bridestones Moor, Ripon Cathedral, Whitby, Settle and, of course, York itself.

HARROGATE near. Mrs G.A. King, High Winsley Cottage, Burnt-Yates, Near Harrogate HG3 3EP (Harrogate [0423] 770662). 🌸 🌸 High Winsley Cottage is situated in peaceful countryside on the edge of Nidderdale, convenient for both town and country. Many places of interest to explore locally: River Nidd, Pateley Bridge, Brimham Rocks, Ripley Castle and Fountains Abbey. Mr and Mrs King assure their guests of a warm welcome and generous hospitality, good food with fresh home grown garden produce; free range eggs from their own hens; and home baked bread. The accommodation is in three twin bedrooms and two double rooms, all with en-suite facilities. Guests' own sittingroom, colour TV, log fires and central heating. Open all year. Telephone or SAE, please, for brochure and terms.

HELMSLEY. Mrs Margaret Wainwright, Sproxton Hall, Sproxton, Helmsley YO6 5QE (Helmsley [0439] 70225). 🌸 🌸 *Commended.* **Working farm.** Enjoy the peaceful atmosphere, magnificent views and comfort of Sproxton Hall, a 17th century Grade II listed farmhouse on a 300 acre family farm. A haven of peace and tranquillity, lovingly and tastefully furbished to give the warm and cosy elegance of a country home. Set amidst idyllic countryside, one and a half miles from Helmsley. Excellent base for touring North Yorkshire Moors, Dales Coast, National Trust properties and York. One twin and one double bedded rooms with colour TV, central heating, electric blankets, drinks facilities, washbasins and razor points. Luxury shower room and bathroom. Laundry facilities. Pay phone. A "Non-Smoking" household. Please send stamp for brochure.

HELMSLEY. Mrs Sally Robinson, Valley View Farm, Old Byland, Helmsley, York YO6 5LG (043-96 221). 🌸 🌸 **Working farm.** A working family farm on the edge of a small village with outstanding views across beautiful countryside. One double, two twin and one family bedrooms each with en-suite shower/bath, washbasin and toilet, tea/coffee making facilities and central heating. Guests' sittingroom furnished traditionally with your comfort always in mind. Separate diningroom. All public rooms recently refurbished. Old-fashioned farmhouse meals; substantial breakfasts and leisurely dinners served (cream teas in season). We are open all year. Bed and Breakfast from £18; Evening Dinner from £9. Children and dogs welcome. Telephone or write for brochure.

HELMSLEY. Mrs Elizabeth Easton, Lockton House Farm, Bilsdale, Helmsley YO6 5NE (Bilsdale [04396] 303). Working farm, join in. 16th century farmhouse on mixed family run farm of 400 acres with sheep, cattle and ponies. Ideally situated for touring North Yorkshire moors and the many other attractions of this area. There are peaceful panoramic views from the farm. Guest accommodation is in two double and one family rooms all with washbasins; lounge with colour TV. Good home cooking in abundance. Open March to October. Bed and Breakfast from £11; Evening Meal (optional) from £7. Reduced rates for children. Tourist Board registered.

HELMSLEY. Mr and Mrs Tim Rowe, Spring Farm Cottages, Cawton, Near Hovingham, York YO6 4LW (Hovingham [065-382] 555). Twixt Helmsley and Castle Howard — half an hour from York and Heritage Coast. Ideal centre for touring North York Moors or visiting one of the many stately homes and gardens. Spring Farm, located down a quiet leafy lane, near to picturesque village of Hovingham, offers two twin-bedded rooms each with private bathroom; central heating; colour TV and tea making facilities. Delightful lounge, log fire. Stands within own gardens and paddock. Tennis court, with coaching available. Open all year. Idyllic setting, peaceful village. Tourist Board registered. Please send enquiries to **Mr and Mrs Tim Rowe.**

HELMSLEY. Mrs J. Milburn, Barn Close Farm, Rievaulx, Helmsley YO6 5LN (Bilsdale [043-96] 321).

👑👑 **Working farm.** Farming family offer homely accommodation on mixed farm in beautiful surroundings near Rievaulx Abbey. Ideal for touring, pony trekking, walking. Home-made bread, own home produced meat, poultry, free range eggs — in fact Mrs Milburn's excellent cooking was praised in "Daily Telegraph". Modern home — two double bedrooms with washbasins, one family room; with tea/coffee making facilities. TV lounge; diningroom. Children welcome, babysitting. Sorry, no pets. Open all year round. Open log fires. Storage heaters in bedrooms. Car essential — parking. Reduced rates for children under 10 sharing parents' room. Terms on request. SAE.

INGLETON. Mrs Nancy Lund, Gatehouse Farm, Far Westhouse, Ingleton, Carnforth LA6 3NR (05242 41458). Bryan and Nancy (formerly of Lund Holme) welcome old and new customers to their new home, GATEHOUSE, which was built in 1740 and faces south with views of the Bowland Fells. Situated on the edge of the Yorkshire Dales National Park, one and a half miles from Ingleton in the little hamlet of Far Westhouse just off the A65. Good home cooking and a warm welcome.

INGLETON. Mrs Mollie Bell, "Langber Country Guest House", Ingleton (Via Carnforth) LA6 3DT (Ingleton [05242] 41587). 👑👑 Ingleton, "Beauty Spot of the North", in the National Parks area. Renowned for waterfalls, glens, underground caves, magnificent scenery and Ingleboro' mountain — 2,373 ft. An excellent centre for touring Dales, Lakes and coast. Golf, fishing, tennis, swimming and bowls in vicinity. Pony-trekking a few miles distant. Guests are warmly welcomed to "Langber", a detached country house, having beautiful views with 57 acres of gardens, terrace and fields. Sheep, lambs and goats kept. There are three family, two double and one single bedroom — all with washbasins and razor points. En-suite rooms available. Bathroom, shower and three toilets. Sunny, comfortable lounge and separate diningroom. Central heating and fitted carpets. Babysitting offered. Open all year except Christmas. Fire certificate granted. AA and RAC listed. Tourist Board registered. SAE for terms for Evening Dinner, Bed and Breakfast or Bed and Breakfast only. Reductions for children under 13 sharing parents' room.

JERVAULX. Mrs C.R. Marshall, Kilgram Grange, Jervaulx, Masham, Ripon HG4 4PQ (0677 60212). 👑👑 50 metres from the River Ure and Kilgram Bridge set amidst stunning scenery and varied birdlife. A short walk from Jervaulx Abbey — Masham, Ripon, Leyburn, Richmond and Herriot Country are all within easy reach. The house has been competely modernised and offers every comfort. One double, one very large twin (can take extra child's bed) and one twin bedrooms; two private bathrooms; separate drawing room with TV. Separate diningroom. Dinner, three courses with wine and cheese (24 hours notice). Pets by prior arrangement. Packed lunches free for stays in excess of three days. A family house where a warm welcome is assured. Bed and Breakfast from £12.50 per person to £16 per person; Dinner £15 per person. Small child in extra bed half adult price.

NORTH YORKSHIRE – RICH IN TOURIST ATTRACTIONS!

Dales, moors, castles, abbeys, cathedrals – you name it and you're almost sure to find it in North Yorkshire. Leading attractions include Castle Howard, the moorlands walks at Goathland, the Waterfalls at Falling Foss, Skipton, Richmond, Wensleydale, Bridestones Moor, Ripon Cathedral, Whitby, Settle and, of course, York itself.

KETTLEWELL (Skipton). Scargill House, Kettlewell, Skipton BD23 5HU (075-676 234). Scargill House, in the Yorkshire Dales, is a beautiful country house, with excellent accommodation for 90 guests and is run by a community of 40 Christians. Come as a couple, individual, family or group and join a Holiday Week in the Summer, a mid-week break in the Spring and Autumn, or a Festival Houseparty. Exceptional walking country, organised days out, plenty of entertainment and for those who wish, an opportunity to join with others in worship in the Chapel, and to explore the reality of the Christian faith in today's world. For further information and tariff contact **The Bookings Secretary.**

KETTLEWELL. Mrs B. Lambert, Fold Farm, Kettlewell, Skipton BD23 5RJ (075676 886). ☙ ☙ Fold Farm is a hill sheep farm situated in a quiet backwater of Kettlewell, within easy walking distance of all village amenities. The house dates back to the 15th century and some of its original beams are still in evidence. There are tea-making facilities in all bedrooms and there is a separate guests' sittingroom. Children over 10 years welcome. Bed and Breakfast from £15. Also two self catering cottages available.

KETTLEWELL-WITH-STARBOTTON. Mrs M.L. Rathmell, Hilltop Country Guest House, Starbotton, Near Skipton BD23 5HY (Kettlewell [075-676] 321). ☙ ☙ ☙ *Commended.* RAC Highly Acclaimed. AA Selected. Superbly situated small 17th century country guest house in three acres of beckside grounds overlooking unspoilt Dales village in the heart of the National Park. Beautifully appointed and immaculate bedrooms all have bath or shower and WC en-suite, also colour TV and tea-making facilities. There is a sittingroom with log fires and a wide selection of books and a bar which is well-stocked and often lively. Fine food is served by candlelight in the oak beamed diningroom. And by day, Hilltop is perfectly situated for circular fell and riverside walks and for touring some of England's loveliest countryside. Brochure available. "This delightful house ... offers the warmth and hospitality of a house party ...".

KIRKBYMOORSIDE. Mrs M.P. Featherstone, Keysbeck Farm, Farndale, Kirkbymoorside YO6 6UZ (Kirkbymoorside [0751] 33221). Working farm, join in. Friendly accommodation on a 200 acre farm. There are one double, one single or twin bedrooms; diningroom with open log fire where good home cooking is served. Car essential, parking. Children and pets welcome; babysitting available. Open all year round. Evening Meal, Bed and Breakfast £12; Bed and Breakfast £8.50. Reduced rates for children and weekly terms. Tourist Board registered.

KNARESBOROUGH. Mrs Barbara Robinson, Lingerfield House, Lingerfield, Knaresborough HG5 9JA (0423-863842). ☙ ☙ Barbara Robinson will extend a warm welcome to Lingerfield House. The main part, almost 300 years old, lies in a rural area between the old villages of Farnham, Scotton and old Scriven, only two miles to the centre of the historic market town of Knaresborough. Open views from all the spacious rooms. Guests accommodated in twin, double and family rooms, all with hot and cold water, shaver points, colour TV and beverage facilities. Colour TV lounge and diningroom. Children are welcome with high chairs and cots available. Various diets can be catered for. Large gardens and orchard offer guests outdoor freedom. Pets welcome by prior agreement. Knaresborough has a market place with Buttercross and boasts the oldest chemist shop in England, plus the Castle and its grounds and boating on the River Nidd. We are well placed for visits to York, the Minster and historic Walls, numerous castles, abbeys and stately homes. The beautiful Yorkshire Dales are on the doorstep. Nature reserve and Sailing Club in Farnham. Bed and Breakfast from £14; Evening Meal from £6.50. Reductions for children. Our brochure available and sent on request.

YORK PLACE · KNARESBOROUGH
Nr HARROGATE · N.YORKSHIRE HG5 0AD
TELEPHONE: (0423) 863539

Privately owned and run by Len and Jackie Cohen, a Grade II Listed Georgian Hotel only two minutes' walk from the market square and castle. Built with stones from the castle ruins and used to house prisoners en-route to York (12 miles away) to be hanged. ALL ROOMS EN-SUITE and individually designed with complimentary beverages; TV, telephone and mini bars. You can stay in one of our four-poster rooms. Two rooms are approved for handicapped folk and we also have four large family rooms. Price from £50 per room (ie £25 each) including full English Breakfast. November to March stay Friday/Saturday or Saturday/Sunday and Dinner for two is FREE on Saturday; or stay two nights Sunday-Thursday and third night FREE (not Friday/Saturday). Not Bank Holidays and trade fairs.

LEN & JACKIE COHEN
(0423) 863539

AA RAC Highly Acclaimed　　　🐾🐾🐾 Recommended

LOTHERSDALE. Gwyneth and Richard Dover, Harrow Ings Country House, Mitton Lane, Lothersdale, Near Skipton BD20 8HR (0535 636658). 🐾🐾

"Shangri-La is true — it's here" one of our guests remarked. Charming old farmhouse, barn and shepherd's cottages, lovingly restored, boasting exposed stonework, beamed ceilings, mullions, polished floors and antiques. Set in two acres surrounded by beautiful Dales countryside. Breathtaking views. The area is steeped in history, perfect for sightseeing Bronte, Herriot and Pendlewitch country, golfing, walking — Pennine Way half a mile — or relaxing in our peace and tranquillity. Luxurious accommodation decorated to the highest standard in Laura Ashley. All rooms have tea making facilities, TV and most are en-suite. No smoking. You will adore the unique "Harrow Ings" experience — everyone does! Terms from £15.

GREENACRES

Greenacres is set in over 2½ acres of beautiful gardens and woodland. HEATED INDOOR SWIMMING POOL.

All nine bedrooms are en suite with colour TV, tea/coffee making facilities, hair dryers and full central heating. Separate lounge, diningroom and conservatory. Residential licence. We are centrally situated in Ryedale, close to Castle Howard, York, East Coast and the North Yorkshire Moors. Ample car parking. Bed and Breakfast from £20; Evening Meals. Bargain Breaks off season. *Please write or phone for brochure and details* **Margaret and Martyn Goodwill, Greenacres Country Guest House, Amotherby, Malton YO17 0TG. Tel: 0653 693623.**

MALTON. Mrs C.P.H. Murray, Manor Farm, Little Barugh, Malton YO17 0UY (Kirby Misperton [065386] 262).

18th century Manor Farm house has recently been extensively modernised with full central heating, AGA, double glazing, etc. Both double and single rooms with bath are available. Guest sittingroom with open fire and colour TV, plus use of large garden and tennis court. Little Barugh is equidistant — eight miles — from Malton, Pickering and Kirkbymoorside and close to Castle Howard, Flamingoland, Eden Camp, North Yorkshire Moors and the historic railway; Scarborough and York are 25 miles. Well behaved children and dogs welcome. Open all year except Christmas. Bed and Breakfast from £16 per person per night; Evening Meal upon request.

OTLEY. Mrs Cheri Beaumont, Paddock Hill, Norwood, Otley LS21 2QU (0943 465977). Converted barn and farmhouse in traditional style. Entirely rural location but within easy reach of Harrogate, Otley and the Yorkshire Dales. B6451 south of Brand Hill. A wealth of history and superb scenery on the doorstep. Open fires. Good food. Fly fishing on nearby reservoirs. Excellent walking and bird watching. Pub food within one mile. Terms from £11.50. Children welcome. Pets by arrangement. ETB listed.

PATELEY BRIDGE. Mrs Joan Simmons, Moorhouse Cottage, Pateley Bridge, Harrogate HG3 5JF (Harrogate [0423] 711123). Restored 18th century farmhouse set in quiet picturesque location with open views over Nidderdale. Central for the beautiful Yorkshire Dales, numerous market towns, abbeys, castles and historic York. The house is furnished in keeping with its age with many original features, including a range with open fire in the guests' lounge. One family, one double, one single room. Guests' own bathroom. Good varied wholefood cooking with home grown produce. Vegetarian meals on request. Tea/coffee making facilities and home made biscuits always available. Colour TV. Children welcome. Sorry no smoking and no pets. Car advisable. Ample parking. Evening Meal, Bed and Breakfast £17. Bed and Breakfast £11.

PICKERING. Mrs Livesey, Sands Farm, Wilton, Pickering YO18 7JY (0751 74405). Enjoy a relaxing holiday in a friendly atmosphere where food, rooms and service are of the highest standard. Laura Ashley style bedrooms, with flowers, colour TV and tea-making facilities; some en-suite. Full English Breakfasts; tea-trays in front of a log fire. Evening Meals on request. Many sporting facilities and places of interest nearby — we are happy to suggest places to eat and places to visit. No smoking. No dogs. Terms from £12.50 per person per night. Self-catering Cottages also available set in 15 acres.

PICKERING. Mrs Ella Bowes, Banavie, Roxby Road, Thornton Dale, Pickering YO18 7SX (Pickering [0751] 74616). 🌑🌑 A warm welcome awaits all guests at Banavie, a stone-built semi-detached house situated in a very nice part of Thornton Dale which, with the stream flowing through the centre, is one of the prettiest villages in Yorkshire. Nearby are four restaurants and three pubs which provide meals. Ideal centre for touring coast, moors, forest, Scarborough, Castle Howard, Flamingo Park and Eden Camp. One family and two double bedrooms, all with washbasins, shaver points and tea making facilities. Bathroom, toilet. Diningroom and lounge with colour TV. Central heating. A real Yorkshire breakfast is served by Mrs Bowes. Visitors' book reads "excellent", "Real Yorkshire Hospitality", "Wonderful holiday; will come again". Large car park. Children made very welcome; cot, high chair, babysitting provided. Dogs welcome. Open all year. Bed and Breakfast from £9.50 (including light supper). SAE, please, for early reply.

PICKERING. Mrs June Carter, Grove House, Levisham Station, Pickering YO18 7NN (Pickering [0751] 72351). Gracious living at the old Manor House. A beautiful old stone country house set in an acre of gardens bounded by woodlands, pine forest and moorland, making an idyllic base to explore North Yorkshire. All rooms furnished to a high standard with sensitive regard for the period of the house. Each bedroom has washbasin, one room has en-suite bathroom, all rooms are centrally heated. We take pride in our excellent home cooking from fresh produce with varied menus. Full Board; Dinner, Bed and Breakfast from £23; Bed and Breakfast from £15. No pets. Unsuitable for children. Car essential, ample parking. Open Easter to October. Non-smoking establishment.

👑👑👑 Highly Commended

BRIDGEFOOT GUEST HOUSE
Thornton Le Dale, Pickering, North Yorkshire YO18 7RR
Telephone 0751 74749

Bridgefoot House is situated in the village of Thornton-le-Dale, by the trout stream in a wall-enclosed garden next to the thatched cottage. Ideal touring base for the moors, east coast, countryside, forestry and York. Centrally heated throughout, open fires in season. Family room; several double and twin-bedded rooms; ground floor double (most rooms en-suite), tea and coffee facilities, shaver points, electric blankets. Colour TV. Guest lounge; diningroom and bar. Bed and Breakfast from £12.50 (en-suite £14.50). Bar meals available. Registered with ETB. Car parking. Open Easter to October. Winter weekends November to Easter. Contact **Mr and Mrs B. Askin** for brochure.

PICKERING. Mrs Carol E. Brisby, White House Farm, Great Barugh, Malton YO17 0XB (Kirby Misperton [065-386] 317). 👑👑👑 **Working farm.** White House Farm is a beautiful rambling 17th century oak-beamed farmhouse. Pleasantly situated in open countryside approximately six miles from the market towns of PICKERING, MALTON and KIRKBYMOORSIDE. The farm nestles on a southern slope of Ryedale and has extensive views towards Yorkshire Wolds, Howardian Hills and Moors. Private fishing in River Seven. Large gardens. The accommodation comprises two large, attractive rooms (one twin-bedded room with private bathroom, one double room with en-suite facilities), all with tea and coffee making facilities. Sittingroom with colour TV, diningroom. Ample safe parking. First-class food is varied and plentiful, choice of menu, own produce. Slimmers beware! Friendly atmosphere. Ideal base for York, coast and moors. Car essential. Open April to October. Bed and Breakfast £13 per person, Dinner £7.50. Weekly rates available.

PICKERING. Mrs J. Avison, Chester Villa, Thornton Dale, Near Pickering YO18 7RB (Pickering [0751] 74513). Chester Villa is a small farm one mile from the village with fishing available in the stream flowing behind the house. Riding school half a mile away. Convenient for visits to the Yorkshire Moors, East Coast, historic houses and Flamingo Park Zoo. All bedrooms have washbasins. One twin, one double and one family rooms; bathroom, two toilets; sittingroom, colour TV; diningroom. Cot. Plenty of parking space. Reductions for children sharing bedroom. Open from Easter to November. Prices from £9. SAE, please, for reply.

PICKERING. Mrs Sue Cavill, Badger Cottage, Stape, Pickering YO18 8HR (Pickering [0751] 76108). Small farm offering comfortable accommodation in a peaceful relaxed setting amidst the glorious scenery of the North Yorkshire Moors National Park. Ideal centre for touring and walking the moors, forests and coast. Within easy reach of York and numerous other historic attractions. Our comfortably furnished guestrooms, all on the ground floor, have en-suite shower rooms, colour TV and tea/coffee making facilities. Delicious home cooked food of high standard making maximum use of farm fresh produce. Bed and Breakfast from £12. Evening Meal optional. Self catering accommodation available. Open all year. Pets welcome.

PICKERING. Stan and Hilary Langton, Vivers Mill, Mill Lane, Pickering YO18 8DJ (Pickering [0751] 73640). Vivers Mill is an ancient watermill situated in peaceful surroundings, quarter mile south of Pickering Market Place on Pickering Beck. The Mill is a listed building constructed of stone, brick and pantiles, part of which possibly dates back to the 13th century. The Mill with its characteristic beamed ceilings is being renovated, whilst maintaining most of the machinery, including the water wheel and millstones. Pickering is an excellent centre from which to explore the North Yorkshire Moors National Park, Ryedale and the spectacular Heritage Coast. It is the terminal station for the preserved North Yorkshire Moors Railway and is only 26 miles from historic York. Visitors are assured of a friendly welcome with nourishing, traditional food. Large lounge and comfortable bedrooms, most with WC, shower or bath. Tea/coffee making facilities. Terms on request. Reductions for family room. Pets welcome.

PICKERING. Mrs J. Allanson, Rains Farm, Allerston, Pickering YO18 7PQ (Scarborough [0723] 859333). Rains Farm is a comfortable modernised farmhouse, situated in the peaceful Vale of Pickering. The ideal base, offering easy access to the coast, Moors as well as York. Traditional farmhouse meals served, using fresh locally grown produce whenever possible. Good food and warm welcome is assured. The centrally heated accommodation comprises double and twin rooms, the majority en-suite, including ground floor with own facilities. Beamed dining-room, lounge with colour TV. Tea-making facilities, hair dryer, iron etc. Car essential, parking. No smoking indoors. Bed and Breakfast from £11; en-suite from £15; Evening Meal optional. Write or phone for further details.

RAVENSCAR. Pat and Mick Wheeler, Church Farm, Ravenscar YO13 0NA (0723 870479). Working farm. Church Farm is a small working farm with a variety of animals set within the National Park with panoramic views over Robin Hood's Bay. The 18th century farm offers a friendly informal atmosphere with exposed stone walls, oak beams and log fires. All bedrooms are tastefully furnished and consist of one family room, one twin room and two double rooms, one with four-poster; all have colour TV, washbasins and tea-making facilities. Guests' own bathroom and lounge. Full central heating. Vegetarians catered for. Full breakfast menu. Golf, walks, many places to visit and pony trekking close by. Open all year. Terms on request. Also available, self-catering cottage.

RAVENSCAR. Mrs Joan Greenfield, Smuggler's Rock Country Guest House, Ravenscar YO13 0ER (Scarborough [0723] 870044). ♥ ♥ Smuggler's Rock is a stone built Georgian Farmhouse between Whitby and Scarborough, with panoramic views over surrounding North Yorkshire National Park and sea. The farmhouse has a homely and relaxed atmosphere. Home cooking is served in our old world diningroom, and there is an open fire and colour TV in our beautiful open-beamed lounge. All bedrooms have private facilities, bedroom TV available. We have a Residential Licence and our own car park. This is an ideal country holiday area, with many picturesque seaside villages on the Heritage Coast, and beautiful Dales just a few miles inland. AA listed. Tourist Board approved. Reasonable prices; please send for brochure.

REETH. Mrs K. Bailey, Fremington Mill Farm, Reeth, Swaledale, Near Richmond DL11 6AR (0748 84581). Working farm. A friendly welcome is guaranteed at this traditional farmhouse on a working farm and pony trekking centre. Nestling on the banks of the Arkle Beck, this old corn mill (listed), in the heart of Herriot country, is the perfect holiday base, starting each day with a choice of our superb breakfasts in front of the open fire. The walks are memorable, there is good fishing in the Swale and Arkle and the treks on our horses/ponies are a must (all standards)! All rooms are beautifully appointed with tea/coffee making facilities and colour TV. Children and pets welcome. Terms from £12, reductions for children. Tourist Board registered.

PLEASE SEND A STAMPED ADDRESSED ENVELOPE WITH ENQUIRIES

RICHMOND. Mrs Dorothy Wardle, Greenbank Farm, Ravensworth, Richmond DL11 7HB (Darlington [0325] 718334). This 170 acre farm, both arable and carrying livestock, is four miles west of Scotch Corner on the A66, midway between the historic towns of Richmond and Barnard Castle, and within easy reach of Teesdale, Swaledale and Wensleydale, only an hour from the Lake District. The farm is one mile outside the village of Ravensworth with plenty of good eating places within easy reach. The traditional farmhouse offers guests' own lounge with large window overlooking the valley; diningroom; one double/family bedroom, one double en-suite room, one twin-bedded room and a single room. All have washbasins, tea/coffee facilities, heating and electric blankets. Children welcome. Sorry, no pets. Car essential. Bed and Breakfast from £9 includes light supper/bedtime drink. Reductions for children and Senior Citizens. Open all year.

RICHMOND. Mrs Annie Porter, Oxnop Hall, Low Oxnop, Gunnerside, Richmond DL11 6JJ (0748-86253). ✿✿ Working farm. Come and discover our beautiful dale and stay with us on our working hill farm with beef cattle and Swaledale sheep. Oxnop Hall is of historic interest, listed grade two, with mullioned windows and oak beams, standing in its own grounds with panoramic views. Situated in the Yorkshire Dales National Park, the heart of Herriot Country — an environmentally sensitive area which is renowned for its stone walls, barns and flora. All bedrooms are centrally heated and have tea/coffee making facilities; two rooms have en-suite facilities. Lounge with colour TV. Bed and Breakfast from £13 – £17; Evening Meal from £9.50. Reductions for children. Sorry, no pets. Brochure available.

RIPON near. Peter and Irene Foster, Lime Tree Farm, Hutts Lane, Grewelthorpe, Near Ripon HG4 3DA (Kirkby Malzeard [076-583] 450). ✿✿✿ Working farm, join in. Secluded Dales farm near Ripon where horses are bred; ideal for touring and visiting Yorkshire's many attractions. The farmhouse is almost 200 years old with exposed beams, oak panelling and open fires, clipped rugs, grandfather clocks etc, plus central heating throughout. All bedrooms are en-suite and have colour TV and tea/coffee making facilities. The diningroom has separate tables and guests have their own lounge with access to books and games. Full English Breakfast, good traditional home cooking with four course Evening Meal. Open all year. Bed and Breakfast from £13.50 (reductions for weekly stays). Evening Dinner £8.50. Brochure on request.

ROSEDALE. Mrs B. Brayshaw, Low Bell End Farm, Rosedale, Pickering YO18 8RE (Lastingham [075-15] 451). Working farm. The farm is situated in the North Yorkshire Moors National Park about 15 miles from the nearest seaside resort of Whitby. Scarborough and Bridlington are within easy reach, also York, Pickering and Helmsley, all places of historic interest. The farm, a 173 acre dairy and sheep farm, is one mile from the village of Rosedale Abbey and there are many lovely walks to be taken in the area. A car is essential with ample parking space. Sorry, no pets. One double, one bunk-bedded, one family rooms; bathroom and toilet; combined sitting/diningroom with colour TV. Children welcome at reduced rates. Cot, high chair, babysitting available. Central heating and open fires. Open May to September. Evening Dinner, Bed and Breakfast or Bed and Breakfast. Terms on request. Tourist Board registered.

ROSEDALE ABBEY. Mrs Alison Dale, Five Acre View, Rosedale, Near Pickering YO18 8RE (Lastingham [07515] 213). Working farm. This 150-acre dairy farm is within easy driving distance from Scarborough, Whitby, York and various leisure parks. Nearer to home there is a wide range of walks set in the North Yorkshire Moors National Park. A small golf course within walking distance is a challenge for any enthusiast. Three-quarters-of-a-mile of trout fishing is also nearby. The "Olde Worlde" farmhouse has all modern-day comforts and offers one family and two double rooms, all with washbasins, tea/coffee making facilities. The open-beamed lounge, complete with log fire, has colour TV and is comfortably furnished. Bed and Breakfast £10; Evening Meal £5. Reductions for children. Pets welcome. Yorkshire and Humberside Tourist Board listed.

ROSEDALE ABBEY. Mrs L. Dale, Sycamores Farm, Rosedale Abbey, Pickering YO18 8RE (Lastingham [07515] 448). ✿✿ Commended. Working farm, join in. Welcome to Sycamores Farm, a family-run dairy farm situated in one of the loveliest parts of the North Yorkshire Moors National Park, an ideal location for holidaymakers to walk, fish, ride, golf or visit places of interest including York, Pickering and Helmsley. Comfortable accommodation in two double bedrooms, one twin, all with washbasins and tea/coffee making facilities; bathroom, shower, toilet. Enjoy the panoramic views from the guest lounge (colour TV), and the superb cooking of Mrs Dale who specialises in evening meals. Children welcome at reduced rates (cot available). Pets accepted. Car essential, parking. Fire Certificate. Bed and Breakfast from £10; Evening Meal from £5. Open all year. Tourist Board listed.

ROSEDALE EAST. Maureen and John Harrison, Moordale House, Dale Head, Pickering YO18 8RH (Lastingham [07515] 219). ♥♥ Dating back to the mid 17th century Moordale House once served the local iron ore mining community as a grainery and general stores. Today after extensive refurbishment and modernisation Maureen and John offer you a visit they hope will remain in your heart and memory for years to come. Accommodation is available in three double en-suite rooms, one twin en-suite or two twin-bedded rooms with washbasins. All with tea/coffee making facilities. Full central heating. Separate shower room, bathroom and toilets. Guests are offered Bed and full English Breakfast, five course Evening Dinner optional in the spacious diningroom which benefits from magnificent views over the valley. Comfortable, relaxing lounge with open fire and colour TV. A family run licensed guest house offering good home cooking, every comfort and a happy, friendly atmosphere. Members of the Yorkshire and Humberside Tourist Board. Full Fire Certificate. Brochure and terms on request.

RYEDALE. Mrs Diane Peirson, Low Northolme Farm, Salton, York YO6 6RP (0751 32321). 18th century farmhouse, situated in the heart of Ryedale, between Helmsley and Kirkbymoorside. A working 250 acre arable farm with pigs and sheep. Accommodation comprises one en-suite family room and one en-suite twin room. Fully centrally heated. Sittingroom with colour TV and video, log fire during winter. Guests have use of kitchenette with tea/coffee making facilities, fridge and spin dryer. Close proximity to North Yorkshire Moors and York. Golf and pony trekking nearby. Ideal for a quiet holiday. Bed and Breakfast from £15 per person, Evening Meal available.

SANDSEND. Mrs Ann Hodgson, Low Farm, Dunsley, Whitby YO21 3TL (0947 83218). Low Farm is a working dairy and sheep farm, quietly situated in village of Dunsley, half a mile from good sandy beach, one mile from golf course, two miles from Whitby and five miles from North Yorkshire Moors Railway at Grosmont. Ideal base for touring Moors and coast. Ample car parking. Bed and Breakfast only offered in one double room; bathroom and toilet upstairs; private dining/sittingroom. Sorry, no pets. Open May to October. SAE for terms and further details.

SCARBOROUGH. Mrs Andrea Wood, Wrea Head House, Wrea Head Farm, Barmoor Lane, Scalby, Scarborough YO13 0PB (0723 375844) You are always assured of a warm welcome at Wrea Head Farm. We are situated in a beautiful location with outstanding coastal and country views on the edge of the North York Moors National Park, and only three miles from Scarborough. All bedrooms are en-suite with colour TV, tea/coffee making facilities. Ample parking. Laundry. Pay phone. Lawns. No smoking, please. Sorry, no pets. Open all year. Bed and Breakfast from £15. Self catering accommodation also available. Yorkshire and Humberside Tourist Board member.

SCARBOROUGH. Mrs E. Stafford, Wheatcroft Mini Motel, Filey Road, Scarborough YO11 3AA (Scarborough [0723] 374613). Small unlicensed Motel offering en-suite bedrooms (shower/toilet), each with colour TV, kettle, drinks facilities (biscuits provided), radio alarm, direct-dial telephone, hair dryer, central heating and colour co-ordinated furnishings. Ample parking for guests. Good Continental breakfasts are served to specially constructed hatches in the rooms, giving guests privacy and flexibility. Situated on the South Cliff (A165) away from town centre traffic. Convenient for the sea and for visiting Whitby, Robin Hood's Bay, Filey, Bridlington, York and ideal for exploring the North Yorks Moors. Open all year. Room and Breakfast from £13.75 per person. Brochure sent by return.

WHEN MAKING ENQUIRIES PLEASE MENTION
FARM HOLIDAY GUIDES

SCARBOROUGH. Mrs D.M. Medd, Hilford House, Crossgates, Scarborough YO12 4JU (Scar-

borough [0723] 862262). Detached country guest house, quietly situated in own grounds adjoining Scarborough — Seamer road just off A64. Near Scarborough, but handy for touring all coast and countryside of North Yorkshire. Three double, one single and one family bedrooms all with washbasins and central heating. Bathroom, two toilets; diningroom with separate tables and guests' lounge with colour TV. Cot, high chair and babysitting available. Full fire certificate held. Open all year round. Personal supervision ensures complete satisfaction of guests. Own home grown fruit and vegetables served in season, also fresh Scarborough cod and local meats. Private car parking. Bed and Breakfast from £12; Evening Dinner, Bed and Breakfast from £17. Reductions for children sharing. Member of English Tourist Board.

SCARBOROUGH near. Mrs June Simpson, Hazel Hall Farm, Snainton, Near Scarborough YO13

9PN (Scarborough [0723] 85413). ✿ ✿ Working farm. Stonebuilt in 1700, Hazel Hall is situated on the hillside with panoramic views of the Vale of Pickering. Forest drives north to purple moors, sea to the east and ancient York to the west. Although a working farm with its accompanying tractors the orchard, garden and swimming pool encourage relaxation. Hazel Hall has been discreetly modernised for comfort, without spoiling its old world charm. Fire Certificate held. Each family room has its own shower and WC. Mrs Simpson personally prepares the farmhouse cooking and helps her guests to plan their daily itinerary. Evening Meal, Bed and Breakfast from £100 per week.

SEDBERGH. Jo Woolley, East Mudbecks, Garsdale Head, Sedbergh LA10 5PW (05396-21328). Set amidst beautiful countryside within sight of the North Yorkshire and Cumbrian border, the house stands off the main A684 road from Wensleydale to Kendal. It is convenient for access to both the Dales and Lakes. Garsdale Station on the Settle and Carlisle railway line is just over a quarter-of-a-mile distant, giving a scenic journey to Carlisle, Leeds or intermediate stations. The Moorcock Inn is just a short walk away. East Mudbecks offers a friendly welcome with comfortable accommodation including residents' lounge/diningroom. Open all year except Christmas. Children welcome. Sorry, no pets. Bed and Breakfast £12 per person. Lunch and Dinner also available.

SEDBERGH. Mrs Marlene Williamson, Ivy Dene, Gawthrop, Dent, Sedbergh LA10 5TA (Dent [058-75] 353). Ivy Dene is situated in the Yorkshire Dales within easy reach of the glorious Lake District and ten miles from the M6. Ideal centre for walking and only half-a-mile from the picturesque village of Dent with its cobbled streets. Accommodation comprises two double and one family bedrooms, with washbasins; bathroom; cosy sittingroom with coal fire and TV/diningroom. All home cooking and baking is served. Sorry, no pets. Children welcome at reduced rates. Car essential — parking. Open March to November for Evening Dinner/Meal, Bed and Breakfast or Bed and Breakfast. Terms on request. Also holiday cottage to let.

SETTLE. Mrs L.J. Gorst, Hollin Hall Farm, Rathmell, Settle BS24 0AJ (Settle [072-92] 2523). Working farm. Ideal for touring Dales and other Yorkshire beauty spots, Hollin Hall is a sheep and beef cattle farm of 108 acres in a quiet position overlooking the Ribble Valley two and a half miles from Settle. To reach us, take the Rathmell Exit off the Settle bypass and we are on the right before Rathmell Village. Within easy reach of the Trough of Bowland and the Lake District. Homely and friendly atmosphere and guests are made welcome from Easter to October. Two double-bedded rooms with washbasins, one twin-bedded room. Bathroom, toilet. Sittingroom; diningroom with separate tables where good home-cooked breakfasts are served. Children welcome at reduced rates. Sorry, no pets. Car essential, ample parking. Garden. SAE, please for terms for Bed and Breakfast.

NEW INN
Clapham, Near Settle
North Yorkshire LA2 8HH

Tel: 046-85 203

ETB ♕♕♕

Member of Wayfarer Inns

Keith and Barbara Mannion invite you to their friendly eighteenth century residential coaching inn in the picturesque Dales village of Clapham. Ideal centre for walking the three peaks of Ingleborough, Pen-y-ghent and Whernside. Kendal and Skipton 21 miles. All rooms have full en-suite facilities, colour television and tea/coffee facilities. Enjoy good wholesome Yorkshire food in our restaurant or bar meals in either of our two bars. Dogs welcome. **Ring Barbara for full details.**

SKIPTON. Mrs C.E. Crabtree, Bolton Park Farm, Bolton Abbey, Near Skipton BD23 6AW (Bolton Abbey [075 671] 244). Working farm. A friendly welcome is assured at this 1000 acre working farm, mainly beef and sheep, set amongst some of the finest views and walks in Wharfedale. Within easy travelling distance of other well-known places of interest in the Dales such as Ilkley, seven miles, Haworth (Bronte country) 16 miles, and York, 40 miles. Accommodation comprises one family room, twin-bedded room, and two double rooms, all with H&C; separate lounge and diningroom. Children and babies welcome, some reduced prices. Open May to end October. Bed and Breakfast from £11 per person per night. Light supper included. Recommended by "Traveller's Britain", the guide featured by BBC TV "Holiday" programme. ETB listed.

Bolton Park Farm

SKIPTON. Mrs Christine Clarkson, Bondcroft Farm, Embsay, Skipton BD23 6SF (0756 793371). Bondcroft Farm is a working dairy and sheep farm in the Yorkshire Dales with excellent walks and car drives in all directions. Everyone is welcomed with a cup of tea or coffee on arrival. Mrs Clarkson is an excellent cook and serves all homemade produce. An information pack is sent to you on request telling about all the interesting things to do and see. Open Easter to October. Bed and Breakfast from £12 to £13.

SKIPTON. The Proprietor, Tudor House, Bell Busk, Skipton BD23 4DT (Airton [07293] 301). A converted country railway station on the Leeds-Settle-Carlisle line. The building is centrally heated throughout and the comfortable accommodation comprises three double, one twin, one family and one single rooms, some with en-suite facilities, and all with tea/coffee makers. Lounge with colour TV and games room. Trains regularly pass the diningroom which was once the station platform. Fire Certificate. Residential licence. Ample parking. Extensive gardens overlooking Malhamdale and bordering on the Yorkshire Dales National Park. Within easy reach of Harrogate, York and Bronte Country. Bed and Breakfast from £12.50 with Evening Meal an optional extra. Picnic lunches. Brochure and tariff on request. Tourist Board registered, AA recommended.

TUDOR HOUSE
BELL BUSK
SKIPTON.

SKIPTON near. Mrs J. Robinson, Lindon House, Airton, Near Skipton BD23 4BE (07293 418). Situated between Gargrave and Malham off the A65, Lindon House is converted from an old barn, set in the Yorkshire Dales with beautiful views. Family-run establishment with friendly atmosphere and good home cooking. Evening Meal optional. All bedrooms have washbasins; bathroom/shower room and three toilets. Tea/coffee making facilities in each room. TV lounge and diningroom. Licensed. Superb home cooking, vegetarians catered for.

SLINGSBY. Mrs P.E. Paylor, Holme Lea Farm, Green Dyke Lane, Slingsby, York YO6 7AU (0653 628 753). Farmhouse set in a pretty village near North Yorkshire Moors, near to coast and historic Castle Howard, the North Yorkshire Dales (Herriot country). Golf, fishing and riding nearby. One double, one twin and two single rooms, all with washbasins and central heating. Access to rooms at all times. Sittingroom with colour TV. Late night drink included in price. Ample parking space. Full English Breakfast. Regret, no children under 12. Open early May to October. Bed and Breakfast only. Telephone for terms.

SUTTON BANK. Mrs K. Hope, High House Farm, Sutton Bank, Thirsk YO7 2HA (0845 597557). ⬥⬥ Approved. **Working farm.** Family-run dairy and sheep farm lies in idyllic surroundings on the Hambleton Hills half way between Thirk and Helmsley just half a mile from Sutton Bank and just three-quarters of an hour's ride from North Yorks Moors and Dales, York 22 miles. Magnificent views and walks. Comfortable, well furnished house with washbasins and tea/coffee making facilities in bedrooms — one double, one family. Bathroom, separate toilet. Large lounge and diningroom. Mid-week bookings accepted. Good food and warm hospitality. Bed and Breakfast £12; Evening Dinner optional. SAE for further details.

SWALEDALE. Mrs G. Allison, Telfit Farm, Marske, Richmond DL11 7NG (Richmond [0748] 3769). Working farm. Telfit is a working hill farm set in a secluded valley of its own, surrounded by beautiful countryside. Ideal centre — Marske village three miles, Reeth and Richmond twenty minutes', Leyburn 10 miles, gateway to Swaledale and Wensleydale. The Yorkshire Dales provide good walking, with pony trekking at nearby Fremington. We offer a friendly, relaxed atmosphere with all home cooking. Centrally heated. Two double rooms. Diningroom with lounge and colour TV. Car essential. Dinner, Bed and Breakfast or Bed and Breakfast only. Rates on application. No pets please.

THIRSK. Mrs Tess Williamson, Thornborough House Farm, South Kilvington, Thirsk YO7 2NP (0845 522103). ⬥⬥ **Working farm.** This is "James Herriot's" town! Situated one and a half miles north of Thirsk, a warm welcome awaits you in this 200 year old farmhouse set in lovely countryside. Ideal location for a walking or touring holiday. The bedrooms are warm and comfortable: one family room en-suite, one double and one twin with washbasins. Guests' own sitting and diningroom with colour TV and open fire. Children most welcome. Babysitting available. Pets accepted. Good home cooking is a speciality; special diets catered for. Guests can choose to have Bed and Breakfast or Bed, Breakfast and Evening Meal. The North Yorks Moors, Pennine Dales, York, the East Coast, Scarborough, Whitby, Ripon, Fountains Abbey, Harrogate are all very near. Golf courses, fishing, horse riding available locally. Bed and Breakfast from £10.

THIRSK. Mrs S. Atkinson, Mill Cottage, South Kilvington, Thirsk YO7 2NL (Thirsk [0845] 522796). Lovely, large period cottage with oak beams and pantiled roof is situated in village one mile north of Thirsk overlooking Cleveland Hills. Easy access from A1, A19 and well situated for touring Yorkshire Dales, visiting City of York, Harrogate and the east coast resorts of Scarborough and Whitby. Three double bedrooms with washbasins, guests' bathroom with shower and toilet; sittingroom with colour TV; central heating; log fire. Open from Easter. Warm Yorkshire hospitality, delicious breakfast, tea trays provided. Bed and Breakfast is provided from £10.50 per person per night; Evening Meal available on request. Delightful large garden. Ample private parking. Please phone Mrs Atkinson for further information.

THIRSK. Mrs Helen G. Proudley, Doxford House, 73 Front Street, Sowerby, Thirsk YO7 1JP (Thirsk [0845] 523238.) ⬥⬥ Approved. A warm welcome awaits guests at this handsome Georgian house which overlooks the greens in Sowerby, a delightful village one mile south of Thirsk (James Herriot's Darrowby). Centrally situated for touring the North York Moors and the Dales National Park; within easy reach of York, Harrogate and the East Coast; places of interest include Coxwold, Shandy Hall, Newbrough Priory with beautiful lake and gardens. Ideal walking and riding countryside. Golf at Thirsk. Accommodation has full central heating, all bedrooms have private bath and/or shower, WC, and tea/coffee making facilities; one ground floor bedroom suitable for the disabled. Residents' lounge with colour TV, diningroom, separate games room with snooker, table tennis and darts. Large garden with a paddock

DOXFORD HOUSE

and friendly animals. Children and pets welcome. Cot, high chair, babysitting available. Open all year. Bed and Breakfast from £12.50; Evening Meal £7. Reductions for children and weekly bookings.

WENSLEYDALE. Mr and Mrs A.K. Butterworth, "Greystone", Preston-under-Scar, Near Leyburn DL8 4AQ (Wensleydale [0969] 22042). "Greystone" is a small, comfortable guest house in a peaceful little village (just off the Wensley to Castle Bolton road). Ideal for walks or drives in an area ("Herriot Country") rich in flowers, birds and history. Richmond, Swaledale, Reeth and Hawes are within a half hour's drive. Beautiful, panoramic views are enjoyed from both bedrooms (one double, one twin), with washbasins, tea/making facilities; the twin-bedded room with shower. Cot available. Lounge with colour TV; diningroom. Dogs accepted. Evening Meal with interesting and varied menu (including vegetarian) £6. Bed and Breakfast from £10. Weekly terms available. ETB registered.

WHITBY. Mrs Marion N. Cockrem, Dale End Farm, Green End, Goathland, Whitby YO22 5LJ (Whitby [0947] 85371). Working farm. Comfortable 17th century stone built farmhouse on a moorland farm of 135 acres with sheep, cows, pigs, poultry, etc. We also keep rare breeds of animals, including Vietnamese pot bellied pigs. Situated in the North Yorkshire Moors National Park, making an ideal location for walking, touring and fishing. One double and two family bedrooms, with washbasins, divan beds, bedside lights. The guests' lounge is furnished with antiques, horse brasses, oak beams and inglenook fireplace; TV; background central heating; diningroom, separate tables, serving generous portions of home-produced food with variety in menus. Pets allowed. Children welcome, cot and babysitting. Children's playground. Mrs Cockrem offers hospitality with every home comfort and Dale End Farm is open all year for Bed, Breakfast and Evening Meal from £16 or just Bed and Breakfast. ETB registered. SAE please.

WHITBY. Mrs Doreen Lister, Yew Grange, Glaisdale, Whitby YO21 2PZ (Whitby [0947] 87352). Working farm. Guests are welcome on this 110 acre mixed farm in an ideal location for walking or touring. Whitby 10 miles, and there are many local beauty spots and places of interest within easy reach including North York Moors Steam Railway, Folk Museum at Hutton-le-Hole and the famous City of York. Home produced vegetables and meat are served when available and visitors receive personal and friendly attention. Morning tea and bedtime drink included. One double, one single and one twin bedrooms; bathroom and toilet; sittingroom with TV, diningroom. Sorry, no pets. Car essential, ample parking. Phone or SAE, please, for terms.

WHITBY. Mrs Jean Lister, Browside Farm, Glaisdale, Whitby YO21 2PZ (Whitby [0947] 87228).

Working farm. This 70 acre dairy and mixed farm is 10 miles from the historic coastal town of Whitby. Surrounded by the beautiful North Yorkshire Moors, it is an ideal area for walking. Hutton-le-Hole, Egton Bridge and the North Yorkshire Moors Railway at Grosmont are all within easy reach. A warm friendly atmosphere is assured, with home grown produce from a large garden, our own meat and free range eggs. Accommodation comprises one double and one family bedroom, one with washbasin; bathroom and toilet; diningroom; sittingroom with TV. No pets please. Car essential — parking. Evening Meal, Bed and Breakfast or Bed and Breakfast only. SAE, please, for terms.

WHITBY near. Mrs Avril Mortimer, Hollins Farm, Glaisdale, Whitby YO21 2PZ (0947 87516). Hollins Farm is a smallholding ten miles from the historic coastal town of Whitby, surrounded by beautiful countryside and moorland with lovely walks. Places of interest include Moors Steam Railway, Pickering market town and castle, many scenic villages such as Hutton-le-Hole with its extensive museum, the quaint fishing port of Robin Hood's Bay and a host of others. Choice of pony trekking centres in the vicinity. The 16th century character farmhouse provides comfortable accommodation comprising one large family or double room (sleeps four/five) another large family room (sleeps three plus cot), both with washbasins; also twin-bedded room. Tea/coffee making facilities. Bathroom; sitting/diningroom with colour TV, sun lounge. In winter there are peat and log fires to enjoy. Cot, high chair and babysitting available. Reduced rates for children who will enjoy the farmyard pets. Access to rooms at all times. Bed and Breakfast with optional Evening Meal. Home produced meats and vegetables. Open all year. Phone or send SAE for terms.

WHITBY near. Mrs Pat Beale, Ryedale House, Coach Road, Sleights, Near Whitby YO22 5EQ (0947

810534). Friendly non-smoking Yorkshire house of charm and character at the foot of the moors amid magnificent scenery; picturesque villages, harbours, beaches, two scenic railways, walking in all directions. Whitby three and a half miles. Well equipped bedrooms on first floor (one twin, one single, one double and one double bedsittingroom and single bed); bath/shower/toilet; shower/toilet and ground floor toilet; TV lounge with guide books; light airy diningroom (separate tables) with breathtaking views over Esk Valley. Enjoy our south facing sun terrace and gardens. Noted for good Yorkshire fare in variety; Pat does the cooking (traditional, vegetarian or diet menus) and daughter Rosie is your waitress. Flexible mealtimes, packed lunches, modest prices — everything you want! Car parking, also ample public transport near. Regret, no pets or children under three years. Bed and Breakfast £11.75–£12.75 per night; Evening Meal £6.50. Weekly reductions. Over 60's Bed, Breakfast and Evening Meal holidays special rates spring and autumn. Established 15 years, member of Yorkshire and Humberside Tourist Board and Whitby Hotel and Catering Association.

YORK. Mrs Janet M. Foster, Grange Farm, Bulmer, York YO6 7BN (065381 376). Grange Farm is very much a family farm which is part of Castle Howard (Brideshead) Estate. It is ideally situated for just relaxing in beautiful countryside or exploring North Yorkshire. We have a double/family room, twin rooms and one single room. Lounge with TV. Large garden. Many short walks over the farm. Full English Breakfast. Bed and Breakfast from £11 per person. Tourist Board registered.

YORK. Mrs Jackie Cundall, Welgarth House, Wetherby Road, Rufforth, York YO2 3QB (Rufforth [0904-83] 592 and 595). ♥ ♥ AA Listed. Welgarth House is an individual and most attractive detached house, situated in the delightful village of Rufforth (B1224), five minutes' drive from the historic city of York. Ideal touring base for the North Yorkshire Moors, the Yorkshire Dales and East Coast resorts. All rooms have vanity units, colour TV, tea/coffee making facilities and central heating. En-suite facilities also available. Residents' lounge and separate diningroom. Terms from £13, reductions early and late season. Self-catering holidays are also available, and shooting, fishing and gliding holidays can be arranged. Personal atttention is assured at all times. Telephone or write for a brochure.

YORK. Alan Wright, Grimston House, Deighton, York YO4 6HB (0904 87328). Warm and friendly atmosphere. Set in lovely countryside, four miles from York. Convenient for bus service. All rooms have washbasin, central heating, colour TV and tea/coffee making facilities. Family rooms available. Private parking. Ideal touring base. Within walking distance of pub and restaurant which serves excellent meals. Bed and Breakfast from £13 to £16.

`See also Colour Display Advertisement` **YORK. Mrs Brenda Lazenby, Rossmoor Park, Melbourne, York YO4 4SZ (0759 318410).** Rossmoor Park is a lovely new farmhouse standing in large gardens amidst 30 acres green fields and woodland. 10 miles from York. Accommodation is offered to guests in three luxury en-suite rooms with colour TV, central heating and tea/coffee facilities. There are separate tables in the diningroom which overlooks gardens, park and woodland. Children are welcome. There is swimming, riding and fishing available locally. Lovely woodland walks on the farm with lots of wildlife. Within easy reach of Yorkshire coast, moors, wolds and Dales. Open all year except Christmas. Bed and Breakfast from £15 per person with reductions for children.

`See also Colour Display Advertisement` **YORK. Mrs W. Dale, The Manor Country Guest House, Acaster Malbis, York YO2 1YL (York [0904] 706723, 9am to 9pm).** The Manor is situated near the River Ouse in six acres of delightful woodland gardens. Only four and a half miles from the city of York and ideally situated for touring Yorkshire. 12 bedrooms, some en-suite and all with tea/coffee making facilities. One ground floor room suitable for the disabled. Stairlifts to both floors. Large TV lounge with open coal fire. Unlicensed. Car parking facilities. For details and brochure send SAE or telephone. Overseas enquiries, send four International Reply Coupons.

YORK. Mrs F. Heels, Sandfield Farm, Murton, York YO3 9XF (York [0904] 489919). Guests are welcomed to a small, family-run working farm. Open all year except December 20th – 27th. Approximately four and a half miles from York, within easy reach of many places of interest. Jorvik Viking Centre, Railway Museum, the Coast, North Yorkshire Moors. Comfortable, homely farmhouse with one double bedroom, one small family bedroom with cot if required, and one triple bedroom. Bathroom, toilet. Lounge with colour TV for visitors; separate diningroom. Home produce served. Children very welcome, babysitting arranged if required. Pets accepted free of charge by prior arrangement. Car essential — parking. Public transport one mile. Bed and Breakfast from £12; Evening Meals by arrangement £6. Reduced rates for children under 12 years. Snacks available, tea-making facilities available in all rooms. Central heating. Tourist Board Listed.

YORK. Mrs Gill, Moreby Grange Farm, Stillingfleet, York YO4 6HW (Escrick [090487] 265). For those wishing to visit York and the surrounding areas, Moreby Grange Farm is ideally situated on the B1222 road midway between the villages of Naburn and Stillingfleet. The historic city of York is just seven miles away; York Races and Fulford Golf Course are within easy reach. Accommodation consists of two family and three double rooms, all with vanity units; two bathrooms and three toilets; guest lounge with colour TV. Full central heating. Ample private parking. Fire Certificate. Bed and Breakfast from £12. Member of the Greater York Association of Hotels and Guest Houses.

YORK. Keith Jackman, Dairy Guesthouse, 3 Scarcroft Road, York YO2 1ND (0904 639367). The Dairy Guest House is a tastefully renovated Victorian town house offering thoughtfully planned and individually styled rooms. Situated only 200 yards south of the Medieval City Walls, it is within easy walking distance of the city centre. Decoration and furnishings are in the style of "Habitat — Sandersons — Laura Ashley", tastefully enhanced by plants and natural pine. All bedrooms have colour TV, hot drinks facilities, washbasin and information folders. Some have en-suite bath/shower room, one of which is at ground floor level. The house is centrally heated and has a lovely enclosed courtyard. Breakfast choice ranges from traditional English to wholefood/vegetarian. Highly Recommended. Bed and Breakfast from £13.

DAIRY

GUESTHOUSE
Traditional and Wholefood

YORK. Mrs D.S. Tindall, Newton Guest House, Neville Street, Haxby Road, York YO3 7NP (0904 635627). Diana and John offer all their guests a friendly and warm welcome to their Victorian town house, 10 minutes' walk from York Minster, the City Walls and town centre. The house is situated near an attractive park with good bowling greens. York is within easy reach of Moors, Dales and coast. All bedrooms have washbasins, private showers, colour TV and tea-making facilities. Bathroom, two toilets. Central heating. Breakfast cooked to guests' requirements. Reduced rates for under 12s sharing a room with two adults. Fire Certificate. Private parking provided. Tourist Board listed.

YORK. Mrs Cynthia Fell, The Hall Country Guest House, Slingsby, York YO6 7AL (Hovingham [065-382] 375 changing to 065-3628 375). 🐦🐦🐦 The Hall is a Regency house of character set in five acres of delightful grounds, with croquet lawn and stream, situated in a 'real' English village with a ruined castle. A genuine Yorkshire welcome awaits every guest, many of whom return year after year. Excellent varied cuisine with fresh produce. Ideally situated for visiting York, the North Yorks Moors, coast and also stately homes such as Castle Howard (three miles). We also have bicycles for hire. Five double rooms, two family and one single. Some with showers. Five en-suite. A car is essential. Ample parking. Brochure available. Open Easter to October. Table Licence. Bed and Breakfast from approximately £14; Dinner, Bed and Breakfast from £22 (£115 weekly).

YORK. Mrs J. Fowler, Holtby Grange, Holtby, York YO3 9XQ (York [0904] 489933). 🐦🐦 **Working farm.** Holtby Grange is a 90 acre arable farm set in peaceful countryside and guests are welcome to walk around. York is easily reached, being only five miles away, and the two main roads (A64 and A166) provide easy access to coast, moors and historic places of interest. Hearty Yorkshire breakfasts and tasty evening meals are served in the separate diningroom. Other facilities include full central heating, a spacious lounge open fire when needed, and colour TV. One family, one twin and one double bedrooms, all with washbasins, shaver sockets, electric blankets and teasmades; bathroom with electric shower, two toilets. Large attractive gardens. Pets allowed, but not in house. Cot, high chair provided, and reduced rates for children under 14 sharing parents' room. Babysitting if required. Car essential, parking. Open from April to October. 10 per cent reduction on a full week's booking of Bed, Breakfast and Evening Meal (adults only), or 5 per cent discount on Bed and Breakfast only. Bed, Breakfast and Evening Meal from £15 per person; Bed and Breakfast only £10. Minimum stay two nights. Send stamp only for brochure or telephone for further details.

YORK. Mrs M.J. Robinson, The Grange Farm, Oak Busk Lane, Flaxton, York YO6 7RL (Flaxton Moor [090-486] 219). 🐦🐦 **Working farm.** OPEN ALL YEAR FOR BED AND BREAKFAST. Family-run working farm, 10 minutes from York going towards MALTON on A64, turn left for FLAXTON; pass through village, turn right down Oak Busk Lane. Centrally heated, modernised farmhouse set in its own garden, midway between LONDON and EDINBURGH. All bedrooms have tea-making facilities, washbasins, electric blankets, razor points; twin room has en-suite bathroom/shower; three toilets; TV lounge; separate tables in breakfast room. Ample free parking. Meals available locally. Flemish spoken. Bed and full Breakfast from £11 to £13 per person. Children at reduced price if sharing parents' room. SAE please or telephone between 5.00 pm and 8.00 pm.

YORK. Mrs K.R. Daniel, Ivy House Farm, Kexby, York YO4 5LQ (0904 489368). Working farm. Bed

and Breakfast on a mixed dairy farm six miles from the ancient city of York on the A1079. Central for the east coast, Herriot country and dales. We offer a friendly service with comfortable accommodation consisting of double or family rooms. We provide a full farmhouse English Breakfast served in separate diningroom; colour TV lounge. Ample car parking with play area for children, who are most welcome. We are within easy reach of local restaurants and public houses serving excellent evening meals. AA and RAC listed.

YORK. Mrs P. Stockhill, Marina House, Naburn, York YO1 4RW (York [0904] 627365) Off A19, superior accommodation overlooking York Marina and the River Ouse. Guests are offered a pleasant stay in country surroundings, yet only two and a half miles from the city of York. Superior accommodation with tastefully furnished and decorated rooms. Some have private bathroom or shower, all have central heating. Tea/coffee available throughout the day. Brochure available on request. ETB registered, RAC listed.

YORK. Mrs C.M. Farnell, Beech Tree House Farm, South Holme, Slingsby, York YO6 7BA

(Hovingham [0653] 628257). Working farm. A 260-acre farm with arable crops, cattle, sheep, pigs, poultry, dogs and cats. Situated in a peaceful valley five miles north of Castle Howard, central for York, North Yorkshire Moors, Dales, Yorkshire coastline and Flamingo Park Zoo. Accommodation comprises three double bedrooms (one twin-bedded, one single/bunk room); two guest bathrooms; diningroom; lounge with log fire; snooker/games room and large garden. Children welcome at reduced rates; cot, high chair, baby-sitting available. Tourist Board inspected. Sorry, no pets. Car essential. Open all year except Christmas. Bed and Breakfast £11; Bed, Breakfast and Evening Meal £17. Home cooking — fresh vegetables. SAE, please, for terms.

YORK. Miss Emma Swiers, Fir Tree Farmhouse, Thormanby, Easingwold, York YO6 3NN (0845

401201 or 401220). Attractive 19th century farmhouse situated in the small village of Thormanby in the beautiful countryside of the Vale of York. Three large bedrooms decorated in traditional farmhouse style. An excellent base for touring the charming market towns of Thirsk, Helmsley and Ripon as well as the famous Roman city of York. A very pretty sittingroom with colour TV is available for guests as well as outdoor pursuits such as tennis and riding. The Yorkshire Dales and the North Yorkshire Moors are only 30 minutes away. Open all year except Christmas. Full English Breakfast. Children and pets welcome. SAE for terms or telephone.

YORKSHIRE DALES. Mr and Mrs W.E. Chaney, New Laithe House, Wood Lane, Grassington, Skipton BD23 5LU (0756 752764).

New Laithe House

BED & BREAKFAST

♨ ♨ ♨ New Laithe House is a converted barn situated in the heart of Wharfedale. There is a private car park where you can leave your car and go walking or fishing for the day and enjoy the scenery on foot. Grassington is the ideal base for visiting the many historic towns in north and west Yorkshire. The rooms have lovely views of woodlands and the river Wharfe. There are three spacious bedrooms en-suite, two rooms with showers and washbasins, two family rooms with washbasins. All rooms have colour TV, tea making facilities and central heating. Children welcome. Sorry, no pets. Terms are from £15 to £18 per person.

If you've found
FARM HOLIDAY GUIDES
of service please tell your friends

YORKSHIRE DALES (Horton-in-Ribblesdale). Mr and Mrs Colin and Joan Horsfall, Studfold House, Horton-in-Ribblesdale, Near Settle BD24 0ER (Horton-in-Ribblesdale [07296] 200). ❦ ❦ This Georgian house, standing in one acre of beautiful gardens, has panoramic views and is near the Three Peaks in the Dales National Park. The house is an ideal centre for visiting the Dales, Lake District and Bronte country. There are oak beams in most rooms and there is full central heating. The two double and one family bedrooms have washbasins, colour TV and tea/coffee making facilities. Open all year except Christmas. Vegetarians, children and pets also welcome. Reduced rates for children sharing rooms. Mountain bikes for hire. Pub half a mile away. Bed and Breakfast from £12; four course Evening Meal £6. Also available, self-catering unit. SAE for brochure.

WEST YORKSHIRE

HOLMFIRTH near. Mrs Sue Smith, Marsh Croft, Marsh Hall Lane, Thurstonland, Huddersfield HD4 6XD (Huddersfield [0484] 665181). Peaceful, unspoilt West Yorkshire village nestling on a ridge overlooking the lovely Holme Valley (the heart of "Summer Wine" country) and the Pennine hills beyond. Scenic walks abound in this conservation area, which is ideally situated within easy reach of the Peak District (Chatsworth House), the splendour of the South Pennines and also historic Bronte country. Marsh Croft is a modern house set in large attractive gardens. Accommodation includes one twin-bedded room with adjoining luxury private bathroom and large double-bedded room with en-suite shower facilities. Both rooms on ground floor and a delightful sittingroom and diningroom are available for guests' use. Delicious home cooking is a speciality, often with own garden produce in season. Bed and Breakfast from £12.50. Evening Meal £10 (four courses plus aperitif). Sorry, no pets. No smoking. Children over 10 years welcome. Brochure available.

FOR THE MUTUAL GUIDANCE OF GUEST AND HOST

Every year literally thousands of holidays, short-breaks and overnight stops are arranged through our guides, the vast majority without any problems at all. In a handful of cases, however, difficulties do arise about bookings, which often could have been prevented from the outset.

It is important to remember that when accommodation has been booked, both parties — guests and hosts — have entered into a form of contract. We hope that the following points will provide helpful guidance.

GUESTS: When enquiring about accommodation, be as precise as possible. Give exact dates, numbers in your party and the ages of any children. State the number and type of rooms wanted and also what catering you require — bed and breakfast, full board, etc. Make sure that the position about evening meals is clear — and about pets, reductions for children or any other special points.

Read our reviews carefully to ensure that the proprietors you are going to contact can supply what you want. Ask for a letter confirming all arrangements, if possible.

If you have to cancel, do so as soon as possible. Proprietors do have the right to retain deposits and under certain circumstances to charge for cancelled holidays if adequate notice is not given and they cannot re-let the accommodation.

HOSTS: Give details about your facilities and about any special conditions. Explain your deposit system clearly and arrangements for cancellations, charges, etc, and whether or not your terms include VAT.

If for any reason you are unable to fulfil an agreed booking without adequate notice, you may be under an obligation to arrange alternative suitable accommodation or to make some form of compensation.

While every effort is made to ensure accuracy, we regret that FHG Publications cannot accept responsibility for errors, omissions or misrepresentation in our entries or any consequences thereof. Prices in particular should be checked because we go to press early. We will follow up complaints but cannot act as arbiters or agents for either party.

ISLE OF WIGHT

GATCOMBE. Mrs D. Harvey, Newbarn Farm, Gatcombe, Near Newport PO30 3EQ (0983 721202).

NEWBARN FARM
GATCOMBE, I.W.

Working farm. This 245 acre farm is situated in a secluded downland valley in the centre of the island. Ideal for walking but a car is essential in order to fully enjoy the attractions and beaches. Accommodation is in two double rooms — one with extra bed and both with washbasins, razor points and tea making facilities. Lounge with colour TV. Children over 10 years very welcome. Sorry, no pets. SAE, please, for terms and brochure.

LAKE. Mrs B. Lawson, Lowood Lodge, 5 Cliff Gardens, Lake, Sandown PO36 8PJ (0983 405550). Lowood is situated in the peaceful surroundings of Sandown Bay, off the beaten track, near amenities and close to the famous Cliff Path. Home cooking is our speciality with a real warmth of hospitality. There are no restrictions and our garden can be a restful haven. Children and pets welcome. Lounge with colour TV, diningroom (separate tables), tea-making facilities and car parking. One double room with shower on first floor and two double rooms on ground floor. Fire Certificate. Bed and Breakfast from £9; Bed, Breakfast and Evening Meal from £12.50 (weekly terms available). Open all year. Brochure on request, appropriate discounts.

RYDE. Mrs M.J. Long, The Brambles, Gatehouse Lane, Upton Cross, Ryde PO33 4BS (Isle of Wight [0983] 65556). Private farmhouse accommodation, one mile from Ryde, in a lovely scenic area. Two double rooms and one family room, all with hot and cold water; two bathrooms with showers; lounge with colour TV; separate dining room. Children welcome; babysitting can be arranged. Very homely atmosphere, with good home cooking and a warm welcome to all our visitors. Open all year, with log fires and electric blankets in winter. Bed and Breakfast from £10 per night. Children under 12 half price if sharing parents' room.

CHANNEL ISLANDS

GUERNSEY

GUERNSEY, ST. SAMPSONS. Misses K.O. and N.A. Dennis, Duvaux Farm, Duvaux Road, St. Sampsons, Guernsey (Guernsey [0488] 44022). A holiday home from home, ideally situated for beach jaunts and outings. This typical Guernsey farmhouse (a listed ancient monument), occupied by the same family for hundreds of years, has a rare antique atmosphere and historical links with Guernsey City, Ohio, USA. Four double bedrooms; bathroom, inside and outside toilets; sittingroom and diningroom. Coal and electric heating. Cot and high chair can be hired. Sorry, no pets. Open from May to October. The owners, who live in the house, will provide the food for guests to cook their own breakfast, but food for other meals must be bought and prepared as required. Terms approximately £8 per person per day.

VILLAGE INNS

DEVON, NEWTON ABBOT near. Clay Cutters Arms, Chudleigh Knighton, Near Newton Abbot TQ13 0EY (0626 853345). Highly recommended in the Good Food Guide and the CAMRA Real Ale Guide, this cosy pub provides good food, draught ale and comfortable bed and breakfast. The candlelit restaurant offers a full à la carte menu, as well as traditional Sunday lunches. Interesting bar snacks are also available. Open log fires, live music and traditional pub games all contribute to the friendly atmosphere. Drinks may also be enjoyed outside in the sun garden. Private parties and wedding receptions, etc are catered for — please enquire. Off the A38, take the B3344 between Chudleigh and Bovey Tracey — Find us at the centre of Chudleigh Knighton village near the church and school.

NORTHUMBERLAND, HEXHAM. Mr and Mrs R. Rowland, Battlesteads Hotel, Wark-on-Tyne, Hexham NE48 3LS (0434 230209). Well placed for those wishing to visit unspoilt Northumberland is this comfortable little hotel run by resident proprietors Robert and Doris Rowland, offering service which is both friendly and efficent. The perfect place to enjoy a pleasant break. All eight en-suite bedrooms are well appointed and spick and span, and the hotel offers an excellent base for those wishing to visit Hadrian's Wall, the Kielder reservoir and forest, historic castles and houses, and the nearby beauty spots and places of interest.

THE WHITE HART
Fore Street, Castle Cary BA7 7BQ
Telephone: 0963 50255

17th century Coaching Inn, beautifully renovated, noted for good home cooking, comfortably appointed accommodation and convivial company. Delightfully placed for half-day visits to many beauty spots and places of historic interest. One hour's drive to the coast. Bed and Breakfast from £14 per night, with reductions for a stay of a week or more.

For further information contact The White Hart's welcoming hosts, CHARLIE & FIONA ANDERSON.

SURREY, CHIDDINGFOLD. Crown Inn, The Green, Chiddingfold GU8 4TX (0428 682255). Built in 1253, this ancient hostelry is thought to have played host to Edward VI and Queen Elizabeth I as well as the travelling pilgrims and Cistercian monks for whose shelter it was originally intended. Today's discerning traveller will find beautifully appointed guestrooms offering rest and overnight comfort, some with sumptuous four-poster beds and all with TV and traditional decor. Candlelight is reflected from the polished wood panelling of the restaurant where an extensive wine list complements quality cuisine, and the Huntsman Bar is a popular venue for lighter lunches and snacks. Traditional cream teas are served on the terrace, or, in inclement weather in the cosy lounge.

The Shambles, York, a perfectly preserved medieval street once used by butchers.

SELF-CATERING HOLIDAYS

LONDON

ORSETT VILLAGE. The Cottages, Orsett Village. Cottages sleep 6. ♀ ♀ ♀ ♀ ♀ *Commended.* **Working**

farm. Two delightful cottages situated just 22 miles from the heart of London, yet quietly nestled in the centre of a pretty Essex village. The cottages with spacious lounges, modern fully equipped kitchens and bathrooms won the AA Regional Holiday Home of the Year Award in 1988 and are Tourist Board commended. Each is equipped with telephone, automatic washing machine, dishwasher, central heating, all linen, games, toys and tourist information. Golf, horse riding, sailing, windsurfing, fishing, swimming and tennis available locally. 30 minutes by train to London and Southend-on-Sea. 10 minutes M25 motorway for Cambridge and Canterbury. £220 to £360 weekly fully inclusive. Also single six-berth caravan at Lorkins Farm from £60 weekly. Fullest details: **Mrs M.A. Wordley, Lorkins Farm, Orsett, Near Grays, Essex RM16 3EL (0375 891439).**

AVON

BRISTOL near. Mrs C.B. Perry, Cleve Hill Farm, Ubley, Near Bristol BS18 6PG (Blagdon [0761] 62410). Working farm. This is a dairy farm, set close under the Mendip Hills. Visitors are welcome to explore and watch farm activities. Chew Valley and Blagdon Lakes close, giving trout fishing, birdwatching and walking in beautiful countryside. Bath, Cheddar, Longleat, Wells, Weston, Wookey very near. Two units forming part of main farmhouse. **Belters End,** maisonette with double bedroom, bunk bed on landing, bathroom upstairs. Downstairs kitchen/diner with double bed settee suite. **Cider House,** single level suitable for wheelchairs. Double bedroom, small twin-bedded room. Lounge with bed settee suite. Large kitchen/diner and bathroom. Units fully equipped except linen. Children welcome. Cot, high chair available. Pets by arrangement. SAE for terms. Open all year.

AVON!

With the seaside resort of Weston-Super-Mare, Bath – with both its Roman and its Georgian heritages – the beautiful limestone Cotswolds and of course Bristol, Avon has much to offer. Interesting places to visit include The Mendip Hills, Avon Gorge, Brockley Combe nature trail and the Castle Farm Museum at Marshfield.

Leigh Farm

Pensford, Bristol BS18 4HA
Telephone:
Compton Dando 0761 490281

All Units – ETB ♀♀

BATH 9 MILES

BRISTOL 8 MILES

Leigh Farm is in a superb setting between Bath and Bristol, quietly situated, and guests are welcome to use the large lawns and enjoy the picturesque countryside.

Rabbits are bred at intervals for the children's enjoyment and the pony and donkey are in the orchard adjoining the lawns. Wild life abounds on the one acre trout fly fishery which is adjacent to the farmhouse. The self-catering accommodation is mostly converted from the outbuildings, with grassy courtyard, using the natural pink, grey and white stone and former cobbles. A three-bedroomed oak beamed character cottage sleeping 6/8, with bed settee in lounge. Downstairs night store heating inclusive at certain times of the year. No pets. Bungalow type accommodation sleeping 2/3 persons or 2/4, one unit with a bed-settee and we also have a z-bed for a fifth person. All units have colour TV, metered electricity, shower room with washbasin and toilet. Linen can be hired. Cots can be supplied. Dogs charged. Mid-week bookings and long weekends at short notice. Excellent recommended pubs within 2½ miles. Open all year. Enquiries, please telephone or SAE: **Mrs Josephine Smart.**

POOL HOUSE – CHURCHILL GREEN FARM

Situated in the garden of Churchill Green Farm Guest House this single storey L-shaped cottage, built around the large heated swimming pool, has its own entrance and access to the garden. Private, quiet and ideal for families wishing to stay at reasonable cost in North Somerset, this is a superb position, with open views to the Mendip Hills. Open pastureland surrounds the cottage which is in the garden. There is room for five in two double bedrooms, and possible sleeping accommodation in the lounge. Bathroom, toilet; all-electric kitchen. Bed linen is supplied. Oil-fired heating throughout. Suitable for disabled visitors. Parking. Weekly cleaning is available.

The Farmhouse

The use of the heated swimming pool is included in weekly terms. Oil and electricity are metered and charged at current prices. "The Farmhouse itself" is available for Self-Catering Holidays at certain times of the year.

SAE please for terms and further details to:
Mrs J. A. Sacof, Churchill Green Farm, Churchill, Avon, Somerset BS19 5QH (Churchill [0934] 852438)

BRISTOL. Owls Loft and Swallows Nest. Sleeping 4/6. Two recently renovated apartments adjoining

Brinsea Green Farm, situated at the end of a quiet country lane surrounded by open fields with magnificent views. Bath, Bristol, Weston-super-Mare, Wells, Cheddar and Blagdon Lake are all within easy reach. Fishing, sports, equestrian and dry-ski all close by. Numerous local inns, many with good eating facilities. The apartments have been equipped to a very high standard and have fully fitted kitchens, beamed lounge with colour TV and bed-settee, bathroom, two bedrooms (one twin, one double), storage radiators, automatic washing machine, tumble dryer and iron. All bed linen, towels and electricity inclusive. Sorry, no pets. Car essential. Terms from £130 to £250 per week. Open all year. Apply **Mrs Delia Edwards, Brinsea Green Farm, Brinsea Lane, Congresbury, Near Bristol BS19 5JN (0934 852278).** Also see Bed and Breakfast Section.

CHEW VALLEY. Mrs Jill Quantrill, Bonhill House, Bishop Sutton, Bristol BS18 4TU (Chew Magna [0272] 332546). Working farm, join in. Bonhill House Cottage, a converted coach house originally built in 1842, offers delightful family holiday accommodation and is set in the beautiful Chew Valley area of the Mendip Hills. Standing adjacent to the main farmhouse and surrounded by picturesque countryside, the cottage comprises a fully equipped kitchen/diner, lounge, WC, bathroom, two bedrooms, one with double bed and the other with two singles (cot can be supplied). Off the road parking. Colour TV, drying and freezer facilities. This is a working farm with on-site stabling and livery facilities. Bath, Wells and Cheddar 12 miles; Bristol 10; Weston-super-Mare 20; Longleat 25. Terms approximately £70 – £162 weekly. ETB Approved.

BUCKINGHAMSHIRE

DINTON. Mrs J.M.W. Cook, Wallace Farm, Dinton, Near Aylesbury HP17 8UF (Aylesbury [0296] 748660). Working farm, join in. Sleep 3/5. Two cottages

are now available for weekly rental at Wallace Farm. THE OLD FOALING BOX is a two-bedroomed cottage, with separate livingroom with fireplace, diningroom, kitchen and bathroom. KEEPERS COTTAGE is a smaller cottage, consisting of a double bedroom with en suite bathroom, living/diningroom and kitchen. Both cottages are carpeted throughout, and both have colour TV. Linen is provided, and a telephone is available at the farmhouse. Suitable for disabled. Wallace Farm is a working family farm, and there is always lots of activity and plenty of animals around. Coarse fishing is available on the ponds. Bed and Breakfast accommodation also at the farmhouse. Self catering terms from £130 to £200. Brochure on request.

See also Colour Display Advertisement WOOBURN GREEN. **Thames Valley Holiday Homes. Properties sleep 1/6.** Two holiday homes situated in a picturesque village a short distance from the famous Cliveden Estate, and within easy reach of London (25 miles) and Windsor (10 miles). OVERLEIGH sleeps two to six people and UNDERLEIGH sleeps one to four people. Both properties are fully equipped with central heating, colour TV, telephone, pretty gardens/orchard and plenty of parking. Registered with Tourist Board. For further details send for free colour brochure to **Mrs Griffin, Myosotis, Widmoor, Wooburn Green HP10 0JG (Bourne End [06285] 21594; Fax: 0628 850471).**

CHESHIRE

MALPAS. Gelli Cottage, Tallarn Green, Malpas. Sleeps 6. 18th century detached cottage set in beautiful countryside on Welsh border. Convenient for Chester and touring North Wales. The cottage has been renovated but still retains its original character. It is centrally heated throughout, well furnished and equipped. Linen supplied. Colour TV. Accommodation comprises three bedrooms, bathroom, two toilets, sittingroom, diningroom, kitchen and large garden. Children welcome — cot available. Car essential. Open all year. Terms are from £75 to £150 per week. For further information apply to **Mrs E. Bartlett, The Gelli, Tallarn Green, Malpas SY14 7LE (094-881 613).**

CORNWALL

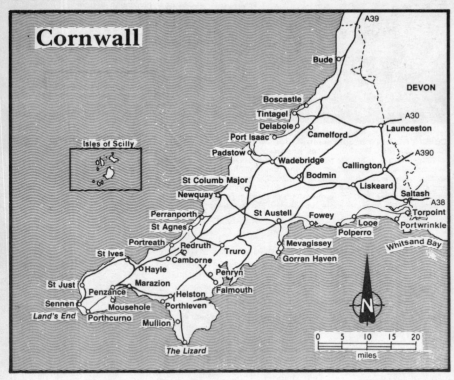

Cornwall

Isles of Scilly

DEVON

A39
Bude
Boscastle
Tintagel
Delabole
Port Isaac
Padstow
Wadebridge
Camelford
Launceston
A30
A390
Callington
Bodmin
Liskeard
Saltash
A38
St Columb Major
Newquay
St Austell
Fowey
Torpoint
Perranporth
Looe
Portwrinkle
St Agnes
Polperro
Whitsand Bay
Portreath
Redruth
Mevagissey
St Ives
Camborne
Truro
Gorran Haven
Hayle
Penryn
St Just
Marazion
Penzance
Helston
Falmouth
Sennen
Mousehole
Porthleven
Land's End
Porthcurno
Mullion

The Lizard

0 5 10 15 20
miles

N

BLISLAND. Mrs Ann Sainsbury, Corwen House, Blisland, Near Bodmin PL30 4JJ (0208 850 485). **Sleeps 2/4 plus cot.** Excellently located in a secluded, sheltered position on the edge of Bodmin Moor, an area of outstanding natural beauty. Under a mile from pretty moorland village of Blisland, perfect location for touring Cornwall. Scrumpy Cottage is a carefully renovated "listed" barn retaining many original features, such as exposed beams and an "A" shaped ceiling. Ideal retreat for a truly rural holiday for birdwatching, sketching, walking and riding with sailing, windsurfing, fishing and golf available close by. Accommodation consists of bedroom with double bed and washbasin, bathroom, sitting room with colour TV and double sofa bed, fully equipped kitchen and diningroom. Child's Z-bed and/or cot available. Babysitting. Electricity on £1 coin meter. Garden. Pets accepted by arrangement. Bed linen supplied at charge. Terms £80 – £200.

CLOAM COTTAGE

BODMIN. Mrs P.A. Smith, Treffry Farm, Lanhydrock, Bodmin PL30 5AF (Bodmin [0208] 74405). **Working farm, join in. Sleeps 2-8.** ♀♀♀♀ *Commended.* Imagine country cottages with thick granite walls, rambling roses, roaring log fires on winter nights, honeysuckle perfume on balmy summer days they're here at Treffry. Our lovely old barns have been converted into delightful stone cottages which are furnished and equipped to an extremely high standard for your holiday. Come and discover the delights of the Cornish countryside with miles of walks along flower-filled hedgerows. Search out granite cliffs and sandy beaches, only 20 minutes' drive away, or relax on our 200 acre dairy farm and meet the farm animals and pony. A warm welcome awaits you. SAE or telephone for brochure and tariff. £80 to £420 per week.

BODMIN. Mrs E. Tidy, Penbugle Farm, Bodmin PL31 2NT (Bodmin [0208] 72844). Working farm.

Sleeps 6 plus cot. This fully modernised medieval cottage is situated on a working farm. It enjoys superb views over open countryside and woodland, and is ideally placed in the centre of Cornwall. The setting is absolutely peaceful but yet not isolated being only one mile from Bodmin, three miles from Bodmin Moor and 12 miles from the north and south coasts. Six people accommodated in one double room and one extra-large room with three single divans plus a further single divan in lounge (downstairs) and cot. Kitchen with electric cooker, fridge and dining area; bathroom, toilet. Lounge. Full central heating and double glazing. Places of historic interest include Lanhydrock House, Pencarrow House, Restormel Castle (National Trust). Leisure activities around Bodmin include trout fishing, indoor and outdoor tennis centre, and a new 18 hole championship golf course available in 1991. Cottage available all year, weekly terms on request. SAE, please for prompt reply. ETB and Cornwall Tourist Board registered.

BODMIN MOOR. Mr and Mrs J. Cooper, Treswigga, Blisland, Bodmin PL30 4LD (Bodmin [0208]

Treswigga Barn

850491). Sleeps 2-4. Treswigga is a small working farm on Bodmin Moor. Treswigga Barn, whilst detached from the house, is very much part of the farm environment. It provides a good base for a couple or small family seeking a moorland walking holiday base or touring centre. Both north and south coasts are within easy driving distance. The Barn contains a large livingroom — the old threshing floor; a spacious bedroom — the former grain store — and bathroom. Terms from £70 to £160 per week, including electricity. Obedient dogs are welcome. Details on request.

BODMIN near. Richard and Jean Crown, Washaway Court, Washaway, Near Bodmin PL30 3AD

(Bodmin [0208] 74951). Enjoy comfort and independence in our delightful cottages, which sleep two/five. They are situated within easy reach of the North and South coasts. Facilities include colour TV and heated swimming pool. Personally supervised by resident proprietors.

Terms quoted in this publication may be subject to increase if rises in costs necessitate

BOSCASTLE. Tresquare, Boscastle. ♀♀♀ *Approved.* **Working farm. Sleeps 2/8.** Superior accommodation, quietly situated, comfortably furnished, carpeted and fully equipped except linen. Delightful dormer bungalow in own grounds with beautiful valley views, within walking distance of Boscastle. Sleeps eight in three bedrooms (two double, one with en-suite shower; one family room); lounge; sunlounge; fitted kitchen/diner, bathroom, two toilets. Open fire. Also two-bedroomed country bungalow for two/five. Sea views, garden, fitted kitchen. Both properties with private parking, colour TV, electric and storage heating, cot, electric cooker, fridge, washing machine, kettle, iron, metered electricity. Picturesque harbour, cliffs, Valency Valley, shops. Tintagel Castle, several sandy surfing beaches nearby. Walking, fishing, golf amidst beautiful scenery. Ideal touring centre. Children welcome. Pets on application. Low season from £80 weekly, high season from £130 weekly. SAE please stating dates, numbers in party etc., to **Mrs G. Congdon, Tremorle, Boscastle PL35 0BU (Boscastle [084-05] 233).**

See also Colour Display Advertisement **BOSCASTLE near. Mrs Russell-Steel, Courtyard Farm, Lesnewth, Near Boscastle PL35 0HR (Otterham Station [08406] 256).** Picturesque group of 17th century luxury stone cottages overlooking beautiful National Trust Valley with fabulous views of the sea. All the cottages are individually designed and furnished and equipped to the very highest standard with colour TV etc. They are warm and comfortable and are open all year round. Virtually all the coastline around Boscastle is National Trust owned and provides fabulous walks and beaches. Our cottages offer you quality and comfort at reasonable rates. For example, our four-bedroomed cottage offers accommodation for eight in two double-bedded rooms, two twin-bedded rooms, sittingroom, diningroom, kitchen, bathroom/toilet. Children welcome, cots and high chairs provided. Pets by arrangement. Please write or phone for our free colour brochure.

BUDE. ♀♀♀♀ *Commended.* LANGFIELD MANOR SET IN ONE ACRE OF GARDENS, complete with solar-heated swimming pool. Carefully converted into seven self catering apartments, including two at ground floor level. Situated overlooking Bude Golf Course, yet only a few minutes' walk to the town centre, shops and central beaches. The swimming pool (complete with diving board and water chute) and sunbathing terraces are floodlit at night. Licensed bar for residents opens onto poolside terrace. Full sized snooker table, pool and table tennis; laundry; car park. Apartments have private hall; lounge/diner; colour TV. Separate fully fitted kitchen with fridge/freezer and microwave oven. Central heating. Choice of one, two or three bedrooms with bath or shower. Open all year for a self catering holiday with the facilities of an hotel. Please send for brochure and price list to resident proprietors: **R. & D. Varley (FHG), Langfield Manor, Bude EX23 8DP (Bude [0288] 352415).**

BUDE. Sharland House, Marhamchurch, Bude. Sleeps 8 adults; 6 children. From A39 take unclassified turning to Marhamchurch. Pleasantly situated, Sharland House overlooks its own lawned garden adjacent to the square of this attractive village and, in a favoured position, is surrounded by white-painted cottages with thatched or slated roofs. The spacious house dates from Victorian and even earlier times with an interesting interior created by thick walls, low beamed ceilings and window seats. Comfortable accommodation for up to 10 persons is provided by two sittingrooms, diningroom and well-equipped kitchen, five bedrooms and a playroom for young children. Ideally placed for exploring with easy access to many good beaches and cliff walks along the beautiful Cornish Coast. Pets welcome. One and a half miles from Bude. Children welcome. Terms from £120 to £336. SAE for further details to **Mrs P. Gilhespy, 2 Church Cottages, Marhamchurch, Bude EX23 0EN (Widemouth Bay [0288] 361570).**

CORNWALL – SOMETHING FOR EVERYONE!

Sea, sand, cliffs and quite often the sun, but that's not all you will find in this interesting county. Cornwall has many fascinating places to visit, such as the Charlestown Shipwreck Centre, the Tropical Bird Gardens at Padstow, Cornwall Aeronautical Park near Helston, Botallack Tin Mine, The Cornish Seal Sanctuary, Perranporth and of course, St. Michael's Mount.

BUDE. Lower Quinceborough, Marine Drive, Widemouth Bay, Bude. Sleeps 6/8. Lower Quinceborough is an extremely attractive character bungalow with many luxury features — double glazing etc. Situated just two minutes' walk from the sandy surfing beach of Widemouth Bay with spectacular uninterrupted views of the sea. Comfortable accommodation for six/eight in two large family bedrooms; all rooms have fitted carpets, are well-decorated and furnished. Fitted kitchen has electric cooker, fridge, washing machine, vacuum, etc. Colour TV. Bed linen. Electric and open fires. Garage. Garden and use of heated outdoor pool, games room, putting green and hard tennis court at Quinceborough Farm (half a mile away) add to your holiday enjoyment. Bude, three miles distant, offers golf, riding, putting, tennis, fishing and boating on canal etc. Good base for touring Cornwall and Devon. Port Isaac, Boscastle, Tintagel, Clovelly, Bideford etc, all within easy reach. Open all year. Children and pets welcome. SAE, please. **Mrs Patricia M. Rowland, Quinceborough Farm, Widemouth Bay, Bude EX23 0NA (Widemouth Bay [0288] 361 236).**

CALLINGTON. Colquite Cottage, Rilla Mill, Callington. Sleeps 5. Perched above the River Lynher in a steep wooded valley, Colquite Cottage offers seclusion, peace and quiet in the midst of the Cornish countryside. Fish for trout and salmon in the river. Riverside and woodland walks, where wild life flourishes. Bodmin Moor is nearby for pony trekking. The Cornish coast is easily accessible for day trips. The cottage is prettily furnished with all you need for a comfortable holiday. Open fire and Rayburn heating. Calor gas cooking, lighting and fridge. All fuel provided. No electricity. Pets welcome. Prices from £120 to £250 per week. Please contact **David Pengelly or Helen Pemberton, Flat 12, 116 High Street, Hadleigh, Suffolk IP7 5EL (0473 823941 or 0305 871284)** for further details.

CAMBORNE. Horsedowns Farm, Drym, Phaze-an-Beeble, Camborne. Sleeps 4 adults; 5 children. Large detached farmhouse halfway between Helston and Camborne. There is a large lounge with open fireplace and storage heater; diningroom with colour TV, electric fire and storage heater; large kitchen with electric cooker, fridge/freezer and washing machine, and rear porch. Upstairs are four bedrooms, one with single bed; one double-bedded; one bedroom with double and single beds and a further bedroom with three single beds. The bathroom has a bath, washbasin, toilet and shower. There is a large rear courtyard with picnic table and benches. A cot and high chair are available. There is plenty of parking space. Electricity by £1 coin meter. Linen and towels are not supplied. A well-behaved dog is normally acceptable. Terms from £145 to £320. Contact: **Mr and Mrs G.N.F. Broughton, Orchard House, Wall, Gwinear, Hayle TR27 5HA (Leedstown [0736] 850201).**

CARBIS BAY. Trenoweth Farm, Carbis Bay. Working farm. Sleeps 6 adults; 5 children. This large attractive modernised farmhouse lies half a mile from Carbis Bay beach and two miles from St. Ives. The accommodation comprises a large lounge/diningroom with wood-burning stove and colour TV; a second small lounge; spacious kitchen; shower room with WC; utility room with washing machine. Upstairs there is one double-bedded room, two twin-bedded rooms, one large bedroom with three single beds; bathroom/WC and an unusual twin-bedded landing. A cot can also be provided. Electricty is included in the rental. Duvets and duvet covers are provided. Well-behaved dogs are normally allowed. The farmyard offers plenty of parking space. There is a small front garden and a sun-soaked patio area at the rear. Terms from £225 to £450. **Mr and Mrs G.N.F. Broughton, Orchard House, Wall, Gwinear, Hayle TR27 5HA (Leedstown [0736] 850201).**

CORNWALL. Cream of Cornwall Farm Holidays. Working farm. Set amidst beautiful scenery, coast and country, 35 carefully inspected working farms. Self-catering, Bed and Breakfast or Half Board. Ranging from gourmet food and en-suite rooms with four-poster to simple Bed and Breakfast, camping or caravanning. A warm welcome and high standards. Further details for self-catering contact: **Katherine Woodley, Degembris Farm, St. Newlyn East, Newquay TR8 5HY (0872 510555)** and for farmhouse accommodation: **Joan Luckraft (0872 510236).**

COVERACK. Sue and Martin Lea, Polcoverack Farm, Coverack TR12 6SP (St. Keverne [0326] 280497). Working farm, join in. Six stone-built one, two and three bedroomed cottages cared for and equipped to a very high standard in sylvan surroundings on this working farm; half mile from safe, sandy beach and unspoilt village of Coverack. Enjoy the best of both worlds — seaside, plus farm. A child's paradise; helping with the animals or exploring fields, woods and stream whilst grown-ups play tennis or soak up the peace and tranquillity of the sunny gardens. Week-day changeovers. Regret no pets. Please send SAE for full details and illustrated brochure. Registered with English Tourist Board.

CRACKINGTON HAVEN. Mr and Mrs O.H.F. Tippett, Trelay, St. Gennys, Bude EX23 0NJ (St. Gennys [084-03] 378). ♀♀♀ *Approved.* Lovely stone cottages converted from traditional barns and period farmhouse (accommodate four, six or eight). Idyllic setting on small working sheep farm at the head of deep wooded valley. Area of outstanding natural beauty. Five minutes to sandy beach at Crackington and coast path along spectacular National Trust cliffs. Ideal area for surfing, walking, bird-watching etc. All cottages furnished in character — much pine and oak, comfortable suites and beds. Log fires, dish-washers, linen, fenced gardens, patios, laundry room and payphone. Pets welcome. Low season from £70 per week, also short breaks. Main season £115 to £390 per week. Colour brochure available.

CRANTOCK. Mr and Mrs R.B. Harty, Treago Mill, Crantock, Newquay TR8 5QS (Crantock [0637] 830213). Accommodation in classified area of outstanding natural beauty and scientific interest for rare flora and wildlife. A 15th century Cornish stone cottage and bungalow each sleeping six and a further two Swedish bungalows each sleeping five — all are fully equipped except for linen. Spacious grounds in quiet, idyllic National Trust coastal setting. Close to lovely sandy Porth Joke beach with safe bathing and surfing. Small quiet camping site with showers, toilets and laundry service. Village one mile. Amenities within easy walking distance — shop, good food pub with twice weekly disco, cafe, golf, riding, fishing, leisure park. Also Bed and Breakfast in our homely 15th century Mill House. SAE for colour brochure with details.

CORNWALL – SOMETHING FOR EVERYONE!

Sea, sand, cliffs and quite often the sun, but that's not all you will find in this interesting county. Cornwall has many fascinating places to visit, such as the Charlestown Shipwreck Centre, the Tropical Bird Gardens at Padstow, Cornwall Aeronautical Park near Helston, Botallack Tin Mine, The Cornish Seal Sanctuary, Perranporth and of course, St. Michael's Mount.

CUSGARNE, near Truro. Joyce and George Clench, Saffron Meadow, Cusgarne, Near Truro TR4

8RW (0872 863171). Sleeps 2. Saffron Meadow Lodge is a cosy chalet in the grounds of Saffron Meadow. Completely secluded with beautiful views, it is surrounded by treed pastureland. Fully tiled heated shower/toilet suite etc; lobby; modern well equipped kitchen; cosy panelled lounge and bedroom. Remote control colour TV. Everything included, except bed linen and towels. Garage adjoining. Post Office, corner shop, inn (providing good meals) within four minutes' walk. Truro, Falmouth five miles; North Coast 25 minutes. Utterly peaceful. Price range during Summer £110 – £180.

FALMOUTH. Nantrissack, Constantine, Falmouth. NANTRISSACK is an impressive farmhouse stand-

ing in a delightful garden. It is ideally situated for touring this lovely southern coast of Cornwall. Being two miles from Gweek — the little creek of the Helford River — it is also ideal for visiting Falmouth and the Lizard Peninsula. The farm and small woodland with a freshwater stream is available for those who wish to walk. The furnishings are nice, and beds have interior sprung mattresses. Bathroom; hot and cold water in all bedrooms. Partial central heating. New 30ft Sun Lounge. Colour TV. Fully equipped with all linen except towels and iron. Kiddies welcome also well-behaved dog. Premises thoroughly cleaned and checked by owners between each let. Sea about four-and-a-half miles. Illustrated brochure available. SAE please. Terms from £120 per week. **Mr T.P. Tremayne, "The Home", Penjerrick, Falmouth TR11 5EE (Falmouth [0326] 250427 and 250143).**

FALMOUTH. Trebarvah Woon Cottage, Constantine, Falmouth. Trebarvah Woon is a modernised

cottage ideally situated for touring the many beauty spots of South Cornwall, being two miles from Gweek, the little creek of the Helford River. Set by the roadside with its own garden, the cottage offers privacy without isolation. Formerly a smallholding there are meadows for children's play or a breath of fresh air before retiring. Two double bedrooms upstairs; one twin-bedded downstairs. Modern kitchen and livingroom with a modern toilet/bathroom. TV. Electric cooker, refrigerator, fires. "Off Peak" electric central heating available as an extra. Nicely furnished. Beds have spring interior mattresses. Cot available. Fully equipped with linen etc., except for towels and iron. Kiddies welcome and also the family dog. Premises thoroughly cleaned and checked by owners between each let. Sea about four-and-a-half miles away. Tourist Board registered. Many guests return year after year. Terms from £120. SAE, please. **Mr T.P. Tremayne, "The Home," Penjerrick, Falmouth TR11 5EE (Falmouth [0326] 250427 and 250143).**

FALMOUTH. Dolvean Holiday Flats, 48 Melvill Road, Falmouth. Flats sleep 2/4/6. Six completely self-contained, well-equipped all-electric flats situated 250 yards from safe, sandy bathing beach and sea front, and within a short distance of Falmouth Town railway station and buses to town centre. Each flat has a full-size cooker and fridge, colour television, lounge or lounge/diner with a double bed-settee, one or two double or twin bedrooms, and a bath or shower room and toilet. Bed linen supplied. Pets permitted. Cot available. Electric coin meter. Four flats each sleep up to six, one takes two to four and one takes two. Open all year. Weekly terms from £65 for the smallest in January up to £285 for the largest in July and August. Tourist Board registered. Stamp, please, for details to **Mr John Myers, 48-50 Melvill Road, Falmouth TR11 4DQ (Falmouth [0326] 313658).**

FOWEY. Mr H.F. Edward-Collins, Lanwithan Farm, Lostwithiel PL22 0LA (0208 872444). 🛉🛉🛉

Approved. **Working farm.** Waterside cottage and house. Fal Estuary or 110 acre Georgian Farm Estate running down to the banks of the River Fowey and private river frontages. We are not a cottage agency. Instead we offer a wide choice of 10 cottages and apartments personally owned and run with good friendly Cornish hospitality and service. We offer *Private quay and dinghies *Private river frontage *Idyllic and unspoilt views *South facing gardens *Laundry and indoor drying facilities *Log fires and central heating *En-suite bathrooms *Telephones *Garage *Games Room *Table tennis *Grass tennis court *Maid service *Baby-sitting. Full colour brochure available.

HAYLE. The Towans, Hayle. Sleeps six. Chalet situated among sand dunes adjoining three miles of golden sands in St. Ives Bay. Ideal spot for touring, or a haven for the family on the sand or grass. Accommodation for six in three double bedrooms; bathroom; toilet; sittingroom; diningroom/kitchen with built-in units and all-electric appliances. Fully equipped except for linen. Sorry, no pets. Shops and sea 200 yards. Car parking. Riding, golfing, fishing all near. Unnecessary to leave the area to enjoy the holiday as shops, post office, hotel and entertainment all within 500 yards. Weekly terms excluding fuel from £50 to £200. SAE, please to **Mrs Enid L. Johns, "Kerana Tiga", 12 Penview Crescent, Grange Road, Helston TR13 8RX (Helston [0326] 572489 — evenings only).**

HELFORD RIVER near. Mrs Anne Matthews, Boskensoe Farm, Mawnan Smith, Falmouth TR11 5JP

(Falmouth [0326] 250257). **Working farm, join in. Sleeps 8.** Picturesque farmhouse set in three acres of garden and orchard on 400-acre farm, accommodation for eight persons. Five minutes' walk to village of Mawnan Smith, with good selection of shops. The lovely river is approximately one mile away and is famous for its beautiful coastal walks and scenery. Several quiet beaches close by for picnicking, bathing; also excellent sailing and fishing facilities. Other properties also available. Cornwall Tourist Board registered. Terms from £95 – £250. Apply for brochure.

HELSTON. Barn Cottage and Parc-an-Fox, Manaccan, Helston. Properties sleep 6/8. Traditional

Cornish stone-built cottage over 250 years old, with beamed ceiling in sittingroom. Also a converted barn comfortably furnished and modernised. One cottage sleeps six and the other sleeps eight. Each has cot; three bedrooms, modern bathroom/shower, shaver points. Spacious sittingroom and dining/kitchen with electric cooker, fridge, immersion heater (50p meter), twin tub washing machine, colour TV. No linen supplied. A car is essential; ample parking; large secluded garden with stream, surrounded by trees. Situated in sheltered valley amid unspoilt countryside, one mile from the sea. Three miles from Helford River, Frenchman's Creek. Boat for hire for sailing and fishing two miles away. Safe bathing from numerous beaches and excellent walking. Very safe for children and pets. Babysitter available. Helston, the home of the Floral Dance, 12 miles. Open all year. SAE, please, stating number of persons and dates required. **Mrs J. Jane, Parc-an-Fox, Manaccan, Helston TR12 6EP (St. Keverne [0326] 280150).**

HELSTON. Mrs A.G. Farquhar, Porthpradnack, Mullion, Helston TR12 7EX (Mullion [0326] 240226). At Mullion Cove on the Lizard Peninsula is Porthpradnack, a well built house with two flats, each with two bedrooms, bathroom and toilet. One has livingroom/kitchen, the other a separate sittingroom and kitchen. Kitchens are fully equipped and have fridges, electric cooker etc., colour TV. Cots, high chair (no extra charge) but linen is not supplied. Each flat has separate front door. A telephone is available to tenants. Flats are available all year. Pets permitted by arrangement. Car essential — parking bay. Weekly terms from £95 to £185 in high season. Tourist Board registered. Enquiries to: **Mrs A.G. Farquhar, as above.**

"HALWYN"
MANACCAN
HELSTON
S. CORNWALL

Situated in an area of outstanding natural beauty, **HALWYN** is an ancient Cornish farmstead with the original old farmhouse and the former farm buildings architecturally converted to a choice of holiday homes. Superbly set in parklike surroundings in an idyllic sunny valley one mile from the sea at Porthallow and two miles from the Helford River.

There is **HALWYN FARMHOUSE**, a spacious six bedroom character house with beams and inglenook, for up to twelve people. **HALVILLA COTTAGE**, a large four bedroom cottage for up to ten. **COURTYARD COTTAGE**, a small single storey three bedroomed cottage. **THE GRANARY** and **THE HAYLOFT** both two bedroom apartments (all sleeping six). All are fully equipped to a high standard with colour TV. Heating and electricity inclusive. NO METERS. Everything is included except linen (which can be hired). There is a laundry room with deep freeze and pay phone.

Two acres of grounds. INDOOR HEATED SWIMMING POOL WITH SAUNA AND SOLARIUM. Small lake with boat, badminton court, children's play area and putting green. Unspoilt coast ideal for those who enjoy a quiet holiday. Many sandy beaches. Safe bathing and boat hire. Open all year round with special low rates and log fires out of season when Cornwall can be at its best. Well behaved dogs welcome. **Stamp for colour brochure to MR & MRS H. DONALD or Telephone ST. KEVERNE (0326) 280359.**

See also Colour Display Advertisement.

See also Colour Display Advertisement. **HELSTON. Mrs H. Lugg, Tregaddra Farm, Cury, Helston TR12 7BB (Mullion [0326] 240235).** This luxury mobile home is tucked away in the grounds of Tregaddra Farmhouse in the centre of the Lizard Peninsula. Furnished to a high standard with one double bedroom and one twin-bedded room. Bathroom with shower and basin, separate toilet. Kitchen, dining area and lounge with colour TV. Linen, gas and electricity included in rental. Open all year. Terms from £100 per week. Colour brochure available.

HELSTON. Mrs Una Harvey, "Menifters", Gillan, Manaccan, Helston TR12 6ER (St. Keverne [0326] 280711). Properties sleep 2/9. MENIFTERS is delightfully set on a hillside one mile inland, with an unobstructed all-round view of the sea and countryside. This area is particularly beautiful, with landscapes ranging from rugged coastline, gently rolling fields to the lovely tranquil Helford River. One mile distant is a small fishing village, and there are miles of coastal footpaths between the secluded coves. The converted HAYLOFT is part of the original granite farm buildings, and sleeps two/four. Our FARMHOUSE sleeps up to nine, and is also tastefully furnished and equipped to make your holiday comfortable and relaxing. Ample parking for cars and boats. Write for brochure, enclosing stamp.

HELSTON. Anne Viccars, Flushing Cottage, Flushing Cove, Gillan, Manaccan, Helston TR12 6HQ (032623 244). Cornwall at its very best. Set in a pretty garden of sloping lawns and many flowering shrubs, right on the beach in the mouth of the Helford River. The area is renowned for beautiful walks, terrific sailing, interesting birds, rare plants and superb fishing. Accommodating six people in three bedrooms, the cottage is fully equipped to a very high standard with dishwasher, microwave, washing machine, tumble dryer. Bathroom, kitchen/diner, lounge with remote control TV and stereo system. Calor gas barbecue and patio furniture. Ideal for out-of-season bookings. Car parking. Cot and high chair. Linen available. Sorry, no pets.

HELSTON. Willow Cottage, Porthallow, St. Keverne, Helston. Sleeps 5. This is a comfortable, homely

cottage set in the little fishing village of Porthallow. Accommodation is for five people in three bedrooms, all with washbasins; upstairs toilet and bath; sittingroom, diningroom and kitchen. Colour TV, electric cooker, fridge and fires (50p meter). Sheets and duvets supplied. The cottage is nicely modernised but still retains character. Own private parking. Local fishing trips, boats for hire, horse riding, golf all within the vicinity. Beautiful countryside and scenery, beautiful walks. This charming cottage would be ideal for a family holiday — children welcome, pets accepted at extra charge. Plenty to do or just relax in comfort and enjoy the peace and quiet of Cornwall. Terms from £75 to £250 weekly. Please apply to **Mrs M. Lugg, Polpidnick Farm, St. Martin, Helston TR12 6DU (0326-23 268).**

HELSTON. Mrs A. Nicholas, Old Mill House, Gweek, Helston TR12 6UA (032622 217). Sleeps 2/6

plus cot. Old Mill Cottage (stream diverted) is situated in a quiet, sheltered but not isolated location. Spring comes early and Autumn late to South Cornwall — so ideal for these times. Three bedrooms, two south-facing with double and twin beds, and back bedroom with large bunk beds. Bathroom, two toilets; kitchen; lounge/diner with hatch. Obedient oil central heating, electric fire; all bedding (duvets, blankets, polycotton sheets etc), colour TV with remote control, four deck chairs, parking on forecourt. You will be as comfortable as at home! Dogs often acceptable by arrangement. Basic rent when only two people. Telephone enquiries only please for July and August. Also a studio (sleeps two) with similar amenities.

HELSTON. The Loft, Tregarne Farm, Manaccan, Helston. Working farm, join in. Sleeps 5. Tregarne

is a small hamlet set in a wooded valley close to the lovely coves and beaches of The Lizard Peninsula and the picturesque Helford River. Part of a stone-built barn 'The Loft' comprises sittingroom (colour TV); all-electric diner/kitchen; one double, one bunk-bedded room (cot); shower room, separate WC, and is fully equipped (including linen) for four/five persons. Situated on a working farm where visitors are welcome to 'muck in', The Loft is ideal for a relaxing family holiday amidst traditional country and close to unspoilt coves. Nearby leisure activities include fishing, sailing, swimming, riding, etc. Available all year. Weekly terms from £80. **Mrs P. A. Lugg, Tregarne Farm, Manaccan, Helston TR12 6EW (St. Keverne [0326] 280304).**

HELSTON. Fuchsia Cottage, Tregarne, Manaccan, Helston. Secluded country bungalow (owner's

home) in large, mature garden, one mile from fishing cove of Porthallow. Lovely area for walking, touring, boating and fishing. Shop, pub and beach one mile. Ideal for a relaxing holiday. The well carpeted, fully equipped accommodation comprises three double bedrooms, two with double beds, one with bunks/twin beds, all with Continental Quilts; large dining room/kitchen with electric cooker, twin tub washing machine, fridge/freezer, electric water heater and toaster. The large lounge has an inglenook with stone fireplace, TV and radio. Bathroom with WC. Ideal for children, cots available on request. Electricity by meter. Car essential, access by private lane; ample parking. Pets by arrangement. Available April to October. Special Rates for Senior Citizens except June, July and August. For dates telephone after four p.m. and weekends to **Mrs P.M. Jones, "Avisford", Chase Road, Brocton, Stafford ST17 0TL (Stafford [0785] 662470).**

FHG PUBLICATIONS LIMITED publish a large range of well-known accommodation guides. We will be happy to send you details or you can use the order form at the back of this book.

HELSTON. Chapel Cottage, Tregarne, Manaccan, Helston. Sleeps 7. Tregarne is a hamlet one mile

from the sea, near the beautiful Helford River, offering safe bathing, boating, fishing and walking. A traditional Cornish cottage with modern single-storey extension. Accommodation for seven (plus cot and folding bed). Large enclosed garden, garage and parking. Children and pets welcome, babysitting available. Comfortable lounge with colour TV, modern kitchen/diner with electric cooker, microwave and fridge-freezer. Bathroom/shower and family bedroom on ground floor. Two bedrooms and toilet with washbasin on first floor. Fully equipped except for linen. Automatic washing machine and three free heatstores October to May. Terms £60-£275. SAE for brochure to **Mrs H. Dagger, Swanpool House, 65 Long Lane, Aughton, Near Ormskirk, Lancashire L39 5AS (0695 423140).**

See also Colour Display Advertisement **HELSTON. Mr and Mrs H. Donald, Halwyn, Manaccan, Helston TR12 6ER (St Keverne [0326] 280359). Properties sleep 2/12.** Situated in an area of outstanding natural beauty, "Halwyn" is an ancient Cornish farmstead with the original old farmhouse and former farm buildings converted to a choice of holiday homes for two to 12. There are two acres of delightful gardens including an indoor heated swimming pool with sauna and solarium, small lake with boat, badminton court, children's play area and a putting green. A perfect away-from-it-all holiday retreat. Open all year with special low rates out of season. Stamp for colour brochure.

HELSTON near. Mrs Pamela M.B. Royall, Glebe Hall, Mawgan, Near Helston TR12 6AB (Mawgan

[032622] 257). Glebe Hall is situated in a quiet sheltered valley on the edge of Mawgan close to the beautiful Helford River. The four cottages are an interesting conversion of the old rectory coach-house and offer well-equipped, all-electric accommodation with two/three bedrooms, kitchen/diner, sittingroom with colour TV and modern bathroom. All linen and towels are provided; cots and high chairs are available; children are most welcome. Two acres of garden include a splendid heated swimming pool, barbecue, swingball, trampoline and games room, with laundry facilities etc. We also have a charming creekside cottage in Helford Village similarly fitted to a high standard. Bookings normally Fridays or Wednesdays, or long weekends early or late season. Registered with the Cornwall Tourist Board.

HELSTON near. Badger Cottage, St. Keverne. Working farm, join in. Sleeps 6. This cottage faces

south overlooking its own private garden which is formed out of an old marl pit and has a lawn running through the length of it. Shrubs on the bank opposite hide the badger holes and there are attractive semi-circular steps leading up to the cottage. Downstairs is one very long (32 foot) room divided, sittingroom from kitchen/dining area, by a curtain. The accommodation is for six people in three bedrooms, cot available; bathroom and two toilets. Well-equipped with everything except linen. Colour TV. Electricity on meter. Tregellast Barton is a lovely Tudor farmstead, near St. Keverne and about one and a half miles from the sea. Cows, donkeys, dogs, cats, etc. Milk is made into cream, many flavoured ice creams, fudges and chocolates. We also make jams and chutneys and have a small shop on the farm. Washing machine, drying space and also use of freezer. Visitors are welcome to watch milking etc. Bring boots! Exclusive information on local walks and drives, etc available. Telephone kiosk. Tourist Board registered. Long SAE, please, or stamps. **Mrs Rachel Roskilly, Tregellast Barton, St. Keverne, Helston TR12 6NX (St. Keverne [0326] 280479).**

HELSTON near. Troon Cottage, Breage, Near Helston. Sleeps 2-5. Take a break in this charming old

cottage, attractively furnished to a high standard, situated in a quiet country lane near the sea. Modern kitchen, colour TV, all equipment provided, beds made up ready. Large storage heaters ensure warmth during cooler months, cost included in rent. Secluded garden, patio, garage. Children welcome, cot provided. Breage is ideal centre for exploring the numerous beaches and National Trust coastal walks in the area, within easy motoring distance of Land's End, The Lizard, Falmouth, St. Ives and many other well known beauty spots. Sorry, no pets. Excellent for spring or autumn holidays. Ring or write to **Mrs A.M. Graham, Long View, Maple Avenue, Bexhill, Sussex TN39 4ST (Cooden [04243] 3182).**

See also Colour Display Advertisement **LANLIVERY. Mr and Mrs C.D. Girdler, Higher Trevilmick, Lanlivery, Bodmin PL30 5HT (0208 872372).** 🐾 Higher Trevilmick Farm overlooks Redmoor Nature Reserve and is set on the side of Helman Tor with impressive views of rural Cornwall in all directions. It is in these peaceful surrounding that a range of old granite farm buildings have been carefully converted into five holiday cottages. Open-plan designs, well equipped kitchens and modern bathrroms. Bed linen supplied. Within easy reach of both north and south coasts and with easy access to all of Cornwall's many tourist attractions. We have information on all of these attractions together with all types of outdoor activities in the area. Terms from £98 to £218.

LAUNCESTON. Mr and Mrs E.J. Broad, Tamar View, Lower Dutson Farm, Launceston PL15 9SP (Launceston [0566] 772607 or 776456). Whether fishing or not, everyone is made equally welcome on this 180 acre family farm where they may feel free to stroll across the fields to the river and/or lake. It is centrally situated for touring the coasts and the counties of Cornwall and Devon. House is comfortably furnished, with colour TV and all equipment, having shower/toilet downstairs and bathroom upstairs and separate room with table tennis, darts, snooker, etc. Terms from £120 per week including heating. There is no close season for fishing the well stocked/matured lake for carp, tench, rudd, etc, or, if preferred, the River Tamar provides good pools for trout and salmon. Bed and Breakfast also available. Space does not allow a detailed description but full particulars will be sent immediately on receipt of SAE.

LAUNCESTON. Mrs E.M. Budge, East Kitcham Farm, St. Giles, Launceston PL15 9SL (0566 84325). Working farm, join in. Enjoy a country holiday in a luxury six-berth caravan, all amenities, equipped and maintained to a high standard, includes two bedrooms, one double, one twin (not bunks). Lounge with colour TV, kitchen with full-size cooker and fridge, shower room with basin and toilet. Linen supplied. The caravan is sited in its own garden (with parking) and has lovely views of the surrounding countryside. Central for coast and Dartmoor; Leisure Centre, golf, bowls, etc. at Launceston (five miles). Visitors are encouraged to enjoy farming activities. Own lake for TROUT FISHING on farm. Pets welcome by arrangement. SAE for terms.

LAUNCESTON near. Mrs A.E. Moore, Hollyvag, Lewannick, Near Launceston PL15 7QH (0566 82309). Working farm, join in. Sleeps 2 adults; 4 children. Part of 17th century farmhouse, self-contained and full of old world charm with own lawns, front and back. Set in secluded position in wooded countryside with views of the moors. Central for North and South coasts. Family farm with ducks on the pond, horses, sheep and poultry. Sleeps four to six, fully furnished with all modern conveniences, folding bed and cot available. Colour TV, fridge, electric cooker, solid fuel heater if needed. Babysitting available free. Linen not provided. Within five miles of market town; golf, fishing and riding nearby. Terms from £70 to £130. Brochure on request.

LAUNCESTON. Dozmary Pool Cottage, Bolventor, Launceston. Enjoy a quiet holiday in a quaint country cottage in this delightful part of Cornwall in the heart of Bodmin Moors overlooking Dozmary Pool and Coliford Reservoir. Approximately one mile Jamaica Inn, 10 miles Launceston, Bodmin and Liskeard. Ideal centre for touring north and south coast and the legendary King Arthur country. The cottage comprises two small double bedrooms, sitting/diningroom; black and white TV; electric coal effect fire. Bathroom, toilet. Kitchen has electric cooker, fridge, etc. Linen supplied on request. Ideal location for children and pets. Car essential — ample parking. Open all year. SAE, please, **Mrs Mary Rich, "Nathania", Altarnun, Launceston PL15 7SL (Pipers Pool [056-686] 426).**

LAUNCESTON. "Beaconsville", South Petherwin, Launceston. Sleeps 8. This holiday bungalow is situated in the village of South Petherwin which is approximately two miles from Launceston. In an ideal position for touring Devon and Cornwall, within easy reach of the north and south Coasts, the bungalow is in its own grounds with plenty of parking space, garage and garden. There are three bedrooms to sleep eight people and a cot is available. The dining/kitchen has electric cooker, fridge, hot and cold water. No linen supplied. There is a lounge; bathroom and toilet. Shops 200 yards away. Sea 15 miles. Car essential — parking and garage. Terms on application to: **Mrs P.J. Parsons, Beacon Farm, South Petherwin, Launceston PL15 7JA (Launceston [0566] 772819).**

LAUNCESTON. Mrs H.H. Rowe, Godcott, North Petherwin, Launceston PL15 8NX (North Petherwin [056-685] 223). Working farm. Sleeps 6. Solid stone farm cottage situated on parish road. The dairy farm is set in beautiful Cornish countryside and fishing, surfing, golf, squash, tennis and leisure centres at both Launceston and Bude, Holsworthy and surrounding districts. Near Devon Border so guests can enjoy the facilities of both Devon and Cornwall. Six people accommodated in one double, one twin and one room with bunk beds and cot. Bathroom and toilet; also Rayburn immersion heater; mains water and electricity (meter 10p). Car essential, parking. Pets welcome. Open January to December; terms from £60 weekly. SAE, please.

PLEASE ENCLOSE A STAMPED ADDRESSED ENVELOPE WITH ENQUIRIES

LISKEARD. Mrs Rosanne Hodin, Lodge Barton Farm, Liskeard PL14 4JX (0579 44432). Lodge

Barton is set in a beautiful river valley flanked by woodland. We keep a milking herd of goats and also have calves, ducks, hens and geese. Everyone can help milk, feed livestock and collect eggs. Our two cottages are full of character and luxuriously equipped with videos, colour TV, woodburners and laundry room. Private gardens and children's playground. Cot available. We are close to sea, moors, sailing, windsurfing, riding, fishing, golf. Open all year. Terms from £80 to £320.

LOWER TRENGALE FARM

ç ç ç ç
Approved

Situated in secluded coutryside overlooking a valley of fields and woods, yet only minutes from Liskeard. Within easy reach of many beaches and tourist attractions. Three comfortable cottages, sleeping 4/5, carefully converted from a stone barn. Furnished and equipped to a very high standard, all linen supplied and beds made up. Home cooked meals available, also cots, high chairs and laundry. Plenty of fun for children with a pony, huge sandpit, swings and table tennis. Farm animals to help feed and space to play in safety.

Mrs L. Kidd, Lower Trengale Farm, Liskeard, Cornwall PL14 6HF   Tel: Liskeard (0579) 21019

LISKEARD. Mrs E. Coles, Cutkive Wood Chalets, St. Ive, Liskeard PL14 3ND (0579 62216).

Properties sleep 4 adults; 2 children. Six only detached, self catering cedarwood chalets in 41 acres of private woodland. Personally supervised; the owners take great pride in the cleanliness and condition of these two and three bedroomed chalets which are fully equipped, including bed linen, colour TV, full size cooker, fridge and microwave oven. Picturesque resorts of Looe and Polperro a short drive away; Plymouth 30 minutes; St. Mellion Championship Golf Course five miles. On-site shop, milk and papers daily. Pets corner with goats, pigs, ducks, hens, geese. Children welcome to help feed the animals and milk the goats. Three-hole golf course, games room, adventure playground. Dogs welcome.

LOOE. Mrs A.E. Barrett, Tredinnick Farm, Duloe, Liskeard PL14 4PJ (Looe [05036] 2997). Working

farm. Sleeps 8. This accommodation is part of a large farmhouse on a mixed farm of dairy, beef, sheep and corn. Situated with beautiful views of the Cornish countryside just four miles from Looe and Polperro. Beaches, swimming, fishing, bowls, golf and horse riding all within easy reach. The house has full central heating and comprises three bedrooms, one with washbasin, sleeping eight, plus cot. Bathroom. Large lounge with woodburner and colour TV. Fully equipped kitchen. Electricity by 50p coin meter. Utility room with automatic washing machine and tumble dryer; extra toilet. Children welcome. Sorry, no pets. Large lawns and ample parking space. Games room. Terms from £95 – £285. Send first class stamp for further details. Cornish Tourist Board member.

See also Colour Display Advertisement **LOOE. Mrs N. Jenkins, Plaidy Beach Holiday Apartments, Plaidy Park Road, Looe PL13 1LG (Looe [050-36] 2044). Flats sleep 2/7.** Situated in a commanding position on the Cornish Riviera overlooking a sheltered beach — eight completely self-contained flats varying in size accommodating from two to seven occupants. About 15 minutes' walk into Looe where shark fishing, boating, tennis are available, while riding stables, golf are about 10 minutes by car. Shops 400 yards. All flats have coastal views and are tastefully decorated. Fitted carpets, colour TV including SKY films; shower/bathroom, toilet. Kitchens have electric cooker, fridge, kettle, generous quantity of equipment. Electricity by coin meters. Blankets, pillows provided, linen by hire. Extra children's beds, cots, high chairs. Launderette/ironing facilities. Free car parking. Pets welcome. Many places of interest to visit. Discounts on golf green fees. Terms from £60 low season; £120 to £320 high season. These rates refer to minimum size up to maximum size of flats. Inspected and approved by English Tourist Board. SAE or telephone for brochure as above.

POLPERRO

WILLY WILCOX and **QUAY**: two beautiful, spacious 400-year-old cottages, just eleven feet from the safe, sandy beach. **LANLAWREN FARM** (Valley of the Foxes): three miles along the coast, mellow old stone barns and granary divided into lovely cottages and apartments.

All properties fully equipped, maintained to a very high professional standard, cleanliness guaranteed; feature exposed beams, stone walls, open log fires, full heating, cosy atmosphere. Personal service: tea/coffee and home made biscuits welcome all guests. Crisply laundered linen on beds; toasters, hair dryers, coffee machines; TV in main bedrooms.

INDOOR HEATED SWIMMING POOL (85°F)

SPA, SAUNA, SOLARIUM, JET STREAM, MINI-GYM and GAMES ROOM PLUS OUTSIDE ACTIVITIES.

For brochure and full details please contact FIONA and MARTIN NICOLLE, BLANCHES WINDSOR, LANSALLOS, LOOE PL13 2PT (0503 72121).

LOOE. Robert and Jean Henly, Bucklawren Farm, St. Martins, Looe PL13 1NZ (Widegates [05034] 738). Bucklawren is situated deep in unspoilt countryside yet only one mile from the beach and three miles from Looe. Delightful cottages recently converted from farm buildings and furnished to a high standard. Large garden with sea views. Ideal position for beach, coastal paths, Woolly Monkey Sanctuary, National Trust properties, fishing trips, golf and water sports. Evening Meal available in the farmhouse.

MARAZION. Trenow Farm Cottages, Perranuthnoe, Marazion, Penzance TR20 9NW. ♛♛♛

Commended. **Sleeps 4-5.** Commanding a superb coastal position with unrivalled views of Mount's Bay and St. Michael's Mount, this barn conversion to two character cottages provides a high standard of accommodation. There are accessible coves along the Coastal Footpath to the picturesque village of Perranuthnoe with pub, shop and Post Office and lovely sandy beach. The magical St. Michael's Mount can be reached from the old Market Town of Marazion (one mile) with a safe beach and watersports facilities. St. Ives, Penzance, Land's End and The Lizard Peninsula are all within easy reach of this ideal holiday location. Both cottages have own garden, patio, barbecue, bath, electric shower, lounge diner, fitted kitchen, electric cooker, fridge/freezer, automatic washing machine, colour TV, night store heaters. Linen provided. Cot and high chair available. Open all year. Terms from £110. Members of Cornwall Tourist Board. Contact **David and Frances Phillips (0736 710421).**

MARAZION near. "Sunnyside", Perranuthnoe, Near Marazion. Sleeps 5. This fully modernised furnished cottage has superb views and is situated in the small, unspoilt village of Perranuthnoe, two miles from Marazion. The village has a shop, pub and ancient church. Sunnyside is only five minutes' walk from the sandy family beach. There are good coastal walks and fishing from the rocks. Nearby are St. Michael's Mount and many tourist attractions, within easy reach of St. Ives, Penzance, the Land's End area, Helston and the Lizard Peninsula. The cottage has fine coastal views from livingroom and bedrooms. The livingroom has sliding glass doors on to a sheltered patio and small secluded garden. Upstairs, the bedroom verandah has a panoramic view of Mount's Bay. It sleeps four, but a fifth folding Z-bed can be supplied. Bed linen is provided but please bring your own towels, otherwise the cottage is fully equipped including TV and a modern all-electric kitchen. Also Night Storage heaters for winter use. SAE please to **Mrs F.S. Roynon, "Treetops", Perran Downs, Goldsithney, Near Penzance TR20 9HJ (Penzance [0736] 710482).**

WHEN MAKING ENQUIRIES PLEASE MENTION
FARM HOLIDAY GUIDES

Coastal Cottages

LOOE, CORNWALL

On the fringe of Looe, a cluster of beautifully furnished cottages, of **rare and exceptional quality**, only 350 yards from the beach and coastal footpath. Country lanes, riding, fishing and golf.

Colour TV and linen included, with beds made up for your arrival. Electric blankets and comprehensive heating for out of season breaks. Regret no pets.

For colour brochure please telephone

Looe (050 36) 2736

MULLION (near Helston). Mr and Mrs R.P. Tyler Street, Trenance Farm, Mullion, Near Helston

TR12 7HB (Mullion [0326] 240639). Trenance Farm Cottages are situated halfway between the village and Mullion Cove. Only half a mile to swimming/surfing beach, plus splendid coastal walks mainly over National Trust land. Golf, fishing and riding locally. The old farm outbuildings have been converted into nine comfortable two/three bedroomed cottages, all fully equipped, with colour TV, etc. Bed linen can be hired. Heated swimming pool, games room, laundry, children's play area, ample parking, metered electricity. Bed and Breakfast available in the farmhouse. Children and pets welcome. Registered with the Cornwall Tourist Board.

NEWQUAY. "The Stable", Lower Trewince Farm, Porth, Newquay. Sleeps 4/6. For your perfect self catering holiday, "The Stable" has a large open-plan lounge with colour TV and luxury kitchen, beamed throughout. The 200 year old stable buildings have been converted into beautifully appointed spacious accommodation for four/six persons. Nestling in farming valley, quiet and secluded. Upstairs two attractive bedrooms (one double and one twin — extra single bed or cot available). Downstairs double bed settee. Luxury bathroom. Linen supplied. Children welcome. Pets accepted. Car essential, parking. Also available "The Bullpen" and "The Dairy" for 1991. All first quality cottages. **Mrs Marnie Beddoe, Lower Trewince Farm, Porth, Newquay TR8 4AW (0637 874650).**

The Stable

LOWER TREWINCE FARM
PORTH   —   NEWQUAY
CORNWALL

NEWQUAY. Mrs Joan Luckraft, Nancolleth Farm Caravan Park (FHG), Newquay TR8 4PN (Mitchell

[0872] 510236). Working farm. ETB √ √ √ √ √, Very Good. Nancolleth is a 250 acre sheep and cereal farm with south-facing caravan park. Cornwall's finest beaches and Newquay only five miles away, ideal touring centre. Accommodation is provided in six deluxe 28' six-berth caravans in garden settings, hardstandings and parking beside. Each caravan is fully equipped with two entrance doors and features which would enhance any home. Each has two bedrooms, colour TV, full size fridge and gas cooker, electric lighting, shaver point, gas fire, hot and cold, shower room with washbasin and toilet. Spacious lounge, dining and kitchen areas. Cleanliness guaranteed. Open May to October. Safe play area with leisure equipment, also Country Trail. Regret no pets. Laundry-auto washing and drying machines. Telephone. Mrs Luckraft's aim is to provide an enjoyable and relaxing holiday, and all visitors are personally welcomed.

NEWQUAY. 59 Carneton Close, Crantock, Newquay. Sleeps 6. This spacious modern first-floor flat with lock-up garage is situated in a peaceful residential cul-de-sac. The village of Crantock is four miles from Newquay and has one of the finest beaches in Cornwall. Tradesmen call, and shops, two inns and a church are within easy walking distance. The accommodation comprises two double bedrooms, one with an extra single bed; bed-settee in dining area of lounge; colour TV; electric heating; bathroom; toilet; kitchen with fridge and electric cooker, etc. No linen supplied. Pets are allowed. Open from Easter to October. There is 50p electric meter. SAE, please, for terms to **Mrs Wendy Carne, "Kalsia", Broadshard, Crewkerne, Somerset TA18 7NF (Crewkerne [0460] 73068).**

PADSTOW. Mrs Caroline Brewer, Carnevas Farm, St. Merryn, Padstow PL28 8PN (0841 520230). √ √ √ √ Situated only half a mile from golden sandy beach, fishing, golf, sailing etc. Quaint harbour village of Padstow only four miles. Bungalows sleep six, have two bedrooms, bathroom, kitchen/diner, airing cupboard, colour TV. Caravans six berth or eight, all have showers, toilets, fridge, colour TV. Also separate camping and caravan facilities. Rose Award Park 1990. E & WCTB also AA three pennant site. Brochure on request.

PADSTOW 1 mile. Wg.Cdr. Pat Patterson, Trevorrick Farm, St. Issey, Wadebridge PL27 7QH (Rumford [0841] 540574). Working farm. Sleeps 2/4. Ideal for peaceful holiday in lovely countryside, with magnificent views overlooking creek and near beautiful beaches. Superb 31 foot long caravan with dining kitchen, lounge with good put-u-up, double bedroom with dressing room, full bathroom, hot and cold water, electric light, cooker, microwave, immersion heater, colour TV, airing cupboard and fridge. Children and well-behaved dog welcome. The caravan is sited in its own fenced garden facing south. Good approach road. Shops, pubs, garages and church within one mile. West Country Tourist Board Member. Registered with English Tourist Board. Weekly terms £75 to £150. Also available, quality farmhouse Bed and Breakfast, and five quality cottages.

PENZANCE. Mr and Mrs S.M. Adey, St. Michael's Farm, Nanceddan, Ludgvan, Penzance TR20 8AW (0736-740 738).

The Croft, adjoining farmhouse, converted from old smoke house, provides cosy accommodation yet retains typical croft character. Loft, double bedroom and ground-floor, open plan, with bunkroom, kitchen/lounge and modern bathroom. Ideal two adults, two children; carpeted throughout, all electric. Situated in beautiful country position overlooking Mount's Bay and St. Michael's Mount — superb sea views. Five minutes by car from beach. Penzance three miles; St. Ives three miles. Numerous country walks including access to wild valley. Favourites with the children are our pony and donkey. Fully equipped except for linen. Shops half a mile away. Car essential. Sorry, no pets. Mini Breaks out of season.

PENZANCE. Mr and Mrs G.B. Hocking, Rospannel, Crows-An-Wra, Penzance TR19 6HS (St. Buryan [0736] 810262). Sleeps 5. Granite farm cottage; situated in centre of quiet 85-acre farm, next to farmhouse, overlooking a peaceful, unspoilt valley. Tarmac drive to garage adjoining cottage, one mile from A30. Ideally situated for touring West Cornwall; many coves and beaches within five miles. Nearest beach, shop, etc. three miles. Ideal for children. Pets allowed. Two bedrooms, electric radiators, washbasin and upstairs toilet. Linen supplied for overseas clients only. Dining/sittingroom has a large granite inglenook fireplace and colour TV. Fully equipped electric kitchen, including fridge and spin dryer. Only one cottage, so personal service guaranteed. SAE, please, for details, stating dates required.

PENZANCE. Mrs James Curnow, Barlowenath, St. Hilary, Penzance TR20 9DQ (Penzance [0736] 710409). Working farm. Cottages sleep 4/5.

These two cottages are on a dairy farm, in a little hamlet right beside St. Hilary Church, with quiet surroundings and a good road approach. A good position for touring Cornish coast and most well-known places. Beaches are two miles away; Marazion two-and-a-half miles; Penzance six miles; St. Ives eight; Land's End 16. Both cottages have fitted carpets, lounge/diner with TV; modern kitchen (fridge, electric cooker, toaster, iron); bathroom with flush toilet, shaver point. Electricity included in the rent, night storage heaters extra. One cottage sleeps five in three bedrooms (one double, twin divans and one single). The second cottage sleeps four in two bedrooms (twin divans in both). Linen not supplied. Cot by arrangement. Available all year. £75 to £230 weekly, VAT exempt.

FOR THE MUTUAL GUIDANCE OF GUEST AND HOST

Every year literally thousands of holidays, short-breaks and overnight stops are arranged through our guides, the vast majority without any problems at all. In a handful of cases, however, difficulties do arise about bookings, which often could have been prevented from the outset.

It is important to remember that when accommodation has been booked, both parties — guests and hosts — have entered into a form of contract. We hope that the following points will provide helpful guidance.

GUESTS: When enquiring about accommodation, be as precise as possible. Give exact dates, numbers in your party and the ages of any children. State the number and type of rooms wanted and also what catering you require — bed and breakfast, full board, etc. Make sure that the position about evening meals is clear — and about pets, reductions for children or any other special points.

Read our reviews carefully to ensure that the proprietors you are going to contact can supply what you want. Ask for a letter confirming all arrangements, if possible.

If you have to cancel, do so as soon as possible. Proprietors do have the right to retain deposits and under certain circumstances to charge for cancelled holidays if adequate notice is not given and they cannot re-let the accommodation.

HOSTS: Give details about your facilities and about any special conditions. Explain your deposit system clearly and arrangements for cancellations, charges, etc, and whether or not your terms include VAT.

If for any reason you are unable to fulfil an agreed booking without adequate notice, you may be under an obligation to arrange alternative suitable accommodation or to make some form of compensation.

While every effort is made to ensure accuracy, we regret that FHG Publications cannot accept responsibility for errors, omissions or misrepresentation in our entries or any consequences thereof. Prices in particular should be checked because we go to press early. We will follow up complaints but cannot act as arbiters or agents for either party.

POLPERRO. Crumplehorn Cottages, Polperro. Cottages sleep 2/7. Dating from early 1700 these traditional Cornish cottages face due south and enjoy maximum sunshine. Catering for two/seven, they have open-beamed ceilings, local stone fireplaces, sun patios, gardens and car parking, and offer the discriminating holidaymaker the unique opportunity of enjoying the comfort of "today" with the charm and character of "by-gone-days". Completely on the level and close to the harbour they blend with the local community and are not part of a "holiday complex". OPEN ALL YEAR with nightstore heating available for out-of-season holiday comfort. CCC and WCTB inspected/approved and under the personal supervision of resident owners to guarantee a high standard of comfort/cleanliness. Also cottages/flats at nearby holiday resort of Looe with similar accommodation/facilities. SAE, please, for illustrated brochure to **Mr and Mrs Murray Collings, Brook Cottage, Longcoombe Lane, Polperro PL13 2PL (Polperro [0503] 72274).**

POLZEATH. Curlew, High Cliff, Polzeath, Near Wadebridge. Sleeps 8. Curlew is in a unique position overlooking the sea and very close to a large sandy beach, ideal for surfing and very good for children of all ages. Pony trekking, sailing and golf at St. Enodoc are within easy reach. Very well situated for cliff walking. Curlew sleeps eight in five bedrooms (all single beds), equipped with hot and cold. Good kitchen facilities — all electric. Sitting room with TV. Parking for cars. Garden. Very safe for children. Close to shops. Ideal as touring centre. West Country Tourist Board registered. Apply **Mr and Mrs Woodcock, 35 Alleyn Park, Dulwich, London SE21 8AT (081-670 7837).**

PORT ISAAC. Mr and Mrs H. Symons, Trevathan Farm, St. Endellion, Port Isaac PL29 3TT (Bodmin [0208] 880248). ♛♛♛♛/♛♛♛♛ *Commended.* **Working farm, join in.** Open all year — Winter Breaks available. A warm welcome awaits you at our working family farm. Our cottages have panoramic views of the countryside and are furnished to a high standard having microwaves, washer/dryers, central heating, double glazing etc. There are glorious walks on the farm and we have very friendly animals which you may enjoy helping to feed. Sea two miles. Golf, sailing, surfing, fishing are all available in the area. Also excellent pubs. We have games and fitness rooms, and a hard tennis court on the farm. Also at Camelford we have a large period house sleeping twelve, plus cots. There are five double bedrooms; two bathrooms, shower room upstairs. Sixty acres of land on which you may wander or perhaps enjoy picnicking by the river. For details telephone or send SAE, please.

PORT ISAAC. Mrs Kathy Alford, Penhill, Pendoggett, Bodmin PL30 3HJ (Bodmin [0208] 880278). Properties sleep 3/4/5. Pendoggett is a small village two miles from the north Cornwall coast and is an excellent centre for touring, walking, surfing and sea fishing. The accommodation, situated at Penhill, commands spectacular views down the valley to Port Gaverne and over Port Isaac Bay. Village stores and Egon Ronay recommended restaurant situated nearby. Available are a cottage and three flats set in large grounds with ample parking space and safe play area for children. The cottage sleeps five, two flats sleep four and the third flat sleeps two/three. All are furnished to a high standard with electric cookers, fridges, TVs, etc. Available April to October. Children and pets welcome. Weekly terms from £60. Electricity by 50p meters. Tourist Board registered.

PORT ISAAC. Mrs M.E. Warne, Tresungers Farm, Port Isaac PL29 3SY (Port Isaac [0208] 880307). Working farm. Sleeps 6. Ideal spot for anyone desiring quiet holiday this farmhouse, on 160 acres of mixed farmland, offers furnished self-contained wing for self catering holidays from March to November. Approximately 400 yards from B3314 coast road, just over two miles from sea at Port Isaac. Accommodation for five/six people in two double bedrooms, one with extra single bed; also cot available; bathroom, toilet; sitting/diningroom; well equipped kitchen with electric cooker, fridge, etc. and including bed linen. Regret, no pets. Shops just over two miles. Car essential — parking. Electricity on meter. Golf, pony trekking, bathing and surfing within easy reach. St. Endellion Church about one and a half miles away. Terms on receipt of SAE, please.

PORT ISAAC. The Lodge, Treharrock, Port Isaac. Sleeps 6. Pleasant, south facing and convenient

bungalow, set in its own small, natural garden and surrounded by fields and woodland with streams. About two miles inland from Port Isaac, a sheltered, secluded spot at the end of driveway to Treharrock Manor. Rugged North Cornish cliffs with National Trust footpaths and lovely sandy coves in the vicinity. Excellent sandy beach at Polzeath (five miles), also pony trekking, golf etc. in the area. South facing sun room leads on to terrace; TV. Accommodation for six plus baby. Bathroom, toilet; sittingroom; kitchen/diner. Open all year. Linen available. Sorry, no pets. Car essential — parking. Terms from £150 to £250 per week (heating included). SAE to **Mrs E.A. Hambly, Home Farm House, Little Gaddesden, Berkhamsted, Hertfordshire HP4 1PN (Little Gaddesden [044-284] 3412).**

PORT ISAAC. Carn Awn, Port Gaverne, Port Isaac. Properties sleep 4/6. Carn Awn stands on its own in the hamlet of Port Gaverne, and overlooks the harbour and sea. Fishing, swimming, boating and delightful rock pools for the children. Magnificent coastline where you can walk for miles along coastal paths. Many other beaches within reach. Plenty of shopping facilities. Car essential, parking. Accommodation for six people in three double bedrooms; cot available; bathroom, separate toilet; large sitting/kitchen/diningroom. All electric. Linen may be hired. Well behaved dogs welcome. Open all year. SAE, please, for terms to **Mrs S.A. May, 24 Silvershell Road, Port Isaac PL29 3SN (Bodmin [0208] 880716).**

PORT ISAAC. Salters Cottage and Penny Cottage, Port Gaverne, Port Isaac. ♀♀ Sleep 4/6. On

National Trust Land. Port Gaverne is a hamlet adjoining Port Isaac on an inlet in the magnificent rugged North Coast, and its shingle beach is one of the safest bathing beaches in Cornwall. Salters and Penny Cottages are about 100 yards from the sea, made from the old fishermen's netting lofts and fish "cellars," dating from the days when Port Gaverne had a flourishing herring and pilchard trade. The cottages are fully equipped and most comfortably furnished and Penny Cottage, being all on the ground floor, is most suitable for the elderly or disabled. Salters Cottage has a piano which is tuned each Spring. I will be most happy to send you full details of rents and all vacant dates on receipt of SAE. **Mrs M.M. Cook, The Beach House, Port Gaverne, Port Isaac PL29 3SQ (Bodmin [020888] 0296).**

PORT ISAAC. The Dolphin, Port Isaac. Sleeps 9. This delightful house, originally an inn, is one of the most attractive in Port Isaac. Fifty yards from the sea, shops and pub. Five bedrooms, three with washbasins. Two bathrooms and WCs. Large diningroom. Cosy sittingroom. Spacious and well-equipped kitchen with electric cooker, dishwasher, washing machine. Sun terrace. Port Isaac is a picturesque fishing village with magnificent coastal scenery all round. Nearby attractions include surfing, sailing, fishing, golf, tennis, pony trekking. The Dolphin sleeps nine but reduced rates offered for smaller families and off-peak season. Weekly terms: £165 to £350 inclusive. SAE for details to **Mrs Thomas, 2 Stephenson Terrace, Worcester, Hereford and Worcester WR1 3EA (Worcester [0905] 20518/21967).**

PRAA SANDS near. Lower Kenneggy Farm, Rosudgeon, Near Praa Sands. Working farm. Sleeps 6. A comfortable, modernised cottage near the farm, with its own garden and ample parking space. The cottage accommodates six persons, with three bedrooms, fully fitted kitchen, diningroom and lounge with TV; bathroom and toilet; airing cupboard with immersion heater. Metered electricity; linen not supplied. Children are welcome, cot provided. Sorry, no pets. Lower Kenneggy is a country area with sea views, but close to Marazion (three miles) and Praa Sands (one mile) beaches; seven miles from Penzance and Helston. SAE, please, for terms to **Mrs P. Laity, Lower Kenneggy Farm, Rosudgeon, Penzance TR20 9AR (Penzance [0736] 762403).**

ST. AUSTELL. Mrs J. King, St. Margaret's Holiday Park, Polgooth, St. Austell PL26 7AX (St. Austell [0726] 74283). Sleep 2/8 Adults. A select family owned and run Holiday Park set in six acres of beautiful parkland offering good quality self-catering accommodation. Our detached bungalows sleep up to six persons and are finished to a high standard. They have colour TV, bathroom, fitted carpets etc. Two bungalows have a third bedroom sleeping up to eight and are suitable for disabled visitors. We also have fully self-contained chalets nestling among the trees, sleeping two to six persons. Laundrette and pay phone on site. The St. Austell Golf Course is 400 yards away and the Polgooth shops and inn are conveniently near. Pets are welcome if kept under control. Special rates for early and late holidays and for two persons. Open 1st March-31st December. Terms from £65-£290 per unit include VAT. Colour brochure from **Mrs J. King.**

See also Colour Display Advertisement **ST. AUSTELL. F.A.M. Milln, Bosinver Farm, St. Austell PL26 7DT (0726 72128).** Quality self catering cottages and bungalows on small rural estate. Relax in seclusion away from the crowds. Close to golf course, village with Post Office/Stores and old world pub. A short drive to many safe beaches, town, recreation centre and horse riding. One property suitable for disabled visitor. Well mannered dogs welcome. Further information on request. ETB approved.

ST. IVES. Higher Trenoweth, Carbis Bay, St. Ives.

A delightfully modernised cottage standing in large secluded garden half a mile from Carbis Bay beach and two miles from St. Ives. There is a large lounge with colour TV, night storage heater and log-burning stove; open plan stairs leading to three bedrooms — one with double bed, one with full sized bunk beds and one with a double and a single bed (a cot can be provided on request); bathroom with bath, WC and washbasin; huge well-fitted kitchen with dining area. Stable doors lead to a sun-soaked patio. There is also a downstairs cloakroom with WC, washbasin and automatic washing machine. Duvets and covers are provided and all electricity is included in the rental. Well-behaved dogs normally allowed. Terms from £145 to £320. Contact **Mr and Mrs G.N.F. Broughton, Orchard House, Wall, Gwinear, Hayle TR27 5HA (0736 850201).**

ST. IVES. Myrtwedhen, Hellesveor, St. Ives. A country cottage and garden, surrounded by farmland, only one mile from St. Ives harbour and beaches; a lovely house in a superb setting, luxuriously equipped for four to six people. Colour TV, central heating, parking for two cars. Children and pets very welcome. We provide cot, high chair and a washing machine. There are country views from the windows, and deck chairs and toys for the garden. Footpaths to the cliffs pass the cottage. Available for full weeks in the summer or off-peak breaks of any length. Whenever you arrive you will find the house warm and welcoming, the beds aired and made up. Tourist Board category 3. Prices from £70 – £320 (including sheets and heating) dependent on season. Details from **Mrs F.H. Seabrook, 30 Newcombe Street, Market Harborough, Leicestershire LE16 9PB (0858 463723).**

CORNWALL – St. Ives Bay

Self-catering Holiday Chalets situated on sand dunes at water's edge. Accommodation sleeps 4-8, fully equipped, colour TV and close to all amenities. Also POTTERIES and PAINTING COURSES offered, flexible to meet all needs – Beginner to Advanced. Accommodation available if required.

John Buchanan

SAE to John Buchanan, St. Ives Craft Centre, Halestown, St. Ives, Cornwall. Tel: 0736 795078.

ST. IVES BAY. Mr and Mrs A. Kay, Cove Bungalow, 33 Riviere Towans, Phillack, Hayle (Hayle [0736] 753673). Sleeps 5. Cove holiday bungalow could not be much closer to the sea, the garden extends down to the Cornish Coastal Footpath and just below is a fine beach of golden sand. Access to the beach is by a short footpath; there are no roads to cross. The bungalow is very well furnished with fitted carpets, colour television and it is double glazed. From the lounge window you will enjoy superb sea views to St. Ives harbour and Godrevey Lighthouse. Will sleep 4/5 maximum. Private car park. SAE or phone for letting rates and available dates. Also Bed and Breakfast accommodation available in luxury bungalow next door.

ST. KEW (North Cornwall). Mr T. Chadwick, Skisdon, St. Kew, Bodmin PL30 3HB (020 884 372). Lovely old country house in extensive gardens and woodlands in peaceful valley four miles from North Coast. Six self-contained, well-equipped apartments for up to seven people (for larger parties communicating doors can be opened). Spacious and comfortable with fully equipped kitchens, colour TV, night store heaters, use of laundry etc. Outstanding coastline and countryside — Camel Estuary, Rock, Polzeath, Port Isaac and Bodmin Moor. Shops at St. Kew Highway, one mile; Wadebridge, a little market town, four and a half miles. St. Kew Inn is only 200 yards away. Bathing, surfing, sailing, golf, hill-walking, fishing, pony trekking and local Leisure Centre all within six miles. Weekly from £84 to £268.

ST. NEOT. Mrs J.H. White, Hilltown Stud Farm, St. Neot, Liskeard PL14 6PT (0579 20565). Close to the moors with superb views, life on this small, peaceful farm revolves around the horses. Two self-catering cottages, carefully converted from old stone barn, make comfortable, friendly holiday homes for all ages. Visitors welcome to join in with farm activities. Drive the pony and trap, go fishing, meet the animals, plus riding for younger visitors. All this and lots more to do in an area that caters for hundreds of different tastes. Colour TV. Babysitting. Home laundry, etc. Phone or write for further details.

HILLTOWN

STITHIANS. Falmouth/Truro area. Pencoose House, Stithians. Sleeps 4/6. Well furnished house on modern farm with pleasant, peaceful garden. Beautiful views, in wooded area. Central for touring, within easy reach of north and south coasts and beaches. Two miles Stithians Reservoir, six miles Falmouth. The house comprises sittingroom with colour TV, diningroom, kitchen, hall, bathroom and two bedrooms. Pets welcome by prior arrangement. Personal supervision. Local Agricultural Show mid-July. Available April to September from £130 to £240 per week (bedlinen and electricity included). **Mrs J. Gluyas, Pencoose Farm, Stithians, Truro TR3 7DN (Stithians [0209] 860388).**

TREBARWITH STRAND near. Mrs Ann Sainsbury, Corwen House, Blisland, Near Bodmin PL30 4JJ

SCRUMPY COTTAGE

(0208 850 485). Sleeps 4/6 plus cot. Cloam Cottage is a pretty "old world" cottage with many character features such as slate floor, beamed ceiling and original fireplace with cloam oven. It lies two miles inland from Trebarwith Strand, a magnificent surfing beach on the spectacular North Cornwall coast. Close by are the picturesque harbours of Port Isaac and Boscastle; Tintagel, the legendary home of King Arthur; and Rock, famous for golf, windsurfing and sailing. Accommodation comprises gallery bedroom with double bed leading to second bedroom with bunk beds. Cot available. Sitting room with an open stone fireplace and colour TV, multi-fuel stove and double sofa bed. Kitchen/dining room with electric cooker and fridge. Bathroom. Electricity on £1 coin meter. Children welcome, pets by arrangement. Garden. Parking. Linen supplied at extra charge. Open all year. £90-£220 per week. Mid-week/weekend breaks November till March. Registered with the Cornwall Tourist Board.

TRURO. Mrs C.M. Penwarden, Garvinack Farm, Truro TR4 9EP (Truro [0872] 560385). Bungalows sleep 4-6. Choice of three farm bungalows available all year round. Situated in the middle of farm with superb views and secluded garden. Off A30 and five miles from Truro and Perranporth coast. All cottages have lounge and TV, separate diningroom, kitchen with electric cooker and fridge; oil fired Aga/Rayburn available in two bungalows with Economy 7 in the third. Two properties have double beds, the other singles and cot. Well equipped to modern standards with duvets in two of the bungalows. Linen supplied on request. Shops two miles. Car essential, garage parking available. Pets by arrangement. Terms from £100 weekly. Leaflet available.

TRURO near. Mrs Hazel Bowerman, Tre-Knoll Farm, Ladock, Near Truro TR2 4QB (St. Austell

[0726] 882451). Working farm. Flat sleeps 4. "Tre-Knoll" was built almost 200 years ago. Situated on a hill above the beautiful Ladock Valley, it offers a first-floor flat overlooking green fields and accommodating four persons. One double bedroom with hot and cold water; studio couch converting to two singles in sitting/diningroom; own bathroom with toilet; fully equipped kitchen, electric cooker, fridge, all cutlery, crockery etc. Linen included. Children welcome. Pets allowed but not female dogs in season. Electric heating throughout. In the centre of Cornwall, ideally placed for touring the whole county. Truro six miles; Newquay 10 miles; innumerable beaches within easy reach. Very informal, quiet and relaxed atmosphere. All animals on this 10 acre smallholding are treated as pets. Terms (including electricity for heating, hot water) on request with SAE. (10p meter for 13 amp sockets).

CORNWALL – SOMETHING FOR EVERYONE!

Sea, sand, cliffs and quite often the sun, but that's not all you will find in this interesting county. Cornwall has many fascinating places to visit, such as the Charlestown Shipwreck Centre, the Tropical Bird Gardens at Padstow, Cornwall Aeronautical Park near Helston, Botallack Tin Mine, The Cornish Seal Sanctuary, Perranporth and of course, St. Michael's Mount.

TRURO near. Mr Chris Warner, The Old Barn, Lower Tresithick Farm, Carnon Downs, Near Truro TR3 6JN (Truro [0872] 863687). Working farm, join in. Sleeps 4. Four persons can be accommodated in The Old

Barn now converted to a self-contained cottage, simple but comfortable; full of character with exposed beams in the upstairs lounge. The cottage has one double bedroom, one bedroom with two 3ft. 6ins. beds, cot; bathroom; sitting-room; diningroom-cum-kitchen which is large and homely with plenty of storage space, electric stove, fridge. Linen, except sheets, supplied; colour TV. Pets permitted. Car not essential but parking available. Lower Tresithick is a small working farm tucked away in a little valley above the creeks of the Fal Estuary. A long, bumpy lane leads only to the farm so peace and privacy are assured, although local shops and the main Truro/Falmouth are reached by a five minutes' walk. The local creek and boatyard are a 10 minute walk away. Mr and Mrs Warner can offer sailing lessons at their own local beach. Lots of space for children to play in surrounding woods and fields. April/October. SAE for terms.

WADEBRIDGE. Down Below. Luxury converted barn with large garden, ample parking space. Situated in its own grounds on 140 acre dairy farm in the centre of beautiful peaceful hamlet of Trewethern. Only four miles from the lovely beaches at Rock, Polzeath, Daymer Bay and Port Isaac, ideal for surfing, fishing, safe bathing and golf. Two local pubs one mile either side with excellent food. Also village stores and Post Office, lovely walk to both and 15th century church of St. Kew. Furnished to a very high standard, accommodation comprises very large lounge featuring open fire with millstone hearth, colour TV. Fully equipped kitchen/diner including fridge, electric cooker, toaster and micro-wave. Three large bedrooms; two twin-bedded, one double. Electric heaters in all rooms. Shower room, separate toilet. Suitable for six people plus baby. Cot and high chair available. 50p slot meter. Laundry room available with automatic washing machine and tumble dryer. Linen on request. Pets by arrangement only; please enquire. Friday to Friday bookings. Open all year. SAE for prompt reply. Details from **Mrs V. Davey, Carns Farm, Amble, Wadebridge PL27 6EB (0208 880398).**

WADEBRIDGE. Gamekeeper's Cottage, Burlawn, Wadebridge. Gamekeeper's Cottage is an 18th century charming Cornish cottage, quietly situated in its own idyllic wooded surroundings, two miles from Wadebridge. Terraced garden with stream and small pond. Tastefully modernised yet retaining original character. Exposed beams, slate floor in diningroom; kitchen; bathroom. Mains water. Attractive diningroom; sittingroom with TV; two bedrooms (one with double and single beds, the other with three singles). Pets welcome. Parking. Sandy beaches, surfing, sailing, fishing, pony trekking, golf at famous St. Enodoc course, all within easy reach. Beautiful walks in Forestry Commission lands bordering cottage. For terms apply **Mr and Mrs P.U.G. Sharp, Tregawne, Withiel, Bodmin PL30 5NR (Lanivet [0208] 831303).**

WADEBRIDGE near. Mrs J. Cherry, Tregawne Farm, Withiel, Bodmin, Near Wadebridge PL30 5NR (Lanivet [0208] 831503). Working farm, join in. Sleeps 2 Adults, 2 Children plus cot. Relax in a comfortable self-contained flat, in dairy farmhouse, surrounded by green fields and birdsong. Sleeps four with facilities for a baby. TV, fridge-freezer and spin dryer. The ancient meadows, hedgerows, streams and wooded valleys are a haven for an abundance of wildlife. The farm was awarded the Cornish Wildlife Trophy for Conservation in 1990. A central position to explore Cornwall's beaches, moors, country houses, golf courses and adventure parks. The River Camel, famed for sea trout in the summer and salmon in the autumn, is only a mile away. Regret no pets. Rates from £50 to £150 weekly.

WHITSAND BAY. Mrs V.J. Andrew, Trewrickle Farm, Crafthole, Torpoint, Whitsand Bay PL11 3BX (St. Germans [0503] 30333). Farmhouses sleep 8. Mid-way between Plymouth and Looe (about seven miles), just off coast road in pleasant country surroundings, two fully furnished, spacious, comfortable farmhouses are available for self-catering holidays from April to November. Both houses accommodate eight people and are well equipped with all modern conveniences. Garden and orchard. Garages. In each house, double and family bedrooms; high chair and cot; bathroom, toilet; sittingroom, diningroom. Electric cooking and heating, plus open fires. No linen supplied. Children and pets welcome. Suitable for disabled visitors. Shops and public transport half a mile, nearest beach one mile. Car essential, parking. Weekly terms from £100 to £180 (peak). Electricity by meter. Further details on request. Tourist Board listed.

WIDEMOUTH BAY, BUDE. Mrs Patricia M. Rowland, Quinceborough Farm, Widemouth Bay, Bude EX23 0NA (Widemouth Bay [0288] 361 236). Working farm, join in. Properties sleep 2/8. A variety of self-catering accommodation is available at Quinceborough Farm, including a hay barn, which has recently been converted into three cottages, each sleeping six to eight persons. These cottages won the CoSira and Country Landowners Cornwall Award for 1982. Also available nearby is a charming character cottage, approximately 200 yards from the beach, sleeping up to six. The sea and country views from all of the properties are magnificent. Each dwelling is equipped and furnished to a very high standard and all have colour TV, fridges, electric cookers, etc. Bed linen is provided and cots and high chairs are available on request, free of charge. Guests are invited to use our heated outdoor swimming pool, games room, hard tennis court and putting green and to

ramble over the fields, etc. Pets and children are welcome but, as this is a working farm of 120 acres, they must be under control. Our best recommendation is that people return regularly for what they consider to be the ideal family holiday. A variety of other self-catering units are available, including a 200-year-old cottage on the outskirts of Bude and an old converted coachouse on the sea front at Widemouth Bay. SAE, please, for further details. ETB registered.

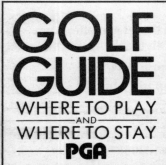

CUMBRIA — English Lakeland

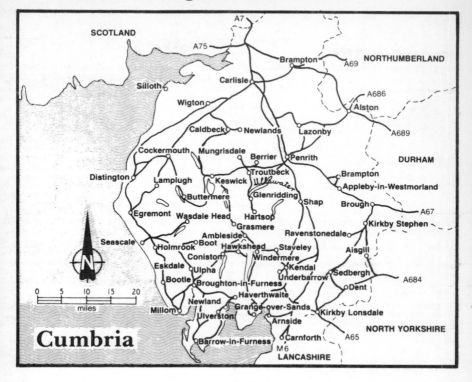

Cumbria

AMBLESIDE. Sally and Anthony Marsden, Betty Fold, Hawkshead Hill, Ambleside LA22 0PS (Hawkshead [096-66] 611). ♀♀♀ *Approved.* **Properties sleep 6.** Betty Fold is a large country house in its own spacious grounds with magnificent views and set in the heart of the Lake District National Park. The quaint village of Hawkshead is nearby and Coniston and Ambleside are within four miles; the beauty spot of Tarn Hows is 20 minutes' walk away. As well as being a Guest House, Betty Fold offers self catering accommodation for up to six persons; "Garden Cottage", in our grounds and a flat which is part of the main house. All accommodation is centrally heated and facilities such as linen, colour TV, and cots are provided, also heating, power and lighting. Pets welcome. Terms approximately £180 to £300 per week, in main season. Dinner available in Guest House. See also advertisement in BOARD SECTION of this guide. Tourist Board registered.

AMBLESIDE AREA. In the conservation village of Near Sawrey made famous by Beatrix Potter as the very essence of the Lake District complete with traditional pub owned by the National Trust. Charming self catering accommodation for five people equipped to a high standard and comprising kitchen/diner; sittingroom with open fire and colour TV; three bedrooms (double, twin and single); bathroom. Outside is a small lawned garden and parking for two cars. Water heating and cooking by electricity (meter), storage heaters included in rental of £140 to £280 per week plus cancellation plan. Regret no pets. Year round letting. **Mrs M.D. Hall, Castle Cottage, Near Sawrey, Ambleside LA22 0LF (Hawkshead [09666] 216).**

AMBLESIDE near. Thrang View, Chapel Stile, Near Ambleside. Sleeps 6. A detached three bedroomed cottage with attractive garden and lovely views of the surrounding fells. Ideally placed for touring, walking and climbing. Accommodation comprises spacious lounge with colour TV and radio; kitchen/diningroom with electric cooker, fridge and microwave; one double and two twin bedrooms; bathroom. Full oil fired central heating included in rental. Bed linen provided. Cot and high chair available. Electricity extra — meter reading. Ample parking. Sorry, no pets. Open all year. ETB and Cumbria Tourist Board Category 3. SAE please for brochure: **Mrs Pat Long, Mill Brow, Skelwith Bridge, Near Ambleside LA22 9NH (Ambleside [05394] 33253).**

APPLEBY-IN-WESTMORLAND near. Milburn Grange, Appleby-in-Westmorland CA16 6DR (07683 61867). ♥♥♥♥ *Approved/Commended.* **Sleeps 2/8.**

Milburn Grange is a tiny hamlet nestling at the foot of the Pennines enjoying extensive views over Lakeland hills and Pennines. Four quality cottages (three beamed) equipped to highest standards set within two acres. All have colour TV, microwaves, all except smallest have washing machines, large cottages have dishwashers. Drying facilities available. All cottages have electric central heating. Linen included. Cots and high chairs available. Safe children's play area with swings, picnic tables, gas barbecue. Shopping/milk/papers may be ordered for arrival. HOME COOKING AVAILABLE. Shop, Post Office, garage close by, public house within walking distance. Well behaved pets accepted. Two other cottages available in nearby idyllic villages. Excellent walking/touring base for couples and families. Ullswater 11 miles, children's fun park 11 miles, Appleby five miles — swimming, golf, fishing, castle etc. Resident owners. BABYSITTING AVAILABLE. TOURIST BOARD MEMBERS. OPEN ALL YEAR — OFF SEASON BARGAIN BREAKS. TERMS from £80 to £300. SAE **Mrs M.J. Burke.**

BASSENTHWAITE. Working farm. Sleeps 4/5. Peter House Farm Cottage, a new 1990 barn conversion with oak beams, is peacefully situated with lovely views. This working farm is an ideal base for touring the Lake District, with fell walking nearby. Accommodation of a high standard, sleeping up to five persons. Log fire, storage heating and hot water, all inclusive. Children welcome. Regret, no pets. Available all year. Short breaks for out of season. Terms from £150 to £200. **Mrs V.A. Trafford, Peter House Farm, Bassenthwaite, Keswick CA12 4QX (Bassenthwaite Lake [059681] 278).**

BOWNESS-ON-WINDERMERE. Self-catering flat. Sleeps 2/4 adults; 2 children. This flat is in a new development with lake views. Ideally placed in the centre of the village for shops, restaurants etc. Parking for tenants. Within easy reach of tennis, boating, fishing, golf. Ideal for touring and walking. Modern self-contained second floor flat comprising lounge/diner with kitchenette; two bedrooms (one twin, one double); bathroom. Furnished and equipped to a high standard for owner's personal use including colour TV, fridge, cooker etc. Continental quilts. Electric heating including storage heaters. Metered electricity. No pets or children under 10. SAE for further details. **Mrs J. Kay, "Fairways", West Lane, High Legh Road, Lymm, Cheshire WA13 0TW (092-575-5612).**

CARLISLE. Mrs Georgina Elwen, New Pallyards, Hethersgill, Carlisle CA6 6HZ (Nicholforest [0228] 77308). ♥♥♥♥ *Commended.* **Working farm, join in.** GOLD AWARD WINNER. Filmed for BBC TV. Relax and see beautiful North Cumbria and the Borders. A warm welcome awaits you on our 65 acre livestock farm tucked away in the Cumbrian countryside, yet easily accessible from M6 Junction 44. In addition to the surrounding attractions there is plenty to enjoy, including hillside walking, peaceful forests and seatrout/salmon fishing — or just nestle down and relax with nature. One comfortable well-equipped bungalow, 3/4 bedrooms. Two lovely, pleasant cottages on a working farm, 1/2 bedrooms. One well-equipped flat. HWFH, ETB, FHB. Video available for small refundable deposit.

See also Colour Display Advertisement **CARLISLE. Mrs Ivinson (FHG), Green View, Welton, Near Dalston, Carlisle CA5 7ES (Raughton Head [069-96] 230).** ♥♥♥♥/♥♥♥♥♥ *Commended.* **Properties sleep 4/6.** Three Scandinavian Pine Chalets, set in our large garden with views over fields to Caldbeck Fells. Sleep four to six in two/three bedrooms, heating in all rooms. Bathroom with heated towel rails including shower, two WCs. Open plan, south-facing sittingrooms with colour TV. All-electric fitted kitchen including fridge/freezer, toaster. All have microwaves and telephones. No. 1 Lodge also includes a dishwasher. Situated on the B5299 in the small, picturesque hamlet of Welton on the northern fringes of the Lake District, 11 miles M6, Exit 41, within 30 minutes' drive from Keswick, Lake Ullswater or Gretna Green. Weekly terms from £136 to £370. Car essential. Suitable for the disabled. Open all year. Member Country Hosts and Cumbria & Lake Self-Catering Association. SAE, please. Some electricity metered.

PLEASE SEND A STAMPED ADDRESSED ENVELOPE WITH ENQUIRIES

CARLISLE. Mrs J. James, Mid Todhills Farm, Road Head, Carlisle CA6 6PF (06978 213). ♀♀♀♀

Commended. **Working farm, join in. Sleeps 2 adults; 3 children.** Riggfoot Cottage is situated on a 280 acre family run farm near the Scottish Border and is an ideal holiday base being within easy teach of the Northern Lakes, Kielder Reservoir, Talkin Tarn as well as numerous other attractions including Hadrian's Wall, Hermitage, Gretna Green and the Alston Miniature Railway. Accommodation comprises two bedrooms; bathroom; open plan kitchen/diningroom. Colour TV. Night storage heaters. Linen supplied but not towels. Parking. Terms from £120 to £250 per week; Breaks from £60. Brochure available.

COCKERMOUTH. Mrs B. M. Chester, Bouch House Farm, Embleton, Cockermouth CA13 9XH (Cockermouth [0900] 823367). Working farm. Sleeps 6. The cottage is situated near the farmhouse and has picturesque views of the Bassenthwaite Valley and surrounding countryside. Own gardens, with deck chairs available. Only one and a half miles from Cockermouth, a pleasant historic market town with good bus service and recreation facilities, including fishing, golf and swimming pool. Well situated for touring Lakes and coastline — nearest Lakes are Bassenthwaite, Buttermere, Crummock and Lowes Water. Accommodates six people, with cot available; bathroom, shower unit, toilet; sittingroom. Colour TV. Fully equipped kitchen. Linen supplied. Pets permitted. Car advisable — parking. Open all year. Terms from £60 weekly. SAE, please.

COCKERMOUTH. Mrs J. Hope, Cornhow Farm, Loweswater, Cockermouth CA13 9UX (Lorton [090-085] 200). Working farm. Sleeps 8. Ideal for a family holiday, spacious, fully modernised house adjoining an 18th-century farmhouse on a 250-acre dairy and stock-rearing farm. Situated in the beautiful Loweswater Valley it is well-placed for all country activities and central for the coast and lakes (Crummock half-a-mile). Fully equipped for eight people, the house is quiet and comfortable and accommodation comprises four double bedrooms; two bathrooms, two toilets; sittingroom. Electric cooking facilities and solid fuel heating. Everything supplied for the ease and enjoyment of your holiday. Private fishing. Children welcome and they may bring their pets. Open all year, a car is essential and there is parking. Three miles from shops. Weekly terms £100 to £210 (inclusive of electricity). No linen supplied. Further details on request with SAE, please.

CONISTON. Clifton Villa, Yewdale Road, Coniston. Sleeps 6. Clifton Villa is situated in the centre of Coniston village, approximately half a mile from Coniston Water. It has all modern amenities including electric cooker, fridge, TV. All beds supplied with linen and continental quilts. There is accommodation for six, in one double bedroom and two twin-bedded rooms. Cot available. Bathroom, toilet, sitting room and kitchen. Electricity by £1 coin meter. Nearby there is fell walking, fishing, boating and pony trekking. Children welcome. Pets by arrangement only. Open all year. Terms from £95 per week. SAE please or telephone **Mrs A.M. Raven, Mountain View, Yewdale Road, Coniston LA21 8DU (05394 41412).**

CONISTON. Mrs Janet Usher, Dixon House, Coniston LA21 8HQ (Coniston [05394] 41217). ♀♀ *Commended.* "Gaythorne" is a stone-built detached bungalow, set in its own garden, in the centre of Coniston village. It is ideally situated with only two minutes' level walk to the shops, whilst enjoying magnificent views of the Coniston fells. The lake is only a 15 minute walk away for sailing, rowing and the beautiful steam yacht Gondola. The accommodation comprises; one double bedroom, one twin bedroom (all beds have continental quilts); lounge with stone fireplace, colour TV, video and radio; fully fitted kitchen; bathroom with shower; private parking. Sorry no pets. For terms/further details please telephone or write for brochure.

CONISTON. Mrs D.A. Hall (FHG), Dow Crag House, Coniston LA21 8AT (05394-41558). Two bungalows to let as holiday chalets, sleeping two/seven. One mile from Coniston village on A593. Resident owner. First bungalow has sittingroom, kitchen/diningroom, three bedrooms sleeping seven; bathroom, separate toilet. Electric cooker, refrigerator. Night store heaters in both bungalows. Second bungalow comprises livingroom/kitchen, three bedrooms sleeping five, bathroom. All equipped with continental quilts. Please bring own linen. Parking space. These holiday chalets are set in private garden with direct access to the Fells and Hills. Superb views overlooking Lake towards Grizedale Forest. Freedom, yet safe for children. Pets welcome by arrangement. Mountain walks, boating, fishing, tennis and bowls in village. Available March till November. Terms on application with SAE, please.

CONISTON. Hanson Ground, Coniston. Sleeps 4. Hanson Ground is situated at the northern end of the road running along the eastern shore of Coniston Lake, two miles from Coniston Village. Set high up amidst the fields with Grizedale Forest behind, it occupies the first floor of a barn on the small agricultural holding of Knipe Ground, standing adjacent to the 16th century farmhouse. Though secluded it is ideal for exploring Lakeland. Two bedrooms, one with twin beds, one with bunk beds, cot; bathroom with toilet; sitting/dining-room with balcony overlooking lake; electric kitchen. No linen supplied. Sorry, not suitable for disabled guests. Terms from £100 to £150. Pets £20. SAE to **Mrs Mary Dutton, Knipe Ground, Coniston LA21 8AE (Coniston [05394] 41221).**

FUN FOR ALL THE FAMILY IN CUMBRIA

Appleby Castle Conservation Centre, Appleby; *Brockhole National Park Visitor Centre*, near Ambleside; *Grizedale Forest Wildlife Centre*, Hawkshead; *Lowther Wildlife Adventure Park*, near Penrith; *Muncaster Castle*, Ravenglass; *Levens Hall*, near Kendal; *Ravenglass & Eskdale Railway*, Ravenglass; *Lakeside & Haverthwaite Railway*, Haverthwaite, near Newby Bridge; *Windermere Steamboat Museum*, Rayrigg Road, near Bowness-on-Windermere; *Fell Foot Park*, Newby Bridge, Lake Windermere.

CONISTON (Lake District). Mrs M. Wilkinson, Station House and Cottage, Torver, Coniston LA21 8AZ ([05394] 41392). Lake District: Country Railway Station. Traditional-style bungalow, detached property in half-acre garden. Accommodates two people. En-suite facilities. Private parking. Low and high level walks. Coniston two miles, Lake walk 20 minutes. Dining facilities in the quiet village of Torver. Sorry, no smokers allowed. Regret no pets. Registered with SLT Board. Rents from £100 to £150. Telephone or write (SAE, please) for full details.

CONISTON near. Mrs J. Halton, Scarr Head Bungalow, Torver, Near Coniston LA21 8BP (Coniston [05394] 41328). Working farm, join in. This delightful self-contained holiday bungalow in quiet picturesque surroundings has a lovely outlook and extensive views of the Coniston Mountains. It is completely detached, and stands in its own half acre of level garden and grounds. Tarmac drive and ample parking. Ideal for walking, touring lakes, etc. Bathroom and toilet; kitchen with electric cooker, fridge, hot and cold water; two double and one single bedrooms; large sitting/diningroom. Fully equipped except linen. Available all year. Village inns very handy, Coniston three miles. SAE, for terms, etc stating number of persons and dates required. English Tourist Board registered.

DENT. Edmondsons, Dent, Sedbergh. This stone built cottage is situated in the main cobbled street of Dent in the Yorkshire Dales. It is an ideal centre for walking or touring and is within easy reach of the Lake District. The fully modernised cottage retains old oak beams and mullion windows. It is comfortably furnished for four people, having two double bedrooms, one with twin beds and vanitory unit; bathroom wtih toilet; lounge/diningroom; fully equipped kitchen; garage. Night storage heaters with electric fire in lounge. Children welcome, pets permitted. Linen included. Open all year. Details from **Mrs B. Bysh, Glebehurst, 24 Church Lane, Southwick, Sussex BN4 4GB (Brighton [0273] 593128).**

TEL. MRS. J. HALL (09403) 319

FISHERGROUND is a lovely traditional fell farm on the quieter, sunnier side of the Lakes. High quality self catering holidays are offered either in three custom built Scandinavian-style Pine Lodges or two traditional stone and slate cottages complete with coal fires. All have colour TV, fully equipped kitchens with microwave ovens and dishwashers, and bathrooms and quality fittings throughout. All have electric central heating which keeps them snug and comfortable on the coldest winter days. FISHERGROUND is a paradise for children and pets and there is an acre of orchard and a natural adventure pool plus an adventure playground. We have our own station on the 7 mile Ravenglass and Eskdale Miniature Railway, and nearby are lakes, boating, walking, climbing, historic castles, forts, horse riding, coastal harbours, fishing and other attractions. Guided adventure days by arrangement. Selection of good bar meals nearby (children welcome). *Brochure on request.*

FISHERGROUND FARM ESKDALE CUMBRIA CA19 1TF

FHG PUBLICATIONS LIMITED publish a large range of well-known accommodation guides. We will be happy to send you details or you can use the order form at the back of this book.

GRASMERE. 3 and 5 Field Foot, Broadgate, Grasmere. Properties sleep 7/8. Two terraced cottages

situated down a private lane in the heart of Grasmere village bordering the River Rothay. Literally one minute from bus route and shops, they are convenient for those without their own transport. Built of traditional Lakeland stone, our fully equipped cottages stay cool in summer but are very cosy in winter. No. 3 sleeps eight, No. 5 sleeps seven and has its own riverside patio. Cots, high chairs and extra camp beds available. Come to Grasmere "the jewel of the Lakes" and enjoy a wonderful holiday. Cumbrian and English Tourist Board listed. Contact **Mrs S.H. Brown, High Dale Park Farm, Satterthwaite, Cumbria LA12 8LJ (0229 860226).**

See also Colour Display Advertisement GRAYTHWAITE. Enjoy a relaxed holiday in the tranquil rural setting of Beatrix Potter country. We offer a range of cottages and apartments sleeping from 2 to 7 people, all equipped and furnished to a high standard. Most accommodation has either a wood burning stove, or open fire (free logs provided). All have night storage heaters. Some have been specially adapted for the accompanied wheel chair user. Free trout and coarse fishing is available on Esthwaite Water. Open all year to enable you to take advantage of the seasonal changes. An ideal base for walking and touring. Please contact **Esthwaite Holidays, Heart of the Lakes, Rydal Holme, Rydal, Ambleside LA22 9LR (05394 32321).**

HARTSOP (Southern Lakes). Mr G.F.C. Mellstrom, The Weaving Cottage, Grove Farm, Hartsop, Patterdale. Working farm. Sleeps 4/6. A traditional Lakeland cottage, modernised to high standard with outstanding views of the fells. Situated in unspoilt peaceful village between Ullswater and Brotherswater, within easy reach of Penrith and Windermere. Fully furnished and well equipped, providing ideal base for self-catering holiday; climbing and walking. Accommodation consists of sitting/diningroom with TV point; electric fire, double settee; double bedroom; second bedroom with two single beds. Kitchen. Bathroom. Night storage heating. Large SAE for details to **Downlands, Bramshott, Liphook, Hants GU30 7QZ (Liphook [0428] 724600).**

HAWKSHEAD. Linda and Alan Bleasdale, Borwick Lodge, Outgate, Hawkshead, Ambleside LA22

0PU (096-66 332). Our 17th century traditional Lakelands cottage of charm and character is in a secluded setting within three acres of beautiful landscaped gardens with magnificent panoramic views of the lakes and mountains. The comfortable three-bedroomed accommodation for up to six persons is of a high standard and centrally heated with bed-linen and colour TV provided. Our central position close to Hawkshead village (good choice of shops, restaurants and inns) is ideal for a pleasant relaxing holiday or numerous outdoor activities. Linda and Alan aim to make you feel welcome and relaxed and especially to make your stay enjoyable in this most beautiful corner of England. Ample parking. Open all year. From £100 per week. Well-behaved dogs accepted by arrangement. Also Bed and Breakfast accommodation available. May we send our brochure?

HOLMROOK. G. and H.W. Cook, Hall Flatt, Santon, Holmrook CA19 1UU (Wasdale [09406] 270). Working farm. Sleeps 7. This comfortably furnished house is set in own grounds with beautiful views. The approach road is a short but good lane off Gosforth/Santon Bridge road. Ideal centre for climbers and walkers. Within easy reach of Muncester Castle and Narrow Gauge Railway from Ravenglass to Eskdale, about three miles from the sea and Wastwater. Accommodation comprises two double bedrooms, two single and child's bed; cot; bathroom, two toilets; sittingroom; diningroom; all electric kitchen with cooker, fridge, kettle, immersion heater, stainless steel sink unit. Fully equipped except for linen. Open Easter to Christmas. Pets by arrangement. Shopping about two miles and car essential. Electricity by 50p meter. SAE, please, for weekly terms.

KENDAL. Mrs E. Bateman, High Underbrow Farm, Burneside, Kendal LA8 9AY (Kendal [0539] 721927). Working farm. Properties sleep 4. This newly converted cottage adjoins the 17th century farmhouse in a sunny position with wonderful views. Ideal spot for touring the Lake District and Yorkshire Dales, with many pleasant walks around. There are two bedrooms (one with double bed, the other with two singles). Children are welcome and a cot is available. Bathroom with shower, toilet. Large livingroom/ kitchen with fitted units, fridge and cooker. Electricity by 50p meter. Understairs store. Fitted carpets throughout. Own entrance porch. Sorry, no pets. Shops at Burneside two miles away, Kendal four miles, Windermere eight miles. Linen optional. Car essential — parking. Terms from £95 weekly. There is also a 6-berth holiday caravan to let from £75 per week.

KENDAL. Mrs E. Barnes, Brackenfold, Whinfell, Kendal LA8 9EF (Grayrigg [053-984] 238). Working farm, join in. Sleeps 6. Brackenfold is a 147-acre dairy/sheep farm set in a quiet country area. There are beautiful scenic views from the farm and also a river running through the middle of the farm which is suitable for paddling and picnicking. Brackenfold is situated centrally for touring the Lake District and the Yorkshire Dales. All children are welcome and babysitting is available. Milk can be obtained from the farm. The accommodation is part of the farmhouse and has two double bedrooms, cot; bathroom, toilet; sitting/diningroom; fully equipped kitchen with electric cooker, fridge, etc. Shops four miles, sea 20. Sorry, no pets. Open March to November. SAE, please, for terms.

KENDAL. Mrs R. Dodgson, Cragg Farm, Bowston, Burneside, Kendal LA8 9HH (0539 821249).

♀♀♀ *Approved.* Cragg Farm Cottage, completely self-contained, adjoins the farmhouse and is set in quiet rural surroundings with ample parking space and opportunity to walk in countryside. It is three-quarters of a mile from main Kendal to Windermere road (A591). Good position for visiting Lakes and Windermere (15 minutes away) and Kendal, a busy market town and good shopping centre, four miles. Villages of Staveley and Burneside two miles. The cottage is comfortable, clean and well equipped. One double and one twin-bedded rooms. Gas fire and central heating, electricity on 50p meter. Bed linen provided. Colour TV. Details on request.

KENDAL. The Barns, Field End, Patton, Kendal. ♀♀♀♀ *Commended.* Two detached barns recently

converted into five spacious architect-designed houses. The Barns are situated on 120 acres of farmland, four miles north of Kendal. A quiet country area with River Mint passing through farmland and lovely views of Cumbrian Hills, many interesting local walks with the Dales Way Walk passing nearby. The Barns consist of four houses with four double bedrooms and one house with three double bedrooms. Each house fully centrally heated for early/late holidays; lounge with open fire, diningroom; kitchen with cooker, fridge and washer; bathroom, downstairs shower room and toilet. Many interesting features include oak beams, pine floors and patio doors. Central to Lakes and Yorkshire Dales, National Parks. Electricity at cost. Pets welcome. For brochure of The Barns apply to **Mr and Mrs E.D. Robinson, 1 Field End, Patton, Kendal (Kendal [053984] 220 or [0539] 21636).**

See also Colour Display Advertisement

KENDAL near CROOK. Plumgarths Holiday Flats, Plumgarths. ♀♀♀♀ *Commended.* **Properties sleep 7.** Plumgarths is

an early 17th century house standing in extensive, peacefully secluded grounds surrounded by open farming country between Windermere and Kendal, just nine miles from M6 exit 36. This picturesque house has been sympathetically converted into six spacious, self-contained flats sleeping up to seven. Also Chalet in the grounds. Choose the one that suits you best — one, two or three bedrooms, first floor or ground floor (no steps). All have colour TV and open fire in the livingroom, fully equipped electric kitchen, bathroom and toilet. Everything is supplied except linen (available for hire). Background central heating October/May. Cot and high chair on request. Dogs by arrangement. We are open all year to welcome you and to care for your comfort. Three-night Breaks November/March. Cumbria Tourist Board member. Write or phone **Jonathan and Fidelia Somervell, Plumgarths Holiday Flats, Crook, Kendal LA8 8LE (Kendal [0539] 821325).**

KESWICK. Mire House, St. Johns-in-the-Vale, Keswick. Sleeps 6. Mire House is a farmhouse situated

in the Vale of St. John four miles from Keswick. The house still retains oak beams in the sittingroom and offers a quiet relaxing holiday in peaceful surroundings. There is accommodation for six people in three double rooms, one single; cot; bathroom; sittingroom with open fire; kitchen with fitted sink and cupboards with utensils; electric cooker, fridge, iron, immersion heater. Linen not supplied. Children welcome and one pet allowed. Ample parking. Available Easter to January. SAE, please, for terms. **Mrs I. Birkett, Birkett Mire, Threlkeld, Keswick CA12 4TT (Threlkeld [059-683] 608).**

Mire House

KESWICK. Mrs Ann Cammack, 7 Grange Park, Keswick CA12 4AY (Keswick [07687] 73849). This centrally heated modern flat is situated in a quiet panoramic location on the outskirts of Keswick, looking over Skiddaw and Bassenthwaite Lake. It comprises lounge (with colour TV); fully fitted kitchen; shower room, toilet; double bedded room with single room annexe; plus garden. Keswick is an excellent centre for touring, hillwalking, water sports and riding. It has several pubs and restaurants, plus a theatre and cinema. Canoes and mountain bikes are available for hire, as well as qualified hillwalking leadership, if required, from the owner. Also gorge walking, scrambling and basic rock climbing for the adventurous.

KESWICK. Horse Shoe Crag, Fieldside Close, Keswick. Flats sleep 6. The property is situated near the Lake District National Park, one mile to the east of Keswick Town Centre. It commands a wonderful and extensive view over the Lakeland Fells. Horse Shoe Crag stands in its own grounds and access is by a private drive with ample parking facilities. The flats are newly built and equipped to provide delightful and carefree holidays involving the minimum of housework. Each flat has full gas central heating for all year round holidays and can accommodate up to six people. Lower flat has two twin and one double bedrooms; upper flat one double, one twin and two single rooms. All with fitted units. Each flat has fitted kitchen with cooker, fridge, etc. Lounge with local stone fireplace, electric fire and colour TV, and bathroom with airing cupboard. SAE for terms and brochure to **Mrs J. Swainson, Lime Grove, Fieldside Close, Keswick CA12 4LN (Keswick [07687] 72150).**

KESWICK. Peter and Jackie Werfel, Fieldside Grange, Keswick CA12 4RN (07687 74444). Apartments sleep 2/6. These fully self-contained and centrally heated apartments have been converted from an old Lakeland farm. Individual units are comprehensively equipped including electric cooker, fridge, bed linen and colour TV. Private grounds of one-and-a-half acres offer magnificent views over Keswick, the Lake and surrounding hills, giving peace and quiet for those who enjoy tranquillity yet plenty of space for children. Full fire precautions. Open all year. Weekly terms from £100 to £265. Members of the Cumbria and Lakeland Self Caterers Association. Tourist Board Inspected and Approved.

Fieldside Grange

KESWICK. Mrs M.R. Tatters, Birkett Bank, St. Johns-in-the-Vale, Keswick (Threlkeld [059-683] 692). The accommodation here is a furnished farm cottage situated in Vale of St. John four-and-a-half miles from Keswick. Two bedrooms (one is large with two double beds, the other has one double bed); bathroom; sittingroom with colour TV; dining/kitchenette with electric cooker, lighting, fridge, immersion heater. Cottage is an old stone one, built in 1787, comfortably furnished. Parking space for cars. Children welcome. Dogs allowed. Penrith 14 miles, Carlisle 28 miles. Terms and further particulars on request with SAE, please, for speedy reply.

KESWICK near. Mrs A.M. Trafford, Bassenthwaite Hall Farm, Bassenthwaite Village, Near Keswick CA12 4QP (07687 76393). Three immaculate cottages of charm and character, near a stream in this tranquil and pretty hamlet. Six miles north of Keswick, off A591 half a mile from village. Children spend many happy hours nearby playing on the swings in the wood whilst the ducks and hens roam freely. Lovely walks to the Lake, Skiddaw, Dash Falls and surrounding hills. Excellent inn nearby serving good food. All cottages are situated around the farmyard. We have small properties for two and family properties sleeping four to 10. Large groups of up to 20 can also be catered for. Reduction off peak. Long weekends, cheap mid-week breaks from November to March. Also farmhouse Bed and Breakfast.

ACORN FLATS

Two new built spacious flats in Hotel grounds. Quietly situated near to town centre and lake, ideal for touring Lake District. Fully equipped modern flats, two bedrooms, lounge with colour TV. Kitchen with fridge/freezer, microwave oven and electric cooker. Cot available on request. All details and prices available. SAE would be appreciated.

Mr & Mrs J. Millar, Acorn House Hotel, Ambleside Road, Keswick, Cumbria CA6 4DL. Telephone: (07687) 72553.

KIRKBY LONSDALE near. Mrs M. Dixon, Harrison Farm, Whittington, Kirkby Lonsdale, Carnforth, Lancashire LA6 2NX (05242 71415). Properties sleep 2/8. Near Hutton Roof, three miles from Kirkby Lonsdale and central for touring Lake District and Yorkshire Dales. Coast walks on Hutton Roof Crag, famous lime stone pavings. Sleeps eight people, one room with double and single bed and one room with double and cot, third bedroom has three single beds. Bathroom. Sittingroom, diningroom and kitchen. Everything supplied but linen. Parking space. Pets permitted. Other cottages available for two to eight people. Electric cooker, fridge, kettle, iron, immersion heaters and TV. Electricity and coal extra. Terms from £100. Member of Cumbria Tourist Board. SAE brings quick reply.

KIRKOSWALD. Crossfield Farm and Sport Fishery. Accessibly secluded tranquil quality cottages overlooking small trout lakes amid Lakeland's beautiful Eden Valley countryside. Only 30 minutes' drive equidistant from Ullswater, North Pennines, Hadrian's Wall and Scotland's Borderlands. *Guaranteed clean. *Well equipped and maintained. *Centrally located. *Good fishing and walking. *Laundry area. *Pets welcome. Relax and escape to "YOUR" home in the country, why settle for less! **Telephone (076883 711) or SAE Crossfield Cottages, Kirkoswald CA10 1EU at any time.**

PLEASE ENCLOSE A STAMPED ADDRESSED ENVELOPE WITH ENQUIRIES

LAKE DISTRICT & EDEN VALLEY. Properties sleep 2/8. Selection of fully furnished Apartments, Cottages and Houses situated in the Lake District and in the popular Eden Valley Villages, all within easy access of the M6 motorway. Pets by arrangement. For Brochure and further details contact **Lowther Scott-Harden with Watson Lewis, St Andrew's Churchyard, Penrith, Cumbria (Penrith [0768] 64541) 24hrs.**

LOWESWATER. Mrs M. Grimshaw, Godferhead Farm, Loweswater, Cockermouth CA13 0RT (Lorton [090085] 661). Working farm. Sleeps 6. Seventeenth century farm cottage with wonderful views of Crummock Lake and Buttermere Fells. Convenient for Loweswater, Crummock and Buttermere Lakes. Bassenthwaite and Derwentwater lakes 12 miles. Keswick 12 miles, Cockermouth seven miles. An ideal centre for walking and climbing. Car essential. Accommodation comprises lounge-diner with open fire and TV; kitchen with electric cooker; bathroom; two double bedrooms and one twin bedded room. Cot and high-chair available. Coal and electricity included. Linen not supplied. Sorry, no pets. £50 deposit per week, balance two weeks prior to arrival. Further details from Mrs Grimshaw.

See also Colour Display Advertisement **PENRITH. The Estate Office, Lisham House, Patterdale Hall Estate, Glenridding, Penrith CA11 0PJ (07684 82308). Apartments** ♀♀♀ *Commended;* **Cottages** ♀♀ *Approved;* **Pine Chalets** ♀ *Commended.* Private 300 acre Estate set between Ullswater and Helvellyn containing a working hill farm, Residential Centre, plantations, ancient woodland, waterfall wood, private fishing/foreshore and 11 self catering units set in various parts of the Estate. This range includes three apartments, two cottages and six pine chalets. Children welcome. Sorry, no animals. Terms from £121 to £305 per week including central heating and one tank of hot water per day. Other electricity metered. Linen hire available. Last minute (within two weeks) short breaks and special offers available. Please phone for detailed brochure.

PENRITH. Thwaite Hall, Hutton Roof, Greystoke, Penrith. Properties sleep 6. This farmhouse is a 16th century listed building which has been modernised but still retains its oak beams and mullioned windows with open fires, overlooking Carrick Fells. Nearby is Keswick and Ullswater Lake for sailing; walking, climbing, golfing, pony trekking and hunting within easy reach in quiet, peaceful, open countryside. Both houses have double bedrooms and one single and both sleep six. There are cots, bathroom, toilet, sittingroom and diningroom in each. Kitchens have cooker, refrigerator, sink unit, fully equipped with plugs. TV. No linen supplied. Pets are allowed. Open all year. Car is essential, parking. SAE, please, for terms. **Mrs E. Taylor, Hill Top Farm, Penruddock, Penrith CA11 0RX (Greystoke [085-33] 340).**

PENRITH. Rampshowe, Orton, Penrith. Working farm, join in. Sleeps 8. Rampshowe is a 150 acre fell farm with sheep, lambs, beef cattle and calves and a riding pony. Delightfully positioned in the peace and quiet of Birkbeck Fells, with a river flowing through the fields, lovely waterfall and pool for bathing. Ideal area for birdwatchers. Local angling club. Shops, post office, pub serving snacks. Unspoilt, rural countryside, yet only five miles from M6 motorway. Accommodates eight people in three double bedrooms, cot; bathroom, toilet; colour TV, sittingroom, diningroom, both with electric storage heaters and open fire with back-boiler. Large kitchen with fridge, cooker, electric kettle, vacuum cleaner, twin-tub washer etc., only linen required. Fitted carpets throughout. Pets must be well-controlled. Car essential — parking. Open all year. Terms include most of fuel. The house stands on its own, with garden and large farmyard. Wood provided for fire. SAE to **Mrs M.E. Mawson, Sproat-Ghyll Farm, Orton, Penrith CA10 3SA (Orton [058-74] 244).**

ULLSWATER. Cottage on a small sheep farm; sleeps 6, adjoining the farmhouse with its own separate

access, parking and playing area, 100 yards from main road A5091. Situated one mile from Troutbeck village and A66, Ullswater Lake four miles, and within equal distance of Penrith and Keswick towns. The cottage consists of two large bedrooms with washbasins; bathroom with toilet; cot available. Large lounge with colour TV, coal fire and also mobile Calor gas heater. Fully equipped kitchen with electric cooker and fridge, electric immersion heater for hot water; electricity included in the price. Linen not supplied. Terms from £100. **Mrs Margaret Wilson, Greenbank Farm, Troutbeck, Penrith CA11 0SS (Greystoke [08533] 259).**

ULLSWATER. South View, Dacre, Penrith. Working farm. South View farmhouse is situated in the small village of Dacre, two miles from Lake Ullswater and four miles from Penrith and M6. There is a large walled garden and plenty of parking space. Car essential. Fully equipped for six people, except linen. Children welcome and cot available on request. Pets allowed if well controlled. The house consists of one double bedded room, two twin bedded rooms; bathroom with toilet; diningroom; sittingroom with electric fire and colour TV. Kitchen with electric cooker and fridge. Water heated by immersion heater. Terms from £90. Metered electricity. SAE, please, to **Mrs N. Bennett, Hollins Farm, Dockray, Penrith CA11 0JY (07684 82374).**

ULLSWATER. Roma Rigg, Greenside Road, Glenridding, Penrith. Sleeps 7. Slate/stone bungalow in large garden, with mountains on all sides and view of Lake Ullswater in front. Fishing, boating (including Lake steamer), ski-ing, fell-walking and sailing in area. Good bar meals and hotels nearby; shops 350 yards. Well-furnished accommodation sleeping seven; cot and high chair available; facilities for disabled. Central heating and open fire. Everything provided except linen. Pets allowed. Terms are from £120 to £245 per week, including central heating and hot water. Other electricity is metered. Tourist Board approved. SAE please to **Mrs M. Matthews, The Rectory, Plains Road, Wetheral, Carlisle CA4 8JY (0228 60216).**

WIGTON near. Dr and Mrs F.M. Elderkin, **The Stables, Rosley, Wigton CA7 8BN (0965 42665).**

♟♟♟♟ *Approved.* A tastefully converted stables, with main living accommodation on first floor; games room with table tennis, darts, snooker table, etc on ground floor. Ideal for a restful or touring holiday in all seasons. Situated near the Lake District, Carlisle and the Borders; Wigton four miles, Carlisle 10 miles, Penrith 15 miles; on B5305 leaving M6 at Junction 41. Fully equipped, with bed linen, towels and electricity included. Fitted carpets throughout and night store central heating. We offer use of automatic washing machine with dryer at small extra charge. Can accommodate up to four adults with two/three children. Cot available. A well trained dog is welcome. Terms approximately from £75 to £225 weekly. SAE please.

THE STABLES

THE HEANING, Heaning Lane, Windermere, Cumbria LA23 1JW
👑👑👑
Windermere (09662) 3453

Beautifully situated country residence, comprising six holiday apartments, sleeping two to six people, and four one-bedroomed cottages each sleeping up to four people. Standing in seven acres of own grounds with formal gardens and extensive unspoiled Lakeland views. The accommodation is comfortably furnished and well equipped. Electric heaters in all rooms. Colour TV. Ample parking for cars and boats. Short breaks out of season. Cumbria Tourist Board approved. Terms from £110-£235.

Proprietors: Mr & Mrs J.N. Pickup

See also Colour Display Advertisement **WINDERMERE. Birthwaite Edge Apartments.** 👑👑👑 *Approved.* Situated in extensive grounds in one of the most exclusive areas of Windermere, ten minutes' walk from village and lake — the perfect all year round holiday base. Ten self-catering apartments for two to six people. Resident proprietors personally ensure the highest standards of cleanliness and comfort. Swimming pool open May to September. Colour TV. Well equipped kitchens. Hot water included. Coin metered electricity for lighting, cooking and electric fires. Background central heating during winter. Duvets, linen (except towels) provided. High chairs and cots extra. Ample car parking. Regret no pets. English Tourist Board Approved. Brochure from **Bruce and Marsha Dodsworth, Birthwaite Edge, Birthwaite Road, Windermere LA23 1BS (09662-2861).**

DERBYSHIRE

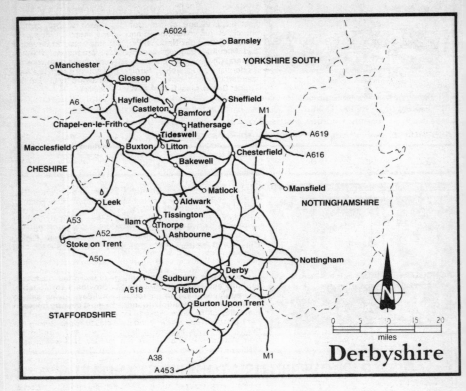

ASHBOURNE. Derbyshire Cottages, Swinscoe, Ashbourne DE6 2HS (0335 300202). "Derbyshire Cottages" are set in the grounds of our 17th century inn overlooking the Staffordshire moorlands and very close to the Peak District, Dovedale, Alton Towers and the quaint town of Ashbourne. Each cottage is stone-built with its own patio and chairs looking onto open countryside. Fully fitted kitchens including fridge and split level cookers. Other facilities include colour TV, radio, direct dial telephones and baby listening. Children and pets are welcome. For further information phone **Mary.**

ASHBOURNE. Mrs Louie Tatlow, Ashfield Farm, Calwich, Near Ashbourne DE6 2EB (Ellastone [033-524] 279 or 443). ♀♀ *Approved.* **Working farm.**

Sleeps 5. Ashfield Cottage is a recently renovated oak-beamed cottage on this working farm well situated for the Peak District and many other places of interest with beautiful views of Dove Valley and Weaver Hills. Accommodation is for five persons in two bedrooms (one family room and one with twin beds). Well furnished and equipped with storage heaters, colour TV, automatic washing machine, tumble dryer, fridge/freezer. Coloured bathroom suite and shower. Linen for hire. Parking space. Terms £60 to £165 per week according to season. Further details and brochure on request.

ASHBOURNE near. Mount Pleasant Farm Cottage, Snelston, Near Ashbourne. Working farm, join in. Sleeps 6. Modern self-catering farm cottage at Snelston (off the A515 Sudbury to Ashbourne road), in beautiful setting ideal for walking and touring in the Peak District. Market town of Ashbourne two miles; Alton Towers eight miles; golf course half a mile. Available all year, the cottage is fully equipped to accommodate six holidaymakers and linen is supplied. Three double bedrooms, plus cot; bathroom, toilet. Large lounge with colour TV; diningroom/kitchen includes refrigerator, electric cooker. Electric heating. Pets welcome. Large garden for the children, also babysitting provided if required. Car essential — parking. Further enquiries and terms (including fuel) to **Mrs A.M. Hollingsworth, Mount Pleasant Farm, Snelston, Near Ashbourne DE6 2OJ (Ashbourne [0335] 42330).**

ASHBOURNE. Alstonefield Holiday Homes, Post Office House, Alstonefield, Ashbourne DE6 2FX (Alstonefield [033527] 201). A choice of five properties sleeping 2/6 people, all situated in the quiet picturesque limestone village of Alstonefield; four times winner of the Best Kept Village award. Complete with a 13th century church, an old coaching inn and village shop. An ideal base to explore the Peak National Park situated between Dovedale and Manifold Valleys, also near the attractions of Alton Towers, Chatsworth House etc. All accommodation recently modernised and tastefully furnished in country style to a high standard having received the Approved award by the English Tourist Board. Ideal for those Winter Breaks.

ASHBOURNE. Dove Cottage, Church Lane, Mayfield, Ashbourne. 🍷🍷🍷 *Approved.* **Sleeps 8.** This modernised 200-year-old cottage in Mayfield village is ideally situated for shops, pubs, busy market towns, sporting facilities, lovely Dove Valley, Alton Towers, Peaks and Staffordshire Moorlands and many other places of interest. The cottage is comfortably furnished and well equipped, TV, fridge, automatic washing machine, gas central heating. The fenced garden overlooks farmland. Garage and parking. Children welcome. Pets by arrangement. Available long and short lets, also mid-week bookings. Terms £60 (low season) to £200 (high season) per week, plus fuel costs. Further details from **Arthur Tatlow, Ashview, Ashfield Farm, Calwich, Ashbourne DE6 2EB (Ellastone [033-524] 443 or 279).**

ASHBOURNE. Clifton Edge, Clifton, Ashbourne. Sleeps 4/5. Groom's cottage of individual character, carefully and tastefully converted to provide a comfortable, well-equipped base for a relaxing holiday. Idyllic setting overlooking the beautiful grounds of a quiet country house in the Valley of the Dove, close to Dovedale, on the edge of the Peak District National Park and well placed for exploring the Derbyshire Dales. Peaceful village just one and a half miles from Ashbourne. Chatsworth and Haddon Hall within easy reach. Alton Towers Leisure Park just five minutes away. Shop and good village pub 200 yards. Twin bedroom with adjacent bathroom; double bedroom with shower room en-suite. Linen provided. Colour TV, dishwasher, woodburner, gas central heating. Garden furniture, barbecue. BARGAIN BREAKS out of season. ETB category 4. Details from **Mr and Mrs B. Davison, Clifton Cottage, Clifton, Ashbourne DE6 2GL (Ashbourne [0335] 43915).**

ASHBOURNE. Mrs J. Audrey Gray, Hayes Farm, Biggin, Hulland Ward, Derby DE6 3FJ (Ashbourne [0335] 70204 or 370204). 🍷🍷 *Commended.* **Working farm, join in.** Relax in our peaceful valley. Superb bungalow for six on small dairy farm. Panoramic views of unspoilt countryside. Join in farm activities. Accommodation includes utility room with automatic washer/tumble dryer; separate toilet. Fully fitted kitchen with microwave, split level electric cooker. Rayburn (free coal). Diningroom, lounge with colour TV. Bathroom with toilet. Two double bedrooms and one twin-bedded room. Heated throughout by storage heaters. Close to Peak District, Dovedale, Chatsworth House. Terms from £95 to £175 all year.

ASHBOURNE near. Tony and Linda Stoddart, Cornpark Cottage, Swinscoe, Near Ashbourne DE6 2BW (Ashbourne [0335] 45041). Overlooking Dovedale with extensive views across three counties, this exciting two storey barn conversion set beside a large pond affords privacy with easy access to all of Derbyshire's attractions. Dovedale eight minutes, Alton Towers 10 minutes. The barn sleeps two/five in an open-plan layout, providing all modern conveniences, in a beamed setting. Large gardens surrounded by open countryside, facilities for children, well behaved pets welcome. Concessions for Senior Citizens, discounts for return bookings. Linen provided, electricity metered, car essential. Terms £60 to £120 per week. Open all year. Phone or write for brochure. Also available, Bed and Breakfast £11.

ASHBOURNE near. Yew Tree Farm, Alstonefield, Near Ashbourne. Sleeps 5. Yew Tree Farmhouse is an attractive 17th century farmhouse with original fireplaces and beams etc. It is ideally situated for touring the Peak District and visiting Alton Towers, as it stands on the edge of the unspoilt village of Alstonefield. There is a large garden with ample parking space and garage. Accommodation for five in two family bedrooms; cot; bathroom, toilet; sitting-room and diningroom; electric kitchen. Storage heaters. Children and pets welcome. Car essential. Shops 200 yards. Open all year. Tourist Board registered. Terms from £75 – £120. **Mr and Mrs K.W. Griffin, Coldwall Farm, Okeover, Ashbourne DE6 2BS (Thorpe Cloud [033-529] 249).**

ASHBOURNE near. Mrs Carolyn Phillips, Culland Mount Farm, Brailsford DE6 3BW (0335 60313). Working farm. Sleeps 6. Guests are very welcome at this family dairy farm in an ideal situation for exploring the Dales, Ashbourne, Derby, Alton Towers and local stately homes. Whilst retaining many original features, the farmhouse is divided, making a large, comfortable holiday home. The lounge has a large bay window with glorious views, colour TV, log fire (logs supplied) and storage heaters; kitchen fully equipped with automatic washing machine, fridge/freezer. Upstairs are two bedrooms with superb views of garden and countryside; bathroom. Linen provided — beds made up before arrival. Prices inclusive of linen and central heating £80 – £180. Sorry, no pets. Farm Holiday Bureau member. OS ref:SK 248 395.

ASHBOURNE near. Throwley Moor Farm and Throwley Cottage, Ilam, Near Ashbourne. ♌♌♌♌ Working farm, join in. Properties sleep 7/12. Self catering farmhouse and cottage on this beef and sheep farm near Dovedale and Manifold Valley. Approached by A52/A53 Ashbourne to Leek road, then via Calton and follow signs for Throwley and Ilam. Within easy reach of Alton Towers, cycle hire and places of historic interest. An ideal touring centre. The cottage accommodates seven people and the farmhouse 12. Ample toilet facilities; sittingrooms and diningroom (kitchen/diner in cottage). Electric cookers; fridges; washing machine and dryer. Pay phone. Pets permitted. Car essential — parking. Available all year; terms according to season. Nearest shops three miles away. Tourist Board registered. SAE, please, for further details to **Mrs M.A. Richardson, Throwley Hall Farm, Ilam, Near Ashbourne DE6 2BB (0538-308 202/243).**

ASHBOURNE near. ROSE COTTAGE, Riverside, Milldale, plus GREEN COTTAGE and COLDWALL COTTAGE, Dovedale. Cottages sleep 6. Very picturesque stone cottages with superb views in delightful settings by river and close to Dovedale. Ideally situated for quiet peaceful holidays walking/touring in the Peak District with stately homes, cycling, trekking, fishing, and Alton Towers close for those seeking a more active holiday. These AA listed and Tourist Board registered properties have recently been sympathetically modernised to a high standard retaining their old beams and character. They sleep up to six and have fitted carpets, electric cooking/heating, all modern conveniences, cots. Terms £75 to £170 per week. Leaflet giving full detailed information about all properties from: **Mrs Y. Bailey, 4 Woodland Close, Thorpe, Ashbourne, Derbyshire DE6 2AP (Thorpe Cloud [033529] 447).**

DERBYSHIRE – PEAK DISTRICT AND DALES!

The undulating dales set against the gritstone edges of the Pennine moors give Derbyshire its scenic wealth. In the tourists' itinerary should be the prehistoric monument at Arbor Low, the canal port of Shardlow, the country parks at Elvaston and Shipley, the limestone caves at Creswell Crags and Castleton and the market towns of Ashbourne and Bakewell. For walkers this area provides many excellent opportunities.

BELPER. Mr and Mrs C. Postles, Chevin Green Farm, Chevin Road, Belper DE5 2UN (0773 822328).

Properties sleep 2/6. Situated in peaceful Derbyshire countryside overlooking the beautiful Derwent Valley, these five cottages with original beams have been tastefully and attractively converted from farm buildings to provide accommodation with character for two/six persons. A laundry room is also provided. The cottages are equipped to a high standard, with colour TV. Arrangements made for riding, golf and fishing. Being on the Gritstone Way, walkers are catered for. Only 30 minutes from Dovedale, Chatsworth, Alton Towers, American Adventure and Matlock. One cottage is equipped for the disabled. Terms from £75 to £205 per week.

CASTLETON (Peak National Park). Sleeps 4/6. Seventeenth century farm cottage restored and maintained to a high standard. Central heating and double glazing. Fitted carpet in living areas, colour TV, radio. Fully equipped, including linen, for up to six persons, but ideal for four. One double and one twin bedded room, two bathrooms, kitchen/diner, lounge. Pets by arrangement. Children welcome. Ample parking. Private terrace with view to Mam Tor — the "Shivering Mountain". Ideal for walking. Terms £90 to £250 (heating and electricity supplied extra through meters). The farm lies half-mile from A625 in the beautiful Hope Valley. ETB registered. **Mrs C. Bell, Spring House Farm, Castleton S30 2WB (Hope Valley [0433] 20962).**

CUTTHORPE. Birley Grange Farm, Cutthorpe. Three cottages and converted Barn, tastefully converted and retaining original beams and stone wherever possible.

Birley Grange Cottages

Bramble Cottage has twin-bedded room; Acorn Cottage has double-bedded room; Haywain Cottage has double-bedded room and room with bunk beds; The Barn has family room and twin-bedded room. All the dwellings are comfortably furnished and carpeted and are completely self-contained, with refrigerator, cooker and television. Heating and cooking by 50p meter. Well-behaved pets welcome. Ample parking space. Situated at the edge of the Peak National Park, eight miles from Bakewell. Many interesting places to visit — Chatsworth House, Matlock, Buxton and Chesterfield. ETB approved. Terms from £70 to £185. Further details from **Mrs M. Ward, Birley Grange Farm, Cutthorpe S42 7AY (0246 583292).**

CUTTHORPE. Mr and Mrs D. Sutton, Cow Close Farm, Overgreen, Cutthorpe, Chesterfield S42 7BA (Chesterfield [0246] 232055).

♀♀♀ A small farm dating from the 17th century, situated in the tiny hamlet of Overgreen. It lies on the B6050, four miles from Chatsworth, on the edge of the Peak. A country inn across the road serves good food and traditional ales. The two fully equipped cottages are renovations of single storey farm buildings, which surround a central courtyard and accommodate six and four persons respectively. Fitted carpets, exposed timbers, central heating, separate kitchen, colour TV, garden sitting areas and ample car parking. Beds made up for your arrival; children, pets welcome. Terms from £70 to £130 per week. Bed and Breakfast also available, £12 to £18. Brochure on request.

DOVEDALE. Mrs Beryl Howson, Hallfields Farm, Wetton, Ashbourne DE6 2AF (Alstonefield [033-527] 282). Properties sleep 3/5. Recently renovated from stables, the first self-catering holiday cottage sleeps 4/5, while the second cottage (suitable for the disabled) sleeps 3/4. Situated in the country with panoramic views overlooking the Manifold Valley and Thor's Cave. A quarter mile from the next residence and the village of Wetton. Central heating is by storage radiators (included in the price). TV supplied. There is unlimited safe parking, an excellent choice of country pubs and inns for your evening meals, some within walking distance. Dovedale is two miles, Ashbourne, Leek and Buxton 10 miles. Open all year. Terms from £70 – £165 per week. Short stay holidays available off season. Pets and children welcome. ETB approved.

HARTINGTON near. Upper Elkstones, Longnor, Buxton. ♀♀♀ *Commended.* Two beamed cottages of charm and character in quiet village with many walks from doorstep. **Grove Cottage** sleeps six in one double, one twin and two single rooms plus cot; spacious diningroom/lounge with inglenook fireplace which overlooks well maintained garden with lawn, rockery and shrubs with uninterrupted view of glorious countryside. **Stable Cottage** sleeps two/three and cot; recently completely renovated lounge, open plan dining/kitchen area, fully fitted with door leading to private garden. Shower room/WC, stairs leading to gallery landing and pretty double bedroom. Both convenient for Dovedale and Staffordshire Moorlands; Alton Towers 15 minutes by car. Further details from **Mrs V. Lawrenson, The Bungalow, Hall Bank, Hartington, Near Buxton SK17 0AT (Hartington [0298] 84223).**

HOPE. Crabtree Cottages, Aston Lane, Hope, via Sheffield. Four Cottages sleep 2/6. Interesting stone-built cottages situated in the grounds of a country house in the Peak National Park. Half a mile from station and bus; three-quarters of a mile from shops. Newly converted to a high standard with central heating, fitted kitchens, carpets and very well equipped. Colour TVs. Cot and high chair available. Laundry for use of tenants. One cottage suitable for the disabled. Ample parking, but car not essential. Facilities for golf, tennis, hill climbing, gliding, fishing, pony trekking, swimming. Open all year. Sorry no dogs. For brochure phone or write. Weekly terms from £80 to £250 including central heating and fuel. **Mrs P. M. Mason, Crabtree Meadow, Hope, via Sheffield S30 2RA (Hope Valley [0433] 20291).**

LONGNOR. Mrs D. Campbell, Oaktree Farm, Longnor, Near Buxton SK17 0QP (0298 83432). In idyllic setting in the heart of the Peak Park amid rolling hills and sweeping dales. Conveniently placed to explore the many attractions of the Peak District, the potteries, Chatsworth and Alton Towers. A luxury cottage on five acre smallholding. Sleeps four plus Z-bed and cot if required. Two bedrooms; fully equipped kitchen/diner; lounge with colour TV; bathroom. Modernised and refurbished, providing comforts and amenities of home whilst retaining old worlde charm, exposed beams, etc. Ideal for walking, touring or just lounging or lazing enjoying clean air and magnificent views. Terms from £80 to £145 per week. Electricity, gas and linen included. Dogs welcome.

MATLOCK. Meadow Cottage, Low Moor, Pikehall, Matlock. ♀♀♀ **Working farm, join in. Sleeps 5.** This semi-detached cottage is situated on owners' 300 acre farm between four market towns in the centre of the Derbyshire Dales. Good walking area. Nature Trails half-a-mile. Many historic houses in the area including Chatsworth and Haddon Hall. The cottage has fitted carpets throughout and lawned garden with parking space. Milk and eggs may be purchased from the farm daily. Accommodation for five in two double and one single rooms, cot; bathroom, toilet; sitting/diningroom with colour TV. Kitchen has sink unit, fridge, electric cooker, kettle and water heater (£1 meter). Pets permitted. Car essential — parking. Available all year. SAE, please, for terms to **Mrs M. Bunting, Low Moor, Pikehall, Matlock DE4 2PP (Parwich [033-525] 234).**

SHIRLEY. Mrs S.R. Foster, Shirley Hall Farm, Shirley, Brailsford, Near Ashbourne DE6 3AS (Ashbourne [0335] 60346). ♀♀♀ **Working farm. Properties sleep 6/4.** This delightful bungalow on the edge of the quiet village of Shirley has a lovely outlook and extensive views of surrounding farmland, with ample parking, large lawned garden and private fishing. Ideal for walking, touring and visiting Chatsworth, Kedleston, Sudbury Hall and Alton Towers. The comfortably furnished accommodation, suitable for six people, is centrally heated with three double rooms; bathroom; lounge with colour TV; dining area and modern kitchen with fridge, automatic washing machine. Price £160 weekly inclusive. Also self-contained first floor accommodation on farm having family bedrooms, kitchen/dining/sittingroom with colour TV, electric heating. Sleeps four. From £110 per week inclusive.

Terms quoted in this publication may be subject to increase if rises in costs necessitate

DEVON

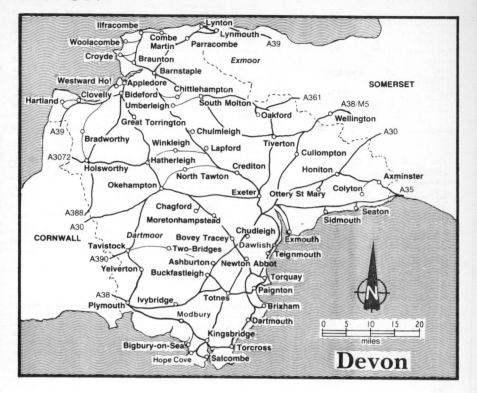

APPLEDORE. **Tides End, Appledore.** Seaside thatched cottage right by the beach in lively area. Historic listed fisherman's cottage, beautifully restored, comprising lounge, diningroom, small snooker table, colour TV, fitted kitchen, bathroom. Downstairs second WC, three double bedrooms and cot; sheltered terrace with picnic table. Tumble dryer. Dogs welcome. Very extensive sea views from most rooms of the beach (sandy at low tide), ships and lighthouses. There is only a quiet approach road between the cottage and beach slipway, and this is the Coastal Path going on to Clovelly and Cornwall. Good local fishing with trips from the quay, championship golf course, historic houses, restaurants, swimming pool, squash, tennis, beaches and surfing. Local quayside inns close by. SAE please for brochure of this and other cottages, with prices and vacancies to **Mrs F.T. Thatcher, Boat Hyde, Northam, Bideford EX39 1NX (0237 473801).**

APPLEDORE. **Mariner's Cottage, Irsha Street, Appledore. Sleeps 6.** Elizabethan fisherman's cottage right at the sea edge — the high tide laps against the garden wall. Extensive open sea and estuary views of ships, lighthouses, fishing and sailing boats. The quayside, beach, ships, restaurants and fishing trips are all close by. Riding, sailing, tennis, golf, sandy beaches, historic houses and beautiful coastal walks, and the Country Park, are all near. Mariner's Cottage (an historic listed building), has three bedrooms, modern bathroom, fitted kitchen with tumble dryer, diningroom and large lounge with colour TV. A modern gas fire makes Mariner's good for winter holidays. Pets welcome. Picture shows view from garden. From £50 per week. SAE, please, for brochure of this and other cottages to **Mrs F.A. Thatcher, Boat Hyde, Northam, Bideford or telephone (Bideford [0237] 473801) for prices and vacancies.**

ASHBURTON. Mr and Mrs C.A. Coulter, 30 East Street, Ashburton, Newton Abbot TQ13 7AZ (Ashburton [0364] 52589). Ashburton is a small charming town, full of historic interest, situated on edge of Dartmoor, within the bounds of Dartmoor National Park. The Parish of Ashburton is surrounded on three sides by moorland, woods and rolling hills and, to the west, some of the most beautiful reaches of the River Dart. It is near Widecombe-in-the-Moor, Haytor Rock, Becky Falls and many other beauty spots and within easy reach of Torbay, Teignmouth and other seaside resorts. Flat is fully furnished and carpeted; lounge with colour TV; kitchen/diner; all essentials; two bedrooms (one double and one twin-bedded). Constant hot water to kitchen and bathroom. Completely self-contained. No linen supplied. Pets allowed. Car desirable — parking. Open all year. Shops nearby. SAE, please, for terms.

AXMINSTER. Mrs L. Hosking, Woodhouse Farm, Hawkchurch, Axminster EX13 5UF (02977 250). Approached down half a mile tree-lined drive, Woodhouse Farm is a 100 acre working farm set in glorious Devon countryside, five miles from Lyme Regis and Charmouth coastline. Excellent walking area including National Trust bridleways and footpaths. Visitors are welcome to explore the farm with its many acres of woodland rich in wildlife and to meet the animals including calves, sheep, pigs, horses and pets. The accommodation consists of a self catering flat comprising one family bedroom sleeping four, sittingroom, bathroom, well equipped kitchen. Full central heating. Colour TV. Bed and Breakfast is available in the farmhouse. Tea-making facilities in all rooms. Children welcome — baby-sitting can be arranged. Play area for younger children. Pets welcome. Open all year. Write or phone for further details. English Tourist Board approved.

AXMINSTER. Cider Room Cottage, Hasland Farmhouse, Membury, Axminster. Sleeps 5. This delightfully converted, thatched cider barn, with exposed beams, adjoins main farmhouse and overlooks the outstanding beauty of the orchards, pools and pastureland, and is ideally situated for touring Devon, Dorset and Somerset. Bathing, golf and tennis at Lyme Regis and many places of interest locally, including Wildlife Park, donkey sanctuary and Forde Abbey. Membury Village, with its post office and stores, trout farm, church and swimming pool is one mile away. The accommodation is of the highest standard with the emphasis on comfort. Two double rooms (sleep five), cot if required; shower room and toilet; sitting/diningroom with colour TV; kitchen with electric cooker, fridge, kettle and iron. Linen supplied if required. Pets by arrangement. Car essential. Open all year. Terms on application with SAE, please to **Mr D.A. Steele, Hasland Farm, Membury, Axminster EX13 7JF (Stockland [040-488] 558).**

BARNSTAPLE. Huish Farm, Marwood, Barnstaple. Working farm. Sleeps 10. This 17th century farmhouse, in a quiet, yet not secluded position is three-and-a-half miles from market town of Barnstaple and five miles from Saunton. A ten-minute walk takes you to Marwood Hill gardens with lakes (open to public from March to October). Four spacious double bedrooms (one room contains four beds). Bathroom, separate toilet; sittingroom; large kitchen with all essentials. Colour TV. Cot and high chair provided. Plenty of room for children to play. Ten people accommodated. Electricity and VAT included in price. No linen supplied, pets permitted. Car essential — parking. Open all year. Terms from £105 to £250 weekly. Out of season daily terms £16 per day including electricity. Fresh milk available daily. Apply to **Mrs. V.M. Chugg, Valley View, Marwood, Barnstaple EX31 4EA (Barnstaple [0271] 43458).**

See also Colour Display Advertisement BARNSTAPLE. North Devon Holiday Homes, 48 Boutport Street, Barnstaple EX31 1SE (0271 76322 24-hour brochure service). With our Free Colour Guide and unbiased recommendation and booking service, we can spoil you for choice in the beautiful unspoilt region around Exmoor and the wide sandy beaches and coves of Devon's Golden National Trust Coast. Over 500 selected properties including thatched cottages, working farms, beachside bungalows with swimming pools, luxury manor houses, etc. From only £55 per week in Spring and Autumn. First class value assured.

BARNSTAPLE. Mrs G.M. Bament, Muxworthy Farm, Brayford, Barnstaple EX32 7QP (0598 710342). Sleeps 6. Muxworthy Cottage is a secluded olde worlde cottage situated on a hill stock farm in the heart of Exmoor, three miles from the village of Brayford. Within easy reach of the sea and Leisure Centre at Barnstaple. Well furnished and maintained, the property is fully equipped and sleeps six. Cot available. Pets welcome. Ideal for a peaceful relaxing holiday and available all year. Terms from £75 to £160 weekly.

BARNSTAPLE. Malt Cottage, Churchill, East Down, Barnstaple. Working farm, join in. This delightful modernised cottage is set amongst the most glorious countryside overlooking the National Trust property of Arlington Court, with Exmoor in the distance. The fine and varied beaches of North Devon are within easy reach. The cottage is attached to a small farm where children are welcome to help with the animals. It comprises kitchen/diner with larder off; beamed sittingroom; two double bedrooms, one single, two with washbasins; bathroom with shower and separate toilet. Outside the kitchen door is a walled courtyard for the exclusive use of the cottage. No linen. Details **Mrs A. Mant, Churchill House, Churchill, East Down, Barnstaple EX31 4LT (Shirwell [027182] 380).**

BARNSTAPLE. Mrs R. Gard, Brinscombe Farm, Arlington, Barnstaple EX31 4SW (Shirwell [0271] 850529). Working farm. Sleeps 6. An 18th century farmhouse situated on a 180-acre hill farm in a peaceful location approached by a concrete drive. It is ideally situated for touring the Exmoor National Park and North Devon beaches. Wistland Pond Reservoir for fishing two miles; Arlington Court, a National Trust property, one and a half miles; Barnstaple with its Leisure Centre nine miles. Nearest beach Combe Martin, six miles. The large self-contained wing of the farmhouse comprises two family bedrooms with washbasins, diningroom, sittingroom with colour TV and electric fire, bathroom and fitted kitchen. Fully carpeted, night storage heaters, large lawn. No linen supplied. Shops three miles. Car essential, ample parking. Open May to September. No pets. Personally cleaned between each booking. A comfortable stay and a warm welcome guaranteed. SAE please.

BARNSTAPLE. Mrs J. Lawson, Smemington Farm, Tawstock, Barnstaple EX31 3JD (Barnstaple [0271] 42485). Working farm, join in. Sleeps 6. Self-contained part of this farmhouse to let for self-catering holidays. Own entrance and driveway. In pleasant rural surroundings, one mile from River Taw (fishing available through local angling club). Accommodation for up to six — two double, one single bedroom; bathroom and toilet; sittingroom; kitchen/diningroom with electric cooker. Night storage heater and iron; TV. Guests supply own bed linen. Pets allowed. Car essential, parking. Shops three miles. Open April/September with special reductions April, May and September. SAE, please, for terms and details.

BARNSTAPLE. Mrs C. Long-Howell, Down Farm, Brayford, Barnstaple EX32 7QQ (0598 710683). Sleeps 4. Set in lovely countryside overlooking the Bray Valley, ideal for walking, we are a small farm of 53 acres including five acres of woodland. Centrally situated for touring, Exmoor only two miles away, Lynton, Lynmouth and the beautiful Doone Valley are 10 miles away, sandy beaches and quaint market towns approximately 12 to 15 miles. Accommodation sleeping four comprises kitchen/dining area, fully fitted and equipped; two bedrooms; bathroom with shower; sittingroom. Cot, high chair and babysitting available. Blankets and pillows provided. Stabling available on negotiation. Parking. Hot water and central heating included in price of £90 to £175 per week. Brochure available.

See also Colour Display Advertisement BARNSTAPLE near. Northcote Farm Cottages. Surrounded by natural gardens, woodlands and streams, three charming character cottages set together with 17th century farmhouse around delightful courtyard. Properties sleep two to five persons. All equipped to a very high standard. Ample car parking. Central for touring. Full details available. Mrs D. Heath and Family, Northcote Farm, Patchole, Kentisbury, Barnstaple EX31 4NR (0271 882376).

BARNSTAPLE. Mr and Mrs C.L. Hartnoll, Little Bray House, Brayford, Barnstaple EX32 7QG (Brayford [0598] 710295). Properties sleep 2/7.

Situated nine miles east of Barnstaple, Little Bray House is ideally placed for day trips to east Devon and Cornwall, the lovely surfing, sandy beaches at Saunton Sands and Woolacombe, and many places of interest including the National Trust house and garden at Arlington Court, the castle at Watermouth, the Honey Farm at South Molton and Exmoor Bird Gardens. Lovely walks abound, and there is a large garden with lawn and woodland, safe for children. Excellent indoor badminton and ping-pong room. Fishing available. The accommodation is in four cottages sleeping from two to seven people, each self-contained and fully furnished with well-equipped kitchens and colour TV. Cot and high chair available on request. Bring own linen and towels. Well behaved dogs allowed, on lead. Terms range from £60 to £170 weekly, depending on cottage and season. Telephone or write for brochure.

BARNSTAPLE near. Mrs Veronica M. Ley, Stock Farm, Brayford, Near Barnstaple EX32 7QQ (0598 710498). Working farm, join in. Sleeps 7.

This completely self-contained part of farmhouse is beautifully situated on 280-acre beef and sheep farm in beautiful countryside with lovely views over the moors and along the Bray Valley. Ideal for touring and walking; two miles from Exmoor and 10 miles from the sea. Visitors are welcome to join in the working life of the farm. The house has three bedrooms, sleeping seven, all fully carpeted. Fitted electric kitchen/diner with microwave and washer/dryer. The oak beamed lounge is full of character. Colour TV. Own garden, lawn and drying area. Adjacent patio and barbecue area. Personally cleaned; bedding available by arrangement. Cot and babysitting. Separate play area where children can play safely with our own family. Pets under supervision. Terms from £80 to £200. Excellent sporting facilities in the area including wind surfing, fishing, riding and golf. SAE please.

BARNSTAPLE near. Mrs J. Tythcott, Churchcombe, Yarnscombe, Near Barnstaple EX31 3NE (Torrington [0805] 23239). Working farm. Sleeps 6. Churchcombe is a 200-acre farm, the highest point between Exmoor and Dartmoor. Torrington three-and-a-half miles, Instow and many other beaches seven miles. Pony available free. Accommodation in farm cottage for six in two double rooms (with two extra single beds); modern bathroom, shaver point, upstairs toilet; kitchen, electric cooker, fridge, electric water heater; sittingroom with TV; diningroom; electric fire. Completely modernised and fully carpeted. Blankets provided and bed linen for double beds. Metered (10p) electricity. Car essential, ample parking. SAE, please, or telephone for further information.

FUN FOR ALL THE FAMILY IN DEVON

Babbacombe Model Village, Torquay; Beer Modelrama, Beer, near Seaton; Dart Valley Steam Railway, Buckfastleigh; Torbay & Dartmouth Steam Railway, Paignton; Bicton Gardens, East Budleigh, near Budleigh Salterton; Grand Western Horseboat Trips, Tiverton; The Shire Horse Centre, Dunstone, Yealmpton, near Plymouth; Farway Countryside Park, near Honiton; Dartmoor Wildlife Park, Sparkwell, near Plymouth; Paignton Zoo, Totnes Road, Paignton; Plymouth Aquarium, Plymouth Hoe, Plymouth; Exeter Maritime Museum, The Quay, Exeter; Torbay Aircraft Museum, Higher Blagdon, near Paignton; Exmoor Brass Rubbing Centre, The Smuggler's Den, Queen Street, Lynton; Dartington Glass, Linden Close, off School Lane, Torrington; Yelverton Paperweight Centre, Leg O'Mutton Corner, Yelverton; Kents Cavern, Ilsham Road, Wellswood, Torquay.

BIDEFORD. Webbery Cottages, Webbery, Alverdiscott, Bideford. Once the home farm and stables of

the old Manor of Webbery, our architect-designed conversions of farm buildings offer a high degree of modern comfort and luxury. In a courtyard setting at centre of private five acre grounds with views extending to Exmoor, Bideford Bay and Lundy Island, two all-electric, two-bedroomed cottages. All tastefully furnished. Colour TV. Fitted carpets. Fridge, toaster, coffee maker, microwave, etc. Separate laundry room. Ample parking. Garden produce in season. Quietly situated between market towns of Bideford and Barnstaple. Beaches, birdwatching, fishing, golf, riding, sailing, surfing, walks nearby. Also Mini Breaks/Weekends. Brochure with pleasure. **Mrs Pamela Andrews, The Garden Cottage, Webbery, Alverdiscott, Bideford EX39 4PU (027-185 430).**

BIGBURY BAY. "Waves Edge", Challaborough, Bigbury Bay. Sleeps 8. "Waves Edge" is a detached four-bedroom bungalow in a magnificent position overlooking the sea. It is situated in a large lawned garden leading on to a low cliff with direct access to the sandy beach. First class furnishings and equipment include a modern kitchen complete with automatic washing machine and tumble dryer, also a large lounge with picture windows. Fully centrally heated. Ample parking. No pets. Challaborough is part of a beautiful coastline including superb sandy beaches such as Bigbury, Bantham, Thurlestone. Walkers can explore for miles along scenic cliffs or surf, sail, swim and fish to their heart's content. SAE **Mrs C. Cooper, The Oaks, Woolston, Loddiswell, Kingsbridge TQ7 4DU (Kingsbridge [0548] 550511/810704).**

BIGBURY near. Buckleys Harraton, Modbury. Properties sleep 6/8. Small bungalow with garden situated on Plymouth — Kingsbridge main road, near Modbury, five miles from sandy beaches of Bigbury Bay. Within easy reach Cornwall (15 miles), Dartmoor (10 miles). Sleeps six. Saturday bookings. Also main part of Bennicke Farmhouse (self contained) in peaceful situation reached by a lane quarter mile from road. Large garden. Three bedrooms sleep eight. Sunday bookings. Both have mains water, electricity and colour TV. Well behaved dogs allowed. Linen is not provided. SAE, for details. Terms from £115 to £175 weekly. No VAT. **Miss C.M. Hodder, Bennicke Farm, Modbury, Ivybridge PL21 0SU (Modbury [0548] 830265).**

BISHOPS TAWTON. Mrs J. Waldron, Court Farm, Bishops Tawton, Barnstaple EX32 0AB (0271

42886). Sleeps 5/8. This is a modern village cottage, the end of a block of three, situated in the centre of the village, which is self-contained with a butcher, Post Office, papershop and general grocery shop. Main shopping centre of Barnstaple is two miles away and also has a Leisure Centre. Coastal resorts and Exmoor are within easy reach. Tidal fishing permitted on river behind the cottage down the Bridle Path. Cottage comprises three bedrooms; bathroom, toilet; livingroom with colour TV; fully equipped kitchen. Pillows and pillowcases, duvets and duvet covers supplied, but no linen provided. Cot available. Pets by arrangement. Prices from £90 to £180, electricity extra. Brochure available.

BRAUNTON. Mrs J.M. Barnes, Denham Farm Holidays, North Buckland, Braunton EX33 1HY

(0271 890297). ♀ ♀ ♀ These newly converted self-catering units are situated in a small hamlet only two miles from the golden sands of Woolacombe and Putsborough and the quaint old village of Croyde. An ideal touring base for walking, surfing, golfing and riding. One unit sleeps eight in four bedrooms; lounge with colour TV and inglenook fireplace with woodburner; the other sleeps four in one family bedroom; downstairs room with kitchen/diner and lounge area with colour TV. Both units have lovely kitchens with electric cooker, fridge, microwave. Bathrooms fitted with showers only. Barbecue area, large lawn with swings/trampoline for children. Some small pets. Linen hire, and evening meals may be obtained (by arrangement) from the licensed farmhouse. Pets taken. Ample parking and some garage space. Send for colour brochure.

CHULMLEIGH near. Sandra Gay, Northcott Barton Farm, Ashreigney, Near Chulmleigh EX18 7PR

(Ashreigney [07693] 259). Northcott Barton is a working farm set amidst green fields, wooded valleys and quiet country lanes where you can explore the farm and see the animals. The holiday wing of our lovely old farmhouse sleeps 7/9 plus cot and offers well equipped "home from home" comfort with oak beams, heating throughout and a log fire to welcome early and late season guests. Bed linen provided. Large south-facing garden. Golf, riding, fishing close by. Handy for sea/moors. Terms from £95 weekly. English Tourist Board approved. Farm Holiday Bureau Member.

Compton Pool Farm – South Devon

E.T.B.

Top E.T.B. Category

A.A. Listed

We warmly invite you to enjoy a country holiday in our
LUXURY PERIOD FARMYARD COTTAGES WITH MANY RECREATIONAL FACILITIES

Attractive stone cottages around central courtyard with fish pond. The cottages have been converted to a very high standard from the old stone barns of an elegant Georgian farmhouse. They are tastefully furnished in farmhouse pine and are fully equipped with modern appliances and linen, including heaters in every room. Some with woodburning stoves. Set in 12½ acres of lovely countryside all cottages have superb views. Our facilities include a heated indoor swimming pool, sauna, trout lakes, tennis court, fully equipped games barn, children's playground, farm animals, colour TV, cots and high chairs, laundry room, public telephone and partial central heating which is free in the low season. Babysitting, in-cottage catering. Close Dartmoor and only 3 miles from sea. Riding and sailing etc. available nearby. Open Jan-Nov for holidays and winter breaks.

JOHN & CATHY SONGER, COMPTON POOL FARM, COMPTON, S. DEVON TQ3 1TA. TELEPHONE: 0803 872241.

COLYTON. Mrs R. Gould and Mrs S. Gould, Bonehayne Farm, Colyton EX13 6SG (040487 396 or

416). Working farm. Bonehayne Farm, situated in the beautiful Coly Valley amidst 250 acres working farmland on the banks of the River Coly. Daffodils are quite a feature in Springtime. Mallard Duck and Kingfishers too are a common sight. Trout fishing freely available and woodlands to explore. This is an annexe of the farmhouse, completely modernised and tastefully furnished, with fitted carpets, to accommodate up to six people. Two double bedrooms and one with bunk beds. Lounge with oak beams, inglenook fireplace, TV and centrally heated, making it really ideal for out of season holidays at no extra cost. Kitchen and dining-room with electric cooker, fridge, electricity by meter; bathroom and toilet; cot and babysitting available. Fully equipped except linen. Parking space. The sea four miles. Weekly terms on application. Caravan also available.

COLYTON. Mrs C.E. Pady, Horriford Farm, Colyford, Colyton EX13 6HW (Colyton [0297] 52316).

Working farm, join in. Sleeps 7. Horriford Farmhouse lies at the end of a winding Devon lane, near a ford. The wing of the farmhouse is let, fully furnished. Accomodation in four bedrooms, sleeping seven. Many original features remain in this ancient house. An oak screen passage, mullion windows, inglenook fireplace with bread oven, newel staircase, oak beams. Close to the sea, yet in secluded valley deep in the peaceful countryside. Walks with fine views close to the farm which is all-grass dairy farm in an area of outstanding natural beauty. A herd of 100 Friesian and Guernsey cows is kept. Visitors are welcome to watch farming activities. Seaton one-and-a-half miles; Beer two miles; Lyme Regis and Sidmouth six miles; Exeter 22 miles. A good base to explore unspoilt East Devon. Easter to end of October. Also available, two bedroomed cottage sleeps six. SAE for details and terms.

PLEASE SEND A STAMPED ADDRESSED ENVELOPE WITH ENQUIRIES

CREDITON. Mrs D. M. Lock, Brindiwell Farm, Cheriton Fitzpaine, Crediton EX17 4HR (Cheriton Fitzpaine [036-36] 357). Working farm. Wing of delight-

ful old farmhouse situated midway between the north and south coasts and the moors with outstanding views to Dartmoor. It is in quiet countryside with superb walks and interesting places to visit. The farmhouse is AA listed and is on a 120-acre sheep farm and offers year round accommodation from £100 to £120 weekly. Double and single bedrooms, cot and high chair provided. Colour TV. Sorry, no pets. Car is essential and there is ample parking. ETB listed. Brochure on request with SAE, please.

CULLOMPTON. Mrs D. Tucker, Woodbeare House Farm, Plymtree, Cullompton EX15 2DD (Plymtree [088-47] 256). Working farm. Sleeps 10. This accommodation is homely and part of the owner's own home. Self-contained and private, it is set in lovely unspoilt countryside with the Blackdown Hills in the background. Enjoy the freedom of the farm. It is an excellent touring centre for Exmoor, Dartmoor. Golf, fishing, riding nearby. The M5 and Cullompton three miles; Honiton, Exeter nine; Sidmouth and Exmouth 12. Registered with English Tourist Board. Accommodation for 10 in three bedrooms; bathroom with toilet; diningroom. All-electric kitchen. Linen not supplied. Children welcome. Car essential — parking. SAE, please, for terms.

CULLOMPTON. Mrs P.M. Chave, Coombe Farm, Butterleigh, Cullompton EX15 1PW (Bickleigh [088-45] 252). Sleeps 6. Yew Tree Cottage on Coombe

Farm is modernised and comfortably furnished. Equipped for six people with two double beds, two single beds, cot; bathroom, separate toilet; sittingroom; diningroom with colour TV. Modern kitchen with electric cooker, fridge, Rayburn, electric fire. No linen supplied. Ideally situated for country walks or touring the countryside by car. Within easy reach of sea and moors. No pets, please. Car essential — parking (two cars). Open from May to September. Quartermile from village with friendly pub, post office. Three miles from M5 at Cullompton, four miles from market town of Tiverton. SAE, please, for further details.

DARTMOOR. Mrs Angela Bell, Wooder Manor, Widecombe-in-the-Moor, Near Ashburton TQ13 7TR (Widecombe-in-the-Moor [036-42] 391). Modern-

ised granite cottages and converted coach house on 108-acre working family farm nestled in the picturesque valley of Widecombe, surrounded by unspoilt woodland, moors and granite tors. Three-quarters of a mile from village with post office, general stores, inn with diningroom, church and National Trust Information Centre. Suitable for children. Excellent centre for touring Devon with a variety of places to visit, and for exploring Dartmoor by foot or on horseback. Clean and well-equipped accommodation. One property suitable for disabled. Facilities include electric cooker, fridge, kettle and fires, colour TV; laundry room, fitted carpets, cot, high chair, ironing board, iron, ample crockery and utensils. Linen hire. Large gardens and courtyard. Easy parking. Open all year and centrally heated. Off-season reduced lets. Weekend lets. SAE, please, for brochure.

DARTMOOR NATIONAL PARK. L.A. Astley, Summersbridge Cottage, Higher Coombe, Buckfastleigh (Buckfastleigh [0364] 42388). Self-catering old world, picturesque, detached country cottage situated in an idyllic spot, surrounded by woodlands, moorland, valleys and rivers. Ideal for walking, horse-riding, fishing and sightseeing. Within easy reach of Torbay and Plymouth for sea and shops. The cottage sleeps four/five, is well equipped, fully modernised, comfortable and has a "fairy-like magic". Pets allowed. Parking. Children over seven years welcome.

DARTMOUTH. The Mates House, 17 Higher Street, Dartmouth. ♀♀♀ Sleeps 4/6. The Mates House is a small cottage situated in the centre of town and originally built in 1628 in the reign of King Charles I. It is about 100 yards from the River Dart frontage. There is one double and one twin-bedded room and a double bed-settee in the lounge. Cot is also available. Colour television. Electric heating, cooking and fridge. Linen provided, towels on request. There are no extra charges for electricity, pets etc. Open all year from £120 per week. **Mr N.P. Jestico, The Captain's House, 18 Clarence Street, Dartmouth TQ6 9NW (Dartmouth [0803] 832133).**

DARTMOUTH near. Mrs B.S. Wall, Lower Fuge Farm, Strete, Near Dartmouth TQ6 0LL (Stoke Fleming [0803] 770541). Working farm. Sleeps 10. A holiday here at Fuge can be peaceful, with picturesque farm walks. We have a 240-acre dairy farm and are only one mile from Strete village, two miles from two pretty beaches, Blackpool and Slapton. This completely self-contained part of a farmhouse has two family and one double fully carpeted bedrooms, sleeping 10 (cots available). Linen provided and beds ready made. Nice bathroom. Fitted electric kitchen/diner with fridge/freezer, automatic washing machine, dishwasher, microwave, tumble dryer, Kenwood Chef, high chairs. Lounge is large, fully carpeted, with three-piece suite, easy chairs, colour TV. Garden with spacious lawn for playing/sunbathing. Electricity metered. Car essential. Pets allowed by prior arrangement. Further details on request.

HOLIDAY ACCOMMODATION
Classification Schemes in
England, Scotland and Wales

The National Tourist Boards for England, Scotland and Wales have agreed a common 'Crown Classification' scheme for **serviced (Board)** accommodation. All establishments are inspected regularly and are given a classification indicating their level of facilities and services.

There are six grades ranging from 'Listed' to 'Five Crowns ♛ ♛ ♛ ♛ ♛'. The higher the classification, the more facilities and services offered.

Crown classification is a measure of *facilities* not *quality*. A common quality grading scheme grades the quality of establishments as 'Approved', 'Commended' or 'Highly Commended' according to the accommodation, welcome and service they provide.

For **Self-Catering**, holiday homes in England are awarded 'Keys' after inspection and can also be 'Approved', 'Commended' or 'Highly Commended' according to the facilities available. In Scotland the Crown scheme includes self-catering accommodation and Wales also has a voluntary inspection scheme for self-catering grading from '1 (Standard)' to '5 (Excellent)'.

Caravan and Camping Parks can participate in the British Holiday Parks grading scheme from 'Approved (✓)' to 'Excellent (✓ ✓ ✓ ✓ ✓)'. In addition, each National Tourist Board has an annual award for high-quality caravan accommodation: in England – Rose Awards; in Scotland – Thistle Commendations; in Wales – Dragon Awards.

When advertisers supply us with the information, FHG Publications show Crowns and other awards or gradings, including AA, RAC, Egon Ronay etc. We also award a small number of Farm Holiday Guide Diplomas every year, based on readers' recommendations.

EXETER near. Mrs R.F. Horsman, George Teign Barton, Ashton, Exeter EX6 7QT (Christow [0647] 52461). Working farm, join in. Sleeps 2 Adults. This fine old thatched farmhouse has within it two units of self-catering accomodation, each suitable for two people. A real home-from-home, with the bed made, and no extra charge for electricity and linen. Totally self-contained. The farm is set in rolling hills, with walks and panoramic views over the Teign Valley. There are sheep, cattle, and a wealth of wildlife, buzzards and badgers. Ashton is noted for its church and unspoilt thatched cottages. It is only eight miles west of Exeter and the M5, yet it is within easy reach of Dartmoor, the coast of Torbay, and many other holiday attractions. West Country Tourist Board approved. Weekly terms from £85 to £115.

EXMOOR. Mrs C.M. Wright, Friendship Farm, Bratton Fleming, Barnstaple EX31 4SQ (Parracombe [059-83] 291). Working farm, join in. Friendship Bungalow is quietly situated down a short drive from the farmhouse, in its own garden, and surrounded by fields. There is ample parking space. The farm is situated 12 miles from Barnstaple and Ilfracombe, at the junction of roads B3226 and B3358, within easy reach of the beaches of Woolacombe and Combe Martin. Exmoor is literally on the doorstep. The accommodation comprises three bedrooms (sleep six), plus cot. Linen supplied. Lounge with colour TV. Well equipped kitchen/diningroom. Bathroom, laundry room, washing machine. Metered electricity. Weekly terms, low season from £95, high season £185.

DEVON – ENDLESS CHOICES!

People never tire of visiting Devon. There's so much to do, like visiting Alscott Farm Museum, Berry Head Country Park, Bickleigh Mill Farm, Farway Countryside Park, Haytor Granite Railway, Kent's Cavern, Dartmoor National Park and of course Plymouth and its Hoe.

FROGMORE. Keynedon Cottage, Frogmore, Kingsbridge. Keynedon Cottage is situated on the road between two villages where there are shops and pubs, backing on to farmland about half-mile from farmstead — visitors are welcome to walk around. The cottage is within two miles of beaches and coves, within easy reach of Dartmoor, Torbay and Plymouth. Accommodation, one family, two double and one single bedrooms, loan of cot, bathroom with toilet. Sittingroom has dining table and chairs, easy chairs, electric fire (log fire if required) and black/white television. Kitchen supplied with electric cooker, heater, fridge, kettle, iron, cleaner and spin dryer. Electricity on 50p meter — linen supplied extra — pets allowed — parking. SAE, please, for terms and brochure: **Mrs M.J. Heath, Higher Oddicombe, Chillington Road, Frogmore, Kingsbridge TQ7 2JD (0548 531247).**

HOLSWORTHY near. Mrs M.G. Axford, Gunnacott Farm, Clawton, Near Holsworthy EX22 6QW

(0409-27273). Self-contained wing in 14th century farmhouse. Guests can walk over farm to nearby river. Very spacious accommmodation, attractively furnished for seven: three bedrooms, plus cot. Livingroom with inglenook, oak panelling, beams, mullion windows and colour TV. Modern kitchen with microwave, automatic washing machine, tumble dryer, dishwasher, freezer, as well as basic equipment. Bathroom with toilet, separate toilet and washbasin. Garden with garden furniture and barbecue. Linen provided. Heating, by meter. No pets! Pony riding available at no extra charge, fishing nearby. Sea and sandy beaches, Bude 15 miles, Dartmoor National Park 19 miles. Small shop two miles, main shop five miles. Rental: £95 to £260 per week.

HONITON. Mrs Sue Wigram, Riggles Farm, Upottery, Honiton EX14 0SP (Luppitt [0404-891] 229). Working farm, join in. Sleeps 8. Four beautifully situated caravans on 450-acre dairy/arable farm, nine miles from Honiton, easy access to many lovely beaches and local attractions. Visitors welcome on farm. Milk and eggs. Children's play area, table tennis; cot and linen hire available; tumble and spin dryer. Caravans are in two peaceful acres near farmhouse. Each is fully equipped for two/eight people, with two separate bedrooms and spacious living areas. Own bathroom with shower, flush toilet, washbasin. Gas cooker, heater, colour TV, fridge. WCTB registered. Terms from £55 per week inclusive (10 per cent reductions for couples, not school holidays). For brochure please telephone or send SAE.

ILFRACOMBE. Mrs M. Thomas, Twitchen Farm, West Down, Ilfracombe EX34 8NP (Ilfracombe

[0271] 862720). Working farm. Twitchen Bungalow is part of the farm and guests have all the advantages of a farm holiday. About three miles from Woolacombe and Ilfracombe, convenient for beaches and day trips to Exmoor, Clovelly, etc.,this 280 acre farm has hundreds of lambs in the spring and plenty of space to roam free from traffic worries. There is one family room and two double rooms, sittingroom with colour TV, log fire in winter and full heating system. Dining/kitchen and scullery; separate bathroom and WC. Drying and airing facilities. Fully equipped except for bed linen. Personal supervision ensures well-aired beds and high standard of cleanliness. Open all year, reduced rates for out of season bookings; suitable for disabled. Electricity on meter. SAE, please, for reply by return.

See also Colour Display Advertisement **ILFRACOMBE. Mrs F.M. Irwin, Smythen Farm Luxury Holiday Cottages, Sterridge Valley, Berrynarbor, Ilfracombe EX34 9TB (Combe Martin [0271-88] 3515). Working farm, join in.** Superior holiday cottages on this Devon family farm situated overlooking the picturesque Sterridge Valley across the sea to Wales. Free pony rides. Central for miles of golden sands, shops and inn two miles. Fully equipped. Cleanliness guaranteed. Brochure and terms available. ETB Category 3. Member WCTB.

ILFRACOMBE near. Dr A.V. Parke, Middle Lee Farm, Berrynarbor, Ilfracombe EX34 9SD (Combe Martin [0271] 882256). Properties sleep 2/6. Luxurious self-catering in six beautifully appointed properties, most with dish-washers, all with fully fitted kitchens and furnished patios (barbecue available). Linen and towels included. Laundry, games barn, beautiful gardens, field to play in (dogs welcome). Farmhouse prepared food available. Ideal for walking, touring, relaxing. Open all year. Cosy short breaks out of season assured by night storage heating and electric blankets. Two cottages for up to six, two farmhouse apartments for five, two studios (ideal for honeymooners) for two-three. Five minutes' walk from Berrynarbor, unspoiled and "Best Kept Village 1985, 1987 and 1988". Good pub, shop, butcher and PO. West Country Tourist Board Registered categories 3 and 4. SAE please for brochure.

ILFRACOMBE near. Mrs M. Cowell, Lower Campscott Farm, Lee, Near Ilfracombe EX34 8LS (Ilfracombe [0271] 863479). Four excellent holiday cottages on a 90 acre dairy farm with a delightful one mile walk down to the beach at Lee Bay. The cottages have been newly converted from the original farm buildings to a high standard. Two of the cottages will accommodate four people, one will accommodate up to six people and the large one will take eight/ten people; laundry room; linen and electricity included in the price. We also have a large, self-contained six-berth caravan to let, with Bed and Breakfast in the farmhouse. Children welcome but regret no pets. Terms from £55 – £409.

KING'S NYMPTON. Venn Farm Cottages. Sleep 2/6 adults; 2/4 children. Delightful holiday cottages converted from old stone barn on small working farm set in beautiful Devon countryside. The children will love to feed the lambs and goat kids. Nearly 50 acres of rolling fields to wander over with views to Exmoor and Dartmoor. The cottages are furnished and equipped to a high standard and have patios with a picnic table and barbecue. Cottages have two or three bedrooms sleeping up to six persons plus cot. One cottage is suitable for disabled visitors. Bed linen provided. Laundry room and children's play area. Pets welcome. For brochure apply to: **Mrs Martin, Venn Farm, King's Nympton, Umberleigh EX37 9TR (07695 2448).**

KINGSBRIDGE. Mr and Mrs M.B. Turner, Cross Farm, East Allington, Near Totnes TQ9 7RW (East Allington [054-852] 327). Working farm, join in. Sleeps 12. For a peaceful holiday in the heart of the South Hams, come to Cross Farm, a mixed working farm situated in beautiful countryside at the head of a valley only four miles from Kingsbridge, and within four to six miles radius of many lovely beaches and coves. East Allington village is just a mile away with shops and character Inn. Good centre for visiting Plymouth, Torbay and Dartmoor. Riding facilities nearby. Lovely farm walks. Rough shooting in season. Accommodation in 17th century self-contained farmhouse wing to sleep 12 persons, plus two cots, in four bedrooms. Accommodation is very comfortably furnished and equipped to a high standard with all modern conveniences including colour TV, shower, automatic washing machine and dishwasher. Duvets and linen provided. Heated for early/late holidays.

Recreation barn with billiards, table-tennis etc, and play area for children. Baby-sitting by arrangement. SAE for brochure and terms, please.

KINGSBRIDGE. Mrs Jill Kerswell, Bearscombe Farm, Kingsbridge TQ7 2DW (Kingsbridge [0548] 852123). Working farm. Sleeps 8. 17th century farmhouse situated in the heart of an open valley rich with wildlife. Traditional family farm just one and a half miles from the market town of Kingsbridge which is central to the wide range of holiday activities in the famous South Hams district. A wealth of interest for the whole family. The first floor flat has three double bedrooms, two with single beds (cot available). Lounge/diningroom with kitchen, breakfast bar, electric cooker, fridge, washing machine. Two bathrooms. The flat is well equipped. Electricity on 50p meter. Children welcome. Sorry, no pets. Babysitting. Open all year. Terms from £150 to £280. SAE for details.

KINGSBRIDGE. Mrs Sarah Hanmer, Buckland Court, Slapton, Near Kingsbridge TQ7 2RE (054-852 366). ♀ ♀ ♀ ♀ Set in nine acres of beautiful South Hams countryside, seven luxury cottages created from 17th century barns and arranged around the courtyard of an old South Devon farm. Situated two miles from Slapton Sands and close to Dartmouth, Dartmoor and Salcombe, the opportunities for all types of outdoor pursuits are endless. The cottages carry the English Tourist Board's highest grade for self-catering accommodation. Gas, electricity, central heating, TV, telephone and laundry room. Linen, cots and high chairs by arrangement. Pets welcome. For colour brochure please write or phone **Mrs Sarah Hanmer.**

KINGSBRIDGE. Mrs Ruth Bate, Woolcombe Farm, East Allington, Near Totnes (East Allington [054-852] 275). Working farm, join in. Sleeps 6. Woolcombe Farm is situated 200 yards off the A381, four miles from the market town of Kingsbridge; Totnes, Plymouth, Torbay and Dartmoor National Park all within easy reach. Visitors welcome around the farmyard. A self-contained part of the farmhouse, sleeping six, plus cot, is available to let. The kitchen/diner has an automatic electric cooker, fridge and is fully equipped. The sittingroom has colour TV and electric fire. On the first floor there are three double bedrooms, one with two single beds and washbasin etc; one with double bed, cot and airing cupboard and the third has two single beds. Toilet and washbasin (bath not included in accommodation, small charge of 20p for use). Sheets and blankets provided, but not for the cot. Babysitting by arrangement. Regret, cannot accept pets. Open from May to September. Tourist Board registered — category 2. Terms £98 to £180 per week (electricity inclusive).

KINGSBRIDGE near. Mrs J. Tucker, Mount Folly Farm, Bigbury-on-Sea, Near Kingsbridge TQ7 4AR (Bigbury-on-Sea [0548] 810267). Working farm. Sleeps 6. A delightful family farm, situated on the coast, overlooking the sea and sandy beaches of Bigbury Bay. Farm adjoins golf course and River Avon. Lovely coastal walks. Ideal centre for South Hams and Dartmoor. The spacious wing comprises half of a farmhouse, self-contained with separate entrance. Large, comfortable lounge with sea views; colour TV. Well equipped kitchen/diner — all electric; metered. Sleeps six persons in three bedrooms — one family, one double and one single; two have washbasins and sea views; bathroom and toilet. All rooms attractively furnished. Visitors made welcome. Nice garden, ideal for children. Cot and babysitting available. Car essential, ample parking. Available all year. SAE for terms please.

KINGSBRIDGE. Mrs D.M. Tolchard, Bickerton Farm, Hallsands, Kingsbridge TQ7 2EU (Chivelstone [054-851] 220). Working farm. Sleeps 6. This is a detached cottage five minutes' walk from the sea at Hallsands, a small, unspoilt village on the coastline between Dartmouth and Salcombe. Four miles from Torcross and the freshwater lake and nature reserve at Slapton Lea. Sleeping six, one double room, one twin bedded room, bunk beds in third room, cot. The kitchen is all-electric with immerser, cooker, fridge, kettle, etc., everything supplied but linen. Colour TV, and night storage heater in the sittingroom for early and late holidays. Car essential — parking. The cottage is open all year round with weekly terms on request. SAE, please.

KINGSBRIDGE. Mr and Mrs A.R. Wotton, "Andryl", Lower Farm, Beeson, Kingsbridge TQ7 2HW (Kingsbridge [0548] 580527). Working farm. Sleeps 4 adults; 2 children. "Andryl" is situated in a sheltered sunny position on Lower Farm, Beeson. The flat is part of "Andryl", with bathroom, separate toilet, airing cupboard and well equipped kitchen/diner/lounge with TV. Linen is optional. The garden has a swing, and there are other attractions for the children including chicks, ducks, goslings and a pony. The countryside around is very picturesque, and there are numerous walks, including the very pleasant coastal paths. Beesands is half-a-mile away, and other beaches are very near; Kingsbridge is the nearest town, while Dartmouth and Salcombe are within easy reach. Babysitting can be arranged. Pets are not allowed. Car essential, parking. Terms from £85 per week including domestic hot water. SAE, please, for brochure.

KINGSBRIDGE. 1 New Buildings, South Milton, Kingsbridge. Sleeps 2 adults; 2 children. This is a modernised end terraced cottage overlooking the little village of South Milton. The cottage is white painted and facing south, with garden running down the hill towards an attractive 13th century church. The cottage dates from about 1830 and has a winding staircase. Lounge has large open Devon fireplace. Sleeps four people. Salcombe is four miles away for sailing and fishing. Dartmoor is 15 miles away; provides excellent game fishing. Nearest rivers Avon and Dart. Kingsbridge is an excellent shopping centre and many villages have delightful eating out places. Thurlestone (one mile) offers magnificent golf course and tennis facilities. Nearest beach, one mile, is ideal for children, very safe bathing and large stretches of rock pools. Let from Spring Bank Holiday to end of August. Terms from £75 – £150. SAE to **Mrs J.M. Turner, Beach Cottage, South Milton, Kingsbridge TQ7 3JR (Kingsbridge [0548] 560354).**

KINGSBRIDGE. "Savernake," Thurlestone Sands, Kingsbridge. Sleeps 10. This substantial house, with a beautiful and unobstructed view of the sea and Thurlestone Rock, stands in its own grounds, adjoining the dunes and beach. The area is of outstanding beauty with wonderful cliff walks. Golf, tennis, quarter mile. Sailing and riding in area. Accommodation for 10 in three twin-bedded double rooms with washbasins; three single rooms (one with washbasin); cot; bathroom, three toilets; lounge and diningroom. Kitchen fully equipped with electric cooker, fridge, kettle and toaster. Linen not supplied. Village shop one mile. SAE to **Mrs M.D. Horsfall, Century Cottage, Foxdon Hill, Wadeford, Chard, Somerset TA20 3AN (Chard [0460] 62475).**

KINGSBRIDGE. Mrs R. Kemsley, Luke's Barn, Addlehole, Kingsbridge TQ7 2DX (0548 853401). Sleeps 5. Situated one-and-a-half miles from the market town of Kingsbridge, ground level flat is offered for self-catering holidays from April to October (inclusive). Accommodation for five people in bedroom with double and single beds, and bedroom with full length bunk beds. Cot on request. Bathroom. Lounge/diningroom. TV. Fully equipped electric kitchen including crockery, cutlery, etc. Electric heating. Linen supplied by arrangement. Electric meter (50p). The flat is annexed to the main house in rural and peaceful surroundings. A separate building with its own entrance, modern and clean. Children are welcome and there is space for them to play. Pets permitted if well behaved. Car essential, parking. Shops, public transport one-and-a-half miles. Weekly terms from £75 to £140 (excluding fuel).

See also Colour Display Advertisement **KINGSBRIDGE. Helen and Peter Mound, Woolston House, Kingsbridge TQ7 4DU (0548 550341).** ♀♀♀♀ Come and share our friendly home: a non-smoking haven of civilised tranquillity. Nature study/hobby craft room for parents. Set in 30 acres of grounds and meadows. Children's playroom and fenced nursery lawn. Bathrooms en-suite. Accommodation for two to six per unit (bedroom/suite of rooms/self catering apartments), maximum nine families. Heated swimming pool, tennis court, adventure playground, picnic areas, walking. FOR ALL AGES: books, jigsaws, board games, deck chairs, easels. Pushchairs, high chairs, bath toys. Guests' kitchen with microwave, washing machine, tumble dryer, fridge, kettle, tea, etc. Easy reach shops, tourist attractions, sailing, pony trekking, leisure centres, etc. Comfortable beds and chairs. Residential licence. Home cooking, special diets prepared fresh daily along with additive-free traditional food (low cholesterol). Seasonal bedding, central heating and log fire. Telephone for brochure. Guesthouse 🐾 🐾 🐾 *Commended.*

EXMOOR VALLEY

Two delightful genuine Devon Cottages and a Modern Bungalow

The two modernised cottages are XVI century and situated in their own sheltered valley yet only half a mile from a main road, facing South, with a trout stream running through the garden. The bungalow sits on a hill behind with superb views of Exmoor. All are located on an 86-acre farm containing riding stables, sheep, cows and plenty of interest for the children, plus all the other attractions and sporting activities of the area. Three miles from sea.

RIVERSIDE COTTAGE sleeps nine in three bedrooms, two with hot and cold; bathroom, separate toilet; kitchen; diningroom and lounge with large open log fire. Terms from £110 weekly off season.
NEW MILL COTTAGE sleeps six in two bedrooms, one with hot and cold; large bathroom; separate toilet; kitchen and lounge with open log fire. Terms from £95 weekly off season.
NEW MILL BUNGALOW sleeps six in three bedrooms; bathroom, toilet; kitchen; diningroom and lounge with open fire. Night storage heaters available if required. Terms from £95 weekly off season.

All have mains electricity, night storage heaters, flush toilet, colour TV, fridge, fitted kitchens, full cooking facilities, spin rinsers and fitted carpets. Furniture is comfortable, interior sprung mattresses, and linen provided, if required. All thoroughly inspected before arrival. Pets are welcome at £15 each weekly. Safe for children and pets to play. Horse riding over Exmoor from farm. Stables are "Ponies of Britain Approved."

SAE to R. J. Bingham, New Mill Farm, Barbrook, Lynton, North Devon EX35 6JR (Lynton [0598] 53341).

See also Colour Display Advertisement KINGSBRIDGE near. Torcross Apartment Hotel, Torcross, Near Kingsbridge TQ7 2TQ (0548 580206). Family self-catering in our luxury Apartment Hotel. Ranging in size from our ground floor Beachside apartments for two, to our really spacious family apartments. Superb sea views. Family owned and supervised ensuring a high standard of cleanliness. Village Inn and Waterside Family Restaurant with an extensive menu including fresh local fish and a Sunday Carvery, light entertainment some evenings. Baby listening. Games room. Launderette/drying/ironing room. Bargain Breaks. Central heating. Car park. Colour brochure with pleasure.

KINGSBRIDGE. Mrs E. Wakeham, Chivelstone Barton, Chivelstone, Kingsbridge TQ7 2LY (054851 222). Self-catering farm cottage between Start Point and Salcombe. Sleeps six. Ideal for walking, two miles of sandy beach and sailing. The cottage is in close proximity to the farm, but has good views to fields where cows and sheep graze. It has three bedrooms with fitted carpets, (one) with double divan, (two) twin divans (three) bunk beds. Cot provided. Bathroom with toilet. Lounge with fitted carpet and colour TV. Kitchen/diner with electric cooker, fridge, immersion heater, electric fires where needed. Meter 50p. Car space and lawns. Many local places of interest to visit including Plymouth, Dartmoor, Dartmouth and all Torbay's attractions.

LYNTON. H.D. King-Fretts, West Lyn Farm, Barbrook, Lynton EX35 6LD (Lynton [0598] 53618).

Working farm. Traditional farmhouse sleeping 8/10, also two recently converted farm cottages to sleep four/five. All are set in 134 acres of secluded and private farm land adjoining coastal footpaths and National Trust woodland. Panoramic views across the Bristol Channel to South Wales. Farmhouse has four bedrooms including one double, one twin, one family, one bunk. Each cottage has one double and one twin (plus one). Pine fitted kitchens (electric) and colour TV in lounges, modern bathrooms/WC. Full double glazing, part central heating. Ample gardens and garaging for the cottages. Shop/laundrette within walking distance. West Country Tourist Board Category 3. SAE for illustrated brochures and tariff for friendly farm holidays.

PLEASE ENCLOSE A STAMPED ADDRESSED ENVELOPE WITH ENQUIRIES

LYNTON near. Mrs Lesley Young, "Moorlands", Woody Bay, Parracombe EX31 4RA (Parracombe [05983] 224).

Set within Exmoor National Park, "Moorlands" nestles in its own extensive, private and very picturesque gardens. The peaceful woodland and gardens are home for many species of birds, trees, shrubs and wild flowers, and offer delightful changes with each season. The surrounding area offers magnificent scenery, peaceful walks, riding, fishing and lovely bays. The self-contained apartments provide clean, modern facilities, colour TV, central heating and lovely outlooks. Swimming pool, croquet, badminton and children's lawned play area within the grounds. Children very welcome; laundry, cots and high chairs available. Pets welcome. Open all year. Weekly terms from £45. Please write or telephone for brochure.

MORTEHOE. Mrs H.F. Lethbridge, Chebenears, Damage Barton, Mortehoe, Woolacombe EX34 7EJ (0271 870712). Working farm. Fully equipped self contained mobile home, sleeps four/six, shower, washbasin, toilet, electricity, heating, fridge and TV. Situated in unique position on working cattle and sheep farm with beautiful views out to the Bristol Channel. Ideal for peaceful relaxing family holidays. Many walks leading directly from farm to Lee Bay, Bull Point lighthouse and Morte Point. Miles of sandy beach at Woolacombe and secluded beaches along coastline. Golf, riding, fishing all available locally. Terms from £150 per week, changeover Friday. Children welcome. Sorry no pets.

NEWTON ABBOT. Averil Corrick, Shippen and Dairy Cottages, c/o Lookweep Farm, Liverton, Newton Abbot TQ12 6HT (0626 833277). Sleeps 1/5.

Come and relax in the peace and tranquillity of these two delightful barn converted cottages. Set within the Dartmoor National Park with easy access to the coast, golf, riding, walking and fishing locally. Sleeps 4/5 fully equipped and well furbished throughout. Own garden with beautiful views. Ample parking. Use of outdoor heated swimming pool. Children welcome, high chairs, cots and linen available. Pets also welcome. Terms from £103 to £295.

NORTH MOLTON. Yen Cottage, Heasley Mill, North Molton. Cottage accommodates six to eight people, is very well equipped and has all modern facilities. Garden. For early and late holidays it's so cosy. Highly recommended. Open all year. Bed and Breakfast accommodation also available. Terms and further details available, contact: **Mary Yendell, Crangs Heasleigh, Heasley Mill, North Molton EX36 3LE (05984 268).**

PAIGNTON. Mrs J. Smerdon, Glenside, Moles Cross, Marldon, Paignton TQ3 1SY (Kingskerswell [0803] 873222). Working farm.

Self-contained, enjoying complete privacy, **The Maisonette,** — Glenside, having been the residence of the former owner of the property, is modern and maintained to a high standard. Comprising three bedrooms, one with balcony; lounge/diningroom with colour TV. Beautifully fitted kitchen with breakfast bar, fridge freezer, washing machine. Bathroom, fully tiled and with shower. Open all year. 100 yards up the lane stands the **Farm Bungalow**, Glenside. Self-contained (owners' living accommodation to one side), well maintained — being the owners' winter residence. Comprises three bedrooms, large lounge/diningroom with colour TV. Kitchen with fridge, electric cooker and washing machine. Bathroom with separate shower. Both properties ideally located for Torbay, three miles, Dartmoor, 12 miles. Many interesting local walks. Farm shop for eggs, fruit, vegetables. Both properties sleep and are fully equipped for up to eight. Large lawn and field for children. Central heating available. Terms £90 low season to £220 high season — inclusive of electricity.

SALCOMBE. Mrs Caroline Jeyes, Beadon Farmhouse, Beadon Road, Salcombe TQ8 8LX (Salcombe [054-884] 3020). Self-contained flat adjoining Victorian farmhouse, set in three and a half acres in quiet position overlooking peaceful valley. Easy reach of beaches, coastal path and beautiful walks. On outskirts fishing/boating town with mild climate, good for early or late holidays. Good parking directly outside property. Double bedroom with en-suite bath/shower room, separate toilet. Large living room with fitted kitchen area, electric cooker and fridge. Colour TV. Night storage heaters. French windows to drive and garden. Cot or extra bed if required. Terms from £120 per week. Also Bed and Breakfast available in farmhouse — see Bed and Breakfast Section for details.

See also Colour Display Advertisement SEATON. Mr and Mrs E.P. Fox, West Ridge, Harepath Hill, Seaton EX12 2TA (Seaton [0297] 22398). ♀ ♀ ♀ *Approved.* West Ridge bungalow stands on elevated ground above the small coastal town of Seaton. On A3052, quarter-mile west of Colyford. It has one and a half acres of lawns and gardens and enjoys wide panoramic views of the beautiful Axe Estuary and the sea. Close by are Axmouth, Beer and Branscombe. The Lyme Bay area is an excellent centre for touring, walking, sailing, fishing, golf etc. This comfortably furnished accommodation is ideally suited for three to five people. Cot can be provided. Available March to October. £95 to £275 weekly (fuel charges included). Full gas central heating; colour TV. AA listed. SAE for brochure.

SEATON near. Mr and Mrs H.J. Pountney, Little Trill, Musbury, Near Axminster EX13 6AR (Axminster [0297] 34731). Little Trill Cottages are situated

in the country on the edge of Musbury Village between Seaton and Axminster, with spectacular views across the Axe Valley. The cottages are set around a cobbled yard and have recently been converted from stone barns about 200 years old, keeping traditional features, to provide three two-bedroomed and one three-bedroomed cottages. Fully furnished including fitted kitchens and bathrooms, gas central heating, cookers, fridges and colour TV. Ample parking. Children and pets welcome. Each cottage has own garden area plus about half an acre of communal grass area. Bed linen available at extra charge. Open all year round. Send SAE for full details.

SIDMOUTH. 4 Hayne Close, Tipton St. John, Sidmouth. Sleeps 5. This modern detached Swedish-

style house is in quiet cul-de-sac on edge of village with front garden and small secluded back garden backing onto a field and open country. Many attractive local walks. Nearby is Newton Poppleford, famous for cream teas; Ottery St. Mary with fine medieval church and the sea at Sidmouth and other beaches. Exeter 14 miles away. House sleeps five and is comfortably furnished with fitted carpets throughout. There are two double bedrooms, and one single; bathroom, two toilets; sittingroom with dining area; modern convenient kitchen with electric cooker, double oven, fridge and washing machine. Everything supplied except linen. Gas central heating. Shop about quarter of a mile, sea four miles. Regret, no pets. Car essential, garage and parking. Available end April to mid-September. Weekly terms from £90 to £210. SAE, please, to **Mr C.H. Silver, 48 Hampden Way, Bilton, Rugby, Warwickshire CV22 7NW (Rugby [0788] 816632).**

WISCOMBE PARK

Southleigh, Near Colyton, Devon

Large private Country Mansion hidden away in own beautiful wooded valley with streams and lakes. Nature lovers' and children's paradise. Wood and parkland walks abounding with wildlife and our own farm animals. Adjoins Countryside Park. Golf and other sports facilities available locally.

★ **Trout and Coarse Fishing** ★ **Pets Welcome** ★ **Near Coast**

Comfortable self-contained cottages/flats with large garden and barbecue area. Colour TV. Central heating. Laundry. Games room with table tennis and toys. Sleep 2/9. Available all year – terms from £80 per week per flat.

For **free brochure**, write or telephone Farway (040487) 474/252.

SOUTH MOLTON. Nethercott Manor Farm, Rose Ash, South Molton EX36 4RE (07697 483). Sleeps 4/8. Denis and Carol Woollacott assure a warm welcome at Nethercott, a 17th century thatched house on a 200 acre working farm. Two comfortable self contained wings sleep 4/8. Pleasant views overlooking woods and trout pond. Pony rides, extensive games room and laundry. Also barbecuing facilities. Six miles from the market town of South Molton, ideal for touring Exmoor and coast. Pets welcome. Terms from £85 to £270. Tourist Board approved.

SOUTH MOLTON. Neildstown, South Molton. Sleeps 10. Modernised farmhouse with spacious rooms; four bedrooms — two double, two with double and single beds. Sittingroom; diningroom; kitchen with electric cooker, fridge etc; bathroom, toilet. Carpeted. Colour TV. Sun porch. No linen supplied. Well controlled pets allowed. Cot, high chair available. Electricity by £1 coin meter. Large lawn and plenty of room for children to play. Car essential, ample parking space. Only one mile from South Molton. Good selection of shops and bus service, yet on its own in quiet countryside. Ideal centre for touring Exmoor, visiting North Devon coast. Lovely walks around the farm and in nearby riverside and wood. Terms on request, with SAE, from **Mrs D.M. Lake, Lordsdown, South Molton EX34 4DU (076-95 2238).**

SOUTH MOLTON. Mrs Sheila M. Coe, Higher Ley Farm, North Molton, South Molton EX36 3JS (05984 281). Working farm. Flats sleep 5 adults; 2 children. Higher Ley Farm is a 75 acre sheep farm on the edge of Exmoor. The holiday flat is part of the farmhouse and is comfortably furnished. It has diningroom, lounge with TV, kitchen, bathroom and three bedrooms sleeping seven. Cot and high chair are provided. Fully equipped except for sheets. Large lawn area outside. Babysitting available. The area offers beautiful countryside for walking and riding and an opportunity to explore an unspoilt coastline from rocky cliffs to long sandy beaches. Sorry, no pets. Open May to October. From £110 per week plus VAT.

**If you've found
FARM HOLIDAY GUIDES
of service please tell your friends**

SOUTH MOLTON. Mrs G.E. Bray, West Millbrook, Twitchen, South Molton EX36 3LP (North Molton [059-84] 382). Working farm, join in. Properties sleep 2/9. Three fully equipped bungalows and one farmhouse annexe at West Millbrook which is a 150 acre stock farm, partly situated in the Exmoor National Park. Ideally situated for touring North Devon and West Somerset and within easy reach of the Lorna Doone Valley. There are many peaceful walks and lovely scenery, North Molton village is only one mile away. The bungalows sleep two, six or nine people — the annexe two. All units are fully carpeted and have electric cookers, fridge-freezers, sink units, irons, TV, cots and high chairs. Linen extra charge. Car essential, parking. Central heating if required. Electricity metered. ETB registered. Beautiful lawns and gardens. Weekly prices from £30 – £115 plus VAT. Stamp for colour brochure.

STOKENHAM. Mrs B. Goodman, Mattiscombe Farm, Stokenham, Near Kingsbridge TQ7 2SR (Kingsbridge [0548] 580442). Working farm. Sleeps 8. Only a mile from the three-mile stretch of beach at Slapton Sands, the self contained flat at Mattiscombe Farm is ideal accommodation for up to eight persons. There are four bedrooms; lounge/diningroom with colour TV; kitchen with electric cooker and fridge/freezer; bathroom with shower, and toilet. Metered electricity (50p). Mattiscombe Farm is a 150 acre mixed farm six miles from Kingsbridge, ten from Dartmouth and close to many beaches. A car is essential, the nearest shops are a mile away as is public transport. Good fishing and many places of interest nearby. Children welcome — cot supplied. Sorry, no pets. Open April — October. SAE please for terms.

TIVERTON. Cider Cottage, Great Bradley Farm, Withleigh Cross, Tiverton. ♀♀♀♀ Commended. Working farm. Sleeps 5. Cider Cottage is a restored 17th century barn on our 155 acre dairy farm in the heart of Devon's countryside. Providing spacious accommodation for five in three bedrooms, two double and one single. Carpeted lounge with colour TV. Excellent kitchen and dining areas. All furnished and equipped to a high standard. Bed linen is supplied and beds made up for your arrival. Heating and cooking by electricity. Ideally situated for exploring coasts, the lovely Exe Valley, Dartmoor and Exmoor, or stay and enjoy the farm! Riding, tennis and swimming nearby. Children welcome. Regret, no pets. Brochure available. Open all year. Weekly terms from £110 to £250. **Mrs Sylvia Hann, Great Bradley Farm, Withleigh Cross, Tiverton EX16 8JL (Tiverton [0884] 256946).**

CIDER COTTAGE

GREAT BRADLEY, WITHLEIGH, TIVERTON

DEVON – ENDLESS CHOICES!

People never tire of visiting Devon. There's so much to do, like visiting Alscott Farm Museum, Berry Head Country Park, Bickleigh Mill Farm, Farway Countryside Park, Haytor Granite Railway, Kent's Cavern, Dartmoor National Park and of course Plymouth and its Hoe.

Mrs Bealey, Week Farm, Torrington, Devon EX38 7HU
Telephone: Torrington (0805) 23354

Excellent accommodation (enjoyed by many) in our farmhouse flat, scenic views and beautiful surroundings. Well equipped kitchen/diner; lounge with colour TV. One room with double bed, one with twin beds; convertible bed and cot if required. Bathroom, WC. Electric cooker, heaters, spin dryer. Linen for hire. Electricity metered. Advance orders. No pets. Children welcome. One mile from Great Torrington with heated swimming pool, tennis, golf, Dartington Glass factory and N.H.S. Rosemoor Gardens. Easy reach beaches, Exmoor, Dartmoor. Terms from £65 weekly. SAE please, or telephone. *ETB registered.*

TOTNES. Mr and Mrs D. Christie-Mutch, Lower Well, Broadhempston, Totnes TQ9 6BD (Ipplepen [0803] 813 417). Charming, comfortable, well equipped self-contained one and two bedroomed cottages, formerly part of Georgian farm. Colour TV; laundry facilities; cot and high chair available. Orchard garden. Linen not provided. Lovely unspoiled Devon village with two pubs, church and shop, situated between Dartmoor and the Torbay coast with easy access to the beautiful South Hams, historic Totnes, Dartington and Exeter etc. Telephone or write for details.

WELLINGTON. Mr and Mrs L.J. Tristram, West End, Holcombe Rogus, Wellington, Somerset TA21 0QD (Greenham [0823] 672384). Working farm, join in. Sleeps 6. This 16th century olde worlde farm cottage in Devon has an inglenook fireplace and bread oven. It is approached by a private tarmac road and surrounded by a large garden. Situated on 120-acre farm, over which guests are free to wander. Half-a-mile from the small village of Holcombe Rogus which has general store with post office, butcher, public house, church. Within easy reach of Exmoor, Taunton, Exeter and the coast. Excellent walks in unspoilt countryside; extensive views. Six people accommodated in three double rooms, cot; bathroom, toilet; sitting/dining-room. Kitchen with electric cooker, fridge, kettle, iron, etc.; glass conservatory at front of house. No linen. Pets allowed. Car an advantage, ample parking. Open all year. TV provided. Tourist Board Registered. SAE, please, for terms.

See also Colour Display Advertisement WESTWARD HO! John and Gill Violet, West Pusehill Farm, Westward Ho! EX39 5AH (Bideford [0237] 475638 or 474622). Cottages sleep 2/8. Our eleven cottages are situated in an idyllic setting in an area of "outstanding natural beauty" and only one mile from Devon's golden coast. Each stone-built cottage is equipped and furnished to a high standard. Varying in size they accommodate from two to eight people. Suitable for holidays throughout the year. Facilities include: heated swimming pool, licensed restaurant and bar, sauna, solarium, children's play area, pets corner, games room and laundry. Prices from £85 — £510. For full colour brochure phone or write to **John & Gill Violet.**

WOODY BAY, near Lynton. Mr and Mrs Hepworth, Martinhoe Manor, Woody Bay, Near Lynton EX31 4QX (Parracombe [059-83] 424). Apartments sleep 1/8. "WHERE EXMOOR MEETS THE SEA". Magnificently situated Manor House set amidst spectacular coastal scenery, 26 acres of lovely grounds, including third of a mile of private coastline, jetty, swimming pool. Superb walking, riding, fishing and touring — the ultimate escape from pressures of modern living. Spacious self-contained apartments for one to eight persons, with breathtaking views and superior facilities, including full central heating and colour TV, laundry room and residents' lounge bar. Children and pets welcome. Cots and high chairs available. Open all year. Apartments from £110 per week INCLUDING central heating and colour TV. We hope to have the pleasure of welcoming you to our lovely home. Please write or telephone for colour brochure. Tourist Board registered.

Terms quoted in this publication may be subject to increase if rises in costs necessitate

DORSET

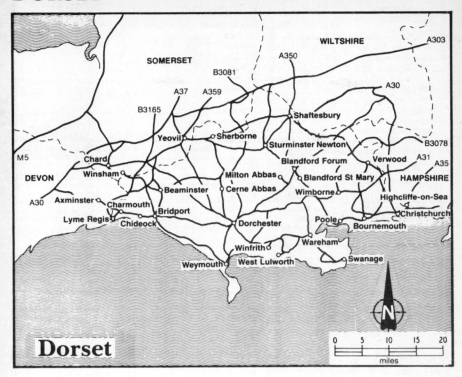

Dorset

ABBOTSBURY. **Mrs Josephine Pearse, Tamarisk Farm, West Bexington, Dorchester DT2 9DF (0308 897784).** On Chesil Beach between Abbotsbury and Burton Bradstock. Spacious and two smaller bungalows and two chalets to let on active mixed farm with sheep, cows, horses and organic market garden — vegetables available. Glorious views along West Dorset and Devon coasts, lovely countryside and coastal walks, fishing, golf, riding nearby. Six miles good local markets, good centre for touring Thomas Hardy's Wessex. Pets and children welcome. Terms from £70 to £450.

BEAMINSTER. **Hursey Farm, Hursey, Broadwindsor, Beaminster DT8 3LN. Cottages sleep 4+.**

Hursey Farm cottages have been skilfully converted from traditional stone farm buildings into three pretty self-contained holiday cottages. Tastefully renovated with natural pine, they retain many character features. Each dwelling has an attractive sittingroom with colour TV; well-appointed kitchen and bathroom and two bedrooms to sleep four plus. Cooking, lighting and heating are all-electric. Pets by arrangement only. Car essential — parking. Hursey is a tiny hamlet on the edge of Broadwindsor situated in the quiet and beautiful Dorset countryside, seven miles from coast. Ideal centre for riding, walking, golfing, fishing and touring. Many places of interest, historic houses and gardens, wildlife park, ancient earthworks and fossil-rich cliffs of Lyme Regis, plus many lovely towns and villages to visit. West Country Tourist Board listed. Terms from £85 to £195 weekly. **Mr and Mrs R.S. and C. Poulton, The Granary, Oldcotes, Over Stratton, South Petherton, Somerset TA13 5LB (South Petherton [0460] 41559).**

FHG PUBLICATIONS LIMITED publish a large range of well-known accommodation guides. We will be happy to send you details or you can use the order form at the back of this book.

BEAMINSTER. Mrs B. Pardey, Sandiford Farm, Mosterton, Beaminster DT8 3HN (Broadwindsor [0308] 68338). Properties sleep 2/10.

Courtyard of four detached natural stone farm buildings, tastefully converted into three cottages and two self-contained flats, situated on the edge of the village. The cottages and flats are comfortably furnished to a good standard, each with small garden, lounge, colour TV, dining area, fully equipped kitchen (electric cooker, fridge, washing machine). Bedrooms, bathroom and toilets. There is a car parking area. Mosterton is on the A3066 within easy motoring distance of the unspoilt Dorset coastline and Thomas Hardy country.

BEAMINSTER. Mrs A.M. Vickery, West Axnoller Farm, Beaminster DT8 3SH (Beaminster [0308] 862331). Working farm.

West Axnoller is a dairy farm situated in West Dorset and set in beautiful countryside with glorious views overlooking the Axe valley. Ideally situated for beach or inland attractions — golf courses, wildlife parks etc. Beaminster three miles, coast 11 miles. Visitors are welcome to look around the farm. The cottage is set in its own large lawned garden. It has three large bedrooms sleeping eight plus a cot. Bathroom and toilet; diningroom; lounge with colour TV; modern kitchen with electric cooker and fridge; utility room. Electric storage heaters. Pets by prior arrangement. Details on request.

BEAMINSTER near (Hooke). "Orchard End", Hooke, Beaminster. ♀♀♀♀ **Working farm. Sleeps 6.**

Hooke is a quiet village nine miles from coast. Good walking country and near Hooke Working Woodland with lovely woodland walks. Trout fishing nearby. Bungalow is stone built and has electric central heating, some double glazing. It is on a working dairy farm and is clean and comfortable. Three bedrooms all with duvets. Cot available. Large lounge/dining room with colour TV. Well equipped kitchen with electric cooker, fridge and automatic washing machine. Bathroom and separate toilet. Carpeted. Payphone. Large garden and garage. Terms from £120 to £240 per week inclusive of electricity, bed linen and VAT. **Mrs P.M. Wallbridge, Bridge Farm, Hooke, Beaminster DT8 3PD (Beaminster [0308] 862619).**

BLANDFORD. Mrs Patricia C.M. Harris, Marsh Farm, Ibberton, Blandford DT11 0EN (Hazelbury Bryan [0258] 817423). Working farm. Self-catering ground floor flat in attractive farmhouse. This old world stock farm is situated in the heart of Dorset in secluded, unspoilt countryside close beneath Bulbarrow Hill, with its incomparable views of the Blackmore Vale. It is ideal for walking, riding or just getting away from it all. Within easy reach of Dorset's beautiful coast. You may pass through "Hardy" country on the way, or visit Dorchester, our historic county town. Two double bedrooms, one with bunk beds; shower room, toilet; kitchen, all-electric; sitting/diningroom. Children and pets welcome. Ponies by arrangement. Milk and eggs from farm. Parking. Weekly terms approximately £80 – £120 (plus VAT). Brochure and terms on request. Available May-October.

BLANDFORD. Mrs M.J. Waldie, The Old Rectory, Lower Blandford St. Mary, Near Blandford Forum DT11 9ND (Blandford [0258] 453220). Sleeps 6. Completely self-contained wing of Georgian Old Rectory, one mile from the market town of Blandford Forum, within easy reach of the south coast, Poole, Bournemouth, Salisbury and Thomas Hardy country around Dorchester. Local fishing and many places of historical interest. Accommodation for six in three rooms, one double bedded, one twin bedded and smaller room with bunk beds. Large well equipped kitchen, spacious sitting/diningroom with colour TV; cloakroom downstairs; bathroom and separate toilet upstairs. All freshly decorated. Pets allowed by prior arrangement. Children welcome. Garage and parking space. Use of secluded garden. Everything provided except linen and towels. Terms from £125 to £185 per week. SAE, please, for further details.

BOURNEMOUTH. Mr H.J. Balestra, "Camellia Court", 5 Milner Road, Westbourne, Bournemouth BH4 8AD (Bournemouth [0202] 761212). Sleep 2-7. "Camellia Court" is a detached property situated on West Cliff, adjacent to Alum Chine and only minutes (300 yards) from the beach. It consists of five spacious self-contained flats sleeping two to seven people, all having separate kitchens with gas cookers and electric fridges, bath, WC; colour TV; visitors' laundry. Linen can be supplied if required, and two of the flats are on ground level. Although a car is not essential, there is a parking space, plus lock-up garages. Ideal for a quiet holiday, there is a large beautiful garden and the property lies in a peaceful cul-de-sac road in between two Pinetree Chines. Buses run nearby. Cots and high chairs are available. Open Easter to September, weekly terms are from £55 – £190 with gas/electricity slot meter, and central heating provided. ETB registered.

Camellia Court

BOURNEMOUTH

Ideal Location

"Camellia Court" is a detached property situated on West Cliff adjacent to Alum Chine and only minutes (300 yards) from the beach. It consists of five spacious self-contained flats sleeping two to seven people, all having separate kitchens with gas cookers and electric fridges, bath, WC. Colour TV supplied. Linen can be supplied if required, and two of the flats are on ground level. Laundry and exterior drying space available. Although a car is not essential, there is a parking space, plus lock-up garages. Ideal for a quiet holiday, there is a large beautiful garden and the property lies in a peaceful cul-de-sac road between two Pinetree Chines. Buses run nearby. Cots and high chairs are available. Open Easter to September, weekly terms are from £55 (£190 High Season) with gas/electricity slot metered, and central heating provided. Member English Tourist Board and Holiday Flats Association. Colour Brochure on request.

Mr H. J. Balestra, "Camellia Court", 5 Milner Road, Westbourne, Bournemouth BH4 8AD (Bournemouth [0202] 761212)

BOURNEMOUTH. Bournemouth Holiday Bureau, Department 24, Cardigan House, Waterloo Road, Bournemouth BH9 1AU (Bournemouth [0202] 518967). For more than a quarter of a century, Bournemouth's oldest self catering holiday accommodation agency has been providing a letting service for scores of privately owned houses, cottages, bungalows, flats, caravans and chalets in Bournemouth, Poole, Ringwood, Christchurch and about 20 miles around. All inspected before acceptance and accurately described. Prices to suit every pocket. Most welcome children and many accept pets. Colour brochure on request.

Happy Holidays

BRIDPORT. Nos. 1 and 2 Marshwood Cottages, Marshwood, Bridport. Properties sleep 5 plus cot.

A pair of fully modernised country cottages of character with their own lawns, situated in the village and within easy reach of the sea. Each provides accommodation for five plus cot. Bathroom, toilet. Sitting/diningroom with colour TV; de-luxe fitted kitchens with electric cookers, fridges, irons etc. Regret no pets. Car necessary, parking. Also available, immaculate bungalow with small field adjoining. Well-maintained and under personal supervision. Marshwood lies on the Dorset/Devon/Somerset border, approximately seven miles from beaches at Lyme Regis and Charmouth. Beautiful surrounding countryside to explore and historic landmarks. Registered with the English Tourist Board. SAE, please, for details to **Mrs P.B. Bowditch, Colmer Farm, Marshwood, Bridport DT6 5QA (Hawkchurch [029-77] 278).**

BRIDPORT Near. Mrs S. Norman, Frogmore Farm, Chideock, Bridport DT6 6HT (0308 56159). Working farm, join in. Sleeps 5 Adults, 1 Child. Delight-

ful farm cottage on ninety acre grazing farm set in the rolling hills of West Dorset. Superb views over Lyme Bay, ideal base for touring Dorset and Devon or rambling the many coastal and country footpaths of the area. This fully equipped self-catering cottage sleeps six, plus cot. Bed linen supplied. Cosy lounge with woodburner and colour TV, french doors to a splendid columned sun verandah. Children and well behaved dogs welcome. Car essential. Open all year. Short breaks available, also Bed and Breakfast in the 17th century farmhouse. Brochure and terms free on request. Tourist Board Approved.

ETB
WCTB

MANOR FARM HOLIDAY CENTRE
Charmouth, Bridport, Dorset

Situated in a rural valley, ten minutes' level walk from the beach.

1983 Built Luxury Two-Bedroomed Houses: *Sleep 4-6 *Lounge with colour T.V. *Fully fitted kitchen/diner *Fitted carpets *Double glazing *Central heating *Parking space.

Three-Bedroomed House and Bungalow: *Sleep 6 each *Lounge with colour T.V. *Central heating available *Parking within grounds *Enclosed garden.

Luxury six-berth Caravans: *One or two bedrooms *Toilet *Shower *Refrigerator *Full cooker *Television *Gas fire.

FULL CENTRE FACILITIES AVAILABLE INCLUDING SWIMMING POOL, SHOP. FISH AND CHIP TAKEAWAY, BAR, LAUNDERETTE, ETC.

Send SAE for colour brochure to Mr R. B. Loosmore or Tel. 0297 60226
See also Colour Display Advertisement in this Guide.

VISA
Access

Dorset & Devon

- Short Breaks ● Longer Stays ●
- Self Catering Cottages, Houses, Flats, etc. ●
- Hotels and Guest Houses ●
☆ *ASK FOR FREE BROCHURES* ☆
Coastal & Country – All Year Round

REGISTERED
WITH THE ENGLISH
TOURIST BOARD

MEMBER

LYME BAY HOLIDAYS

(Dept. FHG)

FINCH & CO., FREEPOST, CHARMOUTH, BRIDPORT, DORSET DT6 3BR TEL: (0297) 60755 (24 hours)

CHARMOUTH. Mrs R. J. White, Little Catherston Farm, Charmouth, Bridport DT6 6LZ (Charmouth [0297] 60550). Working farm. Sleeps 4. Our self-contained holiday flat has superb views over Charmouth and the sea, where the beach is safe and sandy and is well known for its fossils. There are many coastal walks on National Trust land. Golden Cap is the highest point on the South coast. Golf at Lyme Regis and West Bay, also wildlife park near Chard. Accommodation comprises bedroom with two single beds; kitchen; bed sitting room with colour TV; bathroom. Metered electricity. Cot and high chair available. Bed linen supplied. Car parking. Dogs welcome if kept under control. SAE please for terms.

DORSET – RURAL SPLENDOUR!

Absorbing old towns like Dorchester and Shaftesbury, surrounded by panoramic vales, undulating chalklands and peaceful villages contribute to Dorset's great appeal. Included in any tourist's itinerary should be, Abbotsbury Village and Swannery, Ackling Dyke Roman road, Brownsea Island, Lulworth Cove and, of course, the many locations that constitute Hardy's Dorset.

Willowhayne Farm
LUXURY SELF-CATERING MEWS COTTAGES

CHIDEOCK, DORSET Tel: 0297 89042
This exclusive development of 6 Mews cottages opened in 1988, built in mellow stone to a modern design, represents the highest standards in accommodation, furnishing and equipment. The farm nestles quietly in a fold of Dorset's rolling hills only 15 minutes' walk across the fields from the beach at Seatown. The village of Chideock and its services lies half-a-mile away. The cottages, all facing south, have 2 bedrooms, luxury bathroom and a large, comfortable lounge dining/room with french doors to your private patio and formal gardens. The oak kitchens are fully equipped including washing machine and tumble dryer. All heating, electricity and linen are provided free of charge.   ♀♀♀♀ **Commended**

DORCHESTER. Kennel Cottage, Moreton, Dorchester. Semi-detached cottage in quiet setting on 500 acre mixed farm just outside the unspoilt village of Moreton. Recently modernised with one double, one twin and one bunk-bedded rooms (duvets and linen provided). Fully equipped — washing machine, colour TV, night storage heaters, open fire. Ideal for active family holiday or restful break. Children welcome — safe garden, sandpit, swing, climbing frame, cot, highchair and friendly animals! Terms from £150 to £250. Open all year. Apply: **Jim Hosford, Broompound Dairy, Moreton, Dorchester DT2 8RL (0929 462464).**

DORCHESTER near. Pitt Cottage, Ringstead Bay, Near Dorchester. Sleeps 6. An attractive part thatched stone-built cottage, surrounded by farmland and situated on the edge of a small wood about quarter of a mile from the sea, commanding outstanding views of Ringstead Bay on the Dorset Heritage Coast. The cottage has been renovated and is equipped to sleep six; three bedrooms (two beds in each), two bathrooms, sitting room with open fire and large kitchen/dining area. Cot/high chair; washing machine; TV; electric radiators in all rooms. Car essential. Available from £80 per week. For details please send SAE (reference FHG) to: **Mrs S.H. Russell, 14 Brodrick Road, London SW17 7DZ or telephone 081-672-2022.**

PITT COTTAGE

DORCHESTER near. Mr and Mrs Charles Hammick, Higher Waterston Farm Cottages, Piddlehinton, Dorchester DT2 7SW (0305 848208; Fax: 0305 848894). ♀♀♀♀♀ *Commended.* Four superb cottages situated around a lawned courtyard on a sheep farm. 3/3/2/2 bedrooms sleeping 6/6/4/4. One cottage designed for disabled guests on the ground floor. Each cottage has own terrace, colour TV/video, washing machine, dishwasher, microwave, fridge-freezer, electric cooker, central heating and wood burning stove. Fitted carpets in all rooms. Telephones. Tumble dryers. Centre of Hardy's Wessex in lovely country. Sea 10 miles, Dorchester four. New all weather hard tennis court. Games barn with badminton, table tennis, etc. Open all year. Minimum one week in summer; winter breaks. One dog welcome. Member of Country Hosts. Terms from £135 to £360 per week. Brochure available.

DORCHESTER. Mrs R.E. Goldsack, Beech Farm, Warmwell, Dorchester DT2 8LZ (Warmwell [0305] 852414). Working farm. Three miles from the sea, away from the main roads and located close to Egdon Heath in Thomas Hardy country, three well-equipped farm cottages, five miles from Dorchester, the county town of Dorset. The cottages range from one to three bedrooms and are open all year round at prices ranging from £80 in the low season to £195 during high season. All the cottages have colour TV's, automatic washing machines or spin dryers. A grass tennis court is available for visitors. There are excellent coastal walks in an area becoming renowned for its outstanding natural beauty. Sorry, no pets. Children welcome. ETB approved.

See also Colour Display Advertisement **DORCHESTER. Greenwood Grange, Higher Brockhampton, Dorchester DT2 8QH (0305 68874).** ♀ ♀ ♀ ♀ *Commended.* **Cottages sleep 3/6.** This holiday, be a neighbour of Thomas Hardy in beautiul Dorset countryside. Greenwood Grange is an exciting and delightful development. Beautiful self catering luxury holiday cottages converted from magnificent old barns (originally built by Thomas Hardy's father) and set just a stone's throw from Hardy Cottage in the gorgeous Wessex countryside. The unique cottage-style accommodation, sleeping from three to six people, is fully furnished including kitchen with modern cooker and fridge, central heating, colour TV, well appointed bathroom and many other extras. Outside you will find gardens and ample parking near every cottage. Set in a part of Dorset that offers everything. So many things to do and see, from Hardy's Wessex to Roman Dorchester. Hosts of seaside delights, from Weymouth and Lyme Regis to lovely tiny bays and inlets. Prices start from just £90 per week for a one bedroomed cottage for two — linen, lighting and heating inclusive. Telephone for our colour brochure or send your name and address on a postcard.

DORCHESTER. Mrs J.M. Morris, Huish Farm, Sydling St Nicholas, Dorchester (Cerne Abbas [03003] 265). Working farm. Sleeps 2. The perfect place for a peaceful holiday for two people only, this self-contained flat in thatched farmhouse is set amidst beautiful countryside, within easy reach of the coast, and near Cerne Abbas village abounding with historical interest dating back to the 14th century, including remains of the Abbey. The Cerne Giant, 180 feet high, is a curious figure cut in the chalk hillside to the north-east of the village. Upstairs, one very large sunny room with twin beds, private bathroom, toilet; downstairs, large kitchen equipped with large electric cooker, fridge and all utensils. Linen not supplied. No TV. Car essential, ample parking. Own entrance, and sunny corner in garden. Pets are permitted. Weekly terms from £70 including fuel. SAE, please, for further details.

GILLINGHAM. Mrs J. Wallis, Meads Farm, Stour Provost, Gillingham SP8 5RX (East Stour [074-785] 265). Working farm, join in. Sleeps 6. Mead Bungalow is a superior property enjoying outstanding views over Blackmore Vale. Situated one mile from A30 at the end of the lovely village of Stour Provost. Shaftesbury with its famous Gold Hill is nearby and within easy reach are Bournemouth, Weymouth and Bath. Many attractive and interesting places lie a short car ride away. Over one mile of private coarse fishing 160 yards from bungalow. Spacious accommodation sleeps six plus cot. Large lounge with colour TV, diningroom, three double bedrooms, bathroom, luxury oak kitchen with automatic washing machine etc; all electric (no meters), full central heating; linen supplied. Quarter acre lawns. Sorry no pets.

HOLDITCH. Old Forge Cottage, Holditch, Chard. Sleeps 4. Ideal for peace and seclusion in glorious unspoilt countryside within easy reach of the sea. This delightful old world cottage with oak beams stands just outside Holditch on the Devon/Dorset/Somerset borders, affording splendid views over beautiful countryside. Charmouth and its sandy beaches seven miles distant. Lyme Regis, with safe bathing and recreational facilities eight miles. The cottage is completely modernised and tastefully furnished with fitted carpets throughout, for up to four people. One twin-bedded room and two single rooms; sittingroom with colour TV; kitchen with dining area; modern bathroom; second toilet; electric cooker, fridge, vacuum cleaner, modern sink unit, immersion heater, night storage heaters throughout (included in terms). Everything supplied except linen. Electricity charged by meter reading. Phone; walled garden; garage. Chard four and a half miles. Terms £90 to £120 weekly. Open all year. Regret no children under 12 years. No pets. All enquiries to **Mrs P.A. Spice, Orchard Cottage, Duke Street, Micheldever, Near Winchester, Hants SO21 3DF (Micheldever [096-289] 563).**

LULWORTH COVE near. Mr R.W. Canaven, Wynards Farm, Winfrith, Near Lulworth Cove DT2 8DQ (0305 854094). ♀ ♀ **Cottages sleep 2/5.** Furnished to high standards, double glazed. Heating, TV, bedding and linen provided. Set on the edge of conservation village in an elevated position with direct access to Bridleway/footpaths linking to Heritage coastal path. Outstanding views. Two and a half miles Durdle Door, Lulworth Cove; 20 minutes Wareham, Dorchester and Weymouth; 30 minutes Poole and Bournemouth. Three local pubs within walking distance. Local shop/Post Office. Children and dogs welcome. Terms from £99.

LYME REGIS. Mrs S. Denning, Higher Holcombe Farm, Uplyme, Lyme Regis DT7 3SN (Lyme Regis [029-74] 3223). Working farm, join in. Sleeps 7. Completely separate part of farmhouse on dairy farm which was a Roman settlement. Surrounded by pleasant country walks, golf, fishing and safe sandy beaches. Accommodation has three bedrooms, two double and three single beds; lounge with inglenook fireplace, colour TV; kitchen/diningroom with fitted units, microwave oven in kitchen, all amenities. Shower, toilet and washbasin upstairs. Also downstairs bathroom and WC. Linen not provided. Use of washing machine and tumble dryer. Pets by arrangement. Electric heating; 50p slot meter. Babysitting by arrangement. Plenty of parking. Car not essential; one mile from shops and village of Uplyme; two miles from coast of Lyme Regis. Open all year round. Tourist Board approved. SAE for details.

LYTCHETT MINSTER. Mrs Rosemary Williams, Trokes Coppice, Old Wareham Road, Lytchett Minster BH16 6AN (Bournemouth [0202] 622205).

Lovely country setting with magnificent views across open farmland to Poole Harbour and the Purbecks beyond, yet only 30 minutes from Bournemouth with its fine stores and superb entertainment. Trokes Cottage is set in the grounds of Trokes Coppice and has its own small, secluded garden. One mile north of Upton and A35 (Poole to Dorchester road;) four and-a-half miles from Poole and five miles from Wareham (Thomas Hardy country); Wimborne Minster four and-a-half miles. Sleeping accommodation for up to nine in two upstairs bedrooms (one double bed, the other three singles); downstairs bedroom with bunks; double studio couch in lounge/diningroom; bathroom/toilet. Cot and high chair available. Gas central heating. All electric kitchen — cooker, fridge, twin tub washing machine, immersion heater. No linen. TV. SAE for brochure.

MILTON ABBAS. Mrs V.O. Davey, Little Hewish Farm, Milton Abbas, Near Blandford DT11 0LH (Milton Abbas [0258] 880326). Cottages sleep 4/5/6.

Three modernised farm cottages at Little Hewish Farm in Hardy country, situated one mile from the unique village of Milton Abbas with its picturesque thatched cottages, lake and abbey. It is within easy driving distance of the coast with sandy beaches at Bournemouth, Studland, Swanage and Weymouth, with many coastline walks between. The cottages contain two and three bedrooms sleeping four to six persons. Cot if required. Sittingroom, dining/kitchen; bathroom and separate toilet. Cottages are comfortably furnished and fully equipped including fridge, spin dryer and hot water. Fully carpeted. Colour TV. Electricity by 50p meter. Linen extra. Nightstore heaters. Laundry room. Sorry, no pets. Car essential, parking. Available all year. Terms £75 to £185 per week. Tourist Board approved. AA registered. Please phone or send SAE for details.

SHAFTESBURY. Meadow Hayes Cottage, Bedchester, Shaftesbury. Sleeps 7/8. This cottage is situated on the edge of a small village with a large secluded garden, and is about half a mile from the farm with a dairy herd and poultry. It ensures a holiday where comfort and cleanliness are a prime consideration. Tastefully converted from two cottages it comprises hall, lounge with open fire, diningroom, kitchen; three bedrooms, sleeping seven/eight, cot. Bathroom. It is fully equipped and has fitted carpets, colour TV, electric cooker, fridge, washing machine, electric heaters. Parking. Ideally situated for visiting Longleat, Stonehenge, Stourhead, Bournemouth, Poole, Salisbury, five miles from Shaftesbury and nine from Blandford. SAE, please, to **Mrs T. Kendall, Brach Farm, Twyford, Shaftesbury SP7 0JN (Fontmell Magna [0747] 811356).**

STURMINSTER NEWTON. Mrs Sheila Martin, Moorcroft Farm, Moorside, Marnhull, Sturminster Newton DT10 1HH (Marnhull [0258] 820271). Working farm. Sleeps 4.

This is an upstairs flat with own entrance and Yale key. It is part of the farmhouse. Kept very clean, there is a friendly, welcoming atmosphere. We are a 110-acre Dairy Farm, in the Blackmore Vale in Hardy country. Guests are welcome to wander around, watch the farm activities and laze in the large garden. New Forest, Wildlife Park, Cheddar and the coast all within easy reach. Accommodation for four people in two double bedrooms, one with a double bed, the other with two singles. Bathroom, separate toilet. Sitting/diningroom with colour television. Well-equipped kitchen with full-sized electric cooker, fridge, sink unit and wall cabinets. Everything including linen supplied; electric heaters in all rooms. Open Easter-October. Village shop 400 yards. Sea 28 miles. Car essential. Sorry, no pets. Weekly terms from £80 to £145. SAE, please.

WHEN MAKING ENQUIRIES PLEASE MENTION
FARM HOLIDAY GUIDES

STURMINSTER NEWTON. Mrs R.J. Primrose, Lymburghs Farm, Marnhull, Sturminster Newton DT10 1HN (Marnhull [0258] 820310). Sleeps 6. An

attractive modern bungalow on Stock and Stud Farm. Faces south with lovely open views across the peaceful countryside of the Blackmore Vale. Situated between Sturminster Newton and Shaftesbury, 26 miles from the coast and in an ideal position for touring an unspoilt county. Visit the many and varied places of interest which are within easy reach. Coarse fishing available on River Stour. Large restful garden for relaxation or play. There are three bedrooms and the bungalow is fully equipped for all holiday needs including colour TV and spin dryer. Car is essential, good parking. Regret no pets. Tourist Board registered. Please send for details.

VERWOOD. Mr and Mrs R.J. Froud, West Farm, Romford, Verwood BH21 6LE (Verwood [0202] 822263). Working farm. Sleeps 6. The Cottage is situated on West Farm, about 200 yards from the B3081 Verwood to Cranborne road. It is six miles from Ringwood and the New Forest, 12 miles from Bournemouth and its beaches, and 20 miles from historic Salisbury. There are many lovely walks through local surroundings. Cottage has three bedrooms; one double, one single and one twin-bedded, also bed-settee in lounge; sleeps total of six people. Cot and high chair provided on request. All bedding provided, but no linen, towels or tea towels. Downstairs lounge with TV, diningroom, kitchen, bathroom and toilet. Kitchen has electric cooker, kettle, fridge and all crockery, cutlery and cooking utensils for six people. Electricity by 50p meter. Immersion heater, electric fires and night storage heaters. Lawned garden with trees and views over lake, meadows and woods. Car parking. Sorry, no pets. Shops one mile. Terms from £90 plus VAT per week. Phone or send SAE for details.

WAREHAM. Colonel and Mrs A. M. Barne, Culeaze, Wareham BH20 7NR (Bere Regis [0929] 471209 after 6 pm). Working farm. 2 flats sleeping 2 and 4 persons AN UPSTAIRS FLAT attractively decorated and comfortably furnished overlooking a lovely garden. Accommodating four people in two double bedrooms; bathroom, toilet; sittingroom, diningroom. Modern electric kitchen, fully equipped. Also GROUND FLOOR FLAT, self contained, consisting of double bedroom, sittingroom, kitchen, bathroom. Dogs accepted if kept under control. Available April/September. Electricity included in terms during June, July and August. The River Piddle runs through the property and the house is surrounded by farm and "pick your own fruit" farmland. Well off the road. Lulworth Cove, seven miles, is the nearest point of coast; Studland Bay has fine, sandy beach. Dorset is full of beautiful and historic places and buildings, all worth visiting. Bere Regis (one-and-a-half miles) has a few shops. Bournemouth 15 miles, Wareham seven miles. SAE, please, for further particulars, or telephone.

WAREHAM near. Mrs M.J.M. Constantinides, "Woodlands", Hyde, Near Wareham BH20 7NT (0929 471239). Secluded house, formerly Dower House of Hyde Estate, stands alone on a meadow of the River Piddle in four and a half acres in the midst of "Hardy Country". The maisonette comprises upstairs lounge with colour TV; one bedroom (two single beds); downstairs large kitchen/diner, small entrance hall, bathroom; electric cooker (in addition to Aga Cooker), refrigerator. Independent side entrance. Extra bedroom (two single beds) on request at £15 per week. Visitors are welcome to use house grounds; children can fish or play in the boundary stream. Pleasant walks in woods and heath nearby. Golf course half a mile, pony trekking nearby. All linen included, beds ready made and basic shopping arranged on arrival day. Aga will be lit and maintained on request. Ideal for a quiet holiday far from the madding crowd. Linen supplied. Cot and high chair available and children welcome to bring their pets. SAE, please, for terms and further particulars.

GLOUCESTERSHIRE

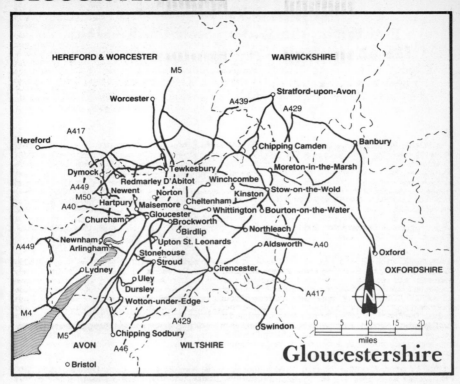

HEREFORD & WORCESTER

WARWICKSHIRE

M5

Worcester

Stratford-upon-Avon

A439

A429

A417

Hereford

Chipping Camden

Banbury

Dymock

Tewkesbury

Moreton-in-the-Marsh

Redmarley D'Abitot

Winchcombe

A449

Newent

Norton

Kinston

Stow-on-the-Wold

M50

Hartpury

Cheltenham

A40

Maisemore

Whittington

Bourton-on-the-Water

Gloucester

Churcham

Brockworth

Birdlip

Northleach

Newnham

Upton St. Leonards

A449

Arlingham

Stonehouse

Aldsworth

A40

Lydney

Stroud

Oxford

Uley

Cirencester

OXFORDSHIRE

Dursley

A417

N

Wotton-under-Edge

M4

A429

0 5 10 15 20

M5

Chipping Sodbury

Swindon

miles

AVON

A46

WILTSHIRE

Bristol

Gloucestershire

CINDERFORD. 7 Silver Street, Littledean, Cinderford. Sleeps 4 Adults, 2 Children. Delightful 17th-century terraced cottage, ideally situated for touring Forest of Dean, Wye valley and Cotswolds. Gloucester 12 miles, Ross-on-Wye 12 miles. Twin bedroom (with children's room off) and double bedroom. Recently renovated but retaining much original character including open beams, inglenook fireplace with bread oven and stone spiral staircase. All electric. Colour TV. Well equipped fully fitted kitchen with cooker and fridge; large lounge/diner; new bathroom; electric heaters. Cottage garden overlooking private parkland. Linen supplied if required. Golf, riding, fishing, swimming and beautiful forest trails nearby. Available all year. Reductions for two person occupancy. For full details contact **Mrs Suzanne Parr, High Gables, Awre Road, Blakeney GL15 4AA (0594 516042 evenings).**

DURSLEY. Stable Cottage, Upper Cam, Dursley. Sleeps 5. Situated in a tiny unspoilt village in the West Cotswolds, this delightful detached cottage was formerly a stable of our 17th century Cotswold farmhouse. Upper Cam is by the Cotswold Way and is surrounded by beautiful countryside for walking, picnics and scenic drives. Golf, gliding, pony trekking and water sports are available nearby and visitors can explore Slimbridge Wildfowl Trust, Berkeley Castle, Westonbirt Arboretum, Wye Valley, Bath and many more places of interest. Accommodation in this carefully converted cottage is for five people, with carpeting throughout, beamed ceilings, pine fittings, tasteful furnishings, storage heating, colour TV etc. Ample parking. Sorry, no pets. Cot and linen available. English Tourist Board registered. Terms from £90, brochure on request, from **Mrs J.T. Whitton, Street Farm, Upper Cam, Dursley GL11 5PG (Dursley [0453] 542837).**

Terms quoted in this publication may be subject to increase if rises in costs necessitate

COTSWOLDS
Bourton-on-the-Water / Stow-on-the-Wold

The **Cotswold Stone Cottages** below are on the outskirts of the small historic market town of Stow-on-the-Wold near Bourton-on-the-Water in the heart of the Cotswolds. They have been tastefully modernised and decorated and are comfortably furnished complete with colour television and central heating. Open all year. Pets permitted. **Winter Weekends** from £58 per cottage October to April.

Charming 17th Century Cottage
with a wealth of oak beams and two inglenook fireplaces. Sleeps 6.

Lovely 17th Century Cottage
with beamed ceilings and inglenook. Sleeps 3/4.

Quaint Little Old Cottage
heated by log fire. Sleeps 2.

Tiny One-Bedroomed Old World Cottage
Sleeps 1/2.

Please phone or write for further details and illustrated brochure.
Mrs. S. Harrison, Olive Hill Farm, Wyck Rissington, Bourton-on-the-Water GL54 2PW. Telephone: Cotswold (0451) 20350.

DURSLEY near. Mrs M.J. Marsh, Downhouse Farm, Springhill, Upper Cam, Dursley GL11 5HQ (Dursley [0453] 546001) Working farm. Downhouse, a listed 18th-century farmhouse with 30 acres of pastureland, is in a quiet rural location at the foot of Peaked Down, yet only one mile from the market town of Dursley. It is an ideal centre for exploring the beautiful Cotswolds by car or on foot. The self-contained wing of the farmhouse has separate access, a lawn and private patio; a large kitchen/diningroom with automatic washing machine; comfortable sittingroom, colour television and telephone for incoming calls. Two twin-bedded rooms with duvets and full linen, cot available; bathroom; cloakroom; central heating. Pets welcome. Telephone or write for brochure.

ILMINGTON (North Cotswolds). Foxglove Cottages, Ilmington. ♀ ♀ ♀ ♀ *Commended*. Single storey Cotswold stone built country cottage accommodation. Situated in a quiet sunny spot overlooking village orchard. Two units sleeping two to five people plus cot, etc, for children. All modern conveniences including microwave, automatic washing machine; bath and shower. Central heating. Electricity and linen included. Extremely well furnished in typical cottage style, with cosy fires, country pine and dried flowers, each with own private garden with sun patio and garden furniture. Easy parking. Suitable for disabled. Ilmington is a delightful Cotswold village nestling at the foot of the Campden Hills, with village shop, Post Office, pub, church, playing fields with tennis, cricket, bowls and children's playground. Ideally placed for visiting Stratford-upon-Avon or surrounding Cotswold villages. £80 to £275 per week. **Mrs S. Lowe, Folly Farm Cottage, Ilmington, Shipston-on-Stour, Warwickshire CV36 4LJ (060882 425).**

PLEASE SEND A STAMPED ADDRESSED ENVELOPE WITH ENQUIRIES

NEWNHAM-ON-SEVERN. Mr G. Tucker, The Granary, Upper Hall, Elton, Newnham-on-Severn

GL14 1JJ (0452 76243). An attractive stone built cottage attached to a former farmhouse in a quiet hamlet nestled between the Royal Forest of Dean and the River Severn. The accommodation is centrally heated, has quality furnishings and comprises a well equipped kitchen with automatic washing machine and dining area; sittingroom with beamed ceiling, Victorian fireplace and colour TV; a large double/family bedroom; bathroom with bath and shower. Private garden with garden furniture and barbecue. Linen and towles provided. Electricity by meter. Sorry no dogs. Sleeps two/four plus cot available. Terms from £100 to £180 weekly.

Relax in comfort at Folly Farm Cottages

Near Tetbury, an ancient Cotswold wool town in 'Royal' Gloucestershire. Tetbury is an ideal touring centre within 1½ hours' drive of Heathrow. Seven skilfully created Cotswold stone cottages border our picturesque farmyard with its imposing tythe barn, circa 1650. The cottages sleep four to ten and have original elm beams; some also have cobbled fireplaces. There is full central heating, modern kitchens and bathrooms, and comfortable furnishings. Linen, logs, a daily newspaper and launderette are provided. Resident hosts. AA listed. Open all year. Low season terms are from £100, high season from £200.

Further information/colour brochure from: Mr Julian Benton, Folly Farm Cottages, Tetbury, Gloucestershire GL8 8XA. Tel: Tetbury (0666) 502475

ULEY near. Mr and Mrs C. N. Mander, Owlpen Manor Cottages, Owlpen, Near Uley GL11 5BZ

(Dursley [0453] 860261). Working farm. Properties sleep 2/10. The tiny hamlet of Owlpen nestles against woods and hills in its own remote and picturesque valley and is one of the treasures of Cotswold scenery. The famous Tudor manor house is the spectacular focus to the group of cottages now restored to very high standards. Guests may enjoy a heritage of peace and beauty in comfort and at leisure throughout the year whether it is a party of two or 10 people. Choose from the enchanting Court House, the elegant Grist Mill, three roomy farmhouses, a smaller weaver's cottage or three cosy retreats for two. Electricity, linen, cleaning after departure, colour TV etc, included in rentals ranging from £120 to £550 including VAT weekly; or try a two-day break from £48. Owlpen carries cattle, plus 245 acres of beechwoods providing logs, walks and shooting. Lake for fishing. Take-away food and wines. Four-poster beds. Golf, gliding and five miles private footpaths. Four-poster beds. Centrally located for touring Cotswolds and Bath. BTA and Tourist Board listed. SAE, please.

UPPER CAM. Mrs Ann Harris, Church Farmhouse, Upper Cam, Dursley GL11 5PB (0453 543165).

Church Farm Cottage is a converted coach-house adjacent to a listed farmhouse in the village of Upper Cam, lying between the Cotswold Escarpment and the Severn Vale in lovely countryside. The Cotswold Way runs through the village. Nearby is Slimbridge Wild Fowl Trust and Berkeley Castle. Within a large radius are Gloucester, Bath, Cheltenham, Wye Valley and Forest of Dean. The well equipped cottage sleeps five in three bedrooms, with extra bed and cot available. A larger comfortable sittingroom has gas fire and colour TV. Bedroom on ground floor has en-suite basin and toilet. Details on request. Terms from £80 to £160 per week.

WHEN MAKING ENQUIRIES PLEASE MENTION
FARM HOLIDAY GUIDES

WINCHCOMBE. Orchard Cottage, Stanley Pontlarge, Near Winchcombe — TEWKESBURY, Magpie Cottage, 4 Chance Street, Tewkesbury. ORCHARD

COTTAGE, set amid pear trees of orchard on Cotswold escarpment, three miles from Winchcombe. Rural privacy, own access and garden. Four people accommodated in two bedrooms; bathroom; sittingroom (log-coal burning stove); night storage heaters; fully equipped except linen; kitchen with electric cooker, etc. Car essential — parking. Shops one mile. Secluded town cottage at 4 CHANCE STREET offers holiday accommodation for four people. Sitting/diningroom (log-coal burning fire); two bedrooms; bathroom; small kitchen (electric cooker); everything provided except linen. Car not essential; shops nearby. Children welcome at both properties — pets by arrangement. Open all year. Ideal centres for exploring, walking, sightseeing, all sports. Stratford-upon-Avon, Cheltenham, other interesting towns and villages within easy reach. English Tourist Board registered. Terms: Orchard Gate from £75 to £160 per week; 4 Chance Street from £70 to £140 per week. **Mrs S.M. Rolt, Stanley Pontlarge, Near Gretton, Winchcombe GL54 5HD (0242 602594).**

HAMPSHIRE

FORDINGBRIDGE. Mrs Sue Sollars, Plum Tree Cottage, Sandleheath, Fordingbridge SP6 1QF (0425 653032). Sleeps 4. Self-contained wing of charming

thatched cottage, set amongst woods and farmland. 10 minutes to the New Forest, half an hour to the sea. Accommodation is furnished, equipped and decorated to a very high standard. Inglenook fireplace with wood stove and storage heaters make it cosy for holidays all year round. Sleeps four people in one double and two single bedrooms. Colour TV, electricity for cooking and heating, and wood for the fire, all included in the rental of £110 to £220 per week. Large, shaggy garden for children to play in, and for parents to relax. Regret, no pets. Leaflet available.

RINGWOOD. Upper Kingston Farm Cottage, Ringwood. Sleeps 4. This furnished cottage set in 100

acre farm, offers a self-catering holiday of complete freedom. Shop one mile away, beach 10 miles. Situated two miles south of Ringwood, bordering the New Forest, it is an ideal centre for the attractions of the Forest, or the resorts of the South Coast. The accommodation consists of two double bedrooms (cot available), large bathroom with toilet, lounge with TV, dining room, kitchen with electric cooker and fridge. Downstairs toilet. Fully equipped, except linen. Electricity included. Economy 7 heating. One dog only permitted, if kept under control. Car essential. SAE, please, for full particulars and terms to **Mrs J. Harlow, "Elsinore", Horsham Road, Rusper, Horsham, Sussex RH12 4PR (Rusper [029-387] 1495).**

SWAY. Mrs H.J. Beale, Hackney Park, Mount Pleasant Lane, Sway, Lymington SO41 8LS (Lymington [0590] 682049). Sleeps 4/6. Situated in commanding and tranquil setting two miles from Lymington and Sway village. Delightful residence in own extensive grounds adjoining New Forest Heath with superb walks, rides and drives. Apartment to sleep six (further bedrooms available), coach-house flat to sleep four. Comfortable and modern, colour TV, bed linen and electricity included. Pets by prior arrangement. First class stables for those wishing to bring own horse and excellent riding facilities within walking distance. Many famous places of interest nearby. Close to Isle of Wight ferry and within six miles of sandy beaches, 15 miles Bournemouth and Southampton. Open all year.

WHEN MAKING ENQUIRIES PLEASE MENTION
FARM HOLIDAY GUIDES

HEREFORD & WORCESTER

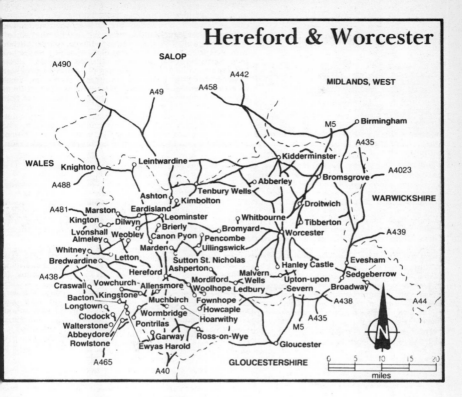

ABBEYDORE. Mrs M. Jenkins, Black Bush Farm, Abbeydore, Herefordshire HR2 0AJ (Golden Valley [0981] 240281). Comfortable farmhouse and cottage on quiet country roadside. Both detached with private gardens and plenty of parking space. Situated amongst farmland 10 miles from Hereford and seven from the Welsh border. Ideal for quiet walks or touring the beautiful and varied countryside. Farmhouse sleeps nine in four bedrooms. Cottage sleeps six in three bedrooms. Cots available. Both properties are fully equipped, except linen which may be hired, and offer bathrooms and well equipped kitchens. Comfortable sittingroom with TV. Electric heating. Carpeted throughout. Children welcome. Pets by prior arrangement. Electricty by 50p meter. Open all year. Terms: Farmhouse from £120; Cottage from £100.

HAY-ON-WYE. Mrs P. Lewer, Glebe Farm, Michaelchurch, Escley HR2 0PR (098123 201). Working farm, join in. Sleeps 4/6. Traditional 40 acre Welsh Border farm (sheep, cattle, goats, free-range hens). Peaceful (no traffic) middle of nowhere! Fringe Brecon Beacons National Park. Wonderful "undiscovered" Herefordshire/Welsh Border countryside, little changed by time. Abundant wild life (including rare Red Kites, Peregrines), buzzards, badgers, etc., wild flowered country lanes. Wealth of Border castles, Offa's Dyke footpath, mountain and valley walks. Abergavenny canal, riding, fishing nearby. Even special off-season charm (late autumn/spring). Large cosy farm caravan, own garden, (WC, fridge, TV, microwave). Friendly animals and owners extend a warm welcome. Free milk, eggs, butter. Full brochure available. discounts for Senior Citizens. Short Breaks available.

HEREFORD. Rose Cottage, Craswall, Hereford. Sleeps 5. Rose Cottage is a modernised stone-built cottage, retaining its original character situated at the foot of Black Mountains, on a quiet country road. Hay-on-Wye, Hereford, Abergavenny easily accessible and ideal base for walking and touring. Many churches and castles of historic interest; close to River Monnow where trout fishing is available. Pony trekking, hang gliding nearby. A car is essential and there is ample parking. Rose Cottage is comfortably furnished with full central heating and wood fire (heating and hot water included). Linen provided free of charge. Electricity by meter reading. Two bedrooms, one with double bed, one with three single beds. Cot can be provided. Bathroom, toilet. Kitchen fully equipped with electric cooker, kettle, fridge etc. Sittingroom; diningroom. TV. Dogs are allowed. Registered with the English Tourist Board. Available all year round. Terms from £85 – £95. **Mrs M. Howard, The Three Horseshoes, Craswall HR2 0PL (Michaelchurch [098-123] 631).**

HEREFORD. Mrs S. Dixon, Swayns Diggins, Harewood End, Hereford HR2 8JU (098-987 358). This

highly recommended first floor flat is completely self-contained at one end of the main house. The bedroom, sitting room and private balcony all face south with panoramic views over farmland towards Ross and Symonds Yat. The fully equipped kitchen overlooks the garden with grand views towards Orcop Hill and the Black Mountains. Open all year, rental from £80 per week includes electricity, linen, heating, colour TV. Ideal base for exploring the beautiful Wye Valley, Herefordshire, Gloucestershire and the historic Welsh Marches. There is much to see and do in the area. Write or phone for further particulars.

KINGTON. The Harbour, Upper Hergest, Kington. Working farm, join in. Properties sleep 5/9. This bungalow is on a good second-class road facing south with beautiful views from its elevated position, across the Hergest Ridge and Offa's Dyke. The Welsh border is a mile away. Shops are two-and-a-half miles away. Kington Golf Club nearby. Accommodation for five/nine in two double rooms (one with extra single bed) downstairs and two double dormer bedrooms; two cots; bathroom, toilet; sittingroom (TV, radio); diningroom; sun porch for relaxing; kitchen with electric cooker, fridge, food store and usual equipment. No linen. Suitable for the disabled. Children and pets welcome. Car essential — parking. Available all year. Also mobile home sleeping two/six with bathroom and flush toilet. SAE, please, to **Mr A.J. Welson, New House Farm, Upper Hergest, Kington, Herefordshire HR5 3EW (Kington [0544] 230533).**

KINNERSLEY. Sunny and Myrtle Cottages, Lower Ailey Farm, Kinnersley. Working farm. Cottages sleep 4/5. Two detached cottages in nice sunny positions away from other houses (except farmhouse). Each is surrounded by lawn and fence and is set away from the road amid quiet countryside. Good approach roads. Near Wye Valley and Welsh hills where pony trekking can be enjoyed. Hereford 12 miles away; Hay-on-Wye nine miles and many surrounding Black and White villages to explore. The farm has chickens, sheep, cattle, cider fruit and cereals, and also two pet donkeys. Fully furnished, the cottages sleep four/five people. Bathroom; sittingroom; kitchen with electric cooker etc. Car essential — parking. Children welcome, cot and high chair supplied if needed. Well controlled pets allowed. Open all year round. Terms from £95 weekly (electricity extra). Tourist Board registered. Details with SAE from **Mrs G.M. Thomas, The Elms Farm, Kinnersley, Hereford HR3 6NY (Eardisley [05446] 480 or 373).**

LEDBURY near. High House Farmhouse, Preston Cross, Near Ledbury. Working farm. Properties

sleep 6. High House Farmhouse (part 13th century), is divided into two holiday houses, equipped to very good standard. Superb views towards Ross-on-Wye (eight miles) and Gloucestershire. Fully electric kitchen/diner; sittingroom; bathroom and toilet; three bedrooms, all with fitted carpets; TV; telephone. Garage (car essential). All rooms have either night storage or electric heaters. Each house sleeps six. No linen supplied. Electricity extra. Farm buildings are nearby (this is a working stock and arable farm). Dogs allowed, under strict control. Children welcome, cot. Historical market town of Ledbury three miles, Malvern eight miles. Weekly terms from £120 to £170; Reductions off season. ETB Approved. CARE Association Approved. **Mrs G.M. Thomas, White House Farm, Preston Cross, Near Ledbury HR8 2LH (Much Marcle [053184] 231).**

LEDBURY near. Homend Bank Cottage,

Stretton Grandison, Near Ledbury. Working farm. A detached fully modernised cottage in the heart of rural Herefordshire. In an elevated position overlooking the Frome Valley, Homend Bank Cottage is quiet and peaceful and offers the perfect base for a relaxed holiday, or for touring Wales, the Cotswolds, the Severn Valley or merely the beautiful local countryside. The accommodation consists of one double, one twin and one single bedroom; bathroom, kitchen, diningroom and sittingroom with colour TV. Electric heating and cooking, through a meter. Telephone. No linen provided. Dogs welcome and cot available. Terms from £140 – £175 per week. Full details from **P.W.A. Hughes, The Estate Office, Madresfield, Malvern WR13 5AU (Malvern [0684] 573614 during office hours).**

LEOMINSTER. The Hollies, Hyde Ash, Ivington, Leominster. Sleeps 6. Leominster three miles, Hereford 10 miles. The Hollies is a fully modernised detached country cottage with fitted carpets, fully equipped for six people. Large modern kitchen with dining area, electric cooker, fridge/freezer, washing machine, spin dryer; bathroom and toilet. Diningroom. Sittingroom with open fire and colour television — logs and coal supplied. Storage heaters all rooms. One double, two twin bedrooms; cot and linen supplied. Immersion heater, airing cupboard; electricity metered. Set in quiet open countryside next to small family farm. Car essential, ample parking. Lawn. Children welcome. Sorry, no pets. Terms **Mrs M. Wood, Little Dilwyn, Dilwyn, Hereford HR4 8EY (Ivington [056-888] 279).**

DOCKLOW MANOR

HOLIDAY COTTAGES IN RURAL HEREFORDSHIRE FOR 2-6 PEOPLE

Quietly secluded in 10 acres of garden/woodland, the delightfully renovated stone cottages are grouped around an attractive stone-walled pond amidst shrubs, roses and honeysuckle. The cottages are homely, cosy and spotlessly clean. Fitted carpets, well equipped kitchens, colour TV, electric blankets. Laundry facilities. Bed linen is provided and beds are made up for your arrival. Wander round our rambling gardens and meet our friendly peacock, ducks, hens and goats. The more energetic can play croquet, lawn tennis, table tennis or take a dip in our **outdoor heated swimming pool**. Docklow is an ideal base for Ludlow, the Welsh border castles and market towns, Wye Valley, Brecon and Malvern hills. OPEN ALL YEAR. Short breaks low season.

For brochure telephone 056 882 643.
Carol and Malcolm Ormerod, Docklow Manor, Leominster, Herefordshire.

LEOMINSTER. Mrs Brooke, Nicholson Farm, Docklow, Leominster HR6 0SL (056882 269). For those seeking a peaceful holiday in the best of self-catering accommodation, we offer 17th century cottage sleeping two/four people and three bungalows sleeping four/seven people, all fully carpeted, storage heaters, colour TV, microwave ovens. Situated in landscaped gardens. Hills, rivers, own fishing lake on farm, golf, tennis, swimming and riding. Wonderful for walking and touring Wales, Brecon Beacons, etc. Meals available at two local hotels. Bed and Breakfast from £11. Stamp for brochure please.

LEOMINSTER. Mrs O.S. Helme, Ford Farm, Fordbridge, Leominster HRS 0LE (Leominster [0568] 2784). Sleep 4/5/6. Riverside apartments with fishing and birdwatching on the picturesque River Lugg. Situated actually on the river bank, these three modern apartments sleeping four, five and six people are skilfully renovated from an old timbered granary. The river, plus the boats and canoes provided (plus life jackets) give hours of fun and for wet days there is a pool table, darts and table tennis. Set in 500 acres of farm and woodland with over one mile of fishing, lovely walks and the nine hole Leominster Golf Course just 200 yards away. Good touring area. Automatic washing machine and dryer.

PLEASE SEND A STAMPED ADDRESSED ENVELOPE WITH ENQUIRIES

MALVERN. Whitewells Farm Cottages. ♀♀♀♀ *Commended.* Seven cottages including one for

disabled guests, full of charm and character, converted from historic farm buildings. Fully furnished and equipped to the highest standards. Exceptionally clean and comfortable. Set in three and a half acres of unspoilt Herefordshire countryside, this is an ideal base for touring Herefordshire, Worcestershire, Gloucestershire, Cotswolds, Welsh mountains, Shakespeare country. All electricity, linen, towels, cleaning materials, central heating in winter months included in price. Laundry room. Open all year. Short Breaks in low season. Dogs welcome. **Mr and Mrs D. Berisford, Whitewells Farm Cottages, Ridgway Cross, Near Malvern WR13 5JS (0886 880607).**

PRESTON WYNNE. The Cyder Barn and The Stables. Two character cottages created from the

conversion of an Elizabethan barn on working dairy farm but separate from the farming activities in the peaceful hamlet of Preston Wynne, seven miles from Hereford. The cottages have been beautifully restored, retaining the charm of the original stone and beamed ceilings and with a very high standard of modern conveniences. Superbly furnished and equipped. Ideally placed to explore the wealth of beauty in this lovely county. Guests are always welcome to join in the daily activities on the farm. We regret no pets. Tourist Board approved. Weekly rates from £150. **Mrs Julie Rogers, New House Farm, Preston Wynne, Hereford HR1 3PE (0432 820 621).**

ROSS-ON-WYE. Mr and Mrs I.J. Morris, Little Wharton Farm, Weston-Under-Penyard, Ross-on-Wye

HR9 5TP (0989 81 221). Sleeps 4/6. Little Wharton Farm is a family owned dairy farm on the edge of the Royal Forest of Dean. Situated three miles from Ross-on-Wye on the A40, near the Herefordshire/Gloucestershire border, it is ideally located for visiting the Wye Valley, Malvern Hills, Cotswolds and South Wales. The accommodation sleeps four (with the possibility of extra space for two). Comfortable sittingroom, modern bathroom, large fitted kitchen with electric cooker, fridge, kettle and iron. Colour television. All linen provided. Children welcome, cot and high chair available on request. Well behaved pets welcome. Fresh milk and bread available. Car parking. Public transport, shop and public house half a mile.

ROSS-ON-WYE. Holly Cottage, Llangrove, Ross-on-Wye. Sleeps 6/7. Holly Cottage is on the edge of a small village, two miles north of A40 at Whitchurch, Herefordshire. It is ideally situated for touring the Wye valley, Black Mountains and Forest of Dean. It is comfortably furnished accommodating 6/7 persons in three bedrooms. Small grassy garden. Ample parking. Electricity charged. Linen supplied. TV. Pets welcome. Cot available. Phone for terms, **Mrs A.C. Williams, The Nurseries, Llangrove, Ross-on-Wye HR9 6ET (Llangarron [098-984] 252).**

ROSS-ON-WYE. Mrs H. Smith, Old Kilns, Howle Hill, Ross-on-Wye HR9 5SP (Ross-on-Wye [0989]

62051]. Sleeps 10/12. 17th century character cottage perched high above the valley has superb views of the surrounding countryside. A short walk away is a magnificent view of Symonds Yat and the ruined 12th century red sandstone Goodrich Castle. Shop and pub half-a-mile. Central for Malverns, Cotswolds and Stratford. Furnished and equipped to high standard with central heating and open fires. One bedroom with kingsize bed and en-suite shower and vanity unit, one double bedroom and one twin-bedded room. Two double bed settees in lounge. Diningroom, fully fitted kitchen with washing machine and fridge/freezer. Colour TV and radio. Garden furniture and barbecue. Cot, high chair, babysitting. Children and pets welcome. Fishing, riding, golf, canoeing, tennis etc. Also smaller properties and smallholding with animals available. RAC.

WORMBRIDGE. Mrs J. Thomas, Granary Flat, Lower Jury Farm, Wormbridge HR2 9EE (Wormbridge [098-121] 229). Working farm. Sleeps 5. Granary Flat is attached to the early 16th century farmhouse on Lower Jury Farm. Situated in a peaceful valley, it is close to the Black Mountains, Golden Valley, market towns and places of historic interest. The flat has a wealth of exposed beams, and the lounge (with colour TV) and bedrooms are fully carpeted. There are lovely views to the distant hills and the Grey Valley. Children are welcome to help with the farm animals and hay-making. Shooting for experienced guns. Accommodates four/five people. Usual conveniences. Kitchen with electric cooker, fridge and dining area. Slot meter (50p) for electricity. Linen supplied. Pets permitted. Car essential — parking. Open April to October. Terms from £70 per week. Registered with the English Tourist Board.

KENT

BENENDEN. Waggon Lodge. Working farm. Sleeps 6. The cottage is situated down a private road. Beautiful and peaceful countryside, much of historic interest in the area. Recently converted to sleep six in three double bedrooms; bathroom, shower and toilet; lounge; dining area; kitchen with electric cooker, fridge, washing machine etc. Linen supplied. Storage heaters and electric fire. Colour TV. Cleaner calls once a week. Shop half a mile. Car essential plenty of parking space. No pets. Terms from £100 to £200. SAE to **Mrs Anne Cyster, Walkhurst Farm, New Pond Road, Benenden TN17 4EN (Cranbrook [0580] 240677).**

DEAL. Miss E.B. Phillips, Clanwilliam House, 1 Marine Road, Walmer, Deal CT14 7DN (Deal [0304] 374059). Sleeps 5. This is a lovely old bungalow built in 1878 and has been well maintained by successive owners. Standing on Walmer seafront it has a verandah with old stone pots and geraniums. Deal Castle is just next to it and Walmer Castle is one mile away. Here Her Majesty the Queen Mother was installed as Lord Warden of the Cinque Ports in 1979. The hovercraft at Dover and Ramsgate are nearby and Canterbury and Sandwich are within easy reach. Five people can be accommodated in two double and one single bedrooms. Fully equipped kitchen; TV and radio; linen can be hired. Dogs permitted at 15p per day. Children welcome and the house is suitable for the disabled. Please book early as this is a popular house and families return regularly. Open Easter to November. Personal service and babysitting (by arrangement). Weekly terms from £100 to £175 approximately. Prefer two weeks minimum. Electricity on slot meter. Deal Music Festival July/August — two weeks. Canterbury Festival September. Tourist Board registered.

FAVERSHAM. 1 Whitehill Cottages, Featherbed Lane, Selling, Faversham. ♀♀♀ *Commended.*

Working farm. Sleeps 5. In the Garden of England, on a traditional East Kent mixed farm with hops, fruit, cattle and cereals, Whitehill is situated in a quiet unspoilt area of the North Downs only six miles from Canterbury and within easy reach of the Channel ports, beaches of Thanet and Weald of Kent. One and a half miles south of junction 7 off M2. A beautiful area during blossom time, fascinating during harvest and peaceful during the winter. The cottage accommodates five with one double, one single and one twin room, cot available. Fully equipped electric kitchen; bathroom; sittingroom with open fireplace and full central heating. Children welcome, dogs by arrangement. Car essential. Available all year. For further details: **Mrs Maggie Berry, Bramble Hall, Brenley Farm, Bushey Close, Boughton, Faversham ME13 9AE (0227 751203).**

MAIDSTONE. Mrs J.M. Higham, Harmony, Pilgrims Way, Trottiscliffe, Maidstone ME19 5EP (Fairseat [0732] 822311). Sleeps 4. Historic Kent. Compact, split-level bungalow with private garden set in two acres, tucked beneath Country Park on North Downs. Superb southerly views. Equidistant London and Kent/Sussex coasts. Ideal touring or walking centre. Comprises bedroom with twin beds, livingroom with radio, TV, bed-settee; all electric kitchen with fridge and freezer; bathroom including bath, toilet, bidet and shower. Linen and electricity included. Private drive. Pets and children welcome. Summer lets from April to October from £90 per week. Winter lets negotiable. Tourist Board registered. Ring or write for details with SAE, please for prompt reply.

TENTERDEN near. Mrs P. Cooke, Great Prawls Farm, Stone-in-Oxney, Near Tenterden TN30 7HB (Wittersham [07972] 70539). Working farm. Detached modern bungalow peacefully set on 160 acre family run sheep and corn farm in an area of outstanding natural beauty. Five miles from medieval Rye or Tenterden, 15 minutes from sea. Comprises one double room, one three-bedded room, plus cot. Large lounge/diner, kitchen, WC, bathroom. Fully furnished, oil central heating, colour TV, washing machine, fridge. Castles, National Trust gardens, animal and craft centres within easy reach. Also London or France day trips. ETB registered. Terms from £120. Also available a brand new conversion of a farm building with oak beams, beautifully furnished, all facilities and environment similar to cottage except sleeps four plus cot and also a quite separate lovely six berth caravan in own half acre, with electricity, TV, WC. Terms from £80. Both personally supervised. Pets by arrangement.

LANCASHIRE

1a NEW MARKET ST.
CLITHEROE.
BB7 2JW.
TEL: (0200) 27310

**English Tourist Board
APPROVED AGENCY**

The **Specialist Agency** for self-catering holidays in the North-West. We offer a warm welcome in our comfortable, selected properties situated in pretty villages, historic towns and beautiful countryside. Children are welcome – often pets too! All properties are personally inspected and have gained Approved or Commended Grades from the English Tourist Board. We will be pleased to send you our free brochure, please write or telephone our office.

Come and discover the beautiful North-West, there's lots to see and do!

CLITHEROE near. Mrs S. Parker, Horns Farm, Church Street, Slaidburn, Near Clitheroe BB7 3ER (02006 288). ♛♛♛ Working farm. Two cosy semi-detached cottages situated in small picturesque village and overlooking farmland, make ideal bases from which to explore the Forest of Bowland, an area of outstanding natural beauty. Within easy reach of Yorkshire Dales, Lake District and seaside. Fishing at Stocks reservoir two miles away. On North Lancashire Cycle Way. Sorry, no pets. No. 24 sleeps five in two bedrooms and No. 22 has just one twin-bedded room. Garden up steps at rear. Linen and electricity included in the rent of £80 to £130 per week or £14 to £24 per night. Open all year. Our farmhouse nearby.

PRESTON. Ash View, Wheel Lane, Pilling, Preston. Working farm. Sleeps 4. This cottage is situated near the 85-acre dairy farm, within easy reach of Yorkshire Dales and Lake District. The attractive market town of Garstang is six miles away; University town of Lancaster 11 miles; Blackpool 12 miles. Lots to see and do in the area. One double and one twin bedroom, plus cot if required. Shower, washbasin, toilet. Lounge with colour TV. Diningroom. Well-equipped kitchen with electric cooker, fridge, iron, etc. Guests must supply their own linen. House is on ground level, though not suitable for wheelchairs. Car essential, parking. Available from Easter to November. Shops three-quarters of a mile. Sea one mile. Terms from £62 per week. SAE, please, or telephone for further details to **D.W.& V. Lawrenson, Bonds Farm, Wheel Lane, Pilling, Preston PR3 6HN (0253-790409).**

LEICESTERSHIRE

ROSE COTTAGE, LYNDON

THE OLD HALL COTTAGE

Lyndon Holiday Cottages
RUTLAND

Nine comfortable and well equipped self-catering cottages in the quiet 17th Century village of Lyndon, one mile south of Rutland Water. All have access to a heated indoor swimming pool and tennis court, both within walking distance. This is a beautiful and unspoilt part of England with many magnificent stately homes and historic towns within easy reach.

Sailing, windsurfing, fishing and bird-watching are all available on and around Rutland Water.

The cottages are registered with and approved by the English Tourist Board. Terms from £105-£195 per week. **For further details contact Lyndon Holiday Cottages, Estate Office, Lyndon Hall, Oakham, Rutland LE15 8TU. (0572 85786 or 0572 85275).**

LINCOLNSHIRE

WOODHALL SPA. Kirkstead Old Mill Cottage, Woodhall Spa. Isolated holiday home which sleeps seven to 10 plus baby, and is only let to NON-SMOKERS. The sunny house is over a mile off the Tattershall road on the outskirts of Woodhall Spa, Lincolnshire. It is set beside the wide but quiet River Witham that is noted for its fishing. A small rowing boat is provided. There is also a large, grassy garden and a three acre nature reserve for picnics. The house is extremely well equipped with colour TV, dishwasher, automatic washing machine, tumble dryer, fridge/freezer, microwave and piano etc. There is plenty of parking space, and a home help is provided for two hours midweek. Membership of local leisure club with swimming pool is included. Contact: **Mrs Hodgkinson, 52 Kelso Close, Worth, Crawley, West Sussex RH10 4XH (0293 882 008).**

**If you've found
FARM HOLIDAY GUIDES
of service please tell your friends**

NORFOLK

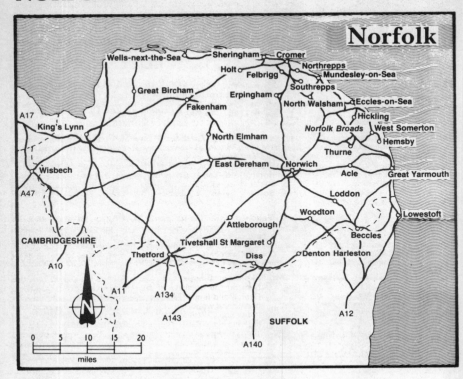

Norfolk

BLAKENEY. 4 Mariners Hill, Blakeney & Starlings, 82 High Street, Blakeney. Properties sleep 6/8.
All year round, beautiful house and attractive cottage available to visitors hoping for a holiday that combines true relaxation, first class accommodation and splendid scenery. MARINERS HILL is a flint/brick-built house sleeping eight, with spectacular views over the quay and marsh. Small, secluded, walled garden. Extremely well furnished and equipped. Colour TV, washing machine and fridge/freezer. STARLINGS is a pink-washed cottage with a part covered courtyard. With accommodation for six, it provides TV, Rayburn for extra warmth in winter. Good dinghy sailing and birdwatching at hand, golf courses nearby. For further details please write to: **Mrs A. Suckling or Mrs B. Marris, The Merchants House, 86 High Street, Blakeney, Holt NR25 7AL. Telephone enquiries: Mrs A. Suckling (Cromer [0263] 515186 — if no reply [0263] 740260).**

BRISLEY. Church Farm Cottages, Brisley, East Dereham, Norfolk NR20 5LL. Properties sleep 6.

These cottages which are clean and well equipped, were originally a 300 year old farmhouse and buildings converted to four three-bedroomed cottages. They stand beside 150 acres of common land in peaceful countryside, just off the B1145/B1146 crossroad. Owner supervised. Less than 15 minutes away is an indoor swimming pool, fishing, race-course and a sports centre offering archery, tennis, squash, bowls, shooting and a 9-hole golf course. Riding available close by also stabling and grazing for own horses from £10 per horse per week. Children and pets welcome. Open all year. Tourist Board approved. Terms £130 – £450. For more details telephone **Gillian V. Howes (036281 332).**

Terms quoted in this publication may be subject to increase if rises in costs necessitate

---

BURNHAM OVERY STAITHE. "Flagstaff House," Burnham Overy Staithe, King's Lynn. Properties sleep 5/7. Flagstaff House is right on the Quay, the old home of Captain Woodgett of the Cutty Sark. Each half of the house sleeps five comfortably in three bedrooms and has wonderful views over the creeks and marshes. Two extra people can be accommodated in summer house. There are also Flagstaff Cottage and Barn, with probably the finest views in Norfolk over the quay and Saltings. All houses are well-equipped with all modern conveniences, including washing machine, dishwasher, colour TV, electric storage heaters, etc. Telephone. The area is well known for dinghy sailing, bird watching, windsurfing, golf, fishing and miles of deserted sandy beaches and sand dunes. Apply to **Mr C.W.C. Green, Red House Farm, Badingham, Woodbridge, Suffolk IP13 8LL (Badingham [072-875] 637).**

CROMER. Hobby Cottage, Driftway Farm, Felbrigg, Cromer. Sleeps 6. Completely modernised, comfortable cottage at the end of a quiet farm lane. Two miles from sandy coast and within easy access of North Norfolk bird sanctuaries, stately homes and Norfolk Broads. The cottage sleeps four/six, having a sitting room with TV and bed settee; two double bedrooms (one with double bed, one with twin beds); diningroom, well-equipped kitchen and bathroom. Garden and parking for two cars. Own transport essential. Available March-October. From £105 — £230 per week, including electricity. No linen. Enquiries, with SAE please, to **Mrs E. Raggatt, The Ferns, Berkley Street, Eynesbury, St. Neots, Cambs PE19 2NE (Huntingdon [0480] 213884).**

FAKENHAM. Hillside Cottage, Colkirk, Fakenham. Built in traditional Norfolk flint, situated in a quiet position on the outskirts of Colkirk village, overlooking farmland. Hillside Cottage sleeps six in one double, one twin and one single bedroom; upstairs bathroom. Downstairs there is a sittingroom with colour TV, large airy kitchen/diningroom with fitted units and washing machine, and a further single bedroom. Cot if required. Linen supplied. Central heating. Children welcome and dogs are allowed. Large fenced garden. Terms on application to **Mrs C. Joice, Colkirk Hall, Fakenham NR21 7ND (Fakenham [0328] 862261).**

FAKENHAM. Saddlery Cottage, Colkirk, Fakenham. Sleeps 7. Saddlery Cottage is situated near the farm on the outskirts of the village overlooking farmland. Garage and fenced garden. Large and light sittingroom with beams and woodburner. Fully fitted kitchen/diningroom with fridge and electric cooker. Utility room with automatic washing machine. Bathroom with toilet and separate shower. Twin bedroom, single bedroom with fitted cupboards, carpets and washbasins. Upstairs double and twin bedrooms with fitted cupboards, carpets and washbasins. Calor gas heating, colour TV. Cot available. Linen included in price. Fuel, gas, electricity etc extra. Dogs allowed. Apply **Mrs C. Joice, Colkirk Hall, Fakenham NR21 7ND (0328 86 2261).**

GELDESTON. Hillside, 15 Kells Way, Geldeston, Beccles. Sleeps 4/6. This bungalow situated in small country village, very quiet and near River Waveney, is within easy reach of Great Yarmouth, Norwich, Lowestoft and seaside. Accommodates four/six people; one double, one twin bedroom; bed settee in lounge, storage heaters, colour TV, wood burner, beams; diningroom; bathroom/shower; toilet; kitchen, electric cooker, microwave, etc. Carpets throughout. Cot available. Sorry, no pets. Bed linen supplied. Open all year. Car essential — parking. Shops nearby. Terms on request. Special winter rates. **Mrs J.A. Rolt, "Conifer", 17 Kells Way, Geldeston, Beccles, Suffolk NR34 0LU (Kirby Cane [050-845] 689).**

GREAT YARMOUTH near. Mrs Jean Lindsay, Clippesby Holidays, Clippesby, Near Great Yarmouth NR29 3BH (Fleggburgh [0493] 369367). √ √ √ √ √ Properties sleep 1/8. In the Norfolk Broads National Park, near nature reserves and coastal resorts, is this quiet family owned park of 34 secluded areas, offering good facilities for family holidays and an ideal base for touring. Courtyard cottages accommodating one to eight persons, and an "EXCELLENT" grade touring park, are set amidst tranquil country surroundings. Swimming, lawn tennis, putting and more in the grounds. Bicycles for hire. Send for colour brochure.

HOLME NEXT THE SEA. Beach Cottage, Holme next the Sea. Sleeps 2/3. Situated in a small coastal

village two miles north of Hunstanton in an area of outstanding natural beauty. The carstone-built Victorian cottage is a two-minute walk from a sandy beach and adjacent to a golf course. The Bird and Nature Reserve, Norfolk Coastal Footpath and riding stables are within walking distance, as are village shop and public house. The cottage includes one twin-bedded room with ensuite bathroom, living room with sofa bed, open fire, colour TV. Fully equipped kitchen. Storage heaters. Cot, high chair. Use of garden. Off street parking. Sorry, no pets. Open all year. Short breaks available. For full details contact **Mrs S. Jones, Beach House, Beach Road, Holme next the Sea, Hunstanton PE36 6LG (Holme [048525] 201).**

KING'S LYNN. Mrs Angela Ringer, The Grange. West Rudham, King's Lynn PE13 8SY (East Rudham [048-522] 229). Working farm. Properties sleep 4/8. Sids Cottage is situated on working arable farm within easy reach of King's Lynn, Sandringham, Walsingham, Fakenham etc. Ideal for a quiet country holiday, the cottage is well equipped and sleeps four people in three bedrooms. Colour TV, washing machine etc. Linen provided. Car essential. Other cottages sleeping five, six and eight people respectively also available. Regret, no pets in smallest cottage. Registered with East Anglian Tourist Board. TELEPHONE ENQUIRIES PREFERRED.

KING'S LYNN. The Manager, The Ken Hill Estate, Ken Hill, Snettisham, King's Lynn PE31 7PG (Heacham [0485] 70001). Cottages sleep 6. Two modernised detached cottages on this estate are offered for holidays. One cottage has two twin bedded rooms, cot: bathroom; sittingroom with studio couch; diningroom; kitchen, electric cooker, fridge, immersion heater; TV. Fully equipped except for linen. This cottage is 150 yards from the shops. The other cottage has three double bedrooms and identical facilities, and is a mile away from the shops. Both are a mile and a half from beach, convenient for Norfolk Coast (sailing, riding, golf, bird watching). Cars advisable, parking. Nearby King's Lynn, Norwich, Ely, Cambridge, Sandringham House, Holkham Hall, wildlife parks and museums. Pets allowed. Fuller information on request.

LODDON. Hall Cottage, Hardley, Loddon. Sleeps 6 adults. Half of an old farmworkers cottage, carefully

converted and modernised, sleeps six, located on a mixed farm on the Norfolk Broads. Large garden, colour TV, Economy 7 heating, payphone and metered electricity. The cottage stands close to Hardley Flood (site of special scientific interest) with excellent coarse fishing from the owner's land and bird watching from two hides supplied by the Norfolk Naturalists Trust. The cottage provides an excellent base for touring Norfolk and Suffolk with Norwich Cathedral and Castle (nine miles), several historic houses and gardens, Pleasurewood Hills Theme Park and the coast all within 15 miles. Full details from **Mr and Mrs D.C. Tabor, Codham Hall, Shalford, Braintree, Essex CM7 5JD (0371 850853).**

MELTON CONSTABLE near. Greenfields, Gunthorpe, Near Melton Constable. Sleeps 5/7. Greenfields is a bungalow in a peaceful rural village, with unspoilt views of green fields and woodland, six and a half miles from Blakeney. The area has many interesting places worth visiting: the City of Norwich (25 miles), National Trust properties, the famous Fair Organ Museum, steam trains, nature reserves, pleasant countryside and sandy beaches. Accommodation for five/seven persons comprises two double and one single bedrooms, plus extra bed and cot if required. Lounge with TV, diningroom, kitchen fully equipped with electric cooker and fridge/freezer. Bathroom with shaver point and toilet. Everything supplied except for linen. Available throughout the year, with reduced rates off season. For further information please contact **Mrs H.J. Craske, 3A Curtis Lane, Sheringham NR26 8DE (Sheringham [0263] 823586) evenings.**

MUNDESLEY-ON-SEA. 47 Seaward Crest, Mundesley-on-Sea. Mundesley-on-Sea is an attractive

seaside village situated centrally on the Norfolk coast, within 10 miles of the Norfolk Broads, seven miles from Cromer and 20 miles from Norwich. The clean sandy beaches stretch for miles with safe bathing and natural paddling pools. This attractive west-facing brick-built chalet is in delightful setting with lawns, flower beds, trees and ample parking. Beach 500 yards away and shops 800 yards. There is an excellent golf course nearby and bowls and riding are within easy reach. Large lounge/diningroom tastefully furnished including easy chairs, settee and colour TV. Kitchenette with electric cooker, fridge, sink unit, etc. One double, one twin-bedded rooms. Fully carpeted. Cot. Bathroom and toilet. Lighting, hot water, heating and cooking by electricity (50p slot meter). Fully equipped except for linen. Weekly terms from £55. East Anglia Tourist Board registered. Details, SAE, please, **Mrs J. Doar, 4 Denbury Road, Ravenshead, Nottinghamshire NG15 9FQ (Mansfield [0623] 798032).**

NORTHREPPS. 1 and 2 Storey's Loke, Northrepps, Cromer. Working farm. Properties sleeps 4.
Cottages available for self-catering holidays in the centre of Northrepps village, three miles from Cromer and 22 miles north of Norwich. The nearest beach is approximately two miles away at Overstrand. The cottages sleep four each and have been extensively modernised. Comfortably furnished sitting/diningroom; well equipped, fitted kitchen with fridge and electric cooker; two bedrooms (one double, two single beds); modern bathroom with heater and shaving point. Hot water and heating by electricity. TV. Milk and eggs available in village. Children are welcome, also pets. Parking. Shops nearby. Open all year. This unspoilt area of Norfolk offers much for the holiday-maker. Many beauty spots, country walks, attractive villages and stately homes. Yarmouth 30 miles. Terms on request from **Mrs B. Roper, Shrublands Farm, Northrepps, Cromer NR27 0AA (Overstrand [026-378] 434/660).**

SWANTON ABBOTT. Near North Walsham. Sleeps 2 adults; 2 children. Self catering, well equipped cottage sleeping four, in quiet village five miles from the coast, clean sandy beaches, six miles from the Broads, footpath walks and within easy reach of stately homes and steam railways. Accommodation comprises two bedrooms, one double and one large bunk-bedded room. Lounge/kitchen; shower, toilet and separate toilet. Central heating. Colour TV. Free electricity. Carpeted throughout. Car essential. Bed linen provided. No pets. Available May to September. Terms from £150 per week. **Mrs C.P. Nockolds, Hill Farm House, Swanton Hill, Swanton Abbott, Norwich NR10 5EA (069269 481).**

See also Colour Display Advertisement **THURNE. Hedera House and Plantation Bungalows, Thurne. Sleeps 12.** Hedera House is a comfortably furnished Georgian-style house comprising spacious lounge and dining area with colour TV, kitchen with split level hob and double oven, breakfast bar, five double (with washbasins) and two single bedrooms, bathroom, shower and two WCs. Heating available for all seasons. Plantation Bungalows are a select group of 10 individual holiday homes, roomy and comfortably furnished and carpeted. Colour TV, fully fitted bathroom and kitchen, electric radiator heating in lounge and bedrooms. Cavity wall insulation. Electric meter. Norfolk is rich in places of historic interest, beautiful beaches, Broads, villages and countryside, all within easy motoring distance of Thurne. Fishing, boating, nearby golf course, horse riding. Free mooring and launching facilities for small craft. SAE to **Miss H.G. Delf, Thurne Cottage, The Staithe, Thurne NR29 3BU (0692 670242 or 0493 844568).**

WALCOTT-ON-SEA. Eryl-Y-Don, Helena Road, Walcott-on-Sea, Norwich. Bungalows sleep 4. TWO

similar chalet-type bungalows side by side, some 40 paces from the sea-front. Set in their own lawned gardens they are completely private and reached by a private road. Fully furnished, each sleeps FOUR persons. Walcott is a quiet village with a clean, sandy beach, about half-a-mile long. WALCOTT, one mile south of Bacton in AA books. Cromer is about 10 miles north of Walcott, Great Yarmouth about 18 miles south. The Norfolk Broads and other places of historic interest are all within easy access from Walcott. EATB registered, "Where to Stay". Enquiries by telephone **(Walcott [0692] 650798)** OR by letter with SAE to **F.A. Webster, Min-Y-Don, St. Helen's Road, Walcott-on-Sea, Norwich NR12 0LU.**

WINTERTON-ON-SEA. Timbers, The Lane, Winterton-on-Sea. Sleeps 5. Comfortable, well furnished

ground floor flat in attractive timber cottage situated in quiet seaside village just eight miles north of Great Yarmouth. Broad sandy beach and sand dunes (nature reserve) for pleasant walks. Three miles from Norfolk Broads (boating and fishing). Flat is carpeted throughout and is fully equipped for self-catering family holidays. Ideal for children, and pets are welcome. One double, one twin-bedded and one single bedroom. Sleeps five plus cot. Bed linen provided and maid service every other day for general cleaning. Beamed sittingroom with colour TV. Secluded garden. Car parking. Available June to September. Terms from £120 to £230 per week. For full details write to **Mr M.J. Isherwood, 79 Oakleigh Avenue, London N20 9JG (081-445 2192).**

NORTHAMPTONSHIRE

HOLIDAY ACCOMMODATION
Classification Schemes in
England, Scotland and Wales

The National Tourist Boards for England, Scotland and Wales have agreed a common 'Crown Classification' scheme for **serviced (Board)** accommodation. All establishments are inspected regularly and are given a classification indicating their level of facilities and services.

There are six grades ranging from 'Listed' to 'Five Crowns 👑👑👑👑👑'. The higher the classification, the more facilities and services offered.

Crown classification is a measure of *facilities* not *quality*. A common quality grading scheme grades the quality of establishments as 'Approved', 'Commended' or 'Highly Commended' according to the accommodation, welcome and service they provide.

For **Self-Catering**, holiday homes in England are awarded 'Keys' after inspection and can also be 'Approved', 'Commended' or 'Highly Commended' according to the facilities available. In Scotland the Crown scheme includes self-catering accommodation and Wales also has a voluntary inspection scheme for self-catering grading from '1 (Standard)' to '5 (Excellent)'.

Caravan and Camping Parks can participate in the British Holiday Parks grading scheme from 'Approved (✓)' to 'Excellent (✓ ✓ ✓ ✓ ✓)'. In addition, each National Tourist Board has an annual award for high-quality caravan accommodation: in England – Rose Awards; in Scotland – Thistle Commendations; in Wales – Dragon Awards.

When advertisers supply us with the information, FHG Publications show Crowns and other awards or gradings, including AA, RAC, Egon Ronay etc. We also award a small number of Farm Holiday Guide Diplomas every year, based on readers' recommendations.

NORTHUMBERLAND

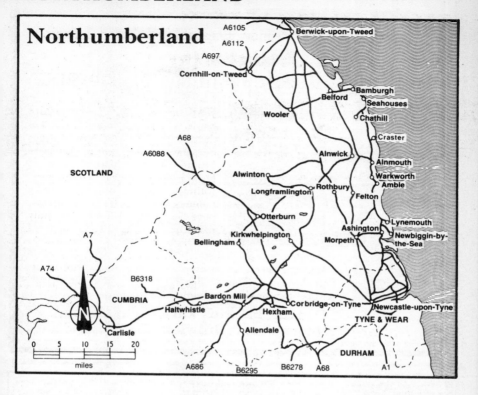

Northumberland

[Map showing Northumberland with locations including: Berwick-upon-Tweed, Cornhill-on-Tweed, Bamburgh, Belford, Seahouses, Wooler, Chathill, Craster, Alnwick, Alnmouth, Alwinton, Warkworth, Amble, Rothbury, Longframlington, Felton, Otterburn, Lynemouth, Ashington, Newbiggin-by-the-Sea, Kirkwhelpington, Morpeth, Bellingham, Bardon Mill, Corbridge-on-Tyne, Newcastle-upon-Tyne, Haltwhistle, Hexham, TYNE & WEAR, Carlisle, Allendale, DURHAM, SCOTLAND, CUMBRIA. Roads: A6105, A6112, A697, A68, A6088, A7, A74, B6318, A686, B6295, B6278, A1]

miles
0 5 10 15 20

ALNWICK. Birling Vale, Warkworth, Alnwick. Birling Vale is an attractive stone-built, detached house standing in a very pleasant, secluded garden, approximately one-third mile from picturesque village of Warkworth which is beside the River Coquet and dominated by an ancient Norman Castle. Birling Vale is only half-a-mile from lovely sandy beaches; 15 minutes from trout and salmon rivers, and within a comfortable drive of many places of interest, including Hadrian's Wall, Holy Island and Scottish Borders. The house which is tastefully furnished and fully equipped including colour TV, has two bedrooms with double beds and a third bedroom with single divans. Oil for full central heating is provided free of charge. Well trained dogs welcome. Weekly terms from £50 low season; £180 mid-season; £240 high season. SAE to **Mrs Janet Brewis, Woodhouse Farm, Shilbottle, Near Alnwick NE66 2HR (Shilbottle [066-575] 222).**

NORTHUMBERLAND – BORDER COUNTRY!

You cannot go any further north and remain in England! There is much outstanding scenery, both inland and on the coast, and a host of interesting places to visit. Border Forest Park has everything you would expect, plus many interesting Roman remains. There are also remains at Housesteads and other places of interest include Lindisfarne, the "conserved" village of Blanchland, Hexham, Heatherslaw Mill and Craster.

BELFORD. Mrs K. Burn, Fenham-le-Moor, Belford NE70 7PN (0668 213247). ♀♀♀ *Approved.* **Working farm. Properties sleep 5/7.** Fenham-le-Moor is a working farm situated half-a-mile from the A1 and half-a-mile from the sea on a quiet road which leads down to the shore on the Lindisfarne Nature Reserve, renowned for sea birds.

Across the water is Lindisfarne Castle on Holy Island. This is an excellent centre for GOOD BEACHES, bird-watching, golf, walking, riding and visiting the many castles in the area. The cottages, numbers two, three and four in a row of five stone-built farm cottages, are adjacent to Fenham-le-Moor farm. Number two sleeps five in one double room, one twin-bedded room and one small single room. Downstairs is livingroom, kitchen/diningroom and bathroom. Numbers three and four will sleep seven in one very large room with double bed and twin beds, one double room and one room with a single bed. Downstairs is a large living room; kitchen/ dining room and bathroom. All cottages are fully furnished and equipped. Coal provided, electricity paid at end of stay. Pets permitted by prior arrangement. Some linen supplied. Terms from £95 to £210 per week.

BERWICK-UPON-TWEED. The Garden Cottage and Nos. 3, 4 and 5 West Ord Farm Cottages, Berwick-upon-Tweed. Working farm. Tourist Board Approved. West Ord is delightfully situated three miles west of Berwick-upon-Tweed, on the banks of the River Tweed. Three of the cottages are on a quiet side road to the river, sleeping two/five persons; all have bathrooms, fully equipped kitchens, sittingroom/ diningroom with colour TV. Bed linen NOT provided. Dogs by arrangement. Terms from £65 to £200 per week. The Garden Cottage has one double and two twin-bedded rooms; luxury kitchen and bathroom; sittingroom/diningroom with colour TV. Central heating and second toilet. No dogs accepted. Bed linen provided. Terms from £145 to £300 per week. Fishing and tennis available. Near to Lindisfarne, Cheviots and Scottish Border. Brochure from **Mrs C.M. Lang, West Ord Farm, Berwick-upon-Tweed TD15 2XQ (0289 86631).**

BERWICK-UPON-TWEED. Mrs R.A. Cadzow, Inland Pasture Farm, Scremerston, Berwick-upon-Tweed TD15 2RJ (Berwick-upon-Tweed [0289] 306072). Working farm. Sleeps 6. No. 5 Inland Pasture Cottages, faces south with beautiful views over beach towards Holy Island and Farne Islands. Situated in a quiet and peaceful area away from traffic and about quarter-mile from all farm buildings. The cottage is Tourist Board approved and sleeps six. Three double bedrooms; bathroom; kitchen with electric cooker and kettle etc. Cot available on request. One dog only allowed. Electric heating and lighting: television. Available April to October. Car advisable — parking. Convenient for golfing, fishing (permits required), climbing, bathing, pony trekking/riding. Many interesting houses and historic places to visit. Terms from £70 to £150 weekly.

CORBRIDGE. Mr F.J. Matthews, The Hayes, Newcastle Road, Corbridge NE45 5LP (Corbridge [0434] 632010). Enjoy your self-catering choice in this picturesque and historic village, an ideal centre for visiting Roman Wall, stately homes, Kielder Dam, Metro centre. Superior flat for four/five and three ground floor cottages for two/five available all year. Luxury six-berth caravan available March to October. Colour TV. Car parking facilities. Riding, fishing, golf, swimming locally. Good walking and exploring countryside and near River Tyne. Children welcome. Pets by arrangement. All accommodation, except flat, suitable for disabled. Awarded two FHG Diplomas. Also Bed and Breakfast accommodation. Full details on application. SAE (ref FHG) or phone.

CORNHILL-ON-TWEED. Mr and Mrs W. Potts, Shidlaw, Cornhill-on-Tweed TD12 4RP (Birgham [089-083] 225). Sleeps 6. Situated on a large, modern, Tweed-side farm, in a beautiful region. The comfortably furnished cottage has a modern kitchen with electric cooker, fridge, water heater, etc. Livingroom/diningroom with open fire, colour TV. Three bedrooms sleeping six; bathroom and toilet. Cot on request. Accommodation suitable for disabled guests. Car essential, parking. Shops six miles, sea 16 miles. Pets allowed. Open May to October. Fishing on the Tweed; golf and racing at Kelso. Tourists can journey through historic, unspoilt Border countryside with abbeys and castles galore. Riding school nearby. SAE for brochure. Terms from £60 weekly.

CORNHILL-ON-TWEED. Mr and Mrs W.G. Clark, Castle Heaton, Cornhill-on-Tweed TD12 4XQ (Coldstream [0890] 2259). Two cottages on large arable farm with breeding cattle located in scenic Borders area with lovely woodland and riverside walks along River Till. A perfect base for the Northumbrian coast with castles, sandy beaches, Cheviot Hills and Border Abbeys. Fishing available on private stretch of River Till. Golf, riding, walking, bird watching available nearby. One cottage (illustrated) sleeps five, the other sleeps four. Both well equipped including electric cooker, fridge, heating and colour TV. Bed linen provided. Cot and high chair available. Electricity by meter reading. Terms from £100 weekly.

HEXHAM (Haydon Bridge). Mrs V.R.A. Drydon, West Deanraw, Langley-on-Tyne, Haydon Bridge, Hexham NE47 5LY (Haydon Bridge [0434-684] 228). Working farm. Detached bungalow situated on a farm in rural Northumberland, approximately three miles from the village of Haydon Bridge, and 10 miles from the market town of Hexham. The property enjoys delightful views of the Tyne Valley, and is an ideal touring base for Hadrian's Wall, Kielder Reservoir, Border country, the magnificent Northumbrian coastline, Cumbria and the Lake District. Accommodation comprises one double and one twin bedrooms (extra children's beds available); livingroom with sofa bed; colour TV; diningroom. Fully fitted kitchen, all-electric, includes microwave, fridge, washing machine, immersion heater, plus open fire-back boiler. Central heating. Dogs allowed. Terms and further details on request.

WOOLER. Mrs E. Logan, East Fenton, Wooler NE71 6JL (Millfield [066-86] 200). Cottages sleep 5/6. Three well-equipped cottages situated on stock farm with quiet country road running past. Overlooking Cheviot Hills. Ideal walking countryside with access to both sea and hills. Farne Islands and Lindisfarne within easy reach. Two cottages sleep five; third sleeps six in three double bedrooms; other two have one double, one three-bedded room. No linen supplied. Sitting/dining room; bathroom and toilet; kitchen with electric cooker and fridge; cot available. Pets permitted. Electric or coal fire. Shops two-and-a-half/three miles. Sea 15 miles. Car essential — parking. Golf two-and-a-half miles; pony trekking two miles. Tourist Board registered. Terms £55 to £90.

OXFORDSHIRE

SHIPTON-UNDER-WYCHWOOD. Paul and Victoria Fletcher, Lane House Farm, Shipton-under-Wychwood OX7 6BD (Shipton [0993] 830348). Working farm. 1985 Henley Award Winning Barn Conversion to Holiday Cottages for the whole of the Eastern Region which comprises 18 counties. There is a delightful bungalow and two cottages on the edge of the Cotswolds, one of England's most attractive holiday areas. Just off the A361, an excellent touring centre within easy reach of the beautiful country villages and Oxford, Cheltenham, Cirencester, Burford, Stratford-upon-Avon. The three properties are carpeted throughout and centrally heated. Fully equipped kitchens with electric cookers, microwave ovens, automatic washing machines. Colour TV. Linen included (towels extra). The bungalow is suitable for wheelchairs. Cots and high chairs available. Dogs welcome. Ample parking. Pubs and shops within a few minutes' walk; children's play area. There is single bank fishing on River Evenlode. Open all year. Brochure and terms on request. Thames and Chiltern Tourist Board Category 3.

PLEASE ENCLOSE A STAMPED ADDRESSED ENVELOPE WITH ENQUIRIES

SHROPSHIRE

BISHOP'S CASTLE. Heblands, Linnet and Lower Lodge, Bishop's Castle. Working farm. Cottages sleep 4/8. Three fully equipped comfortable cottages, Tourist Board approved. Situated about one mile from Bishop's Castle. Ideal for exploring the Clun Forest, Offa's Dyke, the Long Mynd and Stretton Hills. The historic towns of Ludlow and Shreswbury are also near at hand. Cot and high chair available and pets are welcome by arrangement. Weekly terms from £100. Brochure from **Peter Sargent, Camlad House, Lydham, Bishop's Castle SY9 5HB (0588 638 546).**

BISHOP'S CASTLE. Walcot Hall, Lydbury North, Bishop's Castle. Flats sleep 4/9. Spacious flats in Stately Home. Secluded location in own grounds; splendid scenery and ideal area for peaceful holiday for young and old. All flats fully furnished and recently decorated and sleep four/nine. Larger parties by arrangement. Village shop half a mile; local market towns, castles, villages and hill country of the Border Counties provide opportunities for exploration and walking. Coarse fishing in pools and lake. Terms from £105 to £175. **Mrs M. Smith, 41 Cheval Place, London SW7 1EW (071-5812 782).**

BUCKNELL. Church Cottage, Bucknell. ♀♀ *Approved.* **Working farm. Sleeps 6.** This is a tastefully modernised Olde Worlde cottage in small village set in delightful Teme Valley, with easy access to picturesque mid-Wales, Offa's Dyke, Church Stretton Hills, Wenlock Edge and historic towns of Ludlow, Shrewsbury and Hereford. The cottage sleeps six; one double, and two twin-bedded rooms, cot. Modern kitchen with automatic washing machine; lounge; diningroom; TV. Electric fires, storage heaters in cold weather. Private parking, enclosed lawn. Village has General Store, Post Office, butcher, garage and two pubs. Also served by the Central Wales Railway Line. Open all year. SAE for terms and brochure: **Mrs Christine Price, The Hall, Bucknell, Shropshire SY7 0AA (Bucknell [05474] 0249).**

CHURCH STRETTON. Stockhall Cottage and Bartham Cottage, Woolstaston, Church Stretton. Working farm. Two self-contained, semi-detached cottages, in a peaceful country lane on the side of Long Mynd, set in lovely border country in an area of outstanding natural beauty. Panoramic views across Shropshire Hills; farmland, woodland and National Trust moorland all around. There are several country inns nearby serving meals, and many pretty villages and historic market towns. Ironbridge and other museums in the area. Ideal country for walking, bird-watching, sketching, riding, gliding, golf, tennis, bowls, etc., all within easy reach. Each cottage has one double, one twin and one single bedroom; modern bathroom with bath, WC, shaver point, etc. Livingroom with open fire and colour TV, kitchen, pantry, small sun porch. Everything provided except linen and towels. Cooking, immersion heater, heating by electricity (coin meter). Pure spring water is on tap.

Garden and garage/parking. English Tourist Board approved. Terms from £90 to £150 per week. Reduced terms for long lets. **Mrs J. Rowan, Woolstaston Hall, Near Church Stretton SY6 6NN (Leebotwood [06945] 425).**

CLUN VALLEY. Mrs P.E. North, The Old Shop, Clunton, Craven Arms SY7 0HP (Little Brampton [058-87] 327). On B4368 Craven Arms to Clun Road. Self-contained, centrally heated, single storey flat in centre of the small village of Clunton on the River Clun, within six miles of the Welsh Border. Superb walking country with relatively quiet roads and much of historic interest. Sandy beaches within 90 minutes' drive. The flat, a wing of owners' home, is entirely on ground floor and suitable for disabled guests. Entrance hall; comfortable lounge with double bed settee, fitted carpets, central heating, double glazing and open fire; dining kitchen with pine units, electric cooker, kettle, fridge and constant hot water. Shower room with WC and washbasin. Bedroom with two single beds, plus camp bed if required. Cot available, babysitting by arrangement. Linen not supplied. TV, games and books provided. Garden. Pets welcome. Car essential, parking. Village shops one-and-three-quarter miles. Fishing and riding locally. Terms on request. Ideal for winter breaks.

CLUNBURY. Lower Orchard Bungalow at Upper House, Clunbury, Near Craven Arms (058-87 203). ♀♀♀ The Clun Valley — Welsh Borderland, near Ludlow and Offa's Dyke. Lower Orchard Bungalow is a modern luxury bungalow built in the gardens of 17th century Grade II Listed Upper House in picturesque National Parkland village. Sleeps four. Cot and extra camp bed if required. Bedding provided, no towels or linen. Children and pets welcome. Property suitable for elderly/disabled visitors. Fully equipped modern kitchen, fridge, washing machine, electric storage heaters, oil fired central heating, log fires; bathroom, shower; washbasins in bedrooms. Patio with chairs, glorious views. Colour TV provided. Member of the English Tourist Board. Personally supervised by owners. Terms from £115 to £155 per week. Brochure on request. Winter Breaks also available. Write or phone for full details.

CRAVEN ARMS near. Hazel Cottage, Duxmoor, Onibury, Craven Arms. ♀♀♀♀ *Commended.*

Sleeps 4. Beautifully restored semi-detachd period cottage set in its own traditional "cottage" garden with drive and ample parking space. It has panoramic view of the surrounding countryside and is situated five miles north of historic Ludlow. The cottage comprises a comfortable lounge with colour TV, telephone; diningroom; fully equipped kitchen; hall; bathroom; two double bedrooms with washbasins. Electric central heating throughout. Linen provided. No pets. The cottage retains all the original features and has been traditionally furnished to a high standard including antiques. Terms from £110 to £225 per week. **Mrs Rachel Sanders, Duxmoor Farm, Onibury, Craven Arms SY7 9BQ (Bromfield [058-477] 342).**

LUDLOW. Miss H. Morris, Coldoak Cottages, Snitton Lane, Knowbury, Ludlow SY8 3LB (Ludlow

[0584] 890491). The 200-year-old solid stone cottage, four-and-a-half miles from Ludlow, faces south, set well back in field ensuring privacy yet only 130 yards from road. Surroundings are quiet and beautiful and visitors will enjoy extensive views of Herefordshire and Wales beyond. Cottage sleeps visitors in one double bedroom, one twin-bedded and one single bedroom; comfortable sittingroom and diningroom; sittingroom has beamed ceiling, colour TV, well-stocked book shelves. Well-equipped kitchen includes fridge/freezer, microwave oven, automatic washer. Bathroom with shower and toilet, additional shower/toilet on ground floor. Linen supplied. Children over five years welcome. Pets permitted. Large attractive garden with sitting out area. Post Office and village shop, pub; milk and paper delivery. Car essential, parking. Weekly terms from £135 to £150. Metered electricity. Tourist Board registered.

LYDBURY NORTH. Mrs Mary Wall, 6 Lynch Gate, Lydbury North SY7 8AE (Lydbury North [058-88] 267). Old stone cottage, modernised, with unspoilt views. Owner lives next door. One large bedroom with double bed and cot; one bedroom with single bed and one with two single beds. Bathroom, toilet; sittingroom; diningroom; kitchen with electric cooker, fridge, modern sink unit. Electricity on 50p meter. Linen supplied. Pets permitted. Car essential — parking. Shops three miles. Plenty of walks on National Trust property. Borrow with its ancient Roman Fort, Church Stretton for gliding and hang gliding. Historic Ludlow with its castle, and Stokesay Castle with its Elizabethan gateway only a few miles away. The old stagecoach road from London runs by the cottage and less than an hour's ride away by car is the beautiful Wenlock Edge, Bridgnorth and the first ever iron bridge. Terms from £30 to £85. SAE, please.

NEWCASTLE-ON-CLUN. "Ty unllawr", Upper Duffryn, Newcastle-on-Clun, Craven Arms. Working

farm. Sleeps 5. "Ty unllawr" is a modern bungalow situated on a 200 acre mixed farm and provides a very comfortable base for those looking for a peaceful country holiday in an area of outstanding natural beauty. Accommodation comprises three bedrooms (twin, double and single), cot available; large lounge/diner with open fire; well equipped kitchen; bathroom and WC. Blankets and pillows provided but not linen. Large grassed garden with parking and access to small river. Pets by arrangement. Village two miles. Open all year. Terms £80 – £140 per week. ETB Category 2. Further details on request from **Mrs D. Whately, Upper Duffryn, Newcastle on Clun, Craven Arms SY7 8PQ (Clun [05884] 233).**

NEWCASTLE ON CLUN. Mr and Mrs J.K. Goslin, The Riddings Firs, Crossways, Newcastle-on-Clun, Craven Arms SY7 8OT (Kerry [068-688] 467). Sleeps 2 Adults, 3 Children. Ideal holiday location on the Welsh Borders, at 1300 feet, in an area designated as being of outstanding natural beauty. For those seeking complete peace and relaxation, this attractive self-catering family accommodation, for four to five people, is in a self-contained traditional farmhouse annexe with own private entrance. Fully equipped and attractively furnished including colour TV, wood burning stove. Open plan arrangement comprises one double, two bunk beds and bed settee; electric cooker, fridge etc.; shower, toilet, washbasin. Children especially welcome. Pleasantly situated in excellent walking country; several interesting market towns, hospitable inns with dining facilities, Castle within easy reach. Pony trekking and trout fishing can be arranged. Babysitting available. Self-catering terms from £70 per week. Linen supplied at extra cost if required. Out of season and week-end visitors welcome.

PLEASE SEND A STAMPED ADDRESSED ENVELOPE WITH ENQUIRIES

OSWESTRY. Mrs Glenice Jones, Lloran Ganol Farm, Llansilin, Oswestry SY10 7OX (Llansilin [069-170] 287). Working farm. Sleeps 5. A luxury self-catering bungalow on mixed farm in quiet valley. Farm and bungalow are situated over the border in the Welsh hills in Clwyd. Five people accommodated in two double and one single bedrooms; bathroom, toilet; sittingroom, diningroom; colour TV; long kitchen with dining area; automatic washing machine and fridge. Linen supplied. Extra charge for pets. Two and a half miles from the shops. Car essential — parking. Shooting, horse riding and trout fishing on farm; fishing, golf and trekking in surrounding area. Open all year round, the bungalow is suitable for disabled guests. Storage heaters, fitted carpets and garden furniture provided. Glass conservatory. Weekly terms from £70. Bed and Breakfast also available with family in house adjoining from £10 per night, Bed, Breakfast and Evening Meal from £16 per night.

OSWESTRY near. Mrs P. Jackson, Lloran Isaf, Llansilin, Near Oswestry SY10 7QX (069-170 253). Working farm. This beautiful bungalow is set on a working farm in its own valley which has wonderful scenery, walks, trout fishing and shooting. Accommodation comprises fitted kitchen; large lounge and dining area with colour TV and wood-burning stove; three bedrooms one twin, one double and one single (cot available); separate toilet and bathroom. Fitted carpets and electric heating; barbecue area and garden furniture in enclosed garden. One and a half miles from the village, in a wonderful touring area with lots of attractions without the crowds. Open all year. Pets by request only. Prices from £65. Tourist Board registered.

SHREWSBURY. Mrs A. Cartwright, Ryton Farm Holiday Cottages, Ryton, Dorrington SY5 7LY (Dorrington [0743] 73449). Working farm. Properties sleep 2/6. A selection of comfortable country cottages and apartments on the family farm, in a quiet peaceful village close to Ironbridge and the South Shropshire hills. Ideally situated for visiting Shropshire's many attractions, walking or relaxing in our scenic countryside, or sampling quaint friendly pubs and restaurants with good food. The cottages are equipped, furnished and maintained to the highest standards. All linen and towels are included and every effort is made to make your stay with us pleasurable. Well behaved pets welcome. Excellent coarse fishing in owner's pools. Standby holidays and Short Breaks sometimes available. Open all year from £100 to £300 per week. Discounts for couples in larger cottages. English Tourist Board approved.

SHREWSBURY near. Mr T.W.E. Corbett, The Home Farm, Leebotwood, Church Stretton SY6 6LX (Dorrington [074-373] 628). Property is a modernised stone cottage in a magnificent position with extensive views at the foot of Lawley Hill, five miles from Church Stretton, nine miles from Shrewsbury and one mile from the village of Longnor. It is set in one third of an acre of garden and orchard, and offers excellent facilities for walking, riding, golf, tennis and swimming. There are one double and two single bedrooms, with two fold-down beds in addition. Downstairs there is a bathroom, kitchen/diningroom and sittingroom with TV; electric cooker, fridge. Weekly terms include off peak electricity and wood for open fire. Open season from May to October. SAE for terms, please. English Tourist Board approved.

If you've found
FARM HOLIDAY GUIDES
of service please tell your friends

SOMERSET

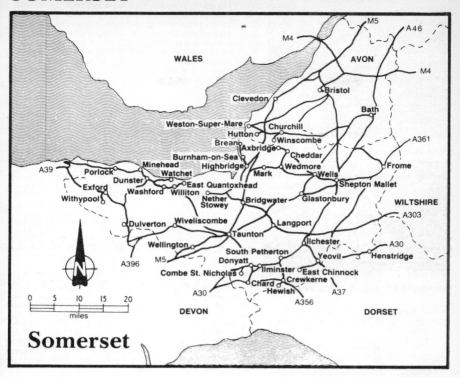

Somerset

BATH near. Mrs Audrey Rich, Whitnell Farm, Binegar, Emborough, Near Bath BA3 4UF (Oakhill [0749] 840277). Working farm, join in. Properties sleep 8. Whitnell Manor is a mixed farm in picturesque setting of peaceful countryside with a relaxed, friendly atmosphere and lawns leading to open fields. Visitors are welcome to participate in farm activities, especially interesting for children, or enjoy the pleasant walks across the farmland. Excellent base for touring the beautiful, unspoilt Mendip Hills, Somerset's towns, villages, wildlife parks, caves, castles, stately homes. Golf, riding, and fishing all within easy reach. Bus service passes the gate every hour. Wells four miles; Bath 14 miles; 20 miles to coast; local shops and Post Office one-and-a-half miles. Properties accommodate four to eight people, fully equipped except linen. Electric cookers, fridges, fires, colour TV, oil central heating for chilly nights. West Country Tourist Board member. Terms from £80 to £250. Bed and Breakfast also available at the farmhouse. SAE, please, for further details.

BRUTON. Cherry Tree Cottage, Henley Grove Farm, Bruton BA10 0QD (Evercreech [0749] 830408). Working farm, join in. Property sleeps 8. Cherry Tree Cottage is situated in the unspoilt countryside of south east Somerset in the midst of a 208 acre dairy farm on which visitors are welcome to wander around to view the various farm animals and pets. Comfortably furnished and fully equipped, with the exception of linen, the cottage has accommodation for eight people plus baby. All appliances are electric and include colour TV. Regret no dogs. Children welcome. Car essential. Local shops two miles. Within short distance of the borders of Wiltshire and Dorset and historic Wells, Cheddar, Bath, Glastonbury. Two miles on the outskirts of Bruton, on the Bruton-Batcombe Road. Terms £120 to £150 per week. SAE, please, for further details to **Mrs M.A. Bown.**

BURNHAM-ON-SEA near. Mrs W. Baker, Withy Grove Farm, East Huntspill, Near Burnham-on-Sea TA9 3NP (Burnham-on-Sea [0278] 784471). Properties sleep 5/6. Six converted holiday bungalows and one barn flat, well-equipped and comfortable. Outdoor heated swimming pool, licensed bar, farm shop, games room and skittle alley. Available Easter to November. Also farmhouse accommodation, all bedrooms with washbasins, guests' lounge with colour TV, separate tables in diningroom. Good country fare.

CHARD. Mrs P.P. Maidment, Manor Farm, Knowle St Giles, Chard TA20 3DA (Chard [046-06] 3102). Working farm. Sleeps 5. Manor Farm is situated

half-a-mile from main A358 road, two miles from Chard and three miles from Ilminster. This is a modernised self-contained farmhouse, dating from 15th century. It is a dairy farm of 100 acres, with a Friesian herd of cows. The spacious lounge has colour TV; sun lounge; bathroom upstairs and cloakroom downstairs; sleeps five, cot; babysitting by arrangement. Modern fully equipped kitchen with electric cooker and fridge. No linen supplied. Pets permitted. Car essential — ample parking. Open all year. Terms on request, with SAE please. It is an ideal centre for touring Somerset, Devon and Dorset. Coast 15 miles. Wildlife Park four miles away; Arts and Crafts Museum half-a-mile.

CHARD near. Mrs Susan J. Adams, Manor Farm, Forton, Near Chard TA20 2LZ (Chard [046-06] 3240). Working farm, join in. Part of 16th century farm-

house (self-contained) of historic importance. Interesting wood structure with murals on walls of large bedroom which will sleep up to three persons. Cot supplied if desired. One medium bedroom with double bed; fully equipped kitchen; separate shower room, toilet; large sitting/diningroom; Super-ser gas heater. Children can play in safe garden and observe life on this Somerset Dairy Farm set in beautiful countryside. Special attractions of the area include Cricket St Thomas Wildlife Park, Forde Abbey and many different seaside resorts. Members of the West Country Tourist Board. No dogs allowed. Shops one mile. There is also a badminton court; rackets provided for grown-ups. Car essential. Weekly terms from £100 to £150; all electricity and linen included.

DULVERTON. Mr and Mrs F.A. Heywood, South Greenslade Farmhouse, Brompton Regis, Dulverton TA22 9NU (Brompton Regis [039-87] 207). Wimbleball Hollow Holiday Homes, South Greenslade Farm: in quiet countryside 200 yards from Wimbleball Lake. Two clean and comfortable holiday houses, each taking six adults plus one or two children. Both with oil-fired cookers, electric storage heaters, fridge/freezers, automatic washing machines, colour TV and microwave ovens. Situated beside Wimbleball Lake and near open moorland of Haddon Hill on the eastern side of Exmoor National Park. Ideal for walking, fishing and countryside activities holidays. Terms from £145 — £225 per week (price includes heating, lighting and electricity). Pets allowed, under control. We aim to make your holiday a success. Please phone for details.

EXMOOR. The Great House, Ross-Lyn, Timberscombe. Situated on the edge of a small village within

the Exmoor National Park and just two miles from Dunster this is the perfect spot to enjoy your stay in this beautiful area. The house, which is of Georgian origins, is listed as being of special architectural interest and provides comfortable and spacious accommodation. It has been split into three flats, one on each floor, each fully fitted and sleeping from two to five people. At the rear is the original portion of the house, this being of Tudor origin, with its beams, inglenook, farmhouse kitchen and walled garden and it will easily accommodate nine or more people. The Tudor portion is fully centrally heated, with gas and electric fires in the Georgian portion. All units have colour TV and are fully equipped, hot water supplied throughout, metered telephone. Ample parking. Horses and dogs by arrangement. Village stores, pub and church within two minutes' walk. Flats from £120 to £245, house from £300 to £490. Breaks available. Apply **Mr and Mrs T. Cadman, Cowbridge House, Timberscombe, Minehead TA24 7TD (0643 841388 24 hours).**

EXMOOR. Roger and Kitty Paul, Whites Farm, Elworthy, Lydeard St Lawrence, Taunton TA4 3PX (0984 56283 after 4.00pm). **Sleeps 4.** Nestling on the edge of Exmoor National Park in the Brendon Hills, within easy reach of moorland, coast and several places of historic interest. The property has been converted from an old cider barn retaining the original beams. French windows lead from livingroom onto a small patio and walled garden. The property is in a hamlet and has beautiful views of surrounding hills. There is a barn for table tennis, snooker, etc. and a tree house, swings and animals. Ideal for a family holiday. OS ref ST 084350. Open all year. Terms from £150 to £180.

The Cider House

EXMOOR. Springfield, Ash Lane, Winsford. Sleeps 6. This cottage stands in a breathtaking position in the heart of Exmoor facing South across the moor. It contains three well furnished bedrooms — one double, one twin and one with full-size bunks and a single bed — a large livingroom with an inglenook fireplace, a modern kitchen/breakfast room with gas cooker and fridge, a well-fitted shower room and automatic washing machine. Central heating and cot available. There is a large garden surrounded by old hedgebanks and parking for two cars. The position is ideal for those wanting to enjoy the peace of this beautiful countryside or to explore Exmoor on foot, on horseback or by car. Prices from £135 — £250 per week. Full details from **Mrs A.P. Hughes, Manor Cottage, Overleigh, Street BA16 0TR (Street [0458] 43556).**

EXMOOR. Pennycombe, Withypool, Near Minehead. Sleeps 6. Pennycombe is a delightful bungalow

set in its own garden which is bounded on one side by a trout stream. It lies on the edge of the picturesque village of Withypool, in the heart of Exmoor, making it an ideal centre for walking and riding, yet is only 16 miles from the sea and beaches. Fully carpeted, the house sleeps six in three double bedrooms; two bathrooms (one en suite with main bedroom); large lounge with TV, open fire. Electric radiators in all bedrooms. Kitchen/diner, well equipped, including split-level cooker and fridge. No linen supplied. Car essential; garage and parking. Village shop. Pony trekking and walking nearby. Electricity extra. Open all year. Suitable for disabled. Weekly terms from £95 to £225. **Mrs M. Rowland, Patch House, Blayney's Lane, Evesham, Worcs. WR11 4TS (Evesham [0386] 446168).**

GLASTONBURY near. Mrs P. Creed, South Town Farm, West Pennard, Glastonbury BA6 8NS (0458 32808). **Working farm.** Detached stone cottage in a quiet situation, four miles from Glastonbury in village with Post Office, Store and Pub. Three bedrooms: a family room with double and single beds, a twin-bedded room and a twin-bedded landing room with steep staircase. Lounge with colour TV and open fire; diningroom; kitchen and bathroom downstairs. Electricity for cooking, heating, hot water, etc by £1 coin meter. Small lawn front and rear. Off road parking. Pets welcome. A cot and high chair available by prior request. Beds have pillow, blankets and bedspread. Linen hire extra £2.50 per person per week. Terms from £75 to £120 per week.

See also Colour Display Advertisement **MINEHEAD. Mrs F.H. Brown, Emmetts Grange, Simonsbath, Minehead TA24 7LD (064-383 282).** ETB APPROVED SELF-CATERING PROPERTIES. Two cottages, one bungalow and one flat sleeping four to eight person. All are centrally heated and have colour TVs. Dinners are available in farmhouse when open. In the heart of Exmoor National Park, near to North Devon and Somerset coast. Beautiful moorland and coastal walks; ideal for riding and trekking (stabling available). Local river, reservoir and sea fishing. Properties available March to November. Apply for detailed brochure, stating which property required.

MINEHEAD. Mrs L.M. Vigars, Honeymead, Simonsbath, Minehead TA24 7JX (Exford [064383] 450). Working farm, join in. Properties sleep 2 adults; 3 children. Two semi-detached cottages on hill farm, four miles from Exford, one-and-a-half miles from Simonsbath. Ideal place for walking, riding, fishing and seaside holidays. Both cottages are well equipped with three large bedrooms, fitted carpets, sitting room with colour TV, log fire, kitchen, electric cooker and washing machine, bathroom. Tennis court, stabling available. Children and pets welcome. Home cooked evening meals by arrangement. Weekly terms from £105 to £200. Tourist Board Registered. Further details on request.

MINEHEAD near. Miss D.M. Deane, The Manor, Wootton Courtenay, Near Minehead (0643 84218). Comfortable 15th century house to let in pretty village on the fringe of Exmoor. Sleeps six. Washbasins in all bedrooms. Colour TV. Ideal centre for walking and pony trekking. Five miles from the coast. Children and dogs welcome. Large garden and grounds for you to relax in. Open all year. Further details and terms on request.

PORLOCK. Lucott Farm, Porlock, Minehead. Sleeps 2/10. Isolated farmhouse on Exmoor, with wood burning fireplaces and all modern conveniences. It lies at the head of Horner Valley and guests will delight in the wonderful scenery. Plenty of pony trekking in the area. Ten people accommodated in four double and two single bedrooms, cot; bathroom, two toilets; sittingroom; diningroom. Kitchen has oil-fired Aga and water heater. No linen supplied. Shops three miles; sea four miles. Car essential — parking. Open all year. Terms (including fuel) on application with SAE please to **Mrs E.A. Tucker, West Luccombe Cottage, Porlock, Minehead TA24 8MT (Porlock [0643] 862810).**

SHEPTON MALLET. Mrs J.A. Boyce, Knowle Farm, West Compton, Shepton Mallet BA4 4PD (Pilton [074-989] 482). ♀♀♀♀ Approved. **Working farm. Cottages sleep 2/5/8.** Knowle Farm Cottages are converted from the old cowstall and stables, set around the old farmyard now laid out as a pleasant garden. Quiet location at the end of a private drive. Excellent views and plenty of wildlife. All cottages furnished to a high standard — bathroom (bath, shower, toilet, washbasin); fully fitted kitchen (automatic washing machine, fridge/freezer, full size gas cooker). Two cottages have kitchen/diner, separate lounge, colour TV, the other two have kitchen, lounge/diner, colour TV. Cot, high chair by prior arrangement. Bed linen and towels supplied. Surrounding area full of interesting places to visit. Good golf courses, fishing, selection of pubs and restaurants. Around the farm plenty of walks, play area for children. Sorry, no pets. Terms: low season £125 — high season £305. Car essential, ample parking. Payphone for guests. Open all year. AA, WCTB.

TAUNTON. Farmhouse Front Wing. Sleeping up to 10. Garden, TV lounge, microwave, electric cooker. Easy reach of the West Somerset/North Devon coast, Exmoor and the Quantock Hills. Fishing and clay shooting can be arranged on the farm. Good bar meals in local villages. Also reasonably priced Bed and Breakfast in other farmhouse. SAE, please, to **Mrs S.J. Watts, Rowdon Farm, Williton, Taunton TA4 4JD (0984 56280).**

SOMERSET – THE CREAM AND CIDER COUNTY!

Wookey Hole, the great cave near Wells, is the first known home of man in Great Britain. Other places of interest in this green and hilly country include The Mendips, Exmoor National Park, Cheddar Gorge, Meare Lake Village and The Somerset Rural Life Museum. The villages and wildlife of the Quantocks, Poldens and Brendons should not be missed.

WEDMORE. Porch Cottage, Blackford, Wedmore. Sleeps 5/6. Pleasantly situated in rural surroundings, adjoining B3139, approximately mid-way between Wells and Burnham-on-Sea. Cheddar, Wookey Hole, Weston-super-Mare quite near, also many other places of interest. Comfortably furnished with large dining/lounge, electric fire, TV. Kitchen has electric cooker, fridge, ample china, cutlery, and cooking utensils. One double and one family bedrooms, both with washbasins. Bathroom, shower. Cot available. Ample parking space. Open all year. Terms vary from £45 to £80 weekly. Apply **Mrs L.G. Callow, Chards Farm, Blackford, Wedmore BS28 4PA (Wedmore [0934] 712262).**

WEDMORE. Mr and Mrs Hugh Tucker, Court Farm, Mudgley, Wedmore BS28 4TY (Wedmore [0934] 712367). Working farm.

Wedmore is a charming Georgian village with historic connections, pleasant shops, banks, post office etc. Accommodation is situated on dairy farm one and a half miles from the village, and comprises two super self-contained, adjacent cottages called "The Hayloft" and "Keepers Cottage" recently tastefully converted from stone-built barn, with superb views over Somerset Levels to Polden Hills. Both consist of lovely open plan kitchen/lounge/diner, delightfully equipped, plus colour TV. Shower room. Family bedroom for four with beamed ceilings. Also sofa-bed in "The Hayloft". Cot and high chair available. Special rates for larger parties (up to eight persons) booking both cottages. Linen available. Patio with garden furniture. Laundry room. Garage. Parking. Well behaved dogs accepted by arrangement. Coarse fishing. Electricity included. Open Easter to October. ETB approved. First-class stamp for brochure, please.

WIVELISCOMBE near. Oddwell and Cridland Cottages, Brompton Ralph, Wiveliscombe. Cottages sleep 6, plus cot.

Standing in a garden at foot of Brendon Hills, charming 300 year old cottages with beamed ceilings and inglenook fireplaces for cosy coal fires. Each equipped for six: two bedrooms (one with three single beds, other with double bed); small bed/sittingroom with put-u-up; modern bathrooms, toilet, plus extra toilet/washroom upstairs; dining/livingroom; kitchen with oil-fired Rayburn, electric cooker, fridge, immerser, iron etc; separate larder. Available all year. Indoor games, books provided. Cot, high chair. Trout fishing, riding, walking, pony trekking. Nine miles to sea and half a mile to shops. Car essential, ample parking, garage in keeping with cottages. Pets by arrangement. ETB/WCTB. Weekly terms from £85 to £180. SAE, please, to **Graham and Joy Durling, Rosewood, 60b Queens Park Avenue, Bournemouth, Dorset BH8 9EZ (0202 302295).**

STAFFORDSHIRE

CROXDEN. Beldene Bungalow, Croxden, Near Uttoxeter. Sleeps 4 adults; 1 child.

A self-catering bungalow set in beautiful rural surroundings close to the Peak National Park, Alton Towers, Gladstone Pottery Museum, the Wedgwood Centre, etc. The accommodation sleeps five person and comprises lounge with colour TV; diningroom and kitchen with electric cooker, fridge and washing machine. Central heating. Fitted carpets. Ample parking space. Children and pets welcome. Terms from £80 to £110. Tourist Board approved. Apply: **Mrs B.J. Barker, Home Farm, Sharpcliffe, Ipstones, Stoke-on-Trent ST10 2LJ (0538 266279).**

NORBURY. Oulton Rock Cottage, Norbury. Sleeps 2 adults; 2 children plus cot.

Relax in my country cottage situated in a southerly elevated peaceful position. Well equipped spacious kitchen with fridge/freezer, washing machine and oil central heating. Comfortable lounge with dining area and open fire. One double and two single rooms, cot available. TV. Pets by arrangement but must be kept under control (livestock). Linen hire £5. Electricity meter reading at end of stay. Babysitting available. Open all year apart from Christmas. Large garden — ideal and safe for children. One mile from busy Shropshire Union Canal Basin and well placed for touring Staffordshire and Shropshire. Terms from £95 to £125 (low season) to £130 to £160 (high season). Member of the Heart of England Board. Apply **Mrs E.G. Palmer, Oulton Firs, Norbury, Stafford ST20 0PG (0785 284405).**

SUFFOLK

HALESWORTH. Beck's End Cottage, Westhall, Halesworth. This delightful red-brick house, converted from the one-time village school, with landscaped gardens and lawns, set on the hillside of a charming Suffolk village overlooking a valley of quiet countryside, is available for holiday letting all year round. Westhall is an interesting village with its 12th century Norman Church, typical village pub and shop and rolling farmlands. Only seven miles from Southwold and Suffolk's Heritage coastline, this is an excellent base from which to tour Norfolk and Suffolk. Many places of interest, both historical and scenic, within easy driving distance. Lovely walking terrain. The accommodation comprises large lounge/diner, entrance hall, two large bedrooms, cot for baby; bathroom, toilet. Modern fitted kitchen with electric cooker, fridge, kettle, toaster, cutlery, crockery and cooking utensils. Electric heating. Car essential, parking. Children welcome. Pets permitted. Bargain breaks November to April. SAE, please, or telephone (evenings) to **O.A. Johnson, Beck's End Farm, Westhall, Halesworth IP19 8QZ (Brampton [050279] 239).**

HALESWORTH near. Old School Cottage, Chediston, Near Halesworth. This charming, 300-year-old detached cottage with beams and inglenook is tastefully furnished and very cosy in winter. Available all year, accommodation includes lounge with TV and multifuel; diningroom with piano and single put-u-up; kitchen/diner with Rayburn, electric cooker, fridge etc. Cottage stairs lead to a landing, double and twin bedrooms and bathroom with storage heaters. Outside is a 'den' for children. The secluded, south-facing garden borders an unfenced stream and farmland. No pets. Three miles from Halesworth, with shops and railway station, it is ideal for touring the Heritage Coastline, Waveney Valley and Broads. EATB approved. Terms from £98 – £192 including electricity, fuel, linen. **Mrs E.A. Barleycorn, 5 Hawkridge, Shoeburyness, Essex SS3 8AU (0702-584514 evenings).**

KESSINGLAND. Kessingland Cottages, Rider Haggard Lane, Kessingland. Sleeps 8. An exciting three-bedroom recently built semi-detached cottage situated on the beach, three miles south of sandy beach at Lowestoft. Fully and attractively furnished with colour TV and delightful sea and lawn views from floor to ceiling windows of lounge. Accommodation for up to eight people. Well-equipped kitchen with electric cooker, fridge, electric immersion heater. Electricity by 50p meter. Luxurious bathroom with coloured suite. No linen or towels provided. Only a few yards to beach and sea fishing. One mile to wildlife country park with mini-train. Buses quarter-of-a-mile and shopping centre half-a-mile. Parking, but car not essential. Children and disabled persons welcome. Available 1st March to 7th January. Weekly terms from £40 in early March and late December to £185 in peak season. SAE to **Mr S. Mahmood, 156 Bromley Road, Beckenham, Kent BR3 2PG (081-650 0539).**

MONK SOHAM, near Woodbridge. Mrs G. Clarke, Monk Soham Hall, Monk Soham, Woodbridge IP13 7EN (072882 358). Situated in the grounds of Monk Soham Hall but with its own private garden, Lodge Cottage enjoys superb Suffolk views. Adjacent to St. Peter's Church and midway between Framlingham and Debenham, this delightful home offers comfortable accommodation for up to six people. The Heritage Coast, Norwich and Constable country are all within easy reach and Cretingham Golf Club is less than five miles away. Lodge Cottage is ideally situated for those wishing either a touring or peaceful relaxing holiday. Please write for further particulars.

SAXMUNDHAM. Mrs Mary Kitson, White House Farm, Sibton, Saxmundham IP17 2NE (Peasenhall [072-879] 260). Working farm, join in. Sleeps 5/6. The flat is a self-contained part of late Georgian farmhouse standing in 130 acres of quiet farmland with pigs, chickens, ponies, donkey. Fishing on farm. Accommodation in three double bedrooms (two double/two single beds) plus cot; livingroom; shower/toilet on first floor. Entrance hall, kitchen/diner on ground floor. Full central heating. Situated one-and-a-half miles from village shops, etc. Ten miles from coast at Dunwich, Minsmere Bird Sanctuary, Snape Maltings. Linen optional. Pets permitted. Car essential — parking. Available all year. SAE, please, for terms. Cottage also available.

WALSHAM-LE-WILLOWS. Bridge Cottage, Walsham-le-Willows, Near Bury St. Edmunds. Sleeps 4.

Bridge Cottage is illustrated in book "English Cottages", with introduction by John Betjeman. Built in the 17th century, it has been attractively modernised. There are fitted carpets and comfortable beds; centrally heated and well furnished. The kitchen is well equipped with electric cooker and fridge. Plenty of hot water. Children and well behaved pets are welcome. Electricity and heating included in rent. Colour TV. Tennis court and swimming pool available by arrangement. Walsham-le-Willows is in the centre of East Anglia (11 miles from Bury St. Edmunds) and has shops and post office. Available all year. Terms from £130 to £170. **Mrs H.M. Russell, The Beeches, Walsham-le-Willows, Near Bury St. Edmunds IP31 3AD (Walsham-le-Willows [0359] 259227).**

SUSSEX

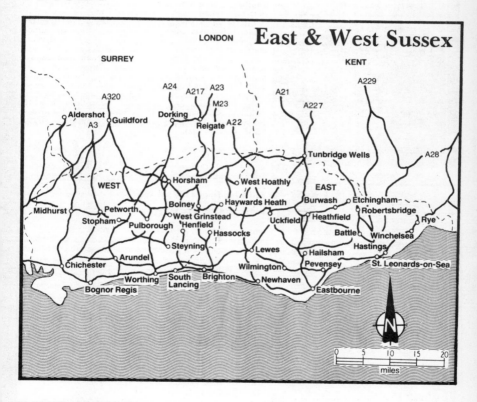

East & West Sussex

EAST SUSSEX

HASTINGS. Mrs Ann Norris, Crowham Manor Farm, Westfield, Hastings TN35 4SR (Brede [0424] 882441). Working farm. Sleeps 6. Crowham Manor is set in the middle of a farm in beautiful countryside. It lies between the historic towns of Battle and Rye, four miles from the sea at Hastings. Holiday guests can fish in the River Brede and have the use of a hard tennis court 100 yards from the house. The maisonette lies at one end of the large house and has its own entrance porch; a staircase leads to spacious accommodation consisting of kitchen, sittingroom, three large bedrooms and a separate bathroom and lavatory. It is well equipped with washing machine and colour TV. Children and pets welcome. Linen and towels can be hired; £2.50 per person. Open all year. Car essential. Shops one mile. Weekly terms £150 to £200.

POLEGATE. Mr M.F. Boniface, Lakeside Farm, Arlington, Polegate BN26 6SB (0323 870111). Sleeps 6. Lakeside Farm is a small working farm situated on the edge of a 150 acre reservoir, with view of the South Downs. Fishing by arrangement; golf, trekking, bathing in the area. Drusilla's Zoo two miles. Beautiful beaches at Eastbourne and Brighton within easy driving distance. Berwick railway station one mile. Shopping three miles. Modern, comfortable accommodation for six in two double rooms and put-u-up in sittingroom; diningroom; bathroom, toilet. Well equipped kitchen with electric cooker. No linen supplied. Open March to October. Car preferable. Parking. Children welcome, cot and high chair available. Well controlled pets allowed. Electric heating. Weekly terms from £115, electricity included.

RYE. "The Annexe", Upper Brook House, Brook Farm, Broad Street, Icklesham, Near Winchelsea.

Self catering farm cottage on working farm with sheep and orchards. Secluded and beautiful surroundings. Half a mile from main road. Garden with superb views. Close to the sea (four and a half miles), Rye and Hasting both six miles away. Also available, semi-detached one bedroomed cottage. Clean, comfortable and well equipped. Sittingroom with open fire, colour TV. Kitchen with electric cooker. Dining area. Upstairs bedroom with twin beds. Bathroom. Sleeps two/five (extra single bed, double Z-bed or cot). Linen provided. Metered electricity. Electric heaters. Pets welcome. Open all year. Weekly terms from £75 to £140. Brochure: **Mrs S. Fovargue, Upper Brook House, Brook Farm, Broad Street, Icklesham, Near Winchelslea TN36 4AX (0424 814266).**

UCKFIELD. Mr & Mrs L.A. Arnold, Whitehouse Farm, Horney Common, Nutley, Uckfield TN22 3EE (Nutley [082571] 2377). ♀ ♀ ♀ *Commended.* Whitehouse Farm Holiday Homes are situated on a small working farm overlooking the beautiful Ashdown Forest, home of that fictional bear Winnie the Pooh. An ideal place for a varied holiday. National Trust properties, castles and gardens abound, and London, Brighton and the coast are within easy reach. Sleeping four with full central heating, double glazing and showers. Large lounge/diners leading to individual patios. Full pine kitchens with washer dryers, fridge/freezers, slow cookers and coffeemakers. Personalised parking. Pets welcome. Full linen supplied. Heating and cots free. Brochure on request.

FOR THE MUTUAL GUIDANCE OF GUEST AND HOST

Every year literally thousands of holidays, short-breaks and overnight stops are arranged through our guides, the vast majority without any problems at all. In a handful of cases, however, difficulties do arise about bookings, which often could have been prevented from the outset.

It is important to remember that when accommodation has been booked, both parties — guests and hosts — have entered into a form of contract. We hope that the following points will provide helpful guidance.

GUESTS: When enquiring about accommodation, be as precise as possible. Give exact dates, numbers in your party and the ages of any children. State the number and type of rooms wanted and also what catering you require — bed and breakfast, full board, etc. Make sure that the position about evening meals is clear — and about pets, reductions for children or any other special points.

Read our reviews carefully to ensure that the proprietors you are going to contact can supply what you want. Ask for a letter confirming all arrangements, if possible.

If you have to cancel, do so as soon as possible. Proprietors do have the right to retain deposits and under certain circumstances to charge for cancelled holidays if adequate notice is not given and they cannot re-let the accommodation.

HOSTS: Give details about your facilities and about any special conditions. Explain your deposit system clearly and arrangements for cancellations, charges, etc, and whether or not your terms include VAT.

If for any reason you are unable to fulfil an agreed booking without adequate notice, you may be under an obligation to arrange alternative suitable accommodation or to make some form of compensation.

While every effort is made to ensure accuracy, we regret that FHG Publications cannot accept responsibility for errors, omissions or misrepresentation in our entries or any consequences thereof. Prices in particular should be checked because we go to press early. We will follow up complaints but cannot act as arbiters or agents for either party.

WEST SUSSEX

HENFIELD. The Holiday Flat, New Hall, Small Dole, Henfield BN5 9YJ (Henfield [0273] 492546).
♀♀♀ Situated just 11 miles north of Brighton, New Hall, the manor house of Henfield, one wing of which dates back to 1600, stands in three-and-a-half acres of mature gardens, surrounded by farmland with abundant footpaths. The holiday flat is completely self-contained being the upper part of the 18th century dairy wing of the house. Its own front door opens from the Georgian Courtyard. Accommodation comprises three bedrooms, one double, one single, one twin-bedded; lounge/diner; fully equipped kitchen; bathroom; comfortably furnished, carpeted throughout; central heating; free hot water; children welcome. Open all year. Terms from £85 to £185 per week. Apply to **Mrs M.W. Carreck.**

STORRINGTON. Byre Cottages. Sleep 2/6. New conversion of farm building into four self-contained

cottages, situated in rural location on working farm, one and a half miles from Storrington and eight miles from Worthing. Each cottage has central heating and is well equipped. Use of outdoor swimming pool during the week in summer. Overnight stays possible. Laundry/drying room and payphone. Gas and electricity charges extra. Prices range from £70 per week in winter for the one bedroomed cottage to £150 per week in July/August for the three bedroomed cottage. No pets. Contact: **Mrs Susan Kittle, Sullington Manor Farm, Storrington RH20 4AE (0903 742469).**

WARWICKSHIRE

Warwickshire Farm Holidays

Warwickshire farming families offer a range of high quality self-catering cottages in beautiful rural locations. Each cottage differs in style, size and price, but all offer excellent value for money for holidays or business travellers. Each holiday home is comfortably furnished, carpeted and equipped to Tourist Board standards, all owners are members of the Farm Holiday Bureau and all properties are inspected and approved by the English Tourist Board, and some participate in the ETB grading scheme. Warwickshire, in the heart of England, has a wealth of attractions, unspoilt countryside, castles, country gardens, stately homes, theatres and picturesque villages.

Places to visit within easy reach include Stratford-upon-Avon, Warwick, Royal Leamington Spa, The Cotswolds, Oxford, Coventry, National Exhibition Centre and National Agricultural Centre.

For further details on self-catering cottages or bed and breakfast please write to:
Warwickshire Farm Holidays (FHG), Crandon House, Avon Dassett, Leamington Spa CV33 0AA.

FARM HOLIDAY BUREAU

SHIPSTON-ON-STOUR. Church View Cottage, Shipston-on-Stour. Sleeps 4. Church View Cottage

adjoins a delightful old Cotswold farmhouse, one of the beautiful original houses in the picturesque little village of Great Wolford. Located on a 90 acre dairy farm, the accommodation comprises 10'6" by 17' lounge with leaded windows and oak beams, comfortably furnished with colour TV and double bed settee; fully fitted kitchen with electric cooker and fridge, ample working surfaces; small bathroom/toilet with linen. Children welcome. Milk provided free. The ideal choice for a family of four looking for a relaxing, comfortable holiday. Three acre lake for coarse fishing. Open April to October. Cot, high chair if required. Babysitting can be arranged. Weekly terms from £70 – £110. **Mrs S. Wrench, Hillside Farm, Great Wolford, Shipston-on-Stour CU36 5NQ (060-874 389).**

FHG PUBLICATIONS LIMITED publish a large range of well-known accommodation guides. We will be happy to send you details or you can use the order form at the back of this book.

WARWICKSHIRE. Warwickshire Farm Holidays. Warwickshire farming families offer a range of high quality self-catering cottages in beautiful locations. Each cottage differs in style, size and price, but all offer excellent value for money for holidays or business travellers. Each holiday home is comfortably furnished, carpeted and equipped to Tourist Board standards, all owners are members of the Farm Holiday Bureau and all properties are inspected and approved by the English Tourist Board, and some participate in the ETB grading scheme. Warwickshire in the Heart of England has a wealth of attractions, unspoilt countryside, castles, country gardens, stately homes, theatres and picturesque villages. Places to visit within easy reach include Stratford-upon-Avon, Warwick, Royal Leamington Spa, The Cotswolds, Oxford, Coventry, National Exhibition Centre, National Agricultural Centre. For further details on self-catering cottages or Bed and Breakfast please write to **Warwickshire Farm Holidays (FHG), Crandon House, Avon Dassett, Leamington Spa CV33 0AA.**

WILTSHIRE

CHIPPENHAM. Mrs C.J. Miles, Middle Farm, Stanley, Chippenham SN15 3RF (0249 650339). Situated outside Chippenham off A4, 13 miles east of Bath. Accommodation for four people, specially designed for handicapped. Easy access, good parking space. Sittingroom with sofa-bed; bedroom with twin beds; fully equipped kitchen; shower room with toilet. Electric central heating. TV. Bed linen, towels provided. Wheelchaired people will find wide doors. Window levels, switches, plugs, hand-basin and kitchen equipment at right height. Shower room has "wheelabout" quarry tile floor, shower seat and adjustable supports. No pets please. Terms from £120 per week including electricity all year round. Minimum stay two nights at £25 per night.

DEVIZES. Mr and Mrs C. Fletcher, Lower Foxhangers, Rowde, Devizes SN10 1SS (0380 828254).

Working farm. Colin and Cynthia Fletcher invite you to enjoy a farm holiday by the Kennet and Avon Canal in Wiltshire. Boating (dinghies or canoes); coarse fishing in season. Walk canal towpath, downland or woods. Easy reach of Bath, Longleat, Stonehenge and the villages of Avebury and Lacock. Horse riding, public golf courses, tennis, heated swimming pool within 15 minutes' drive. Accommodation in large mobile home with two/three bedrooms, bathroom, kitchen, sittingroom with TV; sleeps four. Situated in farm orchard. Open April to September, from £100 to £145 per week. Farmhouse Bed and Breakfast also available. Leaflet and booking form by return. Children and pets welcome.

ROWDE. Miss M.I. Marks, Mulberry Lodge House, Rowde, Devizes SN10 2QQ (Devizes [0380]

723056). Sleeps 5/6. Come and relax in self contained flat with panoramic views, two miles Devizes. Sleeps five/six, furnished, fully equipped wing of Georgian house (own entrance) with seven acres on the Devizes to Chippenham road. Children welcome. Badminton on lawns. Garden available, swimming pool and horse riding nearby. Large bedroom, double and single beds; large sitting/diningroom, TV. Electric and night storage heaters. Kitchen with electric cooker, fridge, spin dryer; toilet and bathroom. 10p meter on first floor. Second bedroom has single beds and cot. Ideal touring centre — Avebury, Wilton House, Longleat, Salisbury and Stonehenge. Fishing, shops and village. Ample parking. Open April to September. Weekly terms from £65 to £125. Brochures on request.

WILTSHIRE – "WHITE" HORSE COUNTY!
Many "White" horses adorn The Wiltshire chalk downs and the prehistoric theme continues with Stonehenge and Avebury. Also of interest are the landscape gardens at Studley, Chiselbury Camp, The Kennet and Avon canal with lock "staircase", Salisbury Plain, and the abandoned city Old Sarum.

YORKSHIRE

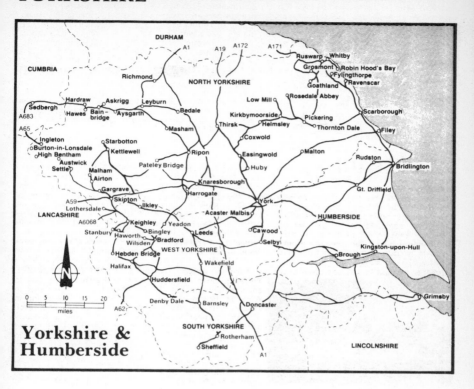

**Yorkshire &
Humberside**

EAST YORKSHIRE

DRIFFIELD near. Manor Farm Cottage, Foxholes, Near Driffield. Working farm. Sleeps 7. Manor Farm Cottage is a detached brick cottage with garage and enclosed garden in small Wolds village 12 miles from East Coast and within easy drive to Yorkshire Moors and York. Three double bedrooms accommodating seven. Bathroom, toilet, sittingroom with colour TV and open fireplace with electric fire. Diningroom. Fully equipped electric kitchen. Immersion heater in bathroom. Economy 7 heating. Registered with English Tourist Board. Open from May to October. Pets welcome. SAE, please, for terms and further details to **Mrs M. Lamplough, Manor Farm, Foxholes, Near Driffield YO25 0QH (Thwing [026-287] 255).**

NORTH YORKSHIRE

ASKRIGG. Fern Croft, 2 Mill Lane, Askrigg. A modern cottage enjoying quiet location on edge of village

with open fields rising immediately behind. Attractive and compact, this Wensleydale village is an ideal centre for Dales, with facilities for everyday needs, including two shops, post office, restaurant and a couple of pubs. Furnished to a high standard for four, ground floor accommodation comprises large, comfortable lounge/diner with colour TV and well equipped kitchen. Upstairs there are two double bedrooms equipped with a double and twin beds respectively, and modern bathroom. Storage heating included, other electricity by meter. Regret, no pets. Terms from £80 to £170 weekly. Brochure: **Mr and Mrs K. Dobson (0689 838450 or 0423 868710).**

AUSTWICK. Blythesgarth Cottage, Eldroth, Austwick. Working farm. Sleeps 6. Detached cottage on a farm two miles from Austwick and six from Settle. Peaceful location with lovely views. Ideal for walking or exploring Yorkshire Dales. Easy reach Lake District and west coast. Three bedrooms, two with double beds, one with two singles. Cot available. Three piece bathroom suite; lounge with colour TV; kitchen/diner. All electric, which is extra. Comfortably furnished and fully equipped (except linen). Garage and parking. Car essential. Part central heating included in rent October to May. Pets by arrangement. Open all year. Personally supervised by owner for 12 succesful years. Stamp only please for brochure and terms to **Mrs M. Booth, Slated House, Eldroth, Austwick, Lancaster LA2 8AG (Clapham [046 85] 365).**

BARTON-LE-WILLOWS. The Old Granary, Green Farm, Barton-Le-Willows, York. Working farm.

Sleeps 5/6 Adults. Barton-Le-Willows is a small, pretty village situated in the vale of York with easy access to Castle Howard, the North York Moors, Yorkshire coast and many other places of interest. Originally an old granary on our working dairy farm, this property has been renovated to a high standard while keeping its original character. Accomodation includes two bedrooms which sleep 5/6; large lounge/diningroom with electric fire, colour TV; fully fitted kitchen; bathroom. Full central heating, electricity, duvets and linen all included in the price. Large garden. Games room with snooker table. Children welcome cot can be provided. Sorry, no pets. Ample car parking space. From £140 per week, £30 deposit confirms booking. For full details concerning tariff and dates, write/telephone **Mrs J.R. Hudson, Green Farm, Barton-Le-Willows, York YO6 7PD (Whitwell [065381] 387).**

BEDALE. Mr F.E. Hudson, Winterfield House, Hornby, Bedale DL8 1NN (Richmond (N. Yorks) [0748] 811619). Cottages sleep 4/5. Two cottages situated in a beautiful parkland setting between Bedale and Leyburn, both facing south. Approached by a long private drive to the main house, they are away from traffic and ideally suited to children. Seven miles from Leyburn, within easy reach of the Moors, two National Parks, Wharfedale, beaches and Lake District etc. Village shop and post office one mile; market town of Bedale four miles. Car essential — parking. Winterfield Cottage, modern, detached with own garden. Kitchen/diningroom, larder, sittingroom, TV; downstairs WC; three bedrooms (one double, one twin, one single). Bathroom. Garden Cottage, older and covered with roses and virginia creeper. Small lawn. Kitchen, diningroom, sittingroom, TV; one double and one twin bedrooms; bathroom, WC; also outside WC. Cots provided. Slot meter (50p) electricity. No linen supplied. Well controlled dogs allowed. Terms from £100 to £150 per week.

BOLTON ABBEY. Skipton. ♀♀♀ *Approved.* Holiday Cottage with panoramic views of Wharfedale. A

delightful cottage close to the river yet accessible to hills and moorland walks. Fully furnished for six persons. Large kitchen, sittingroom, three bedrooms. Central heating, TV, enclosed gardens. For further information on cottage and area, apply: **The Estate Office, Bolton Abbey, Skipton BD23 6EX (075-671 227).**

FILEY near. "The Poop", Watson's Lane, Reighton, Near Filey. Sleeps 6. "The Poop" is situated in its own private garden overlooking the horses' four-acre field. Only one mile from the sea, with outstanding views of Filey Bay. The cedar wood bungalow is an ideal base for those seeking peace and quiet or for touring the Moors and coast. There is accommodation for six people plus a baby. The bungalow is equipped with modern conveniences (colour TV). Holiday facilities are available at nearby Bridlington and Scarborough. Pets by arrangement. Local bus and rail service. Shops five minutes' walk. Suitable for disabled guests — ramp to sun lounge, extra wide doors. Parking. Electricity by 50p meter. Please send SAE or telephone **Mrs R. A. Alderton, "Stubberhill", Watson's Lane, Reighton, Near Filey YO14 9SD (Scarborough [0723] 890394).**

GLAISDALE near Whitby. High Leas Flat, Glaisdale. Sleeps 2. Adjoins the owner's country residence, surrounded by gardens and overlooking the Dales and Moors. Fully equipped kitchenette/diner; sittingroom with colour TV. Electricity included in terms. Open Easter to November, special terms early and late season. Glaisdale is a village 10 miles from Whitby and there are many interesting places to visit including the North Yorkshire Moors Railway, the fishing ports of Staithes and Sandsend and Robin Hood's Bay. High Leas is half a mile from village. Ideal walking country. Tourist Board registered. Weekly terms on request from **Mrs S. Harland, High Leas, Glaisdale, Near Whitby YO21 2PX (Whitby [0947] 87255 or 602059).**

HARDRAW. Cissy's Cottage, Hardraw, Hawes. Sleeps 4. A delightful 18th century cottage of

outstanding character. Situated in the village of Hardraw with its spectacular waterfall and Pennine Way. Market town of Hawes one mile. This traditional stone built cottage retains many original features including beamed ceilings and an open fire. Sleeping four in comfort, it has been furnished and equipped to a high standard using antique pine and Laura Ashley prints. Equipped with microwave and tumble dryer. Outside, a south-facing garden, sun patio with garden furniture, and a large enclosed paddock make it ideal for children. Cot and high chair if required. Open all year. Terms £90-£210 include coal, electricity and trout fishing. For brochure, contact **Mrs Belinda Metcalfe, Southolme Farm, Little Smeaton, Northallerton DL6 2HJ (060981 302).**

HARDRAW. The Homestead, Hardraw, Near Hawes, Wensleydale. A charming 18th century stone

cottage nestling in the heart of the village with church, river, inn, craft/tea shop and the famous "Hardraw Force" waterfall situated under Shunner Fell on the Pennine Way. Lovingly restored, this owner-maintained cottage offers Dales features in warm and luxurious surroundings, each room exuding individual charm and character including original pine doors, mahogany-surround fireplaces, open beams and tastefully furnished with period furniture; fitted carpeting throughout. Fully equipped kitchen with Rayburn for constant hot water, a microwave oven and automatic washer. Bathroom with large claw-foot bath. Walled front garden with seat, patio and large enclosed paddock at rear. Private trout fishing included. Brochure: **Mrs Karen Metcalfe, 62 South Parade, Northallerton DL7 8SL (0609 771973).**

HAWES. River View, Dyers Garth, Hawes. Sleeps 6. A spacious three-bedroomed terraced cottage, River View is situated in a cul-de-sac overlooking "Duerley Beck" an attractive trout stream which runs through Hawes, a market town in the centre of Yorkshire Dales National Park and on the Pennine Way. The cottage has the benefit of storage heaters and also an open coal fire for out of season lets which is an attraction. An ideal situation for walking, fishing and visits to local scenic attractions which include Hardraw Scar, Aysgarth Falls and coach museum, Bolton Castle with the Lake District approximately 30 miles away. The cottage accommodates six plus baby (cot); three double bedrooms, bathroom, sittingroom with TV and fully equipped kitchen/diner. Shops 30 yards. Parking space for one car. SAE, please, for terms to **Mrs Sheila Alderson, "Inverdene," Hawes DL8 2NJ (Wensleydale [0969] 667408).**

Terms quoted in this publication may be subject to increase if rises in costs necessitate

KIRKBY FLEETHAM. Wren Cottage, 25 Forge Lane, Kirkby Fleetham, Northallerton. ♀ ♀ Sleeps 4.

Situated in the heart of "Herriot Country" betwixt the Yorkshire Dales and the Cleveland Hills, this cosy cottage with its traditional oak beams and open fire overlooks the village green where cricket is played in the summer. Nearby is a well-stocked village shop and a local pub which serves meals. The accommodation comprises one double bedroom, one twin-bedded room; fully equipped kitchen; sittingroom and bathroom. A cot and high chair are provided if required and bed linen and towels are available. Terms from £90 to £175. **Mrs J.R. Pybus, Street House Farm, Little Holtby, Northallerton DL7 9LN (0609 748622).**

KNARESBOROUGH. Mr T.M. Hall, Low Hall, Farnham, Knaresborough HG5 9JF (0423 340262). Fully modernised cottage to let, situated in an ideal area for touring, near the Yorkshire Dales and 15 miles from York and many historic houses. Only three miles north-east of Harrogate with its 14th century castle remains. Local fishing and golf; lovely country walks close by. The cottage sleeps five in two double bedrooms, cot; bathroom; sittingroom; all electric dining/kitchen. Fully equipped except for linen. Available all year. Pets allowed. Car essential. SAE, please.

LEYBURN. Lime Tree Cottage, Spennithorne, Leyburn. Sleeps 4. Lime Tree Cottage is situated in

Spennithorne, a beautiful little unspoilt village in Lower Wensleydale two miles from the market town of Leyburn. Spennithorne is well placed as a centre for touring and walking in Yorkshire's two National Parks, The Yorkshire Dales National Park only four miles distant and the North York Moors National Park 25 miles to the east. The cottage has accommodation for four persons, one bedroom with twin beds and one bedroom with two single beds. The furnishings are of high standard and everything is provided with the exception of sheets, pillowcases and towels, which visitors are asked to bring with them. There is car parking available in Spennithorne House Stable Yard behind the cottage. Children are welcome (cot). Pets allowed. Two miles from shops. Available from April to November 1st inclusive. Weekly terms from £90 to £125. Enquiries welcome. Write or phone please — **Colonel P.T. Van Straubenzee, D.S.O.,D.L., Spennithorne House, Leyburn DL8 5PR (Wensleydale [0969] 23200).**

MALTON. Mrs S. Armitage, Mount Pleasant Farm, Swinton, Malton YO17 0SP (0653 695890). Sleeps 5 plus cot. Situated in small village close to pretty market town of Malton. Attractive cottage in courtyard setting adjoining owners' working farm, one of four created by skilful conversion of magnificent barn with splendid views over Ryedale. Harvest Home offers spacious accommodation furnished and equipped to a high standard. Ideal base for exploring North Yorkshire Moors, Heritage Coast, York with Castle Howard only three miles. Golf, riding, swimming and fishing nearby. Pub/restaurant 200 yards. Lounge with open fire, farmhouse-style kitchen, toilet, three bedrooms, bathroom. Central heating, colour TV, automatic washing machine. Own garden. Parking. Linen provided.

MASHAM near. Holly Tree Cottage, Hutts Lane, Grewelthorpe, Near Ripon. Sleeps 5. At the foot of the Dales, Holly Tree Cottage is only 15 minutes from Fountains Abbey and central for the Dales attractions. Set in open countryside Holly Tree is a newly opened and very tasteful barn conversion, fully equipped with central heating, colour TV, microwave, etc. It is cosy with an open fire. Furnished to the highest standard and yet retains much charm and character, with views over a wooded Gill where guests can walk visiting the summerhouse on the way. Linen is provided. Two bedrooms. Open all year. Terms from £85 to £195. Contact: **Irene Foster, Lime Tree Farm, Hutts Lane, Grewelthorpe, Near Ripon HG4 3DA (076583 450).**

NORTHALLERTON. Herriot's Yorkshire Farm and Country Holidays. Farmhouse: farmers' wives offering hospitality in their own homes. Self Catering: owner serviced, warm, well-equipped self catering cottages. Situated in peaceful countryside with market towns, historic cities, stately homes and romantic villages. ETB approved. Send stamp for free brochure to: **Mrs D. Hill, Wellfield House Farm, North Otterington, Northallerton DL7 9JF (0609 2766) or Mrs R. Metcalfe, East Farm, Little Smeaton, Northallerton DL6 2HD (060981 291).**

NORTH YORKSHIRE MOORS. Pickering. Sleeps 7 plus cot. Headlands Farm is situated on a working farm on the edge of the valley of Newton Dale, where runs the North Yorkshire Moors Railway. Just 15 minutes' walk to Levisham Station, only ten minutes' walk from the pretty village of Newton-upon-Rawcliffe with village shop, pub, crafts and bird garden. It is totally surrounded by open countryside with some splendid walks in all directions from the house. Picturesque villages, Flamingo Land Zoo, East coast resorts all within a few miles. The house is comfortably furnished and kept to a high standard with fitted carpets throughout. Fully equipped with fitted kitchen, oven, fridge, washing machine, microwave; two open fires, three storage heaters (all included in the rent). Details from **Mrs J. Holliday, Elm House Farm, Newton-upon-Rawcliffe, Pickering YO18 8QA (0751 73223).**

PICKERING. Grooms Cottage, Grove House, Levisham Station, Pickering. Grove House is a beautiful old country residence set in one acre of garden, bounded by woodland, pine forest and moors; ideal for walkers and nature lovers. A picturesque railway runs through the valley and the car can be left at home for trips to Pickering on market day, and Whitby. The cottage is newly converted from the Groom's cottage in the garden to form a completely self-contained unit which has been restored to a high standard. The accommodation consists of entrance hall and large kitchen with sink unit, electric cooker, fridge and dining area. Separate bathroom with shower and WC. One bedroom, fully fitted, with twin beds. Comfortable lounge with convertible bed-settee. Electricity is charged by meter. Linen is not provided. A warm welcome to all guests. Apply to **Mrs J. Carter, Grove House, Levisham Station, Pickering YO18 7NN (Pickering [0751] 72351).**

PICKERING. Town End Farm Cottage, Pickering. A well appointed south-facing Cottage on the outskirts

of Pickering, with large garden and secluded paved area with garden furniture. Ample parking space and field at the side of the house for games or exercising the dog. Dining kitchen, sittingroom with colour TV and bedsitting room on the ground floor, three bedrooms and bathroom on first floor. Central heating available. Shop and telephone kiosk nearby. The property is thoroughly checked before arrival of visitors as our aim is to cater for those who wish for the best. House trained pets welcome. Pickering is a good centre for touring the North Yorks Moors, Forestry and is 24 miles from York, the ancient capital of the North, dominated by the Minster and steeped in history. Flamingo Park Zoo, riding, fishing and swimming pool in the vicinity. Eighteen miles to the coast. Another self catering property is available, send SAE, or telephone for enquiries. **Mr P.R. Holmes, Town End Farm, Pickering YO18 7HU (Pickering [0751] 72713 or 73983).**

RICHMOND. Mrs Kathleen Hird, Smarber, Low Road, Richmond DL11 6PX (Richmond [0748] 86243). Working farm. Sleeps 7. Spacious stone-built

farm set along a private road high on the north side of Swaledale, overlooking the River Swale, one mile from Low Row. Accommodating seven people in three double bedrooms; cot provided; bathroom, shower; sittingroom. Fully equipped electric kitchen with cooker and fridge. No linen supplied. Part central heating. Sorry, no pets. The cottage has a private garden and is ideal for children. Babysitter available. Many places of historic interest to visit including Folk Museum at Reeth (five miles), Swaledale Woollens at Muker (six miles), Aysgarth Falls (10 miles); Richmond and Barnard Castles. Interesting and scenic walking country. Car essential — ample parking, plus garage. Available from March to November. Weekly terms from £65 (fuel not included).

RIPON area. May Cottage and Braeside, Kirkby Malzeard; Rose Cottage, Winksley. Stone cottages,

very cosy, full of character. Bedrooms — two double; one double; one double and folding beds. Lovely walking, riding, pony trekking, golf, tennis, swimming, fishing nearby. Excellent touring area. 25 miles from York. Many local houses of historical interest. Fully equipped, colour TV, two with central heating. Pets allowed except May Cottage. Bed linen, washing machine, tumble dryer, incoming phone, barbecue (May Cottage only), £85 to £210 including log fire in winter. Tourist Board Inspected. Stamp for brochure, please. **Mrs K. Bailey, Peacock Farm, Winksley, Ripon HG4 3NR (Kirkby Malzeard [076-583] 8801 (ansaphone) or 338).**

ROBIN HOOD'S BAY. Working farm. Near Robin Hood's Bay at Boggle Hole. Five minutes' walk to beach. Between Whitby and Scarborough. Super detached stone cottages and bungalow on dairy farm. Two and three bedrooms and cot. Fully equipped with central heating, fitted carpets, colour TV, fridge, washbasins in bedrooms. Own garden and car parking. North York Moors all around. Pony trekking nearby. Open all year. Sorry, no pets. Terms from £70 to £250. **Mrs N. Pattinson, South House Farm, Robin Hood's Bay, Whitby YO22 4UQ (Whitby [0947] 880243).**

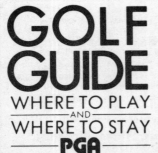

SCARBOROUGH. Mrs R. Pickering, Keasbeck Cottage, Harwood Dale, Scarborough, YO13 0DT (Scarborough [0723] 870311). Sleeps 7. The cottage is situated among the glorious unspoilt countryside which surrounds Scarborough with forest walks and trails nearby. It sleeps seven people comfortably and has been modernised. Three double bedrooms, one single and cot; bathroom with toilet; sittingroom with colour TV; large kitchen with electric cooker, fridge freezer; automatic washing machine; oil central heating. Linen not supplied. Pets are permitted, if kept under strict control. Seven miles from the sea. Stabling can be provided. Car essential, parking. Open May to September. For terms and further details please send SAE.

SCARBOROUGH. Mrs A. Marshall, Spikers Hill Farm, West Ayton, Scarborough YO13 9LB (Scarborough [0723] 862537). ♀♀♀♀ *Approved.* Delightful country cottage and two luxury king size caravans on private 600 acre farm in North Yorkshire National Park. Five miles from Scarborough. Beautifully furnished, every modern convenience. Cleaned to highest standard. Yorkshire and Humberside Tourist Board.

SEDBUSK, near Hawes. Mrs A. Fawcett, Mile House Farm, Hawes DL8 3PT (Hawes [0969] 667481) Sleeps 8. Sedbusk is a peaceful village just over a mile from the market town of Hawes, close to the Pennine Way. "Clematis Cottage" is a delightful old stone cottage tastefully restored with beamed ceilings, open fires and Laura Ashley decoration. Beautifully maintained, the cottage is very warm and cosy with every comfort. Breathtaking views over Upper Wensleydale. The cottage has a lovely walled south-facing garden. Free trout fishing on the farm. Also lovely traditional Dales character cottage in the picturesque village of West Burton, near Aysgarth Falls. Sleeps five plus baby. SAE for terms and prompt reply.

SETTLE. Mrs J. Gray, Yorkshire Properties, Black Carr House, Skipton Road, Trawden, Colne, Lancashire BB8 8QU (Colne [0282] 869404). Properties sleep 2/14. Idyllic stone cottages near Settle, Yorkshire Dales. Excellent base for Lake District, West Coast, York. Renovated to the highest standards. All facilities including central heating, colour TV/video, fridge/freezers, dishwashers, microwaves, automatic washers, bedrooms with en-suite bathrooms. Towels and bed linen provided. Cots and high chairs available — babies, children and pets welcome. Suitable for disabled. Cottages sleep two to 14. ETB, Y&HTB Approved. Prices from £130 per week. **Telephone YORKSHIRE PROPERTIES (0282 869404) for brochure.**

SKIPTON. Mrs Judith M. Joy, Jerry and Ben's, Hebden, Skipton BD23 5DL (Skipton [0756] 752369). Properties sleep 3/6/8/9. Jerry and Ben's stands in two acres of grounds in one of the most attractive parts of the Yorkshire Dales National Park. Seven properties; Ghyll Cottage (sleeps eight); Mamie's Cottage (sleeps eight); Paradise End (sleeps six); Robin Middle (sleeps six); High Close (sleeps nine); Cruck Rise (sleeps six); Raikes Side (sleeps two/three). All have parking, electric cooker, fridge, colour TV, electric heating and immersion heater; lounge, dining area, bathroom or shower; cots if required. Fully equipped, including linen if requested. Washing machine and telephone available. Well behaved pets accepted. Open all year. Fishing and bathing close by. Terms from £55 to £190. SAE, please for detailed brochure. Suitable for disabled.

STUTTON, near York. Cocksford Cottages, Cocksford Farm, Stutton, Tadcaster LS24 9NG

(Tadcaster [0937] 834253). Cocksford Farm stands in its own tranquil valley at the side of Cock Beck adjacent to the site of the famous Battle of Towton (1461) and yet is only 15 minutes' drive to Harrogate and historic York. Free fly fishing is available and for racing enthusiasts the Yorkshire Race Courses are nearby. The cottages have been converted from an old stable block and although fully modernised and centrally heated, they maintain an old world charm. All properties have a large fully fitted kitchen, dining room with electric cooker, refrigerator, washer/dryer and a comfortable beamed lounge with open fire and colour TV. Cottages sleep 4/6. Cot/high chair available. Pets welcome. Terms from £90 to £260. Yorkshire/Humberside Tourist Board Registered. Apply: **Mrs S. Watkinson.**

SUMMERBRIDGE. Mrs Betty Ingleby, Dougill Hall, Summerbridge, Harrogate HG3 4JR (Harrogate

[0423] 780277). 4 Keys. Working farm. Dougill Hall Flat occupies the top floor of the Hall, which is of Georgian design, built in 1722 by the Dougill family who lived on this farm from 1496 to 1803. It is in Nidderdale, half a mile from the village of Summerbridge, just by the River Nidd, where there is fishing available for visitors. There are good facilities for horse riding, tennis, swimming, squash, etc. Well situated for the walking enthusiast and within easy reach of the Dales, the beautiful and ancient city of York, Fountains Abbey, How Stean Gorge and many other places of interest. The flat sleeps up to six people. Well equipped, with electric cooker and fridge, iron, vacuum cleaner. Linen by arrangement. Pets permitted. Car essential, parking. The old Cooling House flat attached to the house is now available and sleeps four. Terms £67 – £134. SAE, please, for details.

WEST SCRAFTON. Mrs Caroline Harrison, Hill Top Farm, West Scrafton, Leyburn DL8 4RU

(Wensleydale [0969] 40663). Working farm, join in. Properties sleep 4/6. Relax in one of our two recently converted traditional dales stone barns, admire the views of Rova Crag and the moors. Inside, the fully equipped kitchens and modern bathrooms retain much character with original exposed beams and open fireplaces. Situated in the heart of the Yorkshire Dales National Park, within easy access of the A1. BARN OWL sleeps from four to six persons and BRACKEN sleeps four. Ensuite bathrooms, central heating, log fires, fitted carpets throughout. Facilities include: colour TVs, shaver points, automatic washing machine, fridge/deep freeze, microwave, electric cooker. Linen provided. Pets and children welcome. Games room, pets corner, rough shooting, fishing, private picnic area by river.

WETHERBY. Mrs M.E. Newby, Rudding Farm, Walshford Bridge, Wetherby LS22 5HR (Wetherby [0937] 63168). A pair of semi-detached bungalows standing in their own well kept gardens, on the side of Cowthorpe Lane on the edge of Rudding Farm, just off the A1 motorway, three miles north of Wetherby roundabout, with York 14 miles and Harrogate only eight miles. Each bungalow has accommodation for five people in one double bedroom, one twin bedded room, and one single room; duvets and clean bed linen are provided but tenants are required to provide their own towels, tea towels, dish cloths etc. The rest of the accommodation consists of a large sitting room with colour TV and open fireplace running five radiators; bathroom; well equipped kitchen with units, electric cooker and fridge; utility room with washing machine and tumble dryer; cloakroom and garage. Electricity is by 50p coin operated meter; two bags of coal will be provided for the fire and included in the rent. Payphone. Fishing is available if required at £1 per session as there is a stretch of the River Nidd running along the farm, with good access. A small barbecue is provided in the garage for tenants' use in fine weather; bungalows are let from Saturday to Saturday and guests are requested not to arrive before 1.00 p.m. and to depart before 10.00 a.m. to allow for cleaning. One dog welcome if well controlled. Regret no cats. Terms: from £120 to £180, 20 per cent deposit when booking.

NORTH YORKSHIRE – RICH IN TOURIST ATTRACTIONS!

Dales, moors, castles, abbeys, cathedrals – you name it and you're almost sure to find it in North Yorkshire. Leading attractions include Castle Howard, the moorlands walks at Goathland, the Waterfalls at Falling Foss, Skipton, Richmond, Wensleydale, Bridestones Moor, Ripon Cathedral, Whitby, Settle and, of course, York itself.

WHITBY. Harbourside Flats, 7 Pier Road, Whitby. Flats sleep 7. Two luxury holiday flats, recently modernised, situated on the harbourside of the picturesque old fishing town of Whitby. The properties, both accommodating seven people, (one two-bedroomed, the other three-bedroomed) are spacious. Lounge bay windows have panoramic views over the harbour; fully equipped kitchen; bathroom; immersion heater; electric fires; TV. Electricity by 50p meter. Children welcome, cot and high chair provided. Pets accepted free of charge. Guests to bring own linen. Whitby, the home of Captain Cook, offers ideal sandy beaches, leisure amenities, fishing trips, golf and tennis. Excellent location for touring North Yorkshire Moors National Park, unique coastal villages and many other places of local interest. Available Easter to September. Terms and further details on request. **Mrs S. Harland, High Leas, Glaisdale, Whitby YO21 2PX (Whitby [0947] 87255 or 602059).**

WHITBY. "The Cottage", Howlet Hall, Ugglebarnby, Whitby. Working farm, join in. Sleeps 5. Situated up a short farm road, three miles from Whitby in the North Yorkshire Moors National Park with views of Abbey, moors and sea. Excellent walking centre and attractions, such as North Yorkshire Moors National Park, railway and sandy beaches are within easy reach. Stone built. Own sheltered garden. Accommodation comprises large lounge/dining room, sittingroom with open or electric fire and colour TV. Three bedrooms upstairs with three single and one double bed. Cot, bathroom, separate WC. Kitchenette with Calor gas cooker, larder, fridge, immersion heater. Parking outside cottage. Sorry no pets. Terms £85 to £185 weekly. SAE, please, to **Mrs A.A.K. Weston, Howlet Hall, Ugglebarnby, Whitby YO22 5HU (Whitby [0947] 810294).**

TERRINGTON HOLIDAY COTTAGES

Come and enjoy comfort and rest in one of our superb holiday cottages, sleeping 2-8 people. A peaceful, unspoilt farming village just 14 miles N.E. of York and within 4 miles of Castle Howard, Terrington is in an ideal position for your discovery of a beautiful area. Illustrated brochure. S.A.E. for full particulars to:
Mrs S. Goodrick, Springfield Court, Terrington, York YO6 4PX. Telephone (065 384) 370 or 268.

YORK. Sunset Cottages, Grimston Manor Farm, Gilling East, York. Working Farm. Six beautiful cottages lovingly converted from the granaries of our family farm. Superbly situated in the heart of the Howardian Hills, on the outskirts of the National Park and only 17 miles north of the historic City of York in Herriot Country. With panoramic views, these warm and comfortable cottages retain their original mellow beams and interesting stonework while still providing all the modern comforts you rightfully expect in a well-designed self-catering cottage. Full central heating. Personally supervised by the resident owners Heather and Richard Kelsey. Sorry, no pets (sheep country). Please phone or write for brochure **Mr and Mrs R.J. and J.H. Kelsey, Grimston Manor Farm, Gilling East, York YO6 4HR (Brandsby [03475] 654).**

YORK. Carr Lynn Apartments, 105 Carr Lane, York. Properties sleep 2/4/7/8. Carr Lynn is an attractive Edwardian Town House recently converted into luxurious self-catering apartments. Located in a well appointed residential area of the historic city of York, one-and-a-half-miles from the centre, yet only a 25 minute walk alongside the River Ouse to the Minster. Convenient local shopping frequent bus service to the city centre with its wealth of attractions: medieval City Walls, Castle Museum, Railway Museum and Jorvik Viking centre. Accommodation comprises three well equipped apartments, with colour TV. Modern kitchens fitted with microwaves, hob units, fridges, kettles, toaster, crockery/cutlery, pans. Iron and board provided. Bed linen, towels and tea towels supplied. All apartments are protected by a monitored fire alarm system. Personally supervised by the proprietor, **Mrs Jackie Cundall, Wellgarth Guest House, Rufforth, York YO2 3QB (Rufforth [0904 83] 595 or 592).**

YORK. West End Mill Farm, Yapham, Pocklington, York. Sleeps 4. The bungalow adjacent to the farmhouse, is on a 76 acre farm situated in the village of Yapham, at the foot of the Yorkshire Wolds and commands a magnificent view of these beautiful wooded hills, two miles from country town of Pocklington, which offers shops, cinema. bingo hall, swimming pool, gardens with lily ponds and museum. Locality provides fishing, boating, country inns, horse riding and is within easy reach of many stately homes, forest drives, moors, dales and zoo. It is 28 miles from the coast and 12 miles from historic York. Bungalow consists of one double bedroom (twin beds) and cot; combined lounge/diningroom with TV, and studio couch which converts into double bed. Bathroom, toilet; kitchen with dining area, electric cooker, immersion heater, washer, fridge, (50p) meter. Farm Cottage available with two bedrooms, bathroom/cloakroom, kitchen/diner and large lounge. Open all year. Children and pets welcome. Parking provided. SAE for terms to **Mrs M.S.A. Woodliffe, Mill Farm, Yapham, Pocklington, York YO4 2PH (0759 302172).**

YORK. Tea Pot Cottage, Meltonby, Pocklington, York. Tea Pot Cottage (the centre one of three) has lawned garden to front, and open views. Situated in Meltonby at the foot of the Yorkshire Wolds, it is near the owners' 170-acre farm. Ideal centre for historic York (13 miles), coast (30 miles), Forest Drives, Moors, Dales, Stately Homes, fishing, boating, country inns, horse riding. Pocklington (two-and-a-half miles) has excellent shopping facilities, supermarkets, cinema, bingo, heated swimming pool, gardens, museum, lily pond. Newly carpeted throughout, the cottage has two double bedrooms plus cot (if required); kitchen with dining area; lounge; bathroom, toilet. Colour TV, immersion and economy water heaters, fridge, washer, automatic double oven, twin tub washing machine, shaving point, etc. Electricity on £1 coin meter. Children, pets welcome. Garage — car essential. Open all year. SAE for terms to **Mrs J. Leach, Fair View House, Meltonby, Pocklington, York YO4 2PW (0759 303433 or 303256).**

YORK. 2 Wandale Cottage, Bulmer, York. Sleeps 5. This lovely cottage is situated in a quiet unspoilt village and is an ideal house from which to tour the Yorkshire Moors and Dales and the East Coast. Near Castle Howard. The historic city of York, with its Tudor houses and cobbled streets, is within easy driving distance. The cottage is available as self-catering accommodation all year. Accommodation for five in two double bedrooms (one with extra single bed); sittingroom (colour TV); bathroom, toilet; well-equipped electric kitchen. Meter for electricity. Everything supplied except linen. Children and pets welcome. Car essential — parking. Electric heating; open fires. SAE, please, to **Mrs J. Goodwill, Wandale Farm, Bulmer, York YO6 7BW (Whitwell-on-the-Hill (065-381) 326).**

YORK near. Mrs V.A. Reed, Field House Farm, Bielby, York YO4 4JR (Melbourne [0759] 318386).

Working farm. This old, but modernised, south-facing, personally cleaned, well-furnished farmhouse and cottage, pleasantly situated on quiet country road, half-a-mile from village, near Yorkshire Wolds, on family run dairy farm. Near to York and Pocklington with Burnby Gardens' famous water lillies, Castle Howard. Within easy reach of Moors, Dales, zoo, coast and Hornsea Potteries. Well-equipped kitchen; sittingroom with patio doors, tidy lawned garden; diningroom with patio doors; colour TV; 3 bedrooms (two double, one twin) ; bathroom, WC upstairs. Bed linen and hot water, inclusive. Full central heating available. No VAT. Fresh milk. Sorry, no pets. Cozy cottage for two also available. Please telephone me for friendly chat.

YORKSHIRE DALES. Near Pateley Bridge, Harrogate. Working farm, join in. Properties sleep 4. English Tourist Board approved. Beautifully situated in 30 acres of undulating green farmland surrounded by woods and streams, two very well furnished, cosy, beamed farm cottages. Both sleeping four. Many original features have been retained with log fires if you wish. Colour TV, washing machine, linen hire, ample parking space. Pets accepted in Well Cottage only. We have many local unspoilt picturesque walks. Near to village and River Nidd. Central for visiting local beauty spots Brimham Rocks, Fountains Abbey, Harrogate, Ripon, York. Terms from £120 to £190 per week. Large SAE please for colour brochure to **Miss Sue Hollings, Well House Farm, Low Laithe, Summerbridge, Harrogate HG3 4DF (Harrogate [0423] 780471/781490).**

PLEASE ENCLOSE A STAMPED ADDRESSED ENVELOPE WITH ENQUIRIES

YORKSHIRE DALES. Wathgill Farm, Downholme, Richmond DL11 6AJ. Sleeps 4 adults; 4 children. The accommodation consists of half a large farmhouse including kitchen, sittingroom-cum-diningroom with open fire and colour TV; two double bedrooms and a downstairs room to sleep four children; bathroom has to be shared with the rest of the house but guests have full use whenever they wish. The farm is situated on a minor road between Leyburn and Reeth. We offer an ideal family holiday with walks around the farm to see our sheep and cows. Prices range from £180 which includes all electricity, full central heating and fuel for the fire. Open all year. **For further details and bookings ring Mark and Judith Stephenson (0748 2939).**

YORKSHIRE DALES NATIONAL PARK. Adrian Cave, Westclose House, West Scrafton, Near Middleham DL8 4RM (081 567 4862 for bookings). With superb views over beautiful and secluded Coverdale, this traditional stone farmhouse with attached barn and garden was the location for Herriot's house (Rowangarth), and other scenes in the BBC TV Vet series. Access via quiet road, quarter of a mile from village, parking for three cars. Three bedrooms (sleep six/eight); living and diningrooms with traditional fireplaces. Ground floor kitchen and bathroom useful for elderly or disabled. Unobtrusively modernised for a real country holiday. Ideal for walkers. Pets welcome. Self-catering from £100 per week.

WEST YORKSHIRE

HAWORTH. 7 Upper Marsh, Oxenhope. A small, stone cottage on the edge of moorland, one mile from Haworth, lovingly renovated, equipped and cared for. Sleeps six in two bedrooms and the lounge. The cottage has sunny rooms, spectacular views, colour TV, gas central heating, well equipped kitchen, washing machine and garden chairs. Waymarked walks start near the cottage or you can take the car to explore the Pennines, Yorkshire Dales and West Riding. Available all year; children and pets very welcome. Tourist Board category 3. Prices £70–£120 (winter) and £110 to £220 (summer) include sheets and heating. For further details contact **Mrs F. M. Seabrook, 30 Newcombe Street, Market Harborough, Leicestershire LE16 9PB (Market Harborough [0858] 463723).**

KEIGHLEY. Mrs W. Cocks, High Hob Cote Farm, Colne Road, Oakworth, Keighley BD22 0RW (0535 642376). Sleeps 5. Situated on the above 30 acre farm, a semi-detached 18th century weaver's cottage, stone mullioned windows, curving stone staircase. Recently modernised, breakfast kitchen, gas cooker, fridge, immersion heater. Modern bathroom. Dining lounge with TV. One double, one twin bedroom, one single put-u-up. Bed linen provided. Three gas fires, electric fires. Small south-facing garden. Dogs by arrangement. Enjoys magnificent panoramic views across fields to Haworth and Haworth Moors. Haworth, home of the Bronte family of "Wuthering Heights" fame (a museum), and the Worth Valley Steam Railway. Ten miles from Skipton, gateway to the beautiful Dales National Park. Open all year. Shops and pub one mile. Registered with Haworth Tourist Board. Terms from £50 to £130 per week.

WHEN MAKING ENQUIRIES PLEASE MENTION
FARM HOLIDAY GUIDES

ISLES OF SCILLY

ISLES OF SCILLY. Mrs R.C. May, Grenofen, St. Mary's, Isle of Scilly TR21 0NE (Scillonia [0720] 22398). Chalet situated in own private surroundings with views of harbour, adjacent to island's nine-hole golf course and Porthloo Beach. Sleeps five in two bedrooms, one with twin beds and one with bunk beds and single bed. Modern all-electric kitchen (cooker, fridge, heater over sink). Shower with toilet and washbasin. Cot, high chair; children welcome. Combined sitting/diningroom. Colour TV. Shops under a mile, sea 100 yards. Pets by prior arrangement only. Parking. Groceries, milk delivered on request. Linen supplied. Motor launch trips from St. Mary's to neighbouring islands — St. Martin's, St Agnes and Bryher, Tresco for gardens and fascinating "Valhalla", also Bishops Rock Lighthouse. Please send SAE for terms which exclude fuel. Registered West Country Tourist Board.

ISLE OF WIGHT

TOTLAND BAY. 3 Seaview Cottages, Broadway, Totland Bay. Sleeps 5. This well-modernised cosy old coastguard cottage holds the Farm Holiday Guide Diploma for the highest standard of accommodation. It is warm and popular throughout the year. Four day winter break — £29; a week in summer £220. Located close to two beaches in beautiful walking country near mainland links. It comprises lounge/dinette/kitchenette; two bedrooms (sleeping five); bathroom/toilet. Well furnished, fully heated, TV, selection of books and other considerations. Another cottage is also available at Cowes, Isle of Wight. Non-smokers only. **Mrs C. Pitts, 11 York Avenue, New Milton, Hampshire BH25 6BT (New Milton [0425] 615215).**

CHANNEL ISLANDS

JERSEY. Nicola Le Boutillier, Woodlands Farm, Mont-a-l'Abbe, St. Helier, Jersey (0534-61345). Our traditional Jersey dairy and new potato farm, situated just two miles from St. Helier in delightful countryside, offers three superior one or two bedroomed apartments, and one cottage. Designed and prepared for your complete comfort and relaxation; linen, towels and household items supplied, personal laundry service, telephone, cots and high chairs all available. Large gardens, barbecues. Open all year. Fully inclusive prices from £109 to £515, depending on length of stay and apartment type. Please write or telephone as above for details.

With beautiful countryside all around, the Poppit Caravan Site at St. Dogmaels, Dyfed, sits in a spacious glade. St. Dogmaels is on the estuary of the River Teifi, near Cardigan.

CARAVAN AND CAMPING HOLIDAYS

CORNWALL

LOOE near. Mrs B.S. Venning, Treire Farm, Lanreath, Near Looe PL13 2PD (0503 20470). Working farm, join in. Sleeps 6. Modern six berth caravan situated in rear of garden of farmhouse with lovely rural view. Turn right off Lanreath to Bodinnick Road, about one and a half miles from Lanreath village. Four miles coast, seven miles Looe and Polperro. Coarse fishing, horse riding, lovely National Trust walks all within easy reach. All electric. Two bedrooms plus one double in kitchen area. Toilet and shower. TV, radio. Linen provided. Electricity on meter. Only caravan on working farm. Regret, no dogs. Available May to October. Terms from £85 per week.

MITHIAN, near St. Agnes. Mrs Mary Thorley, Treleaver, Mithian Downs, Near St. Agnes (St. Agnes [087255] 2486.) Sleeps 6. This modern (1985 model) caravan is situated on a 20 acre smallholding set in sheltered valley two miles from the coast and one mile from the village. A 25' BK Bluebird caravan, with fully fitted and equipped kitchen; shower and flush toilet. Accommodation is suitable for six people in one double bedroom, one bunk bedroom and a pull-down bed in the lounge; mains electricity with Calor gas cooker and heater; television socket. Various farm animals including pony; pet welcome if safe with farm animals. Terms from £70 to £130 weekly (inclusive of gas and electricity used).

MULLION. Mrs P.M. Bennetts, The Friendly Camp & Caravan Park, Tregullas Farm, Ruan Minor, Helston TR12 7LJ (Mullion [0326] 240387). Working farm. Quiet farm site, ideal centre for touring and sea fishing, lovely moorland walks, two and a half miles from good sandy beaches. This site is situated on the left hand side of the main Helston to Lizard road (A3083), about seven miles south of Helston near the junction with the Mullion road (B3296). Six-berth caravans enjoy views over Goonhilly Downs, all with flush toilets and electricity, some with showers, fully equipped except linen. All types of tents and tourers welcome — showers, flush toilets and laundry room on site. Shop nearby. Pets accepted. Open April to November. SAE, please, for brochure and terms for hiring caravans. Car and tent or caravan from £3 per night.

See also Colour Display Advertisement **ST. AUSTELL. Mr D. Borradaile, Trencreek Farm Holiday Park, Hewaswater, St. Austell (St. Austell [0726] 882540).** Trencreek is a small farm with a real farm atmosphere. Wonderful for those who want peace and quiet with lots of space. Quarter of a mile off the main road down our own private lane. The site provides modern fully serviced bungalows; modern caravans; ample wash facilities; laundry and dishwashing rooms; TV and table tennis rooms; heated swimming pool. Terms on application. Special offers early and late season.

ST. IVES. Hellesveor Caravan and Camping Site, St. Ives. Caravans sleep 4/8. Small, secluded farm site on Land's End road (B3306) offers four to eight berth caravans (with electricity) for hire. One mile from St. Ives town centre and beaches. Ideally situated for touring West Cornwall with leisure facilities, pub grub, countryside walks and coastal path nearby. Campers and touring caravans welcome. Special terms early and late season. SAE, please, for further details. **G. and H. Rogers, Hellesveor Farm, St. Ives TR26 3AD (0736 795738).**

PLEASE SEND A STAMPED ADDRESSED ENVELOPE WITH ENQUIRIES

CUMBRIA — English Lakeland

AMBLESIDE. Mrs S.E. Jump, The Grove Farm, Ambleside LA22 9LG (Ambleside [05394] 33074). Caravans sleep 6. Three modern six-berth caravans, available to families only, on private site at The Grove Farm. Each caravan is equipped with shower, toilet, hot and cold water, light, heat, cooker, TV and fridge. The caravans have panoramic views and are situated one-and-a-quarter miles above the village of Ambleside in the beautiful Stock Valley. An ideal spot for walking, touring and boating. ETB registered. Full details and terms on receipt of SAE.

BROUGHTON-IN-FURNESS. Mrs H. Glessal, Whineray Ground, Broughton-in-Furness LA20 6DS

(Broughton-in-Furness [0229] 716500). Working farm. Private, sheltered yet within easy reach of a whole host of facilities — miniature railway, castles, gardens, beach, museum, fishing, bird watching, fell walking — attractive six-berth, 30' modern static caravan set in its own half acre on a working fell farm. Marvellous views and absolute seclusion can be guaranteed. Two bedrooms (one with bunks, one with double bed), spacious living area and separate kitchen; shower and toilet. Fridge, gas fire and cooker — no additional charge for electricity and gas. Hot and cold water. River Duddon close by, indoor swimming pool, village, shops, pub, restaurant and golfing within two miles. Ulverston market town about ten miles. Further details on request. Terms from £70 weekly.

CARLISLE. Mrs P.E. Johnston, Yeast Hall, New House Farm, Newby West, Carlisle CA2 6QZ

(Carlisle [0228] 23545). Two attractive caravans on private farm site — 28 foot Fairview five-berth, 30 foot Willerby six-berth, both with lounge, kitchen, bedroom, bathroom and each completely private in own enclosure. Situated three and a half miles west of Carlisle, a quarter-mile from road down private lane. It is ideally situated for visiting Lake District, Solway coast, Scottish Borders, Roman Wall, Eden Valley, etc. Vans are very well equipped, with everything supplied except linen, and thoroughly cleaned between visitors. Electric lighting, heating. Calor gas cooker, water heater. Terms from £40. Further details with pleasure. Phone or write (SAE please).

CARLISLE near. Mrs W.H. Bolson, Russelgate, Roweltown, Near Carlisle CA6 6LX (Roadhead

[06978] 334). Russelgate is situated on a smallholding in remote, unspoilt countryside. Nearest shops nine miles away so a car is essential. Caravan fully equipped with electricity, gas, fridge, colour TV and flush toilet (all included in price). We offer a typical farm atmosphere, keeping Angora and dairy goats, ducks and hens; we are therefore able to provide you with fresh goats' milk and free range eggs. Conveniently situated for visiting Hadrian's Wall, the Scottish Borders, Kielder Water and Forest, with the Lake District only three-quarters of an hour's drive away. Children welcome. Pets under control welcome. Available all year round from £60–£80 per week inclusive.

CONISTON. Mrs E. Johnson, Spoon Hall, Coniston LA21 8AW (0966 41391). Caravans sleep 6.
Three 33ft caravans situated on a 50 acre working hill farm one mile from Coniston, overlooking Coniston Lake. All have flush toilet, shower, gas cookers, fires and water heaters, electric lighting and fridge. All have colour TV. Children are welcome and there is a cot. Pets are allowed free. Available all year round. Pony trekking arranged from farm. Weekly terms on request.

GRANGE-OVER-SANDS. Greaves Farm Caravan Site, Field Broughton, Grange-over-Sands. Caravans sleep 6. Available March to October, Greaves Farm Caravan Site is situated in a flat, grassy farm orchard. Quiet but not isolated, there are two six-berth caravans for hire, each fully serviced with colour TV, etc., fridge, gas cooker and room heater and electricity for light, as well as sites for 20 caravans. On site there is a toilet block with showers and hot and cold water. Parking alongside caravans. Personally supervised by owner. Children and pets welcome. An ideal base for touring the Lakes. Caravan hire from £110 to £140 weekly and £3.50 per night for touring vans. Tourist Board registered. Contact **Mrs E. Rigg, Prospect House, Barber Green, Grange-over-Sands LA11 6HU (05395 36329).**

KENDAL. Mrs Nancy Waine, Murthwaite Farm, Longsleddale, Kendal LA8 9BA (053983 634).

Come and enjoy a quiet relaxing holiday in our six-berth caravan, sited in its own enclosed and secluded garden, on our traditional Lakeland hill farm nestling in Longsleddale, one of the loveliest valleys in the Lake District National Park. Ideal base for walking or touring. Situated six miles north of Kendal (A6 one and a half miles) and nine miles from Windermere. The caravan is fully equipped (except linen). Calor gas cooker and fire. Electricity for lights, water heater, toaster, fridge and colour TV. Flush toilet. Cleaniness guaranteed. Ample parking. Open March to November. Terms from £65 per week.

KENDAL. Mrs E. Bateman, High Underbrow Farm, Burneside, Kendal LA8 9AY (Kendal [0539] 721927). Working farm. Properties sleep 4/6. The caravan has end bedroom with two single beds, main compartment has two singles and one double bed. It is sited just off our private road before you get to the farmyard on a small piece of ground, fenced and mown. Lovely views and pleasant walks, ideal for touring Lake District and Yorkshire Dales. It has Calor gas cooker and fire, electric lights, fridge, fire, TV and shaving points. Flush toilet in van. Open March 1st to October 31st. Children and pets welcome. Shopping Burneside two miles; Kendal four. Weekly rates from £75. Holiday cottage (sleeps four) also to let from £95 weekly.

KESWICK. Setmabanning Farm, Threlkeld, Near Keswick. At Threlkeld, a genuine farm site, just off the
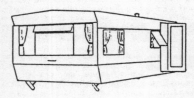
Keswick to Penrith road, with milking cattle and hill sheep, overlooking Saddleback with Helvellyn behind. River Glendermackin runs through the site, marvellous for walkers, within easy reach of Derwentwater, Ullswater, Grasmere and Windermere etc. Sailing, boating, steamer trips can be enjoyed. Wide choice of kingsize, excellently equipped, modern caravans with mains water and gas fires. TV. Flush toilets, hot and cold showers, shaver points, laundry room and pony trekking. Farm and village shop. Parking beside caravans. Special rates early and late, weekends a speciality. Rates from £65 – £159 weekly. SAE to **C.M.C. Holiday Caravans, 23 Brooks Road, Wylde Green, Sutton Coldfield B72 1HP (021-354-1551).**

LOWESWATER. Mrs M. Vickers, Askhill Farm, Loweswater, Cockermouth CA13 0SU (0946 861640). Situated in the beautiful unspoiled valley of Loweswater, four berth caravan on small farm site. 22 foot long, all electric (no meter), flush toilet nearby. Ideal for touring Western Lakes, Crummock, Buttermere, Ennerdale and Wastwater. This area has great appeal for country lovers with many holiday pursuits to enjoy including walking, hill climbing, pony trekking, trout fishing and boating. Within easy reach of the Solway coast (10 miles approximately) and the historic market town of Cockermouth, birthplace of William Wordsworth. SAE for details.

MILLOM. Mrs S.R. Capstick, Whicham Hall, Silecroft, Millom LA18 5LT (0229 772637). Working farm. Sleeps 6. Whicham Hall, situated in Whicham Valley, a beautiful unspoilt part of the Lake District, provides a perfect holiday for those who want a change from a busy noisy life. The large six-berth caravan on quarter-acre, very private site, has water, electricity, gas cooking and fridge and heating, also shower and flush toilet. The 300-acre beef and dairy farm is two miles from Silecroft beach and golf course, and 12 miles from Coniston. Silecroft post office and general store is just a mile away. Children are welcome, as are family pets. Open Easter to October. Weekly from £90. SAE, please, for further details.

NEWBY BRIDGE. Mr and Mrs A.S.N and A. Scott, Oak Head Caravan Park, Ayside, Grange-over-Sands LA11 6JA (Newby Bridge [05395] 31475). Established 1954 — family owned and operated. Select, quiet, clean, wooded site set in picturesque fells of South Lakeland. Easy access from M6, Junction 36; 14 miles to Ayside, 200 yards off main A590 road. Two miles to Lake Windermere and within easy travelling distance of all places of interest in Lake District. Static caravans are sited in wooded area on fully serviced pitches which have been carefully planned for owners' privacy. Tourers — hard standings set in trees, electric hook-ups. Campers — area terraced with pleasant outlook. One caravan to let, six berths; toilet, shower, H/C water, fridge, bunkroom, double bedroom, colour TV, all utensils, bedding. On site are deep freeze, flush toilets, hot showers, deep sinks for washing clothes, spin dryer, tumble dryer. Four-and-a-half miles from sea. Children, pets welcome. Open March to October. Static: £100 plus VAT per week; tourers £3.45 – £4.60 per night. There is also a bungalow to let, sleeps five. Tourist Board registered.

THRELKELD (near Keswick). A good range of well-equipped modern caravans available on a genuine farm site at Threlkeld, near Keswick. They have magnificent views and are most convenient for the northern Lakes. The site facilities include flush toilets, hot and cold showers, shaver points, a laundry room, and an on-site shop. Outdoor activities available nearby include pony trekking. **We specialise in early or late, cheap holidays.** Weekend lets available. Long SAE for details to: **Annable Holiday Caravans, 2 Spring Gardens, Watford, Hertfordshire WD2 6JJ (Garston [0923] 673946).**

DERBYSHIRE

ASHBOURNE. Mrs Louie Tatlow, Ashfield Farm, Calwich, Near Ashbourne DE6 2EB (Ellastone [033-524] 279 or 443). Working farm. Five modern six-berth caravans, fully equipped, each with gas cooker, fridge, TV; shower and toilet; mains electricity and sewer connection. Ashfield Farm overlooks the peaceful Dove Valley and is convenient for the Peak District. The old market town of Ashbourne only two miles away with golf course, swimming pool, squash and bowling. Within easy reach of stately homes like Haddon Hall and Chatsworth, with the Potteries and Lichfield 25 miles distant, Uttoxeter 10, while Alton Towers Theme Park is under five miles away. Write or telephone for further information.

ASHBOURNE. Mr S. Martin, The Alamo, Kniveton Wood, Ashbourne DE6 1JL (Ashbourne [0335] 42276). Situated two miles from Ashbourne, near Alton Towers, Chatsworth House and other beauty spots this six-berth caravan has panoramic views of Dovedale and Derbyshire Peaks. Spacious accommodation in separate bedroom; toilet and shower; full-size cooker, fridge, colour TV; electricity and gas. Children are welcome and babysitting can be arranged. Open all year. Terms from £75 per week, including electricity and gas.

BUXTON near. Mr and Mrs J. Melland, The Pomeroy Caravan Park, Street House Farm, Flagg, Near Buxton SK17 9QG (Longnor [029883] 259). √ √ √ Working farm. Sleeps 6. This newly developed site for 30 caravans is situated five miles from Buxton, in heart of Peak District National Park. Ideal base for touring by car or walking. Site adjoins northern end of now famous Tissington and High Peak Trail. Only nine miles from Haddon Hall and ten from Chatsworth House. Landscaped to the latest model standards for caravan sites; tourers and campers will find high standards here. New toilet block with showers, washing facilities and laundry; mains electric hook-up points. Back-packers welcome. Large rally field available. Tourist Board registered. Children welcome; dogs on lead. We now have six-berth 28ft x 10ft Holiday Van with separate end bedroom; hot and cold water; WC and shower. Fridge, full size gas cooker and fire, TV. Weekly rates only. Fully equipped except linen. Open Easter to end of October. SAE, please, for weekly and nightly rates.

CROMFORD. Mrs Beardsley, Woodseats Farm, Starkholmes Road, Cromford DE4 5JG (Matlock [0629] 56525). Traditional Derbyshire farm situated on a hillside overlooking the valley of the River Derwent and on the borders of the Peak District National Park. One mile distant from Cromford village and Matlock Bath, and two miles from Matlock. Ideally located for Chatsworth House, Haddon Hall, Crich Tramway Museum, and excellent walking country. Self-catering caravan to sleep six persons, set in quiet, secluded woodland, about half a mile from the road. Caravan has gas cooker and fire, electric lights, fridge, TV. Shower and toilet close by. Bed and Breakfast accommodation available in farmhouse, with Evening Meal by arrangement.

DERBYSHIRE – PEAK DISTRICT AND DALES!

The undulating dales set against the gritstone edges of the Pennine moors give Derbyshire its scenic wealth. In the tourists' itinerary should be the prehistoric monument at Arbor Low, the canal port of Shardlow, the country parks at Elvaston and Shipley, the limestone caves at Creswell Crags and Castleton and the market towns of Ashbourne and Bakewell. For walkers this area provides many excellent opportunities.

DEVON

ASHBURTON. Mrs Rhona Parker, Higher Mead Farm, Ashburton TQ13 7LJ (Ashburton [0364] 52598). Six-berth caravans, with showers. Free heating (gas/electric). Set on 270-acre farm on the edge of Dartmoor National Park, 12 miles from Torbay and 20 miles from Exeter and Plymouth, this site is central for touring Devon and Cornwall. Car parking space beside caravans. As the owner lives on site and supervises the cleaning, all caravans are spotless. Children, pets most welcome. 10 per cent reduction if only two occupy the caravan; mid-week bookings out of season. Also available, two three/four bedroom cottages. Please write or phone for free colour brochure.

BIDEFORD. Mrs J. Jackman, Greencliff Farm, Abbotsham, Bideford EX39 5BL (Bideford [0237]

473706). Sleeps 6. Spacious private site on a friendly mixed farm of 150 acres, with outlook to Clovelly, Hartland Point and Lundy Island. A popular pebble beach within 10 minutes' walk. Bideford and Westward Ho! are three miles away, the latter with sandy beach and golf course. Local attractions include leisure centres, riding stables, fishing, working farms and adventure schools. Very pleasant walking area. This six-berth caravan has double bedroom, two bunk rooms, flush toilet. Fully-equipped except linen. Gas cooker, otherwise all electric appliances including colour TV. Children and well-controlled pets welcome. Weekly terms from £65, including electricity and VAT. SAE please.

CHITTLEHAMHOLT (North Devon). Snapdown Farm Caravans, Chittlehamholt. Caravans sleep 6.

Twelve only, six-berth caravans, in two sheltered paddocks in lovely unspoilt countryside, down a quiet lane on a farm, sheltered by trees and well away from busy roads. Each caravan has hard standing for a car. Caravans are equipped with flush toilet, shower, fridge, colour TV, gas cooker and fire . Outside seats, picnic tables, barbecue. Table tennis. Children's play area in small wood adjoining. Laundry room with spin dryer, tumble dryer, iron, etc. Plenty of space field and woodland walks. No commercialism. Within easy reach of sea and moors. Well behaved pets welcome. Two types of caravan available. Terms: £45 to £110 inclusive and £55 to £145 inclusive. REDUCTIONS FOR COUPLES, EARLY AND LATE SEASON. Illustrated brochure from **Mrs M. Bowen, Snapdown, Chittlehamholt, Umberleigh, North Devon EX37 9PF (Chittlehamholt [07694] 708).**

COLYTON. Mrs S. Gould and Mrs R. Gould, Bonehayne Farm, Colyton EX13 6SG (Farway [040487]

416 or 396). Working farm. This is a six-berth B.K. Luxury caravan situated in a secluded spot in the farmhouse garden, overlooking the river, fields and woodlands where foxes, badgers and deer, Mallard duck and Kingfishers too are a common sight. There are farm animals to make friends with on this 250-acre farm and good trout fishing down on the river. The caravan contains a separate double end bedroom, kitchen with electric cooker and fridge. Large lounge dividing into two further double and bunk bedrooms. Mains water and electricity, toilet and shower room facilities. Fully equipped except linen. TV available. Farm produce obtainable from the house. Colyton two miles and the sea four-and-a-half miles. SAE please for full details.

CULLOMPTON. Mrs J. Davey, Pound Farm, Butterleigh, Cullompton EX15 1PH (Bickleigh [08845] 208). Working farm. Sleeps 6. A Pound Farm holiday combines finest English scenery with traditional beauty of village of Butterleigh. Enjoy family break from April to November on this 80-acre sheep and beef farm. Spacious comfortable caravan accommodation for six, in grass paddock with paths and parking for two cars. Enter by road. Well-equipped; linen hire by arrangement. Electric cooker, kettle, iron (plus ironing board), toaster, fridge, heater, electric blanket, colour TV, lights, four power points. All cutlery, utensils, blankets. Adjoining caravan has flush toilet, double drainer stainless steel sink unit in utility room with shaving point, hot/cold water, electric light and two-bar heater. Farmstead within sight of caravans. Four miles from M5, Cullompton, Tiverton, Silverton, Bickleigh; three miles from new North Devon Link road traditional thatched olde worlde village in heart of beautiful Exe Valley. Pets allowed. Our own two ponds (coarse and carp stocked in 1984 ; also roach, tench, perch, rudd) for private fishing only. Terms from £75 to £90. FHG Diploma Winner 1985. Coarse fishing all year round.

PLEASE ENCLOSE A STAMPED ADDRESSED ENVELOPE WITH ENQUIRIES

HOLIDAY ACCOMMODATION
Classification Schemes in
England, Scotland and Wales

The National Tourist Boards for England, Scotland and Wales have agreed a common 'Crown Classification' scheme for **serviced (Board)** accommodation. All establishments are inspected regularly and are given a classification indicating their level of facilities and services.

There are six grades ranging from 'Listed' to 'Five Crowns ♛♛♛♛♛'. The higher the classification, the more facilities and services offered.

Crown classification is a measure of *facilities* not *quality*. A common quality grading scheme grades the quality of establishments as 'Approved', 'Commended' or 'Highly Commended' according to the accommodation, welcome and service they provide.

For **Self-Catering**, holiday homes in England are awarded 'Keys' after inspection and can also be 'Approved', 'Commended' or 'Highly Commended' according to the facilities available. In Scotland the Crown scheme includes self-catering accommodation and Wales also has a voluntary inspection scheme for self-catering grading from '1 (Standard)' to '5 (Excellent)'.

Caravan and Camping Parks can participate in the British Holiday Parks grading scheme from 'Approved (√)' to 'Excellent (√ √ √ √ √)'. In addition, each National Tourist Board has an annual award for high-quality caravan accommodation: in England – Rose Awards; in Scotland – Thistle Commendations; in Wales – Dragon Awards.

When advertisers supply us with the information, FHG Publications show Crowns and other awards or gradings, including AA, RAC, Egon Ronay etc. We also award a small number of Farm Holiday Guide Diplomas every year, based on readers' recommendations.

EXETER near. Mr D.L. Salter, Haldon Lodge Farm, Kennford, Near Exeter EX6 7YG (Exeter [0392] 832312). Working farm. Peace and seclusion are assured

on this private residential site. The Salters offer a family holiday for all ages, with a special invitation to younger members to join in pony riding and enjoy a free and easy farm holiday with them. Exeter four and a half miles, Dawlish (short car drive away) ideal centre for touring all South Devon resorts and Dartmoor. The two luxury six-berth residential holiday caravans adjoin a large lawn with a background of fields, pine trees and rhododendrons. Six comfortable beds, blankets, pillows. Fully equipped kitchen, carpeted lounge with TV, bathroom (hot and cold), flush toilet, electricity and mains connected. Horses and ponies nearby are an interest to everyone. Horse lovers and children are invited to explore the beautiful Teign Valley Forest on horseback. Day pony treks are arranged for small parties. The well-known Nobody Inn is one of the attractive country inns where you can have a drink and a meal in a friendly atmosphere. Pets allowed. Riding and Trekking Holidays can be arranged. Caravans March to December from £65 per week. Tourers and campers at very reasonable daily charge. No extra charge for pets etc.

GOODRINGTON, PAIGNTON. Luxury holiday caravans (one, two and three bedrooms), all with colour television, shower, flush toilet, fridge, full size cooker, hot and cold water. No meters. *Licensed club and restaurant *Heated swimming pool *Supermarket and launderette *Close to beaches. For details send SAE to **Harpers Holiday Homes, Dept. 6, 5 Rydon Acres, Stoke Gabriel, Paignton, Devon TQ9 6QJ (080-428 692).**

HONITON. Mrs Sue Wigram, Riggles Farm, Upottery, Honiton EX14 0SP (Luppitt [0404] 891229). Working farm, join in. Sleeps 8. Four beautifully situated caravans on 450 acre dairy/arable farm, nine miles from Honiton, with easy access to many lovely beaches and local attractions. Visitors welcome on farm, where milk and eggs are sold. Children's play area, table tennis; cot and linen hire available; tumble and spin dryers. Caravans are in two peaceful acres near farmhouse. Each is fully equipped for two/eight people, with two separate bedrooms and spacious living areas. Own bathroom with shower, flush toilet, washbasin. Gas cooker, heater, colour TV, fridge. WCTB registered. Terms from £55 per week inclusive (10 per cent reductions for couples, not school holidays). For brochure please telephone or send SAE.

TEIGN VALLEY. S. and G. Harrison-Crawford, Silver Birches, Teign Valley, Trusham, Newton Abbot TQ13 0NJ (Chudleigh [0626] 852172). Two

luxury 23ft and 29ft four-berth caravans in an attractive two acre garden on the bank of the River Teign. Each has mains water, electricity, shower/bath, flush toilet, washbasin, immersion heater, Calor gas cooker, fridge; TV available. Ideally situated two miles from A38 on B3193. Dartmoor, Exeter, Torquay easily accessible. Sea 12 miles. Car essential, ample parking. Excellent centre for fishing (river and reservoir), bird watching, forest walks; 70 yards private salmon and trout fishing. Golf courses and horse-riding within easy reach. Shops two-and-a-half miles. Milk delivered. We personally clean caravans and ensure your comfort. Pets by arrangement. ETB registered. Open March-October. Terms from £75 per week. Bed and Breakfast available in bungalow from £16 nightly and from £112 weekly.

TOTNES. J. and E. Ball, Higher Well Farm Holiday Park, Stoke Gabriel, Totnes TQ9 6RN (080-428 289). √ √ A quiet secluded farm park welcoming tents, motor caravans and touring caravans. It is less than one mile from the riverside village of Stoke Gabriel and within four miles of Torbay beaches. Central for touring South Devon. Facilities include toilets, showers, launderette, shop, payphone and electric hook-ups. There are also static caravans to let. Enjoy a delightful relaxing holiday in the beautiful Devonshire countryside.

WOOLACOMBE. Caravans at Woolacombe. Well equipped, modern caravans, six-berth, available on well-maintained farm site. Three and a half miles of glorious sand. It is only a 10 minute walk from the site over cliffs to Rockham beach with its rock pools, sand and sheltered beach. Site facilities include a well-stocked shop, excellent toilet/shower block and laundry room. Long SAE for further details, please, to **Annable Caravans, 2 Spring Gardens, Watford, Herts WD2 6JJ (Garston [0923] 673946 after 5.00pm for personal response. 24-hour answering service).**

WHEN MAKING ENQUIRIES PLEASE MENTION
FARM HOLIDAY GUIDES

WOOLACOMBE. Twitchen House and Mortehoe Caravan Park, Woolacombe. LUXURY CARAVANS AT WOOLACOMBE.

Have a carefree and comfortable holiday in one of our Executive, luxury or modern caravans on this attractive, well equipped Rose Award Park graded √ √ √ √. Park facilities include heated pool, licensed club with two bars, snooker, activities room, games and family areas, free entertainment, shop, launderette, putting green, etc. We offer a wide selection of caravans all on concrete bases, having mains water and drainage, flush toilets, hot and cold water to sinks/shower, refrigerators, heating, TV, etc. Terms are fully inclusive from £70 per week, with special low rates/senior citizen discounts out of season. For colour brochure and tariff, SAE or phone **Woolacombe Caravan Hirers, Dept FHG, Garden Cottage, 27 East Street, Braunton EX33 2AE (0271 816580).**

WOOLACOMBE SANDS. CARAVANS TO LET. Farm site above Rockham Beach (only 500 yards).

Delightful situation in the heart of National Trust land, magnificent sea views. Famous three miles of Woolacombe Sands only one mile away. Marvellous walking, surfing. Magnificent coast for lovers of unspoilt beauty. Wide choice of new kingsize caravans (33 ft.) with toilet, shower, hot water, fridge, TV etc. Very well equipped, parking beside caravan. On site shop, laundry, showers, etc. Rates from £75 to £199. SAE, please **Morte Point Caravans, 17 South Road, Stourbridge, West Midlands (0384 395960).**

DORSET

ETB   **MANOR FARM HOLIDAY CENTRE**   WCTB

Charmouth, Bridport, Dorset

Situated in a rural valley. Charmouth beach a level ten minutes' walk away.

Luxury 6-berth Caravans for Hire with toilet/shower, refrigerator, full cooker, colour TV, gas fire.

30-acre Tourist Park for touring caravans, dormobiles and tents.

Centre facilities include * Toilets; * Hot showers; * Fish and chip takeaway; * Licensed bar with family room; * Amusement room; * Launderette; * Shop and off-licence; * Swimming pool; * Electric hook-up points; * Calor gas and Camping Gaz; * Ice pack service; * Chemical disposal unit.

Send SAE for colour brochure to Mr R. B. Loosmore or Tel: 0297 60226
See also Colour Display Advertisement in this Guide.

LYME REGIS. Mr and Mrs Corbin, Carswell Farm, Uplyme, Lyme Regis DT7 3XQ (Lyme Regis [02974] 2378). Carswell Farm is situated in a wooded valley two and a half miles from the sea. A working dairy/sheep farm with traditional jams and marmalades made on the farm. Ideal for family holidays with safe sandy beaches at Lyme Regis and Charmouth. Lovely walks, golf, fishing, riding nearby. Interesting places to visit. Four six-berth caravans (with inside flush toilet and shower). All have hot and cold water. Colour TV. Electric lights, gas fire and cooker, fridge, blankets/sleeping bags. Children are welcome and well controlled pets are allowed. Ample parking. Shops one mile (village). Available May to September. Terms: Weekly rates from £65. SAE for further details please.

LYME REGIS. Mrs C. Grymonprez, Beechfield Cottage, Yawl Hill Lane, Uplyme, Lyme Regis DT7 3RW (Lyme Regis [02974] 3216). Caravans sleep 4/8. Beechfield is a four-acre smallholding situated on Yawl Hill, commanding a truly scenic outlook over Lyme's countryside and the sea. It is conveniently located on the borders of Devon, Somerset and Dorset. To ensure utmost privacy we have a well-kept one acre field, hedge-screened and peaceful, set aside for only two modern caravans. Both are fully equipped (except linen), with fridge, mains electricity and water, inside flush toilet, shower, gas cooker and fire, TV. Cleanliness guaranteed. Lyme Regis is only two and a half miles away. Organically grown vegetables according to season and some herbs, free-range eggs and home-made bread are available. SAE appreciated.

LYME REGIS. Mrs J. Tedbury, Little Paddocks, Yawl Hill Lane, Lyme Regis DT7 3RW (Lyme Regis [029-74] 3085). Sleeps 6.

A six-berth caravan on Devon/Dorset border in a well-kept paddock overlooking Lyme Bay and surrounding countryside. Situated on a smallholding with animals, for perfect peace and quiet. Lyme Regis two-and-a-half miles, Charmouth three-and-a-half miles. Both have safe beaches for children. Easy driving distance to resorts of Seaton, Beer and Sidmouth. The caravan is fully equipped except linen. It has shower room with handbasin and toilet inside as well as flush toilet just outside. Electric light, fridge and TV. Calor gas cooker and fire. Car can be parked alongside. Dogs welcome. Terms from £65. SAE, please.

HEREFORD & WORCESTER

KINGTON. Mrs G. Lloyd, Upper Gwernilla, Colva, Kington HR5 3RA (Gladestry [054 422] 258). Sleeps 6/8. This hill farm, three miles inside Wales, has six/eight berth caravan for holiday letting all year round. Nearest golf course nine miles, though there are eight courses less than 45 minutes' drive away. Pony trekking five miles and ten miles. Offa's Dyke footpath one mile. Beautiful scenery with heather grouse moors. Hay-on-Wye, nine miles, has world's largest second-hand bookshop. Caravan has flush toilet, shower, electricity, gas cooker and TV, and is situated adjoining farmhouse and fields, 1000 feet above sea level. Children are welcome. Pets permitted. Good food can be obtained at local pub. Shopping facilities eight miles. Weekly rates from £90; mid-week bookings accepted.

LEOMINSTER. Miss P. Moore, Meadow Bank, Hamnish, Leominster HR6 0QN (Steensbridge [056-882] 267 or 254).

There are four caravans for hire on this farm, four to eight berths. They have mains water, colour TV, gas cooker, all necessary utensils etc., fridge and everything except personal linen. Flush toilets in all vans and most now have showers. Microwave if required. Small pony usually available and fishing, riding, hacking and driving; golf locally. Children welcome. Pets allowed under proper control. Phone box on site, also games room with snooker table. The only site rules are for reasonable peace and quiet, with friendly atmosphere. Facilities for touring vans and campers. Shops in Leominster, two miles, also swimming pool. Miss Moore enjoys people coming to stay at her caravans and helps in every way she can with information about interesting places to visit. Self-catering Riding Holidays are available most of the year, unaccompanied children catered for. Touring caravans and tents welcome. Terms according to season. Touring caravans available.

NORTHUMBERLAND

ALNWICK. Mrs J.W. Bowden, "Anvil-Kirk", 8 South Charlton Village, Alnwick NE66 2NA (Charlton Mires [066-579] 324). One six-berth caravan on single private site. Hard standing and lovely spacious surroundings. Three-quarters of a mile from the A1; six miles north of Alnwick and six miles also from the lovely clean beaches of Beadnell, Seahouses, Crestor Village; nine miles from the Cheviot Hills. Many castles nearby — Bamburgh and Alnwick being the largest; wild cattle and bird sanctuaries; Ingram Valley for the hill walker, Berwick and Morpeth markets. Holy Island is a must with its tiny castle and harbour with fishing boats. Many places to eat out within a radius of 10 miles. The caravan has mains water and electricity; electric cooker, fridge, TV. End bedroom (bunk beds); flush toilet in bathroom. Open Easter to October. Children and pets welcome. Milk and bread delivered, papers and greengrocery daily. Weekly terms from £75. Tourist Board one Rose award. SAE, please. Also Bed and Breakfast available in house.

SOMERSET

DULVERTON. Mrs M.M. Jones, Higher Town, Dulverton TA22 9RX (Anstey Mills [039-84] 272).

Working farm. Caravans sleep 8. Our farm is situated half a mile from open moorland, one mile from the Devon/Somerset border and four miles from Dulverton. 80 acres of the farm is in the Exmoor National Park. We let **two caravans** which are quarter of a mile apart and do not overlook each other, and have lovely views, situated in lawns with parking space. Both are eight berth, with a double end bedroom, bunk bedroom, shower, flush toilet, hot/cold water. One caravan has colour TV. The caravans are modern and fully equipped except linen. Cot and high chair available. Visitors are welcome to watch or walk over our beef and sheep farm. Riding and fishing nearby. Open May to October. Price from £60, includes gas and electricity.

WIVELISCOMBE. Richard and Marion Rottenbury, Oxenleaze Farm Caravans, Chipstable, Wiveliscombe TA4 2QH (Wiveliscombe [0984] 23427). √ √ √ √ This very picturesque and peaceful site is situated on the Devon/Somerset borders, close to Exmoor, amongst some beautiful countryside. 10 luxury caravans stand on one acre of a working hill farm. Each caravan has its own shower and flush toilet, hot and cold water, cooker, fridge, fire and colour TV. Parking beside each caravan. Car essential. The site offers games room, children's play area, sandpit, swings, barbecue, indoor swimming pool, laundry room, and to keen "Coarse Anglers", free fishing — a "Fisherman's Paradise", one-and-a-half acre ponds stocked with large carp and tench. "No Closed Season". Strictly no pets. Early bookings advised. ETB Rose Award for 1991. Open Easter to end October. Send stamp for colour brochure to **Richard and Marion Rottenbury.**

PLEASE ENCLOSE A STAMPED ADDRESSED ENVELOPE WITH ENQUIRIES

WIVELISCOMBE. Mrs J.P.E. Welch, Washers Farm, Raddington, Wiveliscombe TA4 2QW (Clayhanger [039-86] 269). Working farm, join in. Sleeps 6. Washers Farm is a 220-acre beef and sheep farm in glorious countryside on the fringe of Exmoor, easily accessible but peaceful and unspoilt. Steep combes adjoin the secluded single site where deer and other wildlife may be seen and which slopes down to a stream. The modern caravan is comfortable and spacious. Suitable for two to six persons. Calor gas, electricity and water connected; flush toilet inside. Refrigerator. Separate double bedroom. Children and well-controlled pets are very welcome around the farm. Lots of places to go and things to do, including fishing locally or on the farm. Exmoor a few miles, sea 15 miles. Open May to October from £55 weekly. Please telephone or send SAE.

EAST SUSSEX

BATTLE. Mrs D. Howard, Platnix Farm, Sedlescombe, Battle TN33 0RT (Sedlescombe [0424] 870 214). Large four-berth double caravan on sheep farm. Excellent facilities. Bathroom with flush toilet. Cot available. Only a 15 minute's drive to the sea, seven minutes to golf course and riding school. Good local fishing or free coarse fishing in lake on farm. Stabling available. Further details on request.

YORKSHIRE
EAST YORKSHIRE

·Far Grange Park·

One of the finest caravan parks on the East Coast of Yorkshire, with a superb cliff top location. First class facilities for families including leisure centre with snooker room, family entertainment rooms and lounge bars; adjacent to this is our 1¼ acre coarse fishing lake and children's adventure playground. Amenities include new supermarket, launderette, amusement arcade, fish and chip shops and excellent toilet facilites. 1½ miles south of Skipsea or 4½ miles north of Hornsea on the B1242. Also holiday homes for hire, all mains, 3 bedrooms, colour TV, microwave, fridge/freezer. Please telephone or write for brochure to:

Far Grange Park (Dept. L.), Windhook, Skipsea, Driffield, Yorkshire YO25 8SY.
Telephone: 026286 293-248.   AA ▶▶▶▶

ROSE AWARD CARAVAN HOLIDAY PARKS

NORTH YORKSHIRE

FILEY near. Mrs Joy Pickering, Stockendale Farm, Hunmanby, Near Filey YO14 0LE (Scarborough [0723] 890271). The 25' caravan is on a sheltered, grassy paddock, on an arable-stock farm which is situated on the edge of the Wolds overlooking farmland. It is four miles from Filey and approximately nine miles from both Scarborough and Bridlington. Hunmanby Village is one and a half miles (car essential) with ample shops plus launderette. In good area for touring Dales, Wolds, Moors and Forestry. The accommodation comprises one double and one twin bunk bedroom and two single bunks. It is well equipped except linen. Full cooker and heating by Calor Gas. Fridge, colour TV and shower. Electric lights; outside flush toilet close by. Children and pets welcome. For details send SAE, or telephone.

If you've found
FARM HOLIDAY GUIDES
of service please tell your friends

LITTLE HABTON, near Malton. Sue Thackray, Sunny Brow, Little Habton, Malton (0653 86 407).

Sleeps 2/7. Located in the heart of Ryedale, ideally situated for visiting the coast, North Yorkshire Moors and York. Sunny Brow Caravan is in its own enclosed garden in a quiet, secluded paddock next to the farm, which you are welcome to visit. The River Rye runs close by, ideal for fishing and canoeing (a large canoe is available). The spacious accommodation comprises two bedrooms, lounge with twin beds, kitchen/diner, WC, large porch with shower unit. Laundry facilities available if required. Both caravan and location are ideal for children, and cot, high chair and babysitting are available. Sorry, no pets. Terms from £50 per week, available all year. Phone or write for details.

SLINGSBY. Robin Hood Caravan and Camping Park, Slingsby, York YO6 7AU (Hovingham 0653 628 391). √ √ √ √ Sleeps 6/8. Beautifully situated in rural Ryedale, we offer an ideal touring base for Yorkshire Moors, Wolds and Coast. Castle Howard (Brideshead) is one-and-a-half miles; York is 17 miles; Helmsley 12 miles. Near to stately homes, steam railways, zoo, museums, fun park. Something for everyone! Fishing, golf, cycling, riding and walking all available nearby. Park is in picturesque village its amenities are 200 yards. The two-acre site is a well-sheltered super-dry sun trap offering luxury toilets, showers, laundry, wash-up facilities with hot and cold water, electric hook-ups, good shop, barbecue, separate playground. Disabled facilities. Open March to October. 41 units. Charges from £5 per night. Two hire caravans eight and six berth luxury models. AA three pennants.

THIRSK. Cleavehill Caravan Park, Thirsk. Working farm, join in. On the edge of the Yorkshire Moors and Dales, in the heart of Herriot country, Cleavehill offers 13 six/eight berth caravans sited in a field with uninterrupted views over the Vale of York towards the Pennines. Each is equipped with electricity and Calor gas for heating and cooking. There are toilet and shower facilities, plus a laundry room and freezer available. A truly restful centre for walking or touring. Children welcome. Yorkshire and Humberside Tourist Board registered. Brochure available from **Pamela Hoyle, Low Cleaves Farm, Sutton under Whitestonecliffe, Thirsk YO7 2PY (Thirsk [0845] 597229).**

WHITBY near. Mrs M. Cana, Partridge Nest Farm, Eskdaleside, Sleights, Whitby YO22 5ES (0947

810450). Set in beautiful Esk Valley, six caravans on secluded site in 45 acres of interesting land reaching up to the moors. Just five minutes from the sea and the ancient fishing town of Whitby. The North Yorkshire Moors Steam Railway starts two miles away at Grosmont. Ideal for children, birdwatchers and all country lovers. Each caravan has mains electricity, gas cooker, fire, colour TV, fridge and shower/WC. Ideal touring centre. Riding lessons available on our own horses/ponies. Terms from £85. Telephone or write with SAE, please.

WEST YORKSHIRE

SOUTH PENNINES. Mr Sunderland, Pennine Caravan Site, High Greenwood House, Heptonstall, Hebden Bridge HX7 7AZ (0422 842287). Caravans sleep 4/6. This is a small site overlooking Hardcastle Crags and the wooded Hebden Gorge. Central point for visits to Haworth (Bronte Country), Worth Valley Railway, The Pennine Way, "Emmerdale" and "Compo" country. Towns, cities and sports centre can also be reached as well as many beautiful walks and climbs. Wool and Mill shops. Clog factory. All in the Pennine centre of Hebden Bridge. Two six-berth and two four-berth caravans, all fully furnished, with water installed and having comfort of electric fires, kettles, blankets and lighting. Open all year.

ACTIVITY HOLIDAYS

CORNWALL, ST. NEOT. Mrs J.H. White, Hilltown Stud Farm, St. Neot, Liskeard PL14 6PT (0579 20565). Close to the moors with superb views, life on this small, peaceful farm revolves around its horses. Two self-catering cottages, carefully converted from old stone barn, make comfortable, friendly holiday homes for all ages. Visitors welcome to join in with farm activities. Drive the pony and trap, go fishing, meet the animals, riding for younger visitors. All this and lots more to do in an area that caters for hundreds of different tastes. Colour TV, baby-sitting, home laundry, etc available. Phone or write for details.

HILLTOWN

CUMBRIA, WASDALE. Mr David Killick, Old Strands Cottage, Mountain-Walking Holidays for Children, Wasdale CA20 1ET (09467 26258). Children aged 10–14 can enjoy guided walks to the summits of England's highest mountains, based in the dramatic valley of Wasdale. Superb views of the nearby screes above Wastwater, England's deepest lake; Scafell Pike, England's highest peak and Great Gable. Accommodation is in part of one-time farmhouse, 200 years old, but recently modernised. Only four children accepted at a time. Their guide and host, David Killick, is a very experienced and well qualified mountain leader. Table tennis and other games available. Good food and good fun for energetic and willing children. £98 per week. Phone for brochure (24 hour answering service).

DEVON, ASHBURTON. Mrs Rhona Parker, Higher Mead Farm, Ashburton TQ13 7LJ (Ashburton [0364] 52598). Six-berth caravans, mains services and showers. Free heating gas/electric. Cars park by caravans. Central for touring Devon or Cornwall. Caravans set in 270 acre farm on edge of Dartmoor National Park. Torbay 12 miles, Exeter and Plymouth 20 miles. Shop and laundry on-site. Owner lives on site and supervises cleaning. All caravans spotless. A 10 per cent reduction if only two occupy caravan. Mid week bookings, out of season. Children and pets most welcome. Genuine farm site. Also available, two three/four bedroom cottages. Please write or phone for free colour brochure.

DEVON, EXETER near. Mr D. L. Salter, Haldon Lodge Farm, Kennford, Near Exeter EX6 7YG (Exeter [0392] 832312). Working farm. Peace and seclusion are assured on this private residential site. The Salters offer a family holiday for all ages, with a special invitation to younger members to join in pony riding and enjoy a free and easy farm holiday with them. Exeter four-and-a-half miles. Dawlish (short car drive away) ideal centre for touring all South Devon resorts and Dartmoor. The three six-berth residential holiday caravans adjoin a large lawn with a background of fields, pine trees, rhododendrons. Six comfortable beds, blankets, pillows. Fully equipped kitchen, carpeted lounge (TV), bathroom (H/C), flush toilet, electricity and mains connected. Horses and ponies nearby are an interest to everyone. Horse lovers and children we invite to explore the beautiful Teign Valley forest on horseback. Day pony treks arranged for small parties. The well-known

Nobody Inn is one of the many attractive country inns where you can have a drink and a meal in the midst of a friendly atmosphere. Pets allowed. Riding and Trekking Holidays from £35 per week. Caravans March to December from £40 per week. Tourers from £2.50 per day. Campers from £2 per day. No extra charge for pets etc.

DEVON, NEWTON FERRERS. Mr A. Thomson, Newton Ferrers Sailing School, Yealm Road, Newton Ferrers PL8 1BJ (Plymouth [0752] 872375). Sailing courses for adults and children; RYA approved. Qualified tuition in traditional dayboats and toppers. Accommodation with good food and comfortable beds in The Headquarters, or we will be pleased to advise about other accommodation in the area, and a caravan and campsite is nearby. Tuition is given on the open sea or in the bay, but if the weather conditions do not permit, we can usually sail on the river. River and estuary lie in the midst of National Trust Woodlands and abound in wildlife. Spectacular walks along the coast path and nearby village inns for those who wish to explore in the evenings. Friendly and informal atmosphere and club room. Board from £105 weekly, Bed and Breakfast from £10.50 nightly. Full details on request.

GLOUCESTERSHIRE, DYMOCK. Gill Bennett, Lower House Farm, Kempley, Dymock GL18 2BS (053185-301). Working farm, join in. Children's holiday 6-12 years on family dairy farm. Small number taken as guests of family. Pony riding daily, fishing, swimming, trips to castles, Falconry Centre, Butterfly Farm. Good home cooked food, vegetables from garden. Feed calves, hens, collect eggs. Picnics and barbecues, fun and activities to suit individual children, making their first independent holiday enjoyable. From £150 per week per child all inclusive. Also self-contained wing of farmhouse, sleeps six. Authentic beams, tastefully furnished. Riding or walking in adjoining 1300 acre wood; golf, fishing; visit Malverns, Forest of Dean, Wye Valley and Cotswolds. Bed and Breakfast from £12.50 per day. Self-catering from £130 per week.

NORTH YORKSHIRE, MALTON. Mrs Jenny Floris, Low Easthorpe Farm, Easthorpe, Near Malton YO17 0QX (Malton [0653] 695006). 🐾 🐾 Low Easthorpe Farm is situated in beautiful countryside with splendid views towards Castle Howard. Everything for the happy family holiday with plenty of animals for the children to help feed. Supervised riding available. Comfortable bedrooms, two double, one family with four-poster beds, beamed ceilings, washbasins, tea making facilities and full central heating. Ideal base for visiting York, the coast, Dales, North Yorkshire Moors and many historic sites. Sporting activities nearby include golf, bowling, tennis, swimming etc. Bed and Breakfast from £12.50. Reductions for children. Pets welcome. Babysitting service. Family-run restaurant nearby. Open all year. Car essential.

WILTSHIRE, MARLBOROUGH. Mr David Green, Marlborough College Summer School, Marlborough SN8 1PA (Marlborough [0672] 513888). The Marlborough College Summer School offers over 70 different weekly courses for adults and children (over the age of 7) for residents and non-residents. Courses include Sports, Hobbies and Interests, Music, Languages, Arts and Crafts etc. Accommodation is in the college and consists of mainly single rooms, although some double rooms, family rooms and dormitories are available. All meals are included and a full range of evening activities is available at no extra charge. The Summer School operates during the last two weeks of July and the first week of August. Brochures can be obtained from the Secretary.

Hungry sheep are always ready for roadside titbits on the Horseshoe Pass, near Llangollen, North Wales.

WALES

BOARD ACCOMMODATION

CLWYD

COLWYN BAY. Mrs Webb, Plas Newydd Farm, Llanddulas, Abergele LL22 8HH (Colwyn Bay [0492] 516038). ♥ ♥ A warm and friendly atmosphere awaits you at our 17th century farmhouse set in the lovely Dulas Valley, just one and a half miles from the sea and A55 coast road. Ideal base for touring coast and countryside. Bedrooms are of a high standard, with modern facilities. Cosy evenings can be spent in beamed sittingroom with log fire and colour TV. Open April to October for Bed and Breakfast from £12.50. Children welcome but sorry, no pets. To get here take A55, turn off at Llanddulas, through village, turn right along Beulah Avenue for one and a quarter miles along leafy lane.

CORWEN. Mrs Menna L. Williams, Caenog Farm, Corwen LL21 9DB (0490 2381). Situated two miles from the A5, this 420 acre mixed farm has a big spacious house, parts of which are over 400 years old and oak beamed. Excellent centre for beaches, mountains, lakes, fishing and lovely walks. Sports facilities in the area. Spacious garden with freedom for children who are very welcome. Good farmhouse food and personal attention assures guests of a typical warm Welsh welcome. Free home made cake is served with bedtime drink. Open May to September. Car essential, parking. Cot and babysitting by arrangement. Sorry, no pets. Bed, Breakfast and Evening Meal or Bed and Breakfast only. Reductions for children. Soap and towels provided. SAE, for terms.

FLINT. Mrs J.A. Hulme, Oakenholt Farm, Chester Road, Flint CH6 5SU (03526 3264). ♥ ♥

Commended. **Working farm, join in.** Oakenholt Farm is an active 84 acre dairy and sheep farm, with calves and often pet lambs. 200 yards from the main A584 road, it is quietly situated but convenient for touring North Wales, visiting Chester, 13 miles away, and local places of interest. The farmhouse dates back to 1450 and is a Grade II listed building with beamed hall and TV lounge. Accommodation comprises three bedrooms (two double, one twin), two with washbasins and all with shaver points and tea/coffee making facilities; guest bathroom with shower. Children very welcome — large safe playing area and garden. Sorry, no pets. No smoking. Open for Bed and Breakfast from January to December, with terms from £12 for adults.

CLWYD – MOUNTAINS, RESORTS AND CASTLES

A mountainous county with pleasant resorts such as Colwyn Bay and Rhyl on its north coast and a number of castles, including Chirk, Denbigh, Ewloe, Flint, Hawarden and Ruthin. Gresford parish church, Corwen, Ruthin, the church at Llanrhaeadr and the Pontcysyllte aqueduct are also worth visiting.

AA Listed   **BWLCH Y RHIW FARM**   🌑🌑🌑
Llansilin, Near Oswestry, Shropshire SY10 7PT

FOR THE DISCERNING

Enjoy the peace and tranquillity of this little-known area which is nevertheless so central for North and Mid-Wales, Chester, Shrewsbury, Llangollen, to name only a few of the many places of interest. The 18th century stone farmhouse affords wonderful views over the surrounding countryside and sheep farm. Country lovers can enjoy waterfalls, lakes, forests and excellent scenic walks plus birdwatching, farm activities, etc. We are 4½ miles from Oswestry on B4580, easy to find! The three spacious bedrooms have bathrooms en-suite, are centrally heated, with colour TV, radio and tea/coffee making facilities. There is a large restful lounge and the old oak dining room is full of character. A car is essential here. We offer Bed and Breakfast only, from £15.00 per person. Several good eating places for Evening Meals. Children aged 8 and over are welcome. Sorry, no dogs. Some fishing, horse riding/trekking; pottery and wood turning courses available. Terms on request.

Brochure from Mrs A.M. Gallagher   **(Llansilin [0691 70] 261)**

RUTHIN. Mrs E.O. Jones, Llanbenwch Farm, Llanfair D.C., Ruthin LL15 2SH (Ruthin [08242] 2340). Working farm. 🌑🌑 Situated three miles from Ruthin, on the main (A525) Wrexham road, this is a 40-acre farm amidst beautiful scenery. The old house, oak-beamed and modernised without spoiling its character, is conveniently situated for travelling throughout North Wales. There is a nice garden and quiet roads for evening walks and mountain roads for driving. Good food is assured, with personal attention. One family, two double bedrooms, all with washbasins, TV and tea-making facilities; bathroom, two toilets; diningroom with separate tables, sittingroom with TV. Central heating. Sorry, no dogs in house and no children under five years. Ample parking. Open February to November for Evening Dinner/Meal, Bed and Breakfast £13.50 daily, £90 weekly; Bed and Breakfast from £9. SAE, please, for reply. Wales Tourist Board Farmhouse Award, AA listed, Relais Routiers approved.

ST. ASAPH. Anwen Roberts, Bach-y-Graig, Tremeirchion, St. Asaph LL17 0UH (074-574 627 or

early 1991 0745 730627). 🌑🌑🌑 *Commended.* A 16th century listed farmhouse nestling at the foot of the Clwydian Range with beautiful views of the surrounding countryside. Highest standard of traditional furnishings and decor, en-suite, TVs, brass beds, tea/coffee making facilities in bedrooms; full central heating, beamed inglenook fireplace with log fires. Central for North Wales, Chester, coast nine miles. Games room. 40 acre woodland trail on farm. AA selected award. Bed and Breakfast from £14 to £15; Evening Meal £8. Brochure available.

ST. ASAPH. Mrs Eirlys Jones, Rhewl Farm, Waen, St. Asaph LL17 0DT (0745 582287). 🌑🌑 Enjoy

Welsh hospitality on our 180 acre farm in the beautiful Vale of Clwyd. We are conveniently situated half a mile from A55 expressway, halfway between Chester and Snowdonia in a peaceful setting with extensive views. Comfortable 18th century farmhouse has double, family and twin bedrooms, one with en-suite facilities, all with washbasins, radiators, shaver points and tea-making facilities. Spacious lounge with inglenook fireplace and colour TV. Games room for children. Excellent breakfasts. Ideal base for touring North Wales within easy reach of many top tourist attractions. Pleasant walks nearby including Offa's Dyke path. Free fishing on farm.

🌑🌑🌑🌑🌑
♟♟♟♟♟

HOLIDAY ACCOMMODATION
Classification Schemes in
England, Scotland and Wales

DYFED

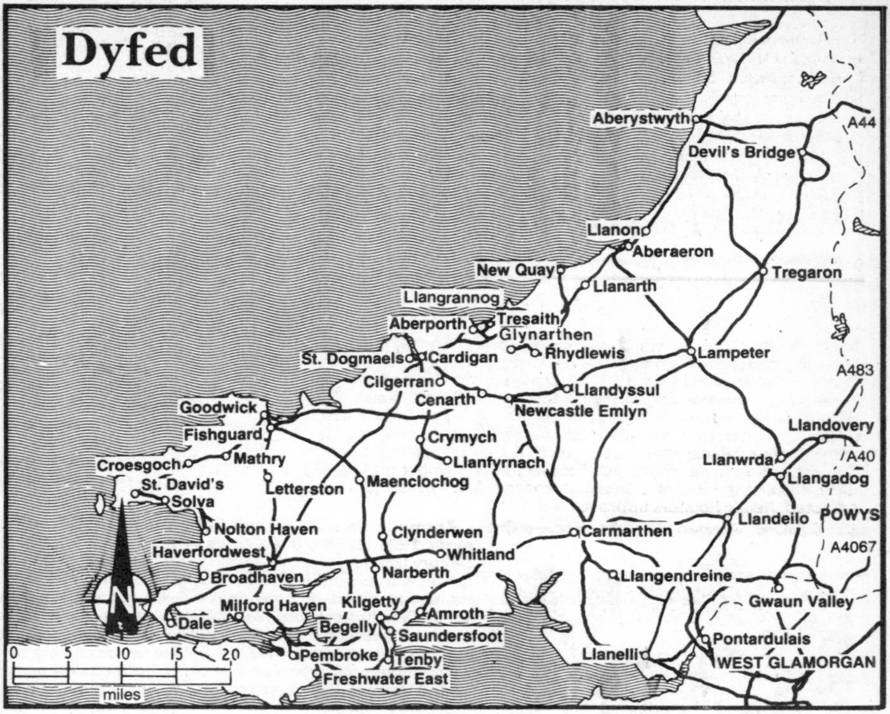

ABERPORTH. Mr and Mrs A.J. Davis, Glandwr Manor Hotel, Tresaith, Aberporth, Cardigan SA43 2JH (Aberporth [0239] 810197). ♛♛♛ Glandwr Manor is a large "listed" 17th century manor house, designed by John Nash, approached by a drive of 400 yards in its own five acres of secluded country. The sea, with beautiful sandy beaches, is five minutes' walk away. Four double, one single bedrooms and two family suites. Most bedrooms have en-suite facilities. Electric wall-heaters and electric blankets for comfort in cold spells during off-peak holidays. Some bedrooms have sea views. Comfortable residents' lounge with colour TV; bar and diningroom with stone fireplace, open log fire, beamed ceiling. The restaurant, popular with locals during the winter, offers a good selection of wines, fresh food, including local salmon and crab, and fresh cream desserts are always on the menu. Children are welcome at reduced rates, cot is available. Car essential, ample parking. Open March to October inclusive. SAE, please. AA One Star.

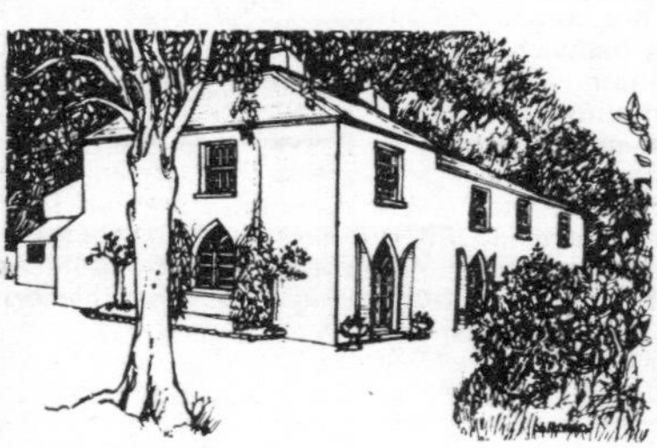

ABERYSTWYTH. Mrs Elaine Lewis, Erwbarfe Farmhouse, Devil's Bridge, Aberystwyth SY23 3JR (Ponterwyd [097 085] 251). ♛♛ Erwbarfe Farmhouse is situated on a 400 acre mixed hill farm set in breathtaking scenery between Devil's Bridge and Ponterwyd. Nearby are the Devil's Bridge Falls and Vale of Rheidol Steam Railway. Fishing at Nant y Moch and Dinas Reservoirs. Pony trekking, bird watching (Red Kite area) and walking are favourite pastimes. An ideal centre for touring Wales, market and University town of Aberystwyth at Cardigan Bay 20 minute drive. Accommodation comprises one double and one family bedrooms with H&C, tea/coffee makers, clock radios; oak beamed lounge with colour TV; separate diningroom. Children welcome. Sorry, no pets. Car essential, ample parking. Good wholesome meals using fresh produce. Wales Farmhouse Award.

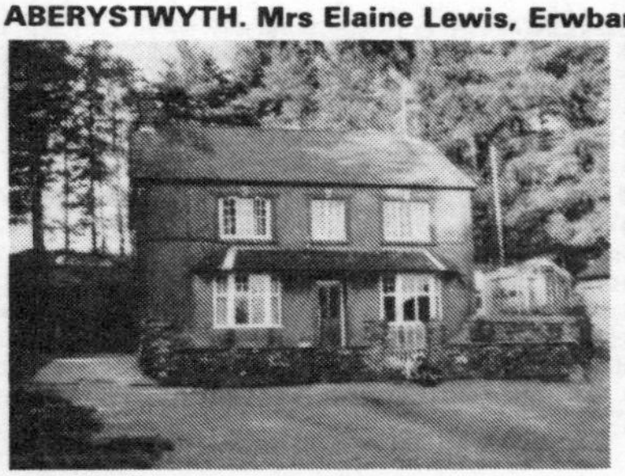

HAVERFORDWEST. Joyce Canton, Nolton Haven Farmhouse, Nolton Haven Farm, Nolton Haven, Haverfordwest SA61 1NH (0437 710263). The farm-

house, on a 170-acre farm, is just 30 yards from Nolton Haven's sandy beach and is ideal for families wishing a restful holiday. Situated on the central St. Bride's Coast, handy for touring and within easy reach of pony trekking, good cliff walks, swimming, fishing, surfing and boating facilities. More than six miles of golden sands within a five mile radius. Children's ponies on farm. Double, single and family bedrooms, some ensuite and all with washbasins; four bathrooms, four toilets; two sittingrooms, one with colour TV, diningroom. Ample facilities and reduced rates for children. Pets allowed. Parking. Open all year. Evening Dinner, Bed and Breakfast or Bed and Breakfast only. SAE, please.

HAVERFORDWEST. Mrs Nesta Thomas, Lower Haythog Farm, Spittal, Haverfordwest SA62 5QL (0437 731 279). ✿ ✿ Working farm, join in. Peace and

relaxation can be enjoyed at our old farmhouse, set in 250 acres of picturesque, unspoilt countryside five miles north of Haverfordwest. Centrally situated for all the beauty spots, on a dairy farm where home cooking, warm hospitality and laughter are assured. Comfortable lounge heated by log fire, with colour TV, books, games for guests' use; separate diningroom. Two family, one double, one single bedroom with washbasins. Cot, high chair, washing and drying facili-ties for guests with small children and babies. Fish for trout in the brook or ponds — abundance of wild life — pony rides. Pets by arrangement. Bed, Breakfast and Evening Meal. Open all year. AA listed, WTB Award. Fire certificate. Brochure on request.

HAVERFORDWEST. Mrs Susan Evans, Spittal Cross Farm, Spittal, Haverfordwest SA62 5DB (0437-87 206). Working farm. A family run dairy farm, in

the heart of the beautiful Pembrokeshire countryside, making it a convenient touring base for the many local activities, beaches and places of historic interest. We offer a full English Breakfast, Evening Dinner is optional, bedtime drinks inclus-ive. Reduced rates for children. Cot, high chair and baby-sitting offered. Accommodation consists of one family and one double rooms, all with washbasins and tea/coffee making facilities; bathroom, two toilets; sitting/diningroom with colour TV; games and books for guests' use. Central heating throughout. A self-catering cottage is also available. Please write or telephone for our brochure.

HAVERFORDWEST. Mrs D.G. James, Woodson, Lower Thornton, Milford Haven, Haverfordwest SA73 3UQ (Haverfordwest [0437] 890358). ✿ Working farm, join in. A warm welcome is assured on this family run farm of 200 acres, situated in a beautiful area for beaches, touring and many other interests. Accommodation comprises two double and two family rooms, all with washbasins and tea making facilities. Children catered for. Pets welcome. Bed and Breakfast and/or Evening Meal. Bed and Breakfast, from £12 for adults. Rates on request for Evening Meal. Reductions for children and OAP's. A car is recommended and there is parking. Open March until October.

HAVERFORDWEST. Mrs M. Lewis, Honey Hook Farm, Portfieldgate, Haverfordwest, Pem-brokeshire (Camrose [0437] 710495). Quietly situated down a tree-lined drive, Honey Hook Farm is three miles west of Haverfordwest and two miles from sandy beaches of the west coast of Pembrokeshire. Central for touring all parts of the county, plenty of space for quiet country walks and for children to play in safety. Car essential. Family room, double and single available; two bathrooms; TV lounge. Ample facilities and reduced rates for children. Open May-September. Bed and Breakfast from £8. Please phone or write for details.

| See also Colour Display Advertisement | **HAVERFORDWEST. Mrs M. Jones, Lochmeyler Farm, Pen-y-Cwm, Near Solva, Haverfordwest SA62 6LL (0348 837724/837705). ✿ ✿ ✿** A 220 acre dairy farm situated in centre of St. David's Peninsula, two and a half miles from coastal path, four miles from Solva Harbour, six miles from St. David's. The 11th century farmhouse has been modernised but still retains its olde worlde character with beams and open fires in early and late season. Five en-suite bedrooms with colour TV, video video library available. Tea making facilities, electric blankets, clock radios, hair dryers and telephone. Some rooms have four poster beds. Two lounges (one for smokers). Spacious diningroom with separate tables. Traditional farmhouse fare and vegetarians can be catered for. Plenty of wildlife trails, pond and streams. Children over 10 years welcome. Dogs accepted free if they stay in the outside kennels or in the owner's car. Open all year round. Brochure available.

HAVERFORDWEST. Mrs Judith Williams, Knock Farm, Camrose, Haverfordwest SA62 6HW (0437

2208). Knock Farm is a 275 acre working dairy farm, situated in a scenic valley, 10 minutes' drive from Pembrokeshire's sandy beaches and two miles from the county town of Haverfordwest. Children welcome, lots of farm animals and pets for them to see. Good home cooking with meals prepared from our home produce. TV lounge available all day and central heating throughout. Babysitting free. Pets welcome. Terms on request. Bedtime drinks free. Reductions for children. Wales Tourist Board approved.

Knock Farm
FARMHOUSE HOLIDAYS
Camrose, Haverfordwest, Dyfed, SA62 6HW.
Proprietors: John and Judith Williams. Tel: Haverfordwest 0437 2208.

HAVERFORDWEST. Mrs M.E. Davies, Cuckoo Mill Farm, Pelcomb Bridge, St. David's Road, Haverfordwest SA62 6EA (0437-76 2139). Working farm. This farm is situated in central Pembrokeshire, two miles out of Haverfordwest on St. David's road. It is within easy reach of many beaches and coastline walks. There are peaceful country walks on the farm, also a small trout stream. Children are welcome at reduced rates and cot, high chair and babysitting provided. The house is cosy with open fires and welcomes guests from January to December. Car is not essential, but parking available. Home-produced dairy products; poultry and meats all home-cooked. Mealtimes arranged to suit guests. Two family, one double, one twin-bedded and one single bedrooms. Two bathrooms. Sittingroom, two diningrooms. Pets permitted. Evening Dinner/Meal, Bed and Breakfast or Bed and Breakfast only. Rates also reduced for senior citizens. Tourist Board listed.

HAVERFORDWEST near. Mrs Gloria Davies, Olmarch Farm, Llandeloy, Near Haverfordwest SA62

6NB (03483 247). Working farm, join in. Recently modernised stone-built farmhouse on a 175 acre mixed dairy farm situated within six miles of St. David's, and ten minutes' drive from many beautiful sandy beaches. Bedrooms are comfortable and spacious, one with en suite shower and washbasin; one family room and one twin-bedded room. Good home cooking is provided using much of our own produce. Lawns for children's use. Open March to October. Bed and Breakfast from £13; Evening Meal from £6. Tourist Board Listed.

FOR THE MUTUAL GUIDANCE
OF GUEST AND HOST

Every year literally thousands of holidays, short-breaks and overnight stops are arranged through our guides, the vast majority without any problems at all. In a handful of cases, however, difficulties do arise about bookings, which often could have been prevented from the outset.

It is important to remember that when accommodation has been booked, both parties — guests and hosts — have entered into a form of contract. We hope that the following points will provide helpful guidance.

GUESTS: When enquiring about accommodation, be as precise as possible. Give exact dates, numbers in your party and the ages of any children. State the number and type of rooms wanted and also what catering you require — bed and breakfast, full board, etc. Make sure that the position about evening meals is clear — and about pets, reductions for children or any other special points.

Read our reviews carefully to ensure that the proprietors you are going to contact can supply what you want. Ask for a letter confirming all arrangements, if possible.

If you have to cancel, do so as soon as possible. Proprietors do have the right to retain deposits and under certain circumstances to charge for cancelled holidays if adequate notice is not given and they cannot re-let the accommodation.

HOSTS: Give details about your facilities and about any special conditions. Explain your deposit system clearly and arrangements for cancellations, charges, etc, and whether or not your terms include VAT.

If for any reason you are unable to fulfil an agreed booking without adequate notice, you may be under an obligation to arrange alternative suitable accommodation or to make some form of compensation.

While every effort is made to ensure accuracy, we regret that FHG Publications cannot accept responsibility for errors, omissions or misrepresentation in our entries or any consequences thereof. Prices in particular should be checked because we go to press early. We will follow up complaints but cannot act as arbiters or agents for either party.

HAVERFORDWEST. Mrs B. Charles, Torbant Farm Guest House, Croesgoch, Haverfordwest SA62

5JN (Croesgoch 0348 831276). ☙☙ Working farm, join in. The 300-year-old farmhouse is situated on a 110-acre mixed farm just off Fishguard/St. David's road. Guests are welcome to explore. The house has been fully modernised for comfort. Large diningroom has separate tables for each family, and leads directly onto sunny patio and garden. Comfortable bar lounge, and also another lounge for peaceful relaxation; colour TV. Six bedrooms (three en-suite). Utility room. Central heating. Cot, high chair and babysitting available. Garden has swings and ample room for children's play. Car essential — parking. Open Easter to October. Sorry, no dogs. There are cliff walks, sandy beaches and much of interest in this beautiful area. Sea one and a half miles. Fishguard nine miles, St. David's six, Croesgoch one. From £115 per week half board. AA/RAC listed.

HAVERFORDWEST. Mrs A.M. Roberts, Haroldston Tongues Farm, Portfield Gate, Haverfordwest SA62 3LE (Broad Haven [0437] 781287). ☙☙ Working farm, join in. This comfortable farmhouse on a working dairy farm with lovely views of the Prescelly Hills is excellently situated being near the sandy beaches; Broad Haven two miles, Newgale three, St. David's 13. Island of Skomer worth visiting especially in May and June. Riding for novice or expert one mile away. Two double rooms, one twin-bedded, one bunk-bedded room, all with washbasins; bathroom, shower room and three toilets; TV lounge; quiet sitting area in large L-shaped diningroom. Children welcome, cot and babysitting. Sorry, no pets in house and no smoking in bedrooms and diningroom. Open March to November with central heating. Car essential, parking. Evening Dinner, Bed and Breakfast; Bed and Breakfast. Rates reduced for children, and for senior citizens in low season. Terms on request. SAE, please.

LAMPETER. Mrs E.M. Davies, Tan-yr-Allt Farm, Ciliau Aeron, Lampeter SA48 8BU (Aeron [0570] 470211). Relax in the homely and luxurious atmosphere of a country farmhouse on a 60-acre mixed farm. Situated in the well known Vale of Aeron on the A482 Lampeter/Aberaeron road, with salmon and trout fishing, four miles from a beach where safe swimming, boating and surfing can be enjoyed. Centrally located for touring in the unspoilt Aeron Valley. Pony trekking locally. Accommodation comprises two bedrooms, heating and washbasins in both. Sittingroom, TV room. Children welcome (reduced rates). Bed and Breakfast only, terms from £10. SAE, please.

LLANARTH near. Mrs K. Dunn, Parc Farm, Derewen Gam, Oakford, Near Llanarth SA47 0RX (0545

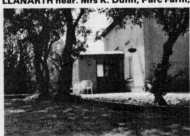

580390). Parc Farm and its holiday cottage are set on a 14 acre working farm, over which there is complete freedom to roam. Situated amidst beautiful farmland and quiet wooded valley close to the sea. Only minutes from Aberaeron and New Quay. Bed and Breakfast accommodation for up to six persons and a fully licensed restaurant provides Evening Meals. Also available Parc Farm Holiday Cottage, tastefully converted and providing all home comforts with central heating and carpets throughout. Fully equipped, sleeping six persons. Brochure available.

LLANDYSUL. Mrs Carole Jacobs, Broniwan, Rhydlewis, Llandysul SA44 5PF (Rhydlewis [023-

975] 261). ☙☙ Broniwan offers a warm welcome and a relaxing holiday to guests, their children and pets. The attractive stone-built farmhouse, ten minutes' drive from Cardigan's sandy coast and standing amidst beech and pine trees, has lovely views from its wood panelled windows. Ideally situated for exploring the West Wales countryside with opportunities for birdwatching, walking, fishing, pony trekking and golf. There are three comfortable bedrooms with washbasins, one with en-suite facilities, sittingroom with log fire and books, games room in barn for children who may join in farm activities. Generous meals, including vegetarian, using fresh home-grown produce. Bed and Breakfast from £13. Guestaccom Good Room Award. WTB Farmhouse Award.

Terms quoted in this publication may be subject to increase if rises in costs necessitate

LLANON. Keith and Christine Chapman, Bikerehyd Farm and Farmhouse Restaurant, Pennant, Llanon SY23 5PB (0974 272 365).

Bikerehyd Farm is part of the remains of a 14th century village. Three quaint cottages with shower and toilet en-suite; TV, etc. Central heating. In the warm and comfortable farmhouse there is an excellent licensed restaurant serving dinners, à la carte menu available (Breakfast and tea/coffee making facilities in rooms). TV lounge for house guests. Ideally situated to enable visitors to see many places of scenic and historic interest; Aberystwyth 12 miles. Children welcome, free accommodation if under 12 years. Car parking. Family cottage also available. Bed and Breakfast from £19.50 to £22.50 per person per day (double room), £135 weekly. AA listed. Wales Tourist Board award.

LLANTOOD. Andy and Sylvie Gow, Croft Farm Guesthouse, Llantood, Cardigan SA43 3NT (Cardigan [0239] 615179). 🌸 🌸 🌸 Working farm, join in.

A warm welcome awaits you at Croft Farm Guesthouse situated in unspoilt countryside near to sandy beaches, coastal paths and National Park. Croft is a working small-holding with farm animals and pets' corner. The guesthouse has been lovingly and beautifully refurbished. All rooms have en-suite or private facilities; tea/coffee trays. There is a relaxing sittingroom and separate TV lounge. Delicious home cooked meals, using fresh local produce where possible. Vegetarians welcome. Licensed. Bed and Breakfast from £12. Dinner three courses, coffee from £6.95. Special weekly and child tariffs. Off season short breaks available. Three miles out of Cardigan on A487 towards Fishguard.

LLAWHADEN. Mrs P.A. Couling, Whiteleys Farm, Llawhaden, Narberth SA67 8DG (Llawhaden [09914] 335 or [0437-541] 335).

Whiteleys Farm, a dairy farm with additional sheep and beef cattle, lies one mile north of the A40 Canaston Bridge. Within easy motoring distance of all Pembrokeshire sandy beaches, Preseli Mountains, forest walks in National Park, Oakwood Leisure Park, and fishing at Llys y Fran Dam. Generous hospitality awaits you in the 100-year-old farmhouse, with colour TVs, hot and cold water, and tea-making facilities in most rooms. All vegetables are organically grown and meat is home produced. We serve typical farmhouse-style meals. There is a lawn for children to play on. Bed and Breakfast from £9, optional Evening Meal from £6.

NARBERTH. Naomi and Ken Jones, Highland Grange Farm, Robeston Wathen, Narberth, Pembrokeshire SA67 8EP (0834 860952). 🌸 🌸 Naomi and Ken Jones and family invite you to visit their 220 acre beef and sheep farm. Excellent situation on the A40 in a central position for touring the Pembrokeshire Peninsula. Superior modern farmhouse. Delicious home cooking with four-course Dinner, Morning Tea, Evening Beverages. Accent on healthy eating. Home-made bread, muesli, gateaux, pate etc. Organic vegetable garden. Log fires, central heating. All ages welcome. Babysitting etc. Accommodation also suitable for elderly or disabled. Beach eight miles. Inn 200 yards. Unique leisure complex. Fishing, golf nearby. Family, double, twin, single bedrooms. Brochure; enclose stamp please.

DYFED – MANY TOURIST ATTRACTIONS!

Dyfed, the largest county in Wales, has for a long time been a popular tourist destination. This is due to the fact that it contains such attractions as Aberystwyth, Cardigan, Carmarthen, Haverfordwest, Pembroke, St. David's and Tenby. The enterprising tourist should also head for the monastery on Caldy Island, the village of Llangrannog, Hafod, the wool museum at Dre-fach Felindre and the village of Laugharne – Dylan Thomas's Wales.

PENUWCH. Mr and Mrs K. Nicholls, "The Edelweiss" Guest House, Penuwch, Near Tregaron SY25 6QZ (Llangeitho [097423] 601). 🌑🌑 Small beamed

country guest house set in one-and-a-half acres of garden, surrounded by beautiful countryside and farmland. Pony trekking and horse riding nearby, lovely walks, wonderful wild flowers and birds to see (red kites, hawks, kestrels breed locally). Situated six miles inland from unspoilt Cardigan Bay. Aberaeron, Aberystwyth, Lampeter and Tregaron are within easy reach. The Edelweiss offers comfortable accommodation for non-smokers throughout the year. All bedrooms have central heating, H&C vanity unit and colour TV. Home cooking with full Breakfast, Evening Dinner available. Morning Coffees, Afternoon Teas served. Terms: Bed and Breakfast £12 daily and £69 weekly per person. Bed, Breakfast and Evening Meal £16.50 daily, £105 weekly per person.

PUNCHESTON. Mrs Betty Devonald, Penycraig Farmhouse, Puncheston, Haverfordwest SA62 5RJ (Puncheston [0348] 881277). Working farm. 🌑🌑

Enjoy a warm welcome here at Penycraig, a dairy farm situated in the North Pembrokeshire village of Puncheston, nestling at the foot of the Preseli Hills. Ideal centre for all of your holiday interests, including walking, fishing, pony riding etc. Also tennis courts nearby. The attractive and prettily furnished bedrooms, one with en suite shower, have washbasins and tea trays. Good wholesome cooking is served in the spacious diningroom; separate TV lounge. Bed and Breakfast from £10; Bed, Breakfast and Evening Meal from £105 weekly. Reductions for children sharing. Pets by arrangement.

SOLVA – UPPER VANLEY FARMHOUSE

Welsh Tourist Board 👑👑👑
AA Listed   RAC Acclaimed

Enjoy an informal and relaxed holiday in our happy, comfortable old farmhouse surrounded by a working farm, fields and hedgerows full of wild flowers. Close to spectacular coastline with safe, sandy beaches, coastal path, castles, lovely Solva harbour and St. David's. Our traditional Breakfasts and Evening Meals are farmhouse cooked and freshly prepared. Sunny dining room and cosy, quiet lounge with open fire. Plenty for the children – large garden and playroom. Some small farm pets. All of the homely bedrooms have private bathroom, colour TV and tea making facilities. Now Licensed.

Run by a young family, we welcome children and quiet pets. Bed and Breakfast from £13.50. Weekly rates available. Reductions for children sharing.

Kevin and Carol Shales, Upper Vanley Farmhouse, Pen-y-Cwm, Near Solva SA62 6LJ
Telephone: 0348 831418

SOLVA. Kevin and Carol Shales, Upper Vanley Farmhouse, Pen-y-Cwm, Solva SA62 6LJ (0348-831418). 🌑🌑🌑 Enjoy an informal and relaxed holiday in our happy comfortable old farmhouse surrounded by a working farm, fields and hedgerows full of wild flowers. Close to spectacular coastline with safe sandy beaches, coastal path, castles, lovely Solva harbour and St. David's. Our traditional Breakfasts and Evening Meals are farmhouse cooked and freshly prepared. Licensed. Sunny dining room and cosy quiet lounge with open fire. Plenty for the children large garden and playroom. Some small farm pets. All the homely bedrooms have private bathroom, colour TV and tea making facilities. Run by a young family, we welcome children and quiet pets. Bed and Breakfast from £13.50 per night. Weekly rates available. Reductions for children sharing. RAC Acclaimed, AA Listed.

SOLVA. Mrs S.C. Griffiths, Llanddinog Old Farmhouse, Solva, Haverfordwest SA62 6NA (Croes-goch [0348] 831224). ✿✿ Working farm, join in. Peacefully situated within easy reach of Solva and St. David's, this 16th century farmstead welcomes guests all year. An ideal base for unspoilt sandy beaches, fishing, surfing, pony trekking and country walks. Spacious grounds for children, and secluded pond with associated plant and animal life is a haven for nature lovers. Llanddinog is a five acre smallholding with small animals and birds. Homely atmosphere (log fires in winter). Substantial meals prepared from home produced meats and vegetables and local fish. Reductions for children. Washbasins; central heating throughout; two bathrooms; colour TV lounge; separate diningroom open to non-residents. Picnics prepared. Ample parking. Special diets. Dogs by arrangement. Terms from £12 for Bed and Breakfast.

TENBY. Mrs S.M. Lewis, Beaconing Farm, Temple Bar Road, Kilgetty SA68 0RD (Saundersfoot [0834] 813296). Working farm. A friendly welcome, beautiful view and pleasing accommodation await you at The Beaconing, a working dairy farm, where good home cooking is assured. Centrally situated for all the beauty spots. Saundersfoot two miles, Tenby four miles. Comfortable lounge with colour TV and a games room with snooker table. Separate tables in diningroom. Double and family bedrooms with washbasins and full central heating. Bathroom, shower and toilet. Senior Citizens special rates off-season. Reduced rates for children. Open for Evening Dinner, Bed and Breakfast or Bed and Breakfast only. Ample private parking. No smoking in farmhouse. Write of telephone for brochure.

TENBY. Mr and Mrs W.H.M. Oxley, Red House Farm, New Hedges, Tenby SA69 9DP (Tenby [0834] 813918). ✿✿ Red House Farm is situated on the A478 near the New Hedges roundabout two miles from Tenby. It is a small family-run farm specialising in vegetable growing, also rearing chickens and ducks. We are a mile from the nearest beach, a lovely area for walking, also watersports, riding, sightseeing. Homely and comfortable accommodation including two family rooms and two double rooms with tea/coffee making facilities. There is a livingroom with open fire and TV. Good home cooking with produce from our farm. Well behaved pets welcome. Bed and Breakfast from £9, children half price. Evening Meal from £3.50. Please write or phone for details.

WHITLAND. Mrs O. Ebsworth, Brunant Farm, Whitland SA34 0LX (0994 240421). ✿✿ Working farm. We offer a warm and friendly welcome at Brunant Farm where guests may enjoy a quiet, peaceful holiday with beautiful views over the picturesque Prescelly Hills. Ideally situated for visiting the beaches of Pendine, Amroth, Saundersfoot and Tenby. Accommodation comprises four comfortable ensuite bedrooms, with tea/coffee making facilities, central heating. Guests may relax in our comfortable lounge with TV. Sorry, no pets.

WHITLAND. Mrs Brenda Worthing, Maencochyrwyn Farm, Login, Whitland SA34 0TN (Hebron [0994] 419283). Working farm. This attractive, well situated farm is located in a quiet, rural area, within two and a half miles of the quaint little village of Llanboidy. Accommodation consists of one double and one family room, both with washbasins; bathroom, separate shower, toilet; sittingroom and diningroom. The farm has every modern amenity the discerning visitor could wish, including fitted carpets, colour TV. Children are very welcome and babysitting available. Open April to October. Ample parking. Enjoy the best of Wales Tenby, Pendine Sands, Saundersfoot, Pembrokeshire coast and the picturesque Prescelly Mountains from a most comfortable, friendly base. Bed and Breakfast from £11; Evening Meal from £5.50. Reduced weekly rates. AA listed and Tourist Board approved. SAE, please, for brochure.

WHEN MAKING ENQUIRIES PLEASE MENTION
FARM HOLIDAY GUIDES

WALES

WHITLAND. Mr & Mrs W.L. Windsor, Forest Farm, Whitland SA34 0LS (Whitland [0994] 240066).

Forest Farm is a mixed livestock farm, situated on the A40 in the rolling hillside of the Taf Valley, with beautiful walks around the farm and woodlands and fishing on the River Taf which runs through the farm (salmon and sewin). Within easy reach of the coastal areas (Tenby, Saundersfoot) and shopping areas of Carmarthen and Swansea. A homely atmosphere, fully centrally heated, TV lounge for guests, dining room with separate tables. One en-suite bedroom, two double bedrooms or two single rooms. Tea and coffee if desired. Ample parking space. SAE for terms or telephone. Also self catering bungalow, fully equipped (sleeps six) available in farm grounds.

GLAMORGAN

WEST GLAMORGAN

GOWER. Mrs D.F. John, Greenways Hills Farm, Reynoldston, Gower, Swansea SA3 1AE (Gower [0792] 390125). Working farm. In beautiful countryside, Greenways is situated adjacent to Cefn Bryn, which is a walker's paradise and is on the main road. Reynoldston is central to all Gower bays. At the guest house own garden produce is served. Open from June to September, there are three doubles and one family room, all with washbasins; bathroom, separate toilet; TV lounge, diningroom. Children are welcome at reduced rates if sharing parents' room. Electric heating. Pets allowed by arrangement. Car essential — parking. The sea is two-and-a-half miles away. Bed and Breakfast only. Tourist Board registered. Terms gladly sent on receipt of SAE, please.

SWANSEA. Mrs E.P. Clark, Winston Private Hotel, 11 Church Lane, Bishopston, Swansea SA3 3JT (Bishopston [044128] 2074).

♥♥ This medium sized, comfortable hotel is set in quiet wooded surroundings at the entrance to a National Trust Valley. Convenient for the beautiful beaches of Gower, it is just six miles from Swansea and three-and-a-half from Mumbles with its watersports, dancing etc. Most bedrooms have showers, some have en suite facilities and all have washbasins. Two lounges (one with TV). Indoor heated swimming pool. Billiards Room, sauna and solarium. Residential Licence. Excellent Welsh cooking. AA Listed, RAC Acclaimed. SAE please, for terms to **Mrs E.P. Clark.**

Coynant Farm

**Felindre
Swansea SA5 7PU**

**Telephone:
0269 595640/592064**

Coynant Farm Guesthouse is a cosy 18th century farmhouse offering a high standard of accommodation with inglenook log fires and homely atmosphere. An idyllic setting amidst 200 peaceful acres with magnificent views. Secluded yet convenient for the many beaches, castles and other attractions. An interesting livestock farm with horse riding, beautiful walks, games room and a number of picturesque lakes stocked with trout for guests' fishing. Five bedrooms all with private bathrooms, colour TV, video, tea/coffee making facilities. Fresh home produce. Separate tables with good food and a wide choice of wines. Peace, comfort and a warm welcome. Residential licensed bar for guests, open all year. Child reductions. 4 course Dinner, Bed and full Breakfast from £17.50 daily, £119 weekly. AA, RAC Recommended. Brochure available. Proprietor Mrs M. Jones.

GWENT

ABERGAVENNY. Mr and Mrs S. Watkins, Treloyvan Farm, Llantillio, Crossenny, Abergavenny NP7 8UE (060085 478). Friendly family-run 113 acre working farm in beautiful rural setting mid-way between Abergavenny and Monmouth on B4233. Within walking distance of White Castle: Offa's Dyke the long distance footpath runs by the castle, also three Castles of Gwent White, Skenfrith and Grosmont, another nice long walk. Nearby you will find golf, fishing and canoeing. Magnificent views. Children welcome, lots of farm animals and pets to see. Bed and Breakfast from £11 to £12; weekly from £70. Evening Meal available; good home cooking with a Swiss cook. Cot and high chair available. Reductions for children. Bedrooms with shower and washbasin. Family speaks German and a little French. Wales Tourist Board registered. For further details write or phone **Mrs S. Watkins.**

ABERGAVENNY. Mrs E.M. Davies, Crossways Farm, Llangattock Lingoed, Abergavenny NP7 8RR (Cross Ash [0873] 821395). Working farm. The farm bungalow is situated in a beautiful part of Wales, often missed by many visitors. The interesting market towns of Abergavenny, Brecon and Hay-on-Wye, renowned for its second-hand bookshops, are an easy drive away. The locality makes an ideal base for exploring the Wye Valley, Llanthony Valley and Black Mountains, where there is superb hill walking and ponytrekking. Miles of quiet country lanes and footpaths with plenty of opportunities to observe wildlife. There are family and double bedrooms. Open January to December, with central heating. Car essential — parking. Children welcome but sorry, no pets. Bed and Breakfast from £11. Tourist Board listed.

See also Colour Display Advertisement BLAINA. Malcolm and Betty Hancock, Chapel Farm, Blaina NP3 3DJ (0495 290888). Guests are assured of a warm welcome when they visit this 15th century renovated farmhouse and many return each year. A good base for touring Big Pit Blonovan, Bryn-Bach Park, Brecon Beacons, Abergavenny. Only four miles from the 1992 Garden Festival site. Packed lunches available; Evening Meal on request. There is a drinks licence but no bar, though there is an unusual drinks cupboard. Full details available.

MONMOUTH. Rosemary and Derek Ringer, Church Farm Guest House, Mitchel Troy, Monmouth NP5 4HZ (Monmouth [0600] 2176). 🐝🐝 A spacious and homely 16th century former farmhouse with oak beams and inglenook fireplaces, set in large attractive garden with stream. An excellent base for visiting the Wye Valley, Forest of Dean and Black Mountains. All bedrooms have washbasins, tea/coffee making facilities and central heating; some are en-suite. Own car park. Colour TV. Non-smoking. Tasty alternatives to English breakfast available. Bed and Breakfast from £13.50 per person. Evening Meal by arrangement. We also offer a programme of guided and self-guided Walking Holidays and Short Breaks. Separate "Wysk walks" brochure on request.

MONMOUTH near. Mrs Linda Gleed, The Old Barn, Trellech, Monmouth NP5 4AF (0600 860469). 🐝 In tranquil setting on the edge of Tintern forest, this small working farm is situated between Chepstow and Monmouth beside the B4293 with panoramic views of the Welsh mountains. Ideal for touring Wye Valley, Forest of Dean, Brecon Beacons. Activities include fishing, golf, walking. Guest TV lounge with log fire. Breakfast/sun room. One en-suite bedroom, one double, one twin and one single, all with vanity units and tea/coffee making facilities. Guest bathroom. Centrally heated. Ample parking. Access at all times. SAE for terms or telephone.

MONMOUTH (Wye Valley). Mrs Rosemary Townsend, Lugano, Llandogo NP5 4TL (Dean [0594] 530496). Modern dormer bungalow set in pleasant gardens just off the A466 in the centre of the picturesque village of Llandogo. Here in the heart of the Wye Valley you will enjoy walks along the banks of the Wye or through the woods to many of the local beauty spots. Within easy reach of the Black Mountains, Forest of Dean, Bath, Slimbridge, the M50 and the Severn Bridge. The area is well served by inns, hotels and restaurants and guests have access to bedrooms and gardens at all times. All bedrooms (one with en-suite bathroom) have washbasins, tea/coffee making facilities and TV sets. Brochure available on request.

PENRHOS. Mrs J.E. Thom, The Grange, Penrhos, Raglan NP5 2LQ (Llantilio [0600] 85202). Working farm, join in. Situated between Monmouth and Abergavenny near Rivers Wye and Usk. Traditional mixed farm in quiet unspoilt country with fantastic views. 115 acres with trees, streams and animals. Walk or picnic on farm, or on Offa's Dyke Path. Centrally placed for touring. Car essential since we are deep in the country. Visit deep coal-mine, castles, little railways, take river trips. Local golf, fishing, riding. Children love the farm. Bring dogs and horses (by arrangement), we have stabling. New large rooms, some en-suite. Bed and Breakfast from £12.50 to £15. Reductions for children and longer stays. Come and share this beautiful place. Welsh Tourist Board listed.

WYE VALLEY. Anne and Peter Howe, Valley House, Raglan Road, Tintern, Near Chepstow NP6 6TH (0291 689652). Valley House is a fine Georgian residence situated in the tranquil Angidy Valley 800 yards from the A466 Chepstow to Monmouth road and within a mile of Tintern Abbey. Numerous walks through picturesque woods and valleys right from our doorstep. The accommodation is of a very high standard; all rooms are en-suite, have tea/coffee making facilities and colour TV. The guests' lounge has a wealth of exposed beams and a working range whilst the diningroom has an arched stone ceiling. Evening Meals and packed lunches are available by arrangement. Bed and Breakfast from £15 per person. Open all year.

GWENT – BORDER COUNTY
Nestling in the south-east corner of Wales, Gwent is an undulating county which includes the ever popular Wye Valley. Other attractions are Chepstow, Abergavenny, Tintern Forest and Tredegar.

GWYNEDD

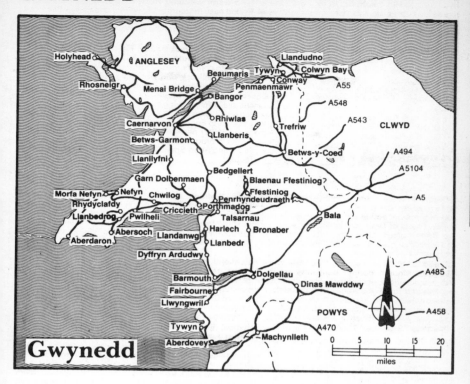

Gwynedd

ABERDARON. Barbara and David Marshallsay, Carreg Plas, Aberdaron, Pwllheli LL53 8LH (Aberdaron [075886] 308). 🏵🏵 17th century manor house of historic interest in sheltered position on west side of Lleyn Peninsula, set in five acres of secluded wooded grounds, and surrounded by National Trust land. Only half a mile from the well-known Whistling Sands Beach, and two miles from the picturesque village of Aberdaron. Lovely coastal scenery and sandy beaches nearby. Seven bedrooms available with washbasins and tea-making facilities, five en-suite or with private bath/shower room. Large lounge; separate TV lounge; two diningrooms. Cots, high chairs provided, children especially welcome. Pets by arrangement. Ample car parking. Open all year. Reduced rates for children. Bed and Breakfast (from £13) or Evening Meal, Bed and Breakfast (from £20). Publicity gladly sent on request.

ANGLESEY. Mrs M.E. Williams, Llanerch, Pendref Street, Newborough, Anglesey LL61 6SY (Newborough [024-879] 235). Llanerch is situated in a quiet part of a country village. It used to be the village rectory and stands in an acre of ground with excellent panoramic views of Snowdonia Mountain Range and the Menai Straits and has plenty of room for children to play in. It is only minutes from Llanddwyn beach which has over four miles of golden sands, is close to forest walks, picnic areas and nature reserves and is ideal for fishing and birdwatching. Llanerch has one double and three family bedrooms, all with washbasins; two bathrooms and toilets; TV lounge; diningroom; central heating throughout. Children welcome, cot, high chair and babysitting offered. Small pets permitted. Plenty of parking space. Evening Meal, Bed and Breakfast from £12.50 or Bed and Breakfast from £10. Late night cup of tea and packed lunches available on request. Reduced rates for children. SAE brings prompt reply.

DRWS Y COED
🐦🐦🐦

Llannerch-y-Medd, Isle of Anglesey LL71 8AD

Drws y Coed, a modern farmhouse on 550 acres of beef, sheep and arable farm is set in beautiful wooded countryside with panoramic views of Snowdonia, near to picturesque Bodafon Mountain. Centrally located for beaches, fishing, golf, riding, leisure centres. Tarmac drives. A warm welcome awaits our guests who are accommodated in well-appointed bedrooms, all en suite with colour TV's, tea making facilities and clock radios. Full central heating. Two lounges, one with log fire. Diningroom with separate tables. Good home cooking with ample portions. Games room. Lovely walks in vicinity. Fire Certificate held. WTB Rural Tourism Award. Farm Holiday Guide Diploma Award. Reductions for children. Bed and Breakfast (Evening Meal optional). Open all year. Brochure available from: **Mrs J. Bown (Llannerch-y-Medd [0248] 470473).**

BALA. Mr T.G. Jones, Frondderw Private Hotel, Bala LL23 7YD (Bala [0678] 520301). 🐦🐦

Delightful period mansion on the hillside five minutes from the town of Bala and within the boundaries of Snowdonia National Park. There are lovely walks, boating, swimming, fishing and picnic facilities, golf and magnificent scenery. The accommodation is well maintained and consists of eight bedrooms, some en-suite, all with washbasins, central heating and tea/coffee making facilities. Guests' lounge with books, separate TV lounge and diningroom. Residential licence. Parking. Sorry, no pets in the house. Open all year. Bed and Breakfast from £10 to £13 daily, £63.50 to £81.50 per week; Dinner optional. Dinner, Bed and Breakfast from £116 to £134 per person per week. AA listed.

BALA. Mrs E. Jones, Eirianfa, Sarnau, Bala LL23 7LH (Llandderfel [06783] 389). 🐦 **Working farm.** This mixed farm of 150 acres is situated four miles from Bala on A494 with splendid views of Berwyn Mountains; fishing and pony trekking nearby. There is a private lake on the farm. Ideal spot from which to tour mid-Wales and north Wales. Good centre for visiting castles, little railways, lakes and waterfalls, slate mines and woollen mills. Home cooked food, and guests are made welcome and assured of every comfort. One family, one double, one twin-bedded rooms, all with washbasins; bathroom, two toilets, one single room with no washbasin; tea/coffee making facilities in bedrooms; sittingroom, diningroom with TV. Children welcome at reduced rates and cot, high chair and babysitting provided. Central heating. Sorry, no dogs. Car essential, parking. Open March to November. Evening Dinner, Bed and Breakfast, or Bed and Breakfast. SAE, please, for terms.

BALA. Mrs C.A. Morris, Tair Felin Farm, Frongoch, Bala LL23 7NS (0678 520763). A warm welcome awaits you at Tair Felin Farm situated three miles north of Bala on the A4212 road and in the Snowdonia National Park. Beamed ceiling in sittingroom, homely atmosphere, good home cooking. Colour TV, log fires when wet and cold. Tea/coffee facilities in bedrooms one family and one double. Mid-week and weekend breaks available. Working farm with sheep and cattle. Ideal for touring North and Mid-Wales. Bed and Breakfast from £11.

BALA. Mrs S.E. Edwards, Bryn Melyn, Rhyduchaf, Bala LL23 7PG (Bala [0678] 520376). Working farm. Bryn Melyn, Rhyduchaf is situated in the beautiful countryside of Bala, and offers accommodation all year. The house is stone-built and stands on 35 acres of mixed farmland. Home cooking and home produced food makes this a real home from home. Two double and one twin bedroom (two with washbasins); two bathrooms, toilet; sittingroom; diningroom; central heating. Children welcome at reduced rates. Sorry, no pets. A car is necessary to ensure that visitors derive all the pleasure that this region offers. Parking space. Sea 28 miles. Good recreation facilities in the area. Evening Dinner, Bed and Breakfast from £95 weekly or Bed and Breakfast from £10 – £11 per person. Mrs Edwards is a Farm Holiday Guide Diploma winner.

BARMOUTH. Mr & Mrs T.L. & S.L. Dyer, Hendreclochydd Hall, Llanaber, Barmouth LL42 1RR (Barmouth [0341] 280242). Situated about two miles from Barmouth on the coast road to Harlech, with superb views of Cardigan Bay and the Lleyn Peninsula. We are practically surrounded by the Snowdonia National Park with Narrow Gauge Steam Railways being only a short drive away. Accommodation is offered in rooms overlooking the sea and with colour TV, easy chairs and beverage facilities, ensuite rooms available. Excellent parking and pleasant garden for our guests' pleasure. Golden sands and safe bathing are not many minutes' walk away. Children welcome at reduced rates. Pets accepted by prior arrangement. Bed and Breakfast from £12.50. Welsh Tourist Board registered. Our aim is to give you a holiday to cherish!

BEAUMARIS. Mrs E. Roberts, Plas Cichle, Beaumaris, Anglesey LL58 8PS (0248 810488). *Commended.* **Working farm.** The beautiful period farmhouse on this 200 acre stock farm, close to the historic town of Beaumaris and the Menai Straits, offers accommodation in spacious, well appointed family, double or twin rooms, all with private facilities, hospitality tray and TV. Large guest lounge. Separate tables in the diningroom, where you may enjoy a hearty Welsh Breakfast or optional Evening Meal. Local activities include water sports, fishing, riding and golf. Close to many attractions — 30 minutes to the heart of Snowdonia. Bed and Breakfast from £14.50; Dinner £9. Weekly terms available. Reductions for children of 12 years and under sharing parents' room. Enjoy the freedom and fine Welsh welcome that awaits you here. WTB Farmhouse Award for serviced accommodation. Brochure available from **Mrs Roberts.**

BEDDGELERT. Joan Williams, Colwyn, Beddgelert (0766-86 276). Welcome to Colwyn. Warm, small and friendly, this 18th century cottage guesthouse, with its original stone fireplace in the low beamed lounge, is restful and unpretentious. Old-fashioned (but modernised of course), licensed, central heating, washbasin, white linen, warm duvets and Welsh tapestry covers. Colwyn overlooks the river in the centre of this picturesque village of Beddgelert, probably the most popular in the area, lying as it does right at the foot of Snowdon and surrounded by wooded mountains, lakes and streams. Spectacular scenery both winter and summer. Ideal base for working, touring or just lazing. There are small shops, inns, cafes in the village. Walkers welcome, group rates off season. Discount on advance bookings of three days or more. Booking advisable especially weekends, Bank/school holidays. Bed and Breakfast from £11 to £15.

BETWS-Y-COED. Mrs E. Jones, Maes-y-Garnedd, Capel Garmon, Llanrwst, Betws-y-Coed (06902 428 or 0690 710 428). Working farm. This 140-acre mixed farm is superbly situated on the Rooftop of Wales as Capel Garmon has been called, and the Snowdonia Range, known to the Welsh as the "Eyri", is visible from the land. Two miles from A5. Surrounding area provides beautiful country scenery and excellent walks. Safe, sandy beaches at Llandudno and Colwyn Bay. Salmon and trout fishing (permit required). Mrs Jones serves excellent home produced meals with generous portions including Welsh Lamb and Roast Beef. Gluten free diets can be arranged. Packed lunches, with flask of coffee or tea. One double and one family bedrooms with washbasins; bathroom, toilet; sittingroom and diningroom. Children welcome, cot, high chair and babysitting available. Regret, no pets. Car essential, ample parking. Open all year. Bed and Breakfast from £11; Evening Meal optional. Gluten-free diets available. SAE brings prompt reply with details and terms. Reductions for children. Bala Lakes, Bodnant Gardens, Ffestiniog Railway, slate quarries, Trefriw Woollen Mills nearby. Member of AA, Tourist Board.

The information in the entries in this guide is presented by the publishers in good faith and after the signed acceptance by advertisers that they will uphold the high standards associated with FHG PUBLICATIONS LIMITED. The publishers do not accept responsibility for any inaccuracies or omissions or any results thereof. Before making final holiday arrangements readers should confirm the prices and facilities directly with advertisers.

BETWS-Y-COED. Mrs Meryl Metcalfe, Tan Yr Eglwys, Lanrhychwyn, Trefriw, Llanrwst LL27 0YJ

(Llanrwst [0492] 640547). ☙☙ 'Tan Yr Eglwys' is a modernised farmhouse where some of the walls are a yard thick! Llanrhychwyn is a little hamlet, conveniently situated above the Conwy Valley between the market town of Llanrwst and Trefriw village. A car is essential, unless very energetic! Ideal haven for country lovers and hill walkers. Central for mountains and lakes of Snowdonia and also the coast. The farmhouse is surrounded by fields and woods. The ancient Church at St. Rhychwyn is about 800 yards up a path leading from the farm. Places of interest include Betws-y-Coed (golf) four miles; Trefriw (Woollen Mill) one mile; Llanrwst two miles, Geirionnydd Lake two miles, Llanberis (Snowdon) 17 miles, Llandudno 10 miles. A homely welcome with log fires available on chilly evenings, and good home cooking is assured. All rooms have washbasins. Open Easter to October. Terms on application. Reduction for children in family rooms. SAE for prompt reply and direction from main road. OS Grid Reference 777616. We also have a static caravan in a lawned garden backed by forest.

BETWS-Y-COED. Jim and Lilian Boughton, Bron Celyn Guest House, Llanrwst Road, Betws-y-Coed

LL24 0HD (Betws-y-Coed [06902] 333 changing to [0690] 710333). ☙☙☙ A warm welcome awaits you at this delightful guest house overlooking the Gwydyr Forest and Llugwy/Conwy Valleys and village of Betws-y-Coed in Snowdonia National Park. Ideal centre for touring, walking, climbing, fishing and golf. Also excellent overnight stop en-route for Holyhead ferries. Easy walk into village and close to Conwy/Swallow Falls and Fairy Glen. Most rooms en-suite, all with colour TV and beverage makers. Lounge. Full central heating. Garden. Car park. Open all year. Full English Breakfast, Packed Meals, Snacks, Evening Meals — special diets catered for. Bed and Breakfast from £12 to £15, reduced rates for children under 12 yrs.

BETWS-Y-COED. Mrs M. Jones, Tyddyn Gethin Farm, Penmachno, Betws-y-Coed LL24 0PS

(Penmachno [06903] 392). Working farm. 80 acre mixed farm situated 200 yards off B4406 half a mile from Penmachno Village, one mile from Woollen Mills, near to Falls and very central for touring. Within easy reach of sea and mountains. Pony trekking nearby. Three and a half miles from Betws-y-Coed. Clean and comfortable, always a welcome and good home cooking. Bathroom, showers and washbasins in all bedrooms, shaving points; separate shower room. Two lounges, one with colour TV. Separate tables in diningroom. Lovely views from the house. Ample parking. Bed and Breakfast from £11; Bed, Breakfast and Evening Meal from £16. SAE brings a prompt reply.

BETWS-Y-COED near. Mrs Eleanore Roberts, 'Awelon', Plas Isa, Llanrwst LL26 0EE (Llanrwst

[0492] 640 047). ☙ 'Awelon' is a small, family-run guest house situated on the edge of the market town of Llanrwst, 200 yards from the A470 and a short walk from the town centre. An ideal base for walking and touring Snowdonia. Three bedrooms (one double, one twin and one family), all have washbasins, shaver points, bedside lights and fitted carpets, also tea/coffee making facilities. Large bathroom has shower. Full central heating. Ample private parking. Good food and cleanliness guaranteed. Bed, Breakfast and Evening Meal from £89 weekly; Bed and Breakfast only from £65 weekly. Daily rates on request. Reductions for children. Pets welcome. Open Easter to October. SAE, please, for brochure.

If you've found
FARM HOLIDAY GUIDES
of service please tell your friends

BLAENAU FFESTINIOG. Mrs G.E. Hughes, Bryn Celynog Farm, Cwm Prysor, Trawsfynydd, Blaenau Ffestiniog LL41 4TR (076-687 378). 🐾 A warm welcome awaits you on this 700 acre working mixed beef and sheep farm with a Welsh-speaking family. Generous home cooked meals. Comfort assured in large stone built farmhouse. Fully carpeted, centrally heated, spacious bedrooms with wash-basins, tea/coffee facilities. Colour TV in lounge; dining-room. Guests have own bathroom. Situated in rural setting but only three miles from village. Ideal spot for relaxing holiday with magnificent views of mountains. Beautiful walks, and fishing available free on farm, also Roman castle (ruin). Ideal for touring Snowdonia National Park. Bed and Breakfast from £12 to £14; Bed, Breakfast and Evening Dinner from £19 to £21 daily. Welsh Tourist Board member.

See also Colour Display Advertisement **BLAENAU FFESTINIOG near. Mrs Paula Williams, Tyddyn Du Farm, Gellilydan, Near Blaenau Ffestiniog LL41 4RB (0766 85281).** 🐾🐾 This delightful 16th century historic farmhouse is in its own extensive grounds on a working farm in the heart of Snowdonia National Park, just off the main A470. Accommodation has inglenook in lounge and a wealth of exposed stonework throughout. All rooms have tea/coffee/drinking chocolate trays, and some are en-suite. There is also one private unit with en-suite facilities. Good whole-some food, packed lunches available. Pets' area with rabbits, ducks, bottle-fed lambs and goats. Free pony rides. Car not essential. Area has beaches, waterfalls, lakes, woods and a wide variety of interesting places to visit. Open all year. Bed and Breakfast from £12 nightly (children reduced rates); Evening Meal from £6; Dinner, Bed and Breakfast from £126 weekly.

CADER IDRIS. CROESO CADER IDRIS! Situated within a 10 mile radius in the Snowdonia National Park between ABERDYFI and DOLGELLAU, we are a group of 10 Welsh speaking (one learner) farmers wives' offering a true Welsh welcome "croeso" at our homes. There are 12 units for self catering, some dating back to the 16th century, from £50 to £350 per week; whilst nine of us cater for Bed and Breakfast from £11 to £14 each daily, some with optional Evening Meals prepared from local homegrown produce. We offer a substantial reduction for weekly rates. All properties are WTB verified. For colour folder of brochures, SAE please to: **Mrs M. Pughe, Dolffanog Fach, Tallyllyn Corris, Tywyn LL36 9AJ or telephone (0654 73235).**

CAERNARFON. Mrs Linda Williams, Pant-yr-Afallen Farm, Portdinorwic, Caernarfon LL56 4QN (Portdinorwic [0248] 670654). Bed and Breakfast, with optional Evening Meal, available on this 250 acre centrally situated farm, only three miles from Caernarfon's lovely castle and six miles from Snowdon. As there are only two letting bedrooms (family or double), both with washbasins, guests are assured of personal attention at all times. Guests' sittingroom with colour TV and separate diningroom. Farm fresh produce is used as much as possible for the good home cooking. Car essential, parking. Sorry, no pets. Terms on request. Open March to October. SAE, please or telephone. WTB listed.

GWYNEDD – OUTSTANDING NATURAL BEAUTY!
With Snowdonia National Park and the Lleyn Peninsula, Gwynedd well deserves its designation as an 'Area of Outstanding Natural Beauty'. The tourist is spoiled for choice in this county but should endeavour to visit the hill-fort at Tre'r Ceiri, the Llugwy Valley, Cwm Pennant, Dinas Dinlle hill-fort, the gold mine at Clogau and the railways and quarries at Blaenau Ffestiniog.

CAERNARFON. Mr and Mrs S. Fry, Gorffwysfa Hotel, St. David's Road, Caernarfon LL55 1BH (0286 2647). 👑👑 Former Victorian Rectory boasting numerous original features such as ornate pine stairway and stained glass windows, standing in own grounds in quiet residential area of this historic town. Magnificent views of Menai Straits and Anglesey, yet only minutes from famous Castle and harbour. Ideal sightseeing and activity centre for Portmeirion Village, Ffestiniog and Snowdonia Railways, Copper Mines, Slate Caverns, Anglesey beaches, National Watersports Centre, fishing, golf and pony trekking. Bedrooms are large and well furnished with TV, radio, drinks facilities, etc. Several are en-suite. Snacks and Dinners always available, with bar facilities and pool table in large TV lounge. For terms write or telephone.

CAERNARVON. Mrs B. Cartwright, "Tan Dinas", Llanddeiniolen, Caernarvon LL55 3AR (Port Dinorwic [0248] 670098).

A modernised stone farmhouse situated in a picturesque, secluded, yet very central location and surrounded by typical Welsh scenic beauty and with a pleasant garden sloping down to a small stream running alongside the woods. Guests have their own private and centrally-heated lounge and diningroom. The area is ideal for touring, all types of fishing, walking and pony trekking if required. Caernarvon, Bangor, Anglesey and Snowdon itself are all within very easy reach. Take the B4366 out of Caernarvon. One mile through Bethel come to the "Gors Bach Inn". Turn into lane by side of Inn and travel on for half a mile. Children welcome, cot, high chair, babysitting available. Car essential — parking. Open April to October with central heating and open fires. Pets accepted. Bed and Breakfast £11, with Evening Dinner £14. Reductions for children. Tourist Board listed.

CAERNARVON near. Mrs J.A. Rees, Plas Cae'r Pwsan, Clynnogfawr, Near Caernarvon LL54 5PF (Clynnogfawr [028-686] 529).

👑👑 Plas Cae'r Pwsan is a pleasant country house in a wooded garden with sea views from all bedrooms. Close to safe sandy beaches. Fishing, pony trekking, golfing and climbing. Good walking centre; ideally situated for touring Snowdonia and Lleyn Peninsula. Friendly atmosphere. Good varied cooking; four-course dinner freshly prepared home baked bread. Comfortable accommodation offered from May to September in double room, twin-bedded room and interconnecting family room, all with tea trays, washbasins and shaver points. Bathroom with shower, two toilets. Colour TV lounge with log fire. Centrally heated throughout. Sorry, no pets. Car essential — parking. Reduced rates for children. Dinner, Bed and Breakfast or Bed and Breakfast only. SAE, please, for terms.

CAERNARVON near. Paula and David Foster, Tan y Gaer, Rhosgadfan, Near Caernarvon LL54 7LE (Caernarvon [0286] 830943).

Set in spectacular scenery with views to the top of Snowdon and over the Irish Sea, this farmhouse with beams and open fires offers a restful atmosphere from which to enjoy beautiful North Wales. Riding, climbing, walking and beaches are all close by. The homemade bread and farmhouse cooking are done on the 'Aga' and much of the food is home produced. Guests have their own diningroom and lounge with TV, books, etc. The ensuite bedrooms are spacious and the family room is comfortable with double bed and bunks. Evening Meal with Bed and Breakfast from £15. Reductions for weekly stays. Telephone/SAE for details, please.

CONWY. Mrs Baxter, Glyn Uchaf, Conway Old Road, Dwygyfylchi, Penmaenmawr, Conway LL34 6YS (0492 623737). ☙ ☙ Enjoy a quiet, peaceful holiday at this old mill house set in 11 acres of National Parkland in beautiful mountainous countryside. Ideal touring centre for Snowdonia. Accommodation comprises three bedrooms, all with washbasins, razor points and lovely views. Lounge with colour TV; diningroom. Excellent cuisine with varied menus and home produce. Tea/coffee making facilities available. Children welcome. Two-and-a-half miles to Conway, five to Llandudno and Colwyn Bay — three minutes' walk to village. Pony trekking and fishing locally. Also stabling available for those wishing to bring their own horses. Ample parking. Guests have access to house at all times. Bed and Breakfast or Bed, Breakfast and Evening Meal. Moderate terms, reductions for children under 12. Also small camping area available. WTB registered. Highly recommended. SAE or phone please.

CONWY. Mrs C. Roberts, Henllys Farm, Llechwedd, Conwy LL32 8DJ (0492 593269). ☙ ☙ **Working farm.** This 200 acre working sheep and cattle farm is situated one and a half miles from Conwy in the heart of beautiful countryside. Accommodation comprises one double and one family room, both with washbasins, tea/coffee making facilities and shaver points; two bathrooms, both with toilets; colour TV lounge; diningroom. Ideally placed for touring Snowdonia and the North Wales coast. Conwy Castle, town walls and fish quay are within easy reach, as are Llandudno, Betws-y-Coed, Caernarvon and Bodnant Gardens. Pony trekking nearby. Good home cooking. Children welcome and pets by arrangement. Bed and Breakfast from £10.50; Bed, Breakfast and Evening Meal from £16.50. Farm House Award.

CONWY near. Mrs Margaret C. Waddingham, "Cefn", Tyn-y-Groes, Near Conwy LL32 8TA (Tyn-y-Groes [0492] 650233). "Cefn" is a lovely 17th century country house set in four acres of grounds, on the edge of the National Park. Quiet and secluded in a rural and picturesque setting with magnificent views of the Conwy Valley and Snowdonia Mountains. Two lovely bedrooms with excellent en-suite facilities, tea-making equipment and TV. Within easy travelling distance of many inland tourist attractions and yet only a short drive to nearby Conwy and seaside towns. Bed and Breakfast from £14. Advance booking essential. Also available, adjoining self-catering holiday flat, ground floor, comfortably furnished, sleeping two persons. Terms from £95 per week. SAE or telephone.

CRICCIETH. Mrs Megan Jones, Tyddyn Felin, Ynys, Criccieth (Garndolbenmaen [076-675] 659). Working farm, join in. Our 150-acre mixed farm is ideal for a family holiday, and everyday activities fascinate youngsters and adults alike, especially when they can lend a hand. We welcome country lovers to our farmhouse which is old, but spacious, comfortable and fully modernised. The bedrooms (two double, one twin) have washbasins and heaters, whilst downstairs are lounge/diningroom; sittingroom with colour TV and sun lounge. We offer farmhouse hospitality and home cooking (Dinner, Bed and Breakfast). Enjoy scenic walks, fishing and rough shooting on the farm which is ideally situated between Snowdonia and the popular beaches, and centrally placed for touring North Wales. Open all year.

CRICCIETH near. Mrs C.S. Lowe, Tyddyn Iolyn, Pentre Felin, Near Criccieth LL52 0RB. Our small 16th century farmhouse stands in quiet farmland with spectacular views of Snowdonia and Welsh coastlines. Ideal base from which to explore: beaches, Snowdonian countryside, castles, slate mines, hillforts, crafts, golf courses, ski slopes and Portmeirion. Comfortable oak-beamed accommodation, double, twin and three-bedded rooms with tea-making facilities, some with private bathrooms; central heating and log fires. Generous Welsh Breakfast, own eggs, spring water. Vegetarian cooking and packed lunches available. Car advisable — limited coastal buses. Sorry, no children or dogs. Cattery. Bed and Breakfast from £10; Evening Meal £5. Bed, Breakfast and Evening Meal from £100 weekly. Open all year. Try our small residential courses: archaeology, history, landscape painting, flora, crafts. All details SAE, please, or telephone **(0766 522509).**

PLEASE SEND A STAMPED ADDRESSED ENVELOPE WITH ENQUIRIES

DOLGELLAU. Mrs Mair Evans, Gwanas, Cross Foxes, Dolgellau LL40 2SH (Dolgellau [0341] 422624). Working farm.  ☙ Peace and comfort with a hearty farmhouse breakfast are assured on this 1100-acre sheep farm; other animals kept too. Gwanas is situated off the A470 Welshpool road, three and a half miles from the quaint old market town of Dolgellau. The region is full of interest — castles, miniature railways, gold mines, slate mines, woollen mills, interesting walks to see waterfalls, torrents and precipices. Pony trekking nearby and safe bathing at Barmouth, Fairbourne, Tywyn and Aberdyfi. The Cross Foxes Hotel is conveniently situated nearby for evening meals. Accommodation in one twin-bedded, one family, one double bedrooms, all with washbasins; two bathrooms with toilets and showers; sittingroom with TV and diningroom. Children welcome. Pets allowed by arrangement. Open from March to November with oil-fired central heating. Cleanliness assured. Car not essential, but there is parking. Bed and Breakfast only from £10.50. Evening refreshments. Rates reduced for children.

DOLGELLAU. Mrs Griffiths, Llwyn Talcen, Brithdir, Dolgellau LL40 2RY (0341-41 276). Situated in  an acre of rhododendron and azalea gardens, Llwyn Talcen offers a warm welcome, outstanding views, together with peace and quiet. Our location, about four miles east of Dolgellau, makes an ideal centre for hill walkers and nature lovers. We offer good fresh food, organic whenever possible. Traditional and vegetarian fare are both available. Bed and Breakfast from £10. Reduced rates are available for children. Ample parking. WTB listed. To find us take narrow lane from the centre of the village of Brithdir (telephone box) past the village hall and wooden houses for about half a mile until you reach a crossroads, turn right, Llwyn Talcen is on the right in the trees after about 200 yards.

DOLGELLAU. Mrs Margaret E. Roberts, Tan-y-Foel, Llanfachreth, Dolgellau LL40 2NA (Dolgellau [0341] 423074). Working farm. Beautifully situated on a 500-acre hill farm, carrying Pedigree Welsh Black cattle and Welsh Mountain sheep, this farmhouse enjoys unrestricted views of Cader Idris and Aran Mountain ranges, and is within walking distance of famous Precipice and Torrent walks. Nearest beaches are at Barmouth and Fairbourne. Pony trekking, fishing, golf courses, old mines, slate caverns, narrow gauge railways, all within driving distance. One double and one family bedrooms; bathroom, toilet; sittingroom; diningroom. Cot, babysitting, reduced rates for children. Sorry, no pets. Car essential — parking. Open from April to November for Evening Meal, Bed and Breakfast, or Bed and Breakfast. SAE, please, for terms.

DOLGELLAU. Mrs G.D. Evans, "Y Goedlan", Brithdir, Dolgellau LL40 2RN (Dolgellau [0341] 423131).  ☙☙ Guests are welcome at "Y Goedlan" from February to October. This old Vicarage with adjoining farm offers peaceful accommodation in pleasant rural surroundings. Three miles from Dolgellau on the B4416 road, in a good position for interesting walks (Torrent, 400 yards from the house), beaches, mountains, narrow gauge railways and pony trekking. All the bedrooms are large and spacious; one double, one twin-bedded and one family rooms all with washbasins, tea-making facilities; bathroom, two toilets; shower; lounge with colour TV; separate tables in diningroom. Reduced rates for children under 10 years; babysitting offered. Central heating. Car essential — parking. Comfort, cleanliness and personal attention assured, with a good hearty breakfast. Bed and Breakfast from £11.

DOLGELLAU. Mrs C.E. Skeel Jones, Arosfyr Farm, Penycefn Road, Dolgellau LL40 2YP (0341 422355). Arosfyr is a 31 acre holding on the way to Dolgellau Golf Course. It has glorious panoramic views of the Cader Idris range of mountains with the quaint old market town of Dolgellau nestling in the valley below. Ideal for touring, walking and climbing for the more energetic. Beaches at Fairbourne (eight miles) and Barmouth (10 miles). Pony trekking three miles, castles, narrow gauge railways, woollen mills, gold mines and slate caverns all within easy reach. Double and family bedrooms, all with heating and washbasins; two toilets, shower and bath; diningroom with separate tables and a comfortable lounge with remote control TV. Bed and Breakfast from £11 per person, inclusive of late evening refreshments and generous cooked breakfast using own free range eggs. Parking available. Personal attention and satisfaction assured. SAE for prompt reply, or telephone.

DOLGELLAU. Mrs A. Jones, Penbryn Croft, Cader Road, Dolgellau LL40 1RN (Dolgellau [0341] 422815). ♛♛ "Penbryn Croft" is almost 200 years old with all modern amenities, situated within two minutes' walk of the centre of Dolgellau. One family and five double rooms, all with washbasins; electric blankets on all beds, heating available when required. Bathroom, toilet. Sittingroom with colour TV; diningroom with separate tables. Access to rooms at all times. Late night drink included in the price. Reputation for high standard of catering and excellent varied menu. Packed lunches on request. Farm Holiday Guide Diploma Award. Open all year, except Christmas. Children welcome, babysitting. Parking. Five-course Evening Dinner, Full English Breakfast. SAE, please, for terms.

DOLGELLAU. Mrs Margaret Westwood, Esgair Wen Newydd, Garreg Feurig, Llanfachreth Road, Dolgellau LL40 2YA (Dolgellau [0341] 423952). ♛♛ Esgair Wen Newydd is a spacious new bungalow on an elevated south facing site overlooking Cader Idris. Situated 10 minutes' walk from Dolgellau town centre in a very quiet cul-de-sac; magnificent mountain views. Ideal for walking, touring, bird watching, gold panning, narrow gauge railways, ski-slope, sandy beaches, pony trekking, fishing, etc. Comfort, cleanliness and personal attention assured. High standard of home cooking. Evening dinner 7.00pm. Two double and one twin bedrooms with washbasins, shaver points, electric blankets, tea/coffee facilities. Guest bathroom with shower, etc. Lounge with colour TV. Central heating. No smoking. Sorry, no pets. Open all year. Parking. Brochure available. Mid-week bookings accepted.

HARLECH. Mrs G.M. Evans, Glanygors, Llandanwg, Harlech LL46 2SD (Lanbedr [034123] 410). The house with two acres of land is situated 400 yards from sandy beach, and has beautiful views of the mountains. It is one and a half miles from Harlech Castle, golf club and swimming pool, and within a quarter mile of train station. Ideal place for bird watching. Presenting good home cooking in a homely and relaxed atmosphere. Welsh speaking family. Open all year. Central heating and electric blankets for Winter months. Accommodation comprises one double, one family and one twin bedrooms. Bathroom, toilet; TV lounge and diningroom. Reduced rates for children. Pets welcome. WTB member. Terms on request for Bed and Breakfast or Dinner, Bed and Breakfast.

HARLECH. Mrs J.T. Jones, Tyddyn Gwynt, Harlech LL46 2TH (0766 780298). ♛♛ Tyddyn Gwynt is beautifully situated within the Snowdonia National Park and three miles inland from Harlech. The farmhouse is fully modernised with storage heaters in public rooms and coal or log fires on chilly evenings. Electric heaters and hot water in the two family and double rooms. Lounge with TV and diningroom with separate tables. Ideal for beautiful sandy beach at Harlech and many tourist attractions within easy reach; for example, the Castles at Harlech and Caernarvon; the Royal St. David's Golf Course, Slate Mines, Narrow Gauge Railways, Portmeirion and many others. Fire Certificate held. A car is essential to make the most of your holiday and there is ample parking space. Rates reduced for children and babysitting is available. Evening Dinner, Bed and Breakfast or Bed and Breakfast only. AA approved and listed. SAE, please, for terms.

WALES

PLEASE SEND A STAMPED ADDRESSED ENVELOPE WITH ENQUIRIES

HARLECH. Mrs Ann Jones, Frondeg, Llanfair, Harlech LL46 2RE (Harlech [0766] 780448). A

beautiful 18th-century house, with magnificent views of Cardigan Bay, within a few minutes' walking distance of the lovely, secluded Harlech beach. An ideal central location for walking, climbing and fishing. Open from March to October, Frondeg comprises two double bedrooms, one twin-bedded room and one single room, all centrally heated and with vanity units. Bathroom with shower. Sittingroom has colour television. Separate diningroom. Pets welcome. Reductions for children under 10 years. Dinner, Bed and Breakfast or Bed and Breakfast only.

HARLECH. Mrs Ruth Owen, "Aris", Pen y Bryn, Harlech LL46 2SL (Harlech [0766] 780409). ♛ ♛ Welcome to our friendly guest house offering comfort and excellent food. Situated in a quiet spot with fine views over Harlech village and its famous castle, golf course, Cardigan Bay and the Snowdonia Mountains. Swimming pool and beach few minutes. Four tastefully furnished bedrooms with washbasins, one with private shower, electric blankets, tea/coffee making facilities, television and central heating. Log fire in lounge with patio to pretty gardens. Open all year. Children welcome. Ample parking. Dogs permitted. Home grown produce. Vegetarians catered for. Bed and Breakfast from £12; Dinner £6. Weekly terms from £100.

See also Colour Display Advertisement **LLANBEDR. Mrs E.L.L. Williams, Gorwel Deg, Hen Dy Farm, Llanbedr LL45 2LT (Llanbedr [034 123] 263).** Gorwel Deg farmhouse, cleverly converted from farm buildings, provides super accommodation. A working farm with a Welsh-speaking family, situated in a rural position in the heart of the Snowdonia National Park in a wealth of unspoilt beauty overlooking Cardigan Bay. The popular golden sands of Harlech and shells of Shell Island beaches are within easy reach. Convenient for golf, fishing, walking etc. An ideal spot for countryside tranquillity and peace. Provides good farmhouse cooking, and guest accommodation in one family, one double and one bunk room. Colour TV. Lounge. Evening Meal optional. Terms from £10.50 per person per night. Children under ten reduced rates.

LLANDUDNO. Mrs E. Jones, Gloddaeth Isa Farm, Derwen Lane, Penrhynside, Llandudno LL30 3DP

(0492 49209). A warm welcome awaits you at Gloddaeth Isa Farm, situated close to the village of Penrhynside, two miles from the popular Victorian holiday resort of Llandudno with its special attractions, The Great Orme and Happy Valley. Ideally located for touring the North Wales coast and Anglesey, within easy reach of the famous Bodnant Gardens and the historic town of Conway. Spacious and comfortable bedrooms with tea/coffee making facilities. TV lounge and two bathrooms. Ample car space. Children welcome. Evening Meal by arrangement only. Enquiries to **Mrs Eirwen Jones.**

WHEN MAKING ENQUIRIES PLEASE MENTION
FARM HOLIDAY GUIDES

LLANGEFNI. Mrs Ann T. Astley, Trer'ddol Farm, Llanerchymedd, Anglesey LL71 7AR (0248 470278). 🏵️ 🏵️ 🏵️ *Highly Commended.* A true Welsh welcome assured at this historic former 17th century manor house with traditional period furniture. Centrally situated off B5109 Llangefni to Holyhead road. 200 acres of freedom with panoramic views of Snowdonia. Ornithologists' paradise. Convenient for beaches and fishing. Free riding for children and participation in farm activities, including preparation of cattle for shows. Spacious en-suite bedrooms with TV and tea-making facilities. Cosy lounge with log fires, utility room for laundry, etc. Homely atmosphere with emphasis on good food and cleanliness. Children welcome at reduced rates. SAE for brochure.

WALES (side tab)

HELP IMPROVE BRITISH TOURIST STANDARDS

You are choosing holiday accommodation from our very popular FHG Publications. Whether it be a hotel, guest house, farmhouse or self-catering accommodation, we think you will find it hospitable, comfortable and clean, and your host and hostess friendly and helpful. Why not write and tell us about it?

As a recognition of the generally well-run and excellent holiday accommodation reviewed in our publications, we at FHG Publications Ltd. present a diploma to proprietors who receive the highest recommendation from their guests who are also readers of our Guides. If you care to write to us praising the holiday you have booked through FHG Publications Ltd. – whether this be board, self-catering accommodation, a sporting or a caravan holiday, what you say will be evaluated and the proprietors who reach our final list will be contacted.

The winning proprietor will receive an attractive framed diploma to display on his premises as recognition of a high standard of comfort, amenity and hospitality. FHG Publications Ltd. offer this diploma as a contribution towards the improvement of standards in tourist accommodation in Britain. Help your excellent host or hostess to win it!

FHG DIPLOMA

We nominate ....

....

Because

Name ....

Address ....

.... Telephone No. ....

LLYN PENINSULA. Mrs F.H. Coker, Mathan Uchaf, Boduan, Pwllheli LL53 6TU (0758 720487 or 0758 612621). OWNER BOOKINGS CUT COSTS. A choice of 37 properties all WTB verified are offered by our group of FARMWIVES. Llyn, an environmentally sensitive area with 50 miles of Heritage coastline, offers an idyllic relaxing holiday away from the madding crowd. Snowdonia National Park, castles, slate and copper mines, woollen mills, railways all within 25 miles. Water sports, pony trekking, sandy beaches, golfing and country lanes with abundance of fauna and flora provide varied interests. Pwllheli Leisure Centre offers sports facilities. Serviced and self-catering accommodation is offered. A warm Welsh welcome awaits all on our farms. Stamp for brochure.

MACHYNLLETH. Mrs Lynwen Edwards, Bryn Sion Farm, Cwm Cywarch, Dinas Mawddwy, Machynlleth SY20 9JG (Dinas Mawddwy [065-04] 251). A very warm welcome awaits you when you visit Bryn Sion Farm which is situated in the quiet, unspoilt valley of Cywarch at the foot of Arran Fawddwy (3,000ft), within easy reach of the beach. Fishing and shooting available on farm. Bryn Sion is a mixed farm of 700 acres offering a variety of good farmhouse meals and bed-time tea/coffee. Log fire in sittingroom in evening. Two double rooms, both with tea making facilities, shaving point, washbasin; bathroom. Cot and high chair available. Car essential — parking. Open all year for Bed, Breakfast and Evening Meal (from £15 per person) or Bed and Breakfast (from £10 per person). Reductions for children under 9. SAE, please, with enquiries.

MACHYNLLETH near. Dave and Ruth Sweeney, Rhianfa Guest House, Corris Uchaf, Near Machynlleth SY20 4BE (Corris [065-473] 283). Rhianfa is situated in beautiful, rugged countryside, on the edge of the Snowdonia National Park. Local attractions include the very interesting Centre for Alternative Technology, Corris Craft Centre and Tal-y-Llyn Railway, whilst lovely sandy beaches are within easy reach. This is a superb area for walking, being just two miles from Cader Idris. Rhianfa offers a friendly, informal atmosphere with good home-cooked food; children, pets and vegetarians are all especially welcome. Cots, toys, babysitting and reduced rates for children under 14. Open all year. Bed and Breakfast from £10.50 per person: optional Evening Meal £6. Special terms for groups.

PWLLHELI. Mrs G.A. Cook, Nantcol Welsh Pony Stud, Ty'n-y-Mynydd Farm, Boduan, Pwllheli LL53 8PZ (0758 720311). Set in the glorious countryside of the Llyn Peninsula enjoying splendid views of both mountains and sea. Situated in idyllic, tranquil and romantic surroundings yet close to all holiday amenities. The farm is also the home of the famous Nantcol Stud and Saddlery offering conducted tours for all ages and gift shop. Bed and Breakfast accommodation available in the farmhouse from £12 per night. For those who prefer self catering there is a cottage sleeping two and a large six berth caravan, both from £15 per night. We also welcome touring caravans and tents and have provided shower facilities for campers. Open all year. Brochure available.

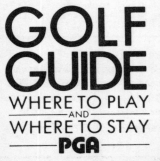

PWLLHELI. Mrs Helen Jones, Castellmarch, Abersoch, Pwllheli LL53 7UE (075881 2242). Castell-

march is a 200 acre beef and sheep farm situated one mile from the yachting village of Abersoch, and only a few minutes' walk from the nearest sandy beach. Accommodation comprises the west wing of Castellmarch, a 16th century farmhouse, which affords a lounge/kitchen with open inglenook fireplace; bathroom; two bedrooms (sleeps four plus cot); all rooms with exposed beams. Also a two bedroomed chalet set in an elevated position (sleeps four adults and two children). Both properties enjoy pleasant sea and countryside views. Bed and Breakfast from £11. Self-catering from £90 to £220. WTB approved.

PWLLHELI. Mrs Ann Williams, Bryn-yr-Aur Farm, Abererch, Pwllheli LL53 6BZ (Pwllheli [0758] 612007). Bryn-yr-Aur is a 75 acre stock rearing farm, situated on a hill overlooking Abererch village and Cardigan Bay about half a mile from A497 road (Pwllheli two miles, Criccieth five miles) and close to Abererch beach. The farm is within easy reach of numerous sandy beaches, the beautiful Llyn Peninsula, rugged mountains of Snowdonia and many interesting historical places. Enjoy fishing on the River Erch which runs through the farm. Friendly welcome awaits guests in comfortable homely accommodation. Two double and one single bedrooms; bathroom and toilet; diningroom and sittingroom with TV. Good home cooking with fresh farm produce and free-range eggs. Bed and Breakfast. Evening Meal (optional). Terms on request.

SNOWDONIA, Porthmadog. Mrs Carol Bain, "Old Mill Farmhouse", Fron Oleu Farm, Trawsfynydd,

Blaenau Ffestiniog LL41 4UN (0766 87 397). Welcome to our 18th century farmhouse in Snowdonia National Park. Working smallholding with goats, sheep, lambs, ducks, chickens, geese, rabbits and a horse. Exposed stonework and beams in bedrooms, with private shower/bathrooms. TV, tea/coffee making facilities, central heating if necessary, own front door in converted farm buildings. Fresh wholesome food. Free range eggs. After dinner, relax with your drink beside inglenook log fires. Scenic drives to castles, lakes, railways, safe sandy beaches. Bird watching, golf, walking, fishing, climbing, water sports, dry slope ski-ing, mountain biking. Pets and children welcome. Help feed the animals. Pony rides. Suitable for disabled guests. Level access. Wales Tourist Board registered. SAE for brochure.

See also Colour Display Advertisement **TALSARNAU. Mr G.J. Williams, Gwrach Ynys Country Guest House, Ynys, Talsarnau LL47 6TS (Harlech [0766] 780742). ✿ ✿ ✿** Country house with all bedrooms en-suite (coffee/tea making facilities); separate tables in diningroom, comfortable lounge, separate TV room. Good, wholesome cooking using local produce. Ideal rambling and birdwatching centre; golf, swimming pool, beach two miles. Children under 12 free accommodation if sharing. Special rates OAPs out of season. AA Listed. Brochure sent with pleasure.

TREFRIW. Mrs K. Jones, Tan-y-Coed, Trefriw LL27 0JU (Llanrwst [0492] 640766). Trefriw is situated between Betws-y-Coed and Conwy, among scenery which ranks with the best in the world. This is a friendly household, overseas visitors and honeymooners especially welcome; many guests return year after year and we receive many letters of recommendation. Only a few visitors received at one time so there is no overcrowding. The house overlooks the village and Conwy Valley, and is very central for both Snowdonia and the coast (eight miles). Llandudno, Colwyn Bay and the famous Bodnant Gardens within a short distance. Fishing lakes and mountains easily accessible. Half hourly bus service. Two double bedrooms and one family room; bathroom, two toilets; sittingroom, diningroom. Central heating. Parking. Bed and Breakfast from £8.50 per night. SAE, please.

GWYNEDD – OUTSTANDING NATURAL BEAUTY!

With Snowdonia National Park and the Lleyn Peninsula, Gwynedd well deserves its designation as an 'Area of Outstanding Natural Beauty'. The tourist is spoiled for choice in this county but should endeavour to visit the hill-fort at Tre'r Ceiri, the Llugwy Valley, Cwm Pennant, Dinas Dinlle hill-fort, the gold mine at Clogau and the railways and quarries at Blaenau Ffestiniog.

POWYS

BRECON. Mrs M.E. Williams, Lower Rhydness, Llyswen, Brecon LD3 0AZ (Llyswen 0874-754264 or 087-485264). Working farm. Lower Rhydness is a 150-acre livestock farm nicely situated in the Wye Valley three miles from main A470 road, 11 miles from the Royal Welsh Showgrounds at Builth Wells, and Brecon. The farmhouse is old and rich in character with oak beams and panelling and offers accommodation in one double, one twin-bedded and one family bedrooms; bathroom with shower and toilet; sittingroom and diningroom. Children are welcome and cot and high chair are provided. Pets allowed. Reduced rates for children. Mrs Williams serves good home produced food in an easy-going atmosphere. Within reach of Brecon Beacons, Black Mountains, Elan Valley, etc. There are lovely walks in the area; pony trekking, sailing at Llangorse Lake. Bed and Breakfast from £10.50 nightly; Bed, Breakfast and Evening Dinner from £105.00 weekly. SAE, please, for brochure. WTB listed.

BRECON. Mrs Ray M. Roderick, Pwllacca Farm, Llanfihangel-Nant-Bran, Brecon LD3 9LY (Sennybridge [087-482] 255). Working farm. Accommodation is offered from Easter to October on this 150-acre livestock farm near the Brecon Beacons. Many beautiful hill, riverside and woodland walks on the farm. Easy reach for walking in Brecon Beacons, Black Mountains and Eypnt. One double/family, one single and one twin-bedded rooms, with washbasins and shaver points. Bathroom, toilet. Sittingroom; diningroom. Children welcome, cot, high chair, babysitting. Sorry, no pets. Log fire in old stone fireplace and storage heaters. Good home cooking served. Bed and Breakfast (Evening Meal optional). Terms from £10 per night. Reductions for stays of five nights or more. Reduced rates for children under 14 years.

BRECON. Mrs Eileen Williams, Upper Farm, Llechfaen, Brecon LD3 7SP (Llanfrynach [087-486] 269). Working farm, join in. A modernised farmhouse offering Bed and Breakfast only, situated just off the A40 Brecon to Abergavenny road, two miles from Brecon town. A 64-acre dairy farm in the heart of the National Park directly facing Brecon Beacons. Ideal for touring, golf, trekking and fishing nearby, with many Welsh craft shops to visit too. Two double, one single and one family bedrooms; bathroom; toilet; sittingroom; diningroom. Cot, babysitting, reduced rates for children. Open all year. Car essential — parking. No pets.

CENTRAL WALES. Victoria Wells Forest Cabin Holiday Motel, Powys. Arguably as like the Canadian

Rockies as you'll find in this country! High in the verdant mountains of Central Wales, situated in 24 acres of woodlands and with miles of natural parkland and riverside walks. Victoria Wells is the ideal holiday location for those who want to unwind and shed the tensions of modern living * Three-quarters-of-a-mile of private fishing * Heated swimming pool * Restaurant and bar * Horse riding and pony trekking centres nearby. All accommodation is ensuite with colour TV, tea-making facilities. Children and pets welcome. Bargain Breaks which includes Bed, full English Breakfast and Evening Meal, £55 for three days. Weekly tariff also available. Bookings by telephone: **Victoria Wells Booking Office, Grosvenor House, 20 St. Andrews Crescent, Cardiff CF1 3DD (Cardiff [0222] 340558 or FAX: [0222] 223692).**

GLADESTRY. Mrs M.E. Hughes, Stonehouse Farm, Gladestry, Kington, Herefordshire HR5 3NU (Gladestry [054-422] 651). Working farm. Large Georgian farmhouse, modernised whilst retaining its character, situated on Welsh border with Offa's Dyke Footpath going through its 380 acres of mixed farming with stream. Beautiful unspoiled area for walking. Many places of interest within driving distance such as Elan Valley dams, Devil's Bridge, Llangorse Lake, Kington golf course, pony trekking. Guests are accommodated in one double, one family and one twin-bedded rooms, two with washbasins; bathroom, two toilets; sitting and diningroom. TV. Homely informal atmosphere with home produced food and home cooking. Vegetarian meals on request. Children welcome. Babysitting available. Evening Dinner/Meal, Bed and Breakfast or Bed and Breakfast. SAE for terms. No pets.

LLANGURIG. Mrs Anna Rollings, The Old Vicarage, Llangurig SY18 6RN (Llangurig [05515] 280).

🐾🐾🐾 Charming Victorian guest house situated in Llangurig — at 100 ft the highest village in Wales. Ideal base for walking, bird watching, fishing and for touring the hills, valleys and lakes of Central Wales. All bedrooms are tastefully furnished with washbasins and heating; some rooms en-suite. Two guests' lounges with colour TV, library of books/maps on Mid Wales; diningroom with separate tables, and fully licensed. Choice of Evening Meals — diets and vegetarians catered for. Pets welcome. Tourist Board Award for high standards and service. AA listed. A warm welcome guaranteed!

MACHYNLLETH. Mrs H. Matthews, Talbontdrain Farm Guest House, Uwchygarreg, Machynlleth SY20 8RR (0654 702192). A 200 year old farmhouse in remote valley surrounded by sheep pastures. Twin, family and single rooms, really good freshly cooked food (no microwave!) and own milk, eggs and honey. Children welcome, dressing up box, dolls house and pianola as well as a friendly dog to throw sticks for. Walking weekends all year, and excellent bird watching from the window! Local attractions include wonderful sandy beaches, the National Centre for Alternative Technology, working mills, golf and fishing as well as a really attractive market town with excellent holiday shopping. Bed and Breakfast from £13; Walking Weekends from £80. Phone for colour brochure.

Talbontdrain

MONTGOMERY. Mrs G.M. Bright, Little Brompton Farm, Montgomery SY15 6HY (Montgomery [0686] 668 371). 🌺🌺 **Working farm, join in.** Little Brompton Farm is a delightful 17th-century farmhouse just two miles east of Montgomery on the B4385. It is our own home and we wish guests to enjoy the peaceful comfortable surroundings. We offer the discriminating guest the unique opportunity of enjoying the comforts of today with the charm and character of "By-gone-days". Our home is furnished in the traditional country style, and has many original oak beams which add to its gracious welcoming atmosphere. Double, twin and family bedrooms, with washbasins, shaver points, tea-making facilities. Two bedrooms with en-suite facilities. Children welcome with all provision made for their needs. Two bathrooms, separate shower room. TV lounge and diningroom with separate tables. Central heating. Good home cooking with fresh farm produce served whenever possible. Guests may try the spinning wheel, browse through the bookcases, sit in the garden or make use of the patio. A peacock roams around the grounds. Excellent selection of brochures, maps and books of the local area. Bed and Breakfast from £12.50. Dinner, Bed and Breakfast available. Comfort, elegance and personal attention with value for money are our priorities.

HOLIDAY ACCOMMODATION
Classification Schemes in England, Scotland and Wales

The National Tourist Boards for England, Scotland and Wales have agreed a common 'Crown Classification' scheme for **serviced (Board)** accommodation. All establishments are inspected regularly and are given a classification indicating their level of facilities and services.

There are six grades ranging from 'Listed' to 'Five Crowns' 🌺🌺🌺🌺🌺'. The higher the classification, the more facilities and services offered.

Crown classification is a measure of *facilities* not *quality*. A common quality grading scheme grades the quality of establishments as 'Approved', 'Commended' or 'Highly Commended' according to the accommodation, welcome and service they provide.

For **Self-Catering**, holiday homes in England are awarded 'Keys' after inspection and can also be 'Approved', 'Commended' or 'Highly Commended' according to the facilities available. In Scotland the Crown scheme includes self-catering accommodation and Wales also has a voluntary inspection scheme for self-catering grading from '1 (Standard)' to '5 (Excellent)'.

Caravan and Camping Parks can participate in the British Holiday Parks grading scheme from 'Approved (√)' to 'Excellent (√ √ √ √ √)'. In addition, each National Tourist Board has an annual award for high-quality caravan accommodation: in England – Rose Awards; in Scotland – Thistle Commendations; in Wales – Dragon Awards.

When advertisers supply us with the information, FHG Publications show Crowns and other awards or gradings, including AA, RAC, Egon Ronay etc. We also award a small number of Farm Holiday Guide Diplomas every year, based on readers' recommendations.

MONTGOMERY. Ceinwen Richards, The Drewin Farm, Churchstoke, Montgomery SY15 6TW (05885 325). 🐾🐾 A family-run mixed farm set on hillside overlooking panoramic views of the most beautiful countryside. The Drewin is a 17th century farmhouse retaining much of its original character with oak beams and large inglenook fireplace, separate lounge. Pleasant bedrooms (one family and one twin, sleep six) with all modern amenities. Fully centrally heated. A games room with snooker table in converted granary for guests' use. Offa's Dyke footpath runs through the farm. Ideal base for touring the many beauty spots around. Good home cooking and a very warm welcome await our visitors. Bed and Breakfast from £12; Bed, Breakfast and Evening Meal from £18. AA and Best Bed and Breakfast in the World Recommended. Holder of Hygiene Certificate and Farmhouse Award from Wales Tourist Board.

RHAYADER. Mr and Mrs Roger Price, Downfield Farm, Rhayader LD6 5PA (Rhayader [0597] 810394). Working farm. Downfield Farm is a 60-acre mixed farm situated one mile east of Rhayader on A44 Crossgates Road, with ample parking space. Surrounded by hills and lakes, fishing, pony trekking and good walking country nearby. We extend a warm welcome to all our guests. There are three double bedrooms, all with washbasins and tea-making facilities; comfortable lounge with colour TV. Children are welcomed and pets allowed. Open from February to November. Car is essential. Bed and Breakfast from £11.50 daily. SAE, please, for details. Tourist Board Listed.

WELSHPOOL. Mrs F.M. Hughes, Plasdwpa, Berriew, Welshpool SY21 8PS (0686 640 298). Plasdwpa is a poultry and dairy farm situated one and a half miles from the pretty village of Berriew. Modern house with panoramic views of the Severn Valley and the Shropshire hills. Three double bedrooms, all with washbasins, and one single room downstairs. Large bathroom and shower; downstairs toilet. Spacious lounge with colour TV. Dining-room. Full English Breakfasts and three course Evening Meals served. Tea/coffee making facilities. Facilities for babies babysitting available. Open Easter to October. Brochure and terms on request.

WELSHPOOL. Mrs Mary Payne, Heath Cottage, Forden, Welshpool SY21 8LX (Forden [0938 76] 453). Our 18th century cottage smallholding is set in over five acres of beautiful Borderland scenery. There are three guest rooms: one family, one double and one single, all with private facilities; central heating throughout; open fire and colour TV in sittingroom. Offa's Dyke goes through the fields. Nearby are a riding stable, River Severn and Powys Castle (National Trust). A car is essential to explore the lakes and mountains, ancient towns and West Wales coast. Bed and Breakfast from £14; Dinner £7. Reduced weekly rate. WTB and AA Listed.

POWYS – MOUNTAINOUS AND LANDLOCKED

With many border castles and the Brecon Beacons, which cover the south of the county, Powys can be very spectacular. You will also find the best stretches of Offa's Dyke, Hay-On-Wye, the steam railway at Llanfair Caereinion, Radnor Forest, the fortified house of Tretower, the farming centre at Builth Wells and the abandoned medieval town of Cefnllys.

SELF-CATERING HOLIDAYS

CLWYD

RUTHIN. Mrs E. Jones, Tyddyn Isaf, Rhewl, Ruthin LL15 1UH (082-42 3367). You can relax in tranquill surroundings of a working farm at Tyddyn Isaf, three miles from historic town of Ruthin, one mile from village shop and pub. The spacious and comfortable holiday accommodation is self contained within the stone built farmhouse, where modern comforts combine with old world charm. Lounge/diner with exposed beams. Colour TV. Kitchen with cooker, fridge, washing machine. Bathroom. Two bedrooms sleep six plus cot. Lawned garden. Convenient for visiting Snowdonia, Bala, Chester and the coast. Central heating in winter months. Also two bedroomed static caravan in its own surroundings.

DYFED

ABERPORTH. Neuadd-Wen Holiday Bungalows, Aberporth, Cardigan. Neuadd-Wen has six holiday bungalows peacefully situated just off the sea-front in the picturesque coastal village of Aberporth, and only 250 yards from sandy beach. Modern brick-built construction and fully equipped for up to five (except linen). Lounge, kitchenette, two bedrooms, bathroom with WC. Fridge, electric cooker, electric fires and colour TV. Cleanliness assured. Private parking. Shops, restaurant, cafe and hotel only three minutes' walk. Golf, squash, fishing, pony trekking/riding within easy reach. These bungalows are also ideal for early/late holidays, for the beach, coastal walks or for touring the surrounding areas of outstanding natural beauty. Tourist Board registered. SAE for brochure to **Mr and Mrs A. Phillips, Orchard House, Aberporth SA43 2HG (0239 811167).**

ABERPORTH. Quality Cottages. Around the magnificent Welsh coast. Away from the madding crowd. Near safe sandy beaches. A small specialist agency offering privacy, peace and unashamed luxury. Wales Tourist Board 1989 Award Winner. Residential standards — dishwashers, microwaves, washing machines, central heating, log fires, no slot meters. Linen provided. Pets welcome free. All in coastal areas famed for scenery, walks, wild flowers, birds, badgers and foxes. Free colour brochure **S.C. Rees, Quality Cottages, Cerbid, Solva, Haverfordwest, Pembrokeshire SA62 6YE (0348 837971).**

BOSHERSTON. Quality Cottages. Around the magnificent Welsh coast. Away from the madding crowd. Near safe sandy beaches. A small specialist agency offering privacy, peace and unashamed luxury. Wales Tourist Board 1989 Award Winner. Residential standards — dishwashers, microwaves, washing machines, central heating, log fires, no slot meters. Linen provided. Pets welcome free. All in coastal areas famed for scenery, walks, wild flowers, birds, badgers and foxes. Free colour brochure **S.C. Rees, Quality Cottages, Cerbid, Solva, Haverfordwest, Pembrokeshire SA62 6YE (0348 837971).**

CARDIGAN. Mrs E. White, Tynewydd, Blaenporth, Cardigan SA43 2AX (Aberporth [0239] 810303). Cottage on smallholding in the village of Blaenporth, six miles north of Cardigan and two miles from sandy beach at Aberporth, with other sandy beaches within few miles. Cottage is single-storeyed, adjacent to house. One double bedroom and one bunk-room which converts to single if necessary. Livingroom with bed-settee and colour TV. Fully equipped kitchen and bathroom. Clean and well aired. Electric heaters in all rooms. Spacious garden with lawn provides safe play area, parking space well away from road. Restaurants, pub, takeaway, shop, Post Office and garage a half a mile. Fishing, castle, railway, swimming pool, tennis within easy reach. On the A487 Aberystwyth/Cardigan road.

CARDIGAN. Mrs B. Davies, Nantycroy Farm, Verwig, Cardigan SA43 1PU (Cardigan [0239] 612506). Working farm. Sleeps 2/8. Accommodation for self-catering holidaymakers in a house on a 191-acre working farm off the main road between Gwbert-on-Sea and Mwnt Beach, overlooking the sea and Cardigan Island. Footpath to Mwnt Beach. Delightful cliff walks and seals can sometimes be seen at play. Golf, fishing, sailing, pony riding and many lovely beaches, woollen and flour mills to visit, all within easy reach. Three double bedrooms; bathroom, toilets; sittingroom with TV; fully equipped kitchen with electric cooker, fridge, hot and cold water. Immersion heater. No linen supplied. Children welcome, cot and high chair available. Pets by prior arrangement. Car essential — parking. Available March to December. Terms from £60 weekly.

CARDIGAN. Mr and Mrs Gow, Croft Farm Guest House and Country Cottages, Llantood, Cardigan SA43 3NT (0239 615179).

You are welcome to stay in one of five newly converted slate farm buildings, sleeping two to six, on croft working smallholding. All cottages are fully furnished and carpeted and have modern well equipped kitchens and central heating. Retaining their character and offering present day comforts including remote control colour TV, flowers and warmth on arrival in cooler months. Children may help feed the animals. Home cooked dinners available in our licensed guesthouse. Pets welcome. Wales Tourist Board Grade 5. Close to market town of Cardigan, sandy beaches, National Park. open all year. Terms from £79 to £325 per week. Short Breaks two to four nights available. Brochure on request.

CARDIGAN COAST (Tresaith/Llangranog). Mrs C. Davies, Brynarthen, Glynarthen, Llandysul SA44 6TG (Rhydlewis [023-975] 783). Cottages sleep 6.

Brynarthen is a small working farm delightfully situated amidst beautiful unspoilt countryside, minutes from sandy beaches, one mile off the A487 Cardigan/Aberaeron coastal road. Within the grounds are two charming traditional stone cottages and one caravan, each surrounded by pleasant lawns and gardens, ideal for those just wishing to relax and take it easy. The Wales Tourist Board assess the cottages as Grade 5 (highest grade possible). They are personally maintained to a high standard and whilst retaining all their charm and character, are comfortably furnished to meet family needs. One is also ideal for the elderly or disabled. Each cottage sleeps six with three bedrooms, bathroom, fully equipped kitchen/diner, lounge with colour TV and fitted carpets throughout. For couples requiring similar accommodation, the 27' caravan has a double bedroom, bathroom, fully equipped kitchen/diner, lounge with colour TV and fitted carpets throughout. Open all year. Brochure on request.

CARDIGAN near. Glandwr, Llangoedmor, Near Cardigan. Glandwr Holiday House is in the Parish of Llangoedmor near Cardigan. Situated on the B4570, one mile from market town of Cardigan. Glandwr is a charming, well-equipped semi-detached holiday house in its own grounds with a small drive. Ample parking space. Sunny position with lawn front and back. Lovely countryside views and walks. Comprising fitted kitchen/dining area, fully equipped with full size electric stove, all utensils etc., two fridges; comfortable sittingroom has 20" colour TV. Two double bedrooms (double bed in each), single bedroom, all well equipped. Bathroom with over bath electric shower, washbasin, toilet; downstairs toilet. Fitted carpets. Central heating, electricity inclusive in charge. Available all year from £80 inclusive per week. Mini breaks any three nights, £48 for two persons, £58 for three persons inclusive. Extra person, additional £10 per week. One well-trained pet £8 per week extra. Sandy beaches two to eight miles; fishing on River Teifi. High standard of comfort, service and heating. SAE to **Mrs B. Evans, Rhydyfuwch Dairy Farm, Near Cardigan SA43 2LB (Cardigan [0239] 612064).**

CARMARTHEN. Mr and Mrs B. and V. Newton, Plasnewydd Farm, Blaenycoed, Carmarthen SA33 6EX (0267-87368). Working farm, join in.

Two attractive self-catering cottages both situated on a small peaceful farm nine miles north of Carmarthen, two miles off A484. Centrally situated, ideal for touring Carmarthenshire, Cardiganshire and Pembrokeshire areas and unspoilt coast line. Local castles, potteries, craft industries, gold mines, adventure parks, pony trekking, steam railway, forestry walks, fishing, golf (Carmarthen Club three miles). Sleeping four/eight, from £90 to £200 per week. Evening Dinner, to a particularly high standard, available from the farmhouse, as are fresh eggs and milk. Welsh Tourist Board registered.

CENARTH. Mrs J. Kelsey, Ffynnonddewi, Cenarth, Newcastle Emlyn SA38 9JK (Llechryd [023-987] 579). Sleeps 4. Close to Cardigan and the seaside village of Aberporth and near the famous Salmon Leap at Cenarth. Modernised Welsh farm cottage with much of its original charm, old beams, inglenook fireplace. Large livingroom; kitchen/diner with gas cooker, fridge and immersion heater; bathroom. Accommodation for four in two comfortable bedrooms, one with double bed and one with two single beds. TV; car parking. An excellent centre for salmon and trout fishing, and for the Preseli National Park with its lovely coastal walks and beautiful sandy beaches. Many interesting tourist attractions and pony trekking nearby. Open Easter to October. Terms from £80 to £150 weekly.

CEREDIGION. Rhysgog, Llanddewi Brefi, Tregaron. Working farm, join in. Properties sleep 6 adults. Modern comfortable accommodation in bungalow and units on Rhysgog, an 800 acre working sheep and beef farm. The accommodation is for six in each, with three bedrooms — two with double beds and one with two single beds; bathroom, toilet; sittingroom/diningroom. Kitchen with electric cooker, etc. TV. Everything supplied except linen. Suitable for disabled or elderly guests. Shop half a mile. Pets are allowed. Car essential, parking. Open all year. The countryside here is really beautiful and unspoilt, with mountains and hills, and within easy distance of the sea. There is something for everyone — fishing (private 14 acre lake), shooting (1000 acres), pony trekking, golf four miles. Ideal walking country. Bird watching also, including the Red Kite. Weekly terms from £80 to £180. SAE, please, to: **Mr D. Gordon Jones, Pant Farm, Llanddewi Brefi, Tregaron SY25 6UQ (0974 298753 or 298311).**

GOODWICK. Mrs Rosemary Johns, Carne, Goodwick SA64 0LB (St. Nicholas [03485] 665). Working farm, join in. Sleeps 5/6. Part of old stone farmhouse in peaceful surroundings on 200 acre dairy and sheep farm. The accommodation sleeps six in three bedrooms; living/diningroom with colour TV; bathroom and fitted kitchen with washing machine. Linen is not supplied. Children are welcome and there is fenced garden where they can play safely. Cot and high chair provided and babysitting available. The farm is three miles from Fishguard, two miles from the sea and within easy reach of many beaches by car. Visitors are welcome to join in farm activities and walk around. Pets welcome if under control. Open all year.

HAVERFORDWEST. Nolton Haven Cottages in the Pembrokeshire National Park. Luxury, recently converted cottages are just 30 yards from the beaches at Nolton Haven in the Pembrokeshire National Park. Equipped with all modern facilities, the open plan lounge and kitchen, two bedrooms (one with balcony), shower and bathroom are also fully carpeted. Private inner courtyard and front grass extending almost to beach. Excellent facilities nearby include hotel with public bar and licensed restaurant. Open all year. Brochure on request with SAE: **D. and J. Canton, Nolton Haven Farm, Nolton Haven, Haverfordwest, Pembrokeshire SA62 1NH (0437-710263).**

HAVERFORDWEST. Mrs E.M. Mathias, Court House Cottages, Wolfsdale, Camrose, Near Haverfordwest SA62 6JJ (Camrose [0437] 710310). Working farm. Cottages sleep 6. Centrally situated for all St. Bride's Bay and close to Prescelli Hills, three homely, stone-built cottages, each sleeping six in three double rooms, plus cots. Well-equipped kitchen area, lounge/diner, colour TV, shower room and toilet. Electricity by 50p meter. Situated in quiet, unspoilt hamlet of Wolfsdale, the owners' 300-acre farm is nearby, and through which flows the Western Cleddau with good trout, sewin and salmon fishing. Lovely country walks, near beautiful sandy beaches and coastal paths. Car essential — parking. Shops half-a-mile. Open all year weekly terms from £80. The market town of Haverfordwest, Cathedral City of St. David's, popular seaside resorts and many places of historic and geological interest within easy driving distance. Further details on request.

HAVERFORDWEST. Lower Cottage, Slatemill, Dale Road, St. Ishmaels, Haverfordwest. Lower Cottage, Slatemill, is quietly situated on a private farm lane in the Pembrokeshire National Park, two miles from the yachting centre of Dale and a similar distance from many delightful beaches and havens. The area is noted for wildlife, particularly in the early Spring, being near the bird sanctuary islands of Skomer and Skokholm. The white painted and beamed farm cottage has been completely modernised and is fully furnished with the exception of personal linen. It comprises sitting room with open fire, dining room and kitchen. The two bedrooms each contain one double and one single divan, plus a cot in one. Separate bathroom and toilet. Other amenitites include large refrigerator, electric cooker and immersion heater with good airing cupboard. Also portable electric fires, electric blankets and TV. Terms on application to **Mrs U.A. Roberts, 27 Wood Lane, Wickersley, Near Rotherham, S. Yorkshire S66 0JT (0709-544660).**

HAVERFORDWEST. Caerhafod House, Henllys, Llanrhian, Haverfordwest. Caerhafod is a private Country House, set in six acres of land within the Pembrokeshire National Park. It is conveniently situated between Fishguard and the Cathedral City of St. David's enjoying breathtaking views of the sea and surrounding coastline and countryside, with numerous safe, sandy beaches within easy reach. The area is completely unspoilt and is of great archaeological interest. A holiday at Caerhafod is ideal for both young and old. There are five bedrooms, bathroom and shower room, all modern conveniences plus colour TV. Ample parking and large lawned area for children to play. Full details and terms from **Mrs A.W.H. Charles, Henllys, Llanrhian, Haverfordwest, Pembrokeshire SA62 5BH (Croesgoch [03483] 364).**

HAVERFORDWEST. Capt. R.W.D. Kenyon, Curlew Cottage, Haverfordwest. Luxury cottage set in large private grounds in the heart of the Pembrokeshire National Park, overlooking sea and open countryside. Five minutes' walk to clean, sandy beach and spectacular coastal path scenery. Modern pine kitchen has fridge/freezer, dishwasher, washing machine and microwave. Sleeps four/five people in two large bedrooms (linen and electric blankets supplied). Swing, and Games Room with table-tennis and darts. Delicious home-cooked meals delivered to your table. Double glazing and heating ensure all year round comfort. Doorstep parking for cars and boats. Weekly terms; £100 to £325. Three night mini-breaks from October to April: £55. Linen, heating, electricity, colour TV etc. inclusive. Telephone bookings recommended. Wales Tourist Board 4 Dragons Award. SAE appreciated. **Capt. R.W.D. Kenyon, Folkeston Hill Farm, Nolton Haven, Haverfordwest SA62 3NL (0437 710621).**

HAVERFORDWEST. Mrs E.M. Thomas, Trewilym Farm, Hayscastle, Haverfordwest SA62 5AA (0348 831381). Nicely situated self catering accommodation for six people on this 300 acre farm where visitors and their children are welcome to walk around. The farm is near Newgale beach and many other beautiful sandy beaches and there are lovely country walks along the coastal path. Accommodation comprises double bedroom and singles, bathroom, sitting room with TV. Well equipped kitchen/dining-room. Car essential — ample parking. Shop half a mile. Market town of Haverfordwest, Cathedral City of St David's and many other places of interest within easy reach. Open from May to September. Linen not provided, cot and high chair available. Sorry no pets. Terms from £80 to £200.

HAVERFORDWEST near. Charles and Joy Spiers, West Lambston, Near Portfield Gate, Haverfordwest SA62 3LG (Camrose [0437] 710038). Sleeps 2 adults; 2 children. Peace and quiet. No early morning tractors on non-working farm. A self contained cottage in 150-year-old farmhouse. Beach within three miles. Many delightful walks — maps provided. Recently fitted kitchen with automatic washer, ironing equipment and fridge; shower and toilet room. Sleeps four in two bedrooms. Gas cast iron stove set in charming oak beamed inglenook, colour TV. Pine furniture, cosy window seat and Laura Ashley fabrics retain the cottage atmosphere. Children welcome; cot, high chair and babysitter available. Swings and climbing frame. Pets permitted by arrangement. Cotton bed linen, beach, bath, hand and tea towels provided. All inclusive from £85 to £195 weekly.

KIDWELLY. Coedadam, Llangendeirne, Kidwelly, Carmarthen. Sleeps 8. Coedadam, standing in 100

acres of grazing land, has been carefully modernised to retain its original character with such homely features as an old inglenook fireplace with a canopy and log fire. Accommodates eight in three double bedrooms, plus cot and high chair; two bathrooms/toilets; sittingroom; diningroom; TV; fitted kitchen with electric cooker, fridge, immersion heater, electric fire. Electricity metered. Economy 7 central heating. Linen not supplied. Car essential — parking. Shops three miles away. Pets allowed. Coin box telephone. Available April to October. This property is suitable for seaside or country holidays with complete privacy not usually obtainable these days. Seven miles from seaside resorts of Ferryside and Cefnsidan. A good touring centre for West Wales. SAE for terms to **Mr S. Thomas, Lletymaelog, Llandeilo SA19 7HY (Llandeilo [0558] 823541) evenings only.**

See also Colour Display Advertisement **LAMPETER near. Tyglyn Holiday Estate (Dept FHG), Ciliau Aeron, Near Lampeter SA48 8DD (Aeron [0570] 470684). Working farm. Bungalows sleep 6.** In the heart of rural Wales and only four miles from the seaside town of Aberaeron: 20 award-winning brick-built semi-detached, two bedroomed Bungalows. All modern facilities and colour TV. Pets welcome. Holders of Wales Tourist Board Self Catering award. Range of outdoor activities locally. For further details contact **Nigel Edkins** for a free colour brochure.

Terms quoted in this publication may be subject to increase if rises in costs necessitate

LLANDOVERY. Tyncoed Farm, Myddfai Road, Llandovery. Sleeps 7+. This spacious and very comfort-

able old farmhouse is beautifully set overlooking the Towy Valley, with magnificent views from the house. Tyncoed is in a secluded and private position, yet very conveniently situated just off the A4069 Llandovery/Llangadog road. The farmhouse retains much character and charm with its original stone fireplace and oak beams. As it is on the fringe of the Brecon Beacons National Park, it makes a perfect base for touring this delightful rural area. Log fires and storage heaters. Fully equipped. Cot and high chair available. Terms from £100 to £200 per week. SAE, please for further details to **Mrs Lewis Jones, Llwynmeredydd Farm, Myddfai, Llandovery SA20 0JE (Llandovery [0550] 20450).**

LLANGADOG. Penmaen, Llanddeusant, Llangadog. Furnished farmhouse situated in the unspoilt countryside of the Brecon Beacons National Park. Visitors can enjoy panoramic views of the Black Mountain and surrounding farms, with cattle, sheep and ponies grazing the fields. Many places of interest in the area including castles, caves and seaside, which is within reach by car. Other activities include pony riding and fishing, and there are lakes and mountain walks to enjoy. Farmhouse sleeps up to 12 people. Oil fired central heating, double glazing, exposed oak beams. Open all year. Please send SAE for further details. Large caravan also available. **Mr W.B. Price, Tybrych, Llanddeusant, Llangadog SA19 9TN (05504 252).**

LLANGADOG. Mrs D.J. Price, Gwydre Farm, Llanddeusant, Llangadog SA19 9YS (Gwynfe [05504]

242). Working farm. Sleeps 6 adults. Gwydre is a comfortable, spacious and well equipped cottage on a working beef and sheep farm at 900 feet situated in the peaceful, beautiful Black Mountain area of the Brecon Beacons National Park. There are extensive views of farmland and mountains. Superb walking from gentle strolls on country lanes to strenuous climbs on the Black Mountain. Fishing in nearby lakes and reservoirs and birdwatching. The cottage has an original inglenook fireplace and woodburner and consists of three bedrooms; two double beds, two single and a cot. Bathroom with hot shower and separate toilet. Fully fitted kitchen and microwave. Large lounge with colour TV. Carpeted throughout. Electricity by 50p meter. Small pets allowed. Linen is supplied. Wales Tourist Board registered. Open April — October from £100 weekly.

See also Colour Display Advertisement MYDROILYN. Blaenllanarth Holiday Cottages, Mydroilyn, Lampeter SA48 7RJ (Lampeter [0570] 470374). Stone farm buildings, newly converted into four cottages, providing a modern standard of comfort in a traditional setting. Sleep two/three (terms £70-£160) or four/eight (terms £110-£280). Gas, electricity and linen included in price. All have shower room and fully equippped kitchen. Colour TV available; laundry room; facilities for children. Open Easter to October. Situated in a secluded rural area, abundant with wildlife and flowers, and only five miles from sandy beaches and picturesque harbours of Cardigan Bay. Within easy reach of National Trust coastal footpaths, sites of historic and cultural interest, steam railways, castles and breathtaking mountain scenery. Bird watching, fishing and pony trekking nearby. Wales Tourist Board and AA approved. Full details from **Gil and Mike Kearney.**

NEW QUAY. Mrs Catherine Davies, Cwmcynon Farm, Llwyndafydd, New Quay, Llandysul SA44 6LE (New Quay [0545] 560426). Working farm, join in. Sleeps 6 Adults, 2 Children. Cwmcynon is a working

family farm with a milking herd and a flock of sheep, guests being welcome to watch or take part in farm activities! Llwyndafydd one-quarter-of-a-mile with shop/post office, village pub, petrol. Accommodation comprising a self-contained part of the owner's farmhouse (private and separate front and back door) includes: large sittingroom with colour TV, electric or open fire; kitchen/diner with electric cooker, fridge/freezer, washing machine, tumble dryer; four bedrooms; large private bathroom. Central heating throughout. Cot, high chair and baby bath available, babysitting by arrangement. Large lawn where children can play. Ample parking. Pets welcome. Open March to October, terms from £120 to £220 weekly. Places of interest, recreation/leisure facilities accommodated nearby. WTB Grade 2.

WHEN MAKING ENQUIRIES PLEASE MENTION
FARM HOLIDAY GUIDES

OAKFORD (near Llanarth). Mrs M. Howell, Cringoed Holiday Cottages, Oakford, Llanarth (0545

580470). Cringoed is an old farmhouse with a 90 foot long stone and slate farm building and two acres of informal grounds surrounded by quiet farmland with lovely views and glimpses of the sea, three miles away. Converted into two flats and two cottages, original stonework and timber features have been retained and modern conveniences and comfort added. Oakford Village with a pub, post office and trout pools is only half a mile away. Lovely beaches, coastal walks, mountain drives, riding and fishing all locally. Children, ornithologists, able and disabled visitors are warmly welcomed.

PENDINE. Mrs Ann Williams, Garness Farm Bungalow, Marros Pendine, Carmarthen SA33 4PL

(Pendine [09945] 277/496). In a superb position overlooking the sea, this modern detached bungalow is situated off a farm trackway between Amroth (four miles), and glorious Pendine (two miles). There are many lovely walks in the area. The accommodation consists of a kitchen/diner with fitted units and a gas cooker, a comfortable lounge with colour TV and a portable gas heater, a bathroom and two bedrooms one double and one twin-bedded. Children welcome. Weekly terms from £80 to £145.

SOLVA. Quality Cottages. Around the magnificent Welsh coast, away from the madding crowd. Near safe sandy beaches. A small specialist agency offering privacy, peace and unashamed luxury. Wales Tourist Board 1989 Award Winner. Residential standards — dishwashers, microwaves, washing machines, central heating, log fires, no slot meters. Linen provided. Pets welcome free. All in coastal areas famed for scenery, walks, wild flowers, birds, badgers and foxes. Free Colour brochure **S.C. Rees, Quality Cottages, Cerbid, Solva, Haverfordwest, Pembrokeshire SA62 6YE (0348 837971).**

ST. DAVID'S. "Llysnewydd", St. David's. Sleeps 4 adults; 3 children. Llysnewydd is a delightful

farmhouse situated in Pembrokeshire's renowned National Park, six miles from ST. DAVID'S, two miles from CROESGOCH, a mile from LLANRHIAN and the picturesque fishing village of PORTHGAIN. Within a mile of numerous safe and sandy beaches. The enchanting coastal path runs through the farmland. Three bedrooms (no linen). Fully equipped and fitted dining kitchen, TV room and pleasant spacious lounge. Carpeted throughout and fresh decor. Washing, ironing and airing facilities. There is a bathroom with toilet upstairs and a toilet downstairs. Storage heating and radiators for your warmth and comfort. Cot available. Ample parking, garage. Secluded sunny lawns with southerly aspect. Open all year, including winter mini breaks, £75 to £245 weekly. Electricity by £1 coin meter. Off peak night storage heaters assessed on meter readings. SAE for prompt reply to **Mrs C.E. Skeel Jones, Arosfyr Farm, Dolgellau, Gwynedd LL40 2YP (0341-422 355).**

ST. DAVID'S. Quality Cottages. Around the magnificent Welsh coast. Away from the madding crowd. Near safe sandy beaches. A small specialist agency offering privacy, peace and unashamed luxury. Wales Tourist Board 1989 Award Winner. Residential standards — dishwashers, microwaves, washing machines, central heating, log fires, no slot meters. Linen provided. Pets welcome free. All in coastal areas famed for scenery, walks, wild flowers, birds, badgers and foxes. Free colour brochure **S.C. Rees, Quality Cottages, Cerbid, Solva, Haverfordwest, Pembrokeshire SA62 6YE (0348 837971).**

ST. DAVID'S (Pembrokeshire). Mrs Jill Morgan, Carnachenwen, Mathry, Haverfordwest SA62 5HL (0348 831636 or 831226). Working farm. Sleeps 10.

Carnachenwen is an 18th century farmhouse of great character, set in a sheltered, wooded valley on a working farm, a mile from the sea, between St. David's and Strumble Head, in the beautiful, unspoilt Pembrokeshire Coast National Park. The self-catering wing sleeps up to 10 people, is comfortably and attractively furnished, and very well equipped. It has a parking area and its own secluded sunny garden. Carnachenwen is an ideal base from which to visit many beaches, walk the famous Pembrokeshire Coastal Path, go birdwatching, study wild flowers, sea-shore life and local history, visit islands, go canoeing, sailing, fishing or riding — all of which we can arrange for you ourselves. Linen supplied. Farm produce available including organically grown vegetables. Ideal surroundings for children. Reductions for small parties. Available all year.

TEGRYN. Trudy and Merv Jones and Roger and Bridget Prideaux, Penbanc, Tegryn, Llanfyrnach SA35 0BP (Llwyndrain [023977] 279 or 666). Working farm. Sheep, cattle (some rare breeds), ponies. Free range hens, ducks, pigeons. The self-catering accommodation consists of half the farmhouse, three bedrooms (sleep five/six); bathroom/WC; kitchen; sittingroom with colour TV; diningroom. Small garden for sitting out. Ample parking. Children welcome to meet animals, and babysitting arranged. Plenty of books to read and piano for wet days. Groceries, stamps, petrol, pub meals — one mile, Cardigan 10 miles, Cenarth Falls six miles. Riding, swimming, fishing, golf and many lovely beaches within easy reach by car (essential). Also available, six berth caravan with all modern conveniences. Open mid-May to end September. SAE or phone for terms.

FOR THE MUTUAL GUIDANCE
OF GUEST AND HOST

Every year literally thousands of holidays, short-breaks and overnight stops are arranged through our guides, the vast majority without any problems at all. In a handful of cases, however, difficulties do arise about bookings, which often could have been prevented from the outset.

It is important to remember that when accommodation has been booked, both parties — guests and hosts — have entered into a form of contract. We hope that the following points will provide helpful guidance.

GUESTS: When enquiring about accommodation, be as precise as possible. Give exact dates, numbers in your party and the ages of any children. State the number and type of rooms wanted and also what catering you require — bed and breakfast, full board, etc. Make sure that the position about evening meals is clear — and about pets, reductions for children or any other special points.

Read our reviews carefully to ensure that the proprietors you are going to contact can supply what you want. Ask for a letter confirming all arrangements, if possible.

If you have to cancel, do so as soon as possible. Proprietors do have the right to retain deposits and under certain circumstances to charge for cancelled holidays if adequate notice is not given and they cannot re-let the accommodation.

HOSTS: Give details about your facilities and about any special conditions. Explain your deposit system clearly and arrangements for cancellations, charges, etc, and whether or not your terms include VAT.

If for any reason you are unable to fulfil an agreed booking without adequate notice, you may be under an obligation to arrange alternative suitable accommodation or to make some form of compensation.

While every effort is made to ensure accuracy, we regret that FHG Publications cannot accept responsibility for errors, omissions or misrepresentation in our entries or any consequences thereof. Prices in particular should be checked because we go to press early. We will follow up complaints but cannot act as arbiters or agents for either party.

GWYNEDD

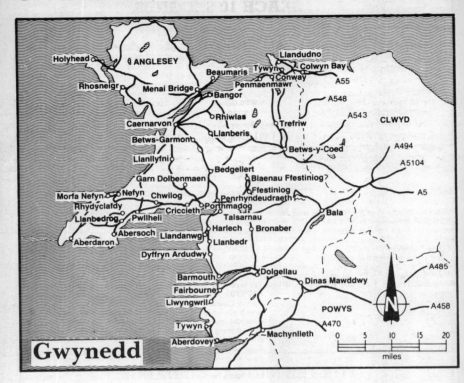

Gwynedd

ABERDARON. Mrs M.P. Roberts and Mrs A. Jones, "Ty Fry", Aberdaron, Pwllheli LL53 8BY (Aberdaron [075-886] 274). Sleeps 5. Completely modernised and fully furnished with linen supplied, this Welsh cottage has exclusive views over Aberdaron Bay. Few minutes' walk from the local grocery shop. Private drive from main road and ample parking space. Convenient for many sandy beaches and coves, including the famous Whistling Sands. Mountain walks where the sea views literally surround you on the extreme tip of the Lleyn Peninsula. Accommodation to let furnished without attendance. Two bedrooms, sleeping five, cot available; bathroom; immerser; large lounge (TV); kitchen/diner with electric cooker, fridge; metered electricity. Pets welcome. Bookings from March to October. For prompt reply SAE, please.

ABERDARON. Mrs J.J. Evans, Bodrydd, Rhoshirwaun, Pwllheli LL53 8HR (Rhiw [075-888] 257). Accommodation for six in self-contained farmhouse, Bodrydd Farm, centrally situated near tip of Lleyn Peninsula, standing back from main road, in lovely Welsh countryside and peaceful surroundings with open view of hills and fields. Within easy reach of Whistling Sands, numerous picturesque sandy beaches. Riding stables at nearby farm. Licensed hotels in Aberdaron (two miles). Small river running through farmland for trout fishing. Small working farm with plenty going on to interest all ages. Comfort and cleanliness guaranteed. Three double bedrooms; cot, high chair; bathroom, toilet; sittingroom with TV; diningroom with electric fire; kitchen all electric with all utensils, etc. No linen. Shop 10 minutes' walk. Sea one and a half miles. Sorry, no pets. Car essential, parking ample. June to September. SAE please for terms and brochure.

ABERDARON. Mrs P.L. Roberts, Tir Glyn Farm, Aberdaron, Pwllheli LL53 8DA (Aberdaron [075-886] 248). Sleeps 6. Tir Glyn is a stone built, well furnished farmhouse, one mile from Aberdaron village. The house, with all modern conveniences, has three bedrooms (plus cot), sleeps six. Bathroom. Sittingroom with TV, dining kitchen; fridge, electric cooker etc. All kitchen utensils supplied. Ideal for children. Milk and eggs from farm. Situated in the National Trust area. Ten minutes' walk from Fisherman's Cove, and within easy reach of other beautiful beaches. Peacocks are one of the many attractions around the farm. Linen not supplied. Sorry, no pets allowed. Shopping five minutes by car. Available March to October. SAE please for terms. Also six berth 1986 model luxury caravan to let, with shower.

ABERSOCH. Quality Cottages. Around the magnificent Welsh coast. Away from the madding crowd. Near safe sandy beaches. A small specialist agency offering privacy, peace and unashamed luxury. Wales Tourist Board 1989 Award Winner. Residential standards — dishwashers, microwaves, washing machines, central heating, log fires, no slot meters. Linen provided. Pets welcome free. All in coastal areas famed for scenery, walks, wild flowers, birds, badgers and foxes. Free colour brochure **S.C. Rees, Quality Cottages, Cerbid, Solva, Haverfordwest, Pembrokeshire SA62 6YE (0348 837971).**

WALES

ABERSOCH near. Mrs J.T. Jones, Trofa, Llanbedrog, Pwllheli LL53 7PA (0758 740806 or 740105). Completely private self-contained part of owners' detached house. Set in the upper part of Llanbedrog village, it is beautifully decorated and furnished to a high standard. Accommodation consists of three bedrooms, two double-bedded and one twin-bedded, cot; bathroom with shower, shaving point and toilet; lounge/diner; fully fitted kitchen. Bedding, including linen, provided at no extra charge. Private entrance and parking for two cars. Lovely flower garden, seat to front. All amenities in village, shop opposite, nice pub serving meals two minutes' walk. Sandy beach close by, easy reach of Snowdonia and Ffestiniog Railways, historic castles, three golf courses, facilities for surfing, board sailing, sea and river fishing, pony trekking. Guaranteed clean and comfortable. Open April to October, reductions for early and late bookings. SAE for full details or telephone.

ANGLESEY. Mr and Mrs Roberts, Plas Trefarthen, Brynsiencyn, Anglesey LL61 6SZ (0248 430379). Plas Trefarthen affords panoramic views of Caernarfon Castle and majestic Snowdonia. Beautiful Llanddwyn beach six miles away. Ideal place for touring, close to Plas Newydd and Penrhyn Castle National Trust properties. The self catering accommodation is in the wing of the large house and has comfortable lounge with colour TV; modern kitchen/diner with fridge, washing machine. Three bedrooms one double, one twin and one single. Bathroom. Bed and Breakfast is also available in the large country house. Most bedrooms with en-suite bathrooms, colour TV and tea-making facilities. Evening Meals available. Home produced meat and vegetables used. Please contact **Martin Roberts** for brochure.

ANGLESEY. "Maen Farm", Maenaddwyn, Llanerchymedd, Anglesey. Working farm. Sleeps 6. "Maen Farm" is about half-a-mile from Clorach Fawr and stands on a 43-acre cattle and sheep farm. Available for self-catering holidays, accommodation is in two double bedrooms and one twin-bedded room. There is a new fitted kitchen with full size cooker, fridge, electric kettle, iron, fires; bathroom, flush toilet; diningroom; TV lounge. Toilet and washbasin downstairs. Cot and high chair available. Fitted carpets throughout. Everything supplied except linen. Regret no pets. Shop a few hundred yards away. Sea approximately three-and-a-half/four miles. SAE for quick reply and terms **Miss Doris P. Williams, "Clorach Fawr", Llanerchymedd, Anglesey LL71 8AD (Llanerchymedd [0248] 470297).**

ANGLESEY. Mrs D. Williams, 1 Fron, Gaerwen, Anglesey LL60 6DP (0248 77 670). Sleeps 2 adults; 3 children plus cot. Situated on the island of Anglesey in the village of Gaerwen which is half a mile from the main A5 Holyhead road. Comfortable accommodation includes two double bedrooms and one single bedroom and cot; bathroom; lounge and kitchen with fridge and automatic washing machine. Pets are welcomed. For the use of electricitu there is a 50p coin meter and there is parking for two cars. Central for shops and 15 minutes from most beaches. From £65.

BALA. Ty-Ucha Farm, Rhosygwaliau, Bala. Sleeps 2. Ty-Ucha Farm is situated in a small quiet valley, amidst some of the most beautiful scenery for miles around.

TY-UCHA FARM

Ideal centre for touring Snowdonia and the coast. Bala is a small country town with largest natural lake in Wales. Facilities for fishing, sailing, windsurfing, golf, pony trekking and there is a miniature railway. The flat is part of farmhouse and accommodates two persons. Fully equipped; colour TV, video and stereo provided; microwave; bed linen provided. Pets are welcome. Ideal for honeymooners. Colourful large garden to relax in. Car essential; ample parking. Own front door. SAE, or telephone in the evenings or weekends. **Mrs S. Lewis, Magsafallen Farm, Rhosygwaliau, Bala LL23 7EY (0678 520373).**

BEDDGELERT. 2 Glanfa, Rhyd Ddu, Near Beddgelert. 150 year old, well-equipped stone cottage in the centre of a pretty village at the foot of Snowdon. In the heart of the National Park, it is an ideal centre for mountains or sea. Suitable for two families, sleeps eight in three bedrooms (two double and four single beds). Large livingroom with exposed beams, Welsh dresser, storage heater, radio and colour TV. Good-sized kitchen with fridge, electric cooker. Bathroom with electric shower. Cot and high chair available. Metered electricity. No pets. Near pub and Post Office/shop. Terms high season from £100 to £175; low season £50 to £80, with short breaks by arrangement in low season. Open all year. Apply **Mr C.R. Vernon, 166 Court Lane, London SE21 7ED (081 693 3971).**

BEDDGELERT. Beudy Coed, Oerddwr, Beddgelert. Sleeps 6. Beautifully renovated shepherd's cottage, one mile from Aberglaslyn Pass and situated on wooded hillside overlooking the Glaslyn River and the Cnicht and Moelwyn Mountain Ranges. Ideal central location for walking, climbing, fishing, yet only four miles from Porthmadog's lovely beaches. The cottage can accommodate six people. Two double bedrooms. Dining/sittingroom with stone fireplace; fully equipped kitchen; shower room. Patio area in the garden with table and benches. Eat out and enjoy the magnificent scenery. Open March to October. Children and pets welcome. Contact **Ann Jones, Frondeg, Llanfair, Harlech LL46 2RE (0766 780448).**

BEDDGELERT. Meillionen, Beddgelert. Farmhouse situated in the heart of Snowdonia within one mile of picturesque village. Large house divided into two units. One consists of large kitchen/livingroom with electric cooker, fridge and Rayburn; stone staircase leading to two double bedrooms and bathroom. Other unit consists of sittingroom; kitchen with fridge and electric cooker; downstairs bathroom; three double bedrooms and single bed. House can be let as one unit sleeping 11. Bed and table linen not provided. Storage heaters in winter. Electricity on meter. Fishing, pony trekking and sports facilities nearby, also beaches within easy reach. SAE to **Mrs S.H. Owen, Cwm Cloch, Beddgelert, Caernarvon (Beddgelert [076-686] 241).**

BEDDGELERT. Bron Eifion, Rhyd Ddu, Beddgelert. Attractive semi-detached stone house on edge of small village in National Park at foot of Snowdon. Splendid valley, pass and mountain walks from village including path up Snowdon. Lakes nearby; excellent centre for riding, fishing, sea and touring. Three bedrooms, two living rooms; bathroom; modern kitchen with fridge, airing cupboard and heaters. Metered electricity. Cot available. Shop and Inn close by. No pets. Open all year. High season rates from £110 to £210 per week; low season £45 to £100 per week. Short Breaks by arrangement. Apply **Davies, 218 Clive Road, London SE21 8BS (081-670 2756).**

CAERNARFON. Mrs Ivy Atkin, Cwm Farm, Clynnogfawr, Caernarfon LL54 5DW (028-686 244). 300 acre mountain farm in an elevated position overlooking Snowdon and Cardigan Bay, eight miles from Pwllheli and Criccieth, four miles from Clynnogfawr, 20 minutes from the beach. Our own trout lake (two acres with island and boat) stocked annually. Large lawned garden and plenty of parking space plus garage. Farmhouse sleeps eight plus cot and high chairs. Sittingroom with colour TV, open inglenook, log fires and exposed beams. Kitchen with modern units, Aga oil-fired cooker, Calor gas cooker, microwave, fridge and freezer. Sun lounge with children's play area, small snooker table. Large bathroom with mixer shower, bath, etc. Two double bedrooms and two single beds in small bedroom. Loft bedroom over bathroom separate from others. Terms from £100 to £200 inclusive. No pets.

CAERNARFON. Mrs M. Gray-Parry, Bryn Bras Castle, Llanrug, Near Caernarfon LL55 4RE (Llanberis [0286] 870210). Properties sleep 2/6. Welcome to beautiful Bryn Bras Castle. Tasteful Castle Apartments, elegant Tower House and mini-cottage, for two to six persons, within unique romantic turreted Regency Castle (Listed building) in the gentle foothills of Snowdonia. Centrally situated, amidst breathtaking scenery, for exploring North Wales' magnificent mountains, beaches, heritage and history. Near local country inns, restaurants and shops. Each apartment is fully self-contained, gracious, peaceful, clean with idyllically individual charming character, comfortable furnishings, generous equipment — dishwasher, microwave, etc. Free central heating, hot water, duvets and bed linen. All highest WTB grade (except one). 32 acres tranquil landscaped gardens, sweeping lawns, woodland walks of natural beauty, panoramic hill walk overlooking the sea, Anglesey and Mount Snowdon. Enjoy the comfort and warmth of this welcoming Castle in truly peaceful surroundings. Always open (including short breaks). Brochure sent with pleasure.

CHWILOG. Pencarth Uchaf, Chwilog, Pwllheli. Sleeps 8 plus cot. Attractive farmhouse situated in the most beautiful part of North Wales. South facing enjoying views of Cardigan Bay, Snowdonia and Rival Mountain Ranges. Ideally placed for touring and beaches. The house sleeps eight plus cot. Fully equipped kitchen including microwave, fridge, freezer. Baby's high chair available. Reading room with telephone; lounge with open fireplace and colour TV; two double bedrooms plus single bed, TV and teasmade. Single rooms all with heating. Bathroom with coloured suite and separate shower unit. Linen, bath and hand towels, tea towels provided. Carpeted throughout. 50p eletric meter. Safe children's play area. Garden furniture, barbecue. Household pets welcome. Ample parking. **Mrs Margaret Evans, 36 High Street, Criccieth LL52 0BT (0766 522805).**

CRICCIETH. Mrs B. Williams, Gaerwen Farm, Ynys, Criccieth LL52 0NU (Chwilog [0766] 810324). Sleeps 7. This 200 acre dairy/sheep farm is situated four-and-a-half miles inland from Criccieth and beaches, within easy reach of Pwllheli, Lleyn Peninsula and Porthmadog. An ideal centre for enjoying climbing, fishing and quiet country walks with extensive views of Snowdonia and Cardigan Bay. Within easy reach of various historic places nearby. Accommodation is self-contained in furnished farmhouse, with TV lounge, electric fire, diningroom, kitchen with cooker and fridge, bathroom/shower and toilet. Children most welcome, plenty of playing space, cot and babysitting available. Pets welcome. Car essential, ample parking space. SAE, please, for terms.

CRICCIETH. Quality Cottages. Around the magnificent Welsh coast. Away from the madding crowd. Near safe sandy beaches. A small specialist agency offering privacy, peace and unashamed luxury. Wales Tourist Board 1989 Award Winner. Residential standards — dishwashers, microwaves, washing machines, central heating, log fires, no slot meters. Linen provided. Pets welcome free. All in coastal areas famed for scenery, walks, wild flowers, birds, badgers and foxes. Free colour brochure **S.C. Rees, Quality Cottages, Cerbid, Solva, Haverfordwest, Pembrokeshire SA62 6YE (0348 837971).**

CRICCIETH. Betws-Bach & Rhos-Ddu, Ynys, Criccieth, Gwynedd LL52 0PB (Nefyn [0758] 720 047) or (Chwilog [0766] 810 295). Wales Tourist Board Grade 5. Old World Farmhouse and Period Country Cottage. Situated just off the B4411 road, in tranquil surroundings. Sleeping 2 – 6 plus cot. Equipped to and above Wales Tourist Board Grade 5 — with washing/drying machines, dishwashers, microwaves, freezers, colour TV; open log fires/inglenook, full central heating. OPEN ALL YEAR — including Christmas. Winter weekends welcome. Ideal for couples. Own fishing and shooting rights, wonderful walks, peace and quiet with Snowdonia and unspoilt beaches on our doorstep. For friendly personal service phone or write to **Mrs Anwen Jones.**

DOLGELLAU. Mrs C.E. Skeel Jones, Arosfyr Farm, Dolgellau LL40 2YP (Dolgellau [0341] 422355). Sleeps 5. "Y Penty" is a farm building coverted into a two bedroomed luxury holiday cottage, half a mile from the quaint market town of Dolgellau, with panoramic views of Cader Idris mountain. Accommodating five persons in two bedrooms; cot available; bathroom, toilet; open plan colour TV lounge and dining area. Kitchen with Hygena fitments, cooker, fridge-freezer, immerser, storage heaters and twin tub washing machine; carpeted throughout. Fully equipped except for linen. Parking. Small lawn and flower borders to the front and grassy area with rotary clothes line at the back. Good centre for visiting castles, slate caverns, gold mines and miniature railways. Walking, golf — Dolgellau Golf Course 400 yards — pony trekking and climbing. Sea eight miles. Weekly terms from £70 to £165 (electricity by £1 meter, but off peak storage heaters are assessed on meter readings). Also luxury flat for two in Dolgellau, convenient on foot to shops etc. SAE for prompt reply.

DYFFRYN ARDUDWY. The Lodge, Cors Y Gedol Hall, Dyffryn Ardudwy. Sleeps 5. Delightful detached 15th century lodge cottage with characteristic beams and stone staircase. Accommodates five people, having two bedrooms with washbasins, small bathroom with shower, one reception room incorporating kitchen units and comfortable living area with TV. All carpeted. Of historic interest and beautifully situated in the peaceful grounds of Cors Y Gedol Hall, an Elizabethan Manor House on the farm. Many scenic walks in the surrounding mountains and adjoining woodland. Village shops, sandy beach and pony trekking a mile and a half away. For further details please send SAE to **Mrs H.E. Bailey, Plas Y Bryn Farm, Llanbedr LL45 2DZ (Llanbedr [034-123] 459).**

LLANBEDR. Mrs G.P. Jones, Alltgoch, Llanbedr LL45 2NA (Llanbedr [034-123] 229). Sleeps 5 adults plus cot. Sheep farm situated two miles from Llanbedr village. Llanbedr is on the A496 between BARMOUTH and HARLECH. The house faces the Lleyn Peninsula in a quiet position with garden and plenty of parking place. Ideally situated for walking the Rhinog range, and paths to woodlands and moorlands for nature lovers. Good trout fishing and private lake. Three miles from the beach. The house sleeps five persons with modern conveniences, new kitchen units, large lounge with colour TV, central heating. Bed linen, cot and high chair. Terms from £60 to £160 per week. WTB Approved.

LLANBEDR. Mrs Moira Holland-Jones, Graig Isaf, Cwm Nantcol, Llanbedr LL45 2PL (0341 23341). Working farm, join in. Sleeps 6. Graig Isaf is four miles from the village of Llanbedr. The cottage is a renovated stable with all modern conveniences, built in traditional stone architecture. All-electric and fully equipped to accommodate six people. Situated amongst the Rhinog Mountains and with a view of the sea, it enjoys splendid scenery and is ideally placed for walking, fishing and birdwatching. Beautiful beaches within easy reach. Places of historic interest include Harlech Castle, slate mines and miniature railway just some of the attractions of this picturesque area. SAE for terms.

LLANBEDR. Mrs O. Evans, Werngron Farm, Llanbedr LL45 2PF (Llanbedr [034-123] 274). Pleasant bungalow on working farm, set in own grounds and enjoying open views of unspoilt countryside. Llanbedr two miles, Harlech three, Barmouth 10. Good touring centre for north and mid Wales; within easy reach of sandy beaches, golf course, indoor swimming pool, pony trekking, fresh water coarse fishing, sea fishing, boat trips and lovely country and mountain walks. Sleeps six, plus cot, in three bedrooms — double, twin and bunks — all with own washbasins. Sittingroom with colour TV; diningroom; well equipped, all electric fitted kitchen; spacious sun lounge; bathroom/shower. Fitted carpets throughout, electric fires, oil central heating. Open all year. Terms from £95 – £160 per week.

LLANBEDROG. Mrs F.H. Jones, Crugan Farm, Llanbedrog, Pwllheli LL53 7LN (0758 740 873 or 0758 81 2570). OWNER BOOKINGS CUT COST! A choice of 37 properties, all Welsh Tourist Board verified, is offered by our groups of FARMWIVES. Llyn, an environmentally sensitive area with 50 miles of Heritage coastline offers an idyllic relaxing holiday away from the madding crowd. Snowdonia National Park, castles, slate and copper mines, woollen mills, railways all within 25 miles. Watersports, pony trekking, sandy beaches, golfing and country lanes with an abundance of fauna and flora provide varied interests. Pwllheli Leisure Centre offers sports facilities. Serviced and self-catering accommodation is offered. A warm Welsh welcome awaits all on our farms. Stamp for free brochure.

MACHYNLLETH. Tyhymaes, Dinas Mawddwy, Machynlleth. Old cottage in the very peaceful area of the Cywarch Valley situated in the Snowdonia area at the foot of Aran Fawddwy near Cader Idris not far from the sea. Fishing rights and shooting. Children and well trained pets welcome. Plenty of space to park cars and for children to play. Very peaceful situation. Car essential. Everything supplied but linen and coal for the open fire. For prompt reply SAE, please, to **Mrs Humphreys, Pencae, Dinas Mawddwy, Machynlleth SY20 9JG (06504 427).**

GWYNEDD – OUTSTANDING NATURAL BEAUTY!

With Snowdonia National Park and the Lleyn Peninsula, Gwynedd well deserves its designation as an 'Area of Outstanding Natural Beauty'. The tourist is spoiled for choice in this county but should endeavour to visit the hill-fort at Tre'r Ceiri, the Llugwy Valley, Cwm Pennant, Dinas Dinlle hill-fort, the gold mine at Clogau and the railways and quarries at Blaenau Ffestiniog.

PORTHMADOG. Mrs A.E. Pugh, Farmyard Cottage, Tremadog, Porthmadog LL49 9PP (Porthmadog [0766] 512338). Working farm, join in. Sleeps 4 Adults. Farmyard Cottage, which adjoins farmhouse, is situated on a working farm one mile from the village of Tremadog. Black Rock Sands are only three miles away and Snowdonia is within easy reach. The farm is an ideal centre for railway enthusiasts, rock climbers and walkers. The cottage itself has two bedrooms: one double, one double and single (cot and high chair available); bathroom; fully equipped kitchen; sittingroom with colour TV. Electrically heated, 50p coin meter. Ample parking space. Children welcome. Sorry, no pets. Terms from £50 to £120, Short Breaks offered during off-peak season. WTB Verified.

PORTHMADOG. Mrs Muriel Parker, Alderley, Borth-y-Gest, Porthmadog LL49 9TP (Porthmadog [0766] 512118). "Alderley" is situated on the shores of the beautiful Glaslyn Estuary with superb mountain views. There are good, sandy beaches in small coves a short distance away. There are many other resorts and excursions in the area as well as many beautiful walks. The ground floor flat comprises two twin bedded rooms, bathroom with WC and washbasin. Modern kitchen with electric cooker and stainless steel sink and fridge. The lounge/diningroom with TV faces the harbour and estuary. There is also a twin bedded room on the first floor available if required, at a small extra charge. Children over five welcome. There is a village shop selling groceries, newspapers etc., also post office, and in Porthmadog (about one mile away) there are usual shops and supermarkets for other items not available in the village. Linen not supplied. Sorry, no pets. Short term winter bookings by arrangement. SAE for brochure. WTB approved.

PWLLHELI. Tai Gwyliau Tyndon Holiday Cottages and Bunglaows, Llanengan, Pwllheli LL53 7LG.

Llyn Heritage Coast. Peaceful, relaxing stone cottages with glorious views overlooking the sea, on a 120 acre sheep farm three-quarters of a mile from Llanengan with 16th century church and country inn. 200 yards Porthneigwl sandy beach with private access. Two miles Abersoch boating resort. Walks, off-shore fishing, surfing, golf, horse riding, sea fishing, pay phone, launderette. Two cottages, suitable for disabled visitors. Personal supervision. reduction for Senior citizens/disabled. Ideal for family holidays. Enquiries to: **Mrs Elizabeth Evans, Penlan, Rhos Isaf, Caernarfon LL54 7NG (0286 831184).**

PWLLHELI. Mrs E. Pierce Jones, Botacho Wyn, Nefyn, Pwllheli LL53 6HA (Nefyn [0758] 720552).

Working farm, join in. Botacho Wyn is a 75-acre farm, situated outside Nefyn within one mile of the shops and a safe sandy beach. The house stands in its own grounds with a view of the sea and mountains. It is comfortably furnished and there are five bedrooms (two with washbasins) to accommodate eight people plus cot if required. Bathroom; sittingroom with colour TV; diningroom; kitchenette with fridge, electric cooker, immersion heater. Parking space. Large, pleasant garden, safe for children. Golf course and riding facilities five minutes by car. There is also a friendly local Inn at the farm entrance, at the end of the 500-yard drive, where good food is available. Fully equipped except linen. Pets allowed if well-behaved. Sea and shops one mile. Weekly terms on request with SAE, please.

PWLLHELI. Mrs M. Adams, Cae'r Ferch Uchaf, Pencaernewydd, Pwllheli LL53 6DJ (0766 810660). Cedarwood Chalet on a secluded working 24 acre smallholding; consists of three bedrooms, all with fitted wardrobes; large lounge with colour TV; luxury shower room with WC, additional WC in boiler room; fully fitted kitchen/diner. The whole cottage is double glazed and centrally heated enabling us to open all year. This area is superb for walking and photography, etc, particularly in early spring or late autumn. We are also central for all beaches and just a few miles from the mountains of Snowdon. Our charges range from £90 to £150 depending on the season. Please write or ring for further details.

PWLLHELI. Mrs C.A. Jones, Rhedyn, Mynytho, Pwllheli LL53 7PS (Llanbedrog [0758] 740669). **Working farm, join in.** Rhedyn is a small dairy farm overlooking the beautiful Nanhoran Valley, and the farm cottage, accommodating four people, is offered for hire between April and November. It is two miles from Llanbedrog and Abersoch, both noted for their safe bathing. Children will enjoy watching the animals, and are made especially welcome. The house has two double bedrooms with cot available. Bathroom and toilet; combined sitting/diningroom with TV; kitchen with immersion heater, washing machine, microwave oven. Calor gas stove and fridge. Linen supplied. Pets permitted. One mile from shops and two from the sea. Car essential — parking. SAE, for further details and terms.

PWLLHELI. Mrs C. Jones, Crugan Farm, Llanbedrog, Pwllheli LL53 7LN (0758 740 873). Crugan is a

traditional Welsh farmhouse, tactfully modernised but unspoilt, retaining all its old world charm. For those seeking a seaside holiday the location is ideal; the sandy Llanbedrog beach is just five minutes' walk from the house along a private path. The house has four bedrooms (two singles and two doubles). Bed linen is provided. There is a bathroom and shower. Downstairs is a lounge with colour TV; diningroom and kitchen with all the essentials including refrigerator and electric cooker. Electricity is charged as extra. A cot and high chair are available. Around the house is a large enclosed garden and patio and there is ample parking space. Llanbedrog village is about three minutes' drive away and there are two pubs and shops, including a chemist. Member of the Wales Tourist Board. Details of terms on request.

PLEASE SEND A STAMPED ADDRESSED ENVELOPE WITH ENQUIRIES

TALSARNAU. Mrs A.M. Wells, Yr-Ogof, Ynys, Talsarnau LL47 6TL (Harlech [0766] 780058). Sleeps 5/6. This comfortable, old fashioned cottage is three miles from Harlech and just five minutes' walk to Ynys Beach. Convenient for shops. Lovely mountain views from cottage windows. Swimming pool at Harlech. Very attractive area with lovely walks. Also fishing nearby. All modern conveniences. Five/six people accommodated in two double bedrooms and one twin-bedded room; bathroom, toilet, also downstairs toilet; lounge with oak beams and colour TV; kitchen/diner with electric cooker, microwave, fridge etc. Everything supplied except linen. Extra charge for electricity used. Economy 7 central heating. Car essential — parking. SAE, please for terms and further details or phone.

TREFRIW. Mrs Mary Griffith, Cae Crwn Farm, Crafnant Lake Road, Trefriw LL27 0JZ (Llanrwst [0492] 640062). Sleeps 4. Hill farm cottage, "Hafod Arthen" in Trefriw close to Crafnant Lake in unspoilt Snowdonia National Park. The cottage sits on the bank of a mountain trout stream amid breathtaking scenery. Enjoy walking, climbing, woollen mills, castles or coast; Llandudno, Conway, Anglesey within easy reach. Good food at three excellent village pubs in Trefriw which is on the B5106. Cottage has three bedrooms. Electric or coal fire; electric cooker; immersion heater, electric blankets. Fully equipped kitchen; bathroom; TV. Ideal for spring/summer/late holidays. If you need peace this is for you. Open March to 1st November. Rates £70 March — £160 August.

TUDWEILIOG. "Hafan", Tudweiliog, Near Pwllheli. Sleeps 6. Comfortable, fully modernised, furnished bungalow situated just 10 minutes' walk from the renowned Towyn beach and from Tudweiliog village. Nefyn three and a half miles away. Accommodation comprises three bedrooms, lounge with colour TV; diningroom; fully fitted kitchen with electric cooker, fridge etc; bathroom. 50p meter for electricity. Lawned garden; garage and parking space. Friday bookings. Wales Tourist Board 4 Dragons. Please contact **Mrs E.C. Llewelyn, Graeanfryn, Morfa Nefyn, Pwllheli LL53 6YQ (Nefyn [0758] 720455).**

TYWYN. CROESO CADER IDRIS. Situated within a 10 mile radius in the Snowdonia National Park between ABERDYFI and DOLGELLAU, we are a group of 10 Welsh speaking (one learner) farmers' wives offering a true Welsh welcome "croeso" at our homes. There are 12 units for self catering, some dating back to the 16th century, from £50 to £350 per week, whilst nine of us cater for Bed and Breakfast from £11 to £14 each daily, some with an optional Evening Meal prepared from local and homegrown produce. We offer a substantial reduction for weekly rates. All properties are WTB verified. For colour brochures, SAE please to: **Mrs M. Pughe, Dolffanog Fach, Talyllyn Corris, Tywyn LL36 9AJ or telephone (0654 73235).**

WALES

POWYS

BRECON. Wern-y-marchog Bungalow, Cantref, Brecon. Sleeps 6. Situated at the foot of the Brecon Beacons amidst picturesque countryside adjoining the farm on quiet country lane. Magnificent views. Accommodation comprises two double bedrooms, one twin-bedded room, bathroom, toilet, hallway, well-equipped kitchen/dining room, electric cooker, fridge, immersion heater, spin-dryer, iron, toaster, storage heaters and electric fires. Spacious sittingroom with TV. Carpeted throughout. Large lawn. Pets by arrangement. Children's play area. Ample parking. Optional hire of bed linen. Fishing, sailing, golf, riding in vicinity. Personally supervised between bookings to ensure comfort and cleanliness. Highly recommended in Visitors' Book. Open all year. Wales Tourist Board Grade 4. Brochure available on request stating number in party and dates required:- **Mrs Ann Phillips, Wern-y-marchog Farmhouse, Cantref, Brecon LD3 8LW (Llanfrynach [087 486] 329).**

BRECON near. Ponde House, Llandefalle, Near Brecon. Sleeps 6. This is a modernised 17th century cottage in spacious grounds a mile from the A4073. A tarmac road winds through a beautiful valley from the main road. The cottage is remote, being only half a mile from the open hillside and yet shops and inn at Llyswen are less than three miles away. Enjoy this unspoilt countryside with its wonderful views, walks and wild life. Open all year, the centrally heated accommodation is for six in two double and two single bedrooms; cot; bathroom, two toilets; sittingroom; diningroom; kitchen, 50p meter for electricity. Fully equipped except linen. Car essential. Weekly terms from £65. A personal interest is taken in the comfort and welfare of visitors. Wales Tourist Board Approved. SAE to **Mrs Mary Edwards, Upper Penwaun, Llanddew, Brecon LD3 9TA (Brecon [0874] 3714).**

PONDE HOUSE

BRECON near. Mrs Iris Lloyd, Talybryn, Bwlch, Near Brecon LD3 7LQ (Talybont-on-Usk [087-487] 278). Sleeps 5. This luxury flat stands in 60 acres of farmland, situated off the A40, looking down on the River Usk. The hills hug the lovely old farmhouse, secluded and "away from it all". Available all year and always warm and comfortable with central heating. This is an area of natural loveliness with green meadows and lush pastures. Nature excels herself at every season here. There is accommodation for five in two double bedrooms and one single bedroom; bathroom and toilet; large sittingroom, colour TV; diningroom; fully fitted all-electric kitchen with all utensils etc.; sink unit and fridge. No meters. Linen supplied. Regret no pets. Shops one mile, the beautiful Gower coast 38 miles. Car not essential (on bus route), though plenty of parking space. A warm welcome awaits you here and brochure gladly sent on request with SAE, please. WTB registered, Farm Holiday Guide Diploma.

TALYBRYN HOUSE

CRICKHOWELL. Mrs B. Broyd, Penrhiw Farm, Llangenny, Crickhowell NP8 1HD (Crickhowell [0873] 810130). Working farm, join in. Teg Fan is a modern bungalow situated beside a quiet country lane on the 112-acre farm (beef, sheep, horses), in a beautiful setting at the foot of the Black Mountains in Brecon Beacons National Park. Pony trekking, fishing, hang gliding, beautiful walks and 10 acres of woodland to hand. Homely village pub serving meals, half a mile away. Crickhowell (one and a half miles) has good shops and the busy market town of Abergavenny is six miles; Brecon 16 miles. Old industrial sites, castles, abbeys, caves to visit. Very good eating places nearby. The bungalow affords every comfort with fitted carpets throughout, colour TV, large livingroom with superb views and three bedrooms sleeping six people. Gas central heating, immersion heater, electric fires; fully fitted kitchen and bathroom. Pleasant garden. Milk delivered. Well controlled pets allowed. Bargain Breaks Spring/Autumn. Terms from £90 to £170.

POWYS – MOUNTAINOUS AND LANDLOCKED

With many border castles and the Brecon Beacons, which cover the south of the county, Powys can be very spectacular. You will also find the best stretches of Offa's Dyke, Hay-On-Wye, the steam railway at Llanfair Caereinion, Radnor Forest, the fortified house of Tretower, the farming centre at Builth Wells and the abandoned medieval town of Cefnllys.

KINGTON. Mrs A.J. Ball, Old Rectory, Newchurch, Kington, Herefordshire HR5 3QF (Gladestry [054-422] 639). Sleeps 4. This is an ideal spot for those wishing a peaceful holiday or who like touring or walking. The "Old Rectory" is situated in the quiet unspoilt little village of Newchurch on the English/Welsh border, near the crossroads between Kington, Hay-on-Wye, Hereford and Builth Wells. Offa's Dyke passes through the centre of the farmland. This is also Rev. Kilvert's country and the Old Rectory is mentioned in his Diary. The accommodation is suitable for four people; two double bedrooms; sittingroom; bathroom and toilet; all electric fully equipped kitchen. Children welcome. Guests must supply own linen. Electric heating and lighting. Fitted carpets throughout.

LLANGORSE. Lower Penllanafal, Llangorse, Near Brecon. Sleeps 6 plus cot. Lower Penllanafal is a lovely superbly furnished cottage situated in beautiful countryside adjoining the farm of 260 acres, being 50 yards off the road with its own private tarmac road leading up to a large yard for parking. It has its own garden with lawn, and orchard with stream. Sleeps six in two bedrooms; upstairs bathroom with toilet. Comfortable lounge and diningroom. Fully equipped kitchen with electric cooker, washing machine, fridge and immersion heater. Three storage heaters, two log fires (logs supplied) and electric fire. TV. Carpets throughout. Highly recommended by visitors. Weekly terms from £95 to £165. Wales Tourist Board Grade 3. SAE for prompt reply to **Mrs S. Hamer, Middle-Penllanafal, Llangorse, Brecon LD3 7UN (0874 84 307).**

LLANRHAEADR-YM-MOCHNANT. Aber-Rhaeadr Cottages, Llanrhaeadr-Ym-Mochnant. Two river-  side cottages in the heart of the Welsh Uplands (renowned for mountain views, lakes, forests and waterfalls) having traditional Welsh cottage charm with pointed riverstone walls, each with beamed inglenook fireplace, open beam ceiling, winding staircase, low doors and sun-trap patio overlooking the riverside lawn and hills to the south. Super- bly furnished, carpeted and equipped, including cot, TV, radio, fridge, washing machine, spin-dryer, airing cupboards etc. (Also sandpit under the damson tree in the riverside garden.) Local attractions include Pistyll Rhaeadr Waterfall, Lake Vyrnwy, Little Trains of Wales, pony trekking, Powys Castle, local markets and character pubs. Associate Members of the Welsh Tourist Board and complying with their standards. Just write for illustrated brochure and terms to **Mr Mark Lucas, 69 Grasmere Avenue, Whitton, Twicken- ham, Middlesex TW3 2JG (081-898 8728).**

WALES

HELP IMPROVE BRITISH TOURIST STANDARDS

You are choosing holiday accommodation from our very popular FHG Publications. Whether it be a hotel, guest house, farmhouse or self-catering accommodation, we think you will find it hospitable, comfortable and clean, and your host and hostess friendly and helpful. Why not write and tell us about it?

As a recognition of the generally well-run and excellent holiday accommodation reviewed in our publications, we at FHG Publications Ltd. present a diploma to proprietors who receive the highest recommendation from their guests who are also readers of our Guides. If you care to write to us praising the holiday you have booked through FHG Publications Ltd. — whether this be board, self-catering accommodation, a sporting or a caravan holiday, what you say will be evaluated and the proprietors who reach our final list will be contacted.

The winning proprietor will receive an attractive framed diploma to display on his premises as recognition of a high standard of comfort, amenity and hospitality. FHG Publications Ltd. offer this diploma as a contribution towards the improvement of standards in tourist accommodation in Britain. Help your excellent host or hostess to win it!

FHG DIPLOMA

We nominate ....

....

Because ....

Name ....

Address ....

.... Telephone No. ....

LLANSANTFFRAID-YM-MECHAIN. Tanybryn, Deytheur, Llansantffraid-ym-Mechain. Tanybryn is a

lovely, spacious, detached cottage, standing in its own lawned grounds in a delightful rural setting. It commands panoramic views over miles of open countryside and adjoins some 17 acres of our farmland. Most guests return year after year — the record so far is fifteen years in a row! Perfect for a relaxing holiday, and ideally situated for touring many beautiful and historic parts of Wales. Convenient for shops, recreation, and all facilities. Fishing available locally. Comfortably furnished and carpeted throughout. Three bedrooms sleeping eight plus cot; bathroom, WC, large airing cupboard with immersion heater on first floor. On ground floor, entrance porch, attractive lounge with open fireplace (log fires add to comfort on cooler evenings). Colour TV. Generously equipped kitchen/diner with electric cooker, fridge, washing machine, solid fuel Rayburn. Second WC and washbasin. Guests refer to Tanybryn as their "Idyllic Cottage". Linen not supplied. House-trained pets welcome. Open all year. Wales Tourist Board member. AA listed. Terms on request. SAE to **Mrs M.E. Jones, Glanvyrnwy Farm, Llansantffraid-ym-Mechain SY22 6SU (Llansantffraid [0691] 828 258).**

MACHYNLLETH. Pengraean, Llanymawddwy, Machynlleth. Sleeps 6. Situated on the upper part of the Dovey Valley, five miles from the Montgomeryshire Border, this cottage is to let from March to November. Surrounded by farms and mountains, it is a haven for walkers and climbers. Sleeping six in three double bedrooms; cot; lounge with black and white TV, diningroom; bathroom, toilet; kitchen with electric cooker, fridge, kettle, immerser, all utensils and hot and cold water. Storage heaters extra. Fully equipped except linen. Pets allowed if under control. Car essential — parking. Fishing by permit. Excellent for touring North and South Wales. Dolgellau 15 miles, Bala Lake 10 miles. SAE please for terms, **Mrs Catherine Roberts, Cerdinn, Llanymawddwy, Near Machynlleth SY20 9AJ (065-04-234).**

NEWTOWN. Mr and Mrs J.R. Pryce, Aberbechan Farm, Newtown SY16 3BJ (0686 630675).

Working farm, join in. Sleeps 10. This part of quaint Tudor farmhouse with its lovely oak beams is situated in picturesque countryside on a mixed farm with trout fishing and shooting in season. Newtown three miles, Welshpool, Powis Castle and Llanfair Light Railway, 14 miles; 45 miles to coast. The sleeping accommodation is for 10 people in four double and two single bedrooms, also cot. Two bathrooms, two toilets. Sitting/diningroom with colour TV. Fully fitted kitchen with fridge, electric cooker, washing machine and dishwasher. Log fires and off-peak heaters. Electricity on meter. Large lawn with swing. Everything supplied for visitors' comfort. Linen available for overseas guests at extra cost. Car essential to obtain the best from the holiday. Farm produce available in season. Village shop one-and-a-half miles away. Open all year. Tourist Board registered. SAE, please.

TALGARTH. Genffordd Cottage, Talgarth. Working farm, join in. Sleeps 9. Wales Tourist Board

approved Grade 4 Self Catering Accommodation. Set in the Brecon Beacons National Park, the cottage is ideal for hill walkers and ramblers. Pony trekking, sailing, canoeing, boating and gliding nearby. The cottage is beautifully furnished with fitted carpets throughout and has double glazing and central heating. Very large lounge with oak beams, open log fires and colour TV. Modern fitted kitchen/diner, fully equipped; bathroom, toilet; three double bedrooms, plus cot (sleeps nine). Linen supplied by request. Children welcome. Pets allowed. Car essential, ample parking. Shop two miles. Available all year. Suitable for disabled guests. Please send SAE or phone for further details to **Mrs Susan Prosser, Genffordd Farm, Talgarth LD3 0EN (Talgarth [0874] 711014).**

POWYS – MOUNTAINOUS AND LANDLOCKED

With many border castles and the Brecon Beacons, which cover the south of the county, Powys can be very spectacular. You will also find the best stretches of Offa's Dyke, Hay-On-Wye, the steam railway at Llanfair Caereinion, Radnor Forest, the fortified house of Tretower, the farming centre at Builth Wells and the abandoned medieval town of Cefnllys.

CARAVAN AND CAMPING HOLIDAYS

CLWYD

CARAVANS

Mr & Mrs R. G. Davies & Son
Caer Mynydd Caravan Park
Saron, Denbigh, Clwyd LL16 4TL
Telephone Nant Glyn 074 570 302

Delightful, small country farm site, a family-run park with personal service. Every caravan is checked and cleaned between lettings. New luxury caravans for hire with electric showers, toilets, mains water (H&C), fridge, microwave oven, Calor gas stoves, ironing facilities and colour TV. Home from home comfort. One pet welcome (under control). Touring, caravans & campers welcome. Modern conveniences including showers/toilets, laundry and drying room. Children's play area, games room and pool room. Well stocked farm shop. Lots of farm animals to see. Excellent centre for walks and for touring North Wales. **WTB APPROVED**

Mr and Mrs Geoffrey Bell,
Glan Lyn, Glyn Ceiriog,
Llangollen, Clwyd LL20 7AB.
Tel: Glyn Ceiriog (069-172) 320.

GLYN CEIRIOG LLANGOLLEN NORTH WALES
Pont Bell, an attractive small park and campsite is family owned and run in sheltered riverside location. Tourers, campers welcome to level grassed pitches. Washrooms, shower with hot and cold, WC, etc. One 32ft luxury 6-berth van for hire, separate bed and bunkrooms. Fully equipped including fridge, shower, TV. Ideal centre for walking, fishing, pony-trekking or enjoying the beautiful Ceiriog Valley. Llangollen with its International Music Eisteddfod (1st week July) four miles, Chirk Castle two. Snowdonia, the coast, Severn Valley Railway and much more within driving distance. Pont Bell is on the B4500, off A5, six miles west of Chirk, on the left through Glyn Ceiriog. Open March – September. SAE please or phone for details.

DYFED

CARAVANS

ABERPORTH. Mrs C. Jones, Manorafon, Sarnau, Llandyssul SA44 6QH (Aberporth [0239] 810564). Sleeps 6. Quiet, peaceful site of 11 caravans, fully equipped except linen, all six-berth with end bedrooms. All essential facilities provided. Running water and toilets inside each van; Calor gas cooker, electric lighting and heating. Toilets and washbasins, showers, shaving points and electric clothes dryer on site, also newly opened shop. Calor and camping gaz sold. Available Easter to October. Children welcome. Dogs must be kept on lead. Dairy produce available. Only half a mile from the pleasant Penbryn beach and nine miles from the market towns of Cardigan and Newcastle Emlyn. One and a half acres for campers and tourers. SAE for further particulars.

ABERYSTWYTH. Mrs Anne Bunton, Cwmergyr, Ponterwyd, Aberystwyth SY23 3LB (Ponterwyd

[097-085] 301). This 40 ft five-berth luxury caravan is sited in own enclosure on a 250-acre farm in the beautiful Cambrian Mountains, 16 miles east of Aberystwyth, off the A44. Accomodation consists of two bedrooms, bathroom (flush toilet); kitchen/diner; spacious lounge with colour TV. Central heating, fridge, gas cooker, hot and cold water, barbecue unit and patio set. No pets allowed. Linen not supplied. Car is essential. Within 15 mile radius there are sandy beaches, fishing, golf, pony trekking, steam railway, scenic drives and walks. An ideal location to explore mid-Wales. Open 1st April to 31st October. Terms £80–£95 per week. Bed and Breakfast available at farmhouse.

CWRTNEWYDD. Mr & Mrs P. Gilbert, Bryn Gwyn, Cwrtnewydd, Llanybydder SA40 9YR (0570-434 263). Four berth caravan on working farm two miles above the village of Cwrtnewydd with fantastic views over the valley towards the Black Mountains. Ideal for walking, hiking, bird watching, touring or just taking it easy. 12 miles New Quay, nine miles Lampeter. Gas heating and cooking. Flush toilet. Shower available. Fresh farm produce. Car essential. Children welcome. Open all year round. Prices from £45 per week (July-August). Please write or phone for further details.

HAVERFORDWEST near. Charles and Joy Spiers, West Lambston, Near Portfield Gate, Haverfordwest SA62 3LG (Camrose [0437] 710038). Sleeps 2 adults; 2 children. Luxury, well equipped six berth caravan in half acre of lush green paddock. Two end bedrooms (one double, the other with bunks); immersion heater for kitchen and bathroom — yes it does have a bath and flush toilet! Gas cooker, gas fire, fridge and colour TV. Cotton bed linen, beach, bath, hand and tea towels provided. Peace and quiet is guaranteed on this non-working farm (no early morning tractors!). Beach three miles; good walking area — maps provided. Tall Ships Race at nearby Milford Haven in July. Children welcome and there are swings and climbing frame. Terms from approximately £65 to £160 per week, all inclusive. Pets accepted by prior arrangement.

TENBY. Mrs J.N. Frazer, Highlands Farm, Manorbier-Newton, Tenby SA70 8PX (Manorbier [0834] 871446). A spacious six berth caravan situated in a quiet three acre meadow. The caravan is fully serviced with electric lighting and TV, also gas cooker and room heater. There are two separate end bedrooms, fully fitted shower room, kitchen/diner and a lounge with panoramic views. The caravan is sited a couple of hundred yards from the main road providing a peaceful countryside setting ideal for children or a well behaved pet. A car is essential. Shopping facilities can be found in nearby Tenby or Pembroke. Please write or phone for details.

TENBY/SAUNDERSFOOT. Mr W.H. Davies, Masterland Farm Touring Caravan and Tent Park, Broadmoor, Kilgetty SA68 0RH (Saundersfoot [0834] 813298). √ √ √ √ "Wales in Bloom" award. Tourist Board registered. Masterland is a perfect spot for a "get away from it all" summer holiday, approximately two miles from Saundersfoot and four miles from Tenby. Both resorts have beautiful beaches. It makes an ideal centre for touring Pembrokeshire, and the many places of historic interest. It is a small, friendly site for ten touring caravans and ten tents. On a private working farm where visitors are made welcome. The proprietor is in attendance to ensure a carefree and enjoyable holiday. Children are welcome and pets are permitted if kept under control. All amenities. Fresh milk daily. Booking essential for July and August. Terms from £2.75 to £6 per night approximately. SAE, please. Also two 6-berth caravans available.

WEST GLAMORGAN

CARAVANS

GOWER. Gower Farm Museum and Caravan Park, Llandewi, Near Reynoldston, Gower, Swansea (0792 391195). Pleasant rural touring and camping facilities on South Gower Britain's first area of Outstanding Natural Beauty. Good views from the park around the Gower countryside and we are close to Port Eynon beach and dramatic Rhossili. Lots of room on the park with the adjoining Gower Farm Museum to enjoy fun for all the family. Farm courtyard, pets' corner, playground, picnic and barbecue area, tearoom. Farm trail walks of two to six miles. Very low rates for short or long term stays, electric hook-ups. Please telephone for brochure. Proprietors: **J.C. Theodore and Sons (Caravans) Ltd, Trecco Bay Leisure Park, Porthcawl, Mid-Glamorgan CF36 5DB (0656 782572/783465).**

GWYNEDD

CARAVANS

ABERSOCH. Mrs Janno Jones, Tynewydd, Sarn Bach, Abersoch, Pwllheli LL53 7LE (Abersoch [075-881] 2446). 1988 modern six berth caravan to let, all modern conveniences. Shower, two flush toilets, colour TV. Sited on our small private site of 28 caravans all well spaced. One mile radius to many sandy beaches. Open from March 1st to November 1st. Terms from £60 to £150.

BALA. Mrs S.E. Edwards, Bryn Melyn Farm, Rhyduchaf, Bala LL23 7PG (Bala [0678] 520376). Sleeps 6. One six-berth caravan is available on Bryn Melyn, a 56-acre mixed farm in the village of Rhyduchaf, two miles from Bala, situated in the beautiful Bala countryside. The caravan has a bathroom, inside flush toilet, hot and cold water, electric light, gas cooker, fridge, TV. Fully equipped with blankets etc. Children are welcome. Sorry, no pets allowed. Quarter of a mile to the nearest shops. Open from April to September. Seaside 25 miles away. Weekly rates from £65. Electricity on slot meter (10p). SAE, please, for further details.

PORTHMADOG. Mrs Rhian Hughes, Carreg yr Eryr, Treflys, Porthmadog LL49 9YL (Porthmadog [0766] 512838). One caravan on mixed working farm. Lovely and quiet with excellent views over countryside. Comprises — lounge with sofa bed, gas fire and colour TV; kitchen with hot and cold water, gas cooker, electric fridge and all cooking utensils. Bathroom with washbasin, shower and flush toilet. Single bedroom with bunk beds and end double bedrooms. Famous Black Rock Sands only five minutes' walk away, and Morfa Bychan village with golf course, shop, pub and garage only five minutes by car. Porthmadog is approximately three miles away and Criccieth five miles. SAE, please.

POWYS

CARAVANS

HAY-ON-WYE. Mrs O. Lewer, Glebe Farm, Michaelchurch, Escley HR2 0PR (098123 201). Traditional 40 acre Welsh Border farm keeping sheep, cattle, goats and free-range hens. Peaceful (no traffic), middle of nowhere! Fringe Brecon Beacons National Park. Wonderful "undiscovered" Herefordshire/Welsh Border countryside, little changed by time. Abundant wildlife including rare Red Kites, Peregrines, Buzzards, Badgers, wild-flowered country lanes. Wealth of Border castles, Offa's Dyke footpath, mountain and valley walks. Abergavenny Canal, riding, fishing nearby. Even special off-season charm (late autumn/spring). Large cosy farm caravan, own garden (WC, fridge, TV, microwave). Friendly animals and owners extend warm welcome. FREE milk, eggs, butter. Full brochure available. Discounts for Senior Citizens.

VILLAGE INNS

CLWYD, LLANSILIN. Mr and Mrs M.S. Gilchrist, The Wynnstay Inn, Llansilin SY10 7QB (069-170 355). ♛ The village of Llansilin is set in picturesque countryside which is ideal for walking, fishing, pony trekking and birdwatching. Wynnstay Inn is a family-run hotel offering comfortable accommodation and a warm, friendly welcome. Lounge with colour TV. Central heating and log fires. Good wholesome food, ranging from bar snacks to à la carte meals. Open all year, except Bank Holidays. Terms: any two days £35 per person, including Evening Meal; Bed and Breakfast from £12.

FOR THE MUTUAL GUIDANCE OF GUEST AND HOST

Every year literally thousands of holidays, short-breaks and overnight stops are arranged through our guides, the vast majority without any problems at all. In a handful of cases, however, difficulties do arise about bookings, which often could have been prevented from the outset.

It is important to remember that when accommodation has been booked, both parties — guests and hosts — have entered into a form of contract. We hope that the following points will provide helpful guidance.

GUESTS: When enquiring about accommodation, be as precise as possible. Give exact dates, numbers in your party and the ages of any children. State the number and type of rooms wanted and also what catering you require — bed and breakfast, full board, etc. Make sure that the position about evening meals is clear — and about pets, reductions for children or any other special points.

Read our reviews carefully to ensure that the proprietors you are going to contact can supply what you want. Ask for a letter confirming all arrangements, if possible.

If you have to cancel, do so as soon as possible. Proprietors do have the right to retain deposits and under certain circumstances to charge for cancelled holidays if adequate notice is not given and they cannot re-let the accommodation.

HOSTS: Give details about your facilities and about any special conditions. Explain your deposit system clearly and arrangements for cancellations, charges, etc, and whether or not your terms include VAT.

If for any reason you are unable to fulfil an agreed booking without adequate notice, you may be under an obligation to arrange alternative suitable accommodation or to make some form of compensation.

While every effort is made to ensure accuracy, we regret that FHG Publications cannot accept responsibility for errors, omissions or misrepresentation in our entries or any consequences thereof. Prices in particular should be checked because we go to press early. We will follow up complaints but cannot act as arbiters or agents for either party.

IRELAND

BOARD ACCOMMODATION

ANTRIM

BUSHMILLS. Mrs Frances Lynch, Carnside House, 23 Causeway Road, Giant's Causeway, Bushmills BT57 8SU (Bushmills [02657] 31337).

Modernised farmhouse on 200-acre dairy farm with magnificent coastal views. Guests welcome from March to October. Accommodation comprises four double, one twin-bedded, one single and two family bedrooms, two ground floor rooms, all with washbasins. Central heating. Babysitting. Bushmills two miles; Ballycastle 12 miles; fishing, golf, water sports easily accessible. The Old Bushmills Distillery, two miles, has open days for visitors. Dogs outside only. Bed and Breakfast from £11; Evening Meal £7.

CORK

BANTRY. Mrs Agnes Hegarty, Hillcrest Farm, Ahakista, Durrus, Bantry (010 353 27 67045).

Seaside dairy farm. Charming old-style farmhouse, newly renovated, retaining traditional character. Situated in picturesque peaceful setting overlooking harbour and Dunmanus Bay, quarter of a mile from Ahakista village on the Sheep's Head Peninsula. Magnificent sea and mountain scenery; swimming, fishing, boating and five minutes' walk to the sea. Irish pubs and restaurant close by. Bantry 12 miles, Durrus six miles. Ideal centre for touring the peninsulas of West Cork and Kerry. Signposted in Durrus. Four guest bedrooms, three with bath/shower en-suite, one with washbasin; two are family rooms. Bathroom; spacious diningroom with stone walls; sittingroom with old world fireplace and log fire. Play/games room, swing, lovely garden with mature trees. Warm hospitality. Fresh farm vegetables and home baking. Babysitting. Irish Tourist Board approved. Bed and Breakfast from (Ir) £10.50; Dinners (Ir) £10. Reductions for one week's stay, 25 per cent reduction for children. Light meals also available. Also to let modern seaside bungalow for self catering. Fully equipped and in superb location.

PLEASE SEND A STAMPED ADDRESSED ENVELOPE WITH ENQUIRIES

IRELAND

FERMANAH

BALLAGH. Mr W.H. Haire, Armagh Manor, Ballagh, Lisnaskea BT92 5BS (Lisnaskea [03657] 21259). Working farm, join in. Ideal for a quiet, peaceful and relaxing holiday surrounded by the undisturbed waterways in the heart of the Fermanagh Lakeland. Enjoy the warm, homely family hospitality with music, folklore and interesting conversation if required. Children welcome, baby sitting services available. Cuisine to suit your palate. Full Board, Half Board or Bed and Breakfast as desired. Pets welcome. Caravan, camping available. Write or phone for full details.

GALWAY

SHRULE. Angela and Ian Pitchford, Shrule Castle, Shrule (Tuam [010-35393] 31277). Fed-up with modern bungalows? The Castle was built in 1238 but has been occupied by our family since 1769. We endeavour to make you part of the family with turf fires and electric blankets. We have a good library and folk museum. Lots of chat, local places to see with maps to follow. A hundred yards from a free fishing trout stream (Rod Licence needed). Lough Corrib is only four miles away and Connemara and Galway/Mayo Coast, a lovely day trip away. We look forward to welcoming you to our home.

KERRY

Welcome to Caragh Lodge!!

Situated in eight acres of award winning gardens on shore of Caragh Lake. Accommodation provided in the main house and garden rooms, each with en-suite bathroom. Diningroom overlooks the lake and the menu features the best of Irish food. Licensed. Located in the gardens are an all weather tennis court and a sauna chalet. Salmon fishing – river, lake or sea, golf, swimming, pony trekking, etc., available nearby. Only four miles to sandy beaches. A full detailed brochure is available.

Caragh Lake, Co. Kerry. Tel: 066 69115 or (from Britain) 010-35366 69115

WHEN MAKING ENQUIRIES PLEASE MENTION
FARM HOLIDAY GUIDES

KENMARE. Mrs Nora May O'Sullivan, Waterfalls Farm, Lackarue, Glengarriff Road, Kenmare (010 35364 41461). Modern farm bungalow in attractive rural setting quarter of a mile off Kenmare/Glengarriff road, four miles from town. River Sheen flows through farm with scenic waterfall. Salmon and trout fishing possible. Ideal for touring Cork and Kerry; good walks on farm or climb surrounding mountains. Horse riding and pony trekking seven miles. Fresh vegetables, home baking, own honey. Four bedrooms with washbasins. Central heating. Pets allowed. Open 1st May to 1st October.

KILLARNEY. Killarney Villa, Waterford Road (N72), Killarney (010-353-64-31878). Killarney Villa is a purpose built holiday villa with all en-suite facilities. It is surrounded by large and beautifully landscaped gardens, offering splendid views of the Kerry Mountains and the River Flesk Valley from its balcony and patio. Ideally located in peaceful surroundings, we are less than four kilometres from Killarney town centre, 200 metres from the junction of the Rosslane and Swansea/Cork ferry routes and 25 minutes' drive from Kerry Airport. Killarney sightseeing Bumper Holiday Break — any three nights Bed and full Irish Breakfast, three dinners at the International Hotel followed by traditional music and song at the hotel. Admission to Muchross House National Park of 10,000 hectares of gardens and lakeshore walks; visit to the National Museum of Irish Transport and one hour all-weather cruise on the Killarney Lakes £78 per person; 40 minute audio/visual introduction to the Killarney area on arrival. Other holiday offers on request. For further information contact **Rosaleen O'Sullivan.** Irish Tourist Board approved. AA listed.

LONDONDERRY

LONDONDERRY/LIMAVADY. Mrs E.M. Hunter, Longfield Farm, 132 Clooney Road, Eglinton, Co. Londonderry BT47 3DX (0504 810210). Working arable farm just off A2 mid-way between Limavady and Londonderry, 30 miles from Giant's Causeway on direct route to Fermanagh and Donegal and six miles from historic Londonderry. Car essential — good parking. Spacious gardens. Large bedrooms with washbasins and central heating. Lounge with TV. Eglinton Airport and Flying Club, an indoor Equestrian Centre and fishing close by. Bed and Breakfast, and tea at anytime. Terms £11 per night. Tourist Board registered.

WEXFORD

ENNISCORTHY. John and Sarah Murphy, Crane Farm, Ferns, Enniscorthy (010-353-54 33476 or 34398). Working farm, join in. Wexford County is steeped in history, and this 120-acre dairy and tillage farm is situated in its centre. Only 20 minutes' drive to safe, sandy beaches. Golf, pitch and putt, tennis, fishing etc. nearby. Beautiful walks, and Wexford, an old county town, is well worth a visit. Donkey for children to ride on farm. Crane Farm boasts landing site of first plane to cross the Irish Sea in 1912 piloted by Mr Dennis Corbet-Wilson. Comfortable accommodation in three double, one single, one family bedrooms, with washbasins; bathroom, toilets; sittingroom, diningroom. Good home cooking, personally served. Cot, high chair, babysitting and half price rates for children. Sorry, no pets. Car essential, parking. Evening Meal, Bed and Breakfast from £80 weekly. Open April to October.

SELF-CATERING HOLIDAYS

CORK

BANTRY. Mrs Agnes Hegarty, Ahakista, Durrus, Bantry (010-353-27-67045). Working farm. Sleeps 6 adults; 2 children. Seaside charming bungalow overlooking harbour and Dunmanus Bay in the "Sheeps Head" peninsula. Magnificent scenery. Excellent bathing, fishing, boating and mountain climbing within 10 minutes' walk. Shops, Irish pubs and restaurants locally. Bantry 12 miles, Durrus six miles, Kilcrochane three miles. Ideal centre for touring West Cork and Kerry. Accommodation comprises three bedrooms (two double and one twin), all with washbasins; bathroom, shower room; large lounge with studio couch, open fireplace and colour TV; spacious fitted kitchen cum diningroom. Solid fuel cooker, electric cooker, fridge, kettle, toaster, fire, etc. Fully equipped for six people. Central heating. Bed linen provided. Donkey on farm. Car park and lovely garden. Irish Tourist Board approved. Terms: April, May, June and September £100 per week; July, August £140 per week. Available rest of year by arrangement. Also available Bed and Breakfast in family farmhouse plus Evening Meals. Superb hospitality, en-suite rooms.

BANTRY. Mrs Sheila O'Shea, Ard-na-Greine, Adrigole, Bantry (010-353-27 60018). Ard-na-Greine is

a furnished holiday house to let without attendance, situated in the Beara Peninsula overlooking Bantry Bay and within easy reach of Glengarriff, Killarney, Ring of Kerry and the Healy Pass. It is an ideal centre for touring, also for mountain climbing as it is situated at the foot of the Hungry Hill. Being on the sea shore, the house is ideally suited for fishing and boating. It consists of five bedrooms, bathroom, sittingroom, diningroom, modern kitchen/diningroom with electric cooker, fridge, etc. Everything supplied except linen. Gardens front and side, including a field suitable as children's playground. Terms £80 to £140.

IRELAND

KERRY

SOUTHERN IRELAND
Abbeydorney, Tralee, Co. Kerry

Situated at the Abbey Tavern in Abbeydorney, these self catering flats are ideally placed for touring County Kerry. Both Tralee and Banna Beach are five miles away and Ballyheigue, Killarney, Dingle and the Ring of Kerry are also within easy reach. Near Tralee, Killarney and Ballybunian Golf Courses. Clean and reasonably priced, the flats have shower, toilet; living room; kitchenette with electric cooker, fridge, heater, etc. Electricity by 50p meter. Linen and towels supplied. Cot on request. A car is essential and there is ample parking. Overnight stops welcome. Evening Meal available for self catering guests. Bed and Breakfast and Partial Board also available. Bar Meals served all day.

Further details from Mrs Mary O'Connor (010-353-6635145).

Mrs M. Sayers
KILMURRY FARM
Minard Castle, Annascaul (010-353 6657173)

Are you looking for a nice, peaceful holiday? All year round self-catering accommodation is offered in the heart of the Dingle Peninsula. One property accommodates six people (three double beds), the other eight people (three double and two single beds). Fully equipped and carpeted. Bathroom, sitting room, dining room; kitchen with electric cooker, fridge, immersion heater. Linen at extra charge. Ideally situated, you can enjoy your meals looking out over Dingle Bay; also magnificent views of mountains all round. Beach within walking distance (safe for children). Minard Castle (famous for its part in "Ryan's Daughter"), and local pub and shops add enjoyment to your holiday. Car essential, parking. Suitable for disabled visitors. Weekly terms: May £100, June £120, July-August £180, September £120, rest of year £80. Electricity extra. International Reply Coupon, please.

LAURAGH. Mrs M. Moriarty, Creveen Lodge, Healy Pass Road, Lauragh (010 353 64 83131) Sleeps 6/8. Attractive two-storey dormer-style farmhouse attached to proprietors' residence, 200 yards from roadside, with magnificent views of sea and countryside. The 80-acre mixed farm is conveniently situated for fishing, mountain climbing, Derreen Gardens, shops and old Irish pub: 16 miles south of Kenmare. Accommodation for six/eight persons in three double and one twin-bedded rooms, all with washbasins; cot. Sittingroom with large stone fireplace, TV; separate diningroom. Kitchen has gas and solid fuel cooker; solid fuel central heating and storage heating; washing machine and dryer. Everything supplied including linen. Solid fuel on sale. Children and pets welcome; high chair, and babysitting arranged. Car essential — parking. Available all year. April, May, June and September £100 to £110 per week; July and August £150 per week; rest of the year by arrangement. Gas and electricity extra. Irish Tourist Board approved.

The information in the entries in this guide is presented by the publishers in good faith and after the signed acceptance by advertisers that they will uphold the high standards associated with FHG PUBLICATIONS LIMITED. The publishers do not accept responsibility for any inaccuracies or omissions or any results thereof. Before making final holiday arrangements readers should confirm the prices and facilities directly with advertisers.

FARM HOLIDAY GUIDE
ENGLAND WALES IRELAND
FARMS HOTELS GUESTHOUSES SELF-CATERING CARAVANS CAMPING
'91
OVER 3000 PLACES TO STAY

FARM HOLIDAY GUIDE
SCOTLAND
FARMS HOTELS GUESTHOUSES SELF-CATERING CARAVANS CAMPING
'91
SELECTED HOLIDAY ACCOMMODATION IN SCOTLAND

RECOMMENDED   £2.99
SHORT BREAK HOLIDAYS
IN BRITAIN   1991

THE FHG GUIDE TO
SELF-CATERING & FURNISHED HOLIDAYS '91
•ENGLAND •SCOTLAND •WALES •Ireland •The Channel Isles
HOUSES • COTTAGES • FLATS • CHALETS CARAVANS & CAMPING

THE FHG GUIDE TO
BED & BREAKFAST STOPS '91
•ENGLAND •SCOTLAND •WALES
WITH SPECIAL WELCOME SUPPLEMENT FOR NON-SMOKERS • THE DISABLED • SPECIAL DIETS

BRITAIN'S BEST HOLIDAYS *1991*
BRITAIN

THE
GOLF GUIDE
PGA
WHERE TO PLAY WHERE TO STAY
OVER 2000 COURSES • HUNDREDS OF HOTELS

1991   FHG
RECOMMENDED
COUNTRY HOTELS OF BRITAIN
COUNTRY HOTELS AND COUNTRY HOUSE HOSPITALITY FOR LOVERS OF GOOD LIVING

1991   FHG
RECOMMENDED
WAYSIDE INNS OF BRITAIN
REFRESHMENTS • FOOD • ACCOMMODATION AND TRADITIONAL GOOD CHEER

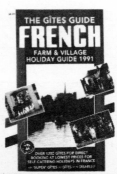

THE GITES GUIDE
FRENCH
FARM & VILLAGE HOLIDAY GUIDE 1991
OVER 1700 GITES FOR DIRECT BOOKING AT LOWEST PRICES FOR SELF-CATERING HOLIDAYS IN FRANCE
• SUPER GITES • GITES • DISABLED

THE ORIGINAL AND UNIQUE   £2.50
PETS *Welcome!* 1991
HOLIDAYS FOR OWNERS & PETS
SUPPLEMENT OF KENNELS & CATTERIES
with maps

CHILDREN WELCOME!
FAMILY HOLIDAY GUIDE
1991
HUNDREDS OF PLACES TO STAY!
WHERE TO GO PLACES TO VISIT MAPS

ONE FOR YOUR FRIEND 1991

FHG Publications have a large range of attractive holiday accommodation guides for all kinds of holiday opportunities throughout Britain. They also make useful gifts at any time of year. Our guides are available in most bookshops and larger newsagents but we will be happy to post you a copy direct if you have any difficulty. We will also post abroad but have to charge separately for post or freight.

The inclusive cost of posting and packing the guides to you or your friends in the UK is as follows:

Farm Holiday Guide
ENGLAND, WALES and IRELAND
Board, Self-catering, Caravans/Camping, Activity Holidays. About 600 pages. **£3.60**

Farm Holiday Guide SCOTLAND
All kinds of holiday accommodation. **£2.60**

SELF-CATERING & FURNISHED HOLIDAYS
Over 1000 addresses throughout for Self-catering and caravans in Britain. **£3.00**

BRITAIN'S BEST HOLIDAYS
A quick-reference general guide for all kinds of holidays. **£2.50**

The FHG Guide to CARAVAN & CAMPING HOLIDAYS
Caravans for hire, sites and holiday parks and centres. **£2.60**

BED AND BREAKFAST STOPS
Over 1000 friendly and comfortable overnight stops. **£3.00**

CHILDREN WELCOME! FAMILY HOLIDAY GUIDE
Family holidays with details of amenities for children and babies. **£2.50**

Recommended SHORT BREAK HOLIDAYS IN BRITAIN
'Approved' accommodation for quality bargain breaks. Introduced by John Carter. **£3.50**

Recommended COUNTRY HOTELS OF BRITAIN
Including Country Houses, for the discriminating. **£3.50**

Recommended WAYSIDE INNS OF BRITAIN
Pubs, Inns and small hotels. **£3.50**

PGA GOLF GUIDE
Where to play and where to stay
Over 2000 golf courses with convenient accommodation. Endorsed by the PGA. **£6.50**

PETS WELCOME!
The unique guide for holidays for pet owners and their pets. **£3.00**

BED AND BREAKFAST IN BRITAIN
Over 1000 choices for touring and holidays throughout Britain. **£2.50**

LONDON'S BEST BED AND BREAKFAST HOTELS
Inspected and recommended with prices. Over 120 safe, clean and friendly small hotels. **£3.25**

THE FRENCH FARM AND VILLAGE HOLIDAY GUIDE
The official guide to self-catering holidays in the 'Gîtes de France'. **£7.50**

Tick your choice and send your order and payment to FHG PUBLICATIONS, ABBEY MILL BUSINESS CENTRE, SEEDHILL, PAISLEY PA1 1JN (TEL: 041-887 0428. FAX: 041-889 7204). **Deduct** 10% for 2/3 titles or copies; 20% for 4 or more.

Send to: NAME ....

ADDRESS ....

....

.... POST CODE ....

I enclose Cheque/Postal Order for £ ....

SIGNATURE .... DATE ....